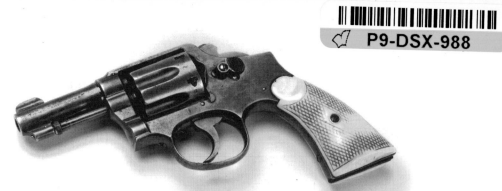

JOHN DILLINGER SLEPT HERE

A CROOKS' TOUR OF CRIME AND CORRUPTION IN ST. PAUL, 1920–1936

JOHN DILLINGER

Minnesota Historical Society Press *St. Paul*

PAUL MACCABEE

SLEPT HERE

A CROOKS' TOUR OF CRIME AND CORRUPTION IN ST. PAUL, 1920–1936

Minnesota Historical Society Press
St. Paul 55102

Manufactured in the United States of America
10 9 8 7 6 5 4 3 2 1

International Standard Book Number 0–87351-315–0 (cloth)
0–87351-316–9 (paper)

∞The paper used in this publication meets the minimum requirements of the American National Standard for Information Sciences— Permanence for Printed Library Materials, ANSI Z39.48–1984.

Maccabee, Paul, 1955–
    John Dillinger Slept Here— : a crooks' tour of crime and corruption in St. Paul, 1920–1936 / Paul Maccabee.
      p.   cm.
    Includes bibliographical references and index.
    ISBM 0–87351-315–0 (alk. paper). — ISBN 0–87351-316–9 (pbk. : alk. paper)
    1. Crime—Minnesota—St. Paul—History—20th century.
2. Criminals—Minnesota—St. Paul—History—20th century.
3. Criminals—Homes and haunts—Minnesota—St. Paul. 4. St. Paul (Minn.)—Description and travel. I. Title
HV6795.S24M33 1995
364.1'09776'58109042—dc20   95–5236

CONTENTS • • • • • • • • • • •

Preface, x

Acknowledgments, xix

ONE: THE SEEDS OF CORRUPTION , 1

1. Home of the Irish Godfather, 2
2. Old St. Paul Police Headquarters, 7
3. Nina Clifford's Brothel and Home, 13
4. Dan Hogan's Final Resting Place, 17

TWO: THE BOTTLING OF FORBIDDEN FRUIT, 22

5. Andrew Volstead's Prohibition Bureau, 24
6. The Murder of Burt Stevens, 29
7. The Hotel St. Paul Headquarters of Leon Gleckman, 34
8. Leon Gleckman's Home, 39
9. The Merchants Bank Building, 41
10. The Mystic Caverns, 44
11. The Castle Royal, 44
12. The Boulevards of Paris and the Coliseum Ballroom, 44
13. The Green Dragon Cafe, 49
14. Bugsy Siegel at the Lowry Hotel, 55

THREE: ORGANIZED CRIME AT YOUR SERVICE, 58

15. Harry "Dutch" Sawyer's Home, 60
16. The Green Lantern Saloon, 64
17. The Hotel St. Francis, 69

FOUR: A BANK ROBBERS' HAVEN, 76

18. The Edgecumbe Court Apartments, 78
19. The Lincoln Oaks Apartments, 85
20. The Cretin Court Apartments, 88
21. The Summit-Dale Apartments, 90
22. The Murder of Sammy Silverman, 92
23. The Plantation Nightclub, 96
24. Keller Golf Course, 99

St. Paul's old Federal Courts Building, site of the 1935–36 trials of Dillinger and Barker-Karpis gang members; (inset) conspirators Elmer Farmer and Volney Davis leaving building after sentencing

FIVE: MURDERING FOR MA, 102

25. Ma Barker's West St. Paul Hideout, 104
26. Summering at the John Lambert Cottage, 112
27. The Third Northwestern National Bank Robbery, 115
28. The Como Park Slaying of Oscar Erickson, 120
29. The Annbee Arms Apartments, 122
30. The Cle-mar Apartments, 124
31. The Barker-Karpis Gang's Grand Avenue Apartments, 127
32. The Commodore Hotel, 129

SIX: A VERY TROUBLING KIDNAPPING, 132

33. The Hollyhocks Club Casino, 134
34. The Barker-Karpis Gang at Idlewild, 141
35. The Hamm Brewing Company, 144
36. Home of Go-Between William W. Dunn, 150
37. The Rosedale Pharmacy, 153
38. Hideout of the "Vernon Street Gang," 155
39. Police Officer Tom Brown's Home, 159
40. The South St. Paul Post Office Robbery, 165

SEVEN: VERNE MILLER'S KANSAS CITY MASSACRE, 170

A Gangster's Brainerd Hideway, 172

EIGHT: ONE KIDNAPPING TOO MANY, 182

41. Fred Barker's Dale Apartments, 184
42. The Jacob Schmidt Brewery, 186
43. Myrtle Eaton's Haven at the Kennington, 189
44. The Holly Falls Apartments, 191
45. The Edward Bremer Kidnapping, 192
46. Home of Go-Between Walter W. Magee, 194
47. Bremer's Abandoned Automobile, 195
48. The Edward G. Bremer Home, 196
49. The Home of Dr. Henry T. Nippert, 197
50. The Home of Adolf Bremer Sr., 199
51. Harry "Dutch" Sawyer's Farm, 203

NINE: JOHN DILLINGER SLEPT HERE, 206

52. Dillinger's Hideout at the Santa Monica Apartments, 208
53. The Charlou and Josephine Apartments, 213
54. The Home of Dr. Nels Mortensen, 216
55. Shootout at the Lincoln Court Apartments, 218

56. Dillinger's Getaway Garage, 221
57. The Dillinger Doctor's Clinic, 224
58. Tommy Carroll's St. Paul Hideout, 226
59. The Dillinger Gang's Minneapolis Mail Drop, 226
60. The Dillinger Gang's Weapons Depot, 232
61. Eddie Green's Ambush House, 234
    The Hastings Spiral Bridge Stakeout, 236
62. Homer Van Meter's Death Site, 240

TEN: THE BIG CLEANUP, 248
63. New St. Paul Police Headquarters, 250
64. The Hamm Building Gambling Den, 255

ELEVEN: FINAL JUDGMENTS, 260
65. Holman Municipal Airport, 262
66. St. Paul City Hall and Ramsey County Courthouse, 265
67. Old Ramsey County Jail, 267
    Old Federal Courts Building (also site 5), 272

EPILOGUE, 278
Crooks' Tour and Maps, 291
Rogues and Reformers Gallery, 306
Twin Cities Crime Chronology, 309
Sources, 314
Notes, 320
Index, 349

John Dillinger in 1934, at his father's home with the wooden handgun used to escape jail in Crown Point, Indiana

"Of all the Midwest cities, the one that I knew best was St. Paul, and it was a crooks' haven," boasted Alvin "Creepy" Karpis, the kidnapper and bank robber whom J. Edgar Hoover anointed Public Enemy Number One. "Every criminal of any importance in the 1930's made his home at one time or another in St. Paul. If you were looking for a guy you hadn't seen for a few months, you usually thought of two places—prison or St. Paul. If he wasn't locked up in one, he was probably hanging out in the other."[1]

Visitors to Minneapolis and St. Paul today see few traces of the years when Karpis, John Dillinger, "Ma" Barker and her sons Fred and "Doc," Lester "Babyface Nelson" Gillis, and George "Machine Gun Kelly" Barnes found refuge in this underworld haven. Instead, travel guides direct tourists to the homes of novelist F. Scott Fitzgerald and railroad magnate James J. Hill. No bronze plaque marks the St. Paul apartment building from which Dillinger machine-gunned his way out of an FBI trap in March 1934. Nor are there any signs identifying the West St. Paul home that served as a hideout for Ma Barker in April 1932. Until now, the locations of dozens of other 1930s gambling dens, Prohibition speakeasies, brothels, Murder Inc. assassination sites, and Dillinger gang safe houses have been known only to a few retired FBI agents and police detectives.

This gangland guide, based on nearly 100,000 pages of FBI files, retraces the steps of those underworld figures and explores the political and social environment that allowed the criminals to flourish in America's Saintliest City. The crooks' tour begins in 1928, with the slaying of Irish syndicate chieftain "Dapper Dan" Hogan, the supervisor of St. Paul police chief John O'Connor's "layover agreement." The agreement guaranteed safe harbor in St. Paul for the nation's bank robbers, stickup artists, kidnappers, extortionists, and killers—with the understanding that they would not commit crimes within the city limits. The tour follows the fuse of civic corruption, lit by the flow of Prohibition bribes. It documents the burgeoning power of gangsters in the 1930s, as St. Paul was transformed into a market for criminal services: the laundering of stolen bank loot and the open sale of getaway vehicles, automatic weapons, and corrupt police officials.

The tour proceeds to the arrival of the Keating-Holden gang, a group as devoted to golf as to bank robbery; the intersecting careers of outlaws Frank "Jelly" Nash and Verne Miller as they collided with bloody consequences in the Kansas City Massacre; the crime waves of the Dillinger and Barker-Karpis gangs, climaxing with the kidnappings of two prominent

St. Paul citizens, William Hamm Jr. and Edward Bremer; and the 1935 and 1936 trials of the surviving gangsters in St. Paul federal court.

To J. Edgar Hoover's disgust, many law-abiding Minnesotans relished the wicked glamour of dancing and dining at the nightclubs—the Hollyhocks, the Boulevards of Paris—patronized by these public enemies. The Great Depression and less-than-great journalists contributed to the perception of sociopathic killers such as Babyface Nelson as outlaw legends. Widespread contempt for Prohibition laws had elevated local bootleggers, among them Benny Haskell of Minneapolis and Leon Gleckman of St. Paul, to the status of illicit entrepreneurs. Anger over banks foreclosing on loans led many people to view the bank robbers flooding St. Paul as machine gun-toting Robin Hoods.

"The papers say he was bad," Dillinger's sister Audrey Hancock told a reporter in 1934, echoing popular sentiment. "No doubt he was. I don't believe in killin' people, but about robbin' banks, well, I don't think Johnny was any worse than the bankers. The bankers robbed people, too, didn't they?"[2]

Adding to the public's confusion was the selective history of J. Edgar Hoover's public relations machine. His FBI ensured that accounts of the Twin Cities underworld remained a cobweb of Hoover-authorized fantasy hung over a skeleton of fact. Hoover, named in 1924 to reorganize and clean up a corrupt Bureau of Investigation in the Department of Justice, built his name and his bureau's image on the capture of flamboyant but relatively petty midwestern gangsters like John Dillinger. That reputation had important consequences: a trusting public believed Hoover when he denied the existence of a national crime syndicate—the Mafia.[3]

"History is always best written generations after the event," suggested journalist and historian Theodore H. White, "when clouded fact and memory have all fused into what can be accepted as truth, whether it be so or not." The absolute truth about the activities of the Barker-Karpis and Dillinger gangs is unknowable because the participants are dead. To construct the most accurate account of the gangster days possible, I began eleven years of research for this book with a review of thousands of pages of FBI files, obtained under the federal Freedom of Information Act (FOIA).

The FBI has been known variously as the Bureau of Investigation (1909), the U.S. Bureau of Investigation (1932), the Division of Investigation (1933), and, finally, the Federal Bureau of Investigation, which has been its name since July 1935. To avoid confusion, all of my references to the agency use the current name, Federal Bureau of Investigation (FBI), a title J. Edgar Hoover secured to reflect the additional powers granted by 1934 legislation in the wake of the Kansas City Massacre, Dillinger, and Lindbergh kidnapping cases.

I expected the files on Dillinger, Karpis, and others released by the FBI to be sanitized, much as Hoover had airbrushed his publicists' accounts of the bureau's pursuit of gangsters during the 1930s. In fact, the FBI's internal memoranda—which Hoover never imagined would be exposed to public view—are remarkably candid. What Hoover allowed to appear in public was often mythology, but what he and his agents wrote for their own consumption was freely peppered with their jealousies and triumphs, the capricious rages of the director, rivalries with local police and other federal agencies, the FBI's frustration with the local news media, and often astounding feats of behind-the-scenes detective work.

Complementing the FBI records that I used were Minnesota Bureau of Criminal Apprehension homicide files, St. Paul and Minneapolis police files, court records, prison inmate files, and federal Prohibition Department documents.

Most importantly, I interviewed more than 250 detectives, gangster family members, FBI agents, prosecutors, judges, gangster girlfriends, and criminal defense attorneys. The vast majority of these people speak here for the first time. Believing, as dramatist John Still wrote, that "the memories of men are too frail a thread to hang history from," I have tried to corroborate each interview with written records from the period. For example, the re-creation in chapter 5 of how the Barker-Karpis gang escaped from its West St. Paul hideout, tipped off by corrupt police, was built from interlocking sources. To the FBI's internal memoranda and newspaper accounts of Ma Barker's flight, I have added the evidence I found in state Bureau of Criminal Apprehension investigative reports and interviews with three surviving members of a family that lived side-by-side with the Barker-Karpis gang.

Preserved within the FBI's files, too, were more than a dozen confessions made by girlfriends and wives of Dillinger and Barker-Karpis gang members, including Paula Harmon, girlfriend of Fred Barker; Edna "the Kissing Bandit" Murray, lover of kidnapper Volney Davis; and Irene Dorsey Goetz, widow of hit man Fred "Shotgun George Ziegler" Goetz. These matter-of-fact accounts provide a unique antidote to Hollywood's portrayal of gangster life: the day-to-day fear of capture, lives marked by furtive abortions and venereal disease, and abandonment and beatings by their men.

I began this book as an investigative reporter in 1981, when a journalist in the newsroom of the *Twin Cities Reader* weekly newspaper mentioned that Isadore "Kid Cann" Blumenfeld—the Godfather of Minneapolis—had died of heart disease. Intrigued that sedate Minnesota had a history of organized crime, I filed the first of more than 200 FOIA requests for crime files possessed by the FBI, the Drug Enforcement Administration, the U.S.

Labor Department, the Immigration and Naturalization Service, and other agencies. A seven-year struggle with the Justice Department led to my testifying before the Senate Subcommittee on Technology and the Law in 1988 about the FBI's reluctance to open its files on mobsters.

My discovery of duplicate—yet uncensored—FBI documents in the National Archives in Washington, D.C., exposed precisely what the FBI was withholding. The National Archives files revealed that the Justice Department was deleting the names of corrupt police and political figures who had accepted bribes from the underworld and acted as "moles" for the gangsters. The FBI cited concern about "invasion of privacy" as justification for protecting the identity of these officials, many of whom had been dead for nearly half a century. Other censored FBI files dealt with law-enforcement strategies that could be embarrassing to the bureau, such as wiretapping, surveillance, and "mail covers" on the correspondence of people who knew the Dillinger and Barker-Karpis gangs.

Probing the history of crime in Minnesota is also complicated by the destruction of much of the written record of the gangster era. At the St. Paul Police Department, limited file space and the renovation of the central police station in the 1980s led to the destruction of thousands of pages of vintage police records. Into the garbage went every page of the files on John Dillinger, Ma Barker, Alvin Karpis, and other gangsters. Thick sheaves of fingerprint and identification records on hundreds of criminals were tossed into the trash; officers wandering by pulled out a few as souvenirs. Even the straw hat that Homer Van Meter of the Dillinger gang had been wearing when police officers shot him to death in 1934, saved for decades, disappeared. A purging of police files occurred in Minneapolis, too, where the entire intelligence file on syndicate boss Isadore Blumenfeld vanished; in Chicago, virtually every police department record from the Al Capone years, including evidence from the St. Valentine's Day Massacre, was thrown out; and in Kansas City, the police department's Kansas City Massacre investigation file has disappeared.[4]

Back in St. Paul, at the site of the old Ramsey County jail, a trash bin was filled with records stretching back to the days of Ma Barker. One witness remembers leaning into the open bin, jammed with city attorneys' records soaked by a light rain, and finding dripping pages of correspondence from the family of Homer Van Meter arguing that city officials should turn over his 1932 Ford coupe. Every page was destroyed.

At the Minnesota Bureau of Criminal Apprehension, when a comprehensive computer system arrived in the 1970s, hundreds of crime documents from the Dillinger era were fed into paper shredders. Index cards to old homicide records were destroyed.[5]

MR. NATHAN
MR. TOLSON
MR. CLEGG
MR. COWLEY
MR. EDWARD
MR. EGAN
MR. QUINN
MR. LESTER
CHIEF CLERK
MR. RORER

Division of Investigation

U. S. Department of Justice

Post Office Box 515,
St. Paul, Minnesota.

May 4, 1934

PERSONAL AND CONFIDENTIAL

Director,
Division of Investigation,
U. S. Department of Justice,
Washington, D. C.

Dear Sir:

With reference to your teletype request to submit all information available concerning ▉▉▉▉ ▉▉▉▉ of the St. Paul Police Department, please be advised that we have no first hand information available concerning this party, as we have never had occasion to investigate this person. The consensus of opinion, however, is that ▉▉▉▉, like ▉▉▉▉ is one of the Leon Gleckman men on the Police Department. Rumors are plentiful to the effect that ▉▉▉▉ is crooked and mixed up with the underworld and the present setup is to the effect that an effort is underway to place ▉▉▉▉▉▉▉▉ and ▉▉▉▉ in charge of the St. Paul Police Department.

▉▉▉▉▉▉▉▉▉▉▉▉▉▉▉▉▉▉▉▉▉▉▉▉▉▉▉▉▉▉▉▉▉▉▉▉

Very truly yours,

WERNER HANNI,
Special Agent in Charge.

RECORDED & INDEXED
MAY 22 1934

62-4100-X12

MAY 7 1934

AIR MAIL - SPECIAL DELIVERY

A 1934 FBI memo about St. Paul bootlegger Leon Gleckman, with censored references to police corruption

According to the Federal Bureau of Prisons, the inmate files for most of the Dillinger and Barker-Karpis gang members imprisoned in Alcatraz and Leavenworth were thrown out in the early 1970s under a statutory thirty-year destruction rule. The handful of Leavenworth and Alcatraz files quoted in this book were saved accidentally, when they were set aside for study and federal officials simply forgot to destroy them.[6]

Why is the historical record of a city's racketeers worth saving? Because the story of Minneapolis and St. Paul, like that of any city, is a mingling of glory and infamy, of people with high integrity and others with low morals. St. Paul was built as much on a legacy of gamblers, scoundrels, and sinners as on a tradition of philanthropists, statesmen, and business barons. By probing the underworld—from homegrown criminals such as fixer Harry "Dutch" Sawyer to imported thieves like Dillinger—one gains a richer understanding of how citizens viewed their police force, their city government, and their vices of alcohol, gambling, and prostitution. St. Paul's experiment in accommodating the underworld also provides a lesson in the consequences of a government forging a partnership with criminals.

The story of the St. Paul underworld also offers a magnifying glass with which to view a defining moment in law enforcement. It was here, from 1933 to 1936, that J. Edgar Hoover demonstrated the viability of the national police force that he craved and that so many had opposed. The necessary elements rushed together in one city: a local police force so corrupt that it demanded a federal alternative; a series of high-profile interstate crimes that left clues in several parts of the country; a firestorm of media coverage, fed primarily by FBI publicity; and a series of clues that demanded a level of technology that few local police possessed. St. Paul served first as a haven, and then as a burial ground, for many members of the Barker-Karpis and Dillinger gangs, but it was also the birthplace of the modern FBI and the cult of Hoover as the nation's number-one G-man.

This book is organized so that it can be enjoyed in two ways: as a "crooks' tour" of the actual crime sites or as a history book to be read in the safety of your home. You will find the criminal events of *John Dillinger Slept Here* grouped around the underworld sites where they occurred, and as a result the chronology skips around a bit. To help you tell your Babyface Nelsons from your Machine Gun Kellys, miniature biographies of the most prominent St. Paul gangsters are offered in the Rogues and Reformers Gallery section. The Twin Cities Crime Chronology traces the major events of Minnesota gangsterdom.

One objective of this book is to explore the belief, espoused in most histories of the gangster era, that legitimate society remained aloof from the underworld during the 1930s—at least until the Barker-Karpis gang violated the O'Connor agreement by kidnapping businessmen Edward Bremer and William Hamm. But research in Justice Department and police files reveals that the overworld and underworld of Minnesota were far more intertwined than was previously acknowledged. The local banking, brewery, city government, and restaurant industries had found common ground with organized crime more than a decade before the Barker-Karpis and Dillinger gangs moved into St. Paul.

Evil can be enticing. The inherent drama of the lawbreakers' lives has made it easy for Hollywood to focus on their cruel dynamism and ignore their victims. Today, the nickname Babyface Nelson is as recognizable as the names of Harry Houdini and P. T. Barnum. Yet few people could identify Nelson's innocent victims, among them bystander Theodore Kidder and slain FBI agents W. Carter Baum, Herman Hollis, and Sam Cowley. Whenever possible, I have tried to give voice to the victims of the Dillinger and Barker-Karpis gangs. You will find here the fullest account yet published of the terror felt by the abducted Edward Bremer, blindfolded and bound to a point near paralysis, and the shock experienced by the children of Roy McCord, who was machine-gunned by the Barker-Karpis gang because his Northwest Airlines uniform made him look like a police officer.

"God cannot alter the past," quipped Samuel Butler, "but historians can." It is my hope that *John Dillinger Slept Here* will alter how we perceive the public enemies in the 1930s and the men who hunted them—that it will peel away the nostalgic glamour ascribed to the Dillinger and Barker-Karpis gangs; restore to public view the heroes of that tumultuous period (crusading *St. Paul Daily News* editor Howard Kahn, for example); place the triumphs and failures of J. Edgar Hoover and the FBI in perspective; and fully reveal the villainy of gangland collaborators like police chief Thomas Archibald Brown.

Now, pull on that black fedora, pick up your violin case, and prepare to take the crooks' tour.

Paul Maccabee
St. Paul, Minnesota
January 1995

ACKNOWLEDGMENTS • • • • • • • •

John Dillinger Slept Here benefits from the contributions of a network of gangland scholars that stretches from New York to Los Angeles. I owe much to crime historian William J. Helmer for his meticulous dissection of the weaponry and explosives mentioned in this book; also helpful were crime aficionados Rick Mattix, Tim Albright, Ross Opsahl, Jeff Maycroft, Kathi Harrell, Ellen Poulsen, Robert Bates, Dee Cordry of the OklahombreS, and Joe Pinkston of Indiana's John Dillinger Historical Wax Museum.

A tip of the cap to the three Minnesota police departments that opened their 1930s crime files: South St. Paul Police Capt. David Vujovich, who lent his records on the Barker-Karpis gang's payroll robbery; Minneapolis Police Department records officer Bev Johnson and Lt. Gary McGaughey; and St. Paul police librarian Edith Kroner, personnel staffer Mary Zupfer, and records officers Lt. Michael Moorehead and Sgt. Mark Johnston. St. Paul police historian Fred Kaphingst deserves a special epaulet for saving the 1928 file on Dan Hogan's murder from destruction.

Capt. Joseph O'Connor, former commander of the Philadelphia Police Department's Organized Crime Intelligence Unit, shared his files on Murder Inc. hit men George Young and Joseph Schaefer. David Finazzo of the Detroit Police Department provided access to the file on Verne Miller's murder, which contained a 1934 police interview with George "Machine Gun Kelly" Barnes that proved revelatory. Special thanks also go to Ramsey County Medical Examiner Michael McGee for his help in providing reports on the murders and suicides of gangsters.

The Minnesota Bureau of Criminal Apprehension (BCA) was singularly generous in offering unrestricted access to its 1930s murder files and crime identification records. Thanks go to Karen McDonald, BCA director of crime history and fingerprints; agent Mike Campion; and former superintendent Mark Shields.

The FBI's Freedom of Information Unit was most reluctant to release its files on the gangster era. I did, however, appreciate the help of FBI historian Susan Rosenfeld and Lawrence J. Heim, editor of the newsletter of the Society of Former Special Agents of the FBI, *The Grapevine*, in providing material on individual agents and cases.

Mike Robar, Freedom of Information officer with the Federal Bureau of Prisons, dedicated himself to locating critical files from Alcatraz and Leavenworth prisons that the bureau had thought were long destroyed.

More than 250 people offered their memories of the gangster era, often in multiple interviews lasting for hours. I am particularly indebted to Horace "Red" Dupont, employee of gangland fixer Tom Filben; former St. Paul police officers Charlie Reiter and Pat Lannon Sr.; the late Richard Pranke, FBI special agent; and Martin Rohling, Jack Peifer's doorman at the Hollyhocks Club. Members of the gangsters' families who were surprisingly open about their nefarious kin included Bruce Barnes, son of "Machine Gun Kelly" Barnes; Bruce Hamilton, nephew of Dillinger gang member John Hamilton; Albert Grooms, nephew of Alvin Karpis; Carole DeMoss, niece of Harry Sawyer; and Ann Michaud, niece of Dan Hogan.

Among the many librarians who contributed, I would like to give special thanks to the staffs of the Minneapolis *Star Tribune*'s library, the St. Paul Public Library, and the Minneapolis Public Library's Special History Collection for unearthing newspaper clippings and photographs. I am also grateful to the Nita Haley Stewart Memorial Library in Midland, Texas, for permission to quote from portions of J. Evetts Haley's five original interviews with bank robber Harvey Bailey.

Journalist Gareth Hiebert and researchers Jim "The House Detective" Sazevich of St. Paul and Sal Giacona of Detroit brought the outlines of madam Nina Clifford's world to life. Journalist Kara Morrison investigated Harry Sawyer's family in Lincoln, Nebraska; Alison Fitzgerald and *Chicago Tribune* reporter John J. O'Brien probed Alvin Karpis's family in Chicago.

The role of the Minnesota Historical Society (MHS) in the creation of this book has extended far beyond that of a publisher; its archives have been a haven and resource throughout this project. I am grateful for the enthusiasm and dedication of Jean A. Brookins and Ann Regan of the MHS Press, and I am astonished by the commitment of editors Marilyn Ziebarth, John Radzilowski, and Lynn Marasco and volunteer reader Pat Rolewicz. I also received assistance from the historical societies in Hennepin, Ramsey, Koochiching, and Dakota counties.

For his guidance through the jungle of publishing arcana, I appreciate the counsel of my literary oracle, Scott Edelstein, of Minneapolis. My parents, Rose and Ralph Fishman, continue to be my life's anchors.

Most of all, this book could never have been written without the unflagging energy and insight of my loving wife and partner in crime history, Paula. She spent hundreds of hours editing every sentence and reviewing every blurry photograph, providing her unerring advice on issues ranging from the legal, historical, and grammatical to the logical, philosophical, and aesthetic. Paula, this one's for you.

Paul Pioneer Press

Sidelights on
Edgar Markham w
column.
See "Politics and E
editorial page.

ST. PAUL, MINN., WEDNESDAY, DECEMBER 5, 1928.   C   PRICE THREE CENTS IN

HOGAN DIES OF BOMB WOUN

'DAPPER DAN' HOGAN AND HIS BOMB-WRECKED CAR

Scenes of the destruction wrought by the bomb which was planted in the automobile of "Dapper Dan" Hogan, restaurant man and underworld figure, were caught by a Pioneer Press photographer soon after the explosion. In the upper picture the approximate location of the death bomb is shown by the cross. The lines radiating from it show the double course of the explosion. Below the arrow points to the wire where the bomb was grounded on the engine. Inset, "Dapper Dan" Hogan, whose right leg was blown off above the knee by the explosion,

**MUST
MATUM
RNANE**

**t Promised St.
hree Major
r in Day.**

AID POLICE

ncy to Co-op-
rding Life
perty.

st go."
matum of Chief
urnane Tuesday
y of major crime
ch a restaurant
y hurt in a bomb
nd a filling sta-
y a bandit who
the attendant.
Commissioner of
M. Clancy and
ller were shown
ter. oon Dispatch
es of the three
emoval to Brain-
y, suspect in the
robbery. Mayor
be reached.

Enforced.

o be done about
d.
gsters or undesir-
ey'll certainly be
f Murnane said.
t go. We intend
rs and give St.
le policing under

bomb explosion
anny Hogan lost
nane said:
st time we have
of this kind and
will be taken to

e City of St. Paul
nal way as other
er Clancy said.
en unfortunate in
at times, we have
uld. We will con-
st possible service
nd property with
mmand."

d Murnane.

pledged co-opera-
urnane in ridding
rld characters.
we are with a
uipment, and no
oeller said. "we
e the chief all we
ur men, in stamp-
n St. Paul.
orce here in the
rs has been used
ters, the care and
and in patroling
word, we have no
. However, at
of the Minnesota
a department."

**ET PART
,000 ESTATE**

AP—Two average
rls are about to
nobility and be-
a $15,000,000

**MUTTER
REVENG
IN UND**

Auto Blast
Gang; Sla
Police

NO CLUES

Description of
Near Gar
Inves

"Dapper Da
nessman, rest
and smiling arl
underworld, die
pital at 8:55 l
victim of a ga
Word of
rapidly and pol
alike armed fo
war of reprisal
Both believed
are sure to follo
give him a chan
Police were
that the crime
by New York
what was term
most cowardly i
and incited by
tious gang of N
The underworld
theories of its e

Dies Wis

Known throu
and to some e
his power to se
ists and to "kee
town," Hogan
silent as to the
if he knew.
In soft drink
and small hote
ments known
abide, muttered
were heard, as
that they woul
lawless aid in

Mr. Hogan, w
lived only a f
hours after he
by at their hon
street, shortly

GANGLA

"Dapper Da
of attaching
tomobile sta
world's newe
the United
feuds, police
night.
While mach
vogue and pol
into their
method of le
nihilate hims
starter of his
used in but n
cases.
Tuesday's l
such case rep
side large Fa
exception of
his garage a

M'NARY-HAUGEN FIRM
ON ROCKS OVER BILL

Iowan Spurns Oregonian's
Feeless Farm Measure as
Ineffective.

By EDGAR MARKHAM
(Pioneer Press Staff Correspondent.)
Washington, Dec. 4. The farm re-

U. S. DENIED CHANCE   **'Dapper Dan' Was 'King' to Scores**
Who ourn as Death Seals Lips

THE SEEDS OF CORRUPTION

The 1928 car-bomb murder of Dan Hogan stunned the underworld; John J. "the Big Fellow" O'Connor, architect of the O'Connor system.

1 'I Didn't Know I Had an Enemy in the World!'

Home of the Irish Godfather
1607 West Seventh Street, St. Paul

Just before 11:30 A.M. on December 4, 1928, St. Paul underworld czar Daniel "Dapper Dan" Hogan—heavy with a late-morning breakfast—walked toward his Paige coupe. The forty-eight-year-old Irishman had parked the car in the white stucco garage just behind his West Seventh Street home. Awaiting Hogan, hidden between the rear end of the engine block and the bottom of the footboard, was an explosive charge wired to the starter.[1]

Hogan had told a friend that he had seen someone hanging around the alley in back of his house several times and that he thought someone had it in for him. Hogan had installed a burglar alarm to warn of any attempts on his life, but the batteries that powered the garage alarm had expired. So, too, would Danny Hogan.[2]

"Some powerful explosive had been placed under the floor board near the starter," said the 1928 police report. "Wires had been attached to the bolt on the top of the block of the Motor . . . which made a complete electrical circuit to the explosive." Hogan climbed into the coupe, turned on the ignition, and stepped down on the starter pedal. Instantly, the bomb lodged beneath the floorboards detonated. The force of the blast rocketed the auto out of Hogan's garage and into the alley. Hogan's right leg was "practically blown off," said the police report. "The explosion blew the hood off of the car, went thru the top of the car, broke all the windows in the car, flattened the gears, blew the steering wheel completely off, tore part of the rear end of the engine off [and] broke all windows in the Garage."[3]

For a decade, Hogan had ruled the underworld from the tables of his Green Lantern saloon on Wabasha Street, just three blocks from the Minnesota Capitol. The "layover agreement," or O'Connor system of protection, named after Police Chief John O'Connor and supervised by Hogan, ensured that out-of-town gangsters visiting St. Paul would receive police protection if they followed three rules: check in with Hogan, donate a small bribe, and promise to commit crimes only outside the city limits.

Hogan's first arrest—for "room prowling" in Los Angeles—had earned the chunky laborer a stay in San Quentin prison in 1905, followed by time in Wisconsin, South Dakota, and Minnesota jails for robbing banks and stealing furs. Shortly after Hogan was first arrested in St. Paul, on November 29, 1909, he discovered his true calling—organizing major crimes from the sanctuary of St. Paul, selecting the criminal personnel for the job, and laundering stolen merchandise, particularly hard-to-fence government bonds.[4]

FBI files indicate that Hogan masterminded the 1924 robbery of $13,000 from the Finkelstein and Ruben collection wagon at the corner of Eighth and Cedar Streets in St. Paul. The wagon picked up the daily receipts from local movie houses, and Hogan shrewdly planned the robbery for a Monday morning so that he would profit from the Saturday and Sunday movie collections. In exchange for planning the robbery, Hogan and his partner received 10 percent of the loot.[5]

"Danny Hogan . . . today he'd probably be called a Godfather, sort of a father figure for hoods who were climbing the world of hoodlumism," said retired St. Paul newspaper reporter Fred Heaberlin.[6]

In the early 1920s, Hogan allied himself with his underworld counterpart in Minneapolis—a 6-foot, 2-inch Irishman named Edward G. "Big Ed" Morgan—to operate a gambling den under Minneapolis police protection. (Curiously, the FBI noted that "no liquor is allowed on these premises by Dan Hogan."[7]) Hogan and Morgan, a slot machine king and muckraking journalist for the *Twin City Reporter* scandal sheet, developed an amicable split of the Twin Cities underworld. Hogan commanded all of St. Paul, while Morgan, in a loose partnership with bootleggers Tommy Banks and Isadore "Kid Cann" Blumenfeld, handled Minneapolis crime out of the Dyckman Hotel and Brady's Bar on Hennepin Avenue.

"It is common knowledge in Minneapolis and St. Paul that Dan Hogan and Edward Morgan harbor criminals from other parts of the United States," stated a 1926 FBI memo.

> The police of Minneapolis and St. Paul are said not to interfere with these criminals, there being an understanding between Dan Hogan and the St. Paul Police and Edward Morgan and the Minneapolis Police that if the criminal gangs controlled by them refrain from committing crime in the Twin Cities, that they will not be disturbed. It is a well known fact in the community that a very little crime such as bank robberies, etc. is committed here, the criminals are safe as long as they live up to the pledge made by Dan Hogan and Edward Morgan to the local police.

Of special value to visiting hoods was St. Paul's tradition of refusing extradition requests made by cities outside the perimeter of the O'Connor system. "It is further rumored that the police have a tipoff system," explained the FBI file, "by which Dan Hogan or Morgan is informed when a member of the criminal gang controlled by them is wanted by either the U.S. authorities or another State, wherefor it is difficult to make such captures in the Twin cities."[8]

Gradually, the bribes of the O'Connor payoff system overflowed into the pockets of St. Paul police detectives, aldermen, grand jury members, judges, and even federal prosecutors. Hogan "is so entrenched politically and otherwise," lamented post office investigators that same year, "that law enforcement officers in St. Paul and Minneapolis fear him. In fact, give protection to members of his organization."[9]

The O'Connor system is more than a historical curiosity, an amusing interlude in a cartoon cops-and-robbers chase. It provides a cautionary tale about corruption, its corrosive effects on a midwestern city, and the rise of organized crime in America. Hogan's activities were only a small part of the scandal. Prohibition had offered lawbreakers a new industry and a sudden infusion of illicit money. Police had particular difficulty enforcing laws that a significant number of people refused to support. Citizens' tacit acceptance of corruption—and their inclination to romanticize criminals—helped the underworld flourish. Bootleggers began to attack and steal from each other; some moved on to robbing banks and kidnapping. Bystanders, police officers, and FBI agents were killed. J. Edgar Hoover and the FBI rose to prominence fighting these highly visible crooks—and ignored the more sophisticated and dangerous crime syndicates of Charles "Lucky" Luciano, Frank Costello, Meyer Lansky, and others.

By 1927, thanks to Dan Hogan's connections, St. Paul was known across the United States as the Wall Street for laundering hot bonds, stolen securities, and other ill-gotten financial paper. "Hogan is a nationally known character as a 'fence' for the disposal of stolen property and undoubtedly hundreds of thousands of dollars of stolen stamps and bonds and other valuable property have come into his hands," concluded a 1927 Justice Department memo. "He is doubtless one of the most resourceful and keenest criminals in the United States and has always been able to cover his tracks so as to avoid detection."[10]

Just how resourceful was demonstrated when the Hamilton County Bank in Cincinnati was robbed by Oklahoma bank robber Harvey Bailey on September 28, 1922. The Bailey gang jammed three laundry bags with more than $265,000 in securities, virtually cleaning out the bank's financial assets. Hogan's syndicate offered to return some of the stolen bonds in exchange for a cash ransom. When the U.S. Secret Service put Hogan under surveillance in the hope of locating the bonds, Hogan responded in kind, putting the Secret Service agents under the gang's surveillance.[11]

Then the FBI learned from an informant in Leavenworth prison that Hogan had personally handled $80,000 of the money stolen from the Denver Mint on December 18, 1922. That ninety-second robbery, which netted $200,000 in currency and left one bank guard dead, was labeled years later by the *Denver Post* "Denver's biggest robbery—a crime that set a new under-world high in an American era already spectacular with bootleg booze, bank robbery, gun molls and murder."[12]

Stolen bonds traceable to both the Denver Mint and the Hamilton County Bank robberies began to surface in St. Paul. Harvey Bailey, who relieved Upper Midwest banks of almost $1 million in cash and bonds—including $30,000 from the Olmsted County Bank and Trust in Rochester, Minnesota—provided an inside view of Hogan's operations. Decades later, Bailey explained in his autobiography, *Robbing Banks Was My Business*, how he met Hogan to explore a market for his loot and then decided to entrust Hogan with some $80,000 in stolen money. "Now listen, it may take me a month or it may take me six months to dispose of this, but I'll get with it," promised Hogan.[13]

Fixers like Hogan made St. Paul a favorite of expert criminals like Bailey, considered the dean of American bank robbers. "I would be lying if I said that I didn't find a market for that money, because I found the market. . . . I had wonderful connections during them years," wrote Bailey.

The usual underworld rate offered criminals thirty-five to forty cents on the dollar for stolen railroad or security bonds and eighty-five to ninety cents for Liberty Bonds. By August 1923, Hogan had successfully laundered most of the Denver Mint loot for Bailey. "We made him make it good and he did make it good. Oh yes, thieves is thieves, you know," said Bailey admiringly of Hogan. "But there's honesty among us."[14]

Although members of Hogan's gang were caught with portions of the Denver Mint money, none would implicate the boss. A triumphant Hogan gave Bailey a going-away gift—a tip-off that Bailey had been recognized at Jack Dempsey's Brainerd, Minnesota, prizefight—and Bailey left St. Paul to cool off in Chicago.

Nothing demonstrated Hogan's influence better than his response to being indicted in 1927 for a conspiracy to commit a 1924 robbery in which $35,000 was taken from the Chicago Great Western Railroad station in South St. Paul. The gangsters met Hogan at his saloon to plan the robbery, then held up the mail messenger and delivered a 10 percent cut to the Green Lantern. Hogan's robberies, unlike those of Bonnie Parker, Clyde Barrow, and other better-known bandits, nearly always reaped substantial profits and seldom resulted in gunplay.[15]

Hogan was imprisoned in the Ramsey County jail for the South St. Paul score, but his $100,000 bond—the largest ever demanded by a U.S. District Court judge in St. Paul—was covered by twenty-five bondsmen. The case against Hogan began to collapse when a key witness, Chicago robber Tommy O'Connor, escaped from a train. O'Connor went to the newspapers,

Family photo of Dan Hogan (left), relaxing at his Big Bass Lake cabin west of Bemidji with his wife, Leila, and father-in-law, Fremont Hardy

claiming that every word of his grand jury testimony implicating Hogan had been fabricated.[16]

"A few days prior to trial of Subjects at St. Paul, Minn., it was learned that the witnesses, all underworld characters, had changed their stories," an FBI agent wrote in a 1927 memo. "It is believed said witnesses were paid or intimidated after indictment and before trial, through the underworld connections and influence of Subject Hogan." Minneapolis police chief Frank Brunskill suddenly told postal inspectors that he could not help prosecute Hogan's gang, that he wouldn't "double-cross the boys." Postal inspectors were baffled: "Every prospective lead at Minneapolis was bungled in some mysterious way." By July 1927, all robbery charges against Hogan were dismissed.[17]

Those who did choose to speak against Hogan suffered a severely reduced life expectancy. Informant John Moran, reportedly a participant in the South St. Paul robbery who was to serve as a government witness against Hogan, died abruptly in the Atlanta penitentiary a week after Hogan visited him there. After being interviewed in 1927 about a mail robbery, two of the Hogan gang's girlfriends, Ann Grenville and Teddy Du Bois, were shot to death in Grenville's University Avenue apartment. A post office inspector told the FBI that Grenville's suite was a hangout for Hogan's gang. "She and her companion were killed by hirelings of Hogan," the inspector concluded, "because of their belief that she had knowledge of their criminal operations." When a cab driver was asked about his statement that the murdered women had visited Hogan's saloon—and that he saw Hogan on the day of the murder—the eyewitness abruptly changed his story. "I made a mistake," the cabbie protested to police. "I did not see Danny that night."[18]

The Justice Department estimated that in a ten-month span, Hogan's gang robbed seven post offices in Wisconsin and Minnesota, netting more than $250,000. "For years many crimes of violence, including Post Office burglaries, bank robberies and hold-ups within a radius of several hundred miles of St. Paul, upon investigation, have pointed to some complicity or responsibility on the part of the defendant Hogan," said an attorney general's memo.[19]

Now a gangster's car bomb had accomplished what the Justice Department's investigators could not. "One thing nearly saved Uncle Dan's life at the time," Hogan's niece, Ann Michaud, recalled of the explosion. "Danny was short with a big tummy, and to drive his coupe, he had to lean way back in order to reach the pedals. That's how he protected his head—they'd intended to blow his head off!"[20]

More than a hundred of Hogan's friends offered to donate blood for a transfusion; hospital phone lines were jammed by people calling to check on his condition. Going into surgery, Hogan looked up at his physician and quipped, "Doc, you'd *better* be good!" But Hogan slipped into a coma and, nine hours after the explosion, died. To the legions of gamblers, burglars, and con men in St. Paul, Hogan's death was a tragedy—a frightening upset in a universe of orderly corruption.[21]

"Hoarse voices, bearing the accent of the underworld, queried, 'I just heard Danny died. That ain't true, is it?,'" reported the *St. Paul Pioneer Press*. "Men who gathered at out of the way places, hardened men who have seen death before, who have seen their pals go by the hand of the gangster, spoke in hushed voices, punctuated now and then by threats of vengeance."[22]

Uppermost in their minds was this question: With Hogan gone, who could ensure that the corrupt legacy of Chief John O'Connor would continue, and that gangland peace would reign in the mob's capital city?

2   'A Haven for Criminals'

Old St. Paul Police Headquarters
110 West Third Street (now Kellogg Boulevard)
near Washington Street, St. Paul

Among tourists visiting Minnesota in the 1920s, St. Paul evoked images of a gracious metropolis built by railroad barons like James J. Hill, with Victorian mansions spread along Summit Avenue and around Irvine Park, near the rolling beauty of the Mississippi River. But the FBI saw the city as a refuge for gamblers, kidnappers, jewel thieves, and bank robbers who were protected by corrupt local police and politicians.

"This city was a haven for criminals," wrote an FBI agent in a 1934 briefing on crime conditions. "The citizenry knew it, the hoodlums knew it, and every police officer in the city knew. Hoodlums from the entire United States knew that they could come into St. Paul, make their presence known to the Chief of Police, and stay here with immunity, provided that they committed no crimes in the city. Everytime they moved they notified the police department. Other cities could try in vain to extradite or remove criminals from St. Paul."[23]

Bill Greer, a St. Paul crime reporter, explained how criminals and the police collaborated: "Usually you got off the train and there was a policeman at the depot who could recognize every face in crime. He'd say, 'If you're gonna stay here, you'd better go up and see so and so. . . .' We were going to have a clean town, even though they had some dirty birds living in it." Mobsters from Chicago would arrive at the depot with gold watches and chains in hand, ready to trade the jewelry for protection from the police.[24]

The architect of this system of crime containment was John J. "the Big Fellow" O'Connor, who supervised his underworld from police headquarters. Born in Louisville, Kentucky, to Irish immigrant parents in 1855, O'Connor moved to St. Paul in 1857 with his father, politician "Honest John" O'Connor. After a ten-year apprenticeship in the grocery business, the younger O'Connor joined the police, rising from the rank of detective in 1881 to serve as chief for nearly eighteen years (from 1900 to his resignation in 1912, and again from 1914 to his

Old St. Paul Police headquarters during Chief John J. O'Connor's administration; gold police badge presented to O'Connor, Christmas 1900

final resignation in 1920). A horse-racing fan who bet tens of thousands of dollars on a single race, O'Connor had a terrific memory, an obsessive dislike of barbershops and movie theaters, a taciturn personality, a massive physique, and an unhappy marriage. (His wife, Annie, divorced him in 1922 on charges of cruelty.)[25]

O'Connor devised his own system of dealing with the underworld. "If they behaved themselves, I let them alone," he admitted. "If they didn't, I got them. Under other administrations there were as many thieves here as when I was chief, and they pillaged and robbed; I chose the lesser of two evils." The police department's official 1904 souvenir book boasted that "thieves and criminals respect" Chief O'Connor. "When they are in the city they choose to retain him as their friend, and to do so avoid committing acts which will not only make him their enemy, but will be sure to result in their falling into the hands of the 'Big Boy,' as they familiarly call him." As a result of O'Connor's methods, the souvenir book proclaimed, "never in the history of St. Paul has human life and the property of citizens been so safe, and the virtue of women so assured."[26]

Cementing the chief's power was his relationship with his brother, Democratic party boss and former city alderman Richard T. "the Cardinal" O'Connor, who had much the same philosophy toward crime. "Gambling, which was rampant, was not subject to graft" under alderman O'Connor, according to the *St. Paul Daily News*. "Every game was run on the square and frequently visited by the best citizens and looked upon in the same spirit as it is today in our best clubs."[27]

The original go-between for Chief O'Connor, before Dan Hogan's reign in the late 1920s, was a crimson-haired character from New York named William H. "Reddy" Griffin. Born of Irish immigrant parents in 1848, Griffin —a "jeweler" by trade—lived with his daughter and his wife, Cora, in the Elmwood Apartments on prestigious Summit Avenue. Griffin held court during the early 1900s at the Hotel Savoy at 420 Minnesota Street, a gamblers' hangout in downtown St. Paul. (The Hotel Savoy site—near the corner of Seventh Place and Minnesota Street—is now occupied by the Bremer Tower and Metropolitan Building.)[28]

Griffin was responsible for collecting money from the brothels and gambling dens along St. Peter, Hill, and Washington Streets and bringing the crisp green tributes to O'Connor's police station. Through his friendship with O'Connor, Griffin would get visiting crooks inexpensive rooms along Wabasha Street and ensure that criminals checked in at police headquarters within twelve hours of their arrival.

"It was even rumored that pickpockets held practice sessions at the Savoy," wrote a St. Paul reporter. "They'd work on each other. The conmen gilded their bricks there. The yeggs mixed their 'soup'"—the safecrackers mixed their explosives.[29]

By 1912 Griffin had moved his St. Paul office to 14 West Sixth Street (adjacent to today's Garrick parking ramp). Griffin survived at least one underworld shootout, only to die of apoplexy in 1913 at the age of sixty-five in Shakopee, Minnesota, en route to the Mudcura Sanitarium.[30] Dan Hogan took his place as the mob's liaison with Chief O'Connor.

One newspaper noted that O'Connor "was criticized for his methods, the old school kind, by which he kept track of crooks. His enemies charged that he made St. Paul a refuge for crooks, allowing them to stay here and escape arrest as long as they did not commit crimes in this city." O'Connor responded to his critics by insisting that St. Paul was better off if his officers forced criminals to police themselves: "When a man knows that I know who and where he is, and that I can put my finger on him if I want him, he has every reason to behave himself."[31]

Yet the O'Connor system, while it reduced bank robberies and other major crimes during the 1920s, fostered an atmosphere that encouraged open gambling and prostitution. Former St. Paul police officer David Morgan recalled the days when his grandfather, the Reverend David Morgan, ran a downtown St. Paul mission during O'Connor's years as chief: "My grandfather was preaching against the wide open town of St. Paul, and especially preaching about those girls in the whorehouses." Chief O'Connor tried to strike a deal to get Reverend Morgan to ease off on his attacks on the St. Paul brothels, explaining that the men using them were from northern Minnesota, where there were no women. Morgan countered that he would stop preaching against sinful St. Paul if the women stopped walking the streets, kept to the brothels, and turned off their red lights.

A year later, Morgan noticed that the red lights were back on and the women were back on the sidewalks. He stormed up to O'Connor's office at police headquarters, charging him with failing to keep his side of the bargain. "I bet you a gold watch, Reverend, that the girls are *not* back on the street," scoffed the chief. To settle the issue, they stepped outside. The first woman they walked up to propositioned them both. "That Christmas, my grandfather received a large railroad watch," laughed Morgan's grandson. "Engraved on it was 'To Rev. David Morgan from Chief O'Connor, Christmas 1902.' My son, David, still has that watch today."[32]

Controversy dogged O'Connor. In 1910 the Minnesota Federation of Women's Clubs charged that the chief tolerated open dice games at cigar stands throughout St. Paul. (O'Connor replied that "women should attend to their own business in their homes.") An official with the Law Enforcement League sought to have O'Connor fired as police chief for failing to pursue liquor law violators. ("Tell your paper that if a _____ like that can put me out of office, I'll leave the city," O'Connor responded to the *St. Paul Dispatch*). Minneapolis mayor Wallace Nye charged in 1916 that police were unable to stem crime in his city because St. Paul under O'Connor had become a haven for crooks.[33]

New York columnist Westbrook Pegler first brought the O'Connor system to national attention, wryly noting that New York and Chicago would not be bothered by the reputation St. Paul had developed, since "those two cities have been called sinkholes of sin for many years and they have learned to take it, and even like it." Pegler told of the day when Detective Tommy Horn, O'Connor's watchdog on the St. Paul underworld, recognized a visiting pickpocket in Hogan's Green Lantern saloon. Horn asked the pickpocket if he had checked in with O'Connor. Not yet, said the pickpocket—he had just gotten off the train and stopped for a drink. Would Horn join him? The detective and the pickpocket had a drink together and then prepared to leave: "At the door, the visiting pickpocket turned and said mischievously, 'I am on my way, Tommy, and I seem to have your stickpin.' 'Yes,' said Detective Horn, 'I saw you. And you can keep it because it is a phony. And, anyway, I have got your watch.'"

Pegler noted that criminals who violated the O'Connor system would be locked in an office alone with Chief O'Connor. Minutes later, the hoodlums would limp out, savagely beaten. O'Connor, said Pegler, "took great pride in the fact that all this police work of his was done by hand." FBI director J. Edgar Hoover sent this Pegler column to the U.S. attorney general, noting soberly that although the article was meant to be humorous, it might furnish information on organized crime in St. Paul.[34]

Chief O'Connor did not mind if St. Paul's resident felons robbed banks in Minneapolis, kidnapped businessmen in Duluth, or burglarized safes in neighboring Iowa. His job was to keep the streets of St. Paul safe, regardless of the consequences for neighboring cities and states. Both FBI and Prohibition Bureau files suggest that until at least 1931, major criminals did restrict their felonious activity to areas outside St. Paul.

Lesser crimes were controlled by the system, too. After all, why should St. Paul gangsters tolerate a wave of purse snatchings downtown when the resulting uproar could jeopardize next week's $160,000 railroad robbery in South Dakota? "I often heard stories about some ambitious young man who would go out and snatch an old lady's purse on the street," reporter Bill Greer recalled. "Within a few hours . . . one or two rather determined gentlemen [would] walk up beside him and say, 'Son, we believe we'd better teach you some manners.' . . . It was a safer town to live in for most people when you had the criminals making sure that there was no crime."[35]

Police officer David Morgan witnessed an example of the mob's self-policing when he helped investigate a bank robbery in St. Paul's Midway area during the early 1930s. A policeman met with racketeer Leon Gleckman at the Hotel St. Paul and told him, "We're living up to the agreement, but you're not living up to your side." The bank robber was turned over to the police the next morning, ready to accept his punishment. "The gangsters," laughed Morgan, "didn't want the heat."[36]

O'Connor died in 1924 at the age of sixty-eight, from what newspapers termed "general ill health and the infirmities of age." Almost four thousand people attended his funeral at the St. Paul Cathedral, and local newspapers applauded his methods of crime prevention. "If it be said that Chief O'Connor's methods were those of a bygone day," wrote the *St. Paul Pioneer Press*, "the fact remains that they generally accomplished results." As long as the criminals "were on their good behavior, they were not molested. . . . And when they transgressed his unwritten rules, they could not escape him."[37]

Frank Sommers, a former Wisconsin city detective, succeeded O'Connor as chief and maintained O'Connor's system of crime containment. A scandal over Sommers's "vice investigations" forced him to resign. The chief had sent police to raid fifty-five gambling dens, brothels, and moonshine houses but reported that at thirty-five of the sites, no illegal activity could be found. Yet in parallel investigations, federal agents found ample evidence of lawbreaking at the same locations "raided" by Sommers's men. Justice Department files claimed that after Sommers's resignation he became a consultant to Dan Hogan's crime gang and provided Hogan's thieves with top-level protection through federal officials who could "fix" Prohibition cases.[38]

Chief O'Connor's legacy—the bribed police, compromised U.S. attorneys, corrupt judges, and network of fences for stolen property—laid the foundation that attracted the John Dillinger and Barker-Karpis gangs to St. Paul in the 1930s.

"St. Paul has been a sanctuary for the underworld long enough," complained one newspaper. "Do the police run this town, or do the gamblers, bootleggers, gunmen and other racketeers?"[39] Government records suggest that under Danny Hogan and John O'Connor, *both* did. Few members of that underworld flourished as profitably as Nina Clifford, the city's most acclaimed madam.

3 'A Very Respectable Brothel'

Nina Clifford's Brothel and Home
147 and 145 South Washington Street, St. Paul

The intertwining of St. Paul's underworld and overworld was most obvious between the sheets at Nina Clifford's brothel. "The story went that there were three important people in St. Paul," said reporter Fred Heaberlin, who was a teenager during Clifford's heyday. "They were James J. Hill, Archbishop John Ireland, and Nina Clifford."[40]

From the late 1880s through the 1920s, Nina's two-story brick mansion reigned as the most elegant house of sin in St. Paul. "In my younger days," recalled veteran St. Paul police officer Pat Lannon Sr., "Nina ran a very respectable brothel, just down below the police station. She was given some immunity. Nina didn't do anything to upset the apple cart—that is, she didn't do anything against the wishes of the police and the other powers that be. There was a lot overlooked." Clifford's house was well kept but not expensive, recalled Lannon. "Anyone was welcome at Nina's who had the bucks— their charges weren't exorbitant, not like some of these flash places."[41]

Clifford was born Hannah Crowe in Ontario in 1851 to British-Irish parents, Patrick and Ann Crowe. The Crowe family emigrated to the United States when Hannah was nine. She later married Conrad Steinbrecher, was widowed, and moved to St. Paul after her mother died in 1886. Hannah Steinbrecher, who lived on Cedar Street close by Third, a few doors down from the old Minnesota Club (located then at the southeast end of Fourth and Cedar), adopted the name Nina Clifford.[42]

In 1888 Clifford built her three-story brick-and-stone brothel at 147 Washington for a cost of $12,000. She lived next door, at 145 Washington. On her 1888 building permit, she described the purpose of the brothel building as "dwelling house"; a wag scribbled in the words "and seminary."[43]

The "vice districts" of St. Paul had moved away from the Fifth Street houses between Sibley and Cedar Streets toward the Hill and Washington Street district of Nina Clifford. The cheaper flophouses stretched along the 300 and 700 blocks of St. Peter and Wabasha. City plat maps openly refer to the Washington Street area as "female boarding houses," and prostitutes were identified in census records as "sports," "boarders," or "prostitutes."[44]

Clifford's brothel was built directly below the central police station and just across the street from the old county morgue at 164 Washington Street (where, legend has it, the prostitutes could get low-cost checks for venereal disease). Down the street was the infamous Bucket of Blood saloon and Mamie Porter's Chicken Shack, which offered butter-fried chicken to the men recovering from the Hill Street brothels.[45]

By the year 1900, census records show, Clifford's brothel—with nine prostitutes ranging in age from eighteen to thirty-eight, a cook, a Norwegian housekeeper, three chambermaids, a male porter, and a Scottish musician—was thriving. The women came from England, Scotland, Arizona, New York, and Michigan.[46]

Former St. Paul police officer and cab driver David Morgan remembered that Clifford hired Blue and White taxis to drive the women who worked for her to Lake McCarron beach, first warning them not to sunburn their backs. Unlike the grim brothels along St. Peter Street, which were little more than second-story flophouses with mattresses, Nina Clifford's was an establishment, offering its customers such amenities as a waiting room furnished with lounges.[47]

Arthur Sundberg, who as a fifteen-year-old delivered dresses to the house from Atkinson's store, recounted to St. Paul newsman Gareth Hiebert just how elegant the brothel was:

> The public area downstairs . . . was all carpeted in the finest deep pile. Nina's office . . . was a beautiful large room with a wide, marble fireplace. . . . To the rear of the office was another large room . . . [with a] polished dance floor, lined with chairs and always someone playing piano. . . . All manner of drinks were available, provided by well-dressed help. . . . It was here that the visitors met the girls. . . .
>
> One day, when I was there delivering dresses, she called me to her

desk and opened a cigar box. In it were several hundred unset diamonds . . . no small ones. . . . She also had a dozen or more diamond rings with identification tags on each.

These were all stones that had been left as security for various obligations. Most of them were left by Westerners, cattlemen, miners and lumbermen, who had come to St. Paul on business and looking for big city pleasures which proved to be too much for their purses.

Sundberg claimed that Clifford would twist the stones out of the rings and throw the settings off the High Bridge into the Mississippi River so the stones could not be identified.[48]

"Nina Clifford has such a flourishing business at her rooming house . . . that it is necessary for her to maintain two phones," noted Police Chief Frank Sommers in a 1923 letter to the public safety commissioner. Although his officers were unable to enter the brothel, Sommers assured the commissioner that the madam "has a maid and a housekeeper there, but . . . there are no other girls living there."[49]

Such official protection helped guarantee the safety of Clifford's patrons, by legend the most prominent businessmen of her era. In turn, Clifford's women were exquisitely dressed when they rode down Summit Avenue on Sundays and visited the Metropolitan Theater for musical performances.[50]

Howard Guilford, editor of the *Twin City Reporter*, an anti-Semitic scandal sheet, was determined to puncture the women's respectability. In his florid 1920s exposé of Twin Cities brothels, *Holies of Holies of the White Slave Worshipper*, Guilford condemned the "pimps, procurers, white slavers, and bawdy house property owners" by name and identified each brothel. Guilford specifically attacked Clifford—"Nina Clifford is only an alias for a Jew name which is almost unpronounceable"—and described her brothel: "Expensive draperies and trappings are festooned from the walls, and imported rugs are on the floor."[51]

The legends of Nina Clifford are legion: how she adopted homeless women until they got back on their feet, how the sons of St. Paul's wealthy families came of age at Nina's.[52]

Clifford died of a stroke, three weeks short of her seventy-eighth birthday, during a visit to Detroit in July 1929. After a $490 funeral at St. Catherine's Church, she was buried beside her mother in Detroit's Mt. Elliott Cemetery.[53]

Her death was front-page news in St. Paul. The *Daily News* hailed her as "the queen of St. Paul's demi-monde," while the rival *Pioneer Press* referred to her as "a prominent figure in St. Paul's underworld," calling her brothel an "underworld resort."[54]

More than thirty-one relatives from Detroit, Omaha, and Seattle were listed in the probate petition for a piece of what newspapers referred to as Clifford's "large fortune," but all that was left of her estate for the Ramsey County probate court to verify were two fur coats worth a total of $150, $500 in household furniture, and the $8,800 real estate value of her brothel. It was rumored that Clifford gave her wealth to an adopted daughter that she put through an elegant eastern boarding school, while probate records suggest that Clifford invested her money back in Michigan: her Detroit estate included more than 133,000 shares of stock in a variety of gold and copper mines.[55]

Journalist Fred Heaberlin, who lamented that "everybody seems to have known Nina Clifford, except for me," told of a legendary prank on the day of the madam's death: "When word got around that Nina Clifford had died in Detroit, a bunch of movers and shakers who used to have fun together rented a room at the Lowry Hotel to . . . [play] practical jokes." The pranksters called St. Paul's most eminent politicians, attorneys, and businessmen (including Roy Dunlap, Heaberlin's managing editor) to inform them sadly that Clifford had passed away. But in her will, each victim was told, Clifford specified that he should be one of the pallbearers at her funeral. Those who caught on to the joke promptly joined the group at the Lowry Hotel for more phone calls to unwary pallbearers. "The fictional part of the story is that the night trains to Chicago were filled with prominent businesspeople who did not want to be pallbearers at Nina Clifford's funeral," Heaberlin said.[56]

Immediately after Clifford's death, claims one source familiar with St. Paul's underworld, Minneapolis gangster Isadore "Kid Cann" Blumenfeld installed his own girlfriend to operate the brothel. City directories indicate that one Lillian Lee, "saleswoman," ran it from 1931 through 1934.[57]

In the summer of 1933, Clifford's heirs, hoping to open a nightclub in her house, tried unsuccessfully to get a restaurant license for her 147 Washington property. Police Chief Thomas E. Dahill, the Guild of Catholic Women, and Mayor William Mahoney vigorously opposed reopening Nina's as a nightclub. In 1936 the house was put up for auction; the next year, St. Paul's most famous brothel was condemned and razed. The curious scavenged bricks from Clifford's house, and her doorknob and bell were salvaged by a Ramsey County engineer.[58]

Long after the destruction of Clifford's house, rumors persisted that the Minnesota Club, at 317 Washington Street, was connected by an underground tunnel extending from the club's basement to Clifford's back door, barely a block away. An underground passage extending from the Minnesota

Club to the site of what once was Clifford's brothel does exist. St. Paul utility maps document a six-foot-high water tunnel stretching from the basement of the Minnesota Club to within a hundred feet of what was once Clifford's back door. (One can still see the New Hill Street entrance to the tunnel just under Kellogg Boulevard, across from the Ramsey County medical examiner's office.)[59]

The Minnesota Club has continued to fan the flames of its connection with Nina Clifford. A portrait of a woman identified as Clifford hangs on the Washington Street wall of the club's main bar, the oval frame enclosing a demure, black-haired beauty in a silver-gray dress. The painting was donated to the club in 1980 through the efforts of *St. Paul Dispatch* columnist Gareth Hiebert.[60]

In the hallway outside the bar is a framed photograph of the first Minnesota Club, on Cedar Street, with a caption noting the apartment where Nina Clifford lived from 1887 to 1889. Attached to a red-brown brick allegedly salvaged from the ruins of Clifford's brothel is a plaque that reads: "This brick from Nina Clifford's house is presented to the Gentlemen of the Minnesota Club for their great interest in historic buildings."[61]

Legendary portrait of "Nina Clifford" hanging in St. Paul's Minnesota Club

4 'I Am Sure There Will Be Justice'

Dan Hogan's Final Resting Place
Calvary Cemetery, 753 Front Avenue, St. Paul

The bomb that killed Danny Hogan in 1928 failed to upset the corrupt traditions of the O'Connor system, the heritage of cooperation between police and the gangsters, gamblers, and madams of St. Paul.

More than three thousand mourners paid tribute before Hogan's casket at the O'Halloran and Murphy funeral home. Hogan's coffin and his grave were bedecked with five thousand dollars' worth of lilies, roses, and gold and white chrysanthemums sent by underworld friends in New York, Chicago, and the Twin Cities.[62]

"Hogan had one of the grandest funerals ever staged in St. Paul—the Chicago gangland-type funeral, with huge masses of flowers and a funeral mass at St. Mary's," reporter Fred Heaberlin recalled. "Somehow, one would rather be in Mr. Hogan's place than [in] that of his murderers," preached Father Nicholas J. Finn. Police detectives flooded the church as mobsters and businesspeople paid their last respects.[63]

"I am sure there will be justice," said Hogan's widow, Leila. "If Danny had lived, he would have gone on the one leg they left him and would have taken care of it himself."[64]

As if in tribute, the St. Paul underworld briefly went dark: slot machines were removed, brothels were demurely closed, gambling dens were emptied. George "Bugs" Moran, the Minnesota-born rival to Al Capone and a friend of Hogan, was seen pacing back and forth in front of Hogan's West Seventh Street residence, apparently to protect the Hogan family from further underworld attacks.[65]

Dan Hogan's grave is in Calvary Cemetery, on the north end of St. Paul. Two other architects of the O'Connor system—William Griffin and Chief John O'Connor—lie nearby. A cemetery staff member says that one of O'Connor's relatives visits to leave the chief a pint of Irish whiskey.[66]

A five-inch portion of the bell wire that connected the bomb to the starter of Hogan's car can be seen today—by special appointment—in the St. Paul Police Department's history exhibit at 110 East Eleventh Street. Although the police had this evidence, the investigation sputtered and Hogan's assassin or assassins were never caught.

"I don't believe the police *made* an attempt to find out who killed Dan Hogan," said retired officer Pat Lannon Sr., who joined the force the year that Dan Hogan was slain. "There were people who had a reason to do it, and the other people figured it was good riddance to eliminate a bad influence!"[67]

"I don't know who could have done it," protested Hogan on his deathbed. "I didn't know I had an enemy in the world." The underworld seethed with theories. "Mr. Hogan always told me everything with which he was connected in the Twin Cities," his widow told the *Minneapolis Tribune*. "He had no serious quarrels with anyone here. He had eastern connections though, which I didn't know much about."[68]

Many suggested that the bomb was long-distance vengeance from the East Coast syndicate. Perhaps the mob held Hogan responsible for the sawed-off pistol—traced to a St. Paul sporting goods store—that had been used to kill gambler Arnold "the Brain" Rothstein in New York one month earlier. If Rothstein's murder had been planned in St. Paul, New York gangsters could have concluded that Hogan must have known about it.[69]

"Uncle Danny knew who had killed him, but he'd never tell his family, because he was afraid the gangsters would come after *us*," said Hogan's niece, Ann Michaud. "Dan Hogan ruled the roost in St. Paul. When my uncle Danny was blown up, we learned that he'd told these small-time gangsters from Chicago that they could not rob a bank in St. Paul. He wanted to keep the worst element out of St. Paul, so it wouldn't attract attention!"

The most credible murder suspect would have to be Hogan's own underworld protégé, Harry "Dutch" Sawyer, a Nebraska butcher's son who had served as Hogan's assistant in fencing jewelry and other stolen goods at the Green Lantern saloon. Before his death, Hogan had told his wife that he had put $50,000 in a safe deposit box for her. Only two men had keys to the box—Dan Hogan and Harry Sawyer. When Hogan was killed, "Aunt Lee went to the bank and the money was all gone," recalled Michaud. "Harry Sawyer cleaned out his safe deposit box. I'm surprised that my uncle even gave Harry the key!"[70]

Daniel "Dapper Dan" Hogan

Sawyer felt that he had reason to be bitter about his mentor. Years later, Sawyer's wife, Gladys Rita Sawyer, told FBI agents that when Hogan was arrested for participating in the 1924 robbery of the South St. Paul Post Office, Sawyer raised the $100,000 bond. She said her husband personally furnished $25,000 of this bond. She continued that Hogan "jipped Harry out of this $25,000."[71]

Gladys Sawyer also claimed that Hogan had cheated her husband of his cut from the Hollywood Inn gambling casino in Mendota. "Some years ago Harry Sawyer, Danny Hogan, Fred Ulrich and Red Clare were jointly associated in the operation of a gambling place known as 'Hollywood Inn' near St. Paul," an FBI interviewer noted. Gladys Sawyer told the FBI that "Harry was jipped out of his share of a $36,000.00 cut through the operation of this place by Danny Hogan."[72]

Woody Keljik, a tour guide and historian for the old Federal Courts Building (now Landmark Center) who has studied St. Paul's gangster era, has no doubts about who killed Hogan. "When Dapper Danny Hogan was running the Green Lantern, it was a very profitable place," said Keljik. "The boys came here and instead of putting their money in the bank, they trusted Dan to leave it with him in the Green Lantern safe. Then a guy named Harry Sawyer, a small hood from Omaha, came to St. Paul under the O'Connor system, and Harry coveted the Green Lantern. Sawyer's the guy who fixed the car on Seventh Street with the bomb. Dapper Dan went to gangster heaven, and Harry Sawyer got the Green Lantern."[73]

Dan Hogan was a rarity in the 1920s underworld, a mob peacekeeper with as much clout at police headquarters as in the underworld. From the Green Lantern, Hogan could arbitrate disputes between competing gangs and cool violent tempers in a city jammed with alumni from the country's major prisons.

When Hogan died, Harry Sawyer inherited both the Green Lantern and control of the O'Connor system. In time, Sawyer's friends from across the

CITY OF ST. PAUL, MINN.

DEPARTMENT OF PUBLIC SAFETY—BUREAU OF HEALTH—DIVISION OF VITAL STATISTICS

CERTIFICATE OF DEATH

PLACE OF DEATH....St..Paul..Hospital.....

2881

If death occurred in a hospital or institution, give the NAME instead of street and number.

1 FULL NAME ....Daniel Hogan...... NO............

(2) Residence. No.........1607 W..7th.St..........St.... O' ....Ward............
(Usual place of abode) (If non-resident, give City or Town or State)

Length of residence in city or town where death occurred 13 yrs. mos. ds. How long in U. S., if of foreign birth? yrs. mos. ds.

PERSONAL AND STATISTICAL PARTICULARS	MEDICAL CERTIFICATE OF DEATH
3 SEX Male **4 COLOR or RACE** White **5 Single, Married, Widowed or Divorced (Write the Word)** Married	**16 DATE OF DEATH** (month, day, and year) December 4, 1928
5a If Married, Widowed or Divorced HUSBAND of (or) WIFE of Jane Hardy	**17** I HEREBY CERTIFY, That I attended deceased from ....19.... to.................19.... that I last saw h.... alive on the date stated above, at......m.
6 DATE OF BIRTH (month, day and year) Unknown 1880	The CAUSE OF DEATH was as follows: Multiple injuries - shock right leg torn off 183
7 AGE Years About 48 Months Days If Less than 1 day...hrs. or .....min.	........duration, ...years ....mos. ....ds.
8 OCCUPATION OF DECEASED (a) Trade, Profession or particular kind of work....Restaurant Prop. (b) General nature of industry, business or establishment in which employed (or employer)............ (c) Name of employer............	CONTRIBUTORY caused by bomb in automo- (Secondary) bile ....duration........years ....mos. ....ds. 18 Where was disease contracted, if not a place of death?
9 BIRTHPLACE (city or town) (State or country) California	Did an operation precede death?....yes.. Date 12-4-28 Was there an autopsy? no
10 NAME OF FATHER Daniel Hogan	What test confirmed diagnosis?................
11 BIRTHPLACE OF FATHER (city or town) (State or country) Unknown	(SIGNED) C.A.Ingerson,Coroner.....M. D. ....19...... (Address) M.J.Leonard,Dep..
12 MAIDEN NAME OF MOTHER Unknown	
13 BIRTHPLACE OF MOTHER (city or town) (State or country) Ireland	*State the Disease Causing Death, or in deaths from Violent Causes, state (1) Means and Nature of Injury, and (2) whether Accidental, Suicidal or Homicidal. (See reverse side for additional space.)
14 Informant (Address) Mrs. Jane Hogan (wife) 1607 W. 7th St.	**19 PLACE OF BURIAL, CREMATION, OR REMOVAL** Calvary Cemetery **DATE OF BURIAL** 12-7-28 19....
15 Filed 12-5-28 19. 64461 Registrar.	**20 UNDERTAKER** O'Halloran & Murphy **ADDRESS** St. Paul

Certified to be a true and correct copy of the record on file with the Division of Public Health, City of St. Paul, Minnesota.

Alterations shown made under authority of Minnesota Statute 144.172, and Regulations of State Board of Health.

(Signed) _____ , this __18__ day of __June__ 19_82_.

Deputy Registrar, Vital Statistics

Dan Hogan's death certificate

country—public enemies like John Dillinger, Alvin Karpis, and Fred and Doc Barker—would be drawn to St. Paul, free to begin a five-year crime wave that might have appalled Hogan.

Sawyer had been a petty thief and bootlegger throughout the 1920s. Now, with the coming of Prohibition, Sawyer, like so many other hoodlums, was transformed from a small-time grifter into an underworld potentate.

Hogan's bombed Paige coupe with blown-out windows and cloth roof

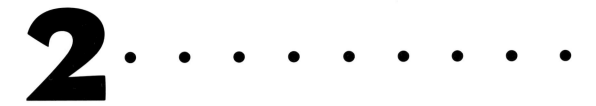

2

THE BOTTLING OF FORBIDDEN FRUIT

Moonshiners Florence Friermuth (at left) and Susie Friermuth Duffing after a 1921 liquor raid; Minnesota Congressman Andrew Volstead, author of the national Prohibition law

5 'Blind Pigs, Beer Flats, and Brothels'

Andrew Volstead's Prohibition Bureau
Old Federal Courts Building
75 West Fifth Street, St. Paul

"On Tuesday next the United States will go 'dry'—the first great nation to undertake this stupendous experiment in behalf of public morals," proclaimed the *St. Paul Pioneer Press* in 1919, in a burst of Prohibition-era optimism. "It has been the experience of those cities which have tried prohibition that crime—petty crime, that is—declines under a dry regime," the article went on. "The probabilities are, however, that little by little everybody will become accustomed to the new order. . . . The best thing for the United States to do is to forget as quickly as possible that it ever enjoyed the stimulation of alcohol."[1]

The naiveté now sounds quaint: in fact, the passage of Prohibition nourished the explosive growth of organized crime in every major city in the United States, turning the trickle of bribes to public officials into a torrent of political corruption. Small-time bootleggers like St. Paul's Jack Peifer, Harry Sawyer, and Leon Gleckman were elevated by Prohibition profits into power brokers who could fix a grand jury, buy off a judge, sheriff, or prosecuting attorney, secure a governor's pardon for a convict, and ensure the appointment of a lenient police chief.

The criminals who later hid out in St. Paul—robbers George "Machine Gun Kelly" Barnes, Alvin "Creepy" Karpis, Lester "Babyface Nelson" Gillis, Harvey Bailey, Frank "Jelly" Nash, Verne Miller, and John "Three Fingered Jack" Hamilton—were initiated into crime and civic corruption through the bootleg liquor trade. "Bootlegging was one of the few crimes in history condoned by the people, ignored by the law, and guaranteed to yield fabulous profit with a minimum of grief," concluded crime writer Dean Jennings. "It made millionaires out of illiterates, heroes out of homicidal Robin Hoods, and corrupt public figures out of honest men."[2]

The Volstead Act, passed by Congress in 1919 over the veto of President Woodrow Wilson, provided for enforcement of the Eighteenth Amendment —Prohibition. The act was named after its author, Republican congressman Andrew John Volstead of Granite Falls, Minnesota. Later appointed special counsel to the Prohibition Bureau at its St. Paul headquarters, Volstead drafted indictments against bootleggers from his office in the old Federal Courts Building.

"In 1925, Mr. Volstead was 65 years old," Prohibition Bureau clerk Helen Warren Pfleger recalled. "He was a dignified gentleman, quiet and unassuming, but most affable. . . . He had been a country lawyer before he became a congressman and was far from the 'hail-fellow, well-met' back-slapping type of politician. . . . I wonder how many of the thousands of persons who passed by Mr. Volstead on the streets of downtown St. Paul recognized him. I don't imagine many did, although his name was well-known all over the world."[3]

Ironically, Volstead's home state was uniquely positioned for maximum participation in the bootlegging industry that resulted from the legislation that bore his name. Because St. Paul was a major railroad center, it was easy for the city's bootleggers to export and import liquor disguised as "timber" or "kerosene." By sheer geographical good fortune, the hundreds of miles of wilderness in northern Minnesota and Canada provided an unpoliceable border for liquor smugglers. Prohibition agents said that every week they stopped about two thousand quarts of liquor from being smuggled across the Ontario-Minnesota line into northern Minnesota or from Manitoba into Bemidji.[4]

The German immigrants who came to the state in the 1800s had used its ample fresh water to found more than a hundred breweries; in 1887 Minnesota was the fifth largest beer-producing state in the country. During Prohibition, at least one major brewery—Schmidt—continued to produce limited quantities of illicit alcohol for sale in speakeasies, although it pretended to be making only soft drinks and nonalcoholic "near beer." In one five-month period in the 1920s, Northwest-area Prohibition agents confiscated 240,569 gallons of moonshine, seized more than fifty automobiles, destroyed 315 stills, and arrested 1,275 people. Minnesota's U.S. marshal made more than a thousand arrests for Prohibition offenses in 1920—a figure that did not include local arrests of bootlegging grocers, cab drivers, railroad cooks and Pullman porters, farmers, drugstore retailers, bartenders, and saloon keepers.[5]

"You could buy it if you knew a druggist. . . . They made their own gin and you could buy it in any drugstore," recalled St. Paul crime reporter Nate Bomberg. "And there were speakeasies and apartment houses where after hours you could buy a bottle and drink all night. . . . In fact, it was a joke. People didn't look down on Prohibition. . . . Forbidden fruit is the sweetest."[6]

Prohibition agents tried to uncover home breweries—hidden in outhouses and basements—by tracking deliveries of the oak chips used to color whiskey. "There will be moon," predicted St. Paul police chief Michael Gebhardt in 1922, "as long as the moon shines and people are just beginning to realize how many persons know how to make it." Gebhardt estimated that 75 percent of St. Paul citizens were distilling moonshine or making wine.[7]

The three dozen agents assigned to Minnesota were overwhelmed: in his *Plain Talk* magazine, crusading reporter Walter Liggett claimed that Minnesota harbored ten thousand bootleggers. The official Prohibition Survey of Minnesota winced over Liggett's charges that the state "is dripping wet; that speak-easies, blind pigs, beer flats, and brothels flourish in abundance . . . that gambling joints operate without fear of molestation; and that police and other local officers protect the bootlegger, the gambler, and the prostitute."[8]

The bootleggers of the 1920s were treated as outlaw folk heroes and tolerated by the wealthiest families. For Minnesota's society matrons and businessmen, the liquor baron of choice was Benny Haskell, who sold fine champagne, scotch, and gin out of the Radisson Hotel in Minneapolis. The Justice Department reported that Haskell catered "to a most exclusive clientele of prominent business and professional people in Minneapolis, St. Paul, and Winona, Minnesota."[9]

Opposing the moonshiners were Prohibition agents with a style reminiscent of the marshals who had patrolled the Wild West. St. Paul had Joseph "Two Gun" Alberts, who shot revolvers out of the hands of bootleggers, Malachi (Mel) Harney, who later helped put Al Capone in prison for tax evasion, and Maurice Silverman, who barely escaped death in 1930 after discovering a moonshine still near Robbinsdale, Minnesota. Attempting to arrest the bootleggers, Silverman jumped onto the running board of their getaway car and grabbed the steering wheel, oblivious to the shots the bootleggers fired at him.[10]

Machine guns were not the only hazard Prohibition agents faced during raids. "The life of a Prohibition agent is a demoralizing one due to the fact that he is necessarily and officially bound to consume considerable intoxicating liquor—good and bad, but mostly bad," noted Minneapolis Judge John McGee in a 1924 letter to the U.S. attorney general. "In time he becomes very much as does a criminal lawyer, about as bad morally as the people he operates among and deals with." The judge noted that one Prohibition agent testified to drinking 700 glasses of alcohol and 700 glasses of moonshine whiskey on the job; not surprisingly, dozens of Prohibition cases were dropped when cases fell apart in court.[11]

Meanwhile, the sheer size of distilling operations in Minnesota towns staggered Prohibition agents. In 1921, agents on power boats found moonshine distilleries built on islands in the Mississippi River, with hundreds of gallons of apricot and corn mash hidden under the greenery. They found distilleries hidden in the St. Paul city dump and on farms in Eagan, Mendota, Rosemount, White Bear Lake, New Brighton, Newport, Forest Lake, North St. Paul, and dozens of other communities.[12]

Prohibition inspired bootleggers to new heights of imagination. Gangsters smuggled liquor into Minnesota on railroad cars, disguising the alcohol as scrap iron shipments, hair tonic, castor oil, paint, varnish, "printer's supplies," and even "saddlery." Federal agents found illicit liquor hidden inside steam radiators. In April 1924, federal "dry agents" found a St. Paul bar owner hiding six pints of moonshine whiskey in bottles suspended from her girdle—three pints dangling against each leg.[13]

From stills in Minnesota's Stearns and Morrison Counties sprang a whiskey so popular it had a trade name—Minnesota 13—that came from its chief ingredient, Northern Dent No. 13 corn. Sold to retailers at up to $6.50 a gallon, Minnesota 13 was reportedly tastier than much of the whiskey available legally before Prohibition. "The best moonshine you could buy was made up around St. Cloud; they called it Minnesota 13," recalled Bob Burns, a former club musician. "They made it clean. Some of the moonshine made up in Minneapolis . . . it was so rotten that you'd take the cork out and just the smell of it would make you sick. But you'd hold your nose and gargle it down and throw up a couple of times and try to get some of it to stay down!"[14]

From Wisconsin came shipments of "miniature"—moonshine redistilled for a higher-proof kick. Best of all was 39B, alcohol legally delivered to cosmetics and pharmaceutical companies for hair tonic or perfume. The liquor syndicates diverted the "perfume" for redistillation, after which it become 139-proof "bang-up" liquor sold at up to fifteen dollars a gallon. Much of this imported liquor was spirited into Minneapolis and St. Paul in the railroad cars arriving daily in the Midway "Transfer District." Not surprisingly, some of the state's busiest redistillation factories and speakeasies sprouted along University Avenue in the Midway.[15]

The liquor syndicates discovered that the odoriferous process of creating moonshine from fermenting fruit in a still was inefficient. Instead, they could buy tax-free denatured alcohol from the federal government for "industrial" purposes and then redistill the poisonous mixture for sale to thirsty consumers.[16]

U.S. attorney Lafayette French admitted privately that Minnesota had "become flooded with various forms of specially denatured alcohol under the designation of body rub," thanks to a loophole in the Volstead Act that enabled drugstores in Minneapolis and St. Paul to legally import railroad cars full of Formula 39 "body rub." "Frankly," wrote French, "I believe it is futile to furnish this office with a prosecution broom and ask us to sweep back the sea of body rub which the government, through its permits, allows to come into the district."[17]

One of the more colorful bootleggers in the Midway area was boxer Sammy "the Fighting Tailor" Taran. In 1925 agents raided Taran's distillery at 817 North Wheeler Avenue (a brown-and-cream bungalow that still stands between Hubbard and Hewitt Avenues). The agents claimed that

Dumping illegal liquor at Pillsbury and Charles Streets, St. Paul, about 1925

Taran's distillery was part of a million-dollar alcohol ring that used the bungalow to redistill "body-rub alcohol" into "high-grade whiskey." But the liquid evidence against Taran disappeared: nearly every bottle of the alcohol seized from his home in 1925 was inexplicably destroyed by Prohibition agents. The jury was forced to acquit him of bootlegging charges, a verdict that inspired Judge Hugo Hanft to rail against the agents for failing to preserve the evidence against Taran. The incident reflected the most corrosive by-product of the bootlegging business—the tens of thousands of dollars in protection money required for local police, sheriffs, judges, prosecutors, and even Prohibition agents. The city of St. Paul, with its twenty-year tradition of corruption through the O'Connor system, provided rich soil for Prohibition bribery.[18]

As early as 1920, northwest Prohibition chief Paul D. Keller admitted that bootleggers had been "tipped off" to virtually every major raid he had undertaken in Minnesota during the previous fourteen days, inspiring an investigation of his entire Prohibition staff. In 1926 a liquor baron told Treasury agents that corruption was so complete in St. Paul that a local bootlegger was able to walk freely into the central police station and steal back his own confiscated liquor. Newspapers reported that when federal agents raided bars and distilleries, they found empty warehouses—and were jeered by moonshiners who had been notified that they were coming. It was only years later, when the FBI questioned Dillinger gang girlfriend Beth Green, that the government learned that in the late 1920s, Dan Hogan had installed a woman informant in the Prohibition Bureau in the Federal Courts Building.[19]

Then, on February 16, 1925, the murder of a St. Paul liquor hijacker named Burt Stevens split open the largest liquor conspiracy in the United States. The killing revealed the breadth of corruption extending from the St. Paul Police Department up to the most powerful federal prosecutors in Minnesota.

6   'A Lawless Business Grown to Gigantic Proportions'
The Murder of Burt Stevens
465 St. Peter Street, St. Paul

The *St. Paul Dispatch* described the 1925 slaying of liquor hijacker Burt Stevens and the revelations of corruption that followed as "the most scandalous episode that has ever disgraced these twin communities." The article noted that the scandal was "prohibition in its finest flower—larceny, banditry and murder superimposed upon bribery and violation of the liquor law."[20]

With 112 indictments for Prohibition violations, the Cleveland liquor case that followed the killing of Stevens became the largest liquor conspiracy case in the history of Prohibition. The collapse of the liquor syndicate began when Stevens was shot outside the Dreis Brothers' Drug Store on the southwest corner of the intersection of Seventh (then Ninth) Street and St. Peter, adjacent to what is today Mickey's Diner.

The reasons for the slaying went back to 1923, when St. Paul bootlegger Bennie Gleeman and Harry Gellman, a tailor from Minneapolis, formed the Gleeman-Gellman alcohol ring. Joining these underworld entrepreneurs were poolroom proprietor Morris Roisner, who acted as accountant and office manager; defense attorney Abe Ginsberg, the fixer and political connection; and an up-and-coming liquor mogul named Leon Gleckman, who would become the most powerful syndicate figure in St. Paul. Roisner dreamed up the front names (the Kevin Sweet Grass Developing Company was a poetic one) and rented the ring's headquarters in St. Paul's Builders Exchange Building. The ring began to ship scotch whisky and champagne, disguised as "lubricating oil," in trucks painted with the names of fictitious moving companies.[21]

The rival bootleggers of Minneapolis and St. Paul averted a liquor war by agreeing in 1924 to cooperate in importing liquor. The Minneapolis group, led by Isadore "Kid Cann" Blumenfeld and his friends Abe "Brownie" Brownstein and Edward "Barney" Berman, called themselves "the Minneapolis Combination." The St. Paul bootleggers, whose roster swelled to include Gleeman's brother Abe, now referred to their operation as "the Syndicate." The Syndicate received its liquor through Cleveland, where gangsters purchased denatured grain alcohol legally from the federal government. Organized along the lines of a corporation, the Cleveland liquor ring operated through underworld figures in St. Paul, Duluth, Minneapolis, and dozens of other U.S. cities. The Cleveland ring offered its affiliates protection through the bribery of local police officials and railroad men, warehouses to store the liquor in, and toughs to discourage liquor hijackers.

By the mid-1920s, the St. Paul Syndicate was importing two carloads of Cleveland alcohol a week, producing weekly revenues of between $100,000 and $200,000. With profits of $20,000 a week, the Syndicate decided, according to Bennie Gleeman, to set aside money to buy protection. Gleeman said that a bribery fund of 14 percent of Syndicate profits—nearly $3,000 a week—was turned over to Minnesota law-enforcement officers. One underworld rumor held that in the early 1920s, the Syndicate was paying the chief of the St. Paul police, Frank Sommers, one dollar for every gallon of illegal liquor sold.[22]

The Syndicate demonstrated its influence over local authorities in the winter of 1923–24, when the Prohibition Bureau seized 237 barrels of denatured alcohol from the Syndicate and stored the liquor at the Kedney warehouse in Minneapolis. Unperturbed, the Syndicate simply paid the warehouse clerk a $75-per-barrel bribe. In exchange, the Syndicate was allowed to steal back 170 barrels of its alcohol, replacing the incriminating evidence with tap water.[23]

A local bootlegger, under questioning by assistant U.S. attorney William Anderson, unexpectedly offered to expose the Syndicate members who had stolen back the Kedney liquor. Suddenly, all charges against the Syndicate were dropped, and Anderson ordered the evidence against the Syndicate destroyed. Ben Gleeman later told a grand jury that the Syndicate bribed Anderson to allow the gang to steal the liquor back. Justice Department informants reported that Anderson was taking thousands of dollars from the Syndicate, enabling the modestly paid official to outfit his $30,000 home with expensive oriental rugs and furniture. Anderson left the U.S. attorney's office in 1929 and became defense attorney for Syndicate bootlegger Leon Gleckman.[24]

The Syndicate's most troubling problem was not the police or even Prohibition agents, but the threat posed by hijackers determined to steal the Syndicate's liquor or extort hush money. Two Syndicate enforcers, Tommie

Webber and Morrie Miller, guarded liquor shipments as they were unloaded. In a prophetic aside, Morris Roisner said that they were "such bad men that they would not hesitate to shoot in broad daylight on as thickly a traveled street as Seventh and Wabasha in St. Paul." If Miller had killed one man, Roisner said, he had killed twenty.[25]

In February 1925 members of the Syndicate were at St. Paul's Milwaukee freight yards to load the latest shipment of alcohol. They were surprised by hijacker Burton Stevens, a twenty-two-year-old hoodlum from Chrechtenville, Iowa, and an accomplice. Stevens warned that Prohibition agents had spotted the liquor and would arrest them unless they paid Stevens a protection fee. The Syndicate guessed that Stevens's warning was a hoax, and Miller had to be restrained from killing Stevens on the spot.[26]

Days later, Bennie Gleeman, driving a truck carrying more than seventy-five cases of scotch whisky, found that he was being followed by Stevens. Gleeman confronted Stevens, saying, "You fellows put a scare into us, I thought you were Feds. I have some stuff in the garage, don't touch it."[27]

That afternoon, Stevens called the Syndicate from the Dreis Drug Store in downtown St. Paul. "I heard a couple of Jews are looking for me," he snarled. "Words don't mean anything on the telephone, come on over and see me." Bennie Gleeman and Morrie Miller drove through downtown, where Gleeman spotted Stevens in front of the drugstore. In a confrontation on the street, Stevens and Miller both brandished guns. Miller shouted, "You won't hijack my stuff anymore" and shot Stevens in the head and chest.[28]

The Syndicate assured Gleeman "that they were going to square everything with the Chief of Police in St. Paul and that all I had to do was to keep quiet and not involve anybody in the shooting." Bootlegger Leon Gleckman "had a drag with the St. Paul Police force, [and] would fix everything so that no one would get in trouble," the Syndicate's lawyer assured Gleeman.

The Syndicate shuttled the Gleeman brothers from hideout to hideout, terrified that the ring would be exposed if the police interviewed Bennie. Under pressure from the Syndicate, Abe Gleeman agreed to falsify testimony to protect his brother. As an extra incentive, the gang promised Abe that if he ever exposed the workings of the Syndicate, Morrie Miller would come back to Minnesota and kill him.[29]

Four days after the shooting, the Gleeman brothers turned themselves in. A first trial ended with a deadlocked jury, but in a second trial, in April 1925, with star prosecutor Pierce Butler Jr. at the helm, both Gleemans were found guilty of murder and sentenced to spend their lives in prison. Government prosecutors denied that Miller existed, calling him a "phantom gunman."[30]

The Gleeman brothers, Ben and Abe (at front), with escorts, after being sentenced to life in prison

In September the Gleemans demanded a third trial, filing fifty-six affidavits from eyewitnesses claiming they were innocent and identifying Morrie Miller as the murderer. Abandoned by the liquor ring, the Gleemans decided to split the Syndicate open. They confessed that the St. Paul group was merely a branch of a $140 million alcohol business run out of the Superior Industrial Alcohol Company in Cleveland.[31]

When agents raided Superior Alcohol, they seized 5,865 drums of denatured alcohol, stumbling over evidence that the conspiracy stretched both east and west: to Pittsburgh, Philadelphia, Baltimore, Atlantic City, Detroit, Chicago, St. Paul, Minneapolis, Duluth, and San Francisco. Nearly 900,000 gallons of liquor were distributed to bootleggers across the country each week. Most importantly, the Gleeman trial brought to light the millions of dollars in protection fees paid to corrupt police, railroad staff, and federal agents.[32]

Inspired largely by the Gleemans' confessions, Treasury agents immersed themselves in the Cleveland ring's trail of telegrams, bank transactions, and telephone calls. The government issued a 50,000-word indictment charging more than one hundred defendants with nearly a hundred illegal acts in twelve cities. Ben and Abe Gleeman, under life sentences at Minnesota's Stillwater State Prison, testified before a Cleveland grand jury that indicted more than sixty Minnesota residents tied to the liquor conspiracy. Of the 112 Cleveland liquor case defendants indicted in 1926, an astonishing 41 lived in St. Paul. The chief prosecutor, Cleveland district attorney A. E. Bernstein, called St. Paul "the most flagrant center of the nationwide alcohol ring."[33]

"Here is disclosed amongst us a lawless business grown to positively gigantic proportions," noted the *St. Paul Dispatch*. "According to the Gleemans, it ran in money to something like $200,000 a week, or approximately $10,000,000 a year. This is about as much money as is spent annually by the city of St. Paul." Unsympathetic to the Gleemans' claims that they had been framed, the *Dispatch* declared that if "they are not properly in the penitentiary for murder, by their own confessions they ought to be there for a variety of other crimes. . . . They are behind prison walls and that is surely where they belong."[34]

Throughout the Gleemans' trials, there were barely hidden overtones of anti-Semitism and nativism directed against bootleggers, many of whom were Jewish immigrants. U.S. attorney Lafayette French promised to deport foreign-born members of the alcohol syndicate. French said that "a large percentage of the leading figures in the illicit liquor business in the Northwest are not American citizens," reported the *St. Paul Pioneer Press*, "and the combined effort will be undertaken to drive those aliens convicted of major crimes from the country." One Prohibition Bureau survey of Minnesota analyzed obedience to prohibition laws by "foreign-born units of the population, as well as those of mixed and foreign parentage," noting that in Minnesota "a pronounced foreign strain characterizes the population." "I have no use for foreigners who come to this country and break laws with impunity," agreed federal judge John McGee in 1923, after sentencing soft drink parlor operator Sam Vannovich for Prohibition violations. "In my opinion they all should be sent back to the countries from which they came."[35]

Walter Liggett, in his *Plain Talk* magazine, summed up the attitudes of many Minnesotans toward Jewish bootleggers such as Bennie and Abe Gleeman with this doggerel: "Ten thousand Jews are making booze/ In endless repetition/ To fill the needs of a million Swedes/ Who wanted Prohibition."[36]

The O'Connor system of police protection held fast during the search for gunman Morrie Miller. A Los Angeles district attorney condemned the city of St. Paul for allowing Miller, then suspected of a California drug company robbery, to jump bond and escape prosecution for Stevens's murder.[37]

If "Miller is a phantom, local officialdom made him so," editorialized the

Pioneer Press. "The regular phantom factories are in St. Paul government. The police can make phantoms of criminals while you wait, the best in the business." Finally Miller was apprehended and brought to St. Paul in April 1929, but two Ramsey County grand juries failed to indict him for the Stevens murder. What St. Paul refused to do, the underworld handled on its own. After Miller became an assistant to East Coast bootlegger Irving "Waxey Gordon" Wexler, he was shot to death by New York mobsters in 1933.[38]

Although the O'Connor system could not protect the Syndicate from the Cleveland grand jury, the gang could employ the best defense lawyers in the Upper Midwest to fight the liquor charges. Assistant U.S. attorney M. E. Evans confessed privately that the conspiracy defendants from Minnesota were formidable opponents in court: each of the twenty-three defendants had one to five lawyers, who were remarkable for their "sheer cussedness."[39]

In 1927 thirteen of the defendants pleaded guilty. Morris Roisner and Sammy Harris were sentenced to prison time in Georgia, Harry Gellman was sentenced to fourteen months in an Atlanta prison, and others received workhouse sentences and jail terms.[40]

Although the trials destroyed the Gellman syndicate, two of the Cleveland defendants surfaced later. One was police officer Thomas A. Brown, arrested and temporarily suspended from the St. Paul Police Department when a federal judge ordered him to Cleveland on charges of participating in the liquor smuggling. All charges against Brown were dismissed; he rose to become chief of the St. Paul police from 1930 to 1932 and played a pivotal role in the John Dillinger and Barker-Karpis cases of the 1930s.[41]

In addition, the FBI discovered that Brown had an alter ego in the St. Paul underworld. According to a 1932 FBI report, "Brown, the former Chief of Police at St. Paul . . . [was] known to be intimately associated with Leon Gleckman and to have been controlled by Leon Gleckman while in the St. Paul Police Department." With the Gellman ring gone, Gleckman—bootlegger, power broker, underworld fixer—could step into the vacuum. The bootlegger's target was nothing short of the St. Paul mayor's office.[42]

7 'A Rendezvous for Gangsters'

The Hotel St. Paul Headquarters of Leon Gleckman
363 St. Peter Street, St. Paul

Every American city had its Prohibition beer baron. In Chicago, it was Alphonse "Scarface" Capone. In New York, it was Arthur "Dutch Schultz" Flegenheimer. And in St. Paul, it was Leon Gleckman.

Gleckman "played an active part in politics and in the affairs of this city generally and in that way became a strong factor in the city government," confided U.S. attorney Lewis L. Drill to the U.S. attorney general in 1933. He "was regarded by some as the Al Capone of St. Paul. That he had influence and acquired influential friends there is no doubt. Moreover, these friends and influences were not at all confined to characters of the under-world, so to speak. On the contrary they included bankers, lawyers, and in fact persons in practically all walks of life." Gleckman cultivated friends in very high places: prosecutors found records of phone conversations be-tween Gleckman and the office of U.S. Senator Thomas Schall, prominent bankers, and Republican political leaders. Gleckman was even able to get Congressman Einar Hoidale to intercede with the U.S. attorney general in an attempt to postpone a criminal case against him in 1934.[43]

This unorthodox "politician" was born in 1894 in Minsk, Russia (today in Belarus), the third of eight children raised by Gershon and Nechama Gleck-man. Gershon was described in his son's prison records as "a strict discipli-narian, a total abstainer and law-abiding man." Nechama (Nettie), origi-nally from Austria and the daughter of a rabbi, was described in government files as "a religious, tolerant woman." The Gleckmans came to the United States from Minsk through London, Nova Scotia, and finally Port Huron, Michigan, during the winter of 1903. As a teenager, Gleckman married clerical worker Rose Goldstein, with whom he had three daughters. A salesman by inclination, a bootlegger by vocation, and a sports buff by av-ocation, Gleckman was described in prison records as "self-confident, glib, respectful."[44]

Psychological tests at Leavenworth prison highlighted Gleckman's intel-ligence. The prison analysis said Gleckman's problem-solving abilities and insight exceeded those of 92 percent of the inmates, "showing that this man is of a high degree of planfulness and efficiency." The prison file concluded by observing that Gleckman was "a rather aggressive, pleasant appearing cooperative hebrew. . . . His aggressiveness is characteristic of his general impressions derived from members of his race, but there is nothing offen-sive about them."[45]

Gleckman was first arrested in 1922, when Prohibition agents raided his Minnesota Blueing Company on University Avenue in Minneapolis. The government estimated that Gleckman's two-story factory, equipped with thirteen stills, was generating annual profits of a million dollars.[46]

Right away, Gleckman showed the inclination for bribery that was to ele-vate him to boss of the St. Paul underworld. After pleading guilty in U.S. District Court to liquor conspiracy, he was sentenced to eighteen months in Leavenworth; his attorney later claimed that Gleckman discussed a bribe with the prosecutor before the conviction and afterward paid the prosecutor to file a false confession of error in the Circuit Court of Appeals. But the appeals court did not buy the scheme and affirmed Gleckman's conviction.[47]

Gleckman was philosophical about the failure of the deal, telling his attorney that he would resign himself to serving his time in prison "if he could get his $30,000 back" from the bribery attempts. Imprisoned in Leavenworth in 1927, Gleckman was so well behaved that he was made a trusty and assigned to the greenhouse.[48]

When he was released, Gleckman turned the third floor of the Hotel St. Paul into his headquarters for summit meetings with gangsters and politicians, according to a Treasury Department probe. On January 18, 1930, Gleckman moved into suites 301–303, where, from an unlisted telephone, he made hundreds of phone calls to Chicago, New Orleans, Milwaukee, New York, Havana, and Montreal. His prominence in the underworld was such that in March 1932—at the height of the FBI's hunt for fugitive bank robbers Francis L. "Jimmy" Keating and Thomas Holden—the FBI rented room 309 to spy on Gleckman's visitors. The FBI also targeted the hotel in its search for prison escapee Frank Nash, noting that "the St. Paul Hotel . . . is believed to be a rendezvous for gangsters." On the other side of the law, Michael Malone, the Treasury Department agent who infiltrated Al Capone's syndicate in Chicago, maintained a room at the hotel.[49]

Interviewed by the FBI years later, Gleckman confirmed that he had "maintained offices" at the hotel "for the purpose of carrying on his political enterprises." According to FBI records, Gleckman's "political enterprises" chiefly involved payments of protection money to police, commissioners, city councilors, and other power brokers—which, in turn, gave Gleckman the power to assist others who wanted favors from these figures. An underworld informant told the FBI that Tom Brown, who was then chief of police, rented a room at the hotel to facilitate payoffs. Boxer Walter "Saph" McKenna of the Hollyhocks Club casino delivered weekly payments to Brown's room.[50]

Police officials Charles Tierney and Thomas Dahill told the FBI that from 1930 to 1932, when Brown was chief of police, all gambling in the city was controlled by Gleckman through his suite in the Hotel St. Paul. Gleckman confessed to FBI agents that he had used political connections to help his friend Tom Brown become police chief. Gleckman added that "with the return of legalized liquor [Gleckman] left the racket and, having a large amount of money, entered the political situation in St. Paul with the hope of some day becoming Mayor of St. Paul."[51]

Gleckman told the FBI that "he had excellent contacts in the political setup in St. Paul during that period [1930–32] and that he made more money

Hotel St. Paul in 1933, headquarters for bootlegging king Leon Gleckman (right)

through politically secured contracts than he ever made in the alcohol business." Gleckman boasted that he had purchased several city councilors as a way to "secure a foothold in politics."[52]

While Gleckman was engineering political deals upstairs, the hotel's circular driveway served as a bootleg distribution center. Austin Cravath, a Texaco filling station owner, was recruited by Minneapolis gangster Isadore "Kid Cann" Blumenfeld to manage his St. Paul alcohol operations hidden at the Dexheimer farm near Mendota and the Fransmeyer farm just off Highway 110 near Fort Snelling. Cravath's son Calvert, now a resident of Stillwater, Minnesota, recalled that "everybody either made it, sold it or drank it—no matter who they were, from preachers on down. There was no stigma to alcy [alcohol] at that time."

As a teenager, Calvert hid gasoline cans filled with alcohol under the hood of his father's Studebaker. The Cravaths would drive the car—customized with a souped-up engine capable of reaching speeds of a hundred miles per hour—into the curved driveway that still graces the Hotel St. Paul. "It was all arranged with the bellhop," Cravath recalled. The bellmen "knew exactly when you'd be there, they had $100 cash—$25 per gallon. The alcy cost us $3 to make, and sold wholesale for $8 per gallon." Cravath figured that his father's distilling operation made a profit of $2,000 a day—which, Cravath quipped, "gives you quite a cushion for the unexpected expenses."[53]

Protection payments were made at Fort Snelling, near where the liquor was made, Cravath said. Farmers and sheriffs operating near the distillery received a gallon of liquid bribery every week. As a result, the ring enjoyed advance notice of police raids. During these well-rehearsed operations, reporters were invited to watch the police plunge axes into a pair of sacrificial stills; the active stills were hidden behind blankets. When the reporters left, the ring picked up two new stills from a Minneapolis warehouse to guarantee that there would be no interruption in production.

By 1932, Austin Cravath's operations usually produced between 400 and 610 gallons of alcohol every twenty-four hours. The four-hundred-gallon stills had sixteen gas burners to cook the alcohol. ("You wore shorts and tennis shoes, with sweat rolling off you," recalled Cravath.) Guards equipped with submachine guns protected the Cravath operation against hijacking, but on occasion they would slip out to hijack someone else's load of liquor. "We were so big, that [once] one of our semi trucks left, the call [alarm signal] went off, and our hijackers hijacked our own stuff!" said Cravath. Cravath's liquor business operated freely through the fall of 1933. The bootlegging ring was then told the precise date on which its guaranteed police protection would expire. A convoy of trucks guarded by a crew of enforcers with sawed-off pump shotguns brought the surplus alcohol to a customer in Chicago by the name of Al Capone.[54]

8 'The Lousiest Crime in the World'

Leon Gleckman's Home
2168 Sargent Avenue, St. Paul

Leon Gleckman's considerable influence at City Hall and police headquarters could not protect him from an occupational hazard common to bootleggers of the 1930s—gangsters who kidnapped other gangsters. Gleckman was abducted on September 24, 1931, from his home, which he shared with his wife of eighteen years. He was held hostage for eight days in a cottage forty miles from Woodruff, Wisconsin. The initial ransom was thought to be as high as $200,000, but when the kidnappers contacted Gleckman's partner, Morris Roisner, the amount had dropped to $75,000. The final sum was precipitously reduced to $5,000, plus the $1,450 in cash that Gleckman had in his pockets. With the help of go-between John "Jack" Peifer of the Hollyhocks casino—newspapers hailed Peifer for performing an "errand of mercy" in negotiating with the kidnappers—Gleckman was released on October 2.[55]

The FBI discovered that there was far more to the Gleckman kidnapping than had made the newspapers; it involved suspicious intermingling of the underworld and the police. One of the four men who kidnapped Gleckman, Albert Tallerico, told his fellow inmates at Stillwater Prison that casino operator Peifer had engineered the kidnapping. Tallerico said that Gleckman's kidnappers "lived in mortal terror of Jack Peifer," claiming that St. Paul police chief Tom Brown and the county attorney had both warned the kidnappers that "if they knew what was good for them they would not mention the name of Jack Peifer" when the grand jury investigated the abduction.[56]

To be sure, there was no love lost between Leon Gleckman and Jack Peifer. An underworld informant detailed how Gleckman's syndicate had once hijacked Peifer's liquor; Peifer, accompanied by strongman William "Dutch" Canner, met with Gleckman and threatened to kill him if he ever interfered with Peifer's business again. "Some friends had recently told [Gleckman] that he would be surprised to know that some persons whom he regarded as friends had participated in the kidnapping," the FBI learned from Gleckman years later. Gleckman told the agents that he intended to investigate the rumors and "would take care of them in his own way."[57]

One of Gleckman's kidnappers, hotel proprietor Frank LaPre, was found on suburban St. Paul's Lake Vadnais Boulevard on October 3, 1931, dead of multiple gunshots in the face. Immediately after LaPre was killed, the other conspirators were apprehended and convicted of the kidnapping.[58]

Several stories were told to account for these events. Kidnapper Tallerico claimed that Jack Peifer and another member of the kidnap gang had driven out to see LaPre, who was allegedly holding out on returning $5,000 of Gleckman's ransom money. But according to a former St. Paul police officer, a list of the kidnappers was beaten out of LaPre just before he died; then Gleckman himself turned the list over to the police. Chief Tom Brown handed the list of suspects to a pair of officers, who promptly picked them up. "Fellas, you did a great job," Brown reportedly told the officers, relaxing in his office with Gleckman. The Gleckman ransom money, recovered from LaPre's hotel safe, was shifted into Brown's campaign fund to finance his unsuccessful run for Ramsey County sheriff.[59]

An FBI informant confirmed the latter story with a slightly different scenario: saloon keeper Frank Reilly told agents that "La Pre was killed by Brown and others and planted in an automobile to make it look like the kidnapping gang had killed LaPre, because he was thought to have double-crossed them." Taxi driver George Rafferty, Brown's brother-in-law, told the FBI that he too had heard rumors that the police killed LaPre and then planted his body in another car to make it look like he had been murdered by underworld companions.[60]

Improbably, the city's leading racketeer publicly hailed the police department, which Gleckman said "rescued me from possible death at the hands of kidnappers and within 26 hours had captured the gangsters and recovered the $5,000 ransom money." The bootlegger offered special praise for policeman Tom Brown, who had been under attack by mayoral candidate William Mahoney. "During the administration of Chief of Police Thomas A. Brown, there have been no gangland murders," said Gleckman to reporters, "and what few major crimes there have been have been promptly and effectively cleared up. . . . I feel it my duty to defend the department against any slurs that may be cast upon it by mud that is intended to be thrown at me."[61]

After the trauma of being kidnapped, the FBI reported, "Gleckman had a police guard near his house, ostensibly to guard against another kidnapping." For months after the kidnapping, Gleckman's protectors—not his bodyguards, but the St. Paul police—were on edge. One evening, a neighbor looking for his five-year-old daughter passed Gleckman's house a few times. Suddenly, the FBI said, the neighbor was "accosted, kicked around and generally abused by two city detectives who accused him of having designs on Gleckman's life." The man was able to convince the police that he was just looking for his errant daughter. Many underworld bosses across the United

States controlled members of their police departments, but how many gangsters could command police officers to stand guard outside their home?[62]

Despite the security, Gleckman's daughter Florence was kidnapped by gangsters in the summer of 1932 but was released without payment of the $50,000 ransom when the kidnappers ran into problems with their hideout. Gleckman told FBI agents that "kidnapping is the lousiest crime in the world." During the investigation of the William Hamm kidnapping in 1933, Gleckman told agents that he normally would not give them information, but because of his personal experiences with kidnappings he would help the FBI identify Hamm's kidnappers.[63]

After his daughter was kidnapped, Gleckman hired a sixteen-year-old girl to clean, cook, and walk the children home from school each day. Apart from the shock of finding a revolver under Gleckman's bedroom pillow ("I was scared to death, I'd never seen a gun before"), Gertrude Sletner remembered her four years as the Gleckman family's maid with pleasure.

Gleckman spent most of his time away from his Sargent Avenue residence on business. His evenings were spent at local movie theaters with wife, Rose. Gleckman would fall asleep the moment the movie began and wake up for the final credits. "Leon said it was the only way he could get any sleep," said Sletner.

The Gleckmans, for all their wealth, still had the simple tastes of immigrants from the eastern European shtetl; his favorite dishes were raw hamburger and barely cooked rump roast. The Gleckmans once asked Sletner to prepare some chopped liver for their dinner, and Sletner forgot the culinary assignment. Later, Rose Gleckman opened the refrigerator, stuck her finger in a bowl, and told Gertrude how terrific her chopped liver was. Puzzled by the comment, Sletner peeked inside the refrigerator. Mrs. Gleckman had been extolling the fine taste of a bowl of dog food.[64]

9   'See If He Wants to Be Mayor'

The Merchants Bank Building
Fourth and Robert Streets, St. Paul

Determined to break Leon Gleckman's hold on city government, in 1932 federal agents stepped up their surveillance by installing a telephone wiretap at his Republic Finance Company, an auto finance firm located in suite 713 of the Merchants Bank Building. To the Prohibition Bureau's dismay, the tap was located by telephone company representatives only four days after it had been installed at great inconvenience and expense ("four nights being necessary to complete same," noted the Prohibition Bureau director,

Liquor baron Leon Gleckman after his release by kidnappers, with wife, Rose, and daughters Lorraine and Helen Mae at their Sargent Avenue home in 1931

"the work being done at intervals when employees of the building were not present").[65]

Despite the government's electronic intrusion, Gleckman continued as unofficial czar of St. Paul. "Leon kept a jar on the desk where people would drop parking tickets," recalled Max Ehrlich, Gleckman's partner in Republic Finance. "At the end of the week, a big Irish cop would drop by, take a fistful of cigars and bring the tickets to City Hall—and that's the last you'd hear of them. . . . Leon Gleckman *was* the Mayor of St. Paul, at least indirectly!"

"I overheard this conversation with Leon," said Ehrlich. "'So and so doesn't want to be mayor.' And Leon said, 'Go call this fellow and see if *he* wants to be mayor!'" The candidate mattered little; Gleckman was already the chief executive officer of Minnesota's capital city.[66]

Gleckman's political power reached its zenith in early 1932, when Justice Department memoranda admitted that Gleckman "controlled the local government in the City of St. Paul." But then on May 3, 1932, William J. Mahoney was elected mayor after a campaign during which he claimed Gleckman had "one-man control" of the underworld. A Treasury Department agent reported that Mahoney had promised to "eliminate Mr. Gleckman from control in local affairs and rid the City of St. Paul from gangster influences." Gleckman responded by offering to donate $5,000 to charity if Mahoney "could prove his malicious charges." Mahoney called the offer a "gangster trick" and declined to take up Gleckman's challenge.[67]

When a Treasury Department investigation discovered evidence that Gleckman was laundering his income through Republic Finance Company, the business's records suddenly disappeared. Powerful forces pressed hard for a full investigation into Gleckman's power. The publisher of the *St. Paul Dispatch* wrote to the U.S. attorney general

> Gleckman is the real political boss in the city and . . . he controls the police and the Council and probably controls the liquor and gambling traffic. We have reached a point where I think something should be done and I am anxious to have something started in the very near future, because I feel that it is time for St. Paul to be rid of gangs and racketeers and gangsters who are now having so much influence in the political and social life of the city.[68]

Assistant U.S. attorney George A. Heisey seconded the publisher's outrage: "While in the past several years, Special Agents of the Prohibition Service have had the taxpayer [Gleckman] under close surveillance, [and] have had 'taps' on telephone wires at his home and at his office, they never have been able, since his release from the penitentiary in 1928, to connect him with the illegal liquor traffic."[69]

Michael Malone and J. N. Sullivan, the Internal Revenue agents who had helped bust Al Capone, were reassigned to work on Gleckman's tax case in 1932. Gleckman reported paying income taxes of $432, far short of the $69,443 the agents believed Gleckman really owed. Sullivan crisscrossed North America—from the St. Paul Boxing Club to Havana's Mill Creek Distillery—to obtain information on Gleckman's hidden assets. Identifying precisely how much Gleckman owned, and where, and with whom was an enormously complex task. "I am not sure how this case will work out," wrote one worried prosecutor. "We are apparently meeting terrific pressure on witnesses, for their memory is either bad or they are denying facts which our investigating leads us to believe existed."[70]

Gleckman's power was diminished by the repeal of the Eighteenth Amendment in 1933 (passed by Congress in February and ratified by 36 states on December 5), and then permanently limited by his 1934 conviction for tax evasion. The government proved that he had concealed $366,522 in income between 1929 and 1931. Gleckman had been clever enough to make the ledger sheets at the bank that documented his deposits disappear. Unfortunately, his envoys forgot to remove the deposit slips, which tipped off the government to the invisible transactions. He was convicted again in May 1937 in U.S. District Court of attempting to bribe a juror during his earlier tax evasion cases. But even as Gleckman's power waned, he could be found acting the role of "the Al Capone of St. Paul" at the Hotel St. Paul and the Boulevards of Paris nightclub.[71]

10–12 St. Paul's Roaring Nightlife

10. *The Mystic Caverns*
    676 Joy Avenue, St. Paul
11. *The Castle Royal*
    6 West Channel Street, St. Paul
12. *The Boulevards of Paris and the Coliseum Ballroom*
    1100 West University Avenue, St. Paul

The flood of criminal talent drawn by the O'Connor system's leniency toward felons to St. Paul in the early 1930s—from the Ozarks, Los Angeles, Chicago, and New York—produced a roaring nightlife of jazz, fine liquor, and high-stakes gambling. By 1932 the 271,606 residents of St. Paul supported forty-four theaters and fourteen major hotels, along with innumerable speakeasies (or "blind pigs") and casinos.[72]

Among the most unusual of the gambling emporiums were the Mystic Caverns and the Castle Royal, two nightclubs built inside the cool sandstone mushroom caves along the Mississippi River bluffs. The Mystic Caverns, which featured fan dances by stripper Sally Rand, was a multichambered cave casino outfitted with roulette wheels and blackjack tables. Robert Brooks Hamilton, later of gangland's notorious Hollyhocks nightclub, and Chicago pickpocket Robert "Frisco Dutch" Steinhardt supervised gambling at the Mystic Caverns. "In the fall of 1933 Bob Hamilton put up a $500 bankroll to back a gambling game we operated in a cave in the side of a mountain near St. Paul," Steinhardt told FBI agents. "This cave was on the property of two brothers named Fester [actually Foster]," one of whom was director of the St. Paul Police Band.[73]

"The Mystic Caverns was the most beautiful place you ever saw," recalled Sarah Knutson, whose father helped maintain the nightclub, hauling out the white sand that sifted down from the cave walls. "The cavern had a monstrous chandelier, with lights flashing all different colors, [hung] two stories above the polished-wood dance floor. It was a thrill—people would walk from miles to get to the Mystic Caverns." The club boasted a full kitchen, a restaurant with white tablecloths, and a private penthouse for underworld business meetings. Knutson recalled surprises hidden throughout the club

—including men dressed as glow-in-the-dark skeletons and an Egyptian mummy in a casket; the mummy would change into an attractive woman, courtesy of the mirror-and-light illusion known to magicians as "Pepper's Ghost." In 1934 a Ramsey County grand jury investigation led to convictions for running an underground casino, closing the Mystic Caverns forever.[74]

In its heyday the Castle Royal (which most recently reopened as the Wabasha Street Caves) featured rich oriental carpets and glittering chandeliers, gambling in the back room, and performances by Cab Calloway, the Dorsey brothers, and Harry James. Although there is no proof that Dillinger and other gangsters frequented the Royal, current owners Donna and Steve Bremer have heard all of the gangland legends. "Ma Barker and her gang stopped into the club," claimed Donna Bremer. "In the 1930s, the underworld would come to these nightclubs on the weekend, and then the wealthy of Minneapolis and St. Paul would come just to see the gangsters."[75]

"The Castle Royal was built in a mushroom cave," recalled former St. Paul police officer Pat Lannon Sr. "They turned it into a nightclub, put in

Castle Royal nightclub, built into the Mississippi River bluffs; 1933 ad announcing club's grand opening

gambling—craps and poker and cards—in the back end." Lannon claimed that the Castle Royal's gambling operations figured in a scheme by Tom Brown (reassigned as a police detective) to destroy rival George Moeller's campaign for Ramsey County sheriff. Lannon took candidate Moeller on a guided tour of the Royal when the police held a party at the club. "But we skirted the gambling room and didn't take him there," laughed Lannon. "Next day, talk about a con, there's a newspaper article about gambling at the Castle Royal and the article said that [Moeller] was there. They put him on the spot and the grand jury was going to have an investigation to railroad Moeller!" Lannon went to Ramsey County Attorney Michael Kinkead and explained Brown's political maneuvering; formal charges were never brought against Moeller.[76]

When it opened in October 1933, the Castle Royal promoted itself in newspapers as "the World's Most Gorgeous Underground Nite Club." Its motto, "Fit for a King," referred to opening night entertainment by Juan King and his ten-piece Castle Royal Orchestra.[77]

The Mystic Caverns and the Castle Royal were dwarfed by the mammoth Boulevards of Paris nightclub at the southwest corner of Lexington Parkway and University Avenue and its adjacent dancehall, the Coliseum Ballroom. The Boulevards was "the fanciest place this side of New York," recalled Marguerite Junterman, daughter of its proprietor, John Lane. "If you hadn't made it to the Boulevards of Paris, you hadn't seen St. Paul!"[78]

The Coliseum, built as an ice rink in 1918, later got a vast dance floor—at 100-by-250 feet, the largest in the world at that time, its owner claimed. Three thousand revelers would sneak in bottles of ginger ale spiked with bootleg whiskey to enhance their enjoyment of such name acts as Fats Waller and Ben Pollack. The Coliseum catered to what Junterman called "the cheaper crowd," serving hot dogs rather than steaks.[79]

In contrast, the Boulevards of Paris offered elegant cigarette girls, twenty-five stage dancers performing a new show every Friday, and tuxedoed and gowned patrons. When it opened in 1929, the Boulevards promoted chef Karl Seidel's cuisine ("European dishes of Old World Origin and rare delicacy"), a ladies' waiting room decorated with black satin and mirrors, simulated Parisian sidewalks, and a full-scale reproduction of the American Bar in Paris.[80]

A basement casino, ringing with the sounds of poker, roulette, and craps, was supervised by gambling expert "Frisco Dutch" Steinhardt. "In about the year of 1930, Ben Harris and John Lane and Bob Hamilton were operating the Boulevards of Paris, a night club in St Paul," Steinhardt told the FBI. "I went into partnership with them, and we opened up a gambling casino at this place." Gambling executive Ben Harris, a former publicist for

The Coliseum Ballroom; impresario John Lane of the
Boulevards of Paris

Minnesota governor Floyd B. Olson and a close friend of Minneapolis syndicate boss Isadore Blumenfeld, managed the Boulevards of Paris. The FBI
reported that Gladys Sawyer, wife of St. Paul racketeer Harry Sawyer, had
said that in 1930 and 1931, when Tom Brown was chief of the St. Paul police,
"gambling in the city was permitted, but a payoff to the police was required . . . and all of the collecting for the county was handled by Benny
Harris, who was operating the 'Boulevards of Paris.'"[81]

To skirt Prohibition violations, Lane's staff would serve customers setups
(a glass, a bowl of ice, and ginger ale), and the customers brought their own
illicit alcohol. "The customers were pretty savvy, they kept the booze hidden," said Junterman. "The police assigned to the Coliseum were all paid
off, but nothing was flaunted." The police support helped discourage competition. Underworld informant Frank Reilly told the FBI that he had con-

templated opening his own nightclub in St. Paul's Highland Park, but when the Boulevards opened— attracting mobsters from Toledo, Philadelphia, and Chicago—Reilly concluded it was useless to fight a club that "opened with the full consent of the police."[82]

Lane, a former telegram messenger, rose to become a Ramsey County commissioner (1926–30) with a deft skill at cultivating political connections. He brought an extravagant style to his life and to his nightclub: he once purchased a magnum of champagne and Rocquefort cheese for his granddaughter's first birthday, insisting that the girl should have only the best. When the spread of jukeboxes began to cut into venues for live music, Lane often let jazz musicians sleep in his basement while he sought work for them in the Twin Cities.[83]

Musical giants Fats Waller, Benny Goodman, and Louis Armstrong were among those who performed at the Boulevards. Many artists performed surprise shows at the Boulevards after Junterman sneaked backstage at the Orpheum Theatre, asked the entertainers if they wanted a free dinner after their show, and brought the hungry singers, actors, and comics to the Boulevards.

Lane had a genius for imaginative promotions, among them weight-reducing contests and a hundred-dollar bounty offered to anyone who could find a club with a larger dance floor. Junterman recalled another: "The parking lot between the Coliseum dance hall and the Boulevards would flood, so no one could park a car there. My dad capitalized on the flood—he put an advertisement in the newspaper that said, 'Come to Lexington and University and see the new Coliseum Lake!' He even put *rowboats* in the water. People took it seriously and would come to see our lake."

Perhaps most wondrous of all is the story of the installation of the Coliseum's famous dance floor. Lane hired his cousin, a carpenter, to install a dance floor on top of the Coliseum's roller-skating surface in the early 1920s. Thanks to a construction error (the floor supports were placed too far apart) and a damp climate, the floor swayed precariously. For anyone else, the unsteady floor would have spelled disaster, but Lane promptly advertised the world's only "floor that sways with motion." He boasted in posters and advertisements that "you'll never get tired of dancing at the Coliseum, because of our swaying floor—it sways with the dancers!"[84]

Part of the wicked fun of the Boulevards of Paris was the chance that you might bump into a gangster on the dance floor. During the 1932 hunt for Chicago bank robbers Jimmy Keating and Tommy Holden, the FBI learned that the Boulevards was a popular winter hangout for the duo, along with gangsters Frank Nash of Oklahoma and Capone hit man Fred "Shotgun George Ziegler" Goetz. The Boulevards may have played a more sinister role for the underworld: Dillinger gang member Tommy Gannon claimed that the Thompson submachine gun used by gangsters to assassinate Minneapolis journalist Walter Liggett in 1935 was secreted under the dance floor before being dumped in the Mississippi River.[85]

On September 18, 1929, unknown gangsters detonated a bomb inside the Boulevards of Paris. Built of concrete blocks, the building was barely damaged, even though the blast was heard more than two miles away.

Publicly, Lane insisted that the bombing was simply a reprisal for his having ejected some unruly thugs who had indulged in a birthday party brawl. "In attempting to operate a cafe for ladies and gentlemen of the community, it seems I have incurred the displeasure of gangsters," Lane told reporters. "The Boulevards of Paris management will not be intimidated by the racketeers who have adopted the Chicago method of terrorism." Privately, though, Lane told his family he believed that the bombing was the work of a vengeful gangster. (Some say John Dillinger; others claim it was New York beer baron Dutch Schultz.) Apparently Lane had thrown the drunken mobsters out of the Boulevards for playing catch with open ketchup bottles and making unwelcome passes at a waitress.[86]

In 1934 the Boulevards of Paris became the Vanity Fair dance hall; the dance palace degenerated into a ten-cent joint, shambling out of business by 1936. Lane died in 1952. Nine years later, the Boulevards of Paris building was razed. When the neighboring Coliseum was torn down in 1958, *St. Paul Dispatch* reporter Gareth Hiebert wrote: "There are many who still rub their eyes and can't believe that the Coliseum isn't there when they pass by."[87]

The demise of the Boulevards of Paris and the Coliseum coincided with the repeal of Prohibition and the rise of a different kind of criminal—the assassin-for-hire exemplified by Murder Incorporated. The trial of two Murder Inc. hit men in 1932 revealed that killers Joey Schaefer and George Young had visited the Boulevards of Paris to relax before planning their murders. The Murder Inc. enforcers were corporate killers sent across the United States to slaughter hundreds of men for calculated business purposes. One of their most sensational "contracts" occurred a few blocks from the Boulevards of Paris, at the corner of University and Snelling Avenues.[88]

13   A Slaying by Murder Inc.

The Green Dragon Cafe
469 North Snelling Avenue, St. Paul

"Bootlegging called for a more elaborate infrastructure than burglary," wrote crime historian William Weir:

A burglar can break into any place, anywhere. Bootlegging was a business that depended on steady customers. The customers had to know the bootlegger and know that they could depend on him. That tied the bootlegger to the area where his customers lived. Because there were a lot of other bootleggers, he had to defend his territory. That led to something new in American crime—the permanently employed, salaried gunman, the hoodlum.[89]

The practice of employing a stable of professional gunmen who killed for business reasons reached its height in the late 1920s and early 1930s, when labor racketeer Louis "Lepke" Buchalter, Benjamin "Bugsy" Siegel, and Mafia chieftain Meyer Lansky founded an assassination service, Murder Inc., in Brooklyn, New York.

On July 25, 1932, at the intersection of University and Snelling Avenues in St. Paul—in broad daylight, with a police car parked just a block away—a pair of Murder Inc. killers assassinated an underworld fugitive they had tracked across the country. Their target was bootlegger Abe Wagner, the twenty-six-year-old son of Jewish immigrants from eastern Europe. Wagner, who had briefly been a suspect in the murder of Charles Lindbergh's baby boy, narrowly survived a February 1932 attempt on his life by New York's Mazza gang, a syndicate that had already killed his brother Allie. Wagner fled to St. Paul, masquerading as a fruit peddler under the alias Abe Loeb. Five months later, Murder Inc. located Wagner and sent the "contract" for the bootlegger's murder to killers George Young and Joseph Schaefer.[90]

Abe Wagner, a Murder Inc. victim, with his wife

Police intelligence files described Young and Schaefer as "competent and dependable killers for Meyer Lansky, very closely aligned with the Italian element of the Mafia or La Cosa Nostra." George Young (whose real name was Albert Silverberg) was an immigrant from Odessa, Russia (today, Ukraine), with a rap sheet covering thirteen arrests for assault and battery, receiving stolen goods, robbery, and possession of burglar's tools. Joey Schaefer (real name Nathan Winger) was an Austrian-born bootlegger whose seven arrests included charges of carrying a concealed weapon, suspicion of murder, and assault and battery on a policeman.[91]

Both Young and Schaefer were former members of the Irving "Waxey Gordon" Wexler bootlegging mob. Both were being hunted themselves for the murder of Prohibition agent John Finiello, whom they may have killed in December 1930 during a raid on the Rising Sun Brewery in Elizabeth,

New Jersey. Murder Inc. sent Young and Schaefer to the safest city in America for crooks on the lam—St. Paul. During a 1931 visit, Schaefer had stayed in a third-floor apartment at 3310 South Fremont Avenue in Minneapolis—the same apartment building where, two years later, John Dillinger's gang would hide from the FBI. This time the two killers moved to the Hotel St. Paul, Young in room 1032 and Schaefer in 824.[92]

Apparently, the assassins had a series of assignments in Minnesota. The underworld's St. Paul territory had been challenged by Harry "Gorilla Kid" Davis, a small-time Philadelphia hoodlum whose nickname came from his reputation as the homeliest crook in Minnesota. To eliminate this rival who had "muscle[d] in on some of the rackets," according to Minnesota Bureau of Criminal Apprehension (BCA) reports, Murder Inc. arranged to have Davis "taken for a ride." The Gorilla Kid's body was found July 20, 1932, in a ditch near Big Marine Lake about twenty miles northeast of St. Paul. Nattily dressed in a golf suit with a white cap, Davis had two small-caliber bullet holes in the back of his head. The bureau desperately hunted for Abe Wagner for questioning, "but before [he] could be located the police were informed that Loeb [Wagner] had expressed his intention of going to the Police Department to clear himself of suspicion with regard to the [Davis] murder," said an FBI file.[93]

On the evening of July 25 Wagner's partner, Al Gordon, stepped into John Courtney's Drug Store at 1598 University Avenue to have a prescription filled. (Today, the Spruce Tree Center mall covers the entire murder scene.) In walked Wagner, with what the cashier called a "wild look." The two men stepped out of the drugstore and started to walk west along University Avenue; neither noticed Young and Schaefer stalking them.[94]

Seventeen-year-old Ellie Hallberg McLean was meeting her boyfriend at the corner of University and Snelling, a few yards from the pharmacy. A Chrysler coupe drove by the young couple, and McLean saw a passenger frantically waving at them to move away, but they ignored the mobster's warning. "A dark green Packard drove up alongside the coupe and two men got out—Joe Schaefer, with dark pants, blue shirt; and George Young, [who] had a panama suit with panama hat," recalled McLean. "We'd seen gangster movies, and we figured the two were going to rob some place. . . . The two men started walking toward Snelling on University. . . . Like fools, we started walking the same direction they were going. Hey, we were kids— we didn't know what we were going to see!"[95]

McLean saw the two killers run toward the Courtney Drug Store, where they fired .32- and .38-caliber revolvers at Al Gordon, fatally wounding him. The pair then began to chase Wagner east down University Avenue and south on Snelling Avenue toward the Snelling Hotel and the Green Dragon

*The southwest corner of University and Snelling Avenues in about 1932, the
murder site of bootlegger Abe Wagner (Loeb); the Green Dragon Cafe is at the far
left, and John Courtney's Drug Store is at the right. A diagram from the magazine*
Startling Detective Adventures *shows how the murder happened.*

cafe at 469 Snelling (today the site of an Applebee's restaurant), firing as they ran and hitting Wagner, as well as nearby windows and walls. Young and Schaefer followed the bleeding Wagner into the Green Dragon, where they beat him over the head with their gun butts. With six bullets in his chest and stomach, Wagner died at Ancker Hospital without regaining consciousness. Young and Schaefer were immediately caught by a patrolman on Roy Street. Their companions in the Chrysler, parked outside 463 North Snelling to facilitate their getaway, were forced to flee without them.[96]

Dick Pranke, a St. Paul police employee and later an FBI agent, remembered the scene at police headquarters when Young and Schaefer were brought in for fingerprinting: "Half a dozen police officers had grabbed the killer—either Young or Schaefer, I can't remember—by his head and legs and arms and physically forced him to put his fingerprints down on the pad." The fingerprints identified Young and Schaefer as the men wanted for killing a Prohibition agent in New Jersey.[97]

St. Paul police arrest photo of Joseph Schaefer, a Murder Inc. hit man

Gradually the FBI and the St. Paul police traced the killers' movements just before the Wagner and Gordon murders. Their getaway driver, William Weisman, was hiding at the St. Paul home of the Harry Smith family at 1892 Lincoln Avenue (a two-story ivy-covered red-brick and stucco house that still stands near the intersection of Lincoln Avenue and Howell Street). Trial testimony placed Young and Schaefer at 1892 Lincoln just an hour before they murdered Wagner. The FBI also found that they had stayed at the Thomas Edwards cottage at Third Street and Park Avenue in White Bear Lake during the summer of 1932. Their landlady remembered a crowd of men gambling and drinking, their guns scattered on the furniture, running up enormous telephone bills, often leaving the cottage at ten o'clock in the evening and returning at five the next morning.[98]

During a twenty-day trial, extraordinary efforts were made to get the killers acquitted. Two men were offered $100 each to fabricate false testimony for the defense. Horace "Red" Dupont, a former employee of underworld figure Tom Filben, said that the St. Paul police chief was offered a $25,000 bribe to free Young and Schaefer but turned the offer down. The state's four top criminal defense attorneys represented Young and Schaefer, while gangsters in New Jersey raised funds for the legal defense. Most surprisingly, St. Paul police drove to Holman Field on October 13 to welcome an aircraft carrying a strange mix of Young and Schaefer supporters: Congressman Ben Golder of Philadelphia and a then-unknown Meyer Lansky, later to become the most powerful non-Italian figure in organized crime.[99]

Despite their powerful connections, Young and Schaefer were convicted of murdering Wagner in Ramsey County District Court. On November 11, 1932, they were sentenced to life at hard labor in Minnesota's Stillwater Prison. But FBI files suggest that the mob's efforts to free Young and Schaefer had just begun. Burton Turkus, the assistant district attorney who prosecuted Murder Inc., claimed that a Brooklyn gangster named "Dandy Jack" was paid $35,000 to spring Young and Schaefer from Stillwater Prison with dynamite, an effort that was unsuccessful.[100]

While they were in Stillwater, the hit men confided in a gambler named Leonard Hankins, who had been imprisoned for murder related to the Barker-Karpis gang's 1932 robbery of the Third Northwestern National Bank in Minneapolis. Hankins told the FBI a remarkable tale of how the Murder Inc. duo benefited from bribes, favoritism, and underworld deals inside the Minnesota prison system. The bureau learned that when Bugsy Siegel realized that he could not free his two employees, he ensured that they were rewarded for their patience (and silence) in Stillwater.[101]

According to Hankins, the Murder Inc. duo "appear[ed] to run the prison." Young and Schaefer seldom ate what the other prisoners ate and at one time had a private room where they dined on steaks, Hankins said. Both had electric plates in their cell blocks so they could make coffee any time. Files from the Philadelphia Police Department confirm that "there was very little that they did without—with the exception of women. They had money, liquor, and food, as much as they wanted." A prison official confirmed in a 1956 letter to U.S. Senator Hubert Humphrey that Young and Schaefer enjoyed special privileges in Stillwater, including contraband whiskey, money, and fresh meat.[102]

The duo received a fifty-dollar weekly stipend from Murder Inc., which they passed on to prison officials for special privileges. Hankins revealed that in 1949 several Minneapolis nightclubs sent entertainers to put on shows for the Stillwater inmates: "Young, Schaefer and [convicted murderer] Rubin Shetsky were allowed to sit in a special section to watch the show," an FBI document said, "and he [Hankins] later heard through gossip that the women entertainers returned the following day and were taken to the basement of the prison, and thereafter Warden Utecht personally took Young, Schaefer and Shetsky to the basement, where he left them alone with some of the women entertainers."[103]

Most intriguingly, Hankins told the FBI that millionaire Charlie Ward, an ex-convict from Leavenworth who had transformed himself into the president of the printing firm of Brown and Bigelow, was secretly Young and Schaefer's guardian angel." Hankins claimed that Ward provided $100,000 to spring Young and Schaefer from prison. The hit men told Hankins that "a Hollywood, California gangster named Bugs Siegel is . . . the person who made the arrangements to get that money from Charles Ward." The FBI was able to confirm only that Ward "borrowed" $100,000 from Siegel and deposited it in St. Paul's Midway Bank.[104]

Siegel himself visited St. Paul in 1939 for a final attempt to spring Young and Schaefer from prison. His temporary headquarters would be the Lowry Hotel in downtown St. Paul.

14   'A Recognized Member of Murder Inc.'
Bugsy Siegel at the Lowry Hotel
339 North Wabasha Street, St. Paul

It was appropriate that mobster Bugsy Siegel stayed at the Lowry Hotel (now the Lowry Office Building), for it had developed a rich underworld history since its opening in 1927. Alvin "Creepy" Karpis often stayed at the Lowry during his 1932–33 crime sprees with Fred and Doc Barker. When Karpis was held in the Federal Courts Building (now Landmark Center), he gazed longingly out the windows of the FBI office toward the Lowry, three blocks away. Bootlegger Leon Gleckman, recovering from his 1931 gangland kidnapping, hid in a rooftop apartment at the hotel.[105]

But no Lowry Hotel resident was more infamous than Bugsy Siegel. Siegel and Meyer Lansky, youthful partners in the Bugs and Meyer mob of bootleggers, murderers, and extortionists, went on to found a coast-to-coast organized crime syndicate with Lucky Luciano, Frank Costello, and other Italian gangsters. By the time Siegel visited the Lowry Hotel, he was running West Coast criminal activities for the syndicate. An FBI Vice Conditions report confirmed that Siegel, "a recognized member of Murder, Inc.," paid a visit to Minnesota: "On December 4, 1939, [Siegel] was known to have visited St. Paul and stayed at the Lowry Hotel, at which time he attempted to make some sort of deal to have Joseph Schaefer and George Young released from Stillwater State Prison. These individuals were known killers of this Murder, Inc., who were sent to St. Paul to murder another member of the Syndicate."[106]

Young and Schaefer told fellow inmate Leonard Hankins that Siegel had tried and failed to get a $100,000 bribe into the prison to get them out. At that time, Hankins told the FBI, Siegel visited them at the prison about

The Lowry Hotel, Wabasha and Fourth Streets, where syndicate founder Ben "Bugsy" Siegel stayed in 1939

nine times in three months and three times during one week; Siegel's visits took place in private offices behind closed blinds. St. Paul police officer Joe Sherin claimed that the mob offered $100,000 to any Minnesota governor who would pardon Young and Schaefer. The FBI noted that "possibly $200,000 has been spent . . . trying to secure the release of these men from Stillwater."[107]

Young and Schaefer gained a measure of immortality when assistant district attorney Burton Turkus featured their killing of Abe Wagner (Loeb) prominently in his 1951 book, *Murder, Inc.: The Story of the Syndicate*, but even the efforts of Bugsy Siegel failed to get them out of prison. When they were paroled in the early 1960s they had outlived their benefactor, who was shot to death in Beverly Hills, California, in 1947. Siegel had once reassured a construction executive affiliated with the Flamingo Hotel that he and other civilians had nothing to fear from the mob. In the world of organized crime, Siegel said, "We only kill each other."[108]

3 • • • • • • • • •

ORGANIZED CRIME AT YOUR SERVICE

STATE OF MINNESOTA, BUREAU OF CRIMINAL APPREHENSION
ROOM 22 STATE OFFICE BUILDING - ST. PAUL, MINNESOTA

Record from _____ Police Dept. _____ (Address) __ St. Paul Minn. __
On the above line please state whether Police Department, Sheriff's Office, or County Jail

...ived from _____ County

... Received __ 8-21-35

...rge __ Invest Kidnaping.

...ence _____

...e of birth __ Lincoln Nebr.

...ionality _____

... 45-1935 __ Height 5'9"

...ght 200 __ Hair __ Dk Grey Tinge.

...d Med Heavy Eyes __ Brown.

...plexion Med.

...rks and Scars __ Brows Heavy.

Paroled _____

Discharged _____

CRIMINAL HISTORY

35796
9-21-35
St.C.P.

(Please furnish all additional criminal history and police record on separate sheet)

Green Lantern saloon proprietor Harry "Dutch" Sawyer, with his wife, Gladys; Sawyer's Bureau of Criminal Apprehension record

15   'The Fix Was in from Top to Bottom'

Harry "Dutch" Sawyer's Home
1878 Jefferson Avenue, St. Paul

Harry "Dutch" Sawyer—underworld banker and heir to Danny Hogan as supervisor of St. Paul's O'Connor system of collusion between police and gangsters—lived in a two-story home near the corner of Jefferson and Fairview Avenues. For the network of bank robbery gangs flourishing between 1930 and 1934—Dillinger out of Indiana, the Keating-Holden gang out of Chicago, and the Barker-Karpis, Frank Nash, and Harvey Bailey gangs out of Missouri and Oklahoma—men like Sawyer created a handful of safe havens, cities where they would not be picked up or prosecuted by local authorities.

"Criminals used to talk about 'safe cities,'" wrote bank robber and kidnapper Alvin Karpis. "They were places where the fix was in from top to bottom, and guys like me could relax. The chances were slim that in those cities we'd ever get arrested."[1]

In addition to St. Paul, "safe cities" included Kansas City, home of Thomas "Boss" Pendergast's political machine; Joplin, Missouri, where Herbert "Deafy" Farmer harbored Karpis and other outlaws; Reno, Nevada, treasured for its money-laundering facilities; Toledo, Ohio, where members of the Barker-Karpis gang went for plastic surgery on their faces and fingertips; Hot Springs, Arkansas, a vacation spot whose mud baths attracted Charles "Lucky" Luciano; and Cicero, Illinois, headquarters of the Capone syndicate and a city where many members of the Barker-Karpis gang obtained their automobiles.[2]

During an interrogation, Karpis confided to FBI agents that (in the words of an FBI report) if he "only had police officers to worry about he could live in Ohio, Oklahoma or Louisiana the rest of his life; that there is not a town in Ohio above 20,000 population that isn't fixed; that Tulsa and New Orleans are on the clout and Kansas City is a pushover." The safe cities were like "the imaginary bases used by children playing tag," wrote historian Michael Wallis in his biography of Oklahoma bank robber Charles Arthur "Pretty Boy" Floyd. "Once a criminal with local connections made it safely inside one of these cities, he was home free. He was 'on base' and could not be 'tagged' by the authorities."[3]

Under the O'Connor system—buttressed by ten years of payoffs from Sawyer to City Hall and the St. Paul police—detectives were unable to recognize the famous faces on the FBI's "wanted" posters, and authorities inexplicably failed to respond to extradition notices sent from other cities. If a raid was inevitable, Sawyer ensured that the police were courteous enough to call their targets half an hour before the invasion. When a new fugitive slipped off the train, Sawyer would dispatch his errand boy, former boxer William Albert "Pat" Reilly, to arrange a hotel room and introduce the felonious visitor to the local underworld.[4]

Bank robber Eddie Bentz recommended St. Paul as a base for criminal operations:

> Once you get planted in a town, the cops from every other city in the United States can wire your location, but nothing happens. For instance when Leon Gleckman had St. Paul, and Jack Peifer was running the Holly Hocks Inn, all a fellow had to do was to take care of Jack. . . . If a guy paid off, he didn't have any trouble. . . .
>
> If a fellow was going into the bank robbery business . . . I'd say the first thing to do would be to get a place to work from. That was always my system. . . . About the only way a fellow can really operate is to have his headquarters in some place where the police can't find you . . . for instance, there was St. Paul. . . .
>
> Most people think of a "right town" as some place where a yegg like myself walks in and calls up the Chief of Police and then meets him on a dark corner and gives him a wad of dough. Why, nine tenths of the time, you don't even know the Chief's name.[5]

By 1932 Sawyer had developed the O'Connor system into a citywide infrastructure of criminal services. Sawyer knew where gangsters could get a new car or repair a vehicle perforated with bullets, how to find an untraceable automatic weapon, how to launder stolen bonds, how to "finger" a kidnapping victim whose family had the financial resources for an appropriate ransom—and even how to ignite a romance with a new girlfriend. At Sawyer's Jefferson Avenue home, Karpis set up his first romantic rendezvous with Delores (Dolores) Delaney, whom he had met at the home of her brother-in-law Pat Reilly. "I knocked on Reilly's door and this beautiful young girl answered," recalled the smitten Karpis. "I could hardly speak. I just watched her. She was a brunette with brown eyes and a gorgeous figure. She was about sixteen."[6]

Delores Delaney, girlfriend of Alvin Karpis

Delaney was similarly smitten with Karpis, whom she had first glimpsed at Jack Peifer's Hollyhocks casino. (Karpis was not the first wanted man Delores had courted. In 1932 she had kept company with Clarence DeVol, brother of Barker-Karpis gang machine gunner Larry DeVol, and she served as an alibi witness when Clarence was arrested for a Minneapolis bank robbery.) In May 1933, Delaney decided to meet Karpis at Harry Sawyer's house so they could move into their own apartment. "As soon as I walked in, Dolores jumped up and planted a big, juicy kiss on my lips," recalled Karpis. "From then on, until the police finally separated us three years later, Dolores and I were a steady couple." Delaney eventually bore Karpis's only child.[7]

For a crime strategist like Karpis, St. Paul offered a support system matched by few cities. Available for hire were "jug marker" Eddie Green, an expert at identifying a vulnerable bank swollen with deposits; Frank Nash and Harvey Bailey, who provided expertise in escape maps, jailbreaks, and the timing of bank jobs; Dr. Clayton E. May, whose specialties included illegal abortions, sexually transmitted diseases, and gunshot wounds; defense attorneys Tommy McMeekin, Thomas Sullivan, and Tom Newman of St. Paul, and Archibald Cary of Minneapolis; and a rotating supply of freelance gunmen.

To stay in touch as they shifted from one St. Paul apartment to another, the gangsters created a system of telegram codes, mail drops, and safe houses, cloaking their messages to each other with multiple aliases. "All of it's done by word of mouth," said the dean of bank robbers, Harvey Bailey. "Writing is out—o-u-t. And telephone calls are out. . . . We never knew what the other's phone number was and we didn't want to." Instead, gangsters could call from anywhere in the country and leave word for one another through Harry Sawyer.[8]

Although the Dillinger gang was unhappy with Minnesota's climate, Harry Sawyer's valuable services more than made up for the grim weather. "The gang had frequently talked about leaving the Twin Cities," the FBI learned from Beth (Bessie) Skinner, who, as the girlfriend of Dillinger gang member Eddie Green, used the name Beth Green. But "because of Harry Sawyer's connections they decided that this was the safest place for them to be [since] Harry is always tipped off before a raid is made." "I don't know *how* he got connected," said former policeman Pat Lannon Sr., "but Sawyer *was* the connection with the underworld." Sawyer was often a shadowy presence at police headquarters. When newspaper reporter Fred Heaberlin bumped into him there one day, the racketeer warned: "Remember, you never saw me here."[9]

Born Harry Sandlovich into an Orthodox Jewish family in Russian-controlled Lithuania in 1890, Sawyer came to America in 1891 with his mother, Gertrude, and father, David, a cattle buyer. The family settled in Nebraska where Harry, the sixth of nine children, attended a religious school and had a traditional bar mitzvah at age thirteen. He later became a butcher, learning skills that would be useful in the kitchens at Alcatraz prison. Sawyer's criminal record began with a guilty plea in Lincoln, Nebraska, for the 1915 burglary of a Standard Oil office, followed by arrests for auto theft, robbery, and attempted grand larceny (each, notably, committed by Sawyer under a different alias).[10]

Sawyer had visited Minnesota before—under the alias Harry J. Porche, he was arrested by Minneapolis police for attempted grand larceny as early as 1918—and when he was arrested for theft in Lincoln in 1921, he jumped his $1,000 bond and fled permanently to St. Paul.[11]

By 1923 Sawyer had joined forces with underworld boss Danny Hogan at the Green Lantern saloon. "Sawyer handled . . . the disposal of jewelry and stolen goods for Hogan," Beth Green told the FBI. "Upon Hogan's death, the gangs naturally migrated to Sawyer." In addition to running the Green Lantern, Sawyer offered his police connections to a variety of Twin Cities gambling clubs. In Little Canada, six miles north of St. Paul, Sawyer owned part of the Owasso Tavern at Rice Street and Owasso Boulevard. "The gambling [at the tavern] was run on a pay-off basis to the Sheriff," the FBI learned from Sawyer's wife.[12]

Sawyer also provided protection services for the Gleckman liquor syndicate's Brown Derby nightclub at 340–380 Main Street in the Seven Corners section of downtown St. Paul, a favorite among visiting members of Bugsy Siegel's Murder Inc. squad of New York hit men. "The Brown Derby was a nightclub that was run for visiting criminals, sort of a Y.M.C.A. for criminals," recalled reporter Bill Greer, who dined there with Bonnie Parker of Bonnie and Clyde infamy. The FBI learned from a rival saloon keeper that "during the time [Tom] Brown was Chief of Police the Brown Derby . . . would not stand for any competition, and if any place opened . . . a gang of Jews, one of whom was Harry Sawyer, who were interested in the Brown Derby, would immediately go up and shoot up the competitor's place."[13]

The FBI placed Sawyer's home under surveillance during the search for fugitive bank robbers Tommy Holden and Jimmy Keating and again when the FBI was hunting for Barker-Karpis machine gunner Verne Miller. When Prohibition was repealed, Sawyer moved away from the liquor business and into more lucrative crimes; his home became a gathering place for the likes of bank robbers Frank Nash and Verne Miller. On Christmas Day 1933, the Sawyers entertained four of America's most-wanted fugitives: bank robber Fred Barker and his girlfriend, Paula Harmon, and Oklahoma burglar Harry "Limpy" Campbell and his companion Wynona Burdette.[14]

Questioned by FBI agents, more than a few of Sawyer's neighbors expressed anxiety about having an underworld power on the block. "Who knew if someone would bomb the Sawyer house, like they did with Danny

Hogan, or would fire a Thompson submachine gun?" said Jane Resler, who was ten years old when she lived at 1880 Jefferson, next door to Sawyer. One night, Resler's parents whispered, "Come here, come here," and pointed at Sawyer's house. There, through Sawyer's bedroom window, the Reslers could see a large pile of U.S. Post Office mailbags from a recent train robbery. Eventually, two of Sawyer's neighbors confronted St. Paul police official Tom Dahill, who lived nearby, with their suspicions about Sawyer's line of work. Dahill reportedly told them, "You just leave Harry Sawyer alone, and Sawyer will leave you alone." Once when he went hunting, Sawyer brought back ducks for his neighbors, and when he and his wife went to the state fair, he rewarded a neighbor's children with an odd toy monkey that shimmied up a cane.

The local children were fascinated by Sawyer. Resler recalled how Karpis's girlfriend, Delores Delaney, would park her Buick in front of Sawyer's home, usually in Sawyer's personal spot. Sawyer would arrive later, spy Delaney's car parked in his space, and cheerfully ram her automobile, inspiring a wave of obscenities from Delaney. The neighborhood youngsters sat eagerly on their front porches awaiting the spectacle, Resler said.[15]

During the 1933 hunt for gangster Verne Miller in the wake of the massacre of FBI agents and police in Kansas City, the FBI put a "mail cover" on every letter and package delivered to Sawyer's home, interrogated Sawyer's neighbors, and hid an agent in Resler's home for round-the-clock surveillance. The bureau discovered little, though, for Harry Sawyer used his home for gangland entertainment rather than business. Sawyer preferred to conduct the commerce of the underworld in the back rooms of his Green Lantern saloon.[16]

16   A Rogues Gallery of Crooks

The Green Lantern Saloon
545 North Wabasha Street, St. Paul

Bank robber and kidnapper Alvin Karpis described the Green Lantern saloon as "my personal headquarters in St. Paul. . . . Everyone had the same things in common—stealing, killing, and looting." Karpis had a weakness for the Green Lantern's hard-boiled eggs and often visited the saloon to relax, asking a cook to prepare a special milk drink to calm his sick stomach. Safe in his booth at the Lantern, Karpis could socialize with the best stickup men in America.[17]

"Sawyer ran the Green Lantern like a host at a great party," wrote Karpis in his memoirs. "The greatest blowout Sawyer threw in the place, in my experience, was on New Year's Eve, 1932. . . . There was probably never before as complete a gathering of criminals in one room in the United States as there was in the Green Lantern that night. There were escapees from every major U.S. penitentiary. I was dazzled. . . . For a kid like me it was great stuff. Rogues Gallery, or Hall of Fame. It depended on your point of view."[18]

Years later, Sawyer was asked during his kidnapping trial what kind of people frequented the Green Lantern. "All walks of life. State senators, attorneys, bootleggers, business men, lawyers," quipped Sawyer. "I forgot to mention newspapermen, quite a few of them, and printers." Pat Lannon Sr., the policeman who patrolled the beat that included the Green Lantern in 1928, disagreed: "Sure the rank and file could visit the Green Lantern, but they wouldn't get any service to speak of [because Sawyer] didn't want businesspeople in there. Anyone could walk into the Lantern, but everyone was not welcome. They wanted the *bad* boys at the Green Lantern!"[19]

And the bad boys came: racketeers Isadore "Kid Cann" Blumenfeld of Minneapolis; nationally known bank robbers John Dillinger, Verne Miller, and Frank Nash; Ma Barker's sons Fred and "Doc"; and reckless newcomers Volney Davis, Larry DeVol, and Earl Christman. Auto thief Claire Lucas admitted to a weakness for the Green Lantern's spaghetti, and bootlegger Isaac Goodman was partial to its fried pork chop sandwiches.[20]

Federal agents raided the saloon as early as 1923, discovering five barrels of spiked beer and arresting a bartender for violating Prohibition. Under Danny Hogan in the mid-1920s, the Green Lantern expanded both its clientele and its cuisine: a sign read "Dapper Dan, The Hot Dog Man," and hot dogs sizzled on a griddle in the front window. "I suppose some people even went in there for a wiener," said reporter Fred Heaberlin, who knew both Hogan and Sawyer. "But the Green Lantern was a front for bootlegging and whatever else, laundering and receiving stolen property." Behind a false wall was the Blue Room, a speakeasy where the underworld enjoyed liquor, piano music, slot machines, and nude dancers. Customers entered the Green Lantern by the back entrance, opening onto a deserted alley. The front door was locked and seldom used.[21]

From 1926 through 1933, Sawyer was able to offer illicit beer (sold as "near beer") to his Green Lantern customers through a secret arrangement with employees of the Schmidt Brewing Company. According to FBI interviews with his wife, Sawyer got the beer through a tunnel that ran from the Schmidt Brewery to the 339 Erie Street home of Schmidt plumber Carl Schoen. (The Schoen house, once located near the intersection of Erie Street and Jefferson Avenue, has since been razed.)[22]

The Green Lantern's resident professor of criminal techniques was Harvey Bailey, dean of American bank robbers. A safecracker of Scotch-Irish descent, born in West Virginia and raised in Missouri, Bailey discovered the comforts of Minnesota in the early 1920s while he was running bootleg whiskey from Canada into Minneapolis and St. Paul. When he graduated to major bank robberies, Bailey continued to seek rest and ancillary services in St. Paul. On September 17, 1930, Bailey's gang robbed the National Bank and Trust Company in Lincoln, Nebraska, of more than $2.6 million in securities and $24,000 cash, a heist described by the Associated Press as "the greatest bank robbery of all time." The responsibility for laundering the stolen bonds fell to Bailey, and he turned immediately to his fences in St. Paul. Bailey clucked his tongue when a bank robber of his acquaintance laundered some stolen bonds in New York. "I'd have dealt them out in St. Paul and Minneapolis," said Bailey. "I did pert near all my business with them people up there—they was good people."[23]

Camouflaged at the Green Lantern under the alias Tom Brennan, Bailey shared the secrets of his meticulous planning. He would explain to young thieves how to assess the size and financial worth of a town, pinpoint the lo-

Oklahoma's master bank robber Harvey Bailey, a frequent visitor to the Green Lantern

cation of traffic policemen, and figure the precise number of minutes the gang should be inside the bank, as well as how to determine the fastest getaway routes and precisely when a payroll deposit would swell the bank's store of cash. Who else but Harvey Bailey would think to obtain road maps from the county surveyor's office to ensure that the roads were adequate for a perfect getaway? Who else but Bailey would hide sawed-off shotguns in his banjo case and then joke with the landlady that he hoped his "practice" would not bother her? Bailey was also respected for his aversion to unnecessary bloodshed. After masterminding the 1933 Memorial Day prison break from the Kansas state penitentiary, Bailey prevented the escapees from killing the prison warden, to whom he gave five dollars and directions to the nearest bus station, ensuring that the hostage was released unharmed.[24]

If anything of value was stolen in St. Paul, someone in the Green Lantern was likely to know about it. FBI agents noted that racketeer Jack Peifer, owner of the Hollyhocks casino, confessed to FBI agents that whenever his liquor was hijacked, he went to the Green Lantern to arrange to buy it back. When the Barker-Karpis gang was tipped off that police were about to raid their Grand Avenue apartment in 1933, they knew where to meet before fleeing for Chicago: the Green Lantern was where criminals regrouped after a close call.[25]

The Green Lantern was a particular favorite with John Dillinger's gang. The FBI discovered that Pantorium Cleaners and Shoe Repair, next to the Green Lantern at 547 Wabasha Street, had been used by the Dillinger gang as a mail drop for the registration documents they filled out as they sold their getaway cars after each robbery. Visitors to the Green Lantern in fall 1933 included Dillinger's first lieutenant, Homer Van Meter; his partners, John Hamilton, Thomas L. "Tommy" Carroll, and Lester "Babyface Nelson" Gillis; and his errand boy, Pat Reilly, who often served as the Green Lantern's bartender.[26]

George Hurley, a St. Cloud prison alumnus and former driver for the Gleeman brothers' bootlegging syndicate, managed the Green Lantern's restaurant for Sawyer. When Hurley was jailed for his bootlegging work with Sawyer and Dan Hogan, Sawyer gave Hurley's family $100 a week. "My father . . . kept his mouth shut," recalled Hurley's son Harold. "When my father was released from prison, Harry Sawyer took him into the Green Lantern and said, 'How do you like this place?' My father said, 'Fine.' And Sawyer said: 'Then, it's yours.'" Hurley was made manager "as a thank you for being true to the code of the underworld," his son said.[27]

William Albert "Pat" Reilly, bartender at the Green Lantern saloon

By most accounts a meanspirited drunk with a violent temper, Hurley was acquitted of involvement in the murder of liquor hijacker Burt Stevens and then found not guilty of the 1930 shooting of St. Paul contractor William R. Bacheller, who died in a street brawl near the Green Lantern. Just before he was picked up for the Bacheller murder, Hurley threw the murder weapon into a snowbank near the old St. Paul Post Office. When his wife visited him in the Ramsey County jail, he asked her to get a message to Sawyer: "Tell Harry that the snow is melting." The murder weapon was never found.[28]

For many patrons, the air of gangland danger was one of the Green Lantern's attractions. Blanche Schude, who was then dating one of underworld fixer Tom Filben's employees, Horace "Red" Dupont, begged her boyfriend to take her to the Green Lantern: "All the gangsters hung around there, and I wanted to see it. Red said, 'No, I don't want to take you there.'" "And I said: 'Red, if you don't take me there, someone *else* will." Reluctantly, Dupont took Schude into the Green Lantern. "We didn't even have a chance to have a drink," Schude continued, "before there was a fellow at the other end of the room pointing a gun at us! For no reason at all. Red threw me on the floor, threw himself down, and we crawled over to the stairs. His first words to me were, 'Well, are you satisfied?'"[29]

Reporter Fred Heaberlin, who during Prohibition often retired with his colleagues to the Green Lantern at two in the morning in search of beer, remembered another close call: "This fellow pulls out a pouch of jewels taken out of their settings, and wanted to sell them to us cheap. My companion started to make nasty remarks, so this guy carelessly let his suit jacket fall open, and displayed his pistol in a shoulder harness. My friend shut up! After all, the fellow in the Green Lantern was in the legitimate business of selling stolen goods!"[30]

On March 19, 1931, a twenty-seven-year-old cook named Frank Ventress stood up from his Green Lantern dinner and told his wife he would be right back. He walked to the rear door of the Lantern and was shot to death, forcing the temporary closing of the saloon. In another incident, gunmen Clarence Colton and William Weaver, later identified as a conspirator in the kidnapping of Edward Bremer, were arrested at the Lantern during a police raid in August 1932, but they jumped their bond and disappeared. [31]

The growing notoriety of the Green Lantern ultimately rendered it too dangerous for criminal get-togethers. When the FBI questioned Dillinger gang member Tommy Gannon about a meeting agents thought he had scheduled near the Green Lantern with robber Homer Van Meter, Gannon was surprised by the FBI's naiveté: this was "one of the 'hottest' blocks in town and it was not conceivable to him that such a spot could be used for a meeting," the FBI reported.[32]

The Green Lantern also served as a place where gangsters met with crooked police, many of whom befriended Harry Sawyer. FBI agents learned from the porter, Eddie Miller, that "it was not unusual for police officers to visit Sawyer's place from time to time to buy cigars."[33]

St. Paul police detective Tom Brown was a frequent visitor to the Green Lantern, where he chatted openly with gangsters. Years later, when detective Brown was assigned to investigate the William Hamm and Edward Bremer kidnappings, his relationships with the customers at the Green Lantern—many of whom were involved in the abductions—led J. Edgar Hoover to launch a fateful investigation into the corruption of the St. Paul Police Department.[34]

17 Tom Filben, Slot Machine King

The Hotel St. Francis
Old West Seventh between Wabasha and St. Peter Streets, St. Paul

The files of the Federal Bureau of Investigation contain transcripts of a series of remarkable 1936 interviews with half a dozen girlfriends of members of the Dillinger and Barker-Karpis gangs. The young women detail the drawbacks of being in love with a public enemy: physical abuse, furtive moving from city to city, sexual infidelity, venereal disease, abortions, false names, anxiety about capture by FBI agents—and, to top it all off, car trouble.

"The gang loses a car frequently for they are registered under fictitious names," the FBI learned from Beth Green of the Dillinger gang. "When they get a traffic ticket . . . they abandon the car and have to buy a new automobile." When they needed a new car, the gang often turned to Thomas Patrick Filben, the Irish slot machine king who, according to the FBI, was also a dealer in "hot" diamonds and was "considered to be a permanent guest at the St. Francis Hotel."[35]

The St. Francis was so popular with criminals that in 1934 the FBI recruited the hotel's telephone operator as a source. An agent noted that "this informant is located advantageously, in view of the fact that the St. Francis Hotel is looked upon as a gangster hotel." Dice games at the cigar counter in the lobby were a key attraction. Jack Ramaley, assistant manager of the St. Francis cafeteria in 1928, remembered a sharpie who was beating the cigar store clerk. "He was winning like crazy, and had the candy piled up," said Ramaley. Boxing promoter Jerk Doran saw her predicament and took over. He stripped off his jacket, picked up the dice, and won back all of the woman's candy along with all of the patron's money. Slipping his coat back on, Doran told the woman, "That guy was an amateur. He was only holding [concealing] one die. I was holding two!"[36]

Ramaley also recalled a New Year's Eve party at the St. Francis at which a gun dropped out of a gangster's pocket and bounced noisily three times on the floor. "The mobster just scooped the gun up and slipped it back into his coat," said Ramaley. So many underworld figures were visiting St. Paul then that a stray revolver was hardly enough to spark comment or elicit more than a passing glance.

Hotel St. Francis, a popular hostelry which served as headquarters for underworld fixer Tom Filben (inset)

The most powerful of the hoods who frequented the hotel was undoubtedly Thomas Filben—practical joker, slot machine czar, fence, underworld automobile financier, and the Dillinger gang's political campaign collector. Filben was questioned by the FBI during both the Bremer and Hamm kidnapping investigations, but he refused to talk about what he knew. The FBI recognized him as the Twin Cities contact for Lester "Babyface Nelson" Gillis and as a close friend of Fred "Shotgun George Ziegler" Goetz, hit man for Capone's syndicate.[37]

For a week in April 1934, Filben was a sensation when newspapers reported on his interrogation by the FBI for helping John Dillinger purchase getaway cars. The FBI had discovered that Filben, through his Federal Acceptance Corporation finance company, had negotiated the sale of the Hudson sedan used by Dillinger in his March 1934 escape from the FBI shootout at the Lincoln Court Apartments in St. Paul.[38]

Confronted with evidence of his dealings with Dillinger, Filben told the agents with refreshing candor that—in the words of an FBI summary—he "would not furnish the Government any information as he was not on the Government payroll and that was not his business; that he is in a racket and that he has to assist racketeers."[39]

Filben was born in St. Paul in 1890 to Irish parents, Delia and Patrick Filben, who ran a "man's saloon" at Eighth and Robert Streets. At the height of his power as an underworld fixer in the early 1930s, he lived in a two-story beige-and-cream stucco home (still standing at 2133 Fairmount Avenue, near the intersection with Finn Avenue) with his second wife. A Filben family yarn says that, in the wake of Danny Hogan's fiery demise, Filben always asked his first wife to start his car for him. According to family legend, when she discovered why, she divorced him.[40]

Filben's family was often ashamed of his notoriety, particularly when he was publicly identified with John Dillinger. "My father didn't want anything to do with Tom's connections. . . . [He] was a big embarrassment, there'd be these stories about his taxes," said Anita Vogelgesang, a relative of Filben. "My father used to get wild with him, angry with him. Tom's personality, well, some people just seem to enjoy that kind of thing, living on the edge."[41]

Gangsters knew they could find Filben at Patrick Novelty company, his slot machine operation at 518 St. Peter Street, a few blocks from the Hotel St. Francis in downtown St. Paul. The windows of Patrick Novelty (which is no longer standing) were filled with radios, none of which was for sale. Filben's slot machines were installed throughout the city, from the lounges of fine restaurants to the living room of Nina Clifford's brothel. Tom Filben's niece, Jean Preston, once visited Patrick Novelty with her mother. "He had this safe three feet high with drawers," recalled Preston. "Tom said, 'Now you and your mom pick out a ring, any ring in this safe.' He opened a drawer, and there [was] nothing but diamond rings in the safe!"[42]

Like Harry Sawyer, Filben acted as an underworld banker; whenever a St. Paul hoodlum was sent to prison, Filben was available to safeguard his bankroll until his release. "Tom's two safes were *crammed* with money," recalled former Patrick Novelty employee Horace Dupont, who said he helped Filben launder stolen currency through his slot machine company: "Jimmy Keating and Tom Holden would rob banks, and then they'd bring the stolen change to Filben at Patrick Novelty Company, stuffed in the canvas bags that we used to cover up our slot machines. My job was to take the bank identification wrappers off the rolls of stolen coins and reroll them into another wrapper, as if they were just our slot machine proceeds."[43]

According to an FBI informant close to the Dillinger gang, Filben also helped the gang fulfill its political responsibilities. He accepted cash contributions totaling $1,500 from Dillinger, Babyface Nelson, and five other mobsters to benefit police detective Tom Brown's campaign for sheriff.[44]

Filben was known throughout the underworld for his bizarre taste in cruel pranks. "Sit down, have a seat," Filben would say, directing a gangster to an upholstered armchair in his Patrick Novelty offices. Moments later, the thug would leap to his feet howling, for the chair was wired to give him a jolt of electricity. Filben once poured burning oil of mustard on the groin area of a sleeping bootlegger's pants. "Herman [the bootlegger] tore out of the place, yelling," recalled Dupont. "That was a joke, that was all."[45]

The joking Irishman may have been drawn into homicide as well. State crime files suggest that Filben was involved in the deaths of two women who were about to turn witness against the Barker-Karpis gang. It all began on January 5, 1932, when a half-dozen gangsters traveled fifty-five miles north of St. Paul to hold the little town of Cambridge, Minnesota, hostage. The gang stole goods worth $3,000 from Cambridge stores and took a Buick sedan from the Gillespie Auto Company but failed to crack open Gillespie's two-thousand-pound safe. (The safe, which is still owned by the Gillespie family, now sits in the front office of Peter Iten's Auto Center at 115 North Main Street in Cambridge.) The gang kidnapped the town marshal, pistol-whipped an elderly garage attendant, and fled for the Twin Cities.[46]

Two months later, the St. Paul police telephoned George Gillespie of Gillespie Auto in Cambridge and mayor Guy Runyan. Would they enjoy witnessing a double cross? According to Gillespie's son Eben, two women—Margaret "Indian Rose" Perry, an Ojibway from Virginia, Minnesota, and her girlfriend Sadie Carmacher of Duluth—were going to "turn tables and squeal on the boys" in the Barker-Karpis gang. The women never showed

Women's Murder Car Identified As Cambridge Terrorists' Loot

An automobile, stolen by bandits in a raid on Cambridge, Minn., three months ago, was found burning with the bodies of two slain women inside, near Turtle Lake, Wis., Saturday night. It is shown above. Insets are officials of Polk County, Wis., who are conducting the investigation of the double murder. Above left is Sheriff James Olson. Upper right is J. L. McGinnis, district attorney. The lower inset shows Coroner Willis C. Park. The bodies of the women were first disfigured with acid, before being burned in an effort to destroy clues to their identities.

The burned-out car in which police found the bodies of Margaret "Indian Rose" Perry and Sadie Carmacher

up, and on March 7, 1932, their bodies were found near Balsam Lake, Wisconsin, in a burned-out sedan—the Buick that had been stolen at Cambridge. The pair had been shot to death with a .38-caliber pistol, their features obscured by nitric acid, and their bodies burned in the car.[47]

Harry Sawyer told a farfetched story to explain the double homicide: a Twin Cities banker who had laundered the money stolen in December 1922 from the Denver branch of the Federal Reserve Bank of Kansas City had had them killed. (Perry was the girlfriend of "Denver Bobbie" Walker, a suspect in the $200,000 Denver robbery.) More convincing are FBI reports that Jack Peifer of the Hollyhocks casino "had them murdered as Indian Rose was making certain demands on Pfeiffer's friend, Thomas Filben and threatened to expose members of the Cambridge, Minnesota, burglary gang if she were not paid off." The state BCA came to the same conclusion: "Jack Peiffer had had some one kill these women for Thomas Filben." Filben, interviewed by the FBI, would say only that Perry was killed "because it was believed she was threatening certain people."[48]

One obstacle to determining whether Peifer and Filben were involved in the slayings was the fact that the police officer assigned to the murder investigation was none other than Thomas Brown, a friend of both Filben and Peifer. Filben and Brown often vacationed together in northern Minnesota, in a rustic mingling of law enforcement and crime. Filben's extravagantly furnished two-story wood frame summer cottage on Trout Lake, near Crane Lake and the U.S.-Canadian border, even contained a player piano that had been painstakingly transported through the wilderness. "Tom Filben would make one trip up to Crane Lake with his wife and the next trip up with his girlfriend," remembered Crane Lake resident John Bowser. "Tom and his wife came up to the place in a line of five cars, all Packards. Filben was a character."[49]

The Filben cabin on Trout Lake, once owned by post office robber William "Dutch" Canner, now stands abandoned in Voyageurs National Park; local residents inaccurately call it "the Capone cabin." The cottage is so remote that in order to reach it the gangsters had to drive to a fishing lodge, rent an inboard motorboat, travel thirty-five miles by water, and then portage to another boat. But the isolation was worth it: how could FBI agents possibly raid the cottage without being noticed? Near Filben's cottage was a twelve-and-a-half-acre vacation site on Crane Lake owned by Tom Brown. Neighbors told stories of underworld figures hunting wild game with Thompson submachine guns near Brown's cottage. A game warden told FBI agents that he ran into bank robber Harvey Bailey and Brown hunting deer together in 1930.[50]

Police detective Bill McMullen, an associate of bootlegger Leon Gleckman, ran six cottages on the west shore of Sand Point Lake. Crane Lake offered a resort run by Bill Randolph, whom the FBI described as "an underworld character . . . intimately acquainted and associated with Jack Peiffer, Harry Sawyer and Tom Filbin, and others of the St. Paul underworld [who act] as 'lookout' for members of the St. Paul 'mob' when they are at their cottages on Sand Point Lake and Trout Lake."[51]

At least one life was saved by the remote cabins of Tom Filben, Bill McMullen, and Tom Brown. Legendary crime reporter Nate Bomberg, equally trusted by gangsters and police, took time off to show the girlfriend of a Chicago mobster the sights of St. Paul one night. The grateful woman wrote two letters that week—one telling a girlfriend about the marvelous time she had with a handsome bachelor named Nate Bomberg and one to her mobster boyfriend—and accidentally switched them, mailing her breathless account of partying with Bomberg to the gangster.

"This hit man, a friend of Nate's . . . said: 'Nate, I've received a contract on you tomorrow, so make yourself scarce,'" recalled retired St. Paul police officer Ted Fahey. "Nate took off for Crane Lake [where] two St. Paul detectives had a resort. . . . After Nate was gone long enough, the whole thing died [down]."[52]

By June 1932, the nationwide hunt for fugitive bank robbers Jimmy Keating, Verne Miller, Tommy Holden, and Frank Nash led the FBI to recognize that the Trout and Sand Point Lakes area was a gathering place for gangsters. Agents recruited informants throughout the region, interviewing post office inspectors, game wardens, sheriffs, border patrol officers, customs agents, and even members of the Royal Canadian Mounted Police. The FBI was playing on Filben and Brown's territory, though, and was unable to capture any vacationing gangsters.[53]

The relationships between police and criminals—Tom Brown and Tom Filben were a classic pair—forged by the O'Connor system of bribes, became the foundation for the Barker-Karpis gang crime waves of 1933 and 1934.[54]

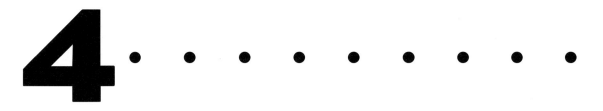

4

A BANK ROBBERS' HAVEN

Thomas Holden (far left) and Francis L. "Jimmy" Keating (left), escapees from Leavenworth prison in 1930

18   The 'Lamsters' Hideout'

The Edgecumbe Court Apartments
1095 Osceola Avenue, St. Paul

The FBI was never able to determine why the Edgecumbe Court Apartments, at the northeast corner of Osceola Avenue and Lexington Parkway, attracted so many Leavenworth prison escapees, but they had no doubt that the building had become a "lamsters' hideout." From 1931 through 1933, the most skillful bank robbers in America paid $85 a month to live in what the FBI called "one of the best furnished apartment houses in the city." Among the Edgecumbe tenants were Oklahoma bank robber Frank "Jelly" Nash; machine gunner Verne Miller; Barker-Karpis gang members Arthur "Doc" Barker, Volney "Curly" Davis and his girlfriend, Edna "the Kissing Bandit" Murray, and con artist Earl Christman; bandit Charles Preston Harmon and his wife, Paula, (later to become Fred Barker's girlfriend); and the two "Evergreen bandits," train robbers Jimmy Keating and Tommy Holden.[1]

The Edgecumbe Court was operated by Henry P. Reed, a former banker from Hibbing, Minnesota, who had no inkling that he was renting to a convention of bank robbers. Reed's other tenants had no difficulty guessing the occupation of their odd neighbors. Robert Seng, who in 1931 lived in apartment 204, across from Frank Nash, recalled the day when another tenant, Esther Haybeck, responded to a knock on her door. "Hi, babe," grinned the visitor, whom Haybeck recognized as the infamous gangster Lester "Babyface Nelson" Gillis. For a moment, Haybeck was speechless, and then she screamed, sending Nelson running for cover. While the gangsters rested during the day, their cars were being polished outside. When night fell, their parties began, and Seng pounded on his apartment walls for respite from the noise.[2]

The influx of gangsters who were sworn under the O'Connor system not to commit crimes within the St. Paul city limits had sparked a wave of bank robberies in rural Minnesota towns such as Hugo, Sandstone, Elk River, Cushing, Savage, Shakopee, and Belle Plaine. In 1930 more than two dozen Minnesota banks were robbed of nearly $214,800; the small communities were not prepared for big-city bandits equipped with machine guns and high-speed cars. In May 1930, after banks in the small towns of Clements, Winthrop, and Bixby were robbed during a three-day period, the Minnesota Bankers Association urged its members to instruct their guards to shoot to kill robbers.[3]

A speaker at the Minnesota Bankers Association's 1933 annual convention noted that 21 percent of all bank holdups in the United States in 1932 occurred in the state of Minnesota—a total of forty-three daylight bank robberies netting $1.39 million.[4]

Just as devastating were the bank robberies in neighboring states. North Dakota banks lost more than $102,000 to robberies in 1930, and robbers struck five North Dakota banks in a thirteen-day span in September 1932. Wisconsin banks in Cameron, Cumberland, Milton Junction, Grantsburg, Stone Lake, Colfax, and other towns suffered similar fates in 1931. During an October 1931 robbery of $5,000 from a Stone Lake bank, four thieves carefully examined the bank's books and determined that there had to be more bonds worth stealing than those they had seized so far.[5]

Police found that some of the Upper Midwest bank robberies were committed by farm youths and desperate amateurs, but others—such as the October 1931 robbery of the Kraft State Bank in Menomonie, Wisconsin, and the Austin, Minnesota, mail robbery of August 1931—clearly involved professionals. Newspaper accounts often noted that the robbers were "last

The Edgecumbe Court Apartments, a hideout for the Barker-Karpis gang; bankrobber Frank "Jelly" Nash (inset)

Aftermath of a Good Thunder, Minnesota, bank robbery in which the safe was blown open with nitroglycerine

seen driving toward St. Paul" or "are believed to be heading toward the Twin Cities."

The most prominent career bank robber living at the Edgecumbe Court Apartments was Frank "Jelly" Nash from Hobart, Oklahoma. An FBI wanted poster listed his occupations as "cook, hotel worker, bank robber." FBI records indicate that Nash lived as "Frank Lee" in apartment 205, rented with his bank-robbing friend from Leavenworth, Charlie Harmon, from June 1 through August 28, 1931.[6]

Born in Indiana in 1887, Nash earned a reputation as a crime strategist with impeccable manners. Like Harvey Bailey, Nash was respected for his detailed planning and daring escapes. In 1913, he broke out of an Oklahoma jail, kidnapped a prosecution witness about to testify against him in a murder trial, and then returned to lock himself in his jail cell the next morning.[7]

"Frank Nash was, perhaps, the most successful bank robber in history . . . [whose] career of bank robbing [was] unparalleled by either old-time outlaw or modern day gangster," wrote his biographers, Clyde Callahan and Byron Jones. Nash, who had a record of more than a hundred successful robberies, was a transitional figure, "a new breed of criminal . . . [with] automobiles rather than horses, automatic pistols and sub-machine[gun]s taking the place of the old fashioned six-shooter [and] urban homes or resorts for hideouts instead of a rough camp in the hills." In contrast to sociopaths like Fred Barker and Larry DeVol, Nash was intelligent and something of a literary aesthete: in prison, he read Dickens and Shakespeare.[8]

Nash was first arrested for a burglary at an Oklahoma store in May 1911. He was picked up for burglary again in June, July, August, September, October, and November of the same year, but none of the arrests led to a conviction. Though Nash generally was poor at evading capture, once he was caught he was adept at cutting his prison sentences short. In 1913, for example, he was sentenced to life in the state penitentiary in McAlester, Oklahoma, for shooting his partner. But in 1918 the governor of Oklahoma commuted his sentence to ten years because officials believed that Nash's victim "was a man of questionable character with a criminal record." Nash was pardoned and freed from prison in July to serve in the U.S. Army.[9]

Convicted in 1924 of an Oklahoma mail train robbery, Nash began to serve a twenty-five-year sentence in Leavenworth prison. He befriended his future partners in crime, bank robbers Jimmy Keating and Tommy Holden, whom he helped escape from Leavenworth in February 1930. In October 1930 Nash walked out of Leavenworth himself, slipping away from the home of the deputy warden, for whom he served as a housekeeper. Nash hid in Joplin, Missouri, vacationed in Hot Springs, Arkansas, and then joined Keating and Holden in Minnesota. When he arrived, Nash first stayed in Minneapolis at the Senator Hotel, run by St. Paul racketeer Jack Peifer and bootlegger Tommy Banks, and then moved to the Edgecumbe Court in St. Paul.[10]

"Since his escape, Nash is reported to have changed his appearance," warned an FBI wanted poster, "having gained approximately 50 pounds, now wears a wig-toupee and has had his nose reshaped by plastic operations." The forty-four-year-old Nash was a balding heavy drinker with an ill-fitting toupee. According to FBI memos, he "apparently did not have any regular woman companion, and was never seen by Mr. Reed [the landlord] in company with any woman other than Mrs. Ryan [Paula Harmon] and her friends."[11]

Then, in late 1931, Nash fell in love with a former schoolteacher and cook from Aurora, Minnesota, a twenty-eight-year-old divorcee named Frances Mikulich. Nash courted Frances using an alias, visiting her family in Aurora as "Mr. Harrison." When they were married in Hot Springs, the fugitive used another alias—George Miller. "After the marriage ceremony I asked

Frances Mikulich Nash, the Aurora schoolteacher who married Frank Nash

Frank why we were married under the name of Miller," Frances told the FBI, "when I thought his name was Frank Harrison."[12]

The residents of the Edgecumbe Court continued to plot new criminal ventures. On April 8, 1931, Nash and Harvey Bailey, using Verne Miller and George "Machine Gun Kelly" Barnes as getaway drivers, stole $40,000 from the Central State Bank of Sherman, Texas.[13]

The tension of the robberies, alternating with the anxiety of life as a fugitive, accelerated Nash's drinking. Miller, a close friend, tried to dry Nash out. "Frank was drinking heavily all during this time," Frances told the FBI, "and every time Verne would see him he would bawl Frank out, but Frank paid no attention, and continued to drink; in fact Frank was a heavy drinker, and indulged freely, and frequently, in intoxicating liquor all during the time I associated with him."[14]

Meanwhile, the FBI was examining every paper, telegram, and telephone call related to Nash's life with Keating, Holden, Miller, and Charlie Harmon. FBI agent Oscar Hall listed the FBI's methods: "surveillance of hangouts of St. Paul hoodlums, covering of their telephones and mail, and the establishing of reliable contacts at what are believed strategic points." During the summer of 1932, FBI agents interviewed dry cleaners, electric utility clerks, tailors, and milkmen who had served Nash and his gang members while they were living at the Edgecumbe Apartments. Agents relentlessly traced their movements through gas, electric, and water records, laundry delivery services, credit bureaus, and auto dealers and registrations. Agents compared the signatures of the gang's girlfriends on utility bills in painstaking efforts to trace forwarding addresses and track their movements from city to city.[15]

Right to the end, Nash lived up to his nickname, "the Gentleman Bandit." When he moved out of the Edgecumbe in August 1931, the FBI learned that Nash had congratulated his landlord "on the manner in which he conducted the apartment house and stated that he enjoyed living there very much."[16] Within two years, the polite bank robber was dead. Nash earned underworld immortality on June 17, 1933, when he was accidentally slain by his friend Verne Miller during the Kansas City Massacre—a botched escape attempt at Kansas City's Union Station.

Even after Nash's departure, crime figures continued to be drawn to the Edgecumbe Court. In mid-December 1933—during the pause between the kidnapping of William Hamm and the abduction of Edward Bremer—Barker-Karpis gang member Volney "Curley" Davis and his girlfriend, Edna Murray, drove into St. Paul from Reno and moved into an Edgecumbe apartment. When Davis met Murray, she was a struggling Oklahoma waitress with a teenage son from a previous marriage. Born in Marion, Kansas, in 1898, Murray was described by moll Beth Green as having a large mouth packed with gold fillings, "small through the back and built like a tent." Murray had an extraordinary history of romancing scoundrels. She fell in love with Davis shortly before he was sentenced to the Oklahoma State Penitentiary at McAlester in 1923 for murdering a night watchman with Doc Barker. While Davis was in prison, Murray lived with jewel thief Fred "Diamond Joe" Sullivan in Kansas City. But in 1924 Sullivan was imprisoned, and ultimately electrocuted, for murdering two Little Rock, Arkansas, police officers. After that, Edna moved in with Kansas City liquor hijacker Jack Murray, with whom she was arrested and convicted of a highway holdup; both received twenty-five-year sentences in the Missouri State Penitentiary in Jefferson City.[17]

Edna "the Kissing Bandit" Murray

The popular media nicknamed Murray "the Kissing Bandit." A 1937 issue of *Official Detective Stories* gave this explanation for her moniker: "It was her habit, in the midst of a hi-jacking job to rush up to the truck-driver or some other male victim and kiss him lustfully. . . . Edna was lavish with her kisses in underworld resorts. She often lulled the suspicions of future victims by this means. . . . While a robbery was in progress, she may have kissed with the idea of keeping the man occupied and blocking a counter-attack." To members of the Barker-Karpis gang, Murray was "Rabbits," a tribute to her ability to escape from prisons. She escaped from the Missouri State Penitentiary in 1927, returned to prison in September 1931, escaped from a Missouri prison farm in November 1931, was returned to prison the next day, and then escaped again by sawing through the bars of her cell in December 1932. Once more a fugitive, Murray arranged a rendezvous in Kansas City with gangster Volney Davis.[18]

Born in Tahlequah, Oklahoma, Davis was a slender man with light blue eyes and chestnut hair, marked by a scar on his forehead. Convicted of grand larceny in Tulsa at the age of seventeen, he was sent briefly to the state prison. In 1925 he escaped from McAlester and joined the Barker-Karpis gang. Murray told the FBI about always being broke, of Davis's having to borrow money from Fred Barker, and of quarreling frequently with Davis "on account of his chasing around with other women."[19]

Far from being a master criminal like Frank Nash, Davis stumbled along on the periphery of the gang. In 1933 he and Murray slipped away to Reno, where he promised to borrow money from his underworld contacts, but as he cruised the streets aimlessly, Murray realized that "he did not know where any of the boys were living." Murray later told FBI agents that Fred Barker's girlfriend, Paula Harmon, would "always bring up the subject that we were living off of Fred's money, which I did not like, and, as a result, I often wanted to get away from them, but Volney and I could not very well afford to do that as . . . we were low on money at that time." During the summer of 1934 Davis loaned Murray money for a cancer operation she urgently needed, but, Murray told the FBI, her doctor "wanted the record of my previous operation, and I could not furnish him with this record without revealing my true identity." She did not have the surgery.[20]

The end for Davis, Murray, and the Edgecumbe Court's lamsters' hideout came in late 1934. On December 26, detective Thomas Brown of the St. Paul police called fixer Harry Sawyer of the Green Lantern saloon with an urgent tip-off. The police were about to raid the Edgecumbe Court, warned detective Brown—were there any members of Sawyer's gang still living there who should be notified? Fred Barker drove to the apartments and warned Davis and Murray, who fled to gangster "Lapland Willie" Weaver's apartment above the Moonlight Gardens on Selby Avenue.[21]

Once again, an O'Connor-system tip had saved a member of the Barker-Karpis gang. But not even the police could save the unluckiest gangster in Minnesota, Charles Preston Harmon.

19 'Unlucky' Charlie Harmon

The Lincoln Oaks Apartments
572 Lincoln Avenue, St. Paul

When the couple calling themselves Thomas and Paula Ryan moved into the Edgecumbe Court Apartments, they told the landlord they were hotel owners from Arkansas. But Charles Preston Harmon, ex-convict and bank robber, and his wife, Paula, were lying. In August 1931 when they told the landlord they were going back to Arkansas, they were lying again: they were moving to the Lincoln Oaks, at 572 Lincoln Avenue.[22]

Texas-born Charlie Harmon was short, slight, scarred (from gunshot wounds in his right leg and abdomen), tattooed (with a bizarre illustration of a man straddling a hog), and unlucky. A U.S. Navy veteran and a carpenter by trade, Harmon was first arrested in 1921 for armed robbery and sent to the Huntsville, Texas, state prison. Released in October 1924, he was identified in prison records as having become a chronic nail-biter. In 1928 Harmon was incarcerated in Leavenworth for a post office robbery in Davenport, Iowa. Typical of his shambling criminal skills, the heist netted barely $174—not in cash, but in postage stamps and C.O.D. parcels. (Harmon later told the prison chaplain he committed the Iowa robbery to "get some clothes.") By the time he was paroled in 1930, Harmon already had been arrested by police in Dallas and Houston, Texas; Chicago and Rock Island, Illinois; and Council Bluffs, Iowa. His bad luck continued on a return stay in Leavenworth in July 1930, when he was injured playing sandlot baseball. A fellow convict's curve ball sailed across the field and struck his left ear; he was hospitalized and had to have stitches. Released again from Leavenworth in January 1931 and discharged to Chicago, Harmon made his way to St. Paul.[23]

The Barker-Karpis gang thought of Harmon as a grumpy hanger-on, wrote Frank Nash's biographers. He "was not considered good company in their leisure hours, was boastful and a poor loser on the golf course. . . . He was included in on bank jobs only because of his persistence and the fact he knew so much about their plans."[24]

Even Charlie's marriage was plagued with missteps. Paula Harmon was raised in Port Arthur, Texas, and educated at a girls' finishing school in Atlanta. She married Charlie in 1925, just after his release from a Huntsville, Texas, prison. According to Beth Green, Eddie Green's girlfriend, Paula was a strange-looking woman: she had false upper teeth, and her face looked flat as a result of automobile-accident injuries. In a 1929 telegram to her imprisoned husband, she cooed, "I just wanted to say I really love you and if I had to do over would be glad to do the same as one hour with you erases all

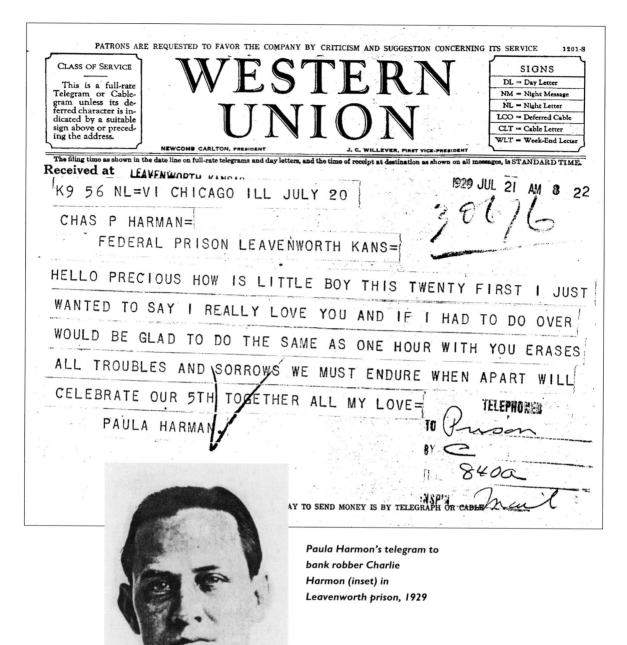

PATRONS ARE REQUESTED TO FAVOR THE COMPANY BY CRITICISM AND SUGGESTION CONCERNING ITS SERVICE 1201-S

WESTERN UNION

CLASS OF SERVICE

This is a full-rate Telegram or Cablegram unless its deferred character is indicated by a suitable sign above or preceding the address.

NEWCOMB CARLTON, PRESIDENT   J. C. WILLEVER, FIRST VICE-PRESIDENT

SIGNS

| DL = Day Letter |
| NM = Night Message |
| NL = Night Letter |
| LCO = Deferred Cable |
| CLT = Cable Letter |
| WLT = Week-End Letter |

The filing time as shown in the date line on full-rate telegrams and day letters, and the time of receipt at destination as shown on all messages, is STANDARD TIME.

Received at LEAVENWORTH KANSAS

K9 56 NL=VI CHICAGO ILL JULY 20   1929 JUL 21 AM 8 22

CHAS P HARMAN=

FEDERAL PRISON LEAVENWORTH KANS=

HELLO PRECIOUS HOW IS LITTLE BOY THIS TWENTY FIRST I JUST
WANTED TO SAY I REALLY LOVE YOU AND IF I HAD TO DO OVER
WOULD BE GLAD TO DO THE SAME AS ONE HOUR WITH YOU ERASES
ALL TROUBLES AND SORROWS WE MUST ENDURE WHEN APART WILL
CELEBRATE OUR 5TH TOGETHER ALL MY LOVE=

PAULA HARMAN

AY TO SEND MONEY IS BY TELEGRAPH OR CABLE

30676

Paula Harmon's telegram to bank robber Charlie Harmon (inset) in Leavenworth prison, 1929

troubles and sorrows we must endure when apart . . . all my love—Paula Harman." But while Charlie was in prison, Paula opened what she termed a "call house" in Chicago; the FBI daintily referred to Paula's business as a "house of ill fame." The brothel became a source of growing tension between the Harmons, and Paula told the FBI that after her husband was released from Leavenworth in 1930, the couple never really got along.[25]

For his part, Charlie was squiring another woman around St. Paul during the summer of 1931. The FBI was later able to convince this woman to talk. When she met Harmon, noted an FBI report, she "did not know that he was a gangster and he conducted himself as a gentleman and always had lots of money and claimed to be an investigator for a nationally known concern. After she had been going with him several months she heard other members of the 'gang' and their sweethearts make comments which led her to believe that her sweetheart was an underworld character." When she confronted him, "he became very angry and denied he associated with any outlaw gang, but admitted that he was a 'fixture' for a liquor ring."[26]

In October 1931, Charlie Harmon made the worst decision of his life. He joined Tommy Holden, Jimmy Keating, and Frankie Webber in taking $130,000 (all but $10,000 in nonnegotiable securities) from the Kraft State Bank of Menomonie, Wisconsin—the thirty-fourth Wisconsin bank robbed in 1931 and the last bank Harmon ever robbed. The Menomonie job was a disaster from the start. Minutes after the robbers entered the bank, the burglar alarm was set off, attracting a swarm of townspeople who fired back at the robbers with deer rifles. Inside the bank, the gangsters were delayed by needless violence. When one of them demanded more money, bank official William Kraft replied, "You have all there is . . . you have every cent in the bank." The gangster yelled "I'll fix you" and fired a bullet into Kraft's chest as he lay helpless on the floor. Twenty-one-year-old cashier James Kraft, son of bank president Sam Kraft, was taken hostage by Harmon, who used him as a shield.

Minutes later, James Kraft was murdered during the getaway ride, his body left on a road just north of Menomonie. Nearby was the bullet-riddled body of the machine gunner who had protected the bank-robbing trio, Utah State Prison alumnus Frank Webber of Minneapolis. Two days later, officials found another body at Shell Lake, Wisconsin. It was Charlie Harmon, shot through the neck and knee—either by the townspeople or his partners. Harmon was buried with Webber in a potter's field grave.[27]

20 Hideout of 'A Very Fine Gentleman'

The Cretin Court Apartments
50 South Cretin Avenue, St. Paul

To the FBI agents hunting them across the United States, gangsters Thomas Holden and Francis L. "Jimmy" Keating were known as the "Evergreen bandits." Their notoriety grew from their robbery of $130,000 from a Port Huron and Chicago Railway train in Evergreen Park, Illinois, for which they had been sentenced in 1928 to serve twenty-five years in Leavenworth prison.[28]

Francis Keating, a muscular former Chicago cab driver and streetcar conductor, was the son of middle-class Irish parents and the youngest in a family of eight. His father died of tuberculosis in 1906, when Keating was just seven years old. Before his conviction, Keating, a U.S. Navy veteran, was married and had two young sons. Holden, two years older, two inches taller, and twenty pounds heavier than his partner, was a former Stutz auto salesman and steam fitter. Neither Keating nor Holden had been convicted of a crime before being apprehended for the train robbery. Keating insisted for decades that they were innocent, their conviction a case of mistaken identity.[29]

While they were in Leavenworth for the Evergreen robbery, Keating and Holden befriended George "Machine Gun Kelly" Barnes and robber Frank Nash. "Frank was deeply interested in what they had to say about crime methods under the Al Capone regime," wrote Nash's biographers, Clyde Callahan and Byron Jones. "They talked of big money, of plush hideouts in large cities . . . of big hauls, of big time bootlegging, bank jobs and gambling. . . . Both Keating and Holden were typical of the coterie that gravitated around Frank Nash. They were intelligent, pleasant, friendly, enjoyed good times, lived in excellent apartment houses and hotels, played golf on exclusive courses, wore good clothes and spent money freely."[30]

In February 1930, Keating and Holden escaped from Leavenworth. With the inside help of Nash, Harmon, and Machine Gun Kelly (who had been assigned to the Leavenworth records room, where fingerprints and photographs were stored), Keating and Holden obtained forged trustee passes. Minneapolis defense attorney Irv Nemerov, who represented Keating years later, recalled their prison-break stratagem: Keating "got himself a pass to get through the prison gate . . . but how was he going to get to the gate? Well, there were signs that said, 'Stay off the Grass.' So he'd run over and step on the grass. The guards would order him off the grass. And he moved off the grass toward the gate."[31]

After the escape, Keating and Holden traveled to Kansas City, Missouri, and Chicago. Bank robber Harvey Bailey suggested they seek haven at the Green Lantern saloon in St. Paul, and like so many gangsters before them, they plugged into fixer Harry Sawyer's contacts there. They stayed for a while in January 1931 at the Admiral Hotel in downtown Minneapolis (also known as the Senator Hotel), which was operated by St. Paul racketeer Jack Peifer and Minneapolis syndicate figure Tommy Banks.[32]

Unfortunately for the gangsters, the O'Connor system of protection did not extend to Minneapolis: an FBI memo noted that "Minneapolis soon became 'too hot' for the Fugitives and they moved to St. Paul and the suburbs near the lakes." By September 1930 Tommy Holden was living on St. Paul's prestigious Summit Avenue; Keating followed in May 1931.[33]

The fugitives were nearly captured early on, when a federal agent recognized them while they were eating in Nelson's Cafe in Minneapolis. Machine Gun Kelly told the FBI that the agent went to bootlegger Tommy Banks, whom Kelly identified as "the town fixer" in Minneapolis, and "told this individual that he had 'spotted' the two fugitives and asked him what it was worth if he took no action." The FBI learned that "through Tommy Banks . . . Keating and Holden paid $5,000 to an agent for protection. This agent . . . understood that he would be 'bumped off' if he double-crossed Keating and Holden on the payoff."[34]

Rescued from the threat of exposure in Minneapolis, Keating and his wife, calling themselves Mr. and Mrs. James Courtney, moved to St. Paul. He drove up to the Cretin Court Apartments in a maroon Buick coupe so fresh the dealer's stickers and tags were still attached. The "Courtneys" were rather fresh, too: an informant told the FBI that "when these people first came to the apartment, they left the impression that they had been recently married." The Keatings pretended to be "show people" performing at the Plantation nightclub in White Bear Lake.[35]

Barber Frank Doran styled Keating's hair every week in the Cretin Court basement. The bank robber "appeared to be a very fine gentleman," Doran told FBI agents. The barber "never saw him under the influence of liquor and he was of good manners and was very likable." Doran noticed that Keating did indulge himself with thick, expensive cigars—"probably they were La Unica cigars, [the] three for 50 cent[s] size." Jimmy Keating was also a terrific dresser. He would take as many as five suits—the finest $125 suits from Minneapolis tailor Ben Millman—to be pressed at Zolly Vetloff's dry cleaners across the street at 2166 Grand Avenue.[36]

The FBI uncovered more information on Keating's personal habits from the Orth family, who ran a delicatessen in the basement of the Cretin Court Apartments. "Keating and his girl would come into our store—we called it the Orth Grocery—and she'd always carry lots of gold coins in her purse," recalled Earl Orth, who managed the deli in the summer of 1931. Keating made long-distance calls from the pay phone to Kansas City—not to plan criminal activity but to make reservations at the golf course there.[37]

Throughout his life, Francis Keating preferred to be known as Jimmy. "I knew him as Jimmy," Charlie Reiter, a former St. Paul police officer who befriended Keating, remembered. "Francis Keating was his real name, but that sounds like a woman."[38] The aliases Keating used during his criminal career included Jimmy Courtney, Jimmy Olson, Jimmy Bates, Jimmy Larson, and Jimmy Stanley. As they searched the Twin Cities for some sign of Keating, the FBI knew that wherever he was hiding, his partner Tommy Holden would be secreted nearby.

21   'Dangerous Men' with Machine Guns

The Summit-Dale Apartments
616 Summit Avenue, St. Paul

"The search for these fugitives [Keating and Holden] led to St. Paul, Minnesota, where it was ascertained that they had taken up their residence and had become associated with the criminal underworld headed by Leon Gleckman," noted a 1934 FBI memo. "Thomas Holden, using the name William McCormick, with his wife, occupied a furnished apartment at 616 Summit Avenue, St. Paul, Minnesota, from September 2, 1930 to August 7, 1931."[39]

Holden lived with his wife in apartment 102 of the twenty-eight-unit apartment building still at the corner of Summit and Dale. Holden's wife Lillian tried to establish a semblance of domesticity in spite of the nationwide manhunt for her husband. She bought a $295 baby grand piano (later repossessed when they failed to keep up the payments) and a fur coat. (Unbeknownst to her, the FBI met with her furrier and piano company in their search for Keating and Holden.) The Holdens' existence was uneasy: Holden's maid told FBI agents that Lillian "had a sullen disposition" and "never appeared happy," and another informant said Jimmy Keating and his wife "quarrelled and cursed each other a great deal."[40]

Both Keating and Holden often left their wives at home to spend winter evenings at the Boulevards of Paris nightclub; during the summer, the pair would gamble at the Plantation nightclub in White Bear Lake. They ate frequently around the corner from the Holdens' Summit-Dale apartment in the French Cafe at 38 South Dale Street (today the site of La Cucaracha restaurant). Anxious about being spotted, Holden always held a hand on one side of his face.[41]

CRIMINAL RECORD

As Thomas Holden, No. 29979, received U. S. Penitentiary, Leavenworth, Kans., May 5, 1928, from Chicago, Ill.; crime, robbery of mails with firearms; sentence 25 years.

Summit-Dale Apartments, hideout for bank robber Tommy Holden (inset record), about 1932

Keating and Holden did not lead bank robberies themselves but were talented freelancers who collaborated with the Barker-Karpis or Frank Nash gangs for a cut of the proceeds. In September 1930 they joined Harvey Bailey, Larry DeVol, Fred Barker, Machine Gun Kelly, and Verne Miller in robbing a bank in Ottumwa, Iowa. The duo also helped Alvin Karpis, DeVol, Bailey, and Barker steal $32,000 from a Fort Scott, Kansas, bank in June 1932.[42]

The FBI did not underestimate the hazards of trying to bring Keating and Holden back to Leavenworth. "Keating and Holden . . . are now classed as dangerous men who are at all times armed, and also have a Thompson sub-machine gun in their possession," warned a 1932 FBI report." An FBI agent noted that

during the stay of Keating, Holden, Nash and their gang in St. Paul, a number of gang murders occurred, but for some reason or another the victims were always dumped in the adjoining counties although every evidence indicated that the men had been murdered elsewhere. In some cases the St. Paul Police would rush to the scene of the "finding of the body," gather up all the evidence and depart before the authorities charged with the solution of the crime could get there. The neighboring County authorities have complained that the case became so garbled they could never solve it.[43]

During the summer of 1932 Jimmy Keating became a prime suspect in the killing of another ex-con from Leavenworth, St. Paul auto thief Eddie Harlow. In December 1931, Harlow's body—with five bullet wounds—had been found in a bullet-riddled convertible seven miles outside Farmington, Minnesota. Shortly before his demise, Harlow had complained to authorities that Keating was "gunning" for him. The Justice Department admitted that Harlow had served as a government informant. Keating, however, was never questioned about the slaying, and Eddie Harlow's murder remained unsolved.[44]

22 'Cold-Blooded Disregard of Human Life'
The Murder of Sammy Silverman
Near Wildwood and Katherine Abbott Parks, Mahtomedi

As the manhunt for bank robbers Jimmy Keating, Tommy Holden, Verne Miller, and Frank Nash accelerated, a number of clues pointed the FBI toward the Mahtomedi area, just fourteen miles northeast of St. Paul. Particularly mystifying to the bureau were the August 1930 murders of gangsters Sammy Silverman, Frank "Weanie" Coleman, and Michael Rusick on a gravel road that ran from Wildwood Road to Long Lake Road, half a mile southeast of Wildwood Park in Mahtomedi.[45]

Weeks earlier, Keating and Holden, grateful to George "Machine Gun Kelly" Barnes for helping them escape from Leavenworth, invited him to join them in robbing the Bank of Willmar, Minnesota. Accompanying the trio to Willmar, about a hundred miles west of St. Paul, were prowler Sammy Silverman, Robert "Frisco Dutch" Steinhardt of Chicago, veteran bank robber Harvey Bailey, and, according to some accounts, machine gunner Verne Miller. The *St. Paul Pioneer Press* called the July 1930 Willmar robbery "one of the most daring bank holdups in the Northwest since the days of the Younger Brothers and Jesse James gangs." W. F. Rhinow, head of the state BCA, said, "I can't remember a holdup in the history of the state since the raids of the Younger Brothers and Jesse James gangs which compares to the one at Willmar for daring and cold-blooded disregard of human life."[46]

During the eight-minute attack, the machine gun-toting bandits demanded that two dozen employees and bank customers lie on the bank floor. A member of the gang pistol-whipped a cashier, yelling, "Lay down or we will kill you. We mean business." A final fusillade of machine-gun fire aimed directly into the crowd of a hundred people surrounding the bank wounded two women, one of them cradling her two-year-old daughter.[47]

The gang left with $142,000 in cash and securities, forcing a man and a

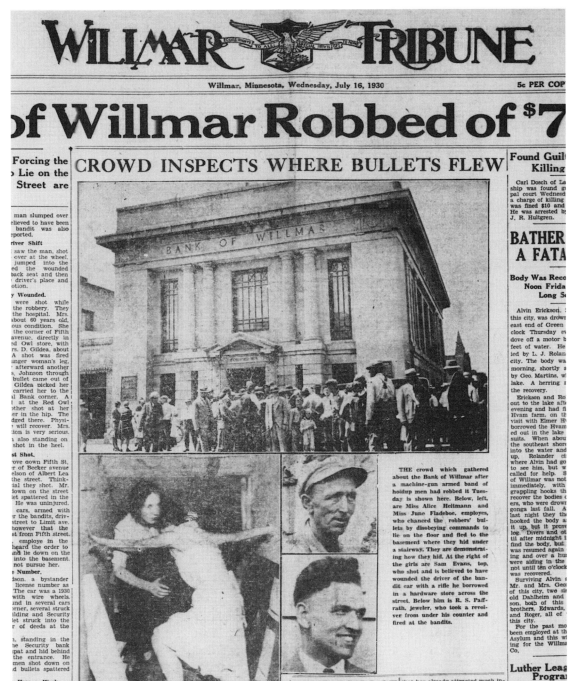

WILLMAR TRIBUNE

Willmar, Minnesota, Wednesday, July 16, 1930

5c PER COP

# of Willmar Robbed of $7

CROWD INSPECTS WHERE BULLETS FLEW

Forcing the Lie on the Street are

man slumped over believed to have been bandit was also reported.

river Shift

saw the man, shot over at the wheel, jumped into the ed the wounded back seat and then driver's place and otion.

y Wounded.

were shot while the robbery. They the hospital. Mrs. about 60 years old, ous condition. She the corner of Fifth avenue, directly in d Owl store, with rs. D. Gildea, about A shot was fired unger woman's leg, afterward another s. Johnson through bullet came out of Gildea picked her carried her to the l Bank corner. A at the Red Owl other shot at her er in the hip. The dged there. Physi-will recover. Mrs. tion is very serious. a also standing on shot in the heel.

st Shot.

ove oown Fifth St, r of Becker avenue elson of Albert Lea the street. Think-ial they shot. Mr. own on the street let spattered in the He was uninjured. cars, armed with r the bandits, driv-street to Limit ave. however that the st from Fifth street, employe in the heard the order to un& lie down on the into the basement. not pursue her.

e Number.

ison. a bystander license number as The car was a 1930 with wire wheels. and in several cars orner, several struck ilding and Security let struck into the r of deeds at the

. standing in the ne Security bank spat and hid behind the entrance. He men shot down on d bullets spattered

Here a Week.

n town claim they well dressed men s during the past

THE crowd which gathered about the Bank of Willmar after a machine-gun armed band of hoidup men had robbed it Tuesday is shown here. Below, left, are Miss Alice Heitmann and Miss June Fladeboe, employes, who chanced the robbers' bullets by disobeying commands to lie on the floor and fled to the basement where they hid under a stairway. They are demonstrating how they hid. At the right of the girls are Sam Evans, top, who shot and is believed to have wounded the driver of the bandit car with a rifle he borrowed in a hardware store across the street. Below him is R. S. Paffrath, jeweler, who took a revolver from under his counter and fired at the bandits.

REHEARSALS OF
PAGEANT ARE ON

that has already attracted much interest is the depiction of the important contributions made to our county's growth by the several ra-

Found Guil
Killing

Carl Dosch of La ship was found g pal court Wednesd a charge of killing was fined $10 and He was arrested by J. R. Hultgren.

BATHER
A FATA

Body Was Reco
Noon Frida
Long S

Alvin Erickson, this city, was drow east end of Green clock Thursday ev dove off a motor b feet of water. He ied by L. J. Rolar city. The body wa morning, shortly by Geo. Martins, w lake. A herring the recovery.

Erickson and Ro out to the lake aft evening and had fi Hvam farm on th visit with Elmer H borrowed the Hvam ed out in the lake suits. When abou the southeast shore into the water and up. Rolander ch where Alvin had go to see him, but w called for help. S of Willmar was not immediately, with grappling hooks th recover the bodies o ers, who were drow gonga last fall. A last night they th hooked the body a it up, but it prove log. Divers and ot til after midnight t find the body, but was resumed again ing and over a hu were aiding in the was resumed about was recovered.

Surviving Alvin Mr. and Mrs. Geo of this city, two si old Dahlheim and son, both of this brothers, Edwards and Roger, all of this city.

For the past mo been employed at th Asylum and this w ing for the Willma Co.,

Luther Leas
Progra

The Tripolis Luth give a program at eran church Wedr

A local newspaper account of the 1930 robbery of the Willmar bank

woman to serve as shields before releasing them. At least two of the robbers were wounded by Willmar residents who fired from nearby buildings, and the windshield and back window of the gang's four-door sedan was shattered by bullets. In what had become an underworld cliché, the *St. Paul Dispatch* reported that "following the robbery, the bandits drove to the Twin Cities." The getaway car was found abandoned in Minneapolis. The robbers switched the Willmar bank loot into another car, which was seen driving from Minneapolis to the safety of St. Paul.[48]

Harvey Bailey's recollections of the Willmar robbery, when he was interviewed some three decades later by biographer J. Evetts Haley, were uncharacteristically confused—he placed the Willmar robbery in "Williston" or "Wilburn":

> We was on a job up there [in Willmar]—this was a help out job, too. On our jobs that we cased, we never did have trouble, but every time we helped somebody else we had trouble. Because the place was not cased down and they didn't know just where they were at, you see. And this boy had got out and got into the car and he got shot right in the back of the neck. . . . They must have got a ring from inside; they must have got a buzzer from the inside that we didn't know about. [The assistant cashier had tripped an alarm bell under the cash drawer with his leg.] When we come out, they showered down on us. . . . The car got shot up pretty bad.[49]

After the Willmar robbery, Sammy Silverman hid in Big Lake, Minnesota, posing as a cattle businessman, and then masqueraded at Lake Minnetonka, just west of Minneapolis, as a Hollywood movie executive. "They lived a peaceful life, spending much of their time boating and swimming," reported the *St. Paul Dispatch* of Silverman and his gangland partners. They "were friendly to the children, buying them candy and ice cream, and intimated they desired seclusion to plan forthcoming motion picture productions."[50]

On August 14, a posse of agents from the BCA, searching for clues to the Willmar robbery, pulled up to examine three fresh bodies found near Wildwood Amusement Park. The agents immediately identified one body as that of Willmar bank robber Sammy Silverman, a former taxi driver known in Minneapolis variously as "the Ten Dollar Kid," "Sammy Stein," and Harry "Heckle" Silberman. Before the Willmar raid, Silverman had been suspected of killing a Kansas City policeman (and wounding four innocent bystanders) when he and four partners held up the Home Trust Company bank during the 1928 Republican National Convention. The FBI heard from informants that "Silverman got away from the [Kansas City] robbery with all of the money, and he was supposed to have been slain by members of the Bugs Moran gang."[51]

Newspaper announcing the triple murders

Silverman, his pockets full of unused .32-caliber bullets, had been shot in the head and neck. Killed along with him were Kansas City hoods Mike Rusick and Frank "Weanie" Coleman. The assailants left the three bloody bodies hanging from willow trees by a lovers' lane near Wildwood Park.[52]

They had left few clues. Police determined that a telephone call had been made from White Bear Lake to a Chicago gambling hall the night of the triple slaying. The FBI paid particular attention to suspicions that Chicago racketeer George "Bugs" Moran may have been involved in the murder. Although the murders were officially unsolved, an interview buried in Detroit police files on the murder of another gangster—Barker-Karpis gang machine gunner Verne Miller—offers the most likely answer. In a 1934 prison interview with police, Machine Gun Kelly identified Miller as the killer who committed the triple slaying near Wildwood Park. According to Kelly, Verne Miller had robbed the Willmar bank with Silverman and other gangsters. Foolishly, Silverman "double crossed Miller"; a few weeks later, "Miller saw this man [Sammy Silverman] with two friends at [White] Bear Lake, and killed all three of them."[53]

As the O'Connor system attracted more gangsters to St. Paul, multiple slayings between feuding criminals became more frequent, and it was not unusual for Minnesotans to stumble over stray corpses along the state's highways. Bank robber Harry "Slim Jones" Morris, for example, was found dead in August 1931 by a group of fishermen on Highway 3, four miles outside of Red Wing, Minnesota. Morris was believed to have robbed the Olmsted County Bank and Trust in Rochester, Minnesota, with Harvey Bailey in December 1926. His lifeless hand still clung to the barrel of a revolver. The FBI learned from Gladys Sawyer, wife of Harry Sawyer, that "the underworld understanding is that [Morris] was killed by 'Old Charlie' Fitzgerald following an argument at the Hollyhocks Inn" in St. Paul.[54]

In a 1966 interview, bank robber Harvey Bailey offered an opinion on how Morris ended up dead: "He was a funny guy, always on the rib. I said to him one time, 'Listen, Slim, you are just going to keep ribbing and somebody is going to shoot you right between the eyes sometime.' And sure enough, that is what happened. Ribbing somebody all the time. You know, it's all right to rib in fun, but when you get down to a man's own personal affairs, leave them alone, because that'll get you in trouble." Bailey's prediction was correct, though Morris was shot not between the eyes, but once in the heart.[55]

23   Ready Money and Riotous Nightlife

The Plantation Nightclub
Old White Bear Avenue, White Bear Lake

Nothing illustrates the prominence of White Bear Lake as a bank robber's playground better than a telegram sent to J. Edgar Hoover by a St. Paul FBI agent on April 1, 1934, the day after John Dillinger machine-gunned his way out of the Lincoln Court apartment house: "Checking each apartment house [in the] Twin Cities," the agent reported. "Also check all houses [in] White Bear Minnesota."[56]

Hoover was infuriated that the gangsters felt so safe they didn't bother to hide from his agents but lived openly in White Bear Lake, partying uproariously at local nightclubs. "With ready money and confidence in their power," said an official FBI summary, the gangs "relaxed vigilance and indulged in riotous nightlife" in White Bear Lake.[57]

The Plantation nightclub, once located at the intersection of Cottage Park Road and Old White Bear Avenue, at what is today Lion's Park, was the mobsters' White Bear Lake headquarters. Among the Plantation's patrons during the summers of 1931 and 1932 were local thugs like fixer Jack

THE PLANTATION

"The Plantation" White Bear's Beautiful Night Club, to be Formerly Opened Wednesday Night, July 2, 9 o'clock

White Bear is to have one of the most beautiful night clubs in the Middle West, and it is to open on Wednesday night, July 2. This is

Manager Harris has succeeded in securing the services of Chris. Gade, who eight years ago was chef at the White Bear Yacht Club, but who of recent years has delighted

Grand opening of the Plantation nightclub, 1930

Peifer and bootlegger Morris Roisner, nationally known bank robbers Jimmy Keating and Tommy Holden, and Capone gunman Fred Goetz.[58]

Frank Nash was also a fan of the Plantation during the summer of 1931, although an FBI informant noted that "Nash, when visiting the beach at White Bear with other members of the gang, could not go swimming because he wore a wig." Gladys Harrington, Holden's girlfriend, remembered that Nash had "a terrible looking" hairpiece. Nash rented the White Bear Lake cottage of Minnella Robertson, a cat fancier whose home was located just off what is today Highway 244 near Rose and Spruce Streets. Nash, who served as croupier at the Plantation, had won $6,000 in a single night's gambling there.[59]

Not everyone was distressed by the presence of mobsters in White Bear Lake. Minneapolis tailor Ben Millman, who provided Keating with his suits, told the FBI that he hung around the Plantation in order to get the gangsters' business and that Ben Harris, Jack Peifer, Tom Filben, and others had bought suits from him.[60]

"When the gangsters took over the Ramaleys' White Bear Castle, they renamed it the Plantation," recalled Walter "Buster" Johnson, a longtime White Bear resident. "They built a gambling hall, with every kind of gambling device available." The Plantation was condemned by White Bear Lake mayor Charles E. Buckbee in 1932 as a rendezvous for gangsters, but it was much more than that.[61]

The Plantation was managed for the underworld from 1930 to 1932 by Ben Harris, a Minneapolis gambling figure the FBI claimed "was directly connected with the Karpis-Barker gang, and with practically all of the well-known crooks in Minneapolis and St. Paul during the prohibition days." Harris told FBI agents he had taken over the Plantation nightclub in 1930 in partnership with impresario John Lane, owner of the Boulevards of Paris dance club.[62]

Robert "Frisco Dutch" Steinhardt was a bouncer and gambling consultant at the Plantation. A friend of the Barker-Karpis and Keating-Holden gangs, the florid-faced Steinhardt had participated in the Willmar bank robbery with Keating, Holden, and the unlucky Sammy Silverman. Steinhardt was a beefy pickpocket who had amassed a record of more than eighteen arrests for petty larceny, disorderly conduct, con-game operations, thievery, and pickpocketing—a series of swindles that took him from Cincinnati to St. Louis to Pittsburgh to Cleveland.[63]

"In the summer of 1931, Bennie Harris and John Lane opened the Plantation Club, a roadhouse at White Bear Lake," Steinhardt told the FBI. "Bob Hamilton and I opened up a gambling casino at the Plantation Club and became partners with Harris and Lane." In 1932 Steinhardt proposed to Harris that he run the gambling at the Plantation for 60 percent of the proceeds; Harris agreed and accepted the remaining 40 percent.[64]

In 1934, after the Plantation had closed, Ben Harris pleaded guilty to gambling violations for operating a roulette wheel at the club. The Plantation reopened as a legitimate restaurant and theater, and was later razed and replaced by a park.[65]

With the passing of the Plantation, its gambling manager, Frisco Dutch Steinhardt, predicted that the casino's underworld patrons—Frank Nash, Jimmy Keating, Tommy Holden—would also be closed down by the FBI. FBI agents learned from Steinhardt that "at the time Hamm was kidnapped, he remarked to his partner in the [Plantation] night club that he supposed they would have to get out of town before very long, because the authorities probably wouldn't let any of the old gang remain in town."[66]

He could not have guessed that one of the last chapters in the saga of Jimmy Keating and Tommy Holden would be played out not during a bank robbery or in a gambling hall but on a golf course.

24   The Golfing Gangsters

Keller Golf Course
2166 Maplewood Drive, Maplewood

Former caddies at the Keller Golf Course in Maplewood, now a St. Paul suburb, claimed that vacationing bank robbers carried two golf bags—one filled with golf clubs, the other with submachine guns and rifles. According to gangland legend, John Dillinger was playing the third hole at Keller in the early 1930s when he saw policemen approaching his party. Dillinger hopped aboard the train that ran adjacent to the links and escaped, leaving only his golf clubs behind.[67]

"It appears from past investigation that wherever [Jimmy] Keating may be he will be a regular patron of some golf course," predicted a 1932 FBI memo, "and . . . in St. Paul he will regularly play at the Keller Golf Course." The FBI considered devoting a full-time agent to the course—at least "on good golfing days between the hours of 11:00 A.M. and 4:00 P.M."—in an attempt to track down the bank-robbing fugitives. During 1931 and 1932, the FBI recruited Keller caddies, golf supply clerks, and a soda jerk in the locker room as informants to keep gangsters under surveillance.[68]

Melvin Passolt, superintendent of Minnesota's Bureau of Criminal Apprehension, knew that the gangsters, like birds, returned to old haunts during the summer. The FBI learned from Passolt that "Holden and Keating may re-appear in the Twin Cities when the weather becomes warmer, and . . . might then be found frequenting golf links." Agent Oscar G. Hall revealed that the FBI, acting on a tip from the doomed Eddie Harlow, once narrowly missed capturing Keating and Holden at Keller.[69]

One FBI agent wrote of the bureau's frustration over the political connections that Keating and Holden enjoyed through their mentor, Leon Gleckman, who in turn was friendly with the county commissioner in charge of the golf course. The agent recounted how Keating and Holden golfed at Keller while they acted as bodyguards for Gleckman. One afternoon, four telephone company employees were playing when a sudden rainstorm soaked them. Two of them decided to return to the clubhouse to change clothing and hitched a ride with a fellow golfer who, unbeknownst to them, was an underworld character. The mobster apparently mistook his passengers for hit men out to kill Gleckman, for a car pulled up and they were pulled out by St. Paul police detectives and Gleckman's bodyguards. The hapless pair was finally able to convince the policemen and the bodyguards that they "had no intention of taking Leon Gleckman for a ride."[70]

FBI surveillance at Keller was so thorough that the agents knew Keating played with Wilson irons purchased from gangster Verne Miller. An agent

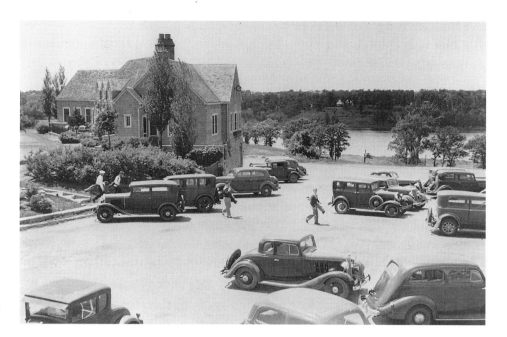

noted disapprovingly that "Keating during the time he played at the Keller
Golf Course played the eighteen holes with a score in the high 90's or between 100 and 112, and showed little improvement in his game."[71]

During the peak of the nationwide manhunt for them, the FBI noted that
"Keating and Holden and their women played golf at the leading public golf
course in St. Paul almost daily during the summer. . . . They all had expensive golf equipment and carried large rolls of money, tipped caddies liber-
ally, drove large cars, and attracted considerable attention on the golf
course." For his games, Jimmy Keating dressed in white linen golf knickers
and a light blue sweater and golf socks, his face obscured behind octagonal
eyeglasses.[72]

Keating and Holden were not the only gang members to court arrest by
playing on a public golf course. An informant told the FBI that Charlie and
Paula Harmon "had expensive clothing and expensive golf equipment and
left the apartment to play golf almost every day." But Frank Nash was puzzled by their golfing. The FBI noted that Nash "did not play golf and chided
the others for their interest in the game." In fact, Keating's and Holden's
love of golf would lead to their capture.[73]

On October 2, 1931, two men (almost certainly Keating and Holden)
robbed a pair of messengers from the First American National Bank of Duluth of $58,000 in front of the Duluth police building. Months later, a St. Paul
bootlegger tried to cash some bonds stolen from the Duluth bank. The bootlegger identified Keating and Holden, calling themselves Jimmy Stanley
and Bill McCormick, as the men who gave him the bonds. Simultaneously,

the FBI identified Charlie Harmon's Edgecumbe Court apartment house and was able to trace a call that Harmon made from a St. Paul telephone to a golf equipment company in Kansas City. Within days, lawmen had the elusive Keating, now living in Kansas City, under surveillance.[74]

Four FBI agents and a police squad waited on July 7, 1932, at the Mission Hills Country Club golf course as Jimmy Keating, Tommy Holden, and bank robber Harvey Bailey walked toward them; mobster Bernard "Big Phil Courtney" Phillips was nearby. Bailey recalled later that he had expected to meet machine gunner Lawrence DeVol that day, so Bailey could deliver a $500 Liberty Bond that had been stolen during the June 17 Fort Scott bank robbery. When DeVol failed to show up, the gangsters decided instead to go golfing at Mission Hills. "When we got around to the 8th hole on the golf course," said Bailey, "up out of the ravine come eight men, Department of Justice and Deputy Sheriffs from Kansas City, Kansas, and Kansas City, Missouri."[75]

After being fugitives for 861 days, Keating and Holden returned to prison on July 8, 1932. Phillips, to the eternal suspicion of the underworld, slipped away without capture. The hapless Harvey Bailey, veteran of more than two dozen bank robberies without an arrest since 1922, was caught with the stolen Liberty Bond and sent to Kansas State Penitentiary at Lansing, convicted of a crime he did not commit.

A jailer reportedly turned down a $15,000 bribe offered by Keating and Holden, refusing to allow them to escape. The golf-loving convicts were finally placed in solitary confinement at an isolation camp, forbidden to talk or have visitors for the next eleven years. They were put to work in Leavenworth's underground rock quarry, locked together with other "incurables." Security precautions included three guards to watch every prisoner.[76] By the time they were released from Leavenworth decades later, the era of tommy guns, speakeasies, and golfing gangsters was long over.

REWARD

$1,200.00 $1,200.0

Twelve Hundred Dollars.

WANTED

For the Murder of C. R. Kelly, Sheriff of Howell County, Missouri, on December 19, 1931

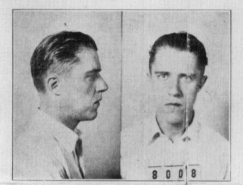

Gangsters of Kimes-Inman Gang of Oklahoma Missouri Kansas and Texas

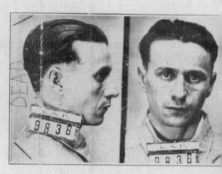

ALVIN KARPIS   **FRED BARKER**

DESCRIPTION: ALVIN KARPIS, alias George Dunn, alias R. E. Hamilton, alias Ray Karpis, alias Raymond Hadle
alias George Haller; Age 22; Height 5-9¾; Weight 130 lbs.; Hair-brown; Eyes-blue; Scars-cut SC base L. hand; Occ
pation, Worked in bakery.   FPC   1-R-II-5
                            1-U-UU-8

Karpis is ex-convict having served State Reformatory Hutchinson, Kansas, 1926, No. 7071   Also State Penitentia
Lansing, Kansas, May, 1930, Crime Burglary.

DESCRIPTION: FRED BARKER, alias F. G. Ward, alias Ted Murphy, alias J. Darrows; Age 28; Weight 120 lb
Height 5-4; Build-slim; Complexion-fair; Hair-sandy; Eyes-blue; Teeth-lower front gold, two upper front gold. Senter
ed State Reformatory, Granite, Oklahoma. Robbery 1923. Sentenced State Penitentiary Lansing, Kan., March, 19:
                     FPC   29-I-20
                         20-O-22

These men acting together murdered Sheriff C. R. Kelly, West Plains, Missouri in cold blood when he attempted
question them.

The Chief of Police and Sheriff at West Plains, Missouri, will pay a reward of $300.00 each for the arrest and s
render of either of these men to Howell County, Missouri officers. $200.00 additional will be paid on conviction.
will come after them any place.

An additional Reward of $100.00 each will be paid for the arrest and surrender to Howell County officers of A.
Dunlop and Old Lady Arrie Barker, Mother of Fred Barker. Dunlop is about 65 years of age; slender, white hair, f
blood Irishman. Mrs. Barker is about 60 years of age. All may be found together on farm. We hold Felony Warra
for each of these parties.

Police and other authorities: Keep this Poster before you at all times as we want these Fugitives. If further
formation is desired Wire Collect Chief of Police or Sheriff at West Plains, Missouri.

James A. Bridges
Chief of Police

Mrs. C. R. Kelly
Sheriff

West Plains, Missouri

5

MURDERING FOR MA

Wanted poster for Alvin Karpis and Fred Barker, 1931; Kate "Ma" Barker

25   'A Vicious, Cold-Blooded Crew of Murderers'

Ma Barker's West St. Paul Hideout
1031 South Robert Street, West St. Paul

Nick Hannegraf recognized the three faces of evil.

They were there in black and white, printed in the pages of the April 1932 issue of *True Detective Mysteries*. The Barker-Karpis gang, a trio of killers from Tulsa, Oklahoma, were wanted for bank robbery and the murder of a Missouri sheriff. The magazine was offering a $100 reward for the apprehension of each member of the gang.

Hannegraf was closing up his Drover's Tavern on South St. Paul's Concord Street on April 25, 1932. It was 1:00 A.M. on a Monday night, Hannegraf's time to escape inside the pages of *True Detective*. As he read about the exploits of the Barker-Karpis gang, it dawned on Hannegraf that he had seen those faces somewhere before. Not in a magazine but in person, that very morning. Those lethal felons were living in his mother's house on South Robert Street. The Barker-Karpis gang, hunted by FBI agents and sheriffs across the country, was driving his children to school!

The gang had moved into Grandma Helen Hannegraf's rental home at 1031 South Robert (still standing near the intersection with Bernard Street) on February 1, 1932. They claimed to be musicians in a local orchestra and carried black violin cases to prove it. To add to the wholesome image, a blonde 5-foot, 4-inch woman in her late fifties accompanied the performers. They called her Mrs. Anderson or Ma, and she was often seen walking her bulldog down Robert Street. The gang was then at the midpoint of a larcenous career that would earn them about $3 million in bank robbery and kidnapping loot. Within months, FBI director J. Edgar Hoover would call them "the most vicious, cold-blooded crew of murderers, kidnappers and robbers in recent history."[1]

Among the "musicians" living in Hannegraf's home was Alvin Karpis, the blue-eyed son of two Lithuanian immigrants, painter John Karpovicz and his wife, Anna. Born Albin Francis Karpovicz in 1908 in Montreal, the slight, 130-pound Karpis spent his early adult years in Topeka, Kansas, working as a baker and shipping clerk. In 1925 his doctor noted a defective heart and advised Karpis to find a less stressful job. Within a year, Karpis had turned to safe blowing and jewel theft—what the FBI called "a career of plunder, pillage and despoilation."[2]

"Alvin was always upset because my grandpa lost his money during the Depression in 1929," recalled Karpis's nephew, Albert Grooms. "Alvin didn't think it was fair, he thought banks should have to be accountable. Alvin thought the banks sort of legally stole my grandpa's money. . . . It was a burr under Alvin's saddle for a long time."[3]

The hallmark of Karpis's career was the leniency of his sentences. In March 1929 he engineered an escape from the State Industrial Reformatory in Hutchinson, Kansas, where he had been serving the fourth year of a sentence for burglary. Karpis was apprehended by Kansas City police a year later and transferred to the state penitentiary in Lansing, Kansas, in May 1930. He was released a year later, only to be arrested in Tulsa in June 1931 and found guilty of burglary, sentenced to four years, and, incredibly, immediately paroled by order of the court.[4]

Karpis met Fred Barker in the Lansing penitentiary in 1930, where Barker was serving a sentence for bank burglary. Released early in May 1931 because of his "good time" effort in the Kansas coal mines, Karpis joined Barker in a string of jewel thefts and robberies in Oklahoma, Missouri, and Minnesota. By the time the twenty-three-year-old Karpis moved into the Hannegraf's house with Barker, his wanted poster warned: "Take no chances with this man. He is a killer."[5]

Sandy-haired Fred Barker was Ma Barker's favorite son. In 1932, Fred was a short (5 feet, 4 inches), slim (120 pounds) thirty-year-old with three

Prison escapees Larry DeVol (left) and Alvin Karpis (right), with guns and burglary tools found in their car in 1930

gold teeth and a scar on his left knee where he had been shot. He had just been released from prison, after nine arrests and convictions for burglary and robbery. "Freddie had a vicious streak," mused Karpis years later. "To be frank, I was sometimes slightly stunned by Freddie's free and easy way with a gun. He never seemed to mind gunning down anybody who stood in his way, whether it was a cop, or a hood or an ordinary guy on the street."

Karpis referred to Katherine "Ma" Barker (born Arizona Clark near Springfield, Missouri, in 1872) as "just an old-fashioned homebody from the Ozarks . . . superstitious, gullible, simple, cantankerous and, well, generally law abiding."[6]

While Ma Barker was married to gas station operator George Barker, their four young sons—Herman, Lloyd, Fred, and Arthur—played in Tulsa parks with junior toughs Harry Campbell and Volney Davis, future members of the Barker-Karpis gang. None of the Barker children was destined for a law-abiding career. Although only Fred and Arthur ("Doc") were active in the Barker-Karpis gang, the eldest son, Herman, killed a Kansas policeman in 1927 and then committed suicide. Lloyd was incarcerated in Leavenworth prison from 1922 to 1947 for a post office robbery and was killed in a domestic dispute in 1949.[7]

J. Edgar Hoover demonized Kate Barker in newspaper interviews and crime books, calling her "the most vicious, dangerous and resourceful criminal brain of the last decade" and claiming she represented "a monument to the evils of parental indulgence." (Hoover always harbored special fury for female criminals. Inspired by Kathryn "Kit" Kelly, wife of Machine Gun Kelly, Hoover declared: "When a woman does turn professional criminal, she is a hundred times more vicious and dangerous than a man.")[8]

Hoover attacked Ma Barker for her sexual immorality, as well; the FBI claimed that before her 1928 separation from her husband, she "became loose in her moral life. She was seen with a neighbor of hers who was having outside dates with other men and was known to have been generally in the company of other men in the vicinity of Tulsa, Oklahoma . . . and cast her lot with [her sons'] lawlessness and criminal activities."[9]

When Karpis defended Ma Barker's innocence in his autobiography, an internal FBI review of his book revealed Hoover's scathing opinion: "Karpis or/and his writer must be on dope." The official bureau line over the past half-century has been that Ma Barker, "an intuitive criminal, with her shrewd thinking and meticulous planning, was responsible for the gang's 'success.'" Oklahoma bank robber Harvey Bailey laughed at the idea of Ma Barker as a criminal mastermind: "The old woman couldn't plan breakfast," said Bailey. "When we'd sit down to plan a bank job, she'd go in the other room and listen to Amos and Andy or hillbilly music on the radio." A review of the FBI's internal files on the Barker-Karpis gang—particularly the confessions of gang members who attended crime-planning meetings—strongly suggests that the FBI knew that Kate Barker had no significant involvement in her sons' criminal activities.[10]

Accompanying Ma Barker to St. Paul was Arthur "Old Man" Dunlop; they masqueraded as "Mr. and Mrs. George Anderson." Ma Barker's seventy-three-year-old lover was described in the acid words of the FBI as a perfect boyfriend for her, since Dunlop "said little and thought less." When his tongue was loosened by alcohol, however, Dunlop could be dangerously talkative. Dunlop was "a pain in the ass," wrote Karpis. "He was a drunk and an ingrate . . . when he was loaded, he'd turn mean and abuse Ma." Ma Barker's daughter-in-law Carol Hamilton called Dunlop "too lazy to work and too scared to steal."[11]

Fred's thirty-two-year-old brother, Arthur "Doc" Barker, was missing from the St. Paul hideout in April 1932. A diminutive (5 feet, 4 inches and 119 pounds) auto thief and convicted murderer easily recognizable by the three moles on his face, Doc Barker was serving a life sentence for murder in the Oklahoma State Penitentiary at McAlester. "Doc was the problem. . . . When Doc got to drinkin', he thought he was king of the world," recalled Karpis's nephew, Albert Grooms. "Doc Barker didn't have all his marbles, he was a little light between the eyes, but Freddie was sharper than the devil."[12]

Kate "Ma" Barker, with boyfriend Arthur Dunlop

Compared to Fred and Doc Barker, whose violent instincts were easily triggered, Karpis demonstrated some restraint. When Gladys Sawyer, wife of St. Paul gangland banker Harry Sawyer, expressed concern that her adopted daughter might get hurt in an FBI raid on the gangsters' hideout, Fred Barker callously replied that "both she and the little girl would have to take their chances and if they got in the line of fire, it would be 'just too bad.'" But Karpis promised "that he would give himself up before he would let anything happen to the child." Sawyer told FBI agents that she thought highly of Karpis ever after.[13]

None of this was known to Helen Hannegraf when she rented out 1031 South Robert to the "Anderson family." Hannegraf lived next door at 1035 South Robert, where she made bootleg whiskey out of sauerkraut in her basement. Nick Hannegraf sold his mother's whiskey through the family's speakeasy, the Drover's Tavern. Eventually, Nick was forced to switch to the St. Paul Syndicate's liquor (with its built-in protection money) after he was raided several times by local police.[14]

The Barkers had been on the lam since December 19, 1931, when Fred Barker had robbed a West Plains, Missouri, store and murdered Sheriff C. Roy Kelly. (An indication of their inept planning at this stage of their career: the gang's take from the Missouri store included fifty neckties.) The Barkers were forced to flee from their hideout near Thayer, Missouri—a ten-acre farm with a cottage, a target practice area, a security fence, and alarms to warn them of police raids.[15]

"Alvin was down the street in Missouri when it [the shooting of Sheriff Kelly] happened," remembered Grooms. "Alvin said there were other ways of doing it—they didn't *have* to kill anyone, they could have dropped the sheriff off in the country without killing him. . . . Ma Barker wasn't too happy with that killing."[16]

According to the FBI, Ma Barker and her sons first fled to Herb Farmer's underworld hideout in Joplin, Missouri. Farmer counseled the Barkers to seek haven in St. Paul through his friend Harry Sawyer of the Green Lantern saloon. "With the assurance of his [Sawyer's] powerful protection," recounted the FBI, the Barker-Karpis gang next "took up residence in a little house in West St. Paul."[17]

While they were living in the Hannegraf home, the gang drove Helen Hannegraf's granddaughter Marian to Catholic school in the rumble seat of their car. When it was time to pick up the children after school, Hannegraf would snare one of her boarders and insist that the gangsters drive her grandchildren home.

Marian Johnson remembered the Barker-Karpis gang as "the nicest people. We'd hurry home from St. Matthews School because if we got home early, we could walk Mrs. Barker's curly-haired dog. Whoever got there first, you'd get a nickel or a candy bar!" The Barker boys would visit the Hannegraf home, sinking deep into Helen's leather rocking chair. But to the gang's growing irritation, Dunlop would drink bootleg whiskey with Nick's brother, Pete Hannegraf.[18]

Inevitably, there were a few suspicious moments. When Marian's ten-year-old cousin Bernice brought some doughnuts over to the Barker boys, they asked her to wait while they gathered up a half-dozen candy bars for her in return. Bernice noticed shotgun shells scattered across a couch. Whenever Dunlop walked Ma Barker's dog behind the Robert Street homes, he kept one hand plunged into his pocket, presumably on a gun.[19]

In the midst of this parody of domesticity, the gang continued to launch criminal forays from the sanctuary of the South Robert Street hideout. They focused on Minneapolis and other cities outside the protection of the O'Connor system. Karpis was particularly pleased when Fred Barker invited him to participate in the robbery of the Northwestern National Bank and Trust Company on March 29, 1932—a milestone the youthful Karpis referred to as "my first genuine major stickup."[20]

The bank, at 1223 North Washington Avenue near downtown Minneapolis (today the bank site, between Twelfth and Plymouth Avenues, is an open lot), was robbed by five men: Karpis, Fred Barker, Tommy Holden, trigger man Larry DeVol, and Bernard Phillips. "It was DeVol's idea to use a big car in honor [of] the big job," recalled Karpis years later. "So we stole a luxury Lincoln with a gorgeous interior and drove up to the Northwestern National." Holding twenty-eight customers and bank employees at gunpoint, the gang escaped safely out the back door into the waiting sedan just as police burst into the front of the bank. "Back at the house we'd rented in St. Paul, the five of us counted out the money," wrote Karpis. "It added up to more loot than I'd ever seen in my life—over $75,000 in paper money, another $6,500 in coins, and $185,000 in bonds."[21]

It is ironic that the Barker-Karpis gang's idyll on South Robert Street would be shattered by the *True Detective* photos of Barker and Karpis, for Karpis told the FBI he bought all the detective magazines, both to read about his activities and to find out which magazines published his photograph. When Karpis had his hair cut, he went to a barbershop in an outlying part of the city; as he entered, "he would glance around to see if a detective magazine containing his picture was in the place, and if he noticed such a publication, he would immediately leave."[22]

After recognizing the faces of his mother's tenants, Nick Hannegraf ran over to her house, rousing her at two o'clock in the morning to show her the photographs. "Nick, those are the boys next door!" she exclaimed. Helen crept into the garage with a flashlight to take down the license numbers of the gang's Chevrolets. Nick borrowed the family's Essex and drove to the central police station, eager to claim a reward. Instead, he drove straight into a demonstration of the O'Connor system's power, still effective twelve years after the death of its architect, police chief John O'Connor.[23]

Hannegraf first approached police inspector James P. Crumley, blurting out that men who looked just like Fred Barker and Alvin Karpis were asleep in his mother's house on Robert Street, just waiting to be arrested. "The police were protecting these gangsters at that time, so they didn't pay too much attention to my dad," recalled daughter Marian Johnson. "They said he was drinking." Impatient, Hannegraf showed detective Fred Raasch the *True Detective Mysteries* photos, but the police made him wait in the Bureau of Records room until eleven o'clock the next morning. "He sat on a bench in an outer office and they said, 'We'll get to you,'" recalled Johnson. "My grandmother called to the police department and said, 'You might as well come home, because they're gone.' They'd been tipped off by the police. My dad was very angry at the police, because he figured he had a good chance at the reward."[24]

Years later, the FBI learned how the tip-off was engineered. Inspector Crumley had buttonholed police chief Thomas Brown, bootlegger Leon Gleckman's old friend from the Cleveland liquor conspiracy days, and told him that a "sucker" had spotted the Barker-Karpis gang on Robert Street. "Jesus Christ," gasped Brown, dashing into his office to make a phone call. "Brown seemed to be greatly disturbed and his face turned white, and he left in a hurry for his office," the FBI learned from Crumley. "A few minutes later a woman called up and asked if her son was there . . . and when this party answered the telephone, he was advised by the woman, his mother, that the people whom he had reported as being next door had just left in a hurry and in fact left so fast that they left the radio turned on."[25]

In his memoirs, Karpis added that Harry Sawyer phoned Chief Brown's warning to the Barker-Karpis gang while "Sawyer's man on the police force was stalling the raid against our house long enough to allow Harry to tip us off." The FBI learned from Gladys Sawyer that "Jim Crumley called Harry Sawyer at the saloon and advised him 'heat' was on the boys and they had better move. Harry telephoned to one of the parties at 1031 Robert Street, with the result they immediately vacated the place."[26]

By eight o'clock that morning, Ma Barker and Karpis were running behind the Hannegraf house to retrieve their car. Fred Barker and Dunlop dashed out in front, jumping into a second car. They "left the door open, the gas on, and the radio running, and part of a cooked dinner on the table," BCA agents noted with palpable frustration.[27]

The gang fled St. Paul, leaving behind a suitcase containing twelve .45 automatic shells, four .16-gauge shotgun shells, and two pistol cleaners. They neglected to pay their final rent and utility bills, and they took Helen Hannegraf's fine silverware. But they left behind Ma Barker's brown fur coat, a pile of Fred Barker's new shoes, a fishing box, a radio, and a camera containing candid photos of Ma Barker. The Hannegrafs also found a closet full of clothes tailored in gangland style: all identifying tags were torn off. Under her rug, Mrs. Hannegraf discovered a final memento—a $500 bond stolen in March 1931 from the Farmers Savings Bank of Alden, Iowa.[28]

Back at the police station, Detective Raasch bumped into Harry Sawyer, who was walking out of Chief Brown's office. Sawyer brashly asked the detective, "Hey, you were sent over to the West Side, weren't you?" Raasch said he had indeed raided the Barker-Karpis hideout. "You found everything all right, didn't you?" Sawyer asked.

"We found everyone gone," Raasch reassured him. "There was nobody there." Sawyer was relieved, until Raasch mentioned that the gangsters had left some ammunition. Sawyer asked the officer for the shells, saying cryptically, "I want to show these guys that that thing was all right—I want to show them their own stuff."[29]

By that time, the gang was driving through Webster, Wisconsin, en route to Kansas City. Unfortunately for Dunlop, they believed that it was his liquor-loosened tongue, not pictures in a detective magazine, that had blown their cover.[30]

On April 25, 1932, the naked body of a 160-pound man with steel-gray hair, a neatly clipped mustache, and a .45-caliber bullet hole in his head was found along the shore of Frenstad Lake, north of Webster. It was Ma's lover, Arthur Dunlop. The BCA concluded that the assassin's car had stopped midway along a short road:

> Here was found a forty-five caliber bullet, together with some blood indicating that the victim had been shot at that point. The evidence further indicated that a body had been dragged from this point through the brush to the lake shore, a distance of about one hundred feet. It seems that they had taken him by the arms, one person on each side of him, and pulled him through the brush. Apparently, they had planned on tossing him into the lake and possibly weighting him down. However, when they reached the shore of the lake, they found it so boggy that it was not possible for them to get the body out into the lake and they dropped it where it was partly submerged on the shore.[31]

Near Dunlop's corpse, the BCA noted, was "a black woman's glove with white trimming, size about eight, covered with blood." Karpis claimed that neither he nor Fred Barker shot Dunlop. "There were plenty of people in St. Paul who wanted to kill him," said Karpis, identifying fixer Jack Peifer as the man who killed Dunlop as a courtesy to the Barker-Karpis gang.[32]

The successful escape of the gang from the Robert Street hideout stunned St. Paul. Mayoral candidate William J. Mahoney charged in a campaign speech that the incident proved that the city was ruled not by law but by the underworld: "Here is a case of fugitives from justice carrying on their nefarious activities in St. Paul for three months, and then, just before they are to be arrested, are mysteriously tipped off, and get away. . . . I cannot complain against the police officers themselves. We have in St. Paul a fine lot of policemen. They would enforce the law if ordered to do so, but they are told to lay off."[33]

On the defensive, Chief Tom Brown made much of the Hannegraf house's location in West St. Paul, part of neighboring Dakota County. "The charges of Mr. Mahoney that St. Paul police are protecting and tipping off criminals are ridiculous," snorted Brown. "It seems strange St. Paul police could offer protection to so-called murderers in another city, where we have no jurisdiction." Still, Brown's behavior during the failed raid was suspicious, and in June he was demoted to the rank of detective.[34]

A week after the Robert Street escape, Helen Hannegraf spied what appeared to be a familiar face in a Woolworth store; she was sure it was Ma Barker. The woman dashed out of the store and disappeared into a waiting automobile while Hannegraf was slowed by the crowds. Gangland history might have been altered dramatically had Hannegraf managed to stop Ma Barker in Woolworth's that day. "My grandmother was a tough old son of a gun," recalled Nick Hannegraf. "Tougher than Ma Barker!"[35]

26   Not the Athletic Type of Gangster

Summering at the John Lambert Cottage
148 Dellwood Avenue, Dellwood

"Mahtomedi is the place to spend your summers," the tourist literature said of the resort community fourteen miles northeast of St. Paul. With "none of the rough crowds found at other resorts [it is] the most beautiful spot in the state. Sundays [are] positively quiet and homelike, with preaching services and Sunday School."[36]

Outlaws Alvin Karpis and Fred and Ma Barker drove to this serene haven on July 9, 1932, and rented the eight-room home of eighty-year-old John Lambert, a retired grocery store owner. In the ten weeks since they fled St. Paul, the Barker-Karpis gang had first stopped in Kansas City, where the gang helped Tommy Holden and Harvey Bailey plan the robbery of the Citizens National Bank in Fort Scott, Kansas. On June 17, 1932, Karpis and Fred Barker joined Bailey, Holden, Bernie Phillips, and Larry DeVol in taking $47,000 from the Fort Scott vault, briefly kidnapping two female bystanders to deter a police shootout and hurling nails onto the road to puncture the tires of pursuing automobiles.[37]

It was to be the last bank robbery of Holden's and Bailey's careers. On July 7, 1932, they were captured—along with veteran bank robber Jimmy Keating—by FBI agents on a Kansas City golf course. Lagging behind on the greens, Phillips witnessed the arrests and warned Karpis and the Barkers, who were living in Kansas City as the "Hunter family." Within thirty minutes of Phillips's alert, the gang was on the run, driving their Auburn sedan toward Mahtomedi. "The gang could afford several hideouts," reported an official FBI summary. "They chose St. Paul, as well as a summer cottage on White Bear Lake, Minnesota."[38]

One of the most popular Mahtomedi gambling spots was the Silver Slipper roadhouse at 230 Warner Road, later known as the King's Horses, and today a private residence near the corner of Warner and Greenwood. The stucco exterior and winding stone walk camouflaged the revelry of the blackjack players inside. The Silver Slipper was considered to be "about the most famous of all speakeasies in this area," recalled Althea Rohlfing, a long-time Mahtomedi resident. "It had the reputation of catering to gangsters and bootleggers of every variety, more specifically, those who were big-time operators. When the state or federal law officers were looking for some nefarious characters and came in the front door, the patrons charged out the back door."[39]

Bootlegger Morris Rutman, kidnapped from his St. Paul home in October 1931, was held prisoner at the Silver Slipper for a $10,000 ransom. Dragged into the basement by a half dozen masked men led by gangster Jack Ferrick, Rutman was beaten and tortured (the kidnappers applied alcohol to his body and lighted it with a match) for three days before being freed. Such displays of violence were anathema to the public enemies relaxing in Mahtomedi, including Chicago robber Lester "Babyface Nelson" Gillis, who lived unobtrusively in the Bauman cottage, dining nearby on pizza and spaghetti at Vince Guarnera's Italian restaurant at 959 Mahtomedi Avenue (Highway 244).[40]

The Barker-Karpis gang, who drove up to the Lambert cottage determined to act the perfect tenants, were just as quiet. "John Lambert and his wife were taking a trip to Scotland, and they were very tight—very particular," remembered their neighbor Evelyn Deyo. "So the Lamberts rented their White Bear Lake home out to these wonderful people—the Ma Barker gang!" Ma Barker told the Lamberts that she was "Mrs. Hunter," and that Fred Barker and Alvin Karpis (posing as "Freddie and Raymond Hunter") were her sons. "When they moved in, we told them we never allowed liquor on the place or late parties or carousing, and there never was any," Mrs. Lambert told reporters. "They were always quiet and very expensively dressed and drove expensive autos."[41]

Neighbors saw the Hunters floating in a rowboat in the middle of White Bear Lake, talking among themselves. The criminals were not difficult to identify. "All of those gangsters were here for vacation," recalled Walter "Buster" Johnson of White Bear Lake. "You could spot them easily because they were pale and sickly looking. The gangsters weren't the athletic type. They wore hats in the summertime—no one wore hats."[42]

During their vacation at Lambert cottage, Alvin Karpis and Fred Barker ventured out to rob the Cloud County Bank in Concordia, Kansas, with machine gunner Larry DeVol, swindler Earl Christman, and Jess Doyle, a thief who had been released in June from the Kansas state penitentiary in Lansing.

Cottage of John Lambert on the east shore of White Bear Lake, headquarters of the Barker-Karpis gang in July 1932

The July 26, 1932, robbery in Concordia, which netted $240,000 in bonds and cash, was meticulously choreographed: the gang had stashed gasoline, coffee, and sandwiches along the getaway route for quick refueling.[43]

"The five of us were living with Ma Barker in a big house out at White Bear Lake . . . when we decided to take the Concordia bank," wrote Karpis. The gang brought $22,000 back to the Lambert cabin after getting lost on the long drive through Kansas and Missouri, during which Doyle and DeVol engaged in a debate on the constellation guiding them back to Mahtomedi.

"There's the Big Dipper," said Doyle. "As a night burglar I know what it looks like."

"You're crazy," argued DeVol. "I've been a night burglar too, and that's the Little Dipper you're pointing to."[44]

Helen Ferguson, Christman's girlfriend, described the gang's return from the Concordia heist: "Kate Barker and I stayed there [in Mahtomedi] while Fred Barker, Karpis and Christman went to Concordia, Kansas. . . . They were away for about five or six days. When they came back, they had a lot of money . . . and the men went into a room to divide it." Christman's share came to about $4,000.[45]

Once again, the O'Connor system's network of fences and money launderers proved valuable to the Barker-Karpis gang. An FBI report noted that many of the bonds stolen from the Cloud County Bank were recovered in St. Paul in August, "through peaceable negotiations by W. S. Gordon of the Burns Detective Agency with some unknown underworld boss in St. Paul." Newspapers reported that the detectives agreed to pay the gangsters a $15,000 ransom for the Concordia securities. Such an arrangement, of course, was safer for the gang than trying to fence the government securities through underworld bankers.[46]

With the burst of activity surrounding the Concordia robbery, neighbors began to notice the odd habits of the tenants in Lambert cottage. "During their stay at White Bear Lake they were visited by many persons in high-powered and expensive automobiles, who usually came very late at night and slept through the morning," reported the FBI. "People in White Bear Lake knew something was going on," said longtime resident Paul Cromer. "The St. Paul newspapers built things up as if everything happened here in White Bear, 'cause they wanted to keep their own name clean!"[47]

The gang's idyll in Mahtomedi ended abruptly on August 12, 1932, when neighbors saw two men park their car outside the Lambert cottage and speak urgently to Karpis. "Mrs. Hunter said they just had had a telegram about some sickness in the family, in the East, and they had to go," Mrs. Lambert told the *St. Paul Dispatch*. Just 48 hours later, agents of the Bureau of Criminal Apprehension burst into the empty cottage. Once again, the gang appeared to have been warned of an upcoming raid.[48]

Karpis and Barker had made sure that the iceman, paperboy, and garbage carrier were paid before they left. Fred Barker casually dropped by the East Side Ice Company in Mahtomedi to pay the gang's final ice bill in person. The inscription remained on the company's books for decades: "Fred Hunter (Lambert Cottage)." The gang had stolen tens of thousands of dollars from banks across the Midwest, yet Barker risked capture to pay a thirty-dollar ice bill.[49]

27   The Routine of Bank Robbery

The Third Northwestern National Bank Robbery
430 East Hennepin Avenue, Minneapolis

"Bank robbery, dangerous as it was, could get to be routine," wrote Alvin Karpis. On the afternoon of December 16, 1932, the Barker-Karpis gang robbed the Third Northwestern National Bank of Minneapolis. Although the bank has been razed, a triangular parking lot at Southeast Fifth Street

A. Wahpeton, N.D. Site of alleged Barker-Karpis gang robbery, Sept. 30, 1932

B. Redwood Falls, Minn. Site of Barker-Karpis gang robbery, Sept. 23, 1932

C. Sioux Falls, S.D. Site of Dillinger gang robbery, March 6, 1934

D. Willmar, Minn. Site of Keating-Holden gang robbery, July 15, 1930

E. Brainerd, Minn. Site of bank robbery by Babyface Nelson and allies, Oct. 23, 1933

F. Cambridge, Minn. Town held hostage by Barker-Karpis gang, Jan. 5, 1932

G. Wyoming, Minn. Site of release of kidnapped brewery executive William Hamm Jr., June 19, 1933

H. Rochester, Minn. Site of release of kidnapped banker Edward Bremer, Feb. 7, 1934

I. Waterloo, Iowa Site of police shooting of Dillinger gang member Tommy Carroll, June 7, 1934

J. Mason City, Iowa Site of Dillinger gang robbery, March 13, 1934

K. Menomonie, Wis. Site of Keating-Holden gang robbery and death of bank robber Charlie Harmon, Oct. 20, 1931

L. Rhinelander, Wis. Site of failed FBI raid on Dillinger gang hideout at Little Bohemia Lodge, Apr. 22–23, 1934

M. Hastings, Minn. Site of police roadblock attempt to stop Dillinger gang after their escape from Little Bohemia Lodge, April 23, 1934

N. Minnesota-Canadian border lakes Site of vacation cabins owned by Twin Cities mobsters and corrupt policemen between Central and Hennepin Avenues retains the distinctive shape that made the robbery so daring.

"You had to be pretty wild and not a little crazy to take a bank like the Third Northwestern National in Minneapolis," recalled Karpis. "It was a triangular building smack on one of the city's busiest streets, with a streetcar stop right in front of it, and practically the whole goddamn place was in glass. . . . We sometimes did things like that deliberately, maybe to inject some extra excitement into our work."[50]

The robbery was among the most violent of the Barker-Karpis gang's escapades, leaving two policemen and one bystander dead, and it proved that innocent citizens could be victims of the gangsters harbored in St. Paul.

During the three months preceding this robbery, the gang had regrouped —Karpis recruited a crack bank robbery team—and waited for Doc Barker to be released from prison in Oklahoma. To ensure that local police would not interfere with their heists, the gang solidified its political alliances. During the Minneapolis mayoral campaign, Karpis said, he loaned supporters of candidate Ralph Van Lear $4,000. Fred Barker kicked in $6,500, his personal contribution toward good government in Minneapolis.[51]

After the election, Karpis told the FBI, he and Fred Barker "were offered 'a piece' in a slot machine concession, but he laughingly refused it. Karpis said he told the syndicate that there was too much work connected with the operation of slot machines." A lifelong brothel customer, Karpis told the Minneapolis mob he preferred to control the "houses of ill fame." As for Barker, Karpis explained to the FBI that "Freddie told them that he wanted nothing but to be left alone while [he was] in the Twin Cities."[52]

On September 10, 1932, Doc Barker was released from prison after serving thirteen years of a life sentence for murdering a night watchman. The FBI suspected that the early release was facilitated by bribing Oklahoma officials. Interviewed by the FBI years later, Karpis suggested that he and Fred Barker had supplied the payoff money that freed Doc Barker.[53]

On September 23, the reunited gang robbed the State Bank and Trust Company of Redwood Falls, Minnesota, displaying the full range of Barker-Karpis techniques: they forced the bank staff to lie face down on the floor, kidnapped bystanders to perch on the running boards of their getaway car, and scattered roofing nails to stop police cars. Careful planning ensured that the robbery was launched on the day the bank contained the most possible currency—$35,000. A newspaper account noted that the "band of swaggering" crooks "snapped through the robbery as if it was so much routine."[54]

"My profession was robbing banks, knocking off payrolls and kidnapping rich men. I was good at it," wrote Karpis in his memoirs. "We were professionals at our work, and we figured out timing, escape routes, each guy's individual job, and all the other details of every robbery or kidnapping as if we were laying out the strategy for a combat attack in a war."[55]

A September 30 robbery of $6,900 from the Citizens National Bank of Wahpeton, North Dakota, also had the gang's signature. Once again, five robbers used machine guns to hold a crowd at bay, pistol-whipped a bank cashier (a Fred Barker trademark), used hostages as shields on the running board of the getaway car, and tossed roofing nails to puncture tires of the posse following them. Police lost the quintet as they left North Dakota at speeds up to sixty miles an hour.[56]

With the November 3 release from the Oklahoma State Penitentiary of convicted murderer Volney Davis, one of Doc Barker's boyhood pals, the gang had grown to nearly full strength. Davis drove to a meeting with Doc Barker in Kansas, then headed for St. Paul to join the rest of the gang.[57]

Curiously, the Barker-Karpis gang declined to work with bank robber John Dillinger. "Alvin told me that Dillinger had a wild idea to merge the [Dillinger and Barker-Karpis] gangs, go into a town and clean the whole damned town out . . . rob eight banks in one day," said Albert Grooms, Karpis's nephew. "Alvin and Freddie Barker said they wanted no part of that idea. It would cause too much heat. Alvin was the quiet type, so he and the Barkers didn't like Dillinger's boastful personality and braggadocio crap." But the Barker-Karpis gang might have benefited from Dillinger's ability to avoid unnecessary bloodshed.[58]

The Third Northwestern National Bank robbery involved Fred and Doc Barker, DeVol, Karpis, Verne Miller, William Weaver, and Jess Doyle. The gang was armed with machine guns and .45-caliber automatics equipped with large-capacity clips. Two of the men entered through the Minneapolis bank's Central Avenue doors, and two others went in on the Hennepin Avenue side. DeVol stayed outside the bank, holding his machine gun. Miller ordered everyone in the bank to lie on the floor face down.[59]

"These men worked so fast and were so professional," remembered Earl Patch, who was then a bookkeeper in the bank. "First thing I heard, a guy said, 'This is a stick-up.' All of a sudden, it became *deathly* quiet in the bank." The gangsters had taken few precautions to hide their identities during a daylight robbery in front of dozens of witnesses. "Freddie Barker was running the show," said Patch. "He had some false teeth stuck in his mouth, but he didn't look much better when he took them out . . . Freddie Barker started screaming, 'Open the vault!'"[60]

Bank teller Paul Hesselroth tried to delay the robbery, protesting that he could not open the door to the vault. Miller beat the teller with a revolver, but not before Patch and Hesselroth tripped silent alarms.[61]

St. Paul Pioneer Press

VOL. 79. NO. 352. Full Leased Wire Service of the Associated Press. ST. PAUL, MINN., SATURDAY, DECEMBER 17, 1932. c PRICE THREE CENTS IN ST. PAUL.

BANDITS KILL POLICEMAN IN MINNEAPOLIS

SWEEPING PLAN DRAWN TO EASE FARM FINANCE

Arbitration Board Would Take Lead in Averting Fore-closures.

IMMEDIATE ACTION AIMED

Agricultural Leaders to Announce Complete Program Today.

By ALFRED D. STEDMAN
(Pioneer Press Staff Correspondent)
Washington, Dec. 16.—Work on emergency legislation to check fore-closures and help farmers keep their farms was virtually completed tonight by agricultural leaders meeting here.

After working almost night and day, farm leaders were putting final touches on the program tonight with formal announcement planned Saturday.

The plan is aimed to ease the farm mortgage situation in Minnesota and neighboring corn and wheat states where it is more acute than elsewhere. It is designed to safeguard not only the interests of farmers, but also those of insurance companies, banks and other investors in farm properties.

Included in the proposed legislation is a plan for official boards of arbitration. These would take the lead in various localities in arranging to save farmers their homes and their lands. Proposals for waivers of heavy principal payments, refunding and amortization over a period of years would come before such boards for decision.

Quick Action Sought.

The farmers' representatives here urge that every effort be made to put the emergency legislation through this short session of Congress. They want to afford thus remedy now, giving the farmers a breathing spell of security sufficient to permit later measures for permanent improvement of agriculture to take good effect.

E. A. O'Neal, L. J. Taber and

ROBBERY SCENE AND GIRLS MENACED BY LOOTERS

3RD NORTHWESTERN NATIONAL BANK

The Third Northwestern National bank in Minneapolis, where bandits shot down two policemen Friday afternoon, is shown at the top. Three girls were among the employes of the bank. In the lower picture they are, left to right, Mildred Lobdell, 3225 West Forty-sixth street, Minneapolis; Amy Birge, 3219 Clinton avenue, Minneapolis, and June Hent-hale, 1606 Carl street, St. Paul.

Killed

Ira Evans, Minneapolis patrolman, shown above, was killed by bullets of a bandit gang which robbed the Third Northwestern National Bank in Minneapolis Friday.

WARM WEATHER HOPE EXPRESSED BY SANTA

"I Don't Mind Cold," but Many Children Are Kept Away, He Says.

TODAY'S PROGRAM
Today's St. Paul Christmas Pageant program is:
10 A. M. to Noon—Santa at his lodge on Third street.
2 to 5 P. M.—Santa at lodge.
Aerial maneuvers by 109th Air Squadron and U. S. Naval Reserve fliers and singing by parks and playgrounds children's chorus.
5 to 7:30 P. M.—St. Nick and reindeer parade in loop.
7:30 to 9 P. M.—Santa at lodge.
An old man who has lived at the North Pole for so long he has for-

ST. PAULITE TELLS OF DODGING BULLETS

Car Driver Shot as He Slowed

SECOND OFFICER AND ST. PAUL MAN NEAR DEATH; 5 ROBBERS ESCAPE WITH BANK'S $20,000

Patrolmen Answering Alarm Met at Door of Third Northwestern National by Withering Fire; Auto Driver Shot as He Watches Holdups Change Cars in Como Park When Machine Is Disabled.

MOTORIST FEARED KIDNAPED BY GANG
TO ENABLE THEM TO GET SECOND AUTO

ST. PAUL POLICE ARREST SUSPECTS

Three men and a woman were arrested as suspects in the Third Northwestern National bank robbery early today after they had tried to catch a train to Montreal. Traveling in a car answering the description of the one in which the bandits escaped, they appeared at the Osceola, Wis., station and asked for tickets to Montreal but were told they had missed the train. They headed back to St. Paul and were arrested on the Stillwater road by St. Paul police.

Five machine-gun bandits raided the Third Northwestern National bank at 430 East Hennepin avenue in Minneapolis Friday afternoon, shot and killed one Minneapolis policeman and critically wounded another and then, fleeing through St. Paul, turned their guns on a St. Paul man because he stared at them.

The St. Paul man, Oscar Erickson, 29 years old, 638 Central Park place, is near death in Ancker hospital.

The slain patrolman is Ira L. Evans, who with Patrolman Leo Gorsky reached the bank as the robbers were leaving and stepped into a fusillade of shots. Gorsky is near death.

The bank was robbed of $20,000, all in currency.

The St. Paul man stepped innocently into the path of the bandits' cold-blooded fire when, driving through Como Park with a friend, he reached the point where the bandits had stopped their disabled getaway car to change to another machine.

Erickson, unemployed, had been selling Christmas wreaths in an effort to make a livelihood. Accompanied by Arthur Zachman, 22 years old, 1232 Grand avenue, he was driving along the Como park road near Monkey island when they saw a group of excited men standing around two cars, one a large green sedan and the other a smaller sedan.

Erickson slowed down and looked in the direction of the men. The men jumped one gun with deadly aims and Erickson slumped in his seat, a bullet through his head. His companion scraped the fire, then

---

Minneapolis policemen Ira Evans and Leo Gorski responded to the call. The officers drove immediately to the Third Northwestern National Bank, even though they had heard the report of the bank alarm going off just three minutes after they were to have quit for a 2:40 P.M. roll call. From a distance of fifteen feet, DeVol opened fired with his machine gun while the other thieves shot at the officers through the bank's plate glass windows. Ten of DeVol's bullets struck Evans, killing him instantly. The mortally wounded Gorski died forty-eight hours later.

"The squad car came down Central Avenue and the machine gunner sprayed them all the way down—ten to twelve bullet holes, each big enough to stick your thumb in, all over the police car," said Patch. "They were shooting from inside the bank and blew the windows away. For years, you could see [bullet] marks left on Arone's Bar across Central."[62]

The Barker-Karpis gang escaped with $22,000 in cash and close to $100,000 in securities. But one of the gang's own bullets had penetrated the front wheel of their getaway Lincoln. As the car pulled away from the bank, heading east on Fifth Street and then along East Hennepin and Larpenteur Avenues into St. Paul, the robbers knew they would have to switch tires soon. The tire change would have lethal consequences for Oscar Erickson, the twenty-nine-year-old son of Swedish immigrants.[63]

Headlines announcing the Third Northwestern National Bank robbery

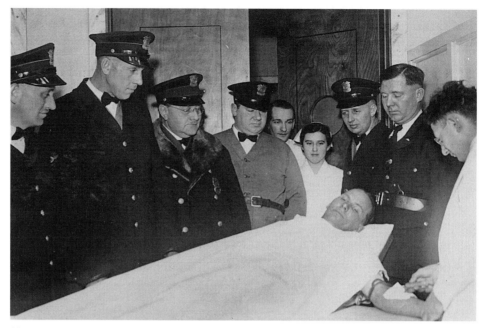

Minneapolis patrolman R. C. Lindvall (on bed) donating blood for Leo Gorski, the policeman mortally wounded in the December 1932 bank robbery

28 He 'Lost His Topper and Started to Fire'

The Como Park Slaying of Oscar Erickson
Near Como Zoo, St. Paul

The Barker-Karpis gang raced from the scene of the December 16 bank robbery to St. Paul's Como Park via "Bank Robber's Row," the route Karpis designed to avoid police roadblocks. The gang's Lincoln lost its tire on the east side of Snelling, just south of Larpenteur. Fortunately, they had left a green Chevrolet in Como Park in case of an emergency.[64]

Unaware of the bank robbers heading toward the "switch car" only blocks away, Oscar Erickson, accompanied by a twenty-two-year-old friend, Arthur Zachman, drove down Lexington to Como in his Chevrolet coupe. It was Erickson's first day selling Christmas wreaths in the neighborhood near the state fairgrounds. Searching for customers, Erickson and Zachman drove through Como Park, turning west past the monkey park and greenhouse. Just after three o'clock, Erickson saw a group of well-dressed men transferring objects from a Lincoln into a Chevy.[65]

"The tire and rim of the Lincoln's wheel were gone," recalled Alvin Karpis. "The Chevy had hot plates. These had to be taken off and the right ones put back on. Ignoring little details like that could result in capture. While this was being done, a jalopy came along with two fellows in it. The

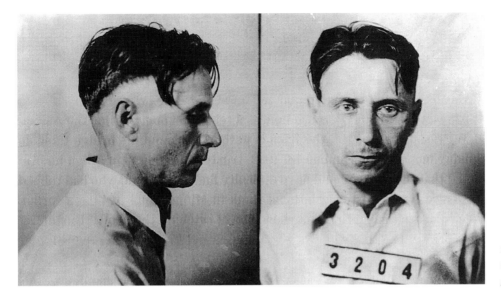

Fred Barker of the Barker-Karpis gang

driver stopped and damn near fell out of the car straining to get a look at the plates on the Chevy."[66]

"We were driving slowly through the park," Arthur Zachman told reporters, "when we noticed two cars standing alongside each other. As we went by, Oscar took his foot off the gas and we slowed down a little, looking out to see what was happening. Then all of a sudden there was a burst of gunfire and a lot of bullets went whistling by."[67]

According to the confession of gang member Jess Doyle, Barker mistakenly thought that Oscar Erickson was trying to catch a glimpse of the gang's license plates. Karpis recalled that Barker shouted, "Get going, or else!" "The guy ignored the warning and Freddie fired," wrote Karpis. "He got him right in the head and the blood streamed out over the side of the car."[68]

"Then Oscar slumped down in the driver's seat," Zachman recalled, "and his foot must have shoved up against the clutch, because the car started to coast." Zachman pulled Erickson onto the passenger side and, holding his bleeding friend with his right arm, drove down Lexington Parkway to the police station at University and St. Albans. Erickson was rushed to the hospital, where he died of a cerebral hemorrhage early the next morning. His wife of barely two years, Delvina Erickson, buried her husband in Roselawn Cemetery, mourning how happy Oscar had been on that first day of work.[69]

Bank robber Larry DeVol later told the St. Paul police that the man who shot Erickson in Como Park must have "been off his nut." Fred Barker just "lost his topper and started to fire," said DeVol. "I tried to stop him, but it was too late. The rest of the mob gave him hell," added DeVol. "That's one shooting that I didn't have a finger in."[70]

The Demise of the Incorrigible Larry DeVol

The Annbee Arms Apartments
928 Grand Avenue, St. Paul

Haskett Burton was a popular tenant at the Annbee Arms Apartments at 928 Grand Avenue. Because he was a telegraph operator for the Associated Press wire service, the friends gathered around his bridge table on Sunday morning, December 18, 1932, trusted his judgment when he predicted that the police would have difficulty finding the men who had robbed the Third Northwestern National Bank in Minneapolis two days earlier. "There doesn't seem to be much chance of catching this mob," Burton reportedly said. "Nobody knows who they are and I reckon they're plenty far away from here by now."[71]

Suddenly, a disheveled stranger wandered into the apartment, staggering and raving. Burton forced the drunk out of his home, which inspired the man to wave a pistol at Burton. Two St. Paul policemen, George Hammergren and Harley Kast, responded to the emergency call to disarm and arrest the drunkard. The officers were told that the man lived in apartment 206, where a search turned up packages of the money that had just been stolen from the Third Northwestern National Bank. Within hours, police identified the drunk in their custody as burglar Larry "the Chopper" DeVol, wanted for his role in killing police officers Evans and Gorski during the Minneapolis bank robbery. The police also found the .45-caliber automatic pistol used during the bank holdup.[72]

DeVol had been living for weeks in the Annbee Arms, a red-brick apartment building near the corner of Grand Avenue and Milton Street. The gang planned the robbery of the Third Northwestern National Bank there and returned to the Annbee hideaway to prepare the stolen bonds for laundering and distribution.[73]

Born in Ohio in 1905, DeVol had been sent to a Texas reformatory and an Oklahoma reform school by the time he was nine, at which time authorities labeled him "incorrigible." DeVol's first arrest was for a 1918 larceny charge in Tulsa, Oklahoma. The first of his three jail escapes occurred when he was fourteen, his first major arrest for burglary when he was sixteen.[74]

By the time the Barker-Karpis gang recruited DeVol, he had amassed a prodigious criminal résumé, including nearly forty safe-blowing jobs and imprisonment in Oklahoma and Kansas. DeVol was also being hunted for an array of homicides, including the double murder of a sheriff and a marshal in Washington, Iowa, in June 1930, a Tulsa murder in August 1930, and the murder of a Missouri policeman in November 1930.[75]

In prison photographs, DeVol's insolent stare overshadows his sunken

MINNEAPOLIS POLICE DEPARTMENT BUREAU OF IDENTIFICATION

Name LEONARD BARTON

Date of arrest 12/19/32

Charge BankRobber, Murder, Fugitiv

Disposition of case *M. S. P. LW 1/10/33*

Residence 928 Grand Ave., St. Pa

Place of birth ?

Nationality

Criminal specialty

Age 27   Build Med.

Height 5-8¼   Comp. Dark

Weight 157   Eyes Dk. Hazel

Hair Med. Dk. Ch.

Scars and marks

23802
12-20-32
Mpls

CRIMINAL HISTORY

With Robert Newburn — Clarence DeVol - Owen Lewis robbed the N. W. branch bank on E. Hennepin ave Mpls. Minn — Eddie DeVol the fifth man was not arrested. He is wanted

12/27/35 Transfered to St. Peter Insane Asylum.

5-7-36, Escaped State Hosp. St. Peter, Minn

DEAD

cheeks and acne. His criminal career had left other marks: a scar over his eyebrows, a gunshot scar on his left hand, a deformed left ring finger, and a knife scar on his right elbow. As for his temperament, a wanted poster described DeVol as "a paranoid maniac [who] suffers from persecutory delusions and is apt to kill associates suddenly without warning."[76]

DeVol claimed in a Stillwater, Minnesota, prison interview that the bonds stolen from the Third Northwestern National bank were taken to Chicago by Verne Miller for "cleaning" and then divided six ways. The FBI heard rumors as late as 1948 that attempts were still being made to launder the stolen bonds. The rest of the Barker-Karpis gang—Alvin Karpis, Jess Doyle, and the Barker brothers—headed for Reno to celebrate another Christmas outside prison walls, fence what they had stolen in Minneapolis, and wait until the newspaper headlines cooled and the Minnesota weather warmed.[77]

DeVol pleaded guilty to the murder of officers Evans and Gorski and in January was sentenced to life in Stillwater Prison. After reviewing DeVol's

Barker-Karpis gang machine gunner Larry DeVol, alias Leonard Barton

extensive criminal record, Stillwater warden John J. Sullivan called his new inmate "probably the most cold blooded man that ever entered the prison." He wrote that "I have not the slightest doubt but that he would take any chance to make a break, and would not hesitate to kill anyone that might stand between him and his freedom." DeVol, restricted to detention, told fellow inmates that he "had friends on the outside and he would get out regardless of the Warden, his deputy or any of his God damn guards."[78]

Declared insane after he claimed that prison guards were attempting to inject poison gas into his cell, DeVol was later transferred to a hospital for the criminally insane in St. Peter, Minnesota, and in June 1936 led a mass escape of fifteen inmates. In attempting to rob three banks, DeVol wounded two police officers and killed a third. He was tracked down by police in Enid, Oklahoma, where he was chased into an alley and killed in July 1936.[79]

30 The Mystery of 'Big Phil' Phillips

The Cle-mar Apartments
2062 Marshall Avenue, St. Paul

After the St. Paul police discovered Larry DeVol's Grand Avenue hideout, they searched without success for the apartment where Karpis and Ma Barker's family had planned the Third Northwestern National Bank robbery. Not until 1936 did the FBI discover that the Barkers made their headquarters at the Cle-mar Apartments, at the southwest corner of Cleveland and Marshall Avenues, where tenants included Ma Barker, swindler Earl Christman, and a disloyal bank robber named Bernard Phillips.[80]

"The Barker gang lived on the third or fourth floor in the back," recalled Jim Lehman, whose mother, Erma, ran a beauty shop in the Cle-mar. "I had mixed feelings about the gangsters as a child. You thought of them as criminals. They were like bad movie stars. . . . [But it] was kind of thrilling, because that was the time when they broadcast radio serials like *Gangbusters*."[81]

Why did so many gangsters live at the Cle-mar? The FBI later uncovered a link between the apartment building and underworld fixer Jack Peifer, who helped many visiting mobsters get settled in their first apartments when they checked into the Twin Cities. Peifer had lived there with his first wife.[82]

Con man Earl Christman of the Barker-Karpis gang and his girlfriend, Helen Ferguson, also lived in the Cle-mar in 1933. But the FBI was most interested in tracking down Doc, Fred, and Ma Barker. FBI investigators interviewed Cle-mar janitor Ed Wiechman about the months when the Barkers lived as "the Gordons" in apartment 37. Wiechman reported that the Barkers "would go away from their apartment for weeks at a time." While they were gone, he found chauffeur caps in the apartment. Apparently these caps were the underworld rage: Jess Doyle wore one during the Third Northwestern robbery, as did Alvin Karpis when he drove the William Hamm kidnap car.[83]

Easily the most intriguing mobster to live in the Cle-mar was an auto thief and former Cicero, Illinois, police officer named Bernard Phillips, also known as Big Phil Courtney. Phillips lived at the Cle-mar as "Mr. Stewart" from October 1931 to January 1932, after his parole from Leavenworth prison. Although he was never considered a gang leader, Phillips participated in a variety of major crimes: he joined veterans Harvey Bailey and Fred Barker in robbing the Citizens National Bank of Fort Scott, Kansas, in June 1932 and helped the Barker-Karpis gang with the March 1932 robbery of Northwestern National Bank and Trust Company of Minneapolis.[84]

FBI files suggest that Phillips was held in low regard by the underworld. From Helen Ferguson the FBI learned that members of the Barker-Karpis gang had said that the reason "Big Phil left St. Paul and went East was because no one would work with him." Gladys Sawyer, wife of Harry Sawyer, was more specific: she told the FBI that the Barkers and Karpis refused to work with Phillips because he was once "an officer of the law."[85]

George "Machine Gun Kelly" Barnes gave Detroit police an idea of how inept a crook Phillips could be. During a 1930 Chicago kidnapping in which Kelly and Phillips were partners, one of the victims taken by Phillips was accidentally killed. Soon after, Phillips asked Kelly to join him in another kidnapping. Kelly declined, concluding that the proposed victim did not have enough money to come up with the ransom. Phillips went ahead with the abduction and discovered that Kelly's assessment had been correct. Phillips released the kidnap victim with the pathetic order to bring his own ransom to a meeting and then borrowed Kelly's Cadillac to collect the ransom. Kelly, now "hot" with police for a kidnapping he had refused to have anything to do with, had to load his coupe into a truck and flee with it to Chicago.[86]

Alvin Karpis was similarly disappointed with Phillips's criminal acumen. In 1931 Karpis loaned Phillips his Buick and was stunned when the burned wreckage of his car appeared on the front page of the St. Paul newspapers in March 1932. Inside were the mutilated bodies of Margaret "Indian Rose" Perry and Sadie Carmacher, whom the underworld had feared would talk about the Barker-Karpis gang's assault on stores in Cambridge, Minnesota. The car was easily recognizable as Karpis's.[87]

Phillips's habit of being the only participant to escape unscathed from a crime scene proved to be his downfall. (In 1932, for example, eyewitnesses identified him as the heavyset man who dashed out of the Green Dragon during the slaying of bootlegger Abe Wagner—just before killers George Young and Joey Schaefer were captured.) Few in the underworld could have been surprised when, during the summer of 1932, Phillips visited a hotel in New York with fellow bank robbers Frank Nash and Verne Miller, received a telephone call, walked out to meet someone, and disappeared.[88]

Years later, Machine Gun Kelly revealed to Detroit police that Phillips had been killed and secretly buried near the Twin Cities. Kelly said that he had heard the story from casino operator Jack Peifer. According to Peifer, the mob never forgot that Phillips was playing just one hole behind Harvey Bailey, Jimmy Keating, and Tommy Holden at the Mission Hills Golf Course in Kansas City when they were arrested by the FBI. The underworld concluded that Phillips had enjoyed more than a lucky break, that in fact he had been allowed to escape because he helped send Bailey, Keating, and Holden to prison.

Police reports and FBI interviews with Phillip's girlfriend, Winnie

Cle-mar Apartments at Cleveland and Marshall, a hideout for Bernard "Big Phil" Phillips (inset) and other members of the Barker-Karpis gang

Williams, indicate that he was stabbed to death with ice picks, covered with lime to prevent identification, and buried on a lonely road. His body was never found. Underworld legend holds that Bernie Phillips got a special treatment reserved for double-crossers: he was buried with his forearm jutting out of the ground. Visible on the exposed arm was a tattoo: a cross with flowers and the words "My Mother" etched in red, blue, and green.[89]

31 Gangland Tip-Off on Grand Avenue

The Barker-Karpis Gang's Grand Avenue Apartments
1290 Grand Avenue, St. Paul

"It was the custom of the gang to immediately install a telephone in their apartments," the FBI learned from Barker-Karpis gang member Jess Doyle. The purpose of the telephone was to receive "telephone calls from Harry Sawyer concerning tip-offs of police raids." But when the members of Ma Barker's gang moved in February 1933 into a four-story brick apartment building near the corner of Grand Avenue and Syndicate Street, they neglected this security precaution.[90]

Doc and Fred Barker rented three apartments; swindler Earl Christman and gunman Jess Doyle joined them. Gradually, other members of the Barker-Karpis gang, who had avoided the Minnesota winter by vacationing in Nevada, drifted back to St. Paul as well. Edna Murray had escaped in December from solitary confinement at the Missouri State Penitentiary and drove to St. Paul to keep company with her beau, Volney Davis.[91]

On March 4, 1933, underworld fixer Harry Sawyer received a tip from a source in the St. Paul Police Department that detectives were about to raid the 1290 Grand apartments. The gang did not yet have a telephone, so Sawyer sent his wife, Gladys, to "tell the boys the 'heat' was on," the FBI reported. Unaware of the unfolding drama, Jess Doyle drove up to the building at about eight o'clock that evening. Three policemen were parked in a squad car in front of the building, Doyle recalled. Gladys Sawyer had already arrived, warning Karpis, Davis, and Christman that the police were outside. Doyle brazenly packed his suitcases, then walked out the front door, sauntering past the police car. The officers courteously waited to raid the building until all of the Barker-Karpis gang had a chance to flee. Doyle, Karpis, and Fred Barker met at Sawyer's Green Lantern saloon, whereupon they all departed for Chicago.[92]

After that brush with capture, the Barker-Karpis gang bounced between the Kansas City, Missouri, and Chicago areas, planning their next major robbery. On April 4, 1933, they struck the First National Bank of Fairbury,

Nebraska. For the Fairbury job, Doyle later told the FBI, the gang consisted of a sprawling conglomeration of hoods: Karpis, Doyle, Volney Davis, Earl Christman, Fred and Doc Barker, Eddie Green (a St. Paul hoodlum then affiliated with Lester "Babyface Nelson" Gillis), and Frank Nash (who usually worked with the Keating-Holden gang).[93]

JESS DOYLE
Age: 26 (1927)
Height: 5' 9¼"
Weight: 151
Build: Medium
Hair: Brown
Eyes: Gray
Complexion: Dark

Jewel thief Jess Doyle of the Barker-Karpis gang

This gang took more than $151,000 worth of government bonds, coin, and silver from the bank vault, but when one of their machine guns jammed, they discovered they were outgunned by the people of Fairbury—and a visiting machine-gun salesman. The looting of the bank, which took just eight minutes, ended in a gory shootout between the gang and a squad of heavily armed townspeople.[94]

Christman, shot in the chest by a Fairbury deputy sheriff, was driven to Verne Miller's bungalow in Kansas City for treatment. Karpis and Eddie Green provided amateur medical care that consisted of injections of morphine and washing the wound with "drugstore prescription whiskey." According to Karpis's confession to the FBI, Christman was recovering so well from the wound that one day, when the doctor was about to lift him out of bed, he got up unaided, reopening the wound and causing a hemorrhage. The doctor said Christman would not live more than an hour, and he was right. Somewhere outside Kansas City, Christman was buried in an unmarked grave.[95]

Doc Barker and Jess Doyle returned to St. Paul, where Barker met with Harry Sawyer to plan the kidnapping of a prominent St. Paul businessman. Fred and Ma Barker drove from Chicago to join Doc in St. Paul in May, bringing Christman's girlfriend, Helen Ferguson, along to the Commodore Hotel. The Barkers told Ferguson that her lover had been wounded during the Fairbury raid—but not too seriously, they reassured her. Christman would have to recuperate in a Kansas City hideout for a few weeks.

Ferguson naively believed them; some of the gang women were hardened, but her background had not prepared her for a lifestyle that involved prison and shootouts. She was described unkindly in FBI files: "pointed nose, prominent big jaw, has dropsy." A former product demonstrator for the H. J. Heinz Company, Ferguson had been married to and divorced from a Prudential insurance salesman before she fell for Christman, a man she knew to be a con man.

Ferguson clearly loved Christman and stuck by him when he was charged with a Seattle mail robbery in 1930 (the charges were dismissed) and again when he was convicted in Michigan of running a confidence game. In the five years she lived with him, Ferguson traveled under a variety of assumed names from Kalamazoo, Michigan, to San Francisco and then to Toledo; Asheville, North Carolina; Hot Springs, Arkansas; Juarez, Mexico; Kirkwood, Missouri; and finally back to St. Paul. Ferguson said of her life as a bank robber's girlfriend: "We had plenty of money and neither Christman nor I ever did any work."

That April 14, Fred Barker took Ferguson aside and told her Christman was dead. His body had already been disposed of. "Fred refused to tell me where he [Christman] was buried," Ferguson bitterly told the FBI, "and refused to permit me to tell Christman's mother, stating that it would put too much 'heat' on the gang." She got $2,000 from Christman's share of the Fairbury money. It was as close to an underworld death benefit as the Barker-Karpis gang ever gave any woman.[96]

32 Ma Barker Meets the Girls

The Commodore Hotel
79 Western Avenue, St. Paul

The Commodore Hotel was widely known as a haven for novelist F. Scott Fitzgerald and his wife, Zelda, in 1921 and 1922. The anonymity cherished by the socialites who sipped at the Commodore's art deco bar also attracted more notorious tenants, Ma Barker and Al Capone among them.

When the Commodore Hotel opened in 1920, it was one of St. Paul's most elegant nightspots for dining and dancing. Patrons were enticed with descriptions of its spacious lobby and ballroom, its "home-like spirit," and its location in "the most aristocratic and quiet section of the city." A city directory ad boasted that "the Commodore has no equal in the Northwest."[97]

Chicago train robber Jimmy Keating, pursued by the FBI for his role in the Menomonie, Wisconsin, bank robbery, stayed at the Commodore in November 1931. Then, in May 1933, Ma Barker moved into the Commodore's apartments 215 to 221, using the alias Mrs. A. B. Gardner. Fred Barker, who was about to have his appendix removed at a Twin Cities hospital, joined her there as Fred E. Gardner. Helen Ferguson was secreted upstairs, in apartment 404. Ma Barker, jealous of any younger women living near her boys, made Ferguson's life miserable at the Commodore.

"Ma Barker was very jealous of her boys and did not wish to have them associate with girl friends," stated a 1936 FBI summary. "She would disclose the conversations had with various women members of the gang to her sons, particularly stressing the women's statements with reference to them. This . . . caused frequent evidence of dissension among the other women of the gang who, in most instances, made every effort to avoid the presence of Ma Barker."[98]

"After Christman died," Helen Ferguson told the FBI, "I was in Kate Barker's company considerably." Ferguson "gradually developed a strong dislike for her company."[99]

At the Commodore, Ma Barker endured her first and last meeting with Fred's new girlfriend, thirty-year-old Paula Harmon. Fred met Paula Harmon at Herb Farmer's gangland hideout in Joplin, Missouri, in the spring of 1931, during one of Paula's frequent marital spats with bank robber Charlie Harmon. When Charlie was shot to death during the robbery of the Kraft

The Commodore Hotel, a haven for Ma and Fred Barker in May 1933

Bank in Menomonie, Wisconsin, in October of that year, Paula was free to explore a relationship with Kate Barker's son.

"Girls liked Freddie and he didn't mind spending money on them," recalled Karpis. "But he wasn't always lucky in the type of broad who hooked him. Paula Harmon turned out to be a rotten choice, though you couldn't tell that to Freddie when he got stuck on her. . . . Paula was a drunk."[100]

On April 5, 1933, Fred Barker, flush with his share of the Fairbury National Bank loot, asked Verne Miller's girlfriend to call the young widow and invite her to meet him in Kansas City. The romance between Barker and Harmon blossomed in May, and Fred decided it was time to introduce Paula to his "Ma."[101]

Whether or not J. Edgar Hoover was correct in believing that Ma Barker "shuddered in jealous trepidation when a new gun moll threatened to steal the love of one of her boys," the first meeting between Ma Barker and Paula Harmon was not a pleasant experience. "The day Fred Barker was taken to the hospital I met his mother, who was living at the Commodore Apartments in St. Paul, under the name of Mrs. Gordon," Paula Harmon told the FBI. "Evidently, I did not make a favorable impression, as I have never seen her since."[102]

Not that it would have been easy for Ma Barker's sons to have found women who pleased their mother. "It was a rare time when she'd let us bring women to the house," mused Karpis. "Whenever Freddie or I got serious about a girl, we'd move out of Ma's place and keep the girls in another hotel or apartment." Doc Barker posed less of a problem for his mother in the arena of female companionship. "Doc Barker never at any time, to my knowledge, was accompanied by a girl," Gladys Sawyer told the FBI, "and apparently has been in the penitentiary so much he does not associate with women." Fred remained Ma's boy throughout his relationship with Harmon, who told the FBI that he kept leaving St. Paul to visit his mother in Chicago. Even though Fred was persuaded to spend New Year's with his girlfriend, he spent Christmas with his mother.[103]

According to legend, Chicago's most notorious gang leader also visited the Commodore Hotel. "Capone, when he came to town the two times that he did, [stayed] in the Commodore Hotel (incognito, of course)," said Bill Greer, veteran St. Paul crime reporter. The gangster era of Al Capone and Ma Barker was the Commodore's heyday, Greer said. "The place has deteriorated," he quipped, "since they've got politicians in there."[104]

Mr. Wm. Dunn

You're so god damed smart that you'll wind up getting both
of you guys killed.It so happened that we taild that cab
last night.

You better take advantage of the time before the papers
get a hold of this.

Heres god news for you. Unless 199 the 100,000 dollars
is delivered as per our instructions on Saturday the
demand will be for 19979   150,000 thereafter.

Furthermore we demand that you personally deliver the
money so that if there is any doble crossing we will
have the pleasure of hitting you in the head.

Prepare to have the cash tomorrow. You will receive new
instructions. If your not going to carry them out fully
don't start. If the coppers succeed in following you it
might prove fatal. You brought the coppers in to this
now you get rid of the assholes.

Hamm is uncomfortable and dissapointed in the way you
bungled this so far.

We won't continue to take these draws forever so dont
spar to long. If we haddVent intended to go thru with
this we would not have started.

I HEREBY AUTHORIZE THE ABOVE PAYMENT TO BE MADE
AND REQUEST THAT ALL INSTRUCTIONS BE FULLY
CARRIED OUT.

M;rWm. Dunn
1916 Summit Ave
St.Paul.

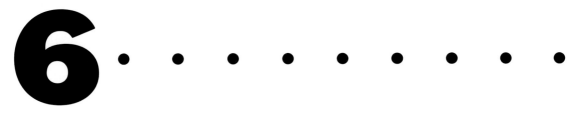

A VERY TROUBLING KIDNAPPING

A Hamm ransom note, as retyped by FBI agents; family photo of fixer Jack Peifer and his wife, Violet, proprietors of the Hollyhocks Club

33   Gangland's Taj Mahal

The Hollyhocks Club Casino
1590 South Mississippi River Boulevard, St. Paul

During the early 1930s, a three-story mansion called the Hollyhocks was filled with tuxedo-clad businessmen and their wives sipping fine liqueurs and rubbing elbows with the most wanted gangsters in America. It was here that the Barker-Karpis gang met to plot the kidnapping that would elevate them to the top of J. Edgar Hoover's list of public enemies.[1]

The host of the Hollyhocks—and the "fingerman" who selected William Hamm as the gang's next victim—was John "Jack" Peifer, a former hotel bellhop and carnival worker turned underworld banker who, in the words of the FBI, "was always out of town whenever anything happen[ed]." A brown-haired, ruddy-skinned German-American from Litchfield, Minnesota, Peifer was 5 feet, 9 inches tall and weighed 189 pounds, with a mole in the center of his left cheek. He lived on the third floor of the Hollyhocks with his second wife, fashion model Violet Peifer, and their dog.[2]

Peifer had run other businesses on the fringes of the underworld, including a gambling operation on the seventh floor of the Radisson Hotel in Minneapolis; a St. Paul hotel (with future Barker-Karpis gang member Larry DeVol); the Senator Hotel in Minneapolis (with bootlegger Tommy Banks), a favorite of bank robbers Frank Nash and Charlie Harmon; and a cigar store/speakeasy on St. Peter Street.

Bank robbers who frequented the Hollyhocks were hesitant to keep their money in a traditional bank account—after all, who knew better how insecure the vaults were than the gangs who pried them open? Barker-Karpis gang members left their money with Peifer for safekeeping. He also made loans: "Some of the gang usually came to him for a 'touch,'" the FBI said. "Any time any hoodlum wanted a loan from him he usually complied with this request in order to keep the Hollyhocks from being held up, as he, Peifer, was operating gambling at the place."[3]

Not all gangsters in the underworld trusted Peifer to keep their money. Alvin Karpis recalled how he had once been forced to flee St. Paul and leave his money behind with a mob "banker" ("Karpis intimated that the man who was holding his money was Peifer," noted the FBI). While he was on the run, he needed the money and thought about going to St. Paul for it, but feared the "banker" might turn him in. Karpis considered kidnapping Peifer's wife to trade for his money but decided it would be too risky.[4]

Hollyhocks dinner guests, served by Japanese waiters on white tablecloths, included Alvin Karpis, Ma Barker and her boys Fred and Doc, bank robbers Verne Miller and Frank Nash, Chicago hoods Robert "Frisco

Dutch" Steinhardt and Fred "Shotgun George Ziegler" Goetz of Al Capone's syndicate, and members of the gangs operated by John Dillinger and Roger "the Terrible" Touhy. Karpis was especially fond of the Hollyhocks, and in May 1933 he romanced his teenaged lover, Delores Delaney, at the casino.[5]

The Hollyhocks site was originally developed by the wealthy family of Henry and Cornelia Boardman, who bought the land in 1904. In 1929 slot machine king Tom Filben, through his Federal Acceptance Corporation, backed the purchase of the property by Harry Silver and boxer Walter "Saph" McKenna, who transformed it into a gambling hall. Silver assured McKenna that the county attorney had told the chief of police to leave them alone, and McKenna told the FBI that 20 percent of the Hollyhocks's net profits were set aside as bribes for local police and politicians.[6]

In March 1931 Jack Peifer bought out McKenna's half share and took over the club with Filben. They named the Hollyhocks after the greenery surrounding the casino. McKenna stayed on to play two roles at the Hollyhocks: funneling weekly payoffs to the St. Paul police and managing the Hollyhocks dining room.[7]

Jack Peifer, manager of the Hollyhocks (below, seen from back), a favorite gangland casino

The Hollyhocks was a sizable operation. FBI agents noted that its garage could hold sixteen automobiles. "On the first floor [was] a large kitchen, butler's pantry, dance floor, semi-private dining rooms, bar, and store room," reported the FBI. "On the second floor . . . was a bedroom which was then occupied by the Japanese house man and a large gambling room." On the third floor were three bedrooms, one of them Peifer's private bedroom, equipped with a safe.[8]

Legend holds that a tunnel, entered through a hidden trap door, extended from the front porch to the Mississippi River below—a route for disposal of gangland victims—and of jewelry and cash stored in the club's walls. The current owners have searched and found no evidence of a tunnel.[9]

Peifer was the Minnesota contact for bank robber George "Machine Gun Kelly" Barnes, for whom he laundered the ransom paid for kidnapped Oklahoma oilman Charles Urschel. FBI agents uncovered Peifer's role in distributing the Urschel ransom through the Minneapolis syndicate of Isadore "Kid Cann" Blumenfeld when they found the Hollyhocks telephone number in the effects of Kelly's wife, Kathryn.

Peifer's menu of criminal services also included supplying alibis. When racketeer John Quinn murdered Frank Ventress at the Green Lantern saloon in 1931, homicide records show that Quinn dashed to the Hollyhocks to hammer out a bogus alibi. How could he have committed the murder, Quinn hoped to argue, if he and his wife were dining at the Hollyhocks at the time of the killing? Peifer's own criminal record was minor: a three-month jail term in 1924 for running illicit liquor out of a St. Paul "soft-drink bar" on St. Peter Street.[10]

Although FBI agents found a .38-caliber police-model revolver, a rusty .38 Colt automatic, and a Browning automatic shotgun when they raided the Hollyhocks, Peifer's value to the underworld was as a political fixer, not as a gunman. Friends claimed that Peifer was much more likely to hire a hit man than commit a murder himself, and in 1931 he demonstrated his incompetence with a gun in a firearms accident of an intimate nature. Precisely what happened is unclear from published reports. The St. Paul newspaper reported that "Peifer said a pistol discharged as he was removing it from his belt" and "a bullet grazed his abdomen," and FBI records showed that Peifer's body bore a scar from an abdominal bullet wound.[11]

Veteran newsman Fred Heaberlin was more explicit about the incident. "There was a telephone call to the St. Paul police one night about a shooting at the Hollyhocks Club," said Heaberlin. "The police detectives poured into their black Cadillac . . . and rushed out to the Hollyhocks. They were met at the door by Jack Peifer, who told them, 'It was nothing at all, boys. Just a scalp wound.' What had happened is that Peifer had a small-caliber pistol in his pocket, and when the derringer went off, the bullet creased the tip of his pecker!"[12]

Peifer's majordomo, Sam Tanaka (his real name was Shigematsu Yukimura), acted as the Hollyhocks chef and handled odd jobs. Peifer liked Japanese servants because, he told his mob associates, "they were very faithful and close-mouthed about what they saw or heard." No request was too unusual to be catered to at the Hollyhocks. When twenty guests asserted a desire for frog legs, Peifer said, "Well, just keep on drinking and I'll have my fellas go to Wisconsin and get frog's legs." Two hours later, Peifer's man "came back with the frog's legs and we ate like King Henry VIII!" recalled patron Blanche Schude. "Oh, the Hollyhocks was out of this world. . . . It was the elite!" The Hollyhocks food was so good, in fact, that Dillinger gang member Homer Van Meter was unable to resist braving a nationwide FBI manhunt to drive to the Hollyhocks with his girlfriend and devour his last Hollyhocks steak, which he ate in his car for security.[13]

"Dinner began at 6:00 P.M. on the first floor," recalled Martin Rohling, who was the Hollyhocks Club doorman during the early 1930s. "They gave food away at the Hollyhocks—you could get a porterhouse steak there for $1.50. . . . But we didn't have many diners at the Hollyhocks. They came to *gamble* . . . craps, roulette, and blackjack," said Rohling. "Once a week, we'd get a hundred women out to the Hollyhocks to play roulette for dimes!" Peifer and his associates "paid off the mayor and everyone else," added Rohling. Early one Sunday morning in July 1934, two policemen raided the club, confiscating two roulette wheels and detaining seven patrons and staff members, including Peifer. Because the roulette wheels were not operating at the time of the raid, the city promised not to charge Peifer with gambling and, Rohling said, two policemen returned the roulette wheels.[14]

In January 1931, the Hollyhocks had faced a crisis: With the election of Michael Kinkead as Ramsey County attorney, the club was temporarily forced to suspend operations, Walt McKenna reported. Interviewed by FBI agents, McKenna claimed that under Kinkead, bootlegger Leon Gleckman was able to tighten his control of gambling rackets. To keep the Hollyhocks gambling operations in business, Peifer would have to ally himself with Gleckman, "the Al Capone of St. Paul," who demanded about 20 percent of the net profits, McKenna told the FBI. The man who would collect Gleckman's $100 weekly payoffs was William W. Dunn, a sales manager for the Hamm Brewing Company. McKenna met Dunn in the lobby of the Hotel St. Paul to schedule payoffs. At the same time that Gleckman was securing his power over gambling payoffs, McKenna noticed another key player in the payoff schemes: St. Paul police chief Tom Brown was often seen speaking quietly with Jack Peifer in the front yard of the Hollyhocks. The payoff arrangement changed abruptly after Peifer negotiated Gleckman's return when the bootlegger was kidnapped in 1931. A grateful Gleckman canceled the Hollyhocks payoffs.[15]

A cast of scoundrels, petty thieves, and roustabouts enlivened the Hollyhocks's party atmosphere. Among them was a former carnival trick shooter nicknamed Tex. Alvin Karpis called Tex the biggest braggart he had ever met in his life, but Tex always lived up to his wildest boasts. He could slash a cigarette in two with a huge bullwhip, shoot six dimes with a gun at a distance of twenty-five yards, and balance six cups of steaming coffee on his arm at one time.[16]

During Christmas 1933 the Hollyhocks was particularly festive. Highway robber Harry Campbell, his girlfriend Wynona Burdette, Doc Barker, Volney Davis, and Edna Murray were all celebrating another holiday outside prison walls. "That [Christmas] night, we all went cabareting at Jack Pfeifer's Hollyhocks Inn," recalled Fred Barker's girlfriend Paula Harmon, "and we all stayed at Jack Peifer's place that night."[17]

Most Hollyhocks regulars were not mobsters. The club catered to businesspeople who enjoyed the thrill of dining and rolling dice in the company of notorious gangsters. "A customer visiting the Hollyhocks recognized as he approached the place that it was 'class' and that his billfold would need to be in a healthy condition," recalled *St. Paul Pioneer Press* crime reporter Nate Bomberg. "Going to the second floor after an excellent dinner, he found a gambling casino with the croupiers, also dressed formally, raking or pushing chips that represented thousands of dollars. If he lost, he knew at least that he had done so at the best illegal operation of its sort in St. Paul during the Prohibition era."[18]

Robert Brooks Hamilton, a white-haired gambling impresario, supervised the Hollyhocks casino with relentless honesty; his staff even supplied gamblers with calipers to test the dice. Hamilton considered it wise to let gamblers win every now and then. "They'll always come back when they win," Hamilton said, "and usually they lose all their winnings and plenty besides before they go home."[19]

Doorman Martin Rohling recalled one morning in 1933 or 1934 when William Mahoney, mayor of St. Paul, knocked at the Hollyhocks, curious to see its luxurious interior: "I had the chain on the door and he said, 'My wife has a headache, I'd like to get a glass of water.' I said, 'I'll bring it to you!' He said, '*I'm the mayor of St. Paul, let me in!*' And I *wouldn't*. The mayor wanted to see the inside of the place, but I never let him in."[20]

By 1932, during the nationwide manhunt for bank robbers Francis Keating and Tommy Holden, the FBI had begun to watch the Hollyhocks. FBI agents obtained a list of all long-distance telephone calls and telegrams charged to the club, documenting Peifer's contact with hoodlums in Miami Beach, Chicago, Montreal, and other cities. New reform-minded police officers—notably Chief Thomas E. Dahill—were now refusing to go along with the corrupt policies of the O'Connor era. In August 1932 he announced a police "drive against hoodlums" and "gun-toters," sparked by the public uproar over the murder of bootleggers Harry "Gorilla Kid" Davis and Abe Wagner by Murder Inc. "Gangsters and would-be gangsters are not wanted here," announced Dahill, "and we intend to do everything in our power to drive them out." A few days after that announcement, police were attracted by a fight outside the Green Lantern. Under Dahill's orders, officers arrested gunmen Clarence Colton, brother of Barker-Karpis gang member Larry DeVol, and William Weaver. Although both enforcers jumped their $500 bail bond and disappeared, a line had been crossed. If Dahill could violate the O'Connor agreement to leave crooks alone, was it time to violate O'Connor's prohibition against major crimes in St. Paul?[21]

The day after Colton's and Weaver's arrest, St. Paul police detective Fred Raasch saw underworld fixer Harry Sawyer sitting in a car across the street from the Public Safety Building on Tenth Street: "Sawyer said that he was in a jam because the police had picked up a couple of fellows in his place the night before. He said he wondered what was the matter with Dahill. . . . that when [Tom] Brown was Chief, he'd always get a call if they were going to come up to his place, and he said: 'If I had got a ring, I'd had those fellows out of there.'" Sawyer warned that he could "keep heat off a town, but he could put it on, too," Raasch told the FBI. "I wonder how Dahill would like a couple of snatches in this town," Sawyer said.[22]

Jack Peifer brought Fred Barker and Alvin Karpis to the Hollyhocks in April 1933 to initiate a "snatch" that would shatter the O'Connor system forever. "Whatever it was he had in mind, I figured it must be a bombshell," Karpis recalled. "Peifer leaned back with an extra-special important look and said, 'How would you boys like to work on a kidnapping?'" Once the kidnapping was set into motion, the Hollyhocks became an unofficial staging area for the abduction.[23]

The victim Peifer had chosen was William Hamm Jr., the young president of St. Paul's Hamm Brewing Company, who was also the president of a department store, a Minnesota Amusement Corporation officer, and a First National Bank board member. Peifer had met Hamm when he was a patron at the Hollyhocks in 1931. The ransom, Peifer said, would be $100,000 in unmarked bills.[24]

Karpis later wondered about the modest ransom amount; after all, Hamm was a brewer and Prohibition had just ended. Twin Cities liquor companies —forced for fourteen years to subsist on manufacturing near beer, malt syrup, and alcohol for industrial purposes—were now brewing money. Because "less money was demanded than the victim was able to pay," Karpis told the FBI years later, he speculated that the motive for the kidnapping was more complex: "[I] thought it was political and had something to do with [the] St. Paul police department and Ramsey County officials."[25]

Kidnapping someone as visible as Hamm was a far cry from kidnapping a racketeer like Leon Gleckman. "Before Prohibition was repealed, the people in rackets were out kidnapping the top bootleggers who were making lots of money," said Pat Lannon Sr., a former St. Paul policeman. "When Prohibition was repealed, those guys didn't have any money—and they had to snatch legitimate people, that's how the Bremer and Hamm kidnappings started."[26]

In the midst of the kidnapping, an act of violence in Kansas City shattered the complacency of every gangster dining at the Hollyhocks. On June 17, 1933, bank robber Verne Miller and two accomplices, armed with submachine guns, attempted to free their comrade Frank Nash from federal custody at Union Station. Instead, Miller slaughtered three policemen, an FBI agent, and Nash. "That damn thing with Frank Nash in Kansas City is going to be the worst thing that ever happened to guys like us," predicted Karpis.[27]

When the FBI launched its massive investigation into what was then dubbed the Kansas City Massacre, agents were curious why the Hollyhocks Club figured so prominently. Nash's wife, Frances, said that she and Frank had enjoyed lunch there in early June, days before the massacre. The agents also learned that gangsters had telephoned the Hollyhocks the morning before the Kansas City Massacre. Two additional phone calls were made to St. Paul from Union Station within hours after the massacre, one to Harry Sawyer's Green Lantern saloon and the other to the Hollyhocks.[28]

By July the FBI had authorized a mail cover on letters and packages delivered to the Hollyhocks and a covert wiretap on its telephone. The St. Paul FBI field office reassured J. Edgar Hoover that "the tapping of this telephone line was conducted entirely unbeknown to the telephone company." Working with a U.S. Army Signal Corps lieutenant at Fort Snelling, across the Mississippi River from the Hollyhocks, FBI agent Oscar Hall tapped Emerson 2121, a phone line at the club.[29]

Within two weeks, the agents learned that the Hollyhocks was far more than just a nightclub; it appeared to be the nerve center linking corrupt Twin Cities police with organized crime. In one wiretapped conversation, Peifer's wife, Violet, telephoned "Maxine," the girlfriend of Minneapolis bootlegger Tommy Banks. The FBI reported that Maxine "told Violet Peifer that their Minneapolis criminal defense attorney Archie Cary 'has been arranging the distribution of the rackets in Minneapolis since the change in police administration,' and proceeded to outline in detail how the rackets were to be divided." The wiretap proved that Peifer was helping mobsters with everything from repairing their getaway cars to dealing with wayward girlfriends.

Harry Sawyer was overheard on a Hollyhocks wiretap complaining to Peifer that criminal defense attorney Tom Newman had referred him to a Ramsey County child welfare agent who was "a bum steer." According to the FBI report, Sawyer said the adoption agent was "investigating more than Newman said she would" when the Sawyers adopted a little girl.[30]

The FBI understood that Peifer's chief value to the underworld was his access to police, judges, and grand juries. When agents raided Vi Peifer's third-floor bedroom at the Hollyhocks, they found a typewritten list titled "Grand Jurors—March-April" with the names of members of a Hennepin County grand jury.[31]

In the most revealing Hollyhocks wiretap, Peifer was overheard negotiating with Jack Lally, junior captain of Minneapolis detectives, precisely how many pickpockets would be allowed on the streets and determining how many pockets had been picked that day. "This is Jack Lally," the policeman said to the gangster. "Have you got any pickpockets working over here? If you have, you better call them off. Things are too hot."[32]

The combined investigations into the kidnapping of Hamm and banker Edward Bremer, and the Kansas City Massacre gradually drew a long shadow over Peifer and the Hollyhocks Club. The club was officially closed in 1934, just after Bremer was kidnapped. FBI agents searched the Hollyhocks for typewriters that might have been used to type the Hamm and Bremer kidnap ransom notes and interviewed a truculent Peifer to determine what he knew about the kidnappings. Peifer boldly claimed that he barely knew the Barkers, but agents retorted that they knew Peifer "was connected with practically every form of racketeering occurring in the Twin Cities."[33]

Although the ransom-note typewriters were never found, the FBI discovered months later that Peifer had not only selected William Hamm as the victim but had also chosen the White Bear Lake Township cottage from which the kidnapping would be launched.

34   Pennies from Gangster Heaven

The Barker-Karpis Gang at Idlewild Cottage
5500 East Bald Eagle Boulevard, White Bear Lake Township

Alvin Karpis and the Barker brothers initiated the June 1933 kidnapping of William Hamm from a Bald Eagle Lake cottage called Idlewild.

When Karpis visited the Hollyhocks Club with Fred Barker, he told Jack Peifer that he would move to Minnesota if he could find "a quiet place out on the lake someplace not too far from St. Paul." Peifer told Karpis to come back after he had had a chance to search the White Bear–Bald Eagle Lake area for a suitable cottage. "I kidded him [Peifer] about it being a racket coming around at dinner time so as I would buy my dinner there instead of some place else," recalled Karpis later. "He just laughed and said I should patronize his place if he was going to the trouble of finding a cottage for me."[34]

White Bear Lake was an ideal spot for the Barker-Karpis gang to blend in with vacationers during the first explosion of "heat" generated by the Hamm kidnapping. Remote from St. Paul and Minneapolis, encircled by winding tree-lined roads and anonymous beach cabins, the resort area was marketed as a place for "people of wealth and refinement"—F. Scott and Zelda Fitzgerald and others attracted by yacht regattas, lawn tennis, and "popular hops and musicales." In fact, it was the playground of the same well-to-do Twin Citians who became the Barker-Karpis gang's kidnapping targets.[35]

Peifer drove up to the Idlewild cottage in a La Salle coupe in May 1933 and paid the $250 cash deposit to rent the home from owner Alex Premo. When the landlord offered a receipt, Peifer declined, preferring that there be no record of the transaction. The Premos had the money, said Peifer, and he had the cottage, "so to hell with a receipt." At that time, Idlewild was a one-and-one-half-story white-and-green building with a thousand-gallon water tank, a screened porch, and a two-car garage where Fred Barker kept his Ford coupe and a Hudson sedan.[36]

Doc and Fred Barker joined Karpis at Idlewild, eager to hammer out the

Idlewild cottage, the Barker-Karpis gang's Bald Eagle Lake headquarters during the Hamm kidnapping

details of the kidnapping. Fred Barker and Karpis followed Hamm as he walked up the hill from the Hamm brewery to his Cable Avenue mansion. "We made almost daily trips into St. Paul to case Hamm's brewery and home," recalled Karpis. "We mastered every last detail of the layouts of both places and spent hours studying Hamm's habits. We got to know so much about the guy that I was sick of him long before the kidnapping."[37]

Meanwhile, the gangsters told their new neighbors that they were entertainers from the Plantation nightclub. "Ma Barker wanted me to mow her lawn with one of our hand mowers," remembered Clifford Lindholm, who lived opposite the Idlewild cottage in 1933. "So I attempted to mow her lawn, and she gave me five dollars. Well, it was the Depression. I didn't know what the hell money was. When my mother saw that, it was like pennies from heaven. . . . And I must have done a horrible job of mowing the Barker-Karpis gang's lawn!" Lindholm tasted his first cream soda pop on the Idlewild back porch with Ma Barker, and when he and other children were selling ten-cent tickets for a community fund raiser, they headed for Idlewild: "I knew [the Barkers] would be very generous. Ma Barker bought the whole roll from me!" She gave the roll of tickets back to Lindholm and let him keep the money. "We thought they were very nice people!"[38]

"They were the perfect neighbors," said Steve Tuttle, whose grandfather had a cottage directly across from Idlewild. "Ma Barker's boys used to hold ice cream socials for the neighborhood kids in the backyard. . . . If people did know who the Barkers were, no one cared—as long as they didn't commit any crimes in the Bald Eagle area!"[39]

Area residents are fond of telling Barker-Karpis stories. It is said that the gang indulged in target shooting at Bald Eagle Lake. Hearing the gunfire, a neighbor ran over to Idlewild and shouted angrily at the gangsters, "You cut this out . . . there are kids around here!" Sheepishly, the story goes, the gang stopped shooting. "Criminals had some kind of ethics in those days," said Lindholm, expressing the lenient view that many citizens of St. Paul and White Bear Lake shared. "Those people would never do things like the drive-by shootings they do today. . . . They'd go into a bar in White Bear and buy everyone a round—which was great, even if the money was stolen from some banker!"[40]

With the gang at Idlewild was a Japanese cook, Henry Kazo Maihori, who had worked for the Nankin Cafe in Minneapolis. A friend of Hollyhocks chef Sam Tanaka, Maihori loved to fish off the nearby dock. He planted radishes and lettuce in a garden outside Idlewild and prepared the vegetables and fruit—sweet corn, potatoes, and strawberries—that children delivered to the gang's back porch. Maihori was paid about fifteen dollars a week for his services, which included fixing breakfast for the gang.[41]

Neighbors interviewed later by FBI agents said that most of the gangsters relaxed in bathrobes and bathing suits, but one plump man sunbathed nude, hoping to heal a rash on his stomach. He was Fred "Shotgun George Ziegler" Goetz, an enforcer for Al Capone's Chicago mob.[42]

White Bear area residents told of hearing loud parties and occasional fights, often fueled by liquor, at Idlewild. Iceman Otto Krause said the Idlewild occupants were "very good beer customers": he "sold them five or six cases of beer at a time and also considerable ginger ale," the FBI reported.[43]

Gradually the gangsters began to attract notice. An FBI report noted that a neighbor said they were "mysterious, as they stayed indoors practically all of the time with the shades of the cottage drawn and did not go swimming as is the custom of the average lake resident." The night William Hamm was released, Idlewild neighbors saw a car light flashing across the lake, as if they were signaling. Three weeks after moving into Idlewild, the gang vanished, leaving Maihori to clean up the emptied cottage.[44]

Steve Tuttle's grandmother Virginia Tuttle had given Ma Barker twenty-five cents to pay the iceman on behalf of the Tuttle family. Suddenly the Barker family fled, FBI agents at their heels. Virginia "lamented how she had given this infamous gangster her quarter to pay the iceman. My gosh, now it won't get paid," Steve Tuttle recalled. She telephoned the iceman to explain her predicament and learned that Ma Barker had stopped on her way out of town to pay the Tuttles' bill. "That was a great relief on my grandmother's part, [because] during the Depression every penny was precious," said Tuttle. "Grandma laughed about Ma Barker, this terrible villain, stopping during her escape from White Bear Lake to pay off the ice bill!"[45]

35   'Like Getting Money from Home'

The Hamm Brewing Company
681 East Minnehaha Avenue, St. Paul

When Fred Barker proposed kidnapping Hamm Brewing Company president William Hamm Jr., Alvin Karpis agreed to participate, on one condition: "I told him as long as it wasn't a woman or child it sounded rather attractive," said Karpis later. To identify their quarry, Barker had Karpis drive by the brewery on Minnehaha Avenue. "Do you think a man that owned a place of that sort," asked Barker, "would be able to pay $100,000 ransom?"[46]

Indeed, the Hamm Brewing Company (today the Stroh Brewery, near Minnehaha and Payne Avenues) was one of the most profitable breweries in the United States. It was founded by Theodore Hamm of Herbolzheim, Germany, who came to St. Paul from Chicago in the 1840s and expanded the brewery dramatically in 1894. The founder's grandson was to be the gangsters' victim.[47]

For this complex kidnapping, Karpis and Barker agreed to call in an experienced strategist from Chicago. Fred Goetz, known to Al Capone's syndicate as "Shotgun George Ziegler," had participated in the 1929 St. Valentine's Day Massacre, which left seven men dead in a garage run by the Bugs Moran gang. ("The object of this wholesale killing was to eradicate 'Bugs' Moran and his mob, who at that time were threatening the dominance of the Capone criminal organization," the FBI learned from the widow of gangster Gus Winkler.) Alvin Karpis claimed that the florid-faced Goetz planned the massacre. Goetz already knew key members of the St. Paul underworld, in particular Harry Sawyer. After meeting Goetz at the Hollyhocks club, Harry and Gladys Sawyer had spent Thanksgiving 1932 with Fred and Irene Goetz at their lodge on Cranberry Lake near Hayward, Wisconsin.[48]

The Hamm Brewery, near which William Hamm Jr. was abducted, and family mansion (far right)

Unique among Capone's enforcers, Goetz freelanced for both the Barker-Karpis and Jimmy Keating–Tommy Holden bank robbery gangs. Other Capone syndicate killers began their careers as petty thugs or bootleggers, but Goetz was once an engineering student and a University of Illinois football player. He even undertook a correspondence course in landscape gardening in 1928. His legitimate career had evaporated in 1925 when, as a lifeguard at a Chicago beach, Goetz was arrested for attempting to rape a seven-year-old girl. He forfeited his $5,000 bond and never stood trial. By October he had resurfaced as a suspect in the killing of a chauffeur during the robbery of a Chicago physician, and then as a hit man of great ingenuity: he invented a time bomb with leather straps that could be bound to a victim, forcing him to give in to demands for money. An FBI agent found that Goetz also invented for himself a belt that contained six steel saws concealed within the leather.[49]

"His character was one of infinite contradictions," wrote FBI agent Melvin Purvis of Goetz. "Well mannered, always polite, he was capable of generous kindness and conscienceless cruelty."[50]

Fred Goetz as a Chicago lifeguard

Irene Dorsey met Fred Goetz, then posing as salesman George Siebert, in an Illinois restaurant in 1924 and married him two years later in Alexandria, Minnesota. "He was changing names constantly," FBI agents learned from Irene Goetz. "He used the moniker Von Ash, because Goetz got a big kick out of using such a high sounding name." To ensure that she did not inadvertently call him by the wrong alias, Goetz trained his wife to refer to him only as her husband. Irene guessed that while her husband was hiding his criminal activities from the FBI, he was also hiding an extramarital affair from her. They vacationed together at the Greenwood Lodge in northern Minnesota to try "to regain their old selves," an FBI report noted.[51]

Summoned by a telephone call from Jack Peifer, Goetz drove to St. Paul in May 1933 to help plan the Hamm kidnapping. He brought along his bodyguard, William Byron Bolton, a tubercular forty-year-old alumnus of Al Capone's syndicate. The nephew of an Illinois police chief and the father of two, Bolton had been a carpenter, auto salesman, and golf teacher; he was honorably discharged from the U.S. Navy in 1919.[52]

Under the alias Monty Carter, Bolton operated on the fringes of Capone's syndicate as a driver for hit man Fred Burke. Bank robber Charlie Fitzgerald told the FBI that Bolton had "messed up" as the lookout during the St. Valentine's Day Massacre by giving an early go-ahead to kill the gangsters, moments before the intended target, Bugs Moran, arrived at the garage. Because his bungling had enabled Moran to escape, Capone demanded that Bolton be killed, according to two FBI sources. Only Goetz's protection kept him alive. The FBI learned from Fitzgerald "that Fred Goetz had implicit faith in [Bolton] but that numerous persons associated with both Goetz and Bolton did not trust Bolton and often tried to persuade Goetz that he should get rid of him."[53]

Alvin Karpis was one of those who distrusted Bolton. Karpis had urged Goetz to abandon him, but Goetz was determined to stick by his ailing partner. (Bolton got tuberculosis during his stint with the navy, and then suffered double pneumonia in 1930.) Karpis's suspicions were confirmed in 1936, when Bolton turned government witness and testified against the Barker-Karpis gang.[54]

Goetz and Bolton visited the Hollyhocks on June 10, 1933, while Peifer was still asleep, so they sat down to breakfast in the dining room. Half an hour later, Peifer joined them, saying that "the rest of the fellows were already in town," recalled Bolton, and "as soon as he got dressed he would take us out to meet them." When they finished breakfast, Peifer, Goetz, and Bolton drove out to a cottage on Bald Eagle Lake. "At the cottage were Alvin Karpis and Fred and Doc Barker."[55]

The gang discussed when and where to snatch their victim, and they decided that Karpis would drive the kidnap car, wearing a chauffeur's cap so as not to alarm Hamm. They planned every detail, from a switch of license plates when they got to Illinois to the three five-gallon cans of gasoline they would carry so they could avoid stopping at a gas station. They determined that Hamm would be held far from St. Paul in Bensonville, Illinois. They would demand a $100,000 ransom payment, with $40,000 earmarked for Jack Peifer to distribute as payoff money in St. Paul. (Karpis had suggested a $250,000 ransom, and Fred Barker argued for at least $200,000, but Goetz overruled the higher figures.)[56]

In this conversation, Bolton learned an astonishing fact that reflected three decades of police corruption: "Peifer had introduced [Goetz] to a police officer of the St. Paul Police Department, who was on the Kidnap Detail . . . and it was the plan to pay him $25,000 of the ransom money; that in return . . . this officer was to keep us advised of the developments at the Police Department" while the victim was being held. Having a high-ranking police officer on the payroll was the fulcrum of the kidnapping plan; the gang would be warned of any mistakes that might lead to capture. "Goetz said that this officer had told him and [Peifer] that we should be careful in telephoning," recalled Bolton. "It took about two minutes to trace a telephone call. . . . Goetz was greatly pleased with this arrangement . . . [since] there was very little chance of a slip-up. . . . It was like getting money from home."

The role of "greeter"—someone who could stop Hamm on the street without alarming him—fell to bank robber Charles "Old Charlie" Fitzgerald, a fifty-seven-year-old native of Missouri. Fitzgerald was gray haired, bull necked, and an imposing six feet tall. "He is an old time criminal, having been first convicted in 1898" for burglarizing a Kansas store, said an FBI

file. "He is one of the shrewdest bank burglars and robbers in the country." By the time he joined the Barker-Karpis gang, Fitzgerald had been imprisoned in Anamosa, Iowa; Hutchinson and Lansing, Kansas; and Atlanta.[57]

Fitzgerald's distinguished appearance in a banker's jacket and tie belied his thirty-five years of blowing bank safes with nitroglycerine. Gang member Jess Doyle told the FBI that Fitzgerald was "an outstanding bank stick-up man, especially good in 'casing' banks." After Fitzgerald agreed to Fred Barker's invitation to join the kidnapping for a cut of up to $8,000, he went to the Bald Eagle Lake cabin for the necessary rehearsals.[58]

At 12:45 P.M., on June 15, 1933, Hamm left his brewing company office to have lunch and crossed the street at the

Charlie Fitzgerald, the Hamm kidnapping "greeter"

corner of Minnehaha and Greenbrier, walking toward his home at 671 Cable. Doc Barker raised his arm to signal that their victim was in view. Karpis was ready, having parked his black Hudson sedan half a block from the brewery. Charlie Fitzgerald stepped up to Hamm, reached out to shake his hand, and gripped Hamm's right elbow. "You are Mr. Hamm, are you not?" asked Fitzgerald. An FBI report documented Hamm's description of what happened next: "I said, 'Yes,' and took hold of [his hand] and he then took my right elbow with his left hand and tightened the grip on my right hand. I looked at him rather astonished and said, 'What is it you want?' The man on his right was then on my left taking hold of my left hand and arm and started pushing me to the curb. Just as we reached the curb, this car drew up right next to us. . . . The door was opened . . . [and] I was pushed into the car."[59]

Doc Barker forced Hamm into the rear seat, where he was sandwiched between Barker and Bolton. A white pillow case was dropped over his head and shoulders. Suddenly, Karpis worried that they had kidnapped the wrong man. With typical Minnesota good spirits, Hamm assured the gangsters that he was indeed William Hamm Jr.—which made Karpis even more suspicious. Fortunately for the gang, Hamm's name was found on the tailor's labels in his coat.[60]

During the drive, the gangsters talked about muskellunge fishing and shared drinks of ice water from a thermos. They told Hamm to be perfectly

Reporters and onlookers at the Hamm residence following the kidnapping

quiet and everything would be all right. "There wasn't much conversation on that trip; we didn't know each other well enough yet," Hamm later recalled. At one point, the hood was removed, and a gangster said, "You are awfully warm down there, aren't you?"[61]

The group traveled on gravel roads until, thirty miles outside St. Paul, they intercepted Fred Goetz and Fred Barker in a Chevrolet sedan. Hamm was given a handful of typewritten ransom notes to sign; one of the gangsters said, "I guess you know what this is all about." They reached the Bensonville, Illinois, hideout that evening. Hamm's blindfold was removed, and he was given a glass of milk and a pork sandwich before being locked in a second-floor bedroom. Fitzgerald, Goetz, and Fred Barker returned to St. Paul that night to begin negotiating the ransom.[62]

36 The Lovable Rogue

Home of Go-Between William W. Dunn
1916 Summit Avenue, St. Paul

With Hamm safely hidden away in Illinois, it was time for the Barker-Karpis gang to concentrate on securing the $100,000 ransom. Hamm was asked for the name of a contact with ties to his brewery, a man he trusted with his life, to serve as the intermediary between the kidnappers and the Hamm family. Hamm suggested William W. Dunn, the brewery's current sales manager.[63]

The gang was overjoyed that Hamm had chosen Dunn, who lived in a two-story white stucco home near the intersection of Prior and Summit Avenues. The FBI later learned from Alvin Karpis that Dunn was the man agreed upon by the gang prior to the kidnapping "because they knew he had contacts and had been the collector for the Police Department at St. Paul, so [he] would be forced to keep his mouth shut."[64]

Most previous accounts of the Hamm kidnapping accept the popular theory that the 1933 abduction was shocking because, for the first time, the "underworld" had dared to intrude upon the "overworld." Yet the FBI files detailing Dunn's career—which straddled the worlds of businessmen like William Hamm and underworld fixers like Harry Sawyer—reveal how permeable the walls were in St. Paul between "civilized" society and the gangsters. Far from holding gangland at arm's length, FBI records suggest, some St. Paul businessmen had profited from associations with underworld figures for decades. Dunn told FBI agents that in about 1920 William Hamm Sr. proposed that Dunn, who had sold billiard and bowling alley equipment for the Brunswick Company, operate the recreation end of his Hamm Building on St. Peter Street in downtown St. Paul. Dunn leased the basement for use as a billiard and pool room and bowling alley and ran the hall until 1929, when he joined Hamm Brewing Company.[65]

During the Hamm investigation, the FBI would learn that Hollyhocks Club manager Walt McKenna had used Dunn to deliver "'pay-off' money which ultimately went to the St. Paul Police Department. . . . Dunn was the contact man between the underworld and the St. Paul Police Department." Businessman Herb Benz, William Hamm's cousin, whose investment company held the mortgage for the Hollyhocks, told the FBI that Dunn was "the payoff between the underworld and the police department during the regime of Tom Brown as chief." (Under oath at Jack Peifer's trial for the Hamm kidnapping, Dunn would say only that he had been "a friend" of Peifer for fifteen years.)[66]

Police officials Charles Tierney and Thomas Dahill told the FBI that

The released William Hamm Jr. (at right) shaking hands with kidnap go-between William Dunn, his brewery sales manager. Hamm did not know that Dunn was also an intermediary between gangsters and corrupt police officers.

Dunn collected for Leon Gleckman, who controlled gambling in St. Paul, in exchange for a share of the proceeds. Gleckman himself was candid about Dunn's role in distributing underworld bribes. "Billy Dunn was very close to him, the reason being that Dunn had only recently entered the employ of the Hamm Brewing Company," the FBI reported after agents interviewed Gleckman in prison, "and was anxious to secure favorable license grants for customers of the company, and was active in having the police lay off of customers who operated their saloons after legal closing hours."[67]

William Figge, former president of the brewing company, remembered Dunn as a lovable rogue. "William Dunn was a refreshing personality," with "a million friends and no enemies," said Figge. "He knew *all* the underworld characters—many of them came to Dunn's pool hall. . . . When bootleggers and thugs came to town with a lot of money, Bill Dunn would put the cash in his safe for them over the weekend!"[68]

Interviewed by the FBI, Dunn denied that he was a payoff man, although "he admitted that he was acquainted with practically every underworld character in the Twin Cities, but claimed that he had met these people through his operation of the St. Paul Recreation Parlor." Dunn said that he had often visited Gleckman at the Hotel St. Paul and the Boulevards of Paris nightclub.[69]

This was the man who received the gang's ransom call at the Hamm brewery.[70]

"Is this W. W. Dunn?" asked the caller.

Dunn replied, "Yes, sir."

"I want to talk to you and I don't want you to say anything until I get all through. We have Mr. Hamm. We want you to get $100,000 in twent[ies], tens and fives."

"Hey, hey, what the hell is going on here?" Dunn blurted out.

"Now shut up and listen to what I have to say." After providing preliminary instructions on the delivery of the ransom, the caller continued, "If you tell a soul about this it will be just too bad for Hamm and you."[71]

Dunn called the St. Paul police; the FBI immediately installed wiretaps on Dunn's home telephone and on the phones at the brewery. Policemen Tom Brown and Charles Tierney of the kidnap squad were assigned to the Hamm case, meeting with Dunn at his Summit Avenue home.[72]

As if the kidnappers were following Dunn's every move—but were not upset by the presence of the police—they called again: "Well, Dunn, you're following instructions very well so far. Now, I have given you time to recover from the shock of the telephone call this afternoon and you must realize that the call was not a joke as you thought. All you've got to do is follow instructions."[73]

The instructions were handed to a Yellow Cab driver by Fred Goetz at the Lowry Ramp Garage in downtown St. Paul. Police detective Tom Brown accepted the note at Dunn's house. "You know your boy friend is out of circulation," it said. "You are to pay off $100,000.00 in the manner explained to you this afternoon. . . . If you fail to comply with our demands, you will never see Hamm, Jr. again."[74]

In Bensonville, the gang promised Hamm that no harm would come to him. They told him to face the wall when they brought him food so that he would not recognize any of them. Hamm admitted later that he peeked at the gang's faces out of the corner of his eye. He also noticed the motto "Mother" on the top of the bed, a crayon sketch of flamingos on the wall, a broken faucet, the volume of traffic on nearby roads, the sounds of children playing, church bells, and the whistles of a nearby freight train. If he survived, William Hamm intended to bring his kidnappers to justice.[75]

37 'Get Away from the Coppers'

The Rosedale Pharmacy
1941 Grand Avenue, St. Paul

Late in the evening of June 16, another ransom demand was delivered, this time to a soda booth at Clarence J. Thomas's Rosedale Pharmacy at the corner of Prior and Grand Avenues. A potbellied, curly-haired blond man sauntered into the pharmacy to buy cigarettes and sulfur ointment, Thomas told the FBI. Based on interviews with kidnappers Charlie Fitzgerald and Byron Bolton, FBI agents were later able to identify the man as Fred Goetz. A few minutes after the shopper left, an unidentified telephone caller directed the Rosedale Pharmacy clerk to the ransom letter, which was delivered to Dunn's home around the corner.[76]

"You're so god dam[n]ed smart that you'll wind up getting both of you guys killed," the note read. "Furthermore we demand that *you* personally deliver the money so that if there is any doble crossing we will have the pleasure of hitting you in the head."[77]

The next day, yet another note was left on the back seat of a car owned by a Hamm Brewing employee. The gang offered precise instructions on how Dunn should deliver the ransom money and demonstrated an intimate knowledge of the Hamm family's contacts with St. Paul police. Dunn was told to drive to Highway 61 and look for five flashes of a headlight, the signal to drop the ransom at the side of the road. "If the coppers succeed in following you it might prove fatal. You brought the coppers in to this now you get rid of the assholes," read the first note. "Hamm is uncomfortable and diss-appointed in the way you bungled this so far."[78]

The FBI and the police considered setting a trap for the kidnappers: an armed policeman could be hidden inside a Hamm brewery truck, ready to ambush the kidnappers when they appeared to collect the ransom. Warned by the police officer of the proposed trap, the gang responded June 17 with a furious note: "If you are through with the bullshit and balyhoo, we'll give you your chance. . . . First of all, *get away from the coppers.* . . . If you try to out *s[m]art* us you only prolong the agony." The note demanded that Dunn remove the doors of his vehicle and hang a red lantern inside "so no one can be concealed."[79]

Clarence Thomas's pharmacy (now Thomas Liquors), where Fred Goetz (inset) dropped off a ransom note

Fred Goetz crowed to the gang that this warning alone made it worth paying the corrupt policeman $25,000, but the investment was about to pay additional dividends, once again saving the gang from virtually certain discovery.[80]

38 'There Goes the Ransom Money'

Hideout of the "Vernon Street Gang"
204 Vernon Street, St. Paul

The thumbprint was barely ½-by-2½-inches in size. Still, FBI headquarters in Washington, D.C., identified the smudge clinging to a beer bottle found at 204 Vernon Street as the print of Frank "Jelly" Nash, the ill-fated bank robber who died in a botched escape attempt that also left an FBI agent and three policemen dead in Kansas City. What had Nash been doing in St. Paul, days before the Kansas City Massacre?[81]

The two-story residence at 204 Vernon Street harbored a convention of public enemies from May 28 to June 19, 1933. Residents included Doc Barker, Fred Barker and his girlfriend Paula Harmon, and Alvin Karpis. Bank robbers Volney Davis, Charlie Fitzgerald, William Weaver, and Fred Goetz also came to do business.

Salesman James MacLaren and his wife, Gertrude, owned the home. They rented it out while summering with their children, Jack and Frances, at a vacation home on Bald Eagle Lake. Fred Barker and Paula Harmon, masquerading as Mr. and Mrs. Stanley Smith, responded to the MacLarens's newspaper ad. "Mrs. Smith . . . was very coy," recalled Frances MacLaren Paul. "'Oh, Mrs. MacLaren,' she told mother, 'I love to cook. Be sure to leave all these pans.' She was putting on an act!"[82]

The "Smiths" inspected the home and offered to rent it through August for forty-five dollars a month. Fred Barker pretended to be a salesman for Federated Metal Company of St. Louis. His "wife," Paula Harmon, was described by the MacLarens as a reddish-blonde with a Southern accent, a ring studded with eight diamonds, and a scarred nose that, in FBI parlance, gave "the appearance of once having been struck by a heavy instrument."[83]

As references, the Smiths offered the names of city health officer Dr. Nels Mortensen and attorney Tom Newman. Only later did the MacLarens learn that Mortensen was to be investigated for tending the bullet wounds of John Dillinger and that Newman was a criminal defense attorney who had represented a variety of underworld characters. The lawyer assured the MacLarens that J. Stanley Smith was "all right as far as [he] knew," the FBI reported. Satisfied with the character of their new tenants, the Mac-

Larens set off for Bald Eagle Lake while the Smiths drove up to 204 Vernon in their new Chevrolet sedan. The Barker-Karpis gang had a nearby drugstore deliver beer and ginger ale, over which they plotted the Hamm kidnapping. On June 15, the day that William Hamm was kidnapped, the Smiths of 204 Vernon ordered a case of Blatz beer to celebrate.[84]

Right away, neighbors noticed that the Smiths were different from most folks on Vernon. When a repairman arrived to fix the MacLarens's gas stove, Harmon refused to let him in until a neighbor intervened. And when a local teenager, John Miller of 211 Vernon, mowed the gang's lawn and trimmed the hedges, they paid him a very conspicuous three dollars—six times the going rate of fifty cents. Iceman Frank Lachowitzer complained that the drawn blinds made it too dark to find the ice box. One of the Smiths grudgingly raised the shade a little but put it down again right away, Lachowitzer recalled.[85]

On June 9 bank robber Frank Nash, accompanied by his wife, Frances, and her young daughter, Danella, drove to St. Paul and stayed overnight at 204 Vernon. During this last week of his life, Nash had dinner at the Hollyhocks Club and enjoyed a final meeting with Alvin Karpis and the Barker boys at the Green Lantern. Nash had intended to spend the night at Harry Sawyer's home, but when Barker and Harmon invited him to spend the night and drink some beer at 204 Vernon, Nash altered his plans.[86]

The girlfriends of the Barker-Karpis gang tried to maintain a semblance of normal family life, but they were always poised on the edge of exposure. Neighbor Helen Fullerton told the FBI that every time a car stopped or a door slammed, the woman at 204 Vernon Street looked out.[87]

Landlady Gertrude MacLaren returned one day for a surprise visit. "My mother was the bane of the existence of those gun molls," said her daughter, Frances MacLaren Paul. "She'd have Dad drive her to the 204 Vernon house, and knock on the door, saying she'd forgotten some bric-a-brac. She had no idea she was walking into a bee's nest." Paula Harmon remembered the shock of having Mrs. MacLaren walk in while Karpis had his gun lying on a chair; he quickly dropped a newspaper over it.[88]

But the gang's stay on Vernon Street was soon to end. Herbert Charles, head of the Hamm brewery's legal department, had brought the $100,000 ransom to the brewery's vaults. On June 17, Dunn drove along Highway 61, saw a car signal him with five flashes of its headlights near Pine City, and dropped the briefcase. In the car to pick up the money were Fred Barker, Fred Goetz, and Charlie Fitzgerald.[89]

In his memoirs, Karpis recalled the day that they returned to the Bensonville hideout with the $100,000 ransom. "You better round up some

Hamm's beer," Goetz told Karpis. "I got a feeling that it'll be my favorite brand for a long time to come."[90]

Hamm was outfitted in new clothes, fed a final ham sandwich, and released at daybreak on June 19 near Wyoming, Minnesota, about fifty miles north of St. Paul, in a vain attempt to convince officials that Hamm had never been taken out of Minnesota.[91]

After Hamm was freed, Fitzgerald and Fred Barker brought the ransom money to 204 Vernon and prepared to drive to Chicago to launder it. Onlookers watched as a Buick drove up to 204 Vernon and five men rushed into the house, one of them carrying a suitcase. Quipped one neighbor: "There goes the ransom money."[92]

The gang's timing was prudent, for a *St. Paul Dispatch–Pioneer Press* editor had informed police chief Tom Dahill and the FBI that a source was reporting strange activity at 204 Vernon. The tipster, according to FBI records, was Charles Bradley, a young man who was keeping company that summer with the niece of the Lester Quick family, then living at 210 Vernon. Intrigued by his girlfriend's stories about suspicious neighbors, Charles spoke to her aunt. Three men and a woman at 204 Vernon were "coming and going at all hours of the night," said the aunt, and she suspected that the small bags they carried with them contained guns. When a roadster drove up to 204 Vernon and a six-foot-tall man rushed out carrying suitcases, "it did enter her mind," the FBI noted, "that these grips might have contained the ransom money."[93]

Alerted to the commotion at 204 Vernon, Chief Dahill drove to police headquarters and asked the head of his kidnap squad, Tom Brown, to investigate the rumors about the occupants. Promising Dahill that he would take care of the situation, Brown left, returning half an hour later. Detective Brown assured Chief Dahill, straight-faced, that "the bunch at 204 Vernon Avenue have nothing to do with the Hamm case." Meanwhile, with all the lights blazing in the house, the Smith family ran upstairs and downstairs, frantically carrying suitcases out to two automobiles. By 2:00 A.M. on June 20, most traces of the gang had vanished.[94]

The FBI learned two weeks afterward "that Tom Brown, member of the St. Paul Police Department, Kidnap Squad, had tipped off the occupants at 204 Vernon Avenue to leave."[95]

Years later, the FBI found out what had really happened. According to Byron Bolton's confession, Tom Brown had called Jack Peifer and told him that the police were suspicious about the house. Peifer sped to 204 Vernon and took Barker and Fitzgerald to the Bald Eagle Lake cottage, then returned to the Vernon Street hideout to strip it of incriminating evidence.[96]

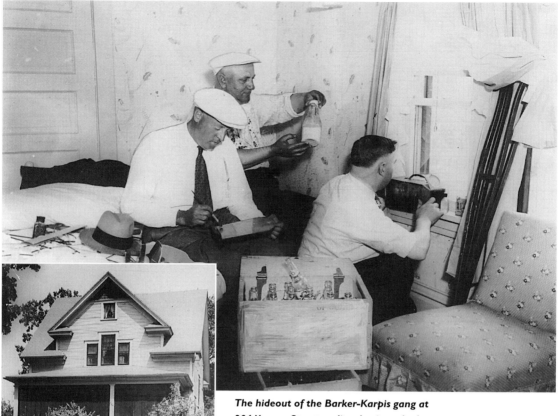

The hideout of the Barker-Karpis gang at 204 Vernon Street; police dusting a bedroom found the right thumbprint of bank robber Frank Nash.

Goaded by the *Pioneer Press* and the *Dispatch*, the police finally descended on the now-empty house, dusting it for fingerprints. True to the protocols of the O'Connor system, though, they did not manage to send the prints to FBI laboratories until eight months had passed.[97]

When the FBI finally searched the house on June 24, all they found was a slip of paper with a grocery list and Peifer's telephone number at the Hollyhocks Club.[98]

The debacle at 204 Vernon convinced the FBI special agent in charge, Werner Hanni, that efforts to apprehend the kidnappers had been thwarted by an inside source. He concluded that he was being betrayed by a police official who was "a close friend and associate of Leon Gleckman, alleged king of the underworld," and who had been tipping off gangsters for years."[99] As the FBI began to track down and arrest the Barker-Karpis gang's girlfriends and accomplices, a growing body of evidence supported Hanni's suspicions that a policeman at the highest level of command had been leaking law enforcement information to the underworld. The disloyal officer was the head of the St. Paul Police kidnap squad, detective Thomas Archibald Brown, the very man entrusted with protecting citizens from kidnappers.

39 'Big Tom' Brown's Kidnap Squad

Police Officer Tom Brown's Home
759 East Maryland Avenue, St. Paul

While he was waiting to divide the Hamm ransom, racketeer Jack Peifer invited the wife of mobster Gus Winkler to visit his casino. When Winkler's wife, Georgette, expressed concern over security, Peifer promised her: "You don't have to be afraid of that. *We've got police protection in St. Paul.*"[100]

That protection was personified by Thomas "Big Tom" Brown, a hulking 280-pound, 6-foot, 3-inch detective, who was forty-four when William Hamm was kidnapped in 1933. Brown lived with his wife, Mary, and five children in a two-story white-stucco home at 759 Maryland Avenue. A former Great Northern Railroad conductor, the West Virginia–born Brown had moved to St. Paul in 1910, joined the police as a traffic patrolman in 1914, rose to detective in 1919, and then served as chief of police from June 1930 to June 1932.[101]

"I'll never forget when my father was nominated to be police chief," said Brown's daughter Vera Peters. "He came home to tell my mother that he was going to get three hundred dollars a month—which was a big sum in those days. . . . My father was the first police chief in the new police station, [so] he took us to the station to have our photos taken like they did with criminals."[102]

Publicly, Chief Brown portrayed himself as a fearless gangbuster. In the summer of 1930, for instance, Brown declared war on Chicago gangsters who were exploring Minnesota's liquor and slot machine rackets: "St. Paul will not tolerate any gangsters. . . . This is an open statement. There is nothing concealed. To all gangsters who may be in St. Paul, get out and stay out."[103]

But Brown's ascent to the chief's office concealed a great deal. An informant, saloon keeper Frank Reilly, told the FBI about "a number of people who had contributed large sums to Brown's campaign," including, Reilly believed, a Dillinger machine gunner, Homer Van Meter, who donated $1,000. "It was understood that after he was appointed Chief of Police they were to be allotted certain rackets in St. Paul," the FBI reported. "During Brown's term it was impossible to run anything without paying off, and according to Reilly, it got to such a point where the various candy companies complained that they were not allowed even to install their merchandise boards in various stores without paying protection."[104]

At home, Brown was a fastidious man. A Baptist whose children were brought up Catholic by his wife, he was a strict disciplinarian. "We knew what was right and wrong in my family," said Peters. "When my brother Jim was engaged to be married, he still had to be home by eleven!" When Brown's daughters visited the state fair, using their father's complimentary tickets, they were free to roam the fairgrounds but forbidden to go to the midway, which was considered sleazy. "So we went to the midway to see the Fat Lady," Peters said. "When we came out of the Fat Lady's booth, there

he was—my father, with police officer [Frank] Cullen. I never had such a ride home. Oh, he put us in his squad car. Oh, was he angry!"

The family heard stories of Tom Brown's generosity to down-on-their-luck criminals. One holiday—"it was either Thanksgiving or Christmas," Peters said—Brown came home late and told his family that he had let all the prisoners go free so they could be with their families for the night. Apart from tales like this, Brown was close-lipped about his police work. "Everything was kept from us kids," Peters said. "Dad was a private person . . . of the old German feeling that kids should be seen and not heard."[105]

Hints of Brown's intimacy with the St. Paul underworld surfaced early. In 1923, St. Paul police chief Frank Sommers was forced to resign in a vice scandal. The furor was sparked when then-detective Tom Brown, head of the "purity squad," raided a series of gambling spots and found no evidence of

Thomas Brown, chief of the St. Paul police, who fed police secrets to gangsters

gambling. "Brown," snarled Mayor Arthur E. Nelson, "it's a remarkable thing that the only ones who look for gambling joints, moonshine parlors and disorderly houses and can't find them are certain St. Paul detectives."[106]

Three years later Brown was suspended for 30 days when a federal judge ordered that he be removed to Ohio to face federal charges that he had participated in the massive Cleveland liquor syndicate conspiracy involving bootlegger Leon Gleckman and the Gleeman brothers. The FBI concluded in 1932 that Brown was "known to be intimately associated with Leon Gleckman and to have been controlled by Leon Gleckman while in the St. Paul Police Department."[107]

When Brown's attorneys protested, District Court Judge John Sanborn noted that in his testimony, Brown (who had headed the purity squad from June 1922 to December 1923) swore that he had no idea what business Leon Gleckman was engaged in. The judge said he did not believe the vice chief's naiveté about the city's leading bootlegger and refused to intercede for Brown. Ultimately, the indictments against Brown were dismissed.[108]

In November 1930, Chief Brown—whose vice squad had seized more than 100 slot machines in five months—was called before a Ramsey County grand jury for questioning about his knowledge of a police protection racket involving illegal slot machines. Harold Heller, a slot machine hijacker, admitted that he had been told to steal some slot machines and "lay off" those with police protection. The Ramsey County attorney expressed concern that "profits from racketeering in St. Paul amount to about $1,000 a day and . . . the temptation for officials is considerable." Once again, no charges were filed against Brown.[109]

Previous police chiefs, notably John J. O'Connor and Frank Sommers, had looked the other way when criminals sought haven in St. Paul. According to testimony gathered by the FBI, Brown took the O'Connor system to new lows, actively supporting the criminal activities of gangsters Leon Gleckman, Harry Sawyer, and Jack Peifer.

Policeman Fred Raasch told the FBI that Brown asked him to commit perjury during the Gleeman brothers' trial for the murder of liquor hijacker Burt Stevens. "Brown asked me to testify that at the time that Stevens was shot, I was talking with the two Gleemans on the West Side at Tubby's place. I told him I would not do it, that I was home in bed at the time and that several witnesses had testified to seeing the Gleemans on St. Peter Street at the time of the murder, and I asked him why he didn't do it himself." Brown was angry at Raasch's refusal and threatened, "I'll get even with you." Raasch believed that when Brown became chief in 1930, he had Raasch demoted to squad car duty in retribution.[110]

Chief Brown himself was demoted to detective in the wake of the Barker-Karpis gang's 1932 escape from West St. Paul. Then, as head of the kidnap squad, Tom Brown led a heavily armed unit to Lake Minnetonka, Minnesota, in mid-June 1933 on a diversionary hunt for the Hamm kidnappers. At the time he knew the actual culprits were living in St. Paul and near White Bear.[111]

Several clues led the FBI to question Brown's integrity as they probed the Barker-Karpis gang. Chief Tom Dahill testified that when he was investigating the Hamm kidnapping, Brown had objected to giving the FBI any information on the grounds that "the government only wanted information and did not give anything in return, and that when the case did break the Federal Agents would get all the glory." During the Bremer kidnapping case in 1934, police officers were asked to supply their fingerprints so that the FBI could eliminate their prints from the ransom notes and identify the prints of the kidnappers. Curiously, Brown was the only one who refused.[112]

Even more revealing was the fact that throughout the Hamm and Bremer kidnappings the Barker-Karpis gang appeared to anticipate every move made by the police. At times, the kidnappers seemed to be playing bizarre games with the FBI, taunting them with information to which only a top police official like Brown had access. Dahill revealed to Brown his secret plan to hide a shotgun-wielding policeman in the truck that would deliver the Hamm ransom. A note from the gang the next day changed the ransom delivery instructions to prevent the involvement of a hidden policeman. When FBI agents displayed four Browning rifles to Dahill and Brown, Chief Dahill caressed the guns, murmuring of the Hamm kidnappers (as an agent later recorded it), "I would like to see one of those _____ now." The next Hamm ransom note teased Dahill: if he was so anxious to meet them, it said, he should come out with the "dough."[113]

During the Hamm kidnapping, "I had a constant feeling of uncertainty and fear of double crossing," FBI special agent in charge Werner Hanni told J. Edgar Hoover, mentioning what appeared to be shadowy friendships between certain police officers and underworld leaders. During the Bremer kidnapping, FBI assistant director Harold Nathan expressed his astonishment at the profusion of police leaks in St. Paul. Nathan noted that in January 1934 four of the Bremer ransom letters were turned over to the chief of police and the FBI and sent by airplane to Washington for laboratory analysis of fingerprints. Dahill told only two people, chief of detectives Charles Tierney and kidnap squad head Tom Brown, about the unusual manner in which the ransom communications had been delivered. Half an hour later, an extra edition of the *St. Paul Daily News* reported that a bottle thrown through the glass door of the vestibule of the house of Dr. R. T. Nippert a few days before contained two of the ransom notes. How could such a breach of secrecy have occurred, asked Nathan? Dahill replied that "there is only one man responsible and he knew it; that it was Tom Brown."[114]

When the Barker-Karpis gang met at Fred Barker's cottage in Illinois to split up the Hamm ransom, one of them asked outright about Tom Brown's share. "Who is Brown?" asked Byron Bolton, who later told the story to the FBI. Brown was the police officer who had given Jack Peifer information for the kidnappers, said one of the gang. Bolton gave a rough accounting for the division of the Hamm ransom money, including $25,000 to Tom Brown; $10,000 to Jack Peifer; $7,800 each to Fred Goetz, Alvin Karpis, Fred Barker, Doc Barker, Byron Bolton, and Charlie Fitzgerald; $2,500 to either Robert "Frisco Dutch" Steinhart or Tommy Banks; and $2,500 to bank robber Jack Davenport. Approximately $1,500 was earmarked for expenses (from gasoline to food), and $7,500 was spent to launder the ransom money in Reno.[115]

Gradually, a parade of FBI informants attested to Tom Brown's involvement in the Hamm kidnapping. Gladys Sawyer reported to the FBI that she overheard a conversation between her husband, Harry, and Jack Peifer, in

```
To the best of my recollection the division of the
ransom money collected in this kidnaping was made in the
following manner:

            TOM BROWN                $25,000.00
            JACK PFEIFFER             10,000.00
            JACK DAVENPORT             8,500.00
            TOM BANKS or "FRISCO       2,500.00
                     DUTCH"
            FRED GOETZ                 7,800.00
            ALVIN KARPIS               7,800.00
            FRED BARKER                7,800.00
            DOC BARKER                 7,800.00
            CHARLES FITZGERALD         7,800.00
            BRYAN BOLTON               7,800.00
            BARTHOLOMEW                  650.00
            VOLNEY DAVIS                 700.00
            HERBERT FARMER             2,500.00
            EXPENSES                   1,500.00
            Cost of exchanging money
            in Reno, Nevada -          7,500.00
```

Kidnap conspirator Byron Bolton provided the FBI with this accounting of the
split of the Hamm ransom between gang members and policeman Tom Brown.

which Peifer said that he and Brown split $36,000 in the Hamm case. She
named Brown, James Crumley, and William McMullen as the sources of police information telephoned to Harry Sawyer and Jack Peifer who delivered
it to "interested parties," and said that the tip-off at the Vernon Street
house traveled this route.[116]

In 1935 the FBI learned from Barker-Karpis gang girlfriend Edna Murray, imprisoned in Missouri State Penitentiary, that while Bremer was
being held by the gang, "Tom Brown was keeping the gang informed of the
activities of the Bureau." In fact, the FBI discovered Brown brought to
Harry Sawyer police pictures of Doc Barker and several other members of
the gang suspected by the FBI. Even more startling was Murray's revela-
tion that when imprisoned gang member Larry DeVol was to be transferred
to testify as a witness at a bank robbery trial, Brown notified Karpis and
"some of the other boys in Chicago" of the route that DeVol was to take
from the Minnesota state prison to Minneapolis, so that they could make
arrangements to release him. (The plans were changed, and DeVol remained in prison.)[117]

Next, the FBI learned from a convicted bank robber in the Wisconsin
state prison that DeVol claimed he paid $100 each week to Harry Sawyer
and that Sawyer then passed the bribe money to Brown and other police
officers. DeVol said that 10 percent of the Barker-Karpis gang's robbery
money was turned over to Brown for protection.[118]

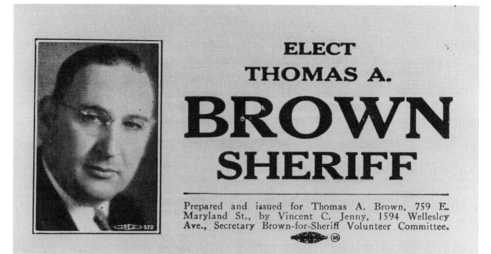

Tom Brown's political campaign card

Finally, government informant Beth Green told the FBI that Dillinger gang members had contributed $1,500, "delivered in cash personally by Eddie Green to Tom Filben," to Tom Brown's campaign for sheriff.[119]

Alvin Karpis was amused by the FBI's shock at Brown's betrayal. "If you are a thief and are fortunate enough to find a copper that is also a thief, you'd be a chump if you didn't get together with him," Karpis told FBI agents in 1936, to which an FBI agent retorted: "Particularly if the thieving copper is head of the kidnap squad and you are in the snatch racket." Karpis, laughing, agreed.[120]

Chief Dahill was tormented by the discovery that his kidnap squad head had leaked the police department's secrets to the underworld. He attended the Bremer kidnapping trial in 1936 to see if testimony would prove Brown's involvement with the gangsters. An FBI memo noted in the same year that "Tom Dahill and Tom Brown are and have been for the past two years, at least, bitter enemies."[121]

Dahill's belief that Brown acted in part out of a desire to embarrass the chief became "an obsession with Dahill, who has spent much of his time in an endeavor to procure information from police officers whom he believes he can trust, which would lead to the prosecution of Brown," reported the FBI. "Neither Dahill nor anyone else has been able to furnish any concrete evidence of these rumors."[122]

With Brown exposed and isolated, the Barker-Karpis gang was forced to use other contacts to prevent Hamm from testifying against them. About a month after the kidnapping, William Hamm Jr. was invited to play golf with his cousin Herbert G. Benz, a liquor and real estate executive.

Peifer told the FBI that Benz's Jackson Investment Company held the mortgage for the Hollyhocks Club, where the Hamm kidnapping had been planned. The Ramsey County auditor confirmed that during the early 1930s Benz was paying taxes on the Hollyhocks, at its height as a gambling casino and underworld hangout, and rented the club out to Jack Peifer. Benz told the FBI that he had frequented the underworld's Plantation nightclub, where he met Peifer. According to the FBI, Benz was "on friendly terms with practically every underworld character in the Twin Cities." Now Benz told William Hamm that Jack Peifer and "the boys" had a message for him: Hamm should be careful about identifying Peifer as part of the Barker-Karpis kidnap gang or "harm might come to him."[123]

After Hamm was released, the Hamm Brewing Company became an informal loan institution for the periphery of the underworld. Gambling figure Ben Harris of the Plantation and Boulevards of Paris nightclubs told the FBI that in 1936 he borrowed $2,000 from the Hamm company through William Dunn, to be paid back in monthly installments.[124]

Dunn told the FBI that after Hamm's kidnapping, a high-ranking police officer had "borrowed $500 from the brewery on three separate occasions. . . . These loans have always been approved by William Hamm, Jr." The police officer was none other than Thomas A. Brown.[125]

The Hamm ransom money was flown to Reno and exchanged for laundered cash, although a conflicting account by Charlie Fitzgerald claimed that the Reno launderers shunned the money because of government interest in the case, and that the gang had to launder the money in Chicago through a mobster for a 10 percent handling fee. In any case, the "clean" money was split up in the bedroom of the Barkers's cottage in Illinois. "Fred Barker took the money out of the briefcase, put it on the bed, and started handing out $100 and $500 bills to each of us," recalled Bolton.[126]

Fitzgerald said that Verne Miller and two other gangsters suspected of involvement in the Kansas City Massacre each received $2,500 of the Hamm ransom as a courtesy to defray their legal costs. To celebrate, on July 4 the Barker-Karpis gang had a fireworks display on the lawn of their cottage.[127]

As late as 1940, the FBI was still hunting for the William Hamm ransom —based on rumors that a gangster had drawn maps showing where it was buried. None of the ransom money has ever been recovered.[128]

40   'Cool and Reckless, Not Giving a Dam[n] Who They Shot'

The South St. Paul Post Office Robbery
236 North Concord Street, South St. Paul

No criminal act illustrated how far the O'Connor system had eroded better than the August 30, 1933, payroll robbery at the South St. Paul Post

Office. In less than ten minutes, bullets from the Barker-Karpis gang's machine guns crashed through businesses in a three-block area, a $33,000 payroll was stolen, one policeman was severely wounded, and another police officer lay dead.

According to Fred Barker's girlfriend Paula Harmon, members of the Barker-Karpis gang returned to the Twin Cities in August 1933 after moving restlessly between Chicago and Long Lake, Illinois, to distribute the Hamm ransom money. Charlie Fitzgerald said his partners in the South St. Paul payroll robbery included Alvin Karpis, Fred Barker, and Chicago gunmen Byron Bolton and Fred Goetz. Karpis drove the heavily armored car with Fred Barker beside him in the front seat, reading the getaway map. Bolton was assigned the role of machine gunner if any policemen intruded during the robbery.[129]

The gang was waiting when a Great Western Railroad train brought the money bags from the Federal Reserve Bank of Minneapolis to South St. Paul. Two policemen were escorting the Swift and Company payroll that day: John Yeaman, father of three; and Leo Pavlak, father of two, who had joined the force in April.[130]

Two of the gangsters waited for the payroll delivery at "Bulldog Mike" Pappas's Depot Cafe on North Concord Street, drinking beer and watching from the window. "Freddie Barker with a machine gun wrapped in a newspaper carrying an account of the William Hamm kidnapping, stood in a beer parlor on the corner north of the post office," Dakota County attorney Harold Stassen told reporters.[131]

Two payroll carriers walked down the front steps of the South St. Paul Post Office at 9:45 A.M., and the robbery commenced. The gang drove up in a black sedan and unloaded Doc Barker, carrying a sawed-off shotgun, just south of the post office entrance. Shouting "Stick 'em up," Barker disarmed Pavlak, forced him to lift his hands above his head, and then shot him in the head, screaming "You dirty rat, son of a bitch!"[132]

"Fred shot Officer Yeaman as he sat in his squad car near the post office," Stassen said. "Doc Barker killed Officer Pavlak without any warning and then the signal man whipped out two .45 caliber pistols from his back pockets and started firing, too."[133]

Yeaman, who had been sitting quietly in his car in the alley between the post office and the Great Western Railway depot, was seriously injured. One bullet plunged through the bill of his cap, just above his right eyebrow. "Dad used to tell me that if that guy had just held his machine gun down, it would have taken Dad's head right off," recalled Jack Yeaman, the officer's son. "The gangsters opened up on my dad; they wanted to put him out of action first, because he had the machine gun."[134]

Newspaper headline after the South St. Paul robbery in August 1933

The choreography was evidence of the gang's careful planning. "The bandits undoubtedly had been watching delivery of that payroll every Wednesday for several weeks," said Melvin Passolt, BCA chief. "They had every movement timed perfectly and the whole thing was over so quickly that many bystanders hardly realized what was happening."[135]

It was, concluded Karpis, "a good day's work, even if it did cost one wounded crook [Charlie Fitzgerald had been shot in the leg] and, as we found out from the papers, one wounded and one dead cop."[136]

"The bandits put on a Jessie James exhibition by shooting up and down Concord St., shooting about a dozen shots into the Postal Building and across the street," noted a BCA report on the robbery. "These bandits used a Thompson machine gun and a sawed off shot gun with which they did their shooting, and it is a miracle that no one else was shot and wounded. They appeared to be cool and reckless, not giving a dam[n] who they shot."[137]

The robbery was so bloody that even Dillinger gang member Eddie Green condemned the assault. An FBI report noted that Green told his wife "how crazy the whole plan was, as they had apparently, without necessity, shot down individuals during the course of that robbery."[138]

South St. Paul Post Office, site of a 1933 stockyards payroll robbery; the Thompson submachine gun taken during the robbery and found in Doc Barker's Chicago apartment

There were rumors that the payroll robbery was an "inside job." James Crumley, former St. Paul inspector of detectives, told the FBI that "Truman Alcorn, former Chief of Police of South St. Paul, is very close to Tom Brown and . . . there is no question but Brown and Alcorn were in on the payroll robbery in South St. Paul."[139]

County attorney Stassen also believed that Alcorn—who had been just a few dozen yards down the street at the time of the robbery—was involved in the crime. "Dad was never bitter about being shot, because you go into police work with the idea that it could happen to you," said Jack Yeaman. But for years, the father and son investigated rumors that police knew in advance that a gang was in town to "make a payroll."[140]

When Doc Barker's Chicago apartment was raided in January 1935, the Thompson submachine gun taken from John Yeaman during the robbery was found. The gun was given to Stassen and then passed along to the South St. Paul police, who store it in the chief's office at police headquarters today.[141]

Robert Pavlak, who became a police officer himself, was nine years old when his father was murdered. Of the day of his father's death, Pavlak said, "I ran home. . . . That's all I remember. My mother was dying of cancer at the time—we had so much grief then." Pavlak knew that his father faced danger, and not just from the underworld. "There was so much criminality then, both within and without the department, that Lieutenant Jeff Dittrich used to tell me, 'You never went to take the garbage out at night without having a gun in your hand.'"[142]

In August 1993, the South St. Paul Police Department paid tribute, awarding the family Pavlak's posthumous Medal of Honor. A wreath was laid at the national law enforcement memorial in Washington, D. C., alongside the name of Leo Pavlak—the only South St. Paul policeman to be murdered while on duty.

Yeaman, despite having twenty-five bullet fragments lodged in his body, survived. When he died in 1971, a number of these fragments were still in his shoulder and neck.[143]

No one was ever charged with the robbery, or with shooting Yeaman and Pavlak. But within three years every outlaw who participated in the South St. Paul robbery was either dead or in federal prison.

7 • • • • • • • • • •

VERNE MILLER'S KANSAS CITY MASSACRE

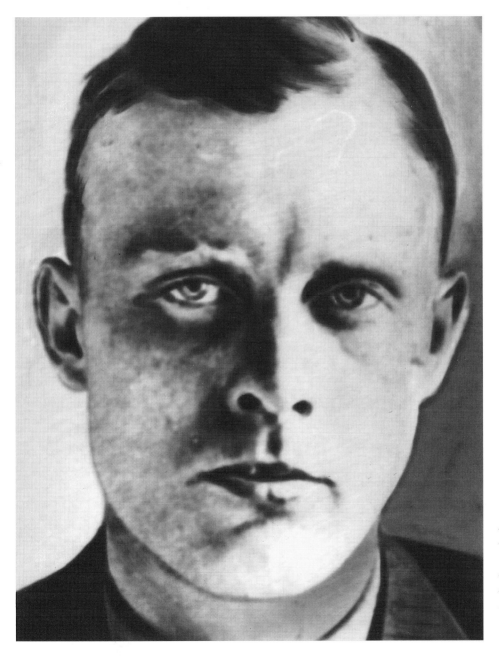

Verne Miller fishing with his girlfriend, Vivian Mathis, near Brainerd, Minnesota; Miller's FBI mug shot

A Gangster's Brainerd Hideaway

6111 Legionville Road, near Brainerd

Vivian Mathis, the daughter of a Brainerd, Minnesota, dairy farmer, was in love with a former South Dakota sheriff—a World War I veteran, boxer, and parachute jumper named Vernon C. Miller.[1]

Mathis told her family that she had been working a carnival concession in the Twin Cities when a belligerent customer refused to leave her booth. The customer hit her, knocking Mathis to the ground, and a stranger—Miller—rushed to her aid. His gallantry led to a friendship, then blossomed into a four-year romance.[2]

"Verne Miller first came to our farm in 1929," recalled Janet Gibson, Mathis's sister-in-law. "He was a very warm person. . . . [He] would take the kids shopping in Brainerd and to the Brainerd county fair." A handsome man of thirty-three, Miller had medium-blond hair and a trim 145-pound, 5-foot, 7-inch physique. His gray eyes had a slightly melancholy expression.[3]

Everything the former sheriff told the Mathis family was technically true. What the family could not know was the darker side of Miller's résumé. Miller—alias Vincent C. Moore—was also a convicted embezzler, bootlegger, and bank robber. His botched attempt to free his friend Frank Nash from FBI custody in June 1933 would result in what newspapers dubbed the Kansas City Massacre, a gangland killing that made Miller the most wanted man in America—by both the FBI and the underworld. But back in 1929, courting Mathis, Miller seemed to be an unlikely candidate to commit a bloodbath. While Fred Barker and other gang members drifted from city to city, restlessly committing petty crimes, Verne Miller relaxed between bank robberies with Vi's family at the Gibson dairy farm, eight miles from Brainerd on Legionville Road, at the south end of North Long Lake. (Today the farm—about three miles from Highway 25—is the Boy Scout's Legionville Camp.)[4]

Miller was born to Scotch-Irish parents in 1896 in Kimball, South Dakota. He left school in the fourth grade, became an auto mechanic, and married his first sweetheart, Mildred, in 1917. He served in the 164th Infantry in France in World War I, distinguishing himself with his machine-gun technique. (FBI special agent Melvin Purvis later claimed that Miller was so expert with a machine gun, he could shoot his initials into the gas tanks of fleeing bootleggers.)[5]

Basking in his wartime glory, Miller was elected policeman in 1920. The people of Huron, South Dakota, made him Beadle County sheriff in 1921 and, in the words of a state's attorney, Miller "made a fine record as a peace officer." But when he was caught embezzling nearly $2,600 in county funds, the disgraced lawman pleaded guilty and was sent to the South Dakota State Prison in April 1923. According to prison records, Miller lost little time in making connections with organized crime: within ninety days he was corresponding with St. Paul fixer Jack Peifer and his wife, the future proprietors of the underworld's Hollyhocks Club.[6]

In October 1925 Miller was indicted in Sioux Falls, South Dakota, for violating the Volstead Act, but he forfeited his bond and the case was dropped. As an ex-convict whose skills included exceptional dexterity with a machine gun, Miller advanced from minor bootlegging to major crimes. The FBI's Purvis claimed that Miller, determined to reassure the Keating-Holden gang that he was ruthless, asked for the name of someone of whom the gang disapproved. "Miller proved his worth by kidnapping the man, taking him out on a country road, and breaking all ten of his fingers," wrote Purvis.[7]

The first public mention of Miller's link to organized crime surfaced on February 3, 1928, when he was identified as a participant in a shooting involving gangster Isadore "Kid Cann" Blumenfeld. A scuffle at the Cotton Club in Minneapolis, incited by an ungentlemanly pass at a female entertainer, erupted into a shootout between bootleggers and policemen. One officer was wounded; another was paralyzed by (and later died from) bullets in his shoulder and stomach. The Minneapolis police quickly called off the search for Miller, claiming a case of "mistaken identity." But in a 1934 police interview in Leavenworth prison, George "Machine Gun Kelly" Barnes said that it was indeed Miller who pulled his gun at the Minneapolis club, adding that Miller had also murdered a police officer in Montreal.[8]

Moving up from bootlegging, Miller tried his hand at running gambling rackets in Montreal in 1930. He developed ties to labor racketeer Louis "Lepke" Buchalter, one of the founders of the national crime syndicate. At the same time, Vivian Mathis formed a close friendship with Lepke's wife, Betty Buchalter. FBI files contend that Miller became a hit man for Buchalter while he was still freelancing as an enforcer for Al Capone's gang in Chicago and the Purple Gang of Detroit. Miller's body bore evidence of his violent trade. Wanted posters identified him by a scar curving over his left eye and an irregular scar on the left side of his head; the end of the third finger on his left hand was missing.[9]

By 1931 Miller had begun to work with a husky Tennessee-born bootlegger who later earned notoriety as "Machine Gun Kelly." "The one man who had the most effect on George [Machine Gun Kelly] was Verne Miller, a machine gun toting desperado," wrote Bruce Barnes, Kelly's son. Miller and other gangsters taught him the intricacies of a successful bank robbery long before Kelly robbed his first bank. "It wasn't only the money" that appealed to his father, wrote Barnes in his book, *Machine Gun Kelly: To Right a Wrong.* "The picture of himself going into a bank, holding a gun and knowing that he had power over those he was robbing appealed to him."[10]

Verne Miller and Mathis lived with Kelly and his wife, Kathryn "Kit" Kelly, in Chicago, Kansas City, and the Twin Cities during the early 1930s. Gradually, Miller's cool under fire led to his involvement with both Kelly and Oklahoma's Harvey Bailey in a series of profitable robberies. Miller was identified as one of those who joined Charlie Fitzgerald and Harvey Bailey in robbing a bank in Lincoln, Nebraska, of $2 million in bonds in September 1930.[11]

"For a criminal, he [Miller] had a peculiar set of morals," mused crime historians Clyde Callahan and Byron Jones. "It was said he had done murder for hire, but at the same time disliked hearing anyone use foul or profane language. He would have nothing to do with kidnappers and dropped the Barkers when they became involved in this sort of business."[12]

In the underworld, Miller's history as a policeman and sheriff was a dirty secret. When Alvin Karpis, suspicious of Miller's background, questioned him about it, Miller denied that he had ever been a sheriff—it was his cousin, he said, who was the white sheep of the family. Karpis, unconvinced, refused to deal with Miller, explaining to the FBI that "he did not care to associate with an 'ex-copper.'"[13]

Miller's retired badge may also have fueled a long-standing feud with bank robber Harvey Bailey. Together, Miller and Bailey had robbed banks in Ottumwa, Iowa, Sherman, Texas, and other cities. But Bailey was perturbed when he found out that, in Kelly's words, "Miller had been the law and then had turned into the racket." Bailey decided that although Miller had "guts," he no longer wanted to work with him.[14]

In his memoirs, Bailey claimed that their falling out had little to do with Miller's law-abiding past. Rather, Bailey distrusted Miller's willingness to tell Mathis about his illegal doings. "If she's not good enough to tell," Miller responded, "she's not good enough to live with." Gradually, Miller grew to distrust Bailey, too. Kelly recounted to police how Bailey had been assigned the job of laundering the nearly $200,000 in bonds stolen by the Barker-Karpis gang in March 1932 from Northwestern National Bank and Trust Company of Minneapolis. Although he'd been advised to cash in the bonds for twenty-five cents on the dollar, Bailey returned to Minnesota, insisting that all he could get from his New York contacts was fifteen cents. With Miller's underworld contacts, it did not take long for him to discover that Bailey was lying: he had received the higher exchange rate for the bonds. Miller forced Bailey to flee to Chicago, and Bailey swore that he would kill Miller in revenge.[15]

Miller did not allow underworld tensions to restrict his increasingly warm relationships with Mathis, her ten-year-old daughter, Betty, and the rest of the family back in Brainerd. Surviving family members and FBI surveillance files confirm that he appeared to be genuinely fond of Betty, who told her grandfather that her "stepdaddy," as she called Miller, had measured her for a set of golf clubs.[16]

Mathis would show up in Brainerd wearing nice clothes, driving a new Cadillac, and bearing expensive gifts for her daughter. Miller went deer hunting at the Brainerd farm, fished for northern pike at North Long Lake, and took Betty golfing at a nearby golf course.[17]

"When I was seven years old I remember playing with one of my neighbors at my grandparents' house in Parkerville, and we were jumping around in Verne Miller's car and the seat came loose. Underneath the seat was an *arsenal*—it was just filled with guns!" recalled Mike Gibson, Vivian Mathis's nephew.

Miller bought the boy his first three-piece suit to wear during a Christmas play. "Verne used to put small coins in my vest pockets as a surprise for me," said Gibson. He "would always bring toys up for us—one time he brought me some toy guns and gave Betty a whole trunk full of doll clothes." When the Mathis family fixed Miller a meal one evening, he noticed that they had few dishes. The machine gunner surprised the family by buying dishes and a tablecloth for their home.[18]

"You could see two sides to Verne," recalled Janet Gibson, Mathis's sister-in-law. At times Miller was "jolly." But on other days, the Mathis family would see him gripped by depression, sitting silently in a lawn chair for hours, his face drawn with tension.[19]

Associating with gangsters, many of whom were emotionally unstable, had its drawbacks. Mathis told FBI agents later that although the Barker boys were "nice little fellows," she felt that Karpis was "a cold proposition" and "she had never felt at ease around him." She clearly loved Miller, whom she always called "Sugar." The FBI observed after he died that "it is apparent from her actions and the way she talks that she is still very much broken up over his death."[20]

Miller's demise was precipitated not by his enemies but by his own loyalty to his longtime friend, Frank Nash. Three years after Nash had escaped from Leavenworth, he was recaptured by FBI agents on June 16, 1933, in the "safe" city of Hot Springs, Arkansas. An underworld contact, "Doc" Stacci, telephoned Miller in Kansas City and alerted him to the arrest; the "feds" would be taking Nash through Kansas City's Union Station en route to prison.[21]

Miller is believed to have called the Dillinger gang's errand boy Pat

Reilly in St. Paul in an attempt to enlist Alvin Karpis and Arthur and Doc Barker to help spring Nash, but the Barker-Karpis gang had its hands full with the William Hamm kidnapping.[22]

On June 17, 1933, Miller and two associates drove up to Union Station minutes before Nash was to arrive. (The FBI insisted that Miller was accompanied by Charles "Pretty Boy" Floyd and Floyd's partner, Adam Richetti; Floyd biographer Michael Wallis believes that evidence of Floyd's involvement is slim.) It is clear from telephone records and other documentation that Miller watched outside Union Station as Nash was forced into the front seat of a police officer's Chevrolet, surrounded by FBI agents and police. Suddenly, Miller, armed with a submachine gun, leaped forward—shouting "Let 'em have it!"—and opened fire on the men guarding Frank Nash. Witnesses heard Nash howl, "For God's sake, don't kill me!" Within thirty seconds, Nash was dead. Other victims of what came to be known as the Kansas City Massacre were FBI agent Raymond Caffrey; Otto Reed, police chief of McAlester, Oklahoma; and two Kansas City police officers, William Grooms and Frank Hermanson.[23]

An alternate scenario for the massacre was posed by gangster Gus Winkler's widow, Georgette, who told the FBI that "Frank Nash and Verne Miller were the best of friends." But after Miller began firing at the guards, Nash exclaimed: "Verne, have you gone crazy?" The question aggravated Miller, who turned his gun on Nash and killed him, Winkler said.[24]

"We heard on the radio about the Kansas City Massacre," recalled Janet Gibson, who had had no hint of the extent of Miller's criminal life. "On the radio they said Verne Miller's gang had killed lots of police and an FBI agent and Frank Nash as well. Oh my, we were dumbfounded."[25]

J. Edgar Hoover said that "no time, money, or labor will be spared toward bringing about the apprehension of the individuals responsible for the cowardly and despicable act. . . . *They must be exterminated and must be exterminated by us, and to this end we are dedicating ourselves.*"[26]

FBI agents swarmed toward Brainerd in the search for Miller, obtaining a mail cover (observation of letters and packages) and telephone surveillance on Mathis's family. When a box of salt water taffy was mailed in July from Atlantic City to Vi Mathis's daughter, the FBI tracked down the clerk in New York who had sold the taffy to Miller. The FBI found that Miller had made two telephone calls to St. Paul on July 15: one to Jack Peifer's Hollyhocks casino, the other to Gladys Sawyer, a close friend of Mathis.[27]

After the massacre in Kansas City, Miller and Mathis fled to Chicago to meet with Volney Davis and Doc Barker and have Miller's hand bandaged. Mathis told her family that Miller intended to spirit her off to Europe. But the nationwide dragnet made escape impossible.[28]

By October, the FBI was hunting Miller with a vengeance, not only for his role in the Kansas City debacle but for nearly every other unsolved crime in the Midwest as well: the kidnapping of oilman Charles Urschel (actually committed by Machine Gun Kelly), the machine-gunning of Chicago policeman Miles Cunningham, the October 1933 robbery of a Brainerd bank (by Babyface Nelson), and the kidnapping of William Hamm. Miller fled first to New York and then shot his way out of a police trap in Chicago on Halloween.[29]

Miller was targeted by the underworld as well, because the furor over the massacre had made life miserable for every gangster in the country. The Detroit police learned from Louis Stacci, one of Miller's underworld contacts, that "any number of people were only too willing to kill Miller, as he was so hot from the law that he was dangerous to everyone." His money dwindling, Miller moved from New York to West Virginia; from Roaring Gap, North Carolina, back to Brooklyn; and then to Lima, Ohio, and Chicago.[30]

Detroit police learned from Machine Gun Kelly that "a number of people, from different gangs, in Chicago and Cicero, were sore at Miller. . . . Not many around Chicago would have much to do with Miller on account of him being so hot with the law and also the gangs." Many gangsters disliked him, Kelly said, because of his habit of avenging underworld assassinations. If a mobster killed a friend of Miller, he felt compelled to track the hit man down and kill him; he confessed to slaughtering three hoodlums in Fox Lake, Wisconsin, in 1930 because the trio had murdered the brother of a friend.[31]

Even Miller's mentor Lepke Buchalter told FBI agents that "no one will have anything to do with Miller now. If he shows up, you will know about it." When an agent asked if Miller was likely to be "bumped off," the mob chieftain "responded with a knowing look" and simply said, "I will have to look into that."[32]

The simultaneous FBI and underworld manhunts ended on November 29, 1933, when Miller's body, nude and mutilated, was found in a ditch along a highway near Detroit. His skull had been crushed by thirteen blows, and he had been strangled with a garrote, then wrapped in a cheap blanket with a fifty-foot sash cord. Miller was so severely beaten that the police could identify him only by his fingerprints. "We wanted Miller badly, but whoever killed him probably saved us from having to do it," the FBI's Werner Hanni told reporters.[33]

Who killed Verne Miller? Machine Gun Kelly suggested to police that he could have been killed only by people he trusted: "Miller never went any place without being armed and never let anyone he did not know real well get close to him on account of there being any number of people who would have taken him. . . . The ones who did get him were real close to him," the Detroit police reported.[34]

Whoever killed Miller, his death was a relief for both the mob and the FBI. "The underworld never forgave Miller for the Kansas City raid," wrote FBI agent Melvin Purvis. "Crime is a business and Verne Miller had become a debit; they wiped him off the ledger and the photograph of his mangled body, which I later saw, told a gruesome story of a cold and bloody murder."[35]

Vivian Mathis had been arrested by the FBI that October in Chicago, where she had been hiding under the alias Mrs. George Hayes. The Minnesota farmgirl pleaded guilty to harboring a criminal and conspiracy to obstruct justice. Mathis told the FBI that she planned to find out who killed Miller and "take care of them." After being released from the federal detention farm at Milan, Michigan, Mathis recuperated in Brainerd for seven months, grieving for Miller. She later married a hotel operator with a penchant for battering women and moved with him to Sioux Falls, South Dakota, where she died in 1940—from complications of domestic abuse, her family suspects.[36]

Verne Miller—ex-sheriff and bank robber, former policeman and assassin—was buried on December 6, 1933. His funeral in White Lake, South Dakota, incorporated the full military rituals of the American Legion: a color guard and an armed escort of Legionnaires.[37]

Mathis's niece Donna Eue recalled the shock her family felt when a detective magazine published photographs of Mathis on the witness stand testifying about Miller. To protect Mathis's daughter, Betty, Grandma Bertha Gibson went into town and bought every available issue of the lurid periodical, brought the magazines home to the farm where Miller had enjoyed dinners with the family, and burned them.[38]

J. Edgar Hoover called the Kansas City Massacre a "turning point in the nation's fight against crime." Indeed, public outrage over the Kansas murders—coupled with the FBI's capture of Machine Gun Kelly in September 1933 and John Dillinger's jail escapes and shootouts in 1934—helped catapult the FBI into national prominence and generated the strong support Hoover needed to overcome opposition to his creation of a federal police force. Agent Purvis wrote in his book, *American Agent*, that "the mad bravado and consummate insolence" of the Kansas City Massacre marked a shift in the public's opinion on gangsters, that it convinced citizens "it was

President Franklin Roosevelt signing new crime bill into law in 1934, watched (left to right) by Attorney General Homer Cummings, Hoover, a senator, and assistant attorney general Joseph Keenan

high time for a new deal on crime. . . . There was no telling who the next victim would be."[39]

Goaded by Hoover's publicity machine, Congress in 1934 passed a series of Justice Department–sponsored initiatives that expanded FBI powers to hunt down criminals. Congress finally made it a federal crime to kill an FBI agent and authorized federal intervention in kidnapping cases a week after the abduction, presuming that by then the victim would have been taken across state lines. The FBI was given the green light to hire two hundred additional agents and to arrest criminals without involving local police, who,

Poster for the 1936 film You Can't Get Away with It (left), which received J. Edgar Hoover's personal support; Hoover, posing on movie camera (above), films his assistant Clyde Tolson, for FBI publicity reels.

attorney general Homer Cummings widely complained, were "hopelessly corrupt."[40]

The attorney general, Hoover's ally, inaugurated a "public enemies" list of ten most-wanted criminals, including Charles "Pretty Boy" Floyd and John Dillinger—a master stroke of publicity that further elevated inept rural hoodlums to national celebrity. The Justice Department in August 1934 hired brilliant public relations man Henry Suydam, while the FBI hired former YMCA publicist Louis Nichols, both of whom promoted Hoover's hunt for the Barker-Karpis gang with a wave of media adulation. By spring 1935, the public was entranced with Jimmy Cagney's portrayal of an FBI agent in the Warner Bros. film *G-Men* and was reading about heroic agents in books like *Ten Thousand Public Enemies*, written by Hoover's ghostwriter Courtney Ryley Cooper.[41]

Hoover vilified gangsters with increased gusto, condemning them as "under-filth. . . . rats crawling from their hide-outs to gnaw at the vitals of our civilization."[42]

The *Chicago Tribune* marveled in 1936 that "in less than three years a tide of printer's ink, accompanied by a roar of sound films and radio programs, has given heroic stature to a relatively obscure burocrat [sic]. . . . Over the air and on the screen the fire was repeated, and out of the welter of dramatic gore Hoover emerged as the leading criminal chaser of all time."[43]

The American public, which Hoover believed had romanticized bank robbers like Pretty Boy Floyd and Dillinger as Dust Bowl Robin Hoods, began to accept the FBI director as a new hero. Now the FBI had to prove that it could destroy the targets it had so avidly pursued in the media—the Barker-Karpis and Dillinger gangs.

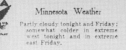

Minnesota Weather

Partly cloudy tonight and Friday; somewhat colder in extreme west tonight and in extreme east Friday.

St. Paul Dispatch

Recognition

The unruly boy may have ideas; don't suppress him, Angelo Patri warns on Page 10 today.

66. NO. 112. 18 PAGES Exclusive Service of the Associated Press. ST. PAUL, MINN., THURSDAY, JANUARY 18, 1934. TWO CENTS IN ST.

EDW. G. BREMER KIDNAPED; $200,000 RANSOM ASKE

ABDUCTION VICTIM, KIN AND KIDNAP SQUAD

Edward G. Bremer, president of the Commercial State bank, and son of Adolph Bremer, part owner of the Schmidt Brewing Co., was kidnaped Wednesday morning. He is in the center above. Police received no official notification of the kidnaping and the family refused to discuss it. Reports were that Mr. Bremer is being held for $200,000 ransom. In the picture above are Walter Magee (upper left) who first was told of the kidnaping. Below is Adolph Bremer, father of the missing man. At the upper right is Charles Tierney, inspector of detectives, and below him is Detective Thomas A. Brown. These two officers comprise the St. Paul police kidnap squad. In the lower center is the Schmidt brewery on West Seventh street. Inset in the brewery picture is Edward Penschuck, who was with Mr. Magee when he was reported to have been notified of the kidnaping.

Women Tossed From Sinking Ship

Secrecy Veil Second Maj Seizure He

Victim Member of One of St. Paul's Wealthies Son of Adolph and Nephew of Otto Bremer, Manager of Home Owners Loan Corporatio Call Gave "Tip."

VANISHED AFTER TAKING HIS DAUGH TO SUMMIT SCHOOL ON GOODRICH

Edward G. Bremer, president of the Co State bank and a member of one of St. Paul's families, was kidnaped for $200,000 ransom W morning.

Police say they have received no official n of the crime and the family refused to discuss it Dahill, chief of police, said he was investigati of the crime.

Mr. Bremer is 37 years old and resides at Mississippi River boulevard. It is known he Tuesday from a business trip to Chicago. Effort his release are reported to have failed thus far.

SECOND MAJOR CASE IN 7 MONTHS.

It was the second big abduction in seven months of a St. Paul brewing family. William Hamm Jr., pre Hamm Brewing Co., paid $100,000 for his release last

Mr. Bremer is the son of Adolph Bremer, 855 W street, part owner of the Jacob Schmidt Brewing Co. and of Otto Bremer, 1344 Summit avenue, a Democratic pow of the American National bank and Minnesota manager

U.S. Agent on Way Here by

Dallas, Jan. 18.—(AP)—Frank J. Blake, Department agent who directed most of the search for the kidnapers F. Urschel, Oklahoma City oil millionaire, left by plane St. Paul.

Owners Loan corporation. He also is a nephew of Paul Amherst avenue.

Kidnapers are reported to have seized him between and 10 A. M. Wednesday, possibly on Summit avenue or St. Paul.

As was his custom, he drove his 8-year-old daughte Summit school, 1150 Goodrich avenue, where she is a third grade, and apparently continued on his way to Sixth and Washington streets to begin his day's work.

His route probably lay east on Summit avenue to and thence to the bank. Somewhere along this line t are believed to have forced his automobile to a halt an

He failed to show up at the bank.

According to reports, the next heard of Mr. Bremer telephone jingled in the office of Walter W. Magee, 118 avenue, general contractor, an associate of the Bremers of the new state office building. Mr. Magee also said he of the affair.

PHONE CALL TELLS WHERE TO FIND CA

A low voice is said to have told Mr. Magee he co Bremer car at the Highland park water tower, Snelli avenues, and a note on the back door step of his office.

The contractor, trying to prolong the conversation to have hastily instructed Ed Penschuck, former city missioner of public utilities, who was in the office, to ge line to trace the call, but the kidnaper clicked his rece effort failed.

Magee found the note under a mat. It was addressed Magee," was written on a typewriter and signed in ink by The signature was shaky, indicating he was nervous.

The man who telephoned Magee is reported to have we've got your friend Bremer and if you are not damn get you, too."

He was warned, it was reported, that any attempts cate with police or newspapers would result in the imm of Bremer.

The note found by Magee apparently had been writ folded and Mr. Bremer forced to sign it, probably with its content.

IN SAFE PLACE, NOTE SAYS.

The note, it was reported, said Mr. Bremer had captive by the kidnap gang and that he was held in a sa was unharmed. A demand for $200,000 for his safe made. Again a threat of death for their victim was ma

4 OTHER KIDNAPINGS IN 30 MONTHS HERE

Obtained $128,400 of $310,000 Demanded; Eight of 20 Suspects in Prison.

St. Paul has been the scene of four other major kidnapings in the past two and one-half years. From their four victims the abductors obtained $128,400 of the $310,000 demanded as ransom. All of the victims suffered physical hardships, but are alive today. Of the approximately 20 suspects in the four abductions, eight have been convicted.

Here are details of the kidnapings in chronological order:

SEPTEMBER 24, 1931—Leon Gleckman, reputed political manipulater, kidnaped by four men. Held approximately a week in a Northern Wisconsin cabin. Ransom first demanded, $75,000; amount paid, $6,400, of which $5,300 was recovered. Five men serving terms in Stillwater for the abduction.

OCTOBER 3, 1931—Morris Rutman, dress shop owner, abducted from his home, 1079 Dayton avenue, by two men. Held for several days and tortured before released. Ransom asked, $100,000. Later reduced to $10,000. Reported to have been paid. Two men convicted and serving prison sentences. A third still sought for complicity in the case.

JUNE 30, 1932—Haskell Bohn, youthful son of a refrigerator manufacturer, kidnaped from garage at his home, 1408 Summit avenue and held until July 6 in a Minneapolis home. Abductors first demanded $35,000, but released Bohn for $12,000. One man convicted and serving sentence, and the wife of another suspect, whom police since have sought, acquitted of complicity.

JUNE 15, 1933—William Hamm Jr., millionaire brewer, kidnaped by two men as he left his office. Believed to have been taken to Wisconsin

The National Whirligig

s Behind The News

WASHINGTON

MONTHS have passed merica took Russia back to om. Ambassadors have changed and preliminary king to the opening of new annels is well under way. dition No. 2 to Washing- gnition of the Soviet gov- President Roosevelt made promise it would not lift by outlay of money or to foment communistic s in the United States. was said about the Am- he agreement Commissar signed but our secret ave good reason to believe ian-controlled New York ing corporation has been many of the principal itators in recent years. communistic demonstra- d activities diminished ember 16." An hour's h federal operatives and icials who check reports over the country proves ng.

NSWER is that agitation ding on about the same before. Organizers and continue to tour from city ttempting to stir up un- ng the poorest classes. arger centers demonstra- more or less consequence staged periodically. dercover men are a little to openly charge a newly d nation with breaking soon but they are con- e old order still prevails, their investigations have pped any change for the

NIST spokesmen un- will seize on this state- proof of the contention never did underwrite the malcontents. They can at the movement in this s 100 per cent domestic ed on only by Americans. here does the jack come k the police. Men and n't be paid regularly and er the country on speak unless a war chest exists

Red leaders would an- the coin comes from tributions collected from umber of sympathizers do say further that the and "sisters" working ose draw mere pittances the movement because of ed conviction.

REPLY the officers, there al treasury organization for collections, a recent Washington is typical. persons were present. e hall was $4. It was the Unemployed council ontribute $2 if the audience in the rest. After the passed a careful count $4. A final stirring ap- ght out another quarter e night. This left up to speaker's traveling ex- and on to the next city.

Turn to Page 4, Col. 7.)

COURT RESTRAINS BANCO STOCK SIFT

Molyneaux Signs Order Halting Action of State Commerce Commission.

Federal Judge Joseph W. Molyneaux of Minneapolis signed today an order temporarily restraining the Minnesota Commerce commission from proceeding with its investigation of sale of stock of the Northwest Bancorporation.

The order was issued at the request of officials of the corporation, and the matter is set for hearing in Federal District court in Minneapolis at 10 A. M., January 27.

At the same time the commission received a notice from the Bancorporation signed by J. C. Thompson, president, stating that the corporation "consents, requests and demands" that the exempt status of its securities be revoked and offering to surrender all rights and privileges under the exempt status.

The commission on November 2 issued two orders against the corporation, one launching an investigation into its stock sales and the other an order to show cause why the exempt status of the corporation's stock should not be revoked, listing as the grounds alleged fraud and other charges.

The commission also temporarily revoked the exempt status which prevented general and open sales in

(Please Turn to Page 2, Col. 5.)

WARRANTS ISSUED FOR SINCLAIR, 24 OTHERS

Tulsa, Okla., Jan. 18.—(AP)—Warrants for the arrest of Harry F. Sinclair, oil magnate, and 24 other men

THE WEATHER

St. Paul Forecast.

8 • • • • • • • • • •

ONE KIDNAPPING TOO MANY

Newspaper announcing kidnap of Edward Bremer, with (clockwise from upper right) Inspector of Detectives Charles Tierney, Thomas Brown, Adolf Bremer, and intermediary Walter Magee; West Seventh Street home of Adolf Bremer Sr.

41 The Gang's All Here

Fred Barker's Dale Apartments
628 Grand Avenue, St. Paul

The Barker-Karpis gang gathered at the Dale Apartments in St. Paul in December 1933 and January 1934 to plot their next kidnapping. The men barricaded themselves in the living room of apartment 103 to debate the abduction of a member of what the FBI would term one of the wealthiest and "most prominent" families of the Twin Cities.[1]

Paula Harmon later told the FBI that she and Fred Barker had "rented an apartment on the corner of Dale and Grand Avenues, just off Summit Avenue, using the alias 'the Bergstroms.'" From January 1 to January 15, 1934, Harmon said, "all of the members of the gang were in St. Paul," having been called back to the Twin Cities from the warmth of Reno and Phoenix. "Several times . . . the gang would have meetings in my apartment," recalled Harmon, who sat with Wynona Burdette drinking beer in the kitchen "while the members of the gang talked. By 'members of the gang,' I mean George Ziegler, Alvin Karpis, Harry Campbell, Volney Davis, William Weaver, Fred Barker and Arthur R. Barker."[2]

At first, the gang considered robbing the Commercial State Bank of St. Paul, but fixer Harry Sawyer argued that kidnapping the bank's president, thirty-seven-year-old Edward Bremer, would be more profitable. Bremer was the son of Adolf Bremer, president of the Jacob Schmidt Brewing Company. The ransom was to be $200,000, double what the gang had demanded when they abducted William Hamm Jr.[3]

The decision to kidnap a second local businessman just seven months after Hamm was ransomed was audacious. The consequences of failure had increased dramatically since July 22, 1933, when Machine Gun Kelly and his wife, Kathryn, kidnapped Oklahoma oilman Charles F. Urschel. The Barker-Karpis gang knew all about the Urschel kidnapping—in fact, about $5,500 of the $200,000 Urschel ransom had been laundered in the Twin Cities. The twenty-dollar ransom bills were passed through the First National Bank and Trust Company and Hennepin State Bank by members of Isadore "Kid Cann" Blumenfeld's Minneapolis syndicate. George and Kathryn Kelly had also visited the offices of Minneapolis bootlegger Tommy Banks to have an additional $30,000 of the money exchanged for "clean" bills.[4]

The Kellys were captured on September 26, 1933, by police and FBI agents in Memphis, Tennessee; the FBI account had Kelly begging, "Don't shoot, G-men!" On October 12 they were convicted and sentenced to life in prison. Two members of Kid Cann's gang, Clifford Skelly and Ed "Barney"

Berman, were among the twenty-one people found guilty in the Urschel kidnapping case; both were sentenced to five years in prison.[5]

The Urschel trial was the first held under the new Lindbergh kidnapping law—federal legislation passed in the wake of the March 1932 kidnapping and slaying of the son of Charles A. Lindbergh Jr.—which allowed life sentences for abductions. After the Urschel verdict, assistant U.S. attorney general Joseph Keenan declared: "This is just the first skirmish. We are going right down the line and every criminal and gangster in the United States may well begin shaking in his boots. This law is a powerful weapon, and we are prepared and eager to wield it to the finish."[6]

The women in the Barker-Karpis gang knew something big was being planned; on January 13, Fred Barker asked Paula Harmon to move from

George "Machine Gun Kelly" Barnes, taken into FBI custody in 1933 for the kidnapping of oilman Charles Urschel

Grand Avenue into the underworld's favorite Edgecumbe Court Apartments with Wynona Burdette and Edna Murray.

When the FBI identified the Dale Apartments hideout during the search for Bremer's kidnappers, agents probed the identities of "Edwin Bergstrom" (actually Fred Barker) and his wife (Paula Harmon), who was described to the FBI as a sandy-haired thirty-year-old Irish woman with crossed eyes and a thick brogue.

The Bergstroms vanished from 628 Grand the evening after Edward Bremer was kidnapped. Their Grand Avenue neighbors extolled the sociability of the mysterious couple. "The people did a lot of drinking and always had friends in their apartment," the building manager told the *St. Paul Dispatch*, "although they never were noisy or troublesome." Apart from an occasional bank robbery or kidnapping, the Barker-Karpis gangsters were ideal neighbors.[7]

42   Beer, Banks, Politics, and Kidnapping
The Jacob Schmidt Brewery
882 West Seventh Street, St. Paul

After the shock of the Hamm kidnapping, the St. Paul Police Department took a decisive step to protect other prominent businessmen: it established a squad whose sole mission was to search out and protect likely kidnap vic-

The Bremer family's Jacob Schmidt Brewery, about 1905; (inset) a Schmidt beer ad shortly after repeal of Prohibition

tims. To head the Kidnap Detail, the police chose Thomas Brown, the officer who had secretly leaked confidential law enforcement information to the Barker-Karpis gang.

Inspector of detectives James Crumley, an ally of Brown's who was dismissed from the police force in 1935 for accepting bribes, revealed to the FBI that it was Brown who gave the Barker-Karpis gang information on the habits of Edward Bremer, as gathered by the Kidnap Detail.[8]

The gang knew that the Bremer family could easily pay the ransom. With the repeal of Prohibition in March 1933, the Schmidt Brewery had returned to night-and-day production of beer. It had been founded as the North Star Brewery in 1855, when Minnesota was a six-year-old territory. By 1872, a German immigrant named Jacob Schmidt was running the company. To ensure that Schmidt would not be hired away by one of North Star's eleven local competitors, he was made half-owner in 1884. With the 1896 marriage of Schmidt's daughter Maria to young Adolf Bremer, a stable family to lead the growing company was established. When a flash fire destroyed the original plant, Bremer purchased the old Stahlman brewery in 1900 and named his new empire the Jacob Schmidt Brewing Company.[9]

During Prohibition, the Bremers weathered the closing of U.S. breweries by producing soft drinks, root beer, and enormously popular malt-based near beer—which enterprising customers could simply spike with their own illicit alcohol. Schmidt's near beer was delivered to the area's private homes, to drug and grocery stores, and to Jack Peifer's Hollyhocks Club casino. "I delivered Schmidt's near beer to lots of bootleg places," recalled Schmidt driver Gordon "Curley" Merrick. "Some bootleg places on Summit Avenue had peepholes, and [they would] look at you, [and] once they knew you were the driver for Schmidt's, they'd open up."[10]

Harry Sawyer's selection of Edward Bremer as the Barker-Karpis gang's next target clearly was not a random choice. "I don't know what Sawyer's beef was," Alvin Karpis wrote in his memoirs, "but he sure didn't like Bremer." Sawyer's wife, Gladys, told gang members that Bremer and Sawyer "once had some differences over some alcohol." Even Bremer himself, interviewed when he was released, said "he knew plenty that he would never tell about banks and politics which caused the kidnapping," the FBI reported.[11]

Years later, Gladys Sawyer, bitter after her husband had been abandoned by the underworld, spoke freely to the FBI of the circumstances preceding the Bremer kidnapping. According to the FBI, "Mrs. Sawyer said that the beer sold by her husband in the Saint Paul [Green Lantern] saloon, during Prohibition Days, was not 'near beer,' but real beer and that it all came from the Schmidt Brewing Company."

From 1926 to 1933, said Gladys, Harry Sawyer had an arrangement with the Bremers' Schmidt Brewery to have real beer delivered for sale at the Green Lantern. The beer was transported through an underground tunnel to the house of brewery employee Carl Schoen on Erie Street. Sawyer sold this illicit Schmidt beer at the Green Lantern as if it were legal near beer. A rival bar owner, Andrew Rothmeyer, stopped handling the Schmidt real beer during Prohibition because of a dispute over money with the brewery. Harry Sawyer became the "exclusive agency for this beer in Saint Paul and bootlegged it through his place of business on Wabasha Street, where he was doing business through virtue of a cigar store license," the FBI reported.[12]

Gladys said that her husband's Green Lantern saloon properties at 545, 543, and 541 Wabasha Street were actually *owned* by the Schmidt Brewing Company. When the Green Lantern was closed in the mid-1930s, a Schmidt truck was dispatched to pick up the fixtures, tables, and chairs. The curious relationship between the Bremer family and Sawyer took its most unusual turn on August 3, 1932, when two gangsters were arrested at Sawyer's Green Lantern bar for possession of firearms. Adolf Bremer requested that a family friend, Walter W. Magee, personally intercede on behalf of the two criminals. "Harry Sawyer is a customer of ours," the elder Bremer told Magee, "and anything that can be done for them will be appreciated." As a result, the gunmen were freed by St. Paul police on $500 bail, after which they vanished. Compounding the irony, one of the two gangsters arrested at the Green Lantern was William Weaver, a Barker-Karpis gang member who was to play a key role in the kidnapping of Adolf's son Edward a year and a half later.[13]

The FBI also learned that the Sawyers banked with Ed Bremer's Commercial State Bank, as did bootlegger Leon Gleckman and slot machine czar Thomas Filben.[14]

In addition, an FBI report noted that while waiting for the kidnapped Bremer's return, the family talked with the FBI. "Reference was made from time to time . . . that Edward Bremer . . . had considerable contact with underworld characters during his business activities at the bank" and that Bremer said he was "perfectly willing to do business with them," noted the report.[15]

In his memoirs, Karpis claimed that during the long wait for the delivery of the ransom money, Bremer confided to his captors that "he was a good buddy of Harry Sawyer's and Jack Peifer's and that either guy would vouch for him." When Dillinger gang member Eddie Green was interrogated on his deathbed in 1934, he stated that Sawyer had fingered Ed Bremer to be kidnapped, remarking, "That's bad, Eddie [Bremer] was a friend of his [Sawyer]."[16]

As the kidnapping of Ed Bremer unfolded, the FBI struggled to uncover the secrets of the police officer who betrayed those he was sworn to protect, and the victim who may have done business with his kidnappers.

43 A Cinch for Two Hundred Grand

Myrtle Eaton's Haven at the Kennington
565 Portland Avenue, St. Paul

Fred and Doc Barker desperately wanted Fred Goetz of Al Capone's Chicago syndicate to help with this second kidnapping. After the Hamm kidnapping, however, Goetz had told the Barkers that he was "through with the kidnapping racket and absolutely would not participate in another as he did not approve of this way of making money," the FBI reported. The Barker brothers enticed Goetz with the promise that their target was "a 'cinch' who was good for two hundred grand." Goetz protested that the Barkers should stay away from St. Paul because another kidnapping there would ruin Jack Peifer and his business. But Goetz finally agreed to participate.[17]

With Goetz on board, the Barker-Karpis gang held final planning sessions in apartment 104 at the Kennington, hosted by kidnap conspirator William "Lapland Willie" Weaver and his girlfriend, Myrtle Eaton. According to the FBI, the meetings in Eaton's apartment involved Karpis, Weaver, Fred and Doc Barker, Volney Davis, Harry Campbell, Fred Goetz, and Harry Sawyer.[18]

Eaton, an Iowa native and the ex-wife of Stillwater Prison parolee Clarence Eaton, was a thirty-one-year-old shoplifter with a taste for fur coats. At the time of the Bremer kidnapping, she was dating Weaver, a Little Rock, Arkansas, gangster who had been paroled in 1931 from a life sentence at the Oklahoma state prison for murdering a member of a posse pursuing him after a bank robbery. Released from prison, Weaver lived in St. Paul in a flat over the Moonlight Gardens saloon at 777 Selby Avenue, a brick apartment building at the intersection of Selby and Avon.[19]

Neighbors noted that Karpis, Weaver, and Fred Barker met at 565 Portland more than a dozen times before the Bremer kidnapping. The FBI reported that Weaver told friends he "had a falling out with Karpis and Barker" after the kidnapping because "Fred Barker was a hot-headed ____; that Fred Barker tried to put him [Weaver] on the spot and bump him off." FBI files suggest that Weaver was finally ordered to leave the hideout where Bremer was being held because he walked back and forth in front of the house, consumed with nervousness over the delays in the delivery of the ransom.[20]

Tensions rose before the Bremer kidnapping. Fred Barker went to Jess Doyle's St. Paul apartment to air another gang dispute. Barker, who had served time in Kansas State Penitentiary with Doyle, told his former partner that he wanted Doyle to leave town. Edna Murray explained that by the fall of 1933 "none of the boys were on speaking terms" with Doyle because "they wanted him to break away from his sister Doris, and he would not do so." The FBI learned from Murray that the Barker brothers felt Doris was "far too outspoken in her manners and also that she knew too much of Jess' business, of which they likewise disapproved." Understanding that the alternative to following the gang's wishes could mean his body being identified by its fingerprints, Doyle left for Oklahoma.[21]

Two days before the Bremer kidnapping was to be carried out, with gang conflicts growing, a figure was seen outside the windows of Eaton's Ken-

Shoplifter Myrtle Eaton (inset) hosted the Barker-Karpis gang at the Kennington (below left); Mr. Cowin and friend Roy McCord in the Holly Falls Apartments (below right) mistook the gang for peeping toms.

nington apartment—a uniformed man who looked very much like a St. Paul police officer to nervous gang members.

44 The Shooting of Roy McCord

The Holly Falls Apartments
562 Holly Avenue, St. Paul

For years, as the O'Connor system drew mobsters to their city, St. Paul citizens comforted themselves with the belief that the criminals would follow an underworld code of conduct: machine guns would be fired only at other gangsters, not at innocent bystanders. The FBI knew that the Barker-Karpis gang offered no such guarantees. After the 1934 shooting of Roy McCord, FBI agent Oscar Hall wrote that the Barker-Karpis gang members "are very reckless in their shooting and it has often been mentioned that they are 'blasters', that is, they shoot at the least provocation."[22]

Early in the morning on January 13, the gang's anxiety over plans to kidnap Bremer led to the shooting of a Northwest Airlines employee, a man who had the misfortune merely to *look* like a policeman. The previous evening, Northwest radio operator Roy McCord had been alerted by neighbors to peeping toms lurking at a friend's Holly Falls apartment, just behind the Kennington. Wearing his aviator's uniform, a peaked hat, and a dark jacket with brass buttons, McCord caught sight of three suspicious-looking men—strangers in a familiar neighborhood—and, just before 1:00 A.M., followed their Ford toward 562 Holly. McCord, accompanied by his friend, "saw a coupe drive down the alley near their home, followed it, and later drove abreast of the coupe," said a 1934 FBI memo. "As soon as their car was stopped, one or more occupants of the coupe fired into McCord's car with one or more machine guns, seriously injuring McCord."[23]

An underworld source told the FBI that "McCord was wearing a radio dispatcher's uniform of the Northwest Airways and was mistaken for a policeman." Karpis described the incident in his autobiography: "We were sitting around an apartment in St. Paul where Bill Weaver lived with a shoplifter named Myrtle Eaton, when someone noticed a guy peeping through the window of an apartment across the alley." Karpis and Fred Barker ran outside and climbed into their Chevrolet sedan, and Karpis pulled out a machine gun. "Freddie was at the wheel," wrote Karpis, "and I told him to pull around a corner and stop suddenly. He did, and I leaped out of the passenger side with a machine gun. I must have thrown twenty or thirty slugs into the cop car. When we drove away that time, nobody was trailing us."[24]

Karpis had fired nearly fifty .45-caliber bullets at McCord's car. "They weren't peeping toms—they were gangsters. . . . A gang like that is not going to be window peeping," said McCord's son Roy Norman McCord, who was then nine years old. "My brilliant father got out of the car with a .32 service revolver and they really let him have it. My dad had a peaked hat with a bill, dark blue suit, like the police."[25]

McCord's daughter Mary Johnson recalled that her father "walked into the hospital himself. Three of the bullets dropped out in the hospital room as they undressed him; these bullets had passed right through him. The doctors went in for the other three bullets."[26]

"I went to the hospital and saw him on the table," recalled Pat Lannon, a former police officer. "He was covered with blood. The doctors were working on him, and he looked up and said, 'Pat, can I have a cigarette?'"[27]

"Here's my first memory of *anything*," said McCord's daughter Colleen McCalla: "I was just two months short of four years old when dad was shot. . . . We drove to the hospital, and I was standing outside the door of my father's room. Then I remember this red bottle and a tube that ran down into his arm, which my father told me was *tomato juice*. Well, I never drank tomato juice until I was nineteen after that!"

Three decades later, McCord died of heart failure in Lancaster, California. "Now that's all ancient history, just a part of our growing up," said McCalla. "We used to go over the Bay Bridge when Alvin Karpis was at Alcatraz, and we'd wave at him."[28]

The uproar over the shooting of McCord proved to be only a minor setback for the gang. At Edna Murray's Edgecumbe Court apartment, Harry Sawyer and Fred Barker discussed a delay in the timing of the Bremer kidnapping: "The shooting of that radio man has made this town hot," Murray heard Sawyer say. "You'd better wait awhile."[29]

45   Threatening the 'Fat Boys'

The Edward Bremer Kidnapping
South Lexington Parkway and Goodrich Avenue, St. Paul

The Barker-Karpis gang was counting on Edward Bremer to follow his usual routine on January 17, 1934, so they could interrupt it. He did not disappoint them. After breakfast at his mansion at 92 North Mississippi River Boulevard, the banker started his Lincoln sedan, bundled his nine-year-old daughter, Betty, into the car, and drove the third-grader to the Summit School at 1150 Goodrich Avenue. Then Bremer began his drive to the Commercial State Bank at Washington and Sixth, braking for the stop sign at the corner of Lexington Parkway and Goodrich Avenue.[30]

Bremer's routine was so precise that students walking to Summit School along Goodrich could time their arrival for morning chapel by watching to see when his car turned onto their street.[31]

When Bremer stopped, Fred Barker and Harry Campbell blocked his car with their black sedan. In another car, Doc Barker, Alvin Karpis, and Volney Davis prevented Bremer's escape from behind. One man opened the front door of Bremer's sedan, stuck a gun in his stomach, and hissed: "Don't move or I'll kill you."

When Bremer began to struggle, the kidnappers bludgeoned him over the head with the butt of a revolver. Blood dripping over his eyes, Bremer attempted to block the closing of the car door with his legs. The kidnappers slammed the door anyway, severely injuring his knee. Forced down to the floor of his car, the banker thought there might still be hope when the gang was unable to start it. But "they continued to beat him over the head so furiously that he decided that he had best start the car, which he did with the starter button on the dash, which they were unable to locate," the FBI reported later.[32]

Veteran crime reporter Nate Bomberg, who covered the kidnapping, remembered how it shocked the ruling families of St. Paul. The abduction of William Hamm Jr. might have been excused as a one-time aberration, but after this second kidnapping, the city's wealthy families—many of whom had connections to the administration of President Franklin D. Roosevelt—demanded a crackdown before another millionaire businessman disappeared. "We had a lot of murders and gangster killings and kidnapping of minor

A reenactment of the January 1934 kidnapping of Edward Bremer at Lexington Parkway and Goodrich Avenue

hoodlums for ransom," recalled Bomberg. "Nobody paid any attention to it. . . . But when you started to pick on the fat boys, then people get alarmed. . . . When a fat boy or a rich man is threatened, he will get action."[33]

46   'A Very Desperate Undertaking'

Home of Go-Between Walter W. Magee
1295 Lincoln Avenue, St. Paul

The action began less than two hours after the gang seized Bremer when contractor Walter W. Magee received an unforgettable telephone call at his St. Paul office. "We've got your friend Bremer and if you are not damn careful, we'll get you too," the caller said. Magee was told to retrieve a ransom note left near the stairway at the office.[34]

"*You* are hereby *declared* in on a very *desperate* undertaking," said the note. "Don't try to cross us. . . . Police have never helped in such a spot, and wont this time either. You better take care of the *payoff first* and let *them do* the *detecting later*. Because the police usually butt in your friend isnt none too comfortable now so don't delay the payment." The payoff demands reflected Fred Goetz's criminal savvy: the $200,000 ransom was to be delivered in used five- and ten-dollar bills. ("*No new money—no consecutive numbers—large variety of issues*," the kidnappers warned.)

The Bremers were to place a personal advertisement ("We are ready Alice") in the *Minneapolis Tribune* to signal their ability to deliver the money. "Dont attempt to stall or outsmart us," read the note. "Dont try to bargain. Dont plead poverty we know how much they have in their banks. . . . Threats arent necessary—*you just do your part*—we *guarantee* to do ours."[35]

Magee notified the St. Paul police and the FBI, but the Barker-Karpis gang had again found a go-between with shadowy connections to the underworld. Magee—an old friend of Adolf Bremer—had risen from an apprentice bricklayer's helper during the construction of the Hotel St. Paul to found the Walter W. Magee Company. The FBI suspected that Magee had also enjoyed contacts with the underworld. A 1934 FBI investigative file claimed that after the Canadian-born Magee arrived in St. Paul in 1914, he had taken over the Tobin family saloon and after the passage of "prohibition, engaged in bootlegging on a large scale." In 1928, six trusted associates had served as pallbearers at the funeral of slain underworld leader Dan Hogan —among them was Magee. In short, concluded the FBI, Magee was "a rather shady character."[36]

As Magee scrambled to maintain contact with the kidnappers, it became clear that the gang had underestimated the firestorm that their abduction of Edward Bremer would ignite. President Roosevelt issued a formal statement deploring the kidnapping of the son of a friend. Governor Floyd B. Olson called the Bremer family to promise the aid of all Minnesota law enforcement agencies. J. Edgar Hoover announced that he was sending a special team of FBI agents. The American Legion offered tens of thousands of Legionnaires to help find their comrade. A thousand mail carriers were ordered to watch for suspicious activity on their routes.[37]

Within hours of Bremer's disappearance, the FBI had the first physical clue to his whereabouts: his blue Lincoln, its interior spattered with blood, was found one mile from St. Paul's Highland Park water tower on Snelling Avenue at Ford Parkway.[38]

47 Blood on the Steering Wheel

Bremer's Abandoned Automobile
1910 Edgecumbe Road, St. Paul

The kidnappers had discarded Bremer's Lincoln sedan here on Edgecumbe Road near the Highland Park golf course. An FBI report described what Walter Magee found in the car: "Bloodstains on the steering wheel, the gear shift lever, the doorsill, the back of the front seat and the floor of the car indicat[ing] . . . that a struggle had occurred." So that Adolf Bremer would not be alarmed, Magee quickly had the bloody Lincoln towed to his Third Street Garage. The FBI had to consider whether Bremer had already been killed. "I can't imagine what my mother felt when they found the car with the blood all over the inside," said Edward's daughter, Betty Bremer Johnson.[39]

Chief of police Tom Dahill confided to his Kidnap Detail supervisor, Tom Brown, his concern that the banker might already be dead. Curiously, the next three ransom notes contained samples of Bremer's handwriting—and Bremer's comment, "I suppose you are worrying about the blood in the car" —as if to reassure Dahill that the victim was still alive.[40]

Meanwhile, J. Edgar Hoover, who had read about the Bremer kidnapping in the Washington, D.C., newspapers, was not happy. He launched a scathing memo to Werner Hanni, the special agent in charge of the St. Paul FBI office: "It appears that it is necessary for me to rely upon the press for information concerning important cases being investigated by the Division under my supervision," Hoover wrote. "It is difficult for me to understand why you neglected, in a case of such significance as the present one, to fully advise me. . . . I must add that I am entirely dissatisfied with the manner in which you have handled this case."[41]

Hoover and the Justice Department were particularly obsessed with the intrusion of the news media into the Bremer case. Assistant attorney general Joseph Keenan confided in a memo that "we are experiencing difficulty in solving the Bremer kidnapping by reason of approximately one hundred newspapermen and photographers gathering in the City of St. Paul and literally pursuing agents of the Government, police and the prosecutor's office. . . . It is almost impossible to make any headway in the solution of the crime."[42]

48   'If That Cheese Moves, It's a Goner!'

The Edward G. Bremer Home
92 North Mississippi River Boulevard, St. Paul

"The telephones of all the relatives of the Bremer family have been tapped and are constantly under surveillance," reported an FBI memo. Indeed, FBI-monitored wiretaps were installed on the telephones at Walter Magee's home, at the Schmidt Brewing Company, and at the home of Edward's uncle, Otto Bremer, at 1344 Summit Avenue.[43]

But most of all, the FBI focused on Edward Bremer's home at 92 North Mississippi River Boulevard. "We had an FBI man living on our second floor

The Mississippi River Boulevard home of Edward Bremer, which the FBI wiretapped after the gang kidnapped the banker in 1934

throughout the time my father was kidnapped," recalled Betty Bremer Johnson. "I thought FBI agents were nice to have around! I thought it was a lark and the agents would play with me." Mike Malone, the Treasury Department agent who went undercover in Chicago to destroy Al Capone, virtually adopted the girl during the ordeal, and the FBI agents tried to amuse her. One night, Betty's grandfather brought some malodorous imported cheese to the house. "I can still see the FBI agent, Brennan, drawing his gun at it and saying: 'If that cheese moves, it's a goner!'" Johnson said.[44]

Although Isadore "Kid Cann" Blumenfeld and other local racketeers were investigated as possible suspects, Mel Harney of the Treasury Department's Alcoholic Beverage Unit in St. Paul guessed early on that "Bremer's kidnapping was not committed by any Twin City talent." Harney reasoned that both kidnapping victims, Hamm and Bremer, were influential and could command police attention, and "for that reason alone, it would indicate that outsiders have committed the crime. Mr. Harney believes that if they were local men they would not tackle families which would have at their disposal the entire police assistance of the Twin Cities."[45]

The day after the kidnapping, gangster Volney Davis took his girlfriend Edna Murray to a safe house, Harry Sawyer's Shoreview farm. "Boy, this town is hot; it's full of G-Men!" a worried Sawyer said to Davis. To reduce the possibility of capture, the gang sent three girlfriends—Murray, Paula Harmon, and Wynona Burdette—to Chicago. The men of the Barker-Karpis gang were forced to remain in St. Paul, even as the investigation intensified. After all, the gang still had Edward Bremer, and the Bremer family still had the ransom money.[46]

49   Delivery of the Bremer Ransom Note

The Home of Dr. Henry T. Nippert
706 Lincoln Avenue, St. Paul

Dr. Henry T. Nippert, the Bremer family's physician, was briefly awakened by a tinkling crash at 6:00 A.M. on January 20. A bottle had been thrown through the glass front door of his home. Although puzzled by the sound, the doctor drifted back to sleep. Then the telephone rang, and an impatient caller told the sixty-five-year-old physician to go downstairs. There, Nippert found the bottle, the shattered pieces of his plate-glass door, and a ransom note for go-between Walter Magee:

You must be proud of yourself by now. If Bremer dont get back his family has you to thank. Youve made it almost impossible but were going to give one more chance—the *last*. First of all *all coppers must be pulled* off. Second *the dough must be ready* . . . the *money must not be hot* as it *will be examined* before bremer is released. If Dahill is so hot to meet us, you can send him out with the dough. Well try to be ready for any trickery if atempted. This is positively our LAST attempt. DONT duck it.[47]

The gang enclosed a letter from Bremer to his wife, Emily ("Patz"), and daughter, Betty ("Hertzy"), reproduced in an FBI memo:

My dearest Patz and Hertzy:

Oh, I've been thinking of you so much, day and night. I'm sure you could nearly feel it. I never knew I could miss you two so much. I can just see you waiting for me to come back—my dears—Dont loose courage, I'll be back with you before long & we'll never be apart again. I'm at a loss what to say—if I could only express my feeling you could understand.

Now my dears pray hard and dont loose courage. I'll be holding you both in my arms before long and that is all that I want in this world is both of you—

Your own, Daddy.[48]

To his sister Lill Bremer he wrote:

I'm sure you'll do just as I ask you to. We always did understand each other. Its a living hell here and the time I've been here seems like ages. Please do your part and I'm assured I'll be home soon.[49]

Bremer was detained in Bensonville, Illinois, blindfolded and bound. The gang stripped him of his rosary, so Bremer said the rosary on his fingers throughout his captivity. "I would be so cramped that they would have to hold me when they bound me up at night to take me to the toilet when I went to bed," Bremer told the FBI. "I couldn't get my limbs apart."[50]

The gangsters fed the banker badly cooked oatmeal, chili, chop suey, and fried chicken, with desserts of strawberry shortcake and apple pie. The FBI reported later that "all of his food was too well seasoned, indicating to him that a man, who was inexperienced, did the seasoning."[51]

The gang quizzed Bremer about how much money was kept in his Commercial State Bank vault; he claimed there was never more than $50,000 in the bank at one time.[52]

On January 25, the Bremer family received another ransom note, this one stuffed inside a coffee can that had been left for the family at the home of John Miller, a pool hall proprietor.

"You better stop listening to those assholes this time do what *we* tell you," said this latest note. "The money *must be delivered tonight*. With all the coniving *we still got the boy. We* keep our word. Either *you* get him back tonight or the coppers bring him back *stiff.*" The Bremer family was to pick up a black zippered bag from St. Paul's Union Bus Depot. The ransom note ended with these words: "Its up to you—you *get* the boy *alive* or *dead.*"[53]

The bag contained yet another note with further instructions. On January 27, when Karpis learned that the Bremers were taking steps to obtain the money to pay the ransom, he prepared for the final act of the kidnapping. Wearing a dark wool jacket, high-topped leather boots, and a wool cap pulled down over his eyes, Karpis visited a St. Paul department store and bought some $3.12 worth of supplies—three flashlights, with bulbs and batteries.[54]

The gang fed Bremer a final dinner of steak, mashed potatoes, and peas. "Eat hearty," they told him, "because this is going to be your last meal here." Throughout his captivity, Bremer had listened to and observed his captors. Interviewed later by the FBI, Bremer recalled the sounds of dogs barking and children playing nearby, the design on the gang's plates, the noise of a coal stove being filled, and even the look of the handle on the toilet: broken enamel over a metal screw. Most importantly, Bremer remembered every detail of the wallpaper pattern adorning the bedroom where he was imprisoned. It was a simple visual clue that—after the FBI sifted through 60,000 wallpaper patterns—would link several of the gangsters to the kidnapping and send them to prison for life.[55]

The banker's wife, Emily Elizabeth Bremer, and their daughter, Betty

50 'Boys, I Am Counting on Your Honor'

The Home of Adolf Bremer Sr.
855 West Seventh Street, St. Paul

The $200,000 Bremer ransom was taken from a bank vault to the West Seventh Street home of Edward's father, Adolf. It was the same house where the newly freed Bremer would later be debriefed by officer Tom Brown after he was released by his kidnappers. The Bremer family later built a safety tunnel from Adolf Bremer's home to the basement of the Schmidt Brewery's Rathskeller bar.[56]

On February 6, 1934, Walter Magee drove a Ford sedan from the parking lot behind the Jacob Schmidt Brewing Company to the corner of St. Clair Avenue and West Seventh Street, where Adolph Bremer Jr., Edward's brother, helped him transfer the ransom money, packed in two suit boxes, to his car. Magee drove on to 969 University Avenue—the intersection of Chatsworth and University—where the gang said he would find a black Chevrolet coupe with Shell Oil signs on the door. Placing the $200,000 inside, Magee followed the instructions in a typewritten note ordering him to drive the Chevrolet to Farmington, Minnesota, and follow the Rochester bus until he saw five flashes of light.

Five miles outside of Zumbrota, at about 11:15 P.M., Magee saw the red lights on the left side of the road; behind him, a car flashed its lights five times. Magee left the ransom on the road, with a note from Adolf Bremer: "I have done my part and kept my word 100 percent, as I said I would. This money is not marked and you have the full amount asked for. Now, boys, I am counting on your honor."[57]

After twenty-one days in captivity, Bremer was released near Rochester, Minnesota, on February 7. His body still sore from being bound, he took a train and a bus to St. Paul, and walked onto the back porch of his father's home just after midnight. He was an apparition to his surprised sister Louise and to the FBI agent on guard. "My father had gone to bed, and suddenly I heard someone at the door," recalled Louise Benz, still moved by the memory nearly sixty years later. "And there was Ed. I had to look twice as he had quite a beard at that time. We brought him inside—and he was scared to death. . . . He was so shaken and . . . frightened."[58]

"When my dad returned he was ashen, very thin," recalled Betty Bremer Johnson. "We tried not to talk about [the kidnapping]. It made dad nervous and his knuckles would whiten."[59]

The FBI interviewed Bremer at his home on February 11 but found him a terrified and sometimes frustrating source of information. "I mentioned the duty which he owed the Government and to the American people," wrote one FBI agent, "whereupon, he remarked: 'To hell with the duty.'" The kidnappers had threatened to kill Bremer's daughter if he talked to the FBI.[60]

The bureau was unmoved by Bremer's distress. After speaking to both kidnap victims—William Hamm Jr. and Bremer—an FBI inspector wrote in May 1934 to J. Edgar Hoover that "I can readily understand why it is called 'kid'naping."[61]

Magee returned with FBI agents to Zumbrota, where they found the three flashlights and a pocket lantern purchased by Alvin Karpis. The bureau's nationwide investigation was astonishingly detailed. Ten agents in New York alone searched through thousands of wallpaper samples to help identify the Bensonville hideout. Others searched for the Sears Roebuck store that sold the Barker-Karpis gang its red signal light. Agents even searched for the store where the gang bought the underwear given to Bremer as his final change of clothes.[62]

The bureau's breakthrough came on February 10, when a Wisconsin farmer discovered four gasoline cans and a tin funnel that had been used to refill the gang's car. The Washington, D.C., crime laboratory identified a fingerprint from a gas can as Doc Barker's. Two days later, an underworld informant told the FBI that the Bremer kidnapping involved "two brothers by the name of Dick and Freddy, who have an ugly old woman with them who poses as their mother"—a passable description of the Barker-Karpis gang. The informant said that the FBI telephones in St. Paul were not secure, warning "that at St. Paul everything is under the control of the syndicate and that it would probably be very unwise to use either the telephone or telegraph between Washington and St. Paul," the FBI noted.[63]

By then policeman Tom Brown, no longer head of the Kidnap Detail and under investigation by the FBI for leaks to the underworld, did not have access to information that could benefit the Barker-Karpis gang. For the first time since 1931, the gang had no inside contact in the police department to warn them of FBI and police raids. The FBI learned that Fred Goetz had revealed that "Harry Sawyer wanted to give Tom Brown his full split out of the Bremer Case, but some of them objected because he wasn't doing them any good, because the Federal officials wouldn't let him sit in on the conferences. And it was finally decided to give him $5,000."[64]

J. Edgar Hoover's public fury was aimed at Ma Barker, but FBI files make clear that it was Goetz, not Doc's and Fred's mother, who directed the Hamm and Bremer kidnappings. Unfortunately, Goetz loved to brag in Chicago pubs about his exploits back in the Twin Cities—regaling his drinking partners with hints about where the Bremer ransom was hidden and the names of his collaborators. On March 20, 1934, the thirty-nine-year-old Goetz walked out of the Minerva Cafe in Cicero, Illinois, and, in the words of FBI agent Melvin Purvis, was "shot directly in the face from close range with a shotgun, which caused considerable disfigurement, and any photographs will very likely be of doubtful value." Agents had to identify the body from the fingerprints.[65]

Newspapers guessed that Goetz was slain by the Barker-Karpis gang in a fight over the Bremer ransom money. Louis "Lefty Louie" Campagna, a Capone syndicate associate of Goetz, told friends that he was killed because "the St. Paul outfit put him on the spot." In his autobiography, Karpis insisted that the murder was a syndicate hit, although he acknowledged that Goetz had been "getting kind of gabby" and could easily have led the FBI to the Barkers. Irene Goetz told the FBI that immediately after her husband's death, Fred Barker heard her speaking of him and muttered, "To hell with George."[66]

Two days after Goetz was shot, the U.S. attorney general publicly

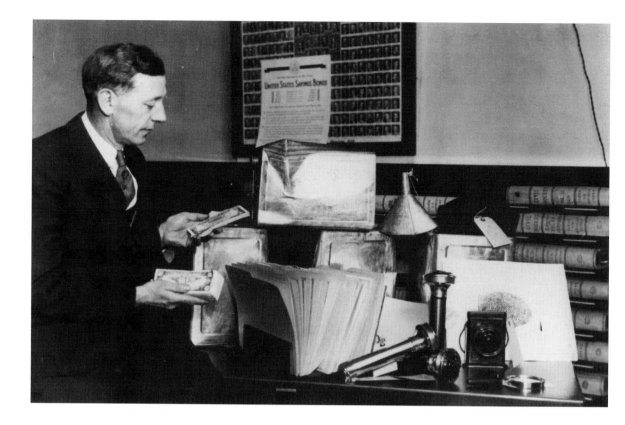

identified Karpis as one of the men who kidnapped Ed Bremer. The next day, the gang retrieved about $100,000 of the ransom money from Goetz's hiding place—wrapped in brown paper in the garage of Irene Goetz's relatives in Wilmington, Illinois—and distributed it to gang members.[67]

By then the gang had begun to splinter. The FBI later learned from Karpis, who had always been fond of Ma Barker, that "towards the last months of her life Kate Barker appeared to be endeavoring to cause trouble between the various members of the gangs, in that she would make statements to one member of the gang derogatory to the other, and that he believed that she was going insane from worry."[68]

In her confession, Edna Murray told the FBI that in July 1934, "I overheard a heated argument between Fred Barker and Volney [Davis]. From their conversation, I believed they were arguing about something that Fred's mother was supposed to have said about Volney, which Volney thought was a lie. I overheard him say, 'I am a man and I cover all the ground I stand on. I wouldn't bring my mother into an argument, you would be a _____ if you didn't hold up for your mother, but I still say she is a damn liar.'" Davis decided to leave the gang to avoid the friction caused by Ma Barker.[69]

While the gang members squabbled, the forensic evidence that would send them to prison was being collected by the FBI crime laboratory. "The Bremer case provided the ultimate justification of a federal police corps which transcends state lines and the rivalries and inefficiencies of local jurisdictions," wrote FBI agent Melvin Purvis.[70]

Many of the clues led directly to the Shoreview farm of Harry Sawyer, the Green Lantern operator, who had chosen Bremer as the gang's second kidnapping victim.

51 Secret Tunnels, Forgotten Dynamite, and Buried Bullets

Harry "Dutch" Sawyer's Farm
305 Snail Lake Road, Shoreview

During Harry Sawyer's trial for kidnapping Edward Bremer, government witness Edna Murray was asked for the name of the first person whom she saw when she and Volney Davis, Paula Harmon, and Fred Barker drove back to Minnesota in August 1933. "Harry Sawyer," answered Murray. "We saw him at this country home, about four or five miles from downtown St. Paul." Sawyer's Shoreview farm operated as a rustic hideout, overnight haven, message drop, and conference center for many of the most wanted gangsters of the 1930s.[71]

FBI files suggest that Sawyer's farm was purchased, in part, with money stolen on April 4, 1933, from the First National Bank of Fairbury, Nebraska. The Fairbury culprits—the Barker brothers and Alvin Karpis, along with Frank Nash, Jess Doyle, and Verne Miller—drove off with more than $151,000. "The money obtained in this robbery was turned over to Harry Sawyer to exchange for cool money," the FBI learned from Beth Green of the Dillinger gang. "Sawyer kept a much larger percentage than they planned for him to take and shortly afterwards bought a farm near the Twin Cities, and the boys frequently laughed about having bought this farm for Sawyer."[72]

Harry Sawyer, then proprietor of the Green Lantern saloon, purchased the ten-acre farm in 1933. He lived there with his wife, Gladys, and Francine, the five-year-old they hoped to adopt, until April 1934, when the Sawyers fled an FBI dragnet. As each of the Barker-Karpis gang's girlfriends was captured and interrogated, the FBI got a fuller picture of the role the farm played for the underworld. The guest list included bank robbers Frank Nash, Alvin Karpis, Fred and Doc Barker, Harry Campbell, Volney Davis, Jack Peifer, and William Weaver, along with Myrtle Eaton, Paula Harmon, and Edna Murray.[73]

The farm offered the mobsters two benefits: advance warnings of police raids and a location remote enough to frustrate surveillance. Immediately after the March 31, 1934, shootout between John Dillinger and St. Paul FBI agents, John "Three Fingered Jack" Hamilton hid at the farm. Hamilton was able to escape when a St. Paul policeman telephoned Sawyer, warning that his fellow officers were about to arrest the Dillinger gang member.[74]

"Dapper Dan" Hogan had succeeded in the 1920s by serving criminals; his protégé, Harry Sawyer, was the fulcrum between gangsters and corrupt policemen in the 1930s. Tom Brown was a frequent visitor to the farm, and other officers often dropped by to discuss the FBI's activities with Sawyer. Finally the FBI struck back, raiding the farm on July 26, 1934, and then again on September 7, 1934. The September raid netted three of Sawyer's helpers—housekeeper Marie McCarthy, handyman Frank Kirwin, and caretaker William Gray—who were wanted for harboring Dillinger gang member Homer Van Meter at a Leech Lake, Minnesota, resort.[75]

When Sawyer discovered that FBI agents were hunting him for questioning in the Bremer case, he fled the farm and met Karpis in Cleveland to retrieve his share of the ransom money. It was a testament to Sawyer's criminal standing that he was entrusted by the gang to launder the remaining $100,000 of the Bremer ransom money for "clean" bills and Cuban gold in Miami.[76]

On September 5, 1934, Gladys Sawyer and two of the farm's most frequent visitors—Wynona Burdette and Paula Harmon—got tipsy in a Cleveland hotel and were arrested by police on drunk and disorderly charges. The trio was nearly freed, but Sawyer's little girl innocently blurted out her mother's identity. The three wanted women were held in the Chicago FBI office and persuaded to provide lengthy confessions that exposed the inner workings of the Barker-Karpis gang. It was the breakthrough the FBI had been searching for.[77]

As the decades passed, the farm disgorged evidence of its gangland legacy. A new tenant, sausage company employee Fred Kohrt, was digging in the garden in May 1936 when he unearthed machine gun cartridges and sticks of dynamite buried in two-gallon pails. His six-year-old son found a pail of .45-caliber machine gun bullets in a nearby grove of trees.[78]

Virginia and Paul Comstock discovered two tunnels in the basement after they moved into the farmhouse in 1963. One tunnel crossed under Highway 49 (Hodgson Road), and the other led behind the barn. "The cement covering the tunnel was so honeycombed, when you tapped on it, it was clearly hollow," recalled Paul Comstock. "I went down with a pickax and broke through that cement. It was only two inches thick and it had been filled out with sand. The tunnel went straight down four or five feet to get under the footings and then veered out toward Hodgson Road."[79]

After purchasing the Sawyer farm in 1985, Dirk Boardsen, a residential contractor, was gutting the upstairs of the farmhouse when he made an odd discovery. "I was doing the upstairs bedroom, insulating the knee walls," he said. He was reaching down in the floor and discovered two pairs of prescription bifocal eyeglasses from the 1930s or 1940s. A few years later, he found three more pairs in the ceiling. "I don't know why they would have hid eyeglasses in the ceiling," Boardsen said, "unless the glasses were from the guys they killed."[80]

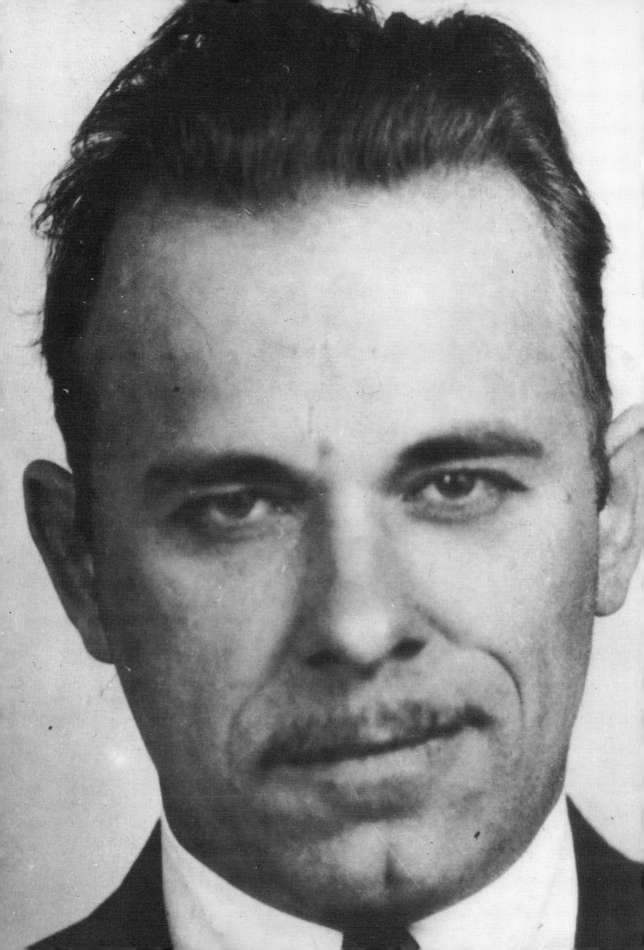

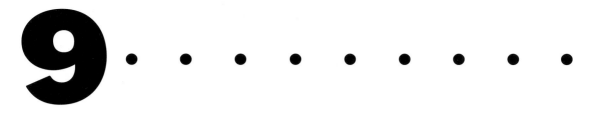

9

JOHN DILLINGER SLEPT HERE

Bank robber John Dillinger; FBI Director J. Edgar Hoover, aiming a submachine gun

52 A Dillinger Mob Reunion

Dillinger's Hideout at the Santa Monica Apartments
3252 South Girard Avenue, Minneapolis

The habits of the couple living in apartment 106 at the Santa Monica Apartments in Minneapolis were strange, all right. It wasn't just how Mrs. Olson paid the fifty-dollar advance deposit on the apartment from a roll of dollar bills. More sinister were the shades in the Olsons' apartment: janitor Silas Lancaster told the FBI that after the Olsons moved in on March 5, 1934, he found the shades wired shut to prevent any light from escaping outside.[1]

But then, the Olsons had good reason to be wary of daylight. Irvin Olson was actually outlaw John Dillinger, then evading a nationwide manhunt after his escape from the Lake County Jail in Crown Point, Indiana.

The thirty-one-year-old Dillinger, held on charges of murdering a police officer during his robbery of $20,000 from the First National Bank of East Chicago, Indiana, had bluffed his way out of the "escape-proof" Crown Point jail on March 3, 1934, with a fake gun he made with wood from a washboard, razor blades, and black shoe polish.[2]

Mrs. Olson was really Evelyn "Billie" Frechette, a twenty-six-year-old Wisconsinite raised on a Menominee Indian reservation, who had fallen in love with Dillinger when she met him in a Chicago nightclub in November 1933. FBI files noted Frechette's "use of a great deal of profanity," describing her as "of the 'hard-boiled' gangster moll type of woman . . . the thrill-seeking type."[3]

When Dillinger met Evelyn, he treated her "like a lady," though his dancing was terrible, she said later: "I didn't know he had been locked up in a prison for years and didn't have a chance to dance. We stepped all over each other's toes, but he said he liked to dance with me." Dillinger confessed to Evelyn, then working variously as a waitress, saleswoman, and nanny, the larcenous nature of his livelihood. The men accompanying them to Minnesota were more than friends, Dillinger admitted. They were thieves, bank robbers, and killers—the Dillinger gang. "What did Dillinger tell you his gang did for a living?" a federal prosecutor asked Frechette during her trial for harboring Dillinger. "Robbing banks, I suppose," she replied.[4]

After his May 1933 parole from Indiana State Prison in Michigan City, Dillinger had launched a career that left at least twelve men dead and at least seven wounded. His violent "withdrawal" of $500,000 from numerous banks resulted in the conviction of twenty-seven people for aiding the Dillinger gang and inspired J. Edgar Hoover to dub him "Public Enemy Number One."

The nation's most famous fugitive had picked up Frechette in Chicago on

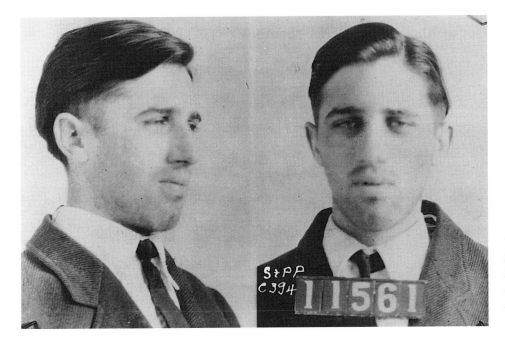

Train robber Homer Van Meter, Dillinger's partner after meeting in an Indiana prison

March 4, 1934, and reunited with gang members Lester "Babyface Nelson" Gillis and John Hamilton. Dillinger drove his partners to the cities that boasted the safest haven in America for mobsters—St. Paul and Minneapolis. By stealing a car from an Indiana sheriff and driving it across state lines to Chicago (thus violating the National Motor Vehicle Theft Act), Dillinger gave the FBI its opportunity to launch a manhunt for his gang. His case was assigned the FBI designation JODIL.[5]

At the Santa Monica Apartments in south Minneapolis, Dillinger hosted a reunion of his gang, and they began plotting bank heists in Iowa and South Dakota. Like Dillinger, who started out as a machinist in Indianapolis, most of the gang gathered there had abandoned legal employment during the Depression, concluding that steady but slow bank deposits were less rewarding than a series of quick withdrawals. Dillinger had been forced to re-create his gang because his original partners—Harry Pierpont, Russell Clark, and Charles Makley—had been jailed in Tucson, Arizona, in early 1934.[6]

Closest to Dillinger was train robber Homer Van Meter, a former waiter from Fort Wayne, Indiana, who had befriended the bank robber while both were serving time in Indiana State Reformatory at Pendleton and the state prison at Michigan City. The twenty-nine-year-old Van Meter was a slender (just over 130 pounds and 5 feet, 10 inches tall), blue-eyed recluse with a scar in the middle of his forehead and "Hope" tattooed on his right forearm.[7]

"Homer Van Meter was more or less a lone wolf," recalled Bernice Clark, wife of Dillinger gang member Russell Clark. "He kept to himself as much as possible." Although Van Meter had a girlfriend, Clark said that "Van was afraid of women—I mean he figured that most of them couldn't be trusted. And I guess he was right. If he had just stuck to that idea maybe he wouldn't have got killed the way he did." An FBI informant who had eavesdropped on the gang recalled, "Van Meter seemed to dominate over Dillinger," who "would ask the advice of Van Meter about different things."[8]

Harry Eugene "Eddie" Green, bank-robbery scout for Dillinger

Of special value to Dillinger was Harry Eugene "Eddie" Green, a St. Paul iron worker who served six months in a Milwaukee workhouse for grand larceny and a state prison term in St. Cloud and Stillwater in 1922 for robbing a cashier of a $2,000 payroll. While he was in St. Cloud, Green was repeatedly locked in solitary confinement for a variety of infractions, including striking an inmate during dinner and causing a disturbance when he returned from chapel "imitating the ladies singing." Describing Green's temperament as "mercurial," the St. Cloud physician's report said that "this is the type with criminal tendencies, selfish, impulsive and hard to manage."[9]

"They were two of the most unruly prisoners we have had any dealing with," said the chief of the Des Moines, Iowa, police, who arrested Green and a companion in 1922 on a charge of grand larceny. "They said they would return and get revenge. I informed them that I would be here when they came. . . . Unless they have changed their attitude wonderfully they would be a menace to society."[10]

Green was born in Pueblo, Colorado; his father died when he was just three. "His mother is a good woman," said Ramsey County judge J. B. Sanborn, "but the rest of the family prefer to live outside of the law." Green became a "jug marker"—a scout who evaluated banks as robbery targets for Dillinger and Babyface Nelson. "You've got to case a jug," advised bank robber Eddie Bentz, a contemporary of Green. "It's a lot like playing solitaire. You drive past the bank a few times and size up the surroundings, whether there are good getaway streets, whether the bank's got a squawker on the outside, whether there's a traffic cop on the corner. . . . Maybe you meet the bank manager. . . . maybe you'll throw out a few hints that you've heard the bank wasn't too solid, and half the time the guy will take you on a personal tour of inspection to show you what a swell lay-out he's got."[11]

Rounding out the Dillinger gang was a quiet but hot-tempered Michigan carpenter named John Hamilton, who received a twenty-five-year prison term for robbing an Indiana gas station. Hamilton was nicknamed "Three Fingered Jack," a reference to his having lost the index and middle fingers on his right hand. Family members attributed the missing digits variously to a factory accident or to an angry girlfriend with a butcher knife. Hamilton owed Dillinger and Van Meter for enabling him to escape from the Indiana State Prison in Michigan City on September 26, 1933, via revolvers hidden in barrels of thread. In turn, Hamilton had proven his worth by helping Dillinger take $74,728 from the Central National Bank of Greencastle, Indiana, and $27,789 from the American Bank and Trust Company of Racine, Wisconsin. Hamilton was also responsible for the brutal murder of Chicago police detective William T. Shanley, who was shot to death in Chicago on December 14, 1933, after he investigated reports that Hamilton's green auto had been seen in an Illinois garage.[12]

Apparently, Hamilton had one major flaw as a bank robber: "Somebody forgot to give John a memory," recalled Bernice Clark. "He'd forget addresses of the places we were staying and he'd even forget the aliases he was using. He'd stumble into trouble and stumble out of it somehow."[13]

Finally, there was jewel thief Lester Gillis, a veteran of Al Capone's syndicate. Just under 5 feet, 5 inches, and weighing barely 133 pounds, he preferred to be called "Big George" but was best known by the nickname he despised: Babyface Nelson. Famous for a near-psychopathic love of machine guns, Nelson was considered a reckless killer.[14]

Reportedly consumed with jealousy over Dillinger's fame, Nelson applied to Homer Van Meter to offer his services to the Dillinger gang. From the day he joined the gang, Nelson proved to be a magnet for violence. On March 4, 1934, a thirty-five-year-old paint salesman named Theodore Kidder had a streetside altercation involving a Hudson sedan at the intersection of Lake Street and Chicago Avenue in Minneapolis. In the Hudson was Nelson and his partner John Paul Chase, who followed the unsuspecting Kidder to his St. Louis Park home. There, as Kidder's wife watched, Nelson stepped out of the car and fired several .32-caliber bullets, killing Kidder. Police were able to identify the shooter's 1934 California license plate, which, according to the FBI, "was traced to James Rogers, the alias used by Gillis [Nelson] in purchasing the Hudson sedan." Not until 1941, when Nelson's partner Joseph "Fatso" Negri talked about his underworld adventures, was an inside account of Kidder's murder released—although Negri mistakenly believed the murder occurred at the scene of the car accident. Nelson had told him, "I and two or three of the boys were driving . . . in Minneapolis . . . and we happened to cut in ahead of another car. The driver, one of those fresh guys, cut right back in front of us. He stopped his car, got out and came back toward us and said to me: 'What the h[ell] do you mean? Get out of that car and I'll slap your face for you.' He had taken a step or two toward us when I leveled on him and hit him. Then we had to tear out of that place."[15]

Uniting the gang was John Dillinger himself, the baseball-loving son of an Indianapolis grocer. Dillinger graduated from car thievery, mugging, and

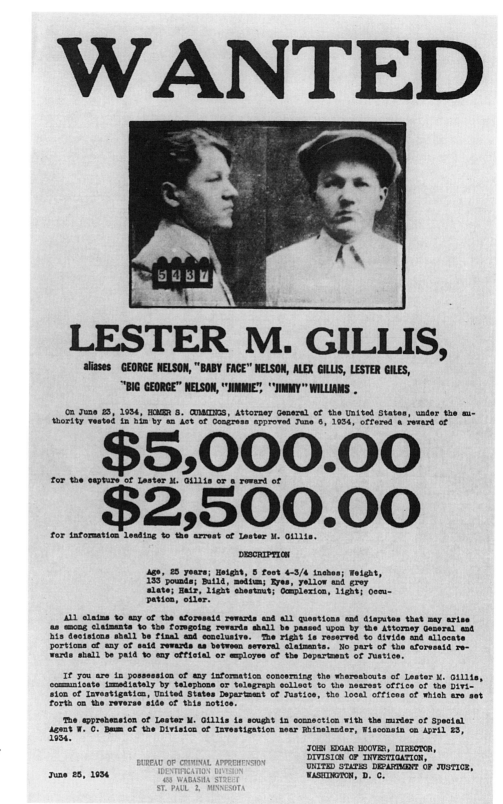

WANTED

LESTER M. GILLIS,

aliases GEORGE NELSON, "BABY FACE" NELSON, ALEX GILLIS, LESTER GILES,
"BIG GEORGE" NELSON, "JIMMIE", "JIMMY" WILLIAMS .

On June 23, 1934, HOMER S. CUMMINGS, Attorney General of the United States, under the authority vested in him by an Act of Congress approved June 6, 1934, offered a reward of

$5,000.00

for the capture of Lester M. Gillis or a reward of

$2,500.00

for information leading to the arrest of Lester M. Gillis.

DESCRIPTION

Age, 25 years; Height, 5 feet 4-3/4 inches; Weight, 133 pounds; Build, medium; Eyes, yellow and grey slate; Hair, light chestnut; Complexion, light; Occupation, oiler.

All claims to any of the aforesaid rewards and all questions and disputes that may arise as among claimants to the foregoing rewards shall be passed upon by the Attorney General and his decisions shall be final and conclusive. The right is reserved to divide and allocate portions of any of said rewards as between several claimants. No part of the aforesaid rewards shall be paid to any official or employee of the Department of Justice.

If you are in possession of any information concerning the whereabouts of Lester M. Gillis, communicate immediately by telephone or telegraph collect to the nearest office of the Division of Investigation, United States Department of Justice, the local offices of which are set forth on the reverse side of this notice.

The apprehension of Lester M. Gillis is sought in connection with the murder of Special Agent W. C. Baum of the Division of Investigation near Rhinelander, Wisconsin on April 23, 1934.

June 25, 1934

BUREAU OF CRIMINAL APPREHENSION
IDENTIFICATION DIVISION
455 WABASHA STREET
ST. PAUL 2, MINNESOTA

JOHN EDGAR HOOVER, DIRECTOR,
DIVISION OF INVESTIGATION,
UNITED STATES DEPARTMENT OF JUSTICE,
WASHINGTON, D. C.

Wanted poster for Lester "Babyface Nelson" Gillis

stealing coal from railroads to become, in the words of *True Detective* magazine, "a by-word in every country of the civilized world. . . . His trail across the black vault of national notoriety has been as spectacular as the rocket-like course of a comet. A red comet!"[16]

Dillinger was embittered by a severe ten- to twenty-year sentence, which he served in the Pendleton, Indiana, reformatory and the state penitentiary in Michigan City, for mugging an elderly grocer. During his imprisonment, his wife, Beryl, filed for divorce. His stepmother died less than an hour before his May 1933 release from a nine-year stretch in prison. Just three weeks after his release, Dillinger robbed a New Carlisle, Ohio, bank of $10,600. During the next nine months, he was believed to have robbed nearly a dozen banks in Indiana, Illinois, Wisconsin, Ohio, and Michigan; escaped a police ambush in Chicago; and raided police stations in Auburn and Peru, Indiana, to acquire bulletproof vests and weapons. By March 1934, Dillinger found himself hiding in Minneapolis—hunted by county sheriffs, state and city police, the FBI, the National Guard, and a forty-member Chicago police "Dillinger Squad."[17]

Evelyn Frechette later told *Startling Detective Adventures* magazine how the gang's stay in the Santa Monica Apartments was cut short: "[John] Hamilton was taking off his coat one evening when he pulled his pistol from its shoulder holster," said Frechette. "The weapon clattered to the floor and discharged. We packed our clothes and were on our way in less than ten minutes."[18] Dillinger next surfaced at the Lincoln Court Apartments in St. Paul. It turned out to be among the most dangerous moves of his career.

53 John Dillinger's Safehouse

The Charlou and Josephine Apartments
3300 and 3310 South Fremont Avenue, Minneapolis

When the FBI raided the Charlou Apartments hideout of the Dillinger gang at 3300 Fremont Avenue in Minneapolis in April 1934, the usually grim bureau offered a glimpse of Justice Department humor. In tallying the armaments they found, the agents counted "one bullet-proof vest, one loaded 50-round machine-gun, one Thompson sub-machine gun and one .45 automatic pistol and one high-powered rifle (nice people)."[19]

Dillinger lieutenant Eddie Green, masquerading as shoe salesman Theodore J. Randall, had rented apartment 207 in the Charlou Apartments in September 1933 to store this weaponry.[20]

Homer Van Meter, newly paroled from Indiana State Prison, lived in the adjacent 3310 Fremont building—the Josephine Apartments. Van Meter stayed in apartment 201 with his twenty-year-old girlfriend Marie Conforti from January to early February 1934. Van Meter, posing as John L. Ober, told Marie that his real name was Ted Ancker, giving her an alias for his alias. "He never told me what his business was," Conforti later told the FBI. "He never told me the address of any business he was connected with, and never introduced me to any of his friends."[21]

From these Fremont Avenue apartment buildings, members of the Dillinger gang executed their March 6 robbery of $49,500 from the Security National Bank of Sioux Falls, South Dakota. On March 13 the gang took $52,000 from the First National Bank of Mason City, Iowa, where they held nearly fifty customers and employees at gunpoint, leaving two innocent by-standers wounded. A telegram from the FBI's Melvin Purvis to director J. Edgar Hoover reveals that the bureau learned from informant Bernice Clark of the Dillinger gang that the "mob now has plenty of money because of Mason City and Sioux Falls Bank jobs[,] also some of mob shot up a little in these jobs but not serious enough for medical attention."[22]

What inspired the gang's girlfriends to risk their lives to follow these armed men from state to state, hunted by police and deceived by their lovers? Conforti, a former department store clerk from Chicago, recalled how Van Meter asked her to leave Illinois and accompany the gang: "Van Meter told me at this time that he was glad to see me again and asked me if I would go with him. At first I was undecided, but later agreed to do so, inasmuch as I did not have any money, and further I did not care to hang around the house."[23]

In other cases, the gangsters may have used force. FBI agents learned from Beth Green, Eddie Green's girlfriend, that Myrtle Eaton, girlfriend of Barker-Karpis gang member William Weaver, "disliked Bill very much, but that Bill would on occasions kidnap her or force her to accompany him on trips at the point of a gun. . . . Myrtle Eaton would welcome Bill Weaver's apprehension [by the FBI] because she is desperately in fear of him."[24]

The lifestyle of the Dillinger gang girlfriends was hardly more glamorous than the tedious jobs they left behind. J. Edgar Hoover publicly reviled them, referring to them in his 1938 book, *Persons in Hiding*, as "dirty, filthy, diseased women." The mobsters often left their women infected with vene-real disease (the FBI files are filled with references to treatment at Twin Cities hospitals for "abdominal and female trouble"), pregnant, battered, and betrayed.[25]

At times, gang members were more frightened of having their illicit af-fairs exposed than of being apprehended by the police. Bank robber Tommy Gannon confessed to FBI agents that he hung out at a root beer stand on Rice Street in St. Paul because he was attracted to a woman there. Having blurted out this admission, Gannon suddenly begged the FBI not to mention it "because it might cause some trouble if his wife found out."[26]

In the end, both Beth Green and Jean Delaney saw their lovers gunned down before their eyes; virtually all of the other Dillinger women were arrested, convicted, and imprisoned. Yet Frechette wrote, "I think I was happier with John Dillinger while we were living in the Twin Cities than I ever was before or since. It wasn't because we didn't have plenty to worry about, because we did. We went out a lot, but it didn't seem the same because— well, we all were getting the jitters. All except John. He was just a little more careful."[27]

The most likely place to spot a Dillinger gang member was not in a bank vault but in a Twin Cities movie house. Green told FBI agents that Dillinger "was crazy about motion pictures." He took in the film *Joe Palooka* in St. Paul and *Fashions of 1933* at a Minneapolis theater. Dillinger warned Eddie Green not to take Beth to see *Fashions* because it would put bad ideas into her head. Frechette wrote that Dillinger's favorite movie was a cartoon, Walt Disney's *The Three Little Pigs*. Tommy Carroll went to the movies about three times a week, and Marie Conforti told FBI agents that Homer Van Meter was particularly fond of Eddie Cantor films.[28]

St. Paul residents were not distressed when they saw John Dillinger and his gang in a Grand Avenue movie theater or in a nightclub like the Boulevards of Paris. "As kids, we thought gangsters were like football players— guys like Dillinger were *heroes* to us," said Charlie Reiter, a former police officer and Bureau of Criminal Apprehension executive. "Those gangsters were glamorized in the newspapers and the detective-story magazines. In those days, kids didn't have many people to admire—we had fighters, baseball players, and gangsters!"[29]

Reiter worked as a fry cook at Frank McCormick's Town Talk Sandwich Shop at 418 Wabasha in downtown St. Paul, a favorite spot for Homer Van Meter. "Three Fingered Jack" Hamilton hid in the Town Talk immediately after Dillinger's 1934 shootout in the Lincoln Court Apartments. "It was nothing in St. Paul to see John Dillinger's men in the Town Talk," said Reiter. "Van Meter would want the special center cut of the ham, the best. He'd tip me a quarter, which was an hour's wage!" As a boy, Reiter sold newspapers; he recalled gangsters who would "give you a quarter for a three-cent paper. They were great people as far as we were concerned!"[30]

Unlike the St. Paul citizens who romanticized the gangsters, the FBI considered Dillinger a "brutal thief and a cold-blooded murderer." He dismissed the threat of local police but viewed the FBI with respect born of fear. Dillinger "made the remark that he got a big kick out of filling station attendants asking him whether he had seen Dillinger," the FBI learned from an informant. He "expressed the utmost contempt for local police departments, calling them a 'lot of clucks,'" but admitted his fear of federal agents because they "had all the money they needed to keep up the search."[31]

On April 3, 1934, the FBI found the address of the Charlou Apartments on a fake driver's license in Beth Green's purse, but when detectives burst into the Charlou, the Dillinger gang was gone. Besides guns and ammunition, they had left behind a first aid kit (morphine, bandages, tape, and cat gut), and eleven notebooks filled with what the FBI called "get-away road charts, generally used in bank robberies."[32]

Those highway maps were vital to the success of Dillinger's vault-busting raids; he had taken to carrying an atlas with him to find the most suitable roads for high-speed getaways.[33]

54   Midnight Medicine

The Home of Dr. Nels Mortensen
2252 Fairmount Avenue, St. Paul

Just after midnight on March 14, 1934, St. Paul physician Nels Mortensen answered the doorbell at his Fairmount Avenue home and discovered four desperate men on his front steps. "I had no thought that these men were criminals or belonged to any gang or underworld group, until they were departing," said Dr. Mortensen in a statement later to authorities. "Then I caught sight of a machine gun under one of the men's coats."[34]

Wounded in the left shoulders by shots fired by a policeman during the Mason City bank job earlier in the day, Dillinger and John Hamilton had driven with Homer Van Meter to St. Paul, seeking emergency medical care. They decided to make an unannounced visit to Dr. Mortensen, an acquaintance of the Dillinger gang's driver, William Albert "Pat" Reilly.[35]

Born in Copenhagen, Denmark, in 1884, Mortensen was a 6-foot-tall war veteran with bushy gray hair. Far from being an underworld sawbones, he was a distinguished physician who had served as president of the state's Board of Health, as city health commissioner, and as a lieutenant colonel in the U.S. Army Reserve Medical Corps.[36]

The two robbers were escorted into the Mortensens' vestibule by Reilly, who was also a bartender at Harry Sawyer's Green Lantern saloon. Reilly was the official mascot and clubhouse boy for two teams, the local American Association baseball franchise and the Dillinger gang. A twenty-seven-year-old Irish American, he had been a petty gambler and bootlegger since 1928. Prison records described his florid face as "slightly pitted, slightly cleft chin, cut scar" and listed his bad habits: "smokes, drinks to excess, sex experience." Reilly "has for many years associated with underworld characters of the worst type," said a Leavenworth prison parole report. "He has never worked, except to sell alcohol. He has also at various times operated a soft drink parlor which has been a rendezvous for criminals and other under world characters." Although authorities admitted that Reilly himself was "not to be regarded as vicious," his association with the Dillinger gang led them to label him "a menace to society."[37]

In 1927 Reilly married into what would become a family trio of gun molls when he wed Helen "Babe" Delaney, the wisecracking sister of Delores Delaney (girlfriend of Alvin Karpis) and Jean Delaney (girlfriend of Tommy Carroll). Reilly's mother-in-law, also named Helen Delaney, was not happy about the marriage. ("She utterly hates Pat Reilly," the FBI noted.) FBI files recorded an incident in which the mother personally served divorce papers for her daughter against Reilly; when the thug drew a pistol on his mother-in-law, she swore at him, walked up, and wrenched the revolver out of his hands.[38]

Dr. Nels Mortensen, president of Minnesota's Board of Health, who tended John Dillinger's wounds

Reilly told Dr. Mortensen that Hamilton and Dillinger had been injured in a gunfight in Minneapolis. Dillinger stripped off his shirt and nearly fainted from the pain when Mortensen probed the wound. Because the doctor did not have his medical bag at home, he asked the quartet to visit his office during the next day. The men did not reappear, but FBI agents did—with a vengeance.[39]

When the FBI interrogated Beth Green, she revealed Mortensen's role in taking care of Dillinger. The FBI "invited" Mortensen, who claimed that he had been too frightened to report the Dillinger visit, to drop by the FBI office on April 20, 1934, for a chat. Mortensen had first come to the attention of the FBI in July 1933, when his name surfaced as a reference for Fred Barker, who rented the Barker-Karpis gang's hideout at 204 Vernon Street. A bottle of medicine for treating venereal disease that was found at 204 Vernon had been prescribed by Mortensen. He also admitted that he had received a contribution toward his campaign for Ramsey County coroner from underworld fixer Harry Sawyer and that he served as physician to both Sawyer and Pat Reilly. The FBI discovered that Alvin Karpis had used Mortensen as a reference when he leased an Illinois apartment in April 1933. Accordingly, the FBI placed the doctor's home under surveillance in the hope that Dillinger might return, but the bank robber had already gone underground on Lexington Parkway.[40]

"An example should be made of this physician," wrote a frustrated J. Edgar Hoover in April, when other FBI officials recommended leniency for the doctor, "particularly in view of his official status in the medical profession in St. Paul. . . . [Mortensen] should be publicly exposed and prosecuted for the action which he has indulged in." The bureau's desperation was reflected in an FBI official's comment that "Pat Reilly was the man to get, that frankly they had been informed that if they drug him in and knocked him in the head with something and waited until he came to and then started talking to him, that he would give them more information than anybody else possesses in the Twin Cities." When the bureau later arrested three Dillinger gang girlfriends at a Wisconsin resort, an FBI official privately advised special agent in charge Sam Hardy "not to give the girls anything to eat and not to let them sleep until they talked."[41]

The FBI knew that the U.S. attorney's office in St. Paul had declared "positively that they had no evidence" that Dr. Mortensen was aware of Dillinger's identity when he examined his wounds, and FBI officials privately admitted that "it would be hard to prove." Still, they recommended on April 24 that agents manufacture negative newspaper publicity against Mortensen through "a statement out of Washington blasting him," which "would no doubt ruin the doctor." One week later, the U.S. attorney general savaged Mortensen publicly: "Excuse me for getting so heated about it," Homer Cummings said to reporters, after he castigated "doctors and lawyers and political bosses [who were] co-operating with criminals."[42]

Mortensen died in 1971 at the age of eighty-seven, insisting to the last that he had no idea that his patients, the men with the poorly concealed machine guns, were public enemies.[43]

55   'I Am Not Going to Let These Cops in Here'
Shootout at the Lincoln Court Apartments
93 South Lexington Parkway, St. Paul

While his gunshot wounds were healing, John Dillinger moved with Evelyn Frechette on March 19, 1934, to the Lincoln Court Apartments, a block from gracious Grand Avenue. It was to be a brief but climactic stay.

Building owner Daisy Coffey noticed something odd about the couple, registered as Mr. and Mrs. Carl P. Hellman, shortly after they moved into apartment 303, and she reported them to the FBI's St. Paul office. "The Hellmans usually remained indoors and when they did go out, they used the rear entrance," the FBI reported. "They lowered their shades just after dusk each evening and kept them lowered until about 10:30 each morning. They

The Lincoln Court Apartments, site of Dillinger's March 1934 shootout with FBI agents and St. Paul police; (insets) Dillinger and his girlfriend Evelyn "Billie" Frechette

refused to allow the caretaker to enter the apartment on one occasion to replace a bathroom fixture, advising him that Mr. Hellman was bathing."[44]

Neighborhood boys also made a noteworthy discovery. "This Evelyn—she was an attractive woman," recalled Louis Schroth, then a fourteen-year-old living next to the Lincoln Court at 105 Lexington. He watched Frechette hang the wash on the clothesline behind her building. "She wore red shorts and a red halter [top] when she did the laundry. We kids in the neighborhood, we'd never *seen* women in shorts and halters before. So we'd whistle at Dillinger's girl from the distance."[45]

Dillinger wrote to his sister Audrey from St. Paul in March:

Dear Sis, I thought I would write you a few lines and let you know I am still perculating, Dont worry about me honey, for that wont help any, and besides I am having a lot of fun. I am sending Emmett my wooden gun and I want him to allways keep it. I see that Deputy Blunk says I had a real forty five[.] Thats just a lot of hooey to cover up because they dont like to admit that I locked eight deputys and a dozen trustys up with my wooden gun before I got my hands on the two machine guns and you should have seen their faces Ha! Ha! Ha! . . .

I got shot a week ago but I am all right now just a little sore I bane one tough sweed Ha! Ha! Well honey I guess I'll close for the time give my love to all and I hope I can see you soon. Lots of love from Johnnie.[46]

Bank robberies and jail escapes may have been thrilling for Dillinger, but Frechette's life as his girlfriend was a bore. She later described her role at the Lincoln Court as "chief cook and bottlewasher" for the Dillinger gang; she also did the grocery shopping and ironed Dillinger's clothes. Her only fun during the two weeks of hiding on Lexington was going to a St. Paul movie theater.[47]

Her dreary existence changed dramatically on March 30, 1934, when the FBI responded to the landlady's tip. For backup, the bureau contacted St. Paul police chief Thomas Dahill, who, admitting that "I have found that I can not trust all my men," sent Henry Cummings, a twenty-seven-year veteran of the force, to accompany the agents. The FBI threw up a ring of overnight surveillance around the Lincoln Court. Two women and a man—later identified as John Hamilton and sisters Bernice Clark and Pat Charrington—walked by without drawing undue attention.[48]

At 10:15 A.M. on March 31, Rufus Coulter, a thirty-one-year-old Tennessee-born law school graduate turned FBI agent, and detective Cummings knocked on the door of apartment 303. Agent Rosser Nalls, Coulter's partner, waited outside the building. Inside, Dillinger and Frechette were in bed, talking. When they heard the police knock, Frechette opened the door the few inches allowed by the chain lock. The agent and the police officer asked to speak with Carl Hellman. "Carl? Carl who?" asked Frechette, who had forgotten Dillinger's alias. "My God, I know I am not going to let these damn cops in here," she thought.

"He's just left and won't be back until this afternoon. Come back then," she improvised.

Cummings asked if she was Mrs. Hellman, and when she answered that she was, said, "We will talk to you."

"I'm not dressed. Come back this afternoon," Frechette said.

Cummings responded, "We'll wait until you dress."

Frechette agreed and closed the door, snapping the night latch closed, and turned to Dillinger, who said calmly, "Keep your shirt on. Grab some clothes, put something in a bag and let's get out of here."[49]

Nalls watched outside as a green Ford coupe stopped by the Lincoln Court; the driver, Homer Van Meter, walked inside toward Dillinger's apartment. Simultaneously, Coulter left Cummings alone to guard apartment 303 and ran downstairs to call for reinforcements. Moments after Coulter rejoined Cummings, Van Meter wandered into the hallway, glibly explaining to the lawmen that he was a soap salesman. Challenged to prove his identity, Van Meter led Coulter down the stairs to see his "soap samples." As they reached the first floor, Van Meter pulled out an automatic pistol. "You want it. Here it is," yelled Van Meter, opening fire. Coulter hurled himself through the outside door, drew his gun, and returned fire as Van Meter chased him across the front lawn and toward the intersection of Lexington and Lincoln. When Nalls joined the gunfight, Van Meter retreated inside the Lincoln Court complex.[50]

Back in apartment 303, Frechette begged Dillinger, "My God, don't shoot. Don't shoot. Try and get out of here, but don't shoot!" The FBI described Dillinger's next actions in slow motion: "When the shooting began, the door of the Hellman apartment was opened slightly and the muzzle of a machine gun protruded and began spraying the hallway with bullets." Detective Cummings flattened himself in an alcove as Dillinger sent bursts of machine-gun fire toward him, splintering walls in a shower of flying plaster. "The bullets were scraping the wall where I had cover and going right past my nose," recalled Cummings, who fired back toward the apartment.[51]

Not a single FBI agent or police officer guarded the rear of the building or Dillinger's path to his getaway car, hidden in a garage just yards away.

56 ‘Something Very Serious Going On'

Dillinger's Getaway Garage
1123 Goodrich Avenue, St. Paul

"A man came out from behind the apartment, dressed in gray clothes," recalled George Schroth, who saw John Dillinger emerge from the Lincoln Court Apartments on March 31. "He was carrying a machine gun. He was not running, however. He was merely walking. . . . [He] took his time and walked up the alley very casually, always keeping a good look behind him as though covering his retreat. When I saw the man with the machine gun, I knew that there was of course something very serious going on."[52]

Moments after Dillinger's gunfire sent the FBI agents running, Evelyn Frechette sprinted to the Halbert family's three-car garage behind the home at 1123 Goodrich Avenue. She backed a black Hudson sedan toward Dillinger.[53] Nearby, young Louis Schroth—who almost became The Teenager Who Killed John Dillinger—was watching.

"I am in my bedroom at this point, a fourteen-year-old kid with a lot of guns in my closet, and [I] saw a man coming out of the door—about fifteen yards from me—with a Thompson submachine gun in his hand," recalled Schroth nearly sixty years later. "I didn't know who he was. I just knew you're not supposed to openly carry a Thompson submachine gun in St. Paul. I was going to shoot Dillinger, but my mother grabbed me by the neck and stopped me! She was worried that if I shot, but hadn't gotten him, Dillinger would have sprayed the whole building with bullets."

Schroth watched from his bedroom window as Dillinger, carrying the machine gun in his right hand and a suitcase in his left, gave Frechette "holy hell" for backing out of the garage the wrong way. Dillinger demanded that she drive into the garage and back out again in the other direction. With a bullet wound in his leg leaving a trail of blood in the snow, Dillinger climbed into the auto, and he and Frechette drove up the alley toward a rendezvous with Eddie Green in Minneapolis.[54]

Van Meter's getaway was even more stylish—he hijacked a garbage collector's horse and, disguised under the hauler's cap, trotted his way to freedom along Lincoln Avenue. For residents of the area it was the finale to an extraordinary afternoon. "We had a quiet, well-to-do neighborhood," said Bob Geisenheyner, who at the time was a seventh grader living across the street from Dillinger's apartment building. "Except for the John Dillinger shootout and the kidnapping of [Edward] Bremer down the block."[55]

Dillinger's sedan resurfaced on April 2 at Clements Auto in Mankato, Minnesota, where it had been taken for repainting by a Mr. Holmes (almost certainly Dillinger gang member Tommy Carroll). The mobster had requested new taillights and license plates attached with wing nuts, for easy removal.[56]

Dillinger's escape stunned St. Paul. The *Pioneer Press* called the city "a happy hunting ground for kidnapers, thugs, thieves, and machine gunners: St. Paul has become a disgrace and a shame before the whole country, because gangsters have been given refuge here. . . . Who brought Dillinger to St. Paul? Let us have an answer to that question." The shootout was a rebuff to a probe into St. Paul's underworld by a Ramsey County grand jury, which had just announced that there was no crime wave in the capital city. It was an embarrassment for Mayor William Mahoney, who had expressed doubts that Dillinger had even visited St. Paul.[57]

But most of all, the escape was a humiliation for J. Edgar Hoover, who vowed that no "rat" would ever take aim at his agents without suffering the consequences. To Hoover's dismay, the newspaper coverage generated by the Lincoln Court shootout made his "Public Enemy Number One" a nationwide antihero.

In its subsequent search for Dillinger, the FBI sent nearly fifty agents to question virtually every underworld figure in the Twin Cities, bunking the agents in hotels and on cots in the Federal Courts Building. Agents stripped the apartment down to the floorboards and found a picture of Dillinger as a three-year-old and a twenty-page guide to getaway routes from an Iowa bank to St. Paul.[58]

Dillinger had left behind a staggering arsenal—including a Thompson submachine gun, two automatic rifles, a 100-round loaded machine gun drum, a .38-caliber Colt automatic with twenty-shot magazine clips, a vertical grip to convert the Colt into a small submachine gun, and two bulletproof vests. In addition, Van Meter's car disgorged a .351-caliber Winchester repeating rifle with thirteen loaded clips, a submachine gun, and a loaded 100-round magazine.[59]

"There is not a big-time gangster who comes to St. Paul but who has more modern, high-powered equipment than the entire St. Paul Police Department," said police chief Tom Dahill. Two St. Paul newspapers responded by raising more than $1,800 to buy machine guns for the police. The FBI privately discussed outfitting its agents with the very .38 Colt automatic pistols and bulletproof vests used by the Dillinger gang.[60]

After the shootout, newspapers were filled with reports of Dillinger sightings. Rose Menke told her family that in 1934 a car filled with steel boxes drove up to her cabin in Rapid River, Minnesota, about thirteen miles south of Baudette. Her husband, a state forestry service employee, was gone at the time. "The men [in the car] asked for a drink of water," recalled Menke's daughter Mary Charlton. "One of the men asked my mother, 'Aren't you afraid out here all by yourself?' And my mother said: 'No, the only thing I'm afraid of is John Dillinger.'" The men roared with laughter and drove away. Menke later discovered that Dillinger was thought to have driven through Rapid River that week. Sightings of Dillinger look-alikes became so frequent that FBI officials discussed the "extreme precaution which we must exercise to prevent any innocent persons being shot in the mistaken belief that they are Dillinger."[61]

At FBI headquarters in Washington, D.C., Hoover's fury was relentless. Publicly, he declared: "In the twenty-odd years of the existence of this division, no one ever has shot at any of our agents and got away with it. We run them to earth. . . . We are going to run down the entire gang." Privately, the director sent scalding memos to the St. Paul field office, expressing his "extreme displeasure" with the agents' handling of every facet of the Lincoln Court shootout, including their having allowed St. Paul police officers to process the fingerprints found in Dillinger's apartment. Hoover seemed to be particularly outraged that his agents allowed evidence to be seen by the police because of the impact on what Hoover termed "the publicity angle" of the case.[62]

In a conversation with agent Melvin Purvis, Hoover raged that the St. Paul office was incompetent, referring to the agents' "atrocious bungling" of the raid on Dillinger's apartment. He asked Purvis to focus all attention on Dillinger and ensure that a copy of any information supplied to the field office be sent to headquarters. Hoover was particularly contemptuous of his agents' decision to bring a police officer with them: "If in order to have some courage it was necessary to have a man in blue uniform along, to go ahead and take one, that if such was the case he, Mr. Hoover, was not going to lay down any rule to forbid it," said a memo documenting a telephone conversation with Hoover. "However, he would not do it and certainly he would not have used a St. Paul policeman."[63]

At the FBI's St. Paul field office—then located in room 203 of the Federal Courts Building at Fifth and Market Streets—the agents fought back against Hoover's condemnations. Special agent in charge Werner Hanni fired off a "personal and confidential memorandum" to headquarters, laying the blame for Dillinger's escape on FBI orders that its agents avoid working with local police officers. "It is not easy for me to make these statements; however, I must do so at this time, for the sake of the good name of the Division," wrote Hanni. "At 93 South Lexington Avenue, in particular, if we had sought the assistance which was readily ours for the asking, Dillinger, undoubtedly, would never have made his escape from that place."[64]

Ironically, the publicity generated by the FBI's failure to stop Dillinger's escape from the Lincoln Court Apartments, and his subsequent flight from Wisconsin's Little Bohemia resort, built support for the FBI as a national crime-fighting organization. During the Dillinger gang furor, U.S. attorney general Cummings recommended adding 270 new Justice Department agents, equipping the G-men with machine guns and faster vehicles, and expanding federal law enforcement powers to capture gangsters operating between states. Police chief Tom Dahill agreed that when "the criminals in question operate all over the country . . . it requires the aid of a national crime-fighting organization to catch them."[65]

Finally, Hoover laid down an order for his agents: they were to find Dillinger at any cost, even if it meant enlisting help from the underworld. "Get the leaders of the gangs," Hoover instructed his St. Paul agents, "and let them know that if they [don't] produce Dillinger, we [will] 'give them the works.'"[66]

57   'I Will Blow Your Head Off!'

The Dillinger Doctor's Clinic
1835 Park Avenue, Minneapolis

The man who limped through the back door of Dr. Clayton E. May's clinic on the morning of March 31, 1934, his arm resting around his girlfriend's shoulder, was no ordinary patient. But then, Dr. May was not operating an ordinary medical clinic.

May was told that his patient had been injured in the explosion of a still, but the doctor soon learned that his business was robbing banks, not bootlegging. The man on his couch, bleeding from an "in-and-out" bullet wound received hours earlier during the Lincoln Court shootout, was John Dillinger.[67]

May had his own secrets to keep. At 1835 Park Avenue, for fifty dollars, he discreetly treated venereal disease and performed abortions, surgery too illicit for his main office. May had cared for the family of Dillinger gang member Eddie Green for more than a decade and had served in 1922 as an alibi witness for Green during his trial for payroll robbery.[68]

From March 31 to April 4, May tended to Dillinger's bullet wound, injecting the gangster's leg with antitetanus serum and bandaging the leg with gauze. When May first met Dillinger, the physician told the mobster he needed full treatment at a hospital. Dillinger pulled out a submachine gun and responded, "To hell with that. You take me where you said you were going to take me to, some private place, or I will blow your head off."[69]

Once he was secure at May's clinic and soothed by nurse Augusta Salt, Dillinger calmed down. When Salt fluffed up his pillow and discovered a pistol there, he assured her that she need not be afraid of it. The nurse made dinner for him and gave Frechette gray thread to mend the holes in his overcoat; Dillinger gave her a hundred-dollar tip in damp five-dollar bills. "I am accused of committing every crime in the country from the East to the West coast," he quipped to Dr. May. "It's a wonder that they don't charge me with crimes in Europe."[70]

With that, Dillinger left the Park Avenue clinic in a Hudson sedan, heading toward a family reunion in Mooresville, Indiana. May had been promised five hundred dollars for helping Dillinger, but instead he got "two telephone calls threatening me with bodily violence . . . if I told about the treatments I had administered to this man."[71]

The FBI learned about Dr. May from the confessions bank robber Eddie Green would make on his deathbed. FBI agent Thomas Dodd (later a U.S. senator from Connecticut) located the doctor by masquerading as a man seeking an abortion for his girlfriend. The FBI put the Park Avenue clinic under surveillance; four agents armed with machine guns apprehended May on April 5. All May earned from his adventure was a two-year stint in Leavenworth prison, the revocation of his medical license, and lifelong notoriety as "the Dillinger doctor."[72]

For five days, Dillinger had enjoyed a rare respite from the FBI's manhunt. He had only three and a half months to live.

58–59 'Lovers Don't Talk about That Kind of Thing'

58. *Tommy Carroll's St. Paul Hideout*
    35 West Isabel Street, St. Paul
59. *The Dillinger Gang's Minneapolis Mail Drop*
    3242 South Sixteenth Avenue, Minneapolis

John Dillinger's front-page exploits in the spring of 1934 overshadowed the extraordinary career of his partner, automobile thief and bank robber Thomas L. Carroll. At 5 feet, 10 inches and a trim 166 pounds, the chestnut-haired, blue-eyed Chicagoan looked roughly handsome in his mug shots, despite what police described as a furrowed upper lip, scars on his jaw and neck, and a mouth that twisted distinctly to the right.[73]

Carroll, one of the few married men in Dillinger's gang, was known for juggling women friends and aliases—which included James Roy Brock, George McLarken, and Frank Sloane. Born in Red Lodge, Montana, Carroll lost his mother when he was two and his father when he was nine. Originally employed as a boilermaker and taxicab driver in Missouri, he was arrested for drunkenness and possession of stolen property, earning his first term in the state prison at Anamosa, Iowa. Two years later, he was returned to Anamosa for auto theft, and in 1927, he was sent to the state penitentiary at Jefferson City, Missouri, for robbery.[74]

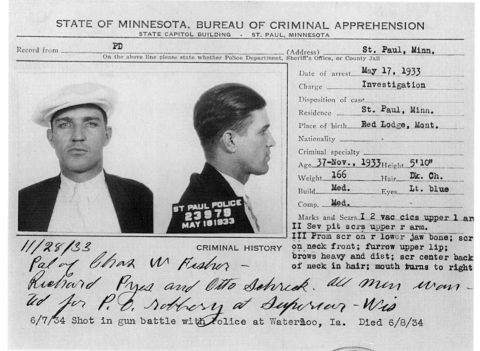

Post office burglar and auto thief Thomas L. Carroll

Finally, in May 1930, Carroll graduated to a twenty-one-month sentence at Leavenworth for transporting a stolen auto across state lines. While he was at Leavenworth, where he used his boilermaking skills as the prison plumber, Carroll was often reprimanded for breaking prison regulations. ("This man is continually loitering and visiting on the gallery," noted his prisoner file, "especially in some other cell. He has been repeatedly warned.") Released in October 1931, he would never again allow himself to be imprisoned.[75]

A 1933 wanted poster described Carroll: "Neat dresser; drives an automobile well; usually resides in an apartment; gambles and is addicted to the use of intoxicants; frequents night clubs; gives his occupation as salesman; is said to be wearing a derby and a reddish mustache."[76]

By that time he had been arrested on charges ranging from concealing weapons to grocery store robberies by police in Omaha, Nebraska; Council Bluffs, Iowa; Kansas City, St. Joseph, and St. Louis, Missouri; and Tulsa, Oklahoma. The U.S. Post Office was particularly eager to capture Carroll, who was suspected of engineering a wave of postal burglaries in Wisconsin, Iowa, and Minnesota.[77]

It is not surprising that when Carroll married his girlfriend, Viola, in 1925, they pledged their marital devotion using aliases: "Beaula Richard" married "Mr. McGuire." The couple moved to St. Paul in 1932, and for a time Carroll attempted to run a Mankato restaurant, briefly trading in his machine gun for a spatula. But that year he met and fell in love with "Radio Sally" Bennett, a twenty-year-old St. Paul nightclub singer, and abandoned his wife. "When I found him with this other girl naturally it was quite a shock to me," Viola told reporters. "After he left I took poison. I loved him. I always loved him."[78]

"Radio Sally" Bennett, girlfriend of Dillinger gang member Tommy Carroll

Bennett was a popular entertainer at John Lane's Boulevards of Paris nightclub. She sang Irish tunes like "Danny Boy," although her specialty was performing virtually any song requested on her ukulele ("like Arthur Godfrey, only she could sing," recalled her son, Kenneth Herschler). Interviewed by FBI agents later, Bennett recalled how Carroll had first walked into St. Paul's Green Gables nightclub with six other men and asked her to sing at his table. Utterly smitten, Carroll returned to the club each night for three weeks. He told Sally that he was a gambler and a bootlegger, and then asked her to marry him. Bennett answered that she could not marry him because of her religion, but she would live with him.[79]

For six months during the spring and summer of 1932, Bennett and Carroll lived in the second-floor apartment at 35 West Isabel Street. Their landlords, who lived on the first floor, were Pete and Mary Vogel, a foundry laborer and a schoolteacher.[80]

"Radio Sally lived with Tommy at our house," said their son Jim Vogel. "My mom referred to women who she didn't think much of, like Radio Sally, as 'frowsies'—let's say she was not the kind of girl you wanted to bring home to mother. . . . Well, that bothered my mother so much that she talked to the parish priest. The priest told mom, 'If you need the money for your income, it's not your problem!'"[81]

"My mom . . . knew Carroll was a criminal and a killer, which they didn't like," said Jim's brother, John Vogel. "But they still talked about the gangsters as refined people. The poor in those days looked up to the gangsters [because they had] money."[82]

Members of the Dillinger gang met regularly in the West Isabel apartment, smoking cigarettes and planning their banking activities. "The whole Dillinger gang . . . would meet in the front room," recalled Loretta Murphy, the Vogel brothers' aunt, who was thirty-one at the time. "They were respectful and wouldn't leave any ashes in the ashtrays—you'd think it was a board meeting for some business." Carroll was a relentless flirt, Murphy said: "He'd come to me and he'd say, 'Don't you think we should have a drink, you know, before you go to bed?'"[83]

Carroll often ate with the Vogels, simple food like potatoes and hamburgers, and always tipped them generously—as much as ten dollars per meal. He came across as a polished gentleman, well-dressed and mannered. Yet he always had to be on guard. When the Vogels' son John was robbed by neighborhood kids of ten dollars in grocery money, the Vogels called the police. Carroll looked out the window and saw the officers. Thinking they were coming for him, he leaped out the window. Later, he told the boy: "Next time that happens, you let me know and I'll just give you the money! We don't want the police here."

There were other clues to Carroll's real vocation. When Mary Vogel peeked inside a violin case in his room, she found it stuffed with hundreds of silver coins. Another day, Carroll left several newspapers open, with articles on local bank robberies underlined; a family member who opened one of his dresser drawers found it filled with U.S. postage stamps.[84]

Even with Bennett, Carroll was evasive about his line of work. She told FBI agents that she often asked about his activities and his friends, and that he always told her it was none of her business. Carroll rarely took Bennett anywhere but to a movie, to a cottage on Lake Owasso for gangster parties, or to the Green Lantern. When he finally brought her to Chicago in the summer of 1933 to enjoy the World's Fair, he was abruptly called back to St. Paul on criminal business.[85]

Carroll had two close calls with police in Minnesota. In May 1933 he was arrested in St. Paul for possession of burglar's tools, but he was released in June. The police, true to the O'Connor system, never pursued the charge. In September, after an auto accident at Rice Street and Wheelock Parkway in St. Paul, he was arrested when police discovered a loaded .45-caliber pistol in his car. Again he was released, despite the fact that he was then out of prison on $15,000 bond for a Wisconsin post office robbery. In October Carroll is believed to have joined Babyface Nelson for a final bank robbery.[86]

The crime may have been inspired by a dinner table conversation between Verne Miller, the Barker-Karpis gang's machine gunner, and the family of his girlfriend, Vivian Mathis, in Brainerd, Minnesota. In early October, the talk between Miller and Mathis's father, farmer John Gibson, turned to money and banks. "That was during the Depression and there were a lot of banks being held up," recalled Janet Gibson, the farmer's daughter-in-law. "John was talking about bank robberies with Verne . . . [and] said, 'I'm telling you, no one will *ever* break into the First National Bank of Brainerd, it's too well protected.' Verne had a snicker on his face. Verne just happened to go to the bank the next day. I think he was checking things out." A few days later, a *Brainerd Daily Dispatch* headline blared: "Daring Machine Gun Mob Robs First National Here," and the bank was $32,000 poorer.[87]

Although the identity of the five Brainerd bank robbers was never determined by police, Fatso Negri, a partner of Babyface Nelson, identified them as Nelson, Tommy Carroll, Homer Van Meter, John Paul Chase, and Charles Fisher.[88]

The Babyface Nelson–Tommy Carroll gang cased the Brainerd bank while they were staying in cabin two at the Sebago Resort, still operating fourteen miles from Brainerd on the north shore of Round Lake. Two black Buick sedans with North Dakota plates drove into the resort in mid-October 1933. "We like it quiet . . . real quiet," said one of the men, whom resort owner Lester Penney instantly recognized as Babyface Nelson. Their arrival pleased Penney: the post–Labor Day slump was on, and the strangers purchased his fresh vegetables and milk, paying him five dollars for fifty cents worth of milk and adding ten dollars extra to the twenty-dollar weekly rent. "They gave him to understand that he was not to even remember that they were there—that he wouldn't say anything about this if he knew what was good for him," recalled Don Fish, the current proprietor of Sebago Resort. "Penney didn't mention it until after Babyface Nelson died!"[89]

Nelson hired a Brainerd plumber to drive him around town, supposedly to look for real estate to purchase, but the tours often circled back to the First National Bank. The morning of the bank robbery, the gang packed up and left Sebago for good.[90]

The building that once housed the First National Bank at the corner of South Sixth and Front in downtown Brainerd now stands vacant, but eyewitnesses have not forgotten how well planned the robbery was. The five thieves, faces obscured by bandannas, knew the name of each bank employee. They methodically broke into the bank and forced everyone to the floor, waiting until the safe's time lock popped open at 8:45 A.M. Outside the bank were two bandits in hunting clothes, hiding a submachine gun under a bushel basket.[91]

One of the only surviving eyewitnesses to the October 23 robbery, Zane Smith, was then a seventeen-year-old collection clerk who had been on the job just twelve months. Arriving at 8:00 A.M., Smith let himself into the bank and headed for the president's office to deliver the day's mail, unaware that Babyface Nelson was crouching behind an ornamental pillar at the bank's main entrance.

"He jumped to his feet . . . took hold of the collar of my topcoat and swung me around and hit my jaw with his fist," recalled Smith. "He . . . dragged me across the bank lobby floor to an office where they had the bank guard and janitor."

Nelson quizzed the teenager on how much money was in the vault. "I didn't know, but he had the machine gun pointed at me. Nelson had the machine gun across his knees, and he'd turn it back and forth. I could hear the cartridges clicking, left and right, left and right. . . . I told them I didn't know. They threatened to put burning cigarettes in my ears to get better answers."

While they waited for the time lock, the gangsters set up a machine gun on a tripod—and then asked the bank employees if they wanted to smoke. The robbers passed out and lit the cigarettes so the hostages would not have to reach into their pockets. Once the money was stuffed into canvas bags, the staff was herded into the bathroom. The gang drove away in a Buick, firing machine gun bullets at the bank windows. "Banking was supposed to be a very tranquil business," said Smith. "It turned out quite differently for me."

"I think of the robbery often," added Smith, who eventually became vice president of the bank. "The strange part of it was, while the robbery was in progress . . . I wasn't frightened. I kept thinking, 'Won't it be fun to tell people this?' After it was over, I realized that those men had horrendous reputations as robbers and murderers. With three machine guns and two pistols, I thought about what *could* have happened that day!"[92]

After the robbery, Carroll hid in the duplex of Sally Bennett's brother, Joseph Bennett, at 3242 Sixteenth Avenue South in Minneapolis, which he used as a mail drop for submachine guns and other weaponry; visitors to the apartment included Homer Van Meter and Babyface Nelson.[93]

On November 11, 1933, two Minneapolis police officers attempted to arrest Carroll on suspicion of participating in the Brainerd robbery. Barefoot and cornered by the armed policemen, he escaped by kicking one officer in the face and punching the other and stealing his gun. Carroll left behind $1,600 in crisp bank notes, a rifle, a machine gun, and a shotgun.[94]

Later that month, Carroll returned to St. Paul, where he met his next lover, twenty-one-year-old waitress Jean Delaney, the sister of Alvin Karpis's girlfriend, Delores Delaney. She moved in with Carroll on Hennepin Avenue. "From the way Carroll talked," Delaney told the FBI, "I believed he was a gambler—he always seemed to have plenty of money." She avoided asking Carroll questions about the Dillinger gang "for fear that Tommy would slap her down," the FBI reported. Carroll told Delaney that one of the reasons he liked her was "because she did not ask questions." Delaney said that Carroll was jealous of her, threatening to "beat up college boys who would pass them in cars and holler, 'Hello, Blondie' and 'Hello, Cutie' at her."[95]

The violent pace of Carroll's life began to accelerate: he was suspected of killing Texas police officer H. C. Perrow on December 11, 1933, and the next year he joined Dillinger in robbing the Security National Bank of Sioux Falls, South Dakota, and the First National Bank of Mason City, Iowa. FBI interviews with Carroll's girlfriends revealed a tense life of incessant travel. On April 19, 1934, Carroll hid in Fox River Grove, Illinois, with Jean Delaney and Babyface Nelson and his wife, Helen. On April 20, 1934, the Dillinger gang moved en masse from Fox River Grove to the Little Bohemia Lodge near Rhinelander, Wisconsin. Three days later, Carroll escaped a shootout with the FBI at Little Bohemia that led to his being sought for the murder of FBI agent W. Carter Baum.[96]

FBI agents thought they came close to snaring Carroll in May 1934, when they received a tip that he was hiding in a lake cottage near Perham, Minnesota. The bureau costumed two of its agents as fishermen pretending to search Perham for a summer fishing cottage. But Carroll and Delaney never showed up; they were staying that month with Nelson at Lake Como in Wisconsin.[97]

Carroll's wanderings ended on June 7, 1934, when a gas station attendant near Waterloo, Iowa, noticed three license plates piled in the rear seat of Carroll's sedan. Two Waterloo detectives were waiting when Carroll and Delaney returned to the car. Delaney, who had been arrested and released by the FBI after the Little Bohemia raid, saw the detectives and volunteered to act as a decoy to climb into the auto to see if the men were police officers, she told the FBI. "But Carroll would not permit her to go alone, and stated that, if there were any danger, he wanted to share it with her," the FBI reported. Delaney added that Babyface Nelson's wife felt the same way about her husband, whom she lovingly called "Jimmy." "They were very devoted to each other and Helen wanted to die at the same time Jimmy died," recalled Delaney.[98]

As Waterloo detectives Paul E. Walker and Emil Steffen identified themselves, Carroll reached for his gun. Walker punched Carroll in the face, knocking him backward, and the officers fired five shots, hitting Carroll four times and mortally wounding him. "I was in love with him," wept Delaney later, explaining why she overlooked his criminal activities. "That was all that mattered to me. Lovers don't talk about that kind of thing." The police arrested Delaney, who was sent to the Alderson, West Virginia, reformatory for women.[99]

"The last thing we heard was that [Carroll] had been shot down in Iowa," recalled Loretta Murphy. Carroll's body was returned to Minnesota, where he was given a Catholic funeral at the Church of the Assumption in St. Paul. "Mary [Vogel] and I went there to be sure that it was our Tommy Carroll. And it was," sighed Murphy.[100]

Carroll and Eddie Green are the only two members of the Dillinger gang to have remained in Minnesota for eternity. Carroll's grave can be seen today in Oakland Cemetery at 927 Jackson. Its marker removed, the grave is located in Lot 279, Block 71.[101]

Startling Detective Adventures magazine offered a colorful eulogy, calling Carroll a "one-time taxi driver who shot himself into the big leagues as Dillinger's ace gunman, but finally was struck out by the great No Hit—No Run Pitcher," and predicted that "the message of blood spells the beginning of the end for John Dillinger and his mob!"[102]

60   Machine Guns for the Gang

The Dillinger Gang's Weapons Depot
2214 Marshall Avenue, St. Paul

John Dillinger's remarkable luck—three jailbreaks and his escape from the Lincoln Court Apartments shootout—began to collapse in April 1934, when the FBI identified his hideout on Marshall Avenue in St. Paul. He had left behind in his Lincoln Court suite a sheet of paper bearing a scribbled telephone number. It was Eddie Green's, traced by FBI agents to a three-story red-brick building in the Merriam Park neighborhood.[103]

The previous month, the Dillinger gang's black sedan ran out of gas a few hundred yards away from the Marshall Avenue safe house. The gangsters pushed the car into the Standard gas station at the intersection of Marshall and Cretin, now the Amoco station at 2178 Marshall. "All of a sudden these three or four guys are pushing a four-door black Pontiac or something into the gas station driveway," recalled Robert Wybest, who was then sixteen years old. "The men—real rugged-looking guys—didn't look like natives with their dark suits and hats, and they didn't smile much. One man got out. I saw that his vest was funny; it was stiff like a board inside his suitcoat."[104]

The gas station attendant, A. L. Martindale, noticed not only the bulletproof vest but also the submachine gun that one of the passengers was nervously covering in the rear seat. Martindale pulled Wybest aside and hissed, "Go across the street and you call the police! Go on!"

"I was trying to be really coy. . . . I put my hands in my pockets and walked across to the drugstore," recalled Wybest. "I should have run across to the drugstore, but then the guys would have blown my head off." By the time the police arrived, the Dillinger gang had refueled and driven away.

Eddie Green, Dillinger's thirty-four-year-old bank scout, rented the Marshall Avenue apartment under the name of D. A. Stevens for two weeks beginning March 15, 1934. Green and his girlfriend, Beth Green, were relieved to move away from Minneapolis, where Dillinger's apartment at Thirty-third and Girard, just one block from Green's Charlou Apartments on Fremont Avenue, was drawing too much attention in the neighborhood.[105]

Green turned the Marshall Avenue apartment over to Dillinger machine gunner Homer Van Meter. On April 3 St. Paul police chief Tom Dahill and a troop of FBI agents raided the apartment, which yielded shotgun shells, machine-gun clips, three notebooks marked "Get Away Charts," and a two-foot piece of dynamite fuse.[106]

While the agents were dusting the apartment for fingerprints, Lucy Jackson and Leona Goodman, sisters who had worked as maids for the Barker-Karpis gang, dropped by during lunch to pick up some baggage for Eddie Green. Greeted by FBI machine guns, the women explained that Green had asked them to clean up the apartment and bring the bags to a home at 778 Rondo. Could the women identify Green? the agents asked. Sure, they said. They had met him face to face in early March.[107]

The agents demanded that Jackson and Goodman carry out their mission —and accompanied them to the Rondo neighborhood where Eddie Green was scheduled to retrieve his suitcases.

61 'This Man Should Be Shot. . . . Kill Him!'

Eddie Green's Ambush House
778 Rondo Ave., St. Paul

Armed with automatic shotguns, rifles, and machine guns, a phalanx of FBI agents staked out the Rondo home on April 3. Backup agents were hidden nearby. The bureau's plan was simple. Leona Goodman was to hail Green at the side porch door and hand him the luggage from the Marshall Avenue hideout. An agent in the bedroom would then fire a .30-caliber rifle into the motor of Green's getaway car to disable it. After that, the instructions were simple. "This man should be shot. . . . Kill him."[108]

At 5:30 P.M., Eddie and Beth Green drove south down Avon and parked their Essex Terraplane across the street. Seeing nothing out of the ordinary, Eddie left Beth in the car and walked to the kitchen door, collected his suitcase from Goodman, and walked back toward the car. Somehow, the mobster then recognized the trap, made what agents later called a "threatening" or "menacing" gesture, and dashed back toward the Terraplane. FBI agent E. N. Notesteen yelled, "Let 'em have it!" Another agent fired at Green through the window of 778 Rondo. The bullets smashed into his shoulders and skull.[109]

Rushed by police ambulance to St. Paul's Ancker Hospital, Green was guarded around the clock by FBI agents. "Honey, back the car to the door," Green moaned wildly, "I've got the keys, he wants them. John . . . Dillinger!" With FBI agent Thomas Dodd transcribing his every delirious word, Green asked for guns and screamed, "Shoot that one!" Whenever Green began to talk, his mother attempted to drown out his confessions by reading from her prayer book, loudly interrupting her son's admissions and entreating, "Eddie, say your prayers." Green's brother Frank warned: "Don't talk, Eddie. Don't talk." The FBI had Frank temporarily barred from the hospital.[110]

When they were alone with Green, the agents' bedside interrogation called upon their acting skills: Green believed in his daze that he had been hit over the head during a robbery attempt, and "the agents played the part of doctors, other gangsters, etc.," in order to get him to talk, reported an FBI memo to J. Edgar Hoover. "Green couldn't see and was in a state of delirium and half the time subconscious and talking."[111]

Another agent reported that "Green did not have his eyes open and, apparently, was under the impression that the police officer was a doctor and . . . [was] advised that there were no police officers, or Agents of the Department of Justice, present." Green asked a police officer if he could perform plastic surgery on the telltale dimple on John Dillinger's chin. No prob-

GANGSTER'S CAR

The Rondo Street home where the FBI shot Dillinger gang member Eddie Green in April 1934. FBI agents fired through the circled windows, and Green was struck by their bullets at the X.

lem, the agent answered, but first Green would have to lead him to where Dillinger was hiding.[112]

"Doc, you sure are a nosey fellow. Give me a shot so I can sleep," begged Green. Promised an injection in exchange for information on Dillinger, Green blurted out the identity of his fellow gang members, the name of Dillinger doctor Clayton May, and the location of the Fremont Avenue safehouse in Minneapolis. His temperature soaring to 105 degrees, Green lived for a week before dying of meningitis on April 11, 1934. He was buried the next day in St. Peter's Cemetery in Mendota, Minnesota.[113]

By then, Dillinger had already left the Twin Cities. He visited his family for a chicken dinner in Indiana, robbed a Warsaw, Indiana, police station on April 3, and drove toward the peace of Little Bohemia Lodge, the setting for one of the bloodiest shootouts in FBI history.[114]

Relieved that the *St. Paul Pioneer Press* had "no unfavorable comment" about the Green shooting, the FBI noted that the newspaper "quote[d] verbatim the release which was furnished them." But *St. Paul Dispatch* reporter Tommy "Buck Tooth" Thompson demanded a Ramsey County coroner's inquest into the propriety of the ambush. The FBI peevishly noted in a memorandum that "Thompson is sometimes referred to as 'Horse Face.'"[115]

One FBI official suggested to J. Edgar Hoover that the bureau "bring pressure to bear to prevent any adverse publicity" and warned that the identity of the agents who participated in the Green shooting should not be disclosed so they could not be subpoenaed. Hoover wrote that an FBI executive had "suggested, in view of the fact that the St. Paul Dispatch has been exerting itself to try to embarrass us, that a confidential tip be given to the rival paper. . . . I approved this suggestion."[116]

Precisely what occurred during the Green shootout is unclear. An April 4, 1934, memo claimed that after agents demanded that he halt, Green made a "suspicious" gesture; "suspicious" was crossed out and changed to "threatening." It is certain from FBI memos that the bureau was determined to stop any investigation into Green's shooting. In a memo to Hoover, an agent noted newspaper coverage expressing "concern over the fact that a gangster was shot down, probably from the back," and reassured Hoover that if the inquest into Green's death were "not held until May 2, the date at which it is now set, it would be given very little consideration and it would probably be a mere formality; that there was a possibility that there would not even be one."[117]

The local police, held in contempt by Hoover, continued to tease the bureau for its inability to capture Dillinger. Hoover was informed after Green's shooting that a law enforcement official had "sarcastically asked if there was any danger of the man getting away from us at the hospital."[118]

Taking no chances, the FBI isolated Beth Green in Chicago for interrogation under the direction of Melvin Purvis. In a series of increasingly open confessions, Green provided many of the FBI's first tips on the Dillinger and Barker-Karpis gangs and the key role played by local fixers Harry Sawyer and Jack Peifer. "There appears to be some friction between this woman and Dillinger," an FBI memo reported happily, although the FBI also noted that her eighteen-year-old son could be "an imposing lever to hold over her head as a means of obtaining information." Through Green, the FBI first learned the identities of each member of the Dillinger gang and the names of the gangsters who had kidnapped Edward Bremer and who committed the Kansas City Massacre.[119]

When the FBI next caught up with Dillinger, Hoover's "shoot to kill" orders would ensure a fusillade of bullets.

John Hamilton's Last Ride

The Hastings Spiral Bridge Stakeout
Finch Drug Store Building
Second and Sibley Streets, Hastings

Dillinger's escape from the Lincoln Court Apartments in St. Paul may have been embarrassing for the FBI, but the Keystone Kops–style fiasco at the Little Bohemia Lodge sparked calls for J. Edgar Hoover's resignation. Had Dillinger's partner John Hamilton not been wounded during a shootout begun at the Hastings Spiral Bridge on the Minnesota-Wisconsin border, Dillinger's gang would once again have slipped away untouched.

On April 22, 1934, a planeload of FBI agents from St. Paul joined Melvin Purvis, then special agent in charge of the FBI's Chicago office, in a surprise raid on Little Bohemia. In the dark, the agents accidentally fired on three innocent visitors to the resort, killing one and wounding another in the belief that they were members of the Dillinger gang. Alerted by the gunfire, Dillinger and his gang slipped out a second-story window and shot their way out of the trap. Babyface Nelson's machine gun left one police officer and one FBI agent, W. Carter Baum, dead. Nelson reportedly sneered at Baum, "I know you have on bulletproof vests, so I will give it to you high and low."[120]

The gangsters got away, but three of their companions—Jean Delaney, girlfriend of Tommy Carroll; Helen Gillis, wife of Babyface Nelson; and Marie Conforti, girlfriend of Homer Van Meter—were arrested. "Three women and a much-shot-up house, which was later to prove of great financial benefit to its proprietors, were all we had to show for our efforts," wrote Purvis. "The raid had failed." The women were tried in Madison, Wisconsin, federal court for harboring Dillinger; they pled guilty and got eighteen months on probation.[121]

The debacle at Little Bohemia was particularly humiliating because Hoover, just before the raid, had boasted to the national news media that his agents had Dillinger surrounded. Distraught over the death of agent Baum, Purvis actually tendered his resignation, but it was refused.[122]

Senator Royal Copeland of New York savaged the FBI for bungling the raid, suggesting creation of a rival crime bureau made up of the best law enforcement officers from each state: "When Dillinger was hidden in the woods of Wisconsin, they brought up a lot of young lawyers from the Department of Justice and armed them and turned them loose. They should have called on local authorities in Wisconsin. . . . They fumbled it again."[123]

Perhaps worst of all, Hoover's men were ridiculed by humorist Will Rogers. "Well, they had Dillinger surrounded and was all ready to shoot him when he came out," quipped Rogers. "But another bunch of folks came out ahead, so they just shot them instead. Dillinger is going to accidentally get with some innocent bystanders some time [and] then he will get shot."[124]

The police figured Dillinger would head across the Mississippi River toward the safety of St. Paul. Alerted by the Justice Department, local sheriffs threw up an armed roadblock in Hastings, Minnesota, on April 23. Two policemen with rifles perched on the roof of the Finch Drug Store, awaiting a clear shot as Dillinger drove over the Hastings Spiral Bridge.[125]

(The magnificent Spiral Bridge, an engineering miracle dedicated in 1895, featured a remarkable 360-degree loop feeding into downtown Hastings. The wooden structure was destroyed in 1951.[126])

Just after 10:00 A.M., Dillinger, Homer Van Meter, and John Hamilton drove south over the bridge toward St. Paul. Recognizing Dillinger as the car crossed the north end of the bridge, the deputies chased it at speeds up to seventy miles an hour. The mobsters lobbed .45-caliber rounds into the police car's windshield; the police fired .30-.30 rifle bullets into the back of Dillinger's 1931 Ford coupe. The car wobbled but sped on, turning at Highway 3 near Newport at the railway station, and then off the highway onto a dirt road at St. Paul Park, eluding the police northwest of Cottage Grove. "The officers trailed this car, shooting at it at every opportunity, but the opportunities were rare because of the rolling land and the numerous curves," explained an FBI report.[127]

A Hastings newspaper account of the gun battle that mortally wounded John Hamilton

Dillinger and Van Meter reached the safe harbor of South St. Paul untouched; Pat Reilly and Tommy Carroll rejoined them there. John Hamilton was not so lucky. One Hastings police bullet had pierced the

HASTINGS GAZETTE

HASTINGS, MINNESOTA, FRIDAY, APRIL 27, 1934.   HASTINGS OFFICIAL NEWSPAPER

Where Officer's Bullet Drew Blood

DILLINGER GANGSTERS IN RUNNING GUN BATTLE WITH LOCAL POSSE; 1 WOUNDED

A. C. Bachman Passes on; Funeral to be Held Mon.

A. C. Bachman, passed away in St. Raphael's hospital Thursday noon from heart trouble and various complications. He had been a patient sufferer in the hospital since February 12.

The funeral obsequies will be held Monday morning from the St. Boniface church. A detailed account of his life will be published in next week's paper.

Petition Asks for Variable Closing Hours for 3.2 Beer

Police Ask City Council for Bullet-Proof Windshield

A petition signed by about 30 people was presented to the City Council at their adjourned meeting last Monday night, asking that the time of ending the sale or consumption of 3.2 per cent beer be extended from the 12 midnight hour to 1:00 o'clock on every night except Saturday and Sunday nights, and on any other nights on which there is a dance in the city which time shall be extended to 2 a. m.

The council received the petition

Hastings Officer Scores In Gun Duel Although Gangsters Escape

A hazardous and exciting bandit chase, in which three Dakota county deputies and a Hastings policeman participated Monday morning, and in which one of a trio of fleeing Dillinger gangsters is thought to have been fatally wounded, came as a swift aftermath of the breaking up of a Dillinger rendezvous in the northern Wisconsin woods late Sunday night.

The bandit pursuit by the local posse culminated a six-hour vigil by Deputy Sheriffs Joe Heisen, Norman Dieters and Larry Dunn and Night Policeman F. H. McArdle, who had been assigned to guard the high bridge on the supposition that some of the Dillinger mob, fleeing from the Little Bohemia lodge from which they were routed by Federal agents Sunday, might try to gain access to the Twin Cities by crossing the river here.

Apprised of this possibility by a call from the Department of Justice in St. Paul at 3:40 Monday morning, Sheriff J. J. Dunn immediately summoned Deputy Sheriffs Heinen and Dieters, and the two officers, with Deputy Sheriff Larry Dunn and Officer McArdle, stationed themselves at the Finch drug store corner, in Heinen's car, to await developments. For six hours their vigil was fruitless, but shortly after ten o'clock, a coupe, containing three men and bearing a Wisconsin license plate, No. 92652, entered the city from the south on high-way No. 3, and turned at the drug store corner, to cross the high bridge, in the direction of St.

Pictured above is the blood soaked interior of the small Ford coupe in which three members of the notorious Dillinger gang staged a running gun fight with Deputy Sheriffs Joe Heinen, Norman Dieters and Larry Dunn, and Officer F. H. McArdle of the Hastings police force, Monday morning.

It was a 30-30 calibre bullet from McArdle's rifle, authorities believe, that tore through the back of the coupe and wounded one of the gangsters severely if not fatally.

The bullet hole in the back of the car seat indicates that a man sitting on that side of the coupe would have probably received the missile in the region of the kidneys, and the amount of blood lost by the wounded bandit is believed to be proof that his injuries were of a fatal nature. The blood-stained coupe was found a short distance outside of South St. Paul where it was abandoned for a faster car which the gangsters commandeered from a South St. Paul couple. One of the outlaw trio was wrapped in a blanket and apparently seriously injured when the gangsters abandoned the coupe and forced the So. St. Paul couple out of their Ford V-8 sedan.

At the right is a picture of F. H. McArdle, Hastings policeman who fired the bullet that is believed to have terminated the career of one of Dillinger's henchmen. The picture of the local officer was snapped at the South St. Paul police station by a Dispatch photographer shortly after the exciting bandit chase.

IDENTIFICATION ORDER NO. 1220
April 2, 1934.

DIVISION OF INVESTIGATION
U. S. DEPARTMENT OF JUSTICE
WASHINGTON, D. C.

Fingerprint Classification
12 29 W 0 13 AMP
19 W 0 12

WANTED
JOHN HAMILTON, with alias,
JOHN CAMPBELL.

MURDER - OBSTRUCTION OF JUSTICE.

AMPUTATED SECOND JOINT

AMPUTATED SECOND JOINT

John "Three Fingered Jack" Hamilton (right), mortally wounded as he and Dillinger drove through a police stakeout in Hastings, Minnesota; Hamilton's identification order (above), noting his two missing fingers

back of Dillinger's automobile, penetrated the rear seat cushion, and plunged into Hamilton's back, mortally wounding him.[128]

Desperate to evade the FBI long enough to find a doctor for Hamilton, Dillinger stopped a car carrying a South St. Paul utilities employee, Roy Francis, and his family at South Robert and Concord Streets. "We're sorry," said Dillinger, "but we have to have your car." Dillinger left his automobile, by then soaked with Hamilton's blood, for the family's Ford Deluxe Coach. The three bank robbers stopped at a filling station two miles from Mendota and bought two-year-old Robert Francis a soda pop. "Don't worry about the kid," one of the Dillinger gang told his mother, before releasing the Francis family. "We like kids."[129]

Hamilton was taken to the Aurora, Illinois, apartment of Barker-Karpis gang member Volney Davis, where he died ten days later. The FBI believed that Hamilton was buried by Davis, Dillinger, Van Meter, Doc Barker, William Weaver, and Harry Campbell in a rare case of cooperation between the Dillinger and Barker-Karpis gangs. The Francis family's car, its window shattered, .45 bullets on the floor, and stained with Hamilton's blood, was found abandoned in the Chicago area several days later. FBI agents searched swamps near Minneapolis for Hamilton's body but returned without a corpse.

In August 1935, more than a year later, the FBI found "Three Fingered Jack" Hamilton's body in a gravel pit in Oswego, Illinois, his face disfigured with lye to make identification difficult. His telltale right hand with its two amputated fingers had been cut off. Hamilton "sure was a hard-luck guy," said John Dillinger. "Whenever we went on a job he came back full of lead. They wounded him at East Chicago, they wounded him at Mason City, and then they killed him in St. Paul. He was a cinch to get it, sooner or later."[130]

62 Death in a Blind Alley

Homer Van Meter's Death Site
Intersection of University Avenue and Marion Street, St. Paul

Federal agents finally ambushed and killed John Dillinger in an alley outside Chicago's Biograph Theater on July 22, 1934. Bystanders dipped their handkerchiefs in his blood, and 15,000 gawkers walked through the morgue to view Dillinger's body.[131]

An exultant J. Edgar Hoover held a press conference to congratulate Melvin Purvis for leading the shootout, dined in triumph with President Roosevelt, and prominently exhibited a plaster death mask as a trophy at FBI headquarters. "I am glad that Dillinger was taken dead. . . . The only good criminal is a dead criminal," said Hoover.[132]

One month later, at an intersection just two blocks from the Minnesota State Capitol, Dillinger's partner Homer Van Meter met a similar end: he was shot to death by police in an alley, betrayed by the underworld. When they heard of Dillinger's death on the radio, Van Meter and his girlfriend Marie Conforti sought refuge in Minnesota. He first hid at Leech Lake Log Cabin Camp on Route 34 near Walker, Minnesota, sneaking into St. Paul for furtive "meets" with his colleagues at bars and bowling alleys along Rice Street.[133]

With the manhunt drawing closer, Van Meter met mob contact Frank Kirwin in St. Paul on August 3, and then hid from August 6 to 14 at Delia and James Coleman's Bear Island View Resort (known then as LeClaire's Resort) on Leech Lake in what is today Longville, Minnesota. Kirwin had recommended Bear Island for its splendid fishing. Visitors to the resort recalled the fugitive pair masquerading as Henry and Ruth Adams; Van Meter fished, Conforti swam, and both devoured the Coleman family's spaghetti.[134]

An FBI agent complained in a memo to Hoover that the search for Van Meter was hampered by "a serious handicap in that since the shootings, about 75 percent of the gangsters and mobsters of the underworld have scuttled out, had their telephones disconnected and have moved, that everybody is on the hideout, knowing that they would be brought in for questioning. There are numerous cottages and places up on the lakes where

The body of Dillinger gang member Homer Van Meter, slain in an alley near University Avenue by St. Paul police; (below) newspaper account of Van Meter's betrayal by the underworld

they have friends or relatives . . . making it doubly hard in carrying out the investigation."[135]

Van Meter moved from Bear Island to the Birches Camp Resort near Grand Rapids for one evening and then to the Green Gables Tourist Camp outside Minneapolis for another night, before heading toward downtown Minneapolis on August 23.[136]

Precisely how the police traced Van Meter has never been determined. Police first claimed that they got a tip from the family of one of Van Meter's girlfriends, a twenty-one-year-old waitress named Opal Milligan. Two days later, they changed their story, insisting that a tip from an auto salesman had led them to ambush Van Meter.[137]

Pat Reilly, interrogated by FBI agents, suggested that the underworld had "fingered" Van Meter for police because he talked too much about upcoming bank robberies. The FBI learned from Reilly that "Van Meter returned to St. Paul and consequently brought heat on the underworld here; that he was advised by the underworld that if he did not keep under cover, he would cause trouble to the remaining members of the underworld. However, according to Reilly, Van Meter was not the type that would stay under cover and that his constant appearance on the streets in St. Paul angered the underworld."[138]

An employee of slot machine king Thomas Filben, a business contact of the Dillinger gang, suggested a very different story. Horace "Red" Dupont, who worked for Filben's Patrick Novelty Company, heard that Van Meter had asked the mob's banker, Harry Sawyer of the Green Lantern saloon, to safeguard $9,000. When Van Meter returned from Illinois and demanded his money back, Sawyer decided to keep it and called police with a tip on Van Meter's location. The *St. Paul Daily News* carried a similar rumor: Van Meter had been turned in by Sawyer's mob after Sawyer was hounded by Van Meter for his cut of the $49,500 stolen by the Dillinger gang from the Security National Bank of Sioux Falls, South Dakota.[139]

Five years after Van Meter's death, the FBI would hear a final hypothesis. An underworld informant told the bureau that Dillinger gang associate Tommy Gannon, a Twin Cities bank robber, had betrayed Van Meter in a conspiracy involving casino operator Jack Peifer. According to this theory, Peifer and members of the St. Paul Police Department divided up Van Meter's bank loot. As a reward, Tommy Gannon was given Van Meter's guns.[140]

The hunt for Van Meter ended at the corner of University Avenue and Marion Street on August 23, 1934. The FBI determined that he had an appointment with Frank Kirwin that day, followed by a meeting with Jack Peifer at the Hollyhocks Club.[141]

Disguised by a mustache, wearing a blue serge suit and a straw hat, Van Meter walked out of the St. Paul Motors auto dealership at 5:12 P.M., ready to hop into a car parked north of University on Marion.[142]

Without warning, Van Meter was confronted by detective Tom Brown, police chief Frank Cullen (who had served under Brown as assistant chief), and two other officers. The police were armed with two sawed-off shotguns, two machine guns, and three words: "Stick them up!" Firing two shots over his shoulder from a .38-caliber Colt automatic, Van Meter ran south on the east side of Marion across University, toward an alley near Aurora. He "either got rattled or didn't know the neighborhood when he turned into that alley, because it's a blind alley," recalled an eyewitness. "If he had turned right, he might have got away."[143]

A blast of buckshot from Brown's shotgun blew Van Meter two feet off the pavement. "As he lay on the ground, he tried to get his revolver up to fire another shot," recalled an eyewitness. "But his hand was mangled by a machine gun blast" that nearly severed his arm. By 5:30 P.M. Van Meter was dead, slumped against a garage wall between Aurora Avenue and Marion Street. He had fifty bullets in his body, $923 in his pocket, and a gold-filled Bulova watch on his wrist. A pistol lay ten feet from his hand.[144]

Paul Presby, the St. Paul beat reporter for the *Minneapolis Journal*, was tipped off that Homer Van Meter had just been shot to death. "Paul Presby was a man who would walk over his grandmother for a scoop. . . . He called the *Journal* office and told them to send a cameraman to University and

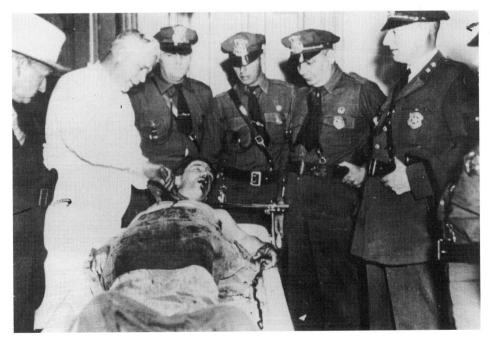

Homer Van
Meter's body at
the Ramsey
County Morgue

Marion," recalled crime buff Woody Keljik. But when Presby arrived, the ward wagon had already come and picked up Van Meter's body. There was still blood in the gutter and a crowd of people there.

"Paul was disappointed he wasn't going to get a picture. He said to his cameraman, 'I'll lie in the gutter, turn up my collar and you take a picture—they won't know if it's Van Meter or Presby.'" He lay down in the gore-filled street and the *Journal* photographer grabbed his shot. "While Presby was lying on the street, a new woman joined the crowd who didn't know what was happening," said Keljik. "They just told her that Homer Van Meter had been shot to death. When the pictures are over, Paul Presby stands up—the woman thinks Van Meter has come back to life and she faints!"[145]

Van Meter's body gave evidence of the lengths to which he had gone to avoid capture. Wax injected under his skin to alter his appearance had begun to deteriorate, turning his face into a lumpy mask. FBI agents discovered scars on his fingertips (Van Meter had paid Chicago doctors $5,000 to obliterate his fingerprints with acid) and an attempt to remove a tattoo ("Hope") on his right arm.[146]

Instead of relishing the triumph, Hoover was furious that the St. Paul police had not notified the FBI until *after* they had killed Van Meter; the bureau learned of the shooting from an Associated Press employee. "The Director is very upset over the fact that that thing could take place in St. Paul without our knowing about it," confessed an FBI memo. The *Minneapolis Tribune* reported that "J. Edgar Hoover . . . had nothing to say about the gangster's death." Privately, Hoover raged at his agents. "I think our St. Paul office has shown utter lack of aggressiveness," he scrawled at the bottom of an August 24 memo. "The Director is rather discouraged about the whole thing," warned FBI executive E. A. Tamm. Although newspapers were reporting Van Meter was "fingered" for death by a girlfriend, "we did not know a thing as they [the police] would tell us nothing."[147]

Hoover's next discovery was even more outrageous: the police version of Van Meter's death, as told to the FBI, appeared to have been fabricated. The police had informed the bureau that they could not have alerted Hoover's men to the ambush because, chief Frank Cullen explained, they had received a tip that Van Meter was at University and Rice just five or ten minutes before the shooting. Yet the manager of the auto dealership at the corner of University and Marion said that plainclothes police officers had kept his garage under surveillance not for ten minutes but for ten *days* prior to the shooting of Van Meter. Even more intriguing, the manager told FBI agents that on the day of the shootout, a mystery man in a Chevrolet sedan had dropped the doomed Van Meter off a few feet from the police. Curiously, the officers allowed the Chevrolet to leave the ambush scene. What was going on under J. Edgar Hoover's nose?[148]

"In the estimation of the Manager, the person who placed Van Meter on the spot was the driver of the Chevrolet car, whom he classified as a 'stool pigeon,'" reported an FBI memo. "The police officers did not fire while the driver of the Chevrolet car was in the line of fire. . . . The whole episode had been put on more or less as a show for the benefit of the Police Department." The FBI believed the Chevrolet driver was Frank Kirwin, Van Meter's trusted mob emissary, but underworld rumor held that Tommy Gannon delivered Van Meter to University Avenue in exchange for protection against being arrested for some burglaries that he was suspected of committing.[149]

The FBI also discovered that detective Tom Brown had visited the manager of St. Paul Motors at 12:30 P.M. that day "and told him that a man would be in there that afternoon to buy an automobile and that they wanted the man. . . . Brown gave him a description of Van Meter." Had the police ambush been a police/underworld setup, with Van Meter as victim and the FBI as patsy?[150]

"A deal was made between some of the 'big shots' and Tom Brown of the Police Department," noted an FBI report of an interview with Pat Reilly, "whereby Van Meter was to be placed 'on the spot.' [Reilly] feels fairly certain that the police were notified of the fact that Van Meter was in town and that he would make his appearance at the corner of University Avenue and Marion Street on the date in question."[151]

Pat Lannon Sr., a patrolman who was present when Van Meter's body was brought to the morgue, asserted that "it was all of Brown's clique, they had Van Meter put on the spot." One FBI informant, a saloon keeper named Frank Reilly, said that "Van Meter was killed . . . to try to put Tom Brown back in a good light, because of certain rumors which had come to the front to the effect that he was a crooked police officer."[152]

Police did not welcome questions about Van Meter's death. "Was Van Meter put on the spot by fellow gangsters?" the *Dispatch* asked chief Cullen days later. "No," answered Cullen. "Is 'No' going to be the answer to all questions?" asked the reporter. "Yes," replied Cullen.[153]

Ironically, Van Meter, who was named by a Dillinger gang girlfriend as one of the gang members who made a donation toward Brown's campaign for sheriff, was shot by his candidate. Both Edna Murray and Byron Bolton of the Barker-Karpis gang told the FBI that Brown lost his $5,000 portion of the Bremer ransom as punishment for shooting Van Meter. The FBI learned that Murray had overheard Doc Barker say of Brown, "I guess you saw where that dirty _____ killed Van Meter." Murray added that "Brown was deprived of his share of the Bremer ransom money because he had double crossed Van Meter."[154]

When FBI agent Richard Pranke was informed that a gangster had been killed by police at University and Marion, he convinced special agent D. Milton "Mickey" Ladd to visit the police station for the first time. "Mickey had never been in the headquarters of the St. Paul police, because they were crooked," said Pranke. "The FBI couldn't trust the police." Of Tom Brown, Pranke said, "It was my ambition to get him indicted."[155]

In the battle between the police and the FBI, the bureau won a single skirmish. After examining Van Meter's body in the morgue, Pranke picked up the mobster's belt. "The belt was rather fat like a fat snake. . . . [I] found a zipper on it and pulled the zipper down and there was a very large bill, and I mean money," recalled Pranke. According to police, the belt contained barely $450. The money apparently was "overlooked by the St. Paul Police Department in their examination of the clothing," gloated an FBI memo. "Some of the members of the St. Paul Police Department hated my guts," wrote Pranke, because "a 'young squirt' like me found the money after the police had searched Van Meter's clothes."[156]

The FBI's satisfaction turned to shock when Van Meter's girlfriend insisted that he had been wearing a money belt containing $2,000 and had driven to the corner of University and Marion with a brown zipped bag containing $6,000—a bag that the manager of St. Paul Motors claimed was under Van Meter's arm just before he was slain. "Evidently the police had disposed of the money," mused J. Edgar Hoover; an agent reported that "the St. Paul Police probably have in their possession $7,000 or $8,000."[157]

Van Meter's body was returned to his birthplace, Fort Wayne, Indiana, and buried by his family in Lindenwood Cemetery.[158]

Three months after Van Meter's death, on November 27, 1934, the FBI caught up with Babyface Nelson on a highway near Fox River Grove, Illinois. Nelson died in a drainage ditch near a cemetery, perforated by seventeen FBI bullets after killing FBI agents Herman Hollis and Samuel Cowley.[159]

The deaths of Dillinger, Van Meter, and Nelson signaled the virtual extermination of the Dillinger gang, yet for years Hoover raged about the tenacity of the public's fascination with the Dillinger legend. "Well, wasn't he a rat?" said Hoover. "Wasn't he everything that was low and vile? Didn't he hide behind women? Didn't he shoot from ambush? Wasn't his whole career as filthy as that of any rat that ever lived?" Dillinger continued to haunt Hoover as the media portrayed the bank robber as a gangland legend, a tommy gun–toting Robin Hood. *True Detective Mysteries* celebrated Dillinger as a "magician who got out of jails as easily as Houdini freed himself from handcuffs; [a] merchant of death who blasted himself and his pals out of one police trap after another."[160]

"Dillinger, who had been glorified by citizens having a distorted sense of values, met a fitting end," countered an FBI report. "And those to whom he had been an objective of hero worship, upon reconsideration, found that their misplaced admiration rightfully belonged with the law enforcement officer who daily risked his life to protect them from the violence of the Nation's Dillingers." The same report maintained that "the Dillinger case contributed greatly in earning for the FBI public confidence and support and caught the imagination of children of the day, many of whom are today devoted FBI employees."[161]

The *St. Paul Pioneer Press* welcomed the killing of Van Meter as "a first class serving of notice on the country at large and on the underworld in particular that St. Paul is really cleaning house and no longer deserves the evil reputation it acquired as a friendly harbor for gangsters." The *Minneapolis Tribune* asserted that "society is well rid of Van Meter. . . . The moral, we suppose, is that the trails of all criminals lead sooner or later to the inevitable 'blind alley' where Van Meter kept his rendezvous with justice."[162]

POLICE SHAKEUP FOLLOWS GRAFT R

Warren
Tieups

providing of most

Detective McGin-
department head
ment. Mr. Crum-
on under various
rtment since Oct.
17 and McGinnis
ve youngster. He

f the department
rved for a short

not fill the va-
public the possi-
oved.

F

s much specula-
Gus Barfus, now
the chief's office
rmanent. It was
the naming of a
t Carr, in charge
Thomas Grace,
ead of the check
was believed.
progress for ap-
s probably never

stalled in a pri-
sensitive instru-
dictograph con-
arks which offi-
e using the tele-
s telephone calls

O

de are said to be

recorded every
was made by the
when suspicious
tigators was de-
ver engagements

may become in-
facilities which
amblers. A fed-
upplied these fa-

E

ors was Wallace
as brought from
police and crime
amie, former fed-
became head of
sible for ridding
oung Jamie was
e University of

News indicated
rtment were far
s assistants were
an undercover

Policemen have
very of a dicta-
ce several weeks
a volcano.

D

es had been tap-
until the monitor
nths.

ayor Gehan, jus-
that it is used in
ficient police de-
d meritorious as
spicion could be

the alleged con-

Commissioner Warren Inspects Recording Instruments

COMMISSIONER OF PUBLIC SAFETY H. E. WARREN, left, is shown above as he this morning inspected the modern scientific equipment which brought about the biggest shakeup in the history of St. Paul's police force. He is placing a record on the phonograph which recorded many of the incriminating conversations. At the rear is WALLACE JAMIE, Daily News investigator, who secured the facts which caused the shakeup.

Scientific Devices Trapped St. Paul Policemen

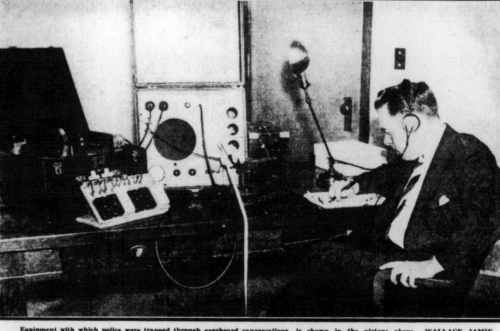

Equipment with which police were trapped through overheard conversations, is shown in the picture above. WALLACE JAMIE, investigator placed on the work by The Daily News, is pictured as he is listening to conversation coming to his office in the public safety building over a dictograph. At the left may be seen the recording phonograph on which much of the important information was recorded.

May
B

tion in this
yours,

"The e
Mayor Geh
present it
ren, and it
of the gran
"I don't
ney or mys
"These
ren's letter
dicted or
sound judg
"I think
service. Th

"If thei
should be s
earliest pos
service."
The ma
be conduciv
in any othe

He imm
and John L
but Mr. Ki
Warren lett
in determin
may be indi
Two m
adopted, th
grand jury
through co

HELD
ty jail, 1
A. Wright
charged
Wright w
by Louis
secret serv
of St. Pa
that he f
half doll
which W
cast the

GOV. OLA
ed a phot
Astor, foun
trading ind
dedication
memorial
Aug. 4, ther
torical colle
came from
on it a repr
trader's sig
ter he signe

UNHA
she fell
window t
Elizabeth
old daugh
William
st. The e
ed upon
screen, le

STATE
Carl Erick
110,000 ton
various sta
capitol duri
The bids w
Last year
to $5.45 pe

Randolp
Plans
On St

There is
steamer C
for the tan
be any.
At least n

Autos Kill 1, | **Kin Knows Nothing Of** | **Tries Jail Suicide** | **Blames Bank**
Lindquist Surrender

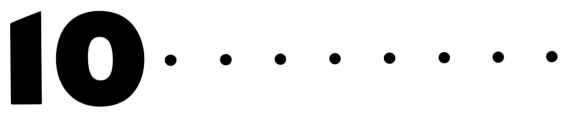

10

THE BIG CLEANUP

The electronic surveillance equipment (far left) that exposed police ties to the underworld also revealed gambling operations housed in the Hamm Building (left).

63 Sweeping the Police Clean

New St. Paul Police Headquarters
100 East Eleventh Street, St. Paul

St. Paul's new Public Safety Building, opened as the police department's headquarters in December 1930, was equipped with a garage, an Identification Division for fingerprints, "show-up" areas for lining up suspects, and three stories of Roman-Doric architecture. In the spring of 1935, the police station also harbored secret telephone wiretaps and microphones installed by the *St. Paul Daily News* and the public safety commissioner to capture corrupt policemen consorting with the underworld.[1]

By 1934 the public could no longer ignore the ties between police and the underworld. City officials were mortified when U.S. attorney general Homer Cummings said, "If there are two cities in America which need cleaning up, they are St. Paul and Minneapolis." Senator Royal Copeland of New York seconded the attorney general, condemning the Twin Cities as "the poison spots of American crime." Police-conducted "cleanup" campaigns had been closing down pinball games, gambling parlors, and brothels

St. Paul Police headquarters, from which investigator Wallace Jamie launched his probe into police corruption

since 1922, but no one had launched a campaign to clean up the St. Paul police themselves.[2]

Werner Hanni, the special agent in charge of the FBI's St. Paul office, reported to J. Edgar Hoover in February 1934 about the ballet the FBI had to dance with corrupt Twin Cities police. "In the Minneapolis Police Department there have always been a limited number that we know of in whom we have been able to place confidence. . . . It has been necessary for this Division, in the nature of investigations, to confine itself to those men of the department . . . whom we have found in the past that we could trust."[3]

Leading the charge for reform in St. Paul was Howard Kahn, the crusading editor of the *St. Paul Daily News*, located then at 55–65 East Fourth Street. A World War I hero who served in the U.S., French, and Italian armies, Kahn became a cub reporter at the *Daily News* in 1918 and rose to the post of managing editor by 1938.[4]

John Dillinger shot his way out of the Lincoln Court Apartments on March 31, 1934, the same day a Ramsey County grand jury report denied that the city was a magnet for gangsters. Kahn answered with the *News* headline, "Machine Guns Blaze as Jury Whitewashes Police." His editorial charged that the mayor "insulted the intelligence of St. Paul citizens" when he insisted that the city had no crime problem.[5]

St. Paul's Mayor William Mahoney angrily dismissed Kahn's relentless editorials. After one Kahn broadside, the mayor proclaimed, "There are no criminals here. They got Machine Gun Kelly in Memphis and Harvey Bailey in Oklahoma. These fellows just come here to visit our lakes. We have 10,000 lakes and a resort for every crook." "The newspapers of St. Paul are endeavoring to picture the Twin Cities as a Mecca for criminals," protested the director of the Minnesota tourist bureau, George Bradley. "Such publicity will irreparably injure the tourist business of this state."[6]

Howard Kahn, newspaper editor and relentless critic of police corruption

Kahn's *Daily News* answered that the public "will find it difficult to understand why such big-time gangsters as Harvey Bailey, Albert Bates, Machine Gun Kelly, Verne Miller, Verne Sankey and others were permitted to hide out in St. Paul. . . . Why shortly after Mr. Mahoney's election in 1932 perhaps the greatest conglomeration of national public enemies ever collected in one city gathered in St. Paul and remained here, unmolested by police."[7]

J. Edgar Hoover, still deeply suspicious of the St. Paul police, appeared reluctant to help the city change its image as a haven for criminals. Reform police chief Tom Dahill asked Hoover to compare street crime rates in

St. Paul to those of other cities. Within three days, the FBI had developed statistical tables of eight cities showing that—in spite of the highly publicized Hamm, Bremer, and Dillinger cases—the rates for everyday murder, assault, and larceny were indeed lower in St. Paul than in comparable cities.[8]

But FBI files show that Hoover lied to chief Dahill, responding that the FBI "has not prepared a compilation of data for individual cities, and that . . . due to the press of current work and limitations of personnel it will not be possible to do so." The FBI also refused requests to allow its agents to testify in the 1934 Ramsey County grand jury probe of civic corruption. Hoover declined to lend support in part because he distrusted the police and the grand jury system in St. Paul: "Within a few hours after any witness appears before the grand jury, the substance of his testimony appears in the local papers," wrote Hoover in a memo to the U.S. attorney general. "Obviously, this situation at St. Paul has degenerated into a publicity campaign and I do not believe that our Agents should become parties to any such spectacle."[9]

The *Daily News* kept up the pressure with a March 8, 1934, editorial headlined "Why Do Big Time Criminals Center Their Activities in St. Paul?" Noting that an Indiana highway patrol captain guessed that the men who robbed a Sioux Falls, South Dakota, bank were from the Twin Cities, the *News* asked: "Can it be mere coincidence that impels big-time criminals to make St. Paul their center of operations? . . . Or is it probable that the underworld knows the St. Paul police are helpless?"[10]

FBI agent Melvin Purvis condemned St. Paul in his 1936 book, *American Agent*. The city's reputation was such, wrote Purvis, "that when the wife of a prominent motion-picture producer was robbed in Chicago, police and federal agents assumed that the thieves would go to St. Paul to make contact with buyers of stolen goods." Tapping a few wires in St. Paul "led to the recovery of the jewels and the arrest of the robbers."[11]

Inside the St. Paul Police Department, Tom Brown and others tied to the O'Connor system battled reformers, among them Tom Dahill, Gustave H. Barfuss, and Clinton A. Hackert. One FBI agent noted that two of the reform policemen "are honest and sincere, but are being 'knifed' by the old outfit that under the civil service rules cannot be entirely eliminated." The agent suggested that the older police "for political and personal reasons, can, through their underworld connections, have crimes committed in this city to embarrass their successors."[12]

Clearly, though, the era of Harry Sawyer, Jack Peifer, and Tom Brown was coming to an end. "St. Paul has paid for its complacency under the O'Connor system, as all must pay who foul their own nest," editorialized the

Police reformers Thomas Dahill (left) and Clinton Hackert (right) , who battled the corrupt followers of former chiefs Tom Brown and John O'Connor

St. Paul Pioneer Press. "St. Paul pays in a vicious underworld that is notorious before the world and in the depredations of these criminals who, no longer under the iron hand of John O'Connor, have since then continually violated this rogues' compact."[13]

One thing was certain: the police could not clean house by themselves. In June 1934, the FBI was amused to hear that the police had created a new crime squad to raid St. Paul's gangster hideouts. The only problem, the FBI noted, was that "the head of this particular squad was Officer [Bill] McMullen, who, according to information furnished by Bessie [Beth] Green [of the Dillinger gang], is a friend of Harry Sawyer and a contact man between the police department and the underworld."[14]

Goaded into action, ten business leaders joined the *Daily News* in raising a $100,000 war chest to finance a campaign against corruption. Leading a team of investigators was a twenty-four-year-old criminologist named Wallace Ness Jamie, the third in a dynasty of gangster fighters. His father was Alexander Jamie of Chicago's "Secret Six," who had tackled Al Capone, and his uncle was Prohibition agent Eliot Ness, the famed head of the "Untouchables."[15]

Arriving in St. Paul in May 1934, Jamie worked with the full authority of public safety commissioner H. E. "Ned" Warren to install telephone taps in police offices to record conversations between officers and gangsters. Microphones were hidden in telephones, furniture, and air shafts throughout police headquarters. "In his preparatory investigations, [Jamie] had found

Wallace Jamie, University-Trained Crime Expert, Obtained Police Corruption Evidence Under Noses of Accused Officers

He Listened In On Talks That Are Made Basis Of Expose

BY JACK WAGNER.

The boys' game of "cops and robbers" has been changed to "cops are

The 27-year-old youth who directed the group of Daily News-Commissioner H. E. Warren investigators in obtaining evidence which led to the ousting and suspension of nine St. Paul policemen and officials and the equipment he used is shown above.

WALLACE JAMIE, son of the famous Alexander Jamie, head of the Chicago "Secret Six," is seen holding one of the numerous aluminum discs on which is recorded the damaging evidence of corruption against policemen. In his left hand Mr. Jamie is holding an expensive little microphone, one of the many which were secreted about the public safety building, in telephone bases, in ventilators and in lamps. It was through these microphones that the conversations of policemen with gamblers

and other underworld characters were overheard and recorded. Recordings were made on pamograph machines, one of which is shown in the lower left corner picture.

The lower right corner picture shows a record being made on one of the machines.

The teletype machine, shown under Mr. Jamie, automatically recorded the telephone numbers of all calls made out of the public safety building over automatic telephones.

In the upper left corner picture is shown the control switch and intake board for the machines.

The center top picture shows a pre-amplifier. One of the concealed microphones is seen in the upper right corner picture, hidden in a "dummy" desk lamp.

Was Regarded As Crank On Survey Work For Warren.

operation. On a white ticker tape, similar to those in brokers' offices, the numbers of all telephone calls made out of the building over auto-

Wallace Jamie (center), holding aluminum disk with damaging evidence revealed by wiretaps on the St. Paul Police Department's telephones

that all the telephone wires at police headquarters entered the building through a single terminal box," one magazine writer recounted. "This box, fortunately, was in a remote corner of the building, and Jamie went to work on it without fear of discovery. Each wire had an identifying tag and, one after another, Jamie cut in on all the wires and led the connection into his own control room which he had set up in a cubby-hole in another deserted part of the building—room 201."[16]

Throughout the spring of 1935, Jamie recorded 2,500 police telephone calls on 400 aluminum pamograph discs. The wiretaps generated 3,000 pages of incriminating evidence, linking police officials to a $2,000-a-day racehorse wire operated out of St. Paul by gambler "Dutch" Otto Cameron and other mobsters with the full protection of police. Among those caught on the wiretaps was police detective Fred Raasch, who warned the

Riverview Commercial Club to hide its slot machines from an impending police raid: "Take the two slot machines down. This is Freddie Raasch. There's a couple of guys coming right over. . . . stick them away in the vault."[17]

Jamie and the *St. Paul Daily News* had finally exposed the ugliness of thirty years of police corruption to the stunned citizens of St. Paul. There on the front page of the *Daily News*, proud residents of Minnesota's capital city read proof of what they had ignored for so long: routine tip-offs to the underworld, payoffs to police officials, and unmistakable camaraderie between gangsters and the police officers the city had hired to stop them.

64 'When Are You Going to Play Santa?'
The Hamm Building Gambling Den
408 St. Peter Street, St. Paul

One of the most striking wiretaps in the 1935 *Daily News* corruption investigation involved conversations between a gambler and James P. Crumley, acting inspector of detectives, who had been a policeman since 1914 and once headed the morals squad. Crumley was heard openly soliciting bribes from Harry Reed, president of the St. Paul Recreation Company, which ran a gambling operation in the basement of St. Paul's Hamm Building.

"Say, when are you going to play Santa?" asked Crumley. "We're all broke up here!"

"Well, you know that there hasn't been anything for the last two weeks," apologized Reed.

"Two weeks, hell, it's been six weeks," roared Crumley, to which Reed replied, "I'll take care of it for you."[18]

The Hamm Building basement was leased by Hamm kidnap intermediary William W. Dunn, who ran a billiards hall, a cigar stand, and a gym with boxing rings and bowling alleys there. One wiretap caught Crumley warning Harry Reed to shut down the Hamm Building's gambling before a police raid. ("Close up that horse book," Crumley said. "Right away . . . no bets, see.") Another wiretap found Reed complaining to Crumley about the success of a rival gambling establishment, Dutch Otto's Royal Cigar Store at 443 St. Peter, which had been kept open while St. Paul Recreation had to lay low. "Did anybody down at the Royal get permission from anybody to open —to run their horse—behind closed doors up there that you know of?" asked Reed. "Well, I just got word that they said they got permission from somebody. I was wondering why the hell we should be closed and they should be open."

Reed agreed to close his gambling operation "tighter 'n a g[od] d[amned] clam," but he was bothered by the bettors gathered at the Royal Cigar Store. Reed asked the officer to assure him that it would be "just a couple days until it cools off and they [St. Paul Recreation] can take the bets in the front there like everybody else is doing. . . . I don't give a damn if they [the Royal Cigar Store] make a million dollars. . . . I aint gonna squawk unless somebody else does."[19]

In June 1935 the scandal exploded on the front pages of the *Daily News*. Public safety commissioner Ned Warren informed Mayor Mark Gehan that the Jamie tapes disclosed "surprising evidence of police ownership of slot machines, police connection with prostitution, police political activities . . . and a sensational connection between police and criminal lawyers." The Jamie investigation forced a Ramsey County grand jury investigation that resulted in twenty-one indictments against officers, detectives, and others. Ultimately, thirteen policemen were either discharged or suspended, and chief Michael J. Culligan was forced to resign.[20]

Crucial to the cleanup was disciplining Crumley, who was exposed in the wiretaps as the "brains" of the network between gangsters and police. The sixty-three-year-old Crumley had joined the force under chief John O'Connor, was appointed inspector of detectives by Tom Brown, and participated in the 1932 police tip-off that enabled the Barker-Karpis gang to escape capture. He was, in short, a living symbol of the corrupt old guard.[21]

During Crumley's 1936 Ramsey County trial for malfeasance in office, his lawyers mounted a spirited defense. The attorneys attacked prosecutors for their technical problems with the wiretaps ("I would like to have seen these amateurs, these investigators, sitting in Mr. Crumley's place at police headquarters, keeping this town clean of murderers, kidnappers and thieves," jeered his lawyer) and defended Crumley's unsavory methods of crime control ("A police station is not a Sunday School"). Although that jury cleared Crumley of criminal charges, he was dismissed from the force and then convicted in 1938 on unrelated charges of fixing a federal drug case. He died of heart disease one year later.[22]

There was still the matter of Thomas Brown, the crucial source of police tip-offs to the Barker-Karpis and Dillinger gangs. "While it is generally rumored in St. Paul that Brown is a crooked police officer," one FBI agent wrote in February 1936, "should he have participated in either the Hamm or Bremer kidnappings . . . he has apparently been smart enough to deal only through Harry Sawyer, as neither Dahill nor anyone else has been able to furnish any concrete evidence of these rumors."[23]

Brown was temporarily suspended during the 1935 trial of the Hamm kidnappers after government witness Byron Bolton testified that Brown had received a $25,000 cut of the ransom money.[24]

The 1935 police cleanup, as announced by the **Daily News**

The FBI wrote that during the *St. Paul Daily News*'s wiretapping of police headquarters, "Thomas Brown was running things in St. Paul and it was hoped ultimately that . . . evidence enough would be secured on him to at least get him out of the Police Department. However, about that time Brown was transferred to some outside detail and had no occasion to make telephone contacts."[25]

Commissioner Warren summoned FBI special agent in charge Clinton Stein to Mayor Gehan's office on April 30, 1936. According to FBI records, Gehan brought up the charge that Brown had received a portion of the Hamm ransom. The commissioner reported that two policemen might be willing to speak out if Brown was removed from the force, but as long as he remained, "they are afraid of being killed if they talk." Dismissed by chief Clinton A. Hackert on July 17, 1936, Brown appealed to the Civil Service Commission, which upheld the dismissal for "breach of duty, misconduct, misfeasance and malfeasance." In a letter written to Brown on August 5, 1936, Warren savaged the detective for his participation in the kidnappings of William Hamm and Edward Bremer, for his role in the Barker-Karpis gang's 1933 escape from 204 Vernon Street, and for his leaks of police information to Harry Sawyer.[26]

The O'Connor system, born in 1900 when John O'Connor became police chief, died on October 9, 1936, when the discharge of Thomas Brown became

permanent. Federal prosecutors were disappointed that the three-year statute of limitations prevented them from charging Brown in the Hamm and Bremer kidnapping cases after June 1936.[27]

Brown died of a heart attack in 1959, at the age of sixty-nine, in Ely, Minnesota, near where he had been running a liquor store. He insisted to the end that his dismissal was the result of political enmity between him and former chief Thomas Dahill.[28]

In a sweep of St. Paul's entire police establishment, reformer Gustave H. Barfuss—who had led the drive to suspend Tom Brown for consorting with gangsters—was installed as acting chief of police and then public safety commissioner. Barfuss then named Clinton Hackert chief of police, and Hackert in turn put detective lieutenant Tom Dahill in charge of five reorganized police districts.[29]

Together, Hackert and Barfuss lobbied successfully for city charter changes designed to depoliticize the job of police chief and cauterize the wounds of corruption. The reforms included changing the process for selecting the police chief to involve merit appointments and extending each chief's term to six years. Given the history of nearly one police chief every twelve months, this change alone was striking. "We had a comic saying in the St. Paul Police," former patrolman Joe Sherin recalled. "You didn't know who was chief until you went to work in the morning."[30] The reforms last to the present day: the St. Paul police chief can only be removed "for cause," and an independent committee selects a field of candidates from which a police chief is appointed.

St. Paul, "long known as a hideout for the nation's desperadoes, has cleaned house," the *Chicago Daily News* cheered. "The chief broom wielder has been—and is—Gus Barfuss, commissioner of public safety."[31]

In the wake of the reforms, Mayor Gehan wrote to Senator Royal Copeland in April 1937, asking that he give the city he had branded a "poison spot of crime" a clean bill of health: "I am very frank in saying that I think your comments at that time were substantially correct, but it did hurt our city a good deal," wrote Gehan. Summarizing the strides made in cleaning up St. Paul, the mayor suggested that "it would be only right now that some short comment be made by the same officials as to the improved conditions."[32]

J. Edgar Hoover, ever mistrustful of city administrations, warned the attorney general against allowing any federal official to satisfy the mayor's hopes: "I think it would be most unwise for you to give St. Paul a 'clean bill of health,'" wrote Hoover. "While I think some improvement has been made . . . it is my opinion that we should make certain that a continued effort will be made so far as crime conditions there are concerned."[33]

The St. Paul police force had been cleansed. Now the last members of the Dillinger and Barker-Karpis gangs had appointments to keep at the Federal Courts Building.

11

FINAL JUDGMENTS

Alvin Karpis, being led by FBI agents into St. Paul's Federal Courts Building while crime reporter Nate Bomberg watches (far right, in profile); a "newsie" hails the **Minneapolis Star** *headlines announcing Harry Sawyer's capture.*

65 'We've Captured Alvin Karpis!'

Holman Municipal Airport
644 Bayfield Street, St. Paul

For members of the Dillinger and Barker-Karpis gangs, Holman Municipal Airport, just outside downtown St. Paul, was the gateway to a cell in the Ramsey County Jail, a trial in the Federal Courts Building, and then a train trip to a federal prison.

FBI agents brought William "Lapland Willie" Weaver and his girlfriend, Myrtle Eaton, to the airport after they were arrested for participating in the Bremer kidnapping. The couple had been hiding near Allendale, Florida, pretending to be chicken farmers. Weaver was apprehended on September 1, 1935, just after he awoke to feed his chickens—a chore that took him far from the two shotguns he stored in his house.[1]

Weaver's arrest was eclipsed by another, exactly eight months later: Alvin Karpis was seized in New Orleans on May 1, 1936. While most other members of the Barker-Karpis gang were being killed or jailed, Karpis—accompanied by Harry Campbell—was robbing jewelry stores, mail trucks, and even a railroad train. The FBI was infuriated that while Karpis was being hunted, he was indulging in "uninterrupted revelry" and "pleasureable activities," including a stay with a madam in Hot Springs, Arkansas, and fishing in the Gulf of Mexico. In January 1935 Campbell and Karpis machine-gunned their way out of a police raid in Atlantic City, New Jersey, but their girlfriends, Wynona Burdette and Delores Delaney, were arrested.[2]

Karpis was finally captured by the FBI, as he walked out of his apartment in New Orleans. "We've captured Alvin Karpis; generally known as Public Enemy No. 1—but not to us," chortled J. Edgar Hoover, who had traveled to New Orleans to participate in the arrest. "Karpis never had a chance." At 6:00 P.M. on May 1, Hoover informed special agent in charge Clinton Stein that Karpis had been seized and was being flown to St. Paul that night.[3]

Hoover ensured that his presence at Karpis's arrest was widely publicized. When the FBI director had testified before Congress in April 1934, he had been shamed by Senator Kenneth McKellar. The Tennessee Democrat had charged that the FBI was "running wild" and forced Hoover to admit he had never made an arrest. "I am talking about the actual arrests," the senator pressed Hoover. "You never arrested them, actually?" According to biographer Curt Gentry, Hoover left the Capitol after McKellar's inquisition and went directly to FBI headquarters, where he issued orders that he be notified the moment Karpis was found so that he could personally attend the arrest.[4]

As FBI publicity executive Louis Nichols told Gentry later, the capture of Karpis "pretty much ended the 'queer' talk"—widespread rumors that Hoover was hiding his life as a homosexual. Back in August 1933, for example, *Colliers* said the never-married Hoover walked "with mincing step." Magazines such as *True Detective* reported that during the arrest Karpis said to Hoover, "Go ahead—kill me. Get it over with." Karpis's nephew Albert Grooms told a different story. "Alvin told Hoover: 'You're a big brave S.O.B., you let these agents do all the work, and you take all the credit. What makes me mad is that the number one queer in the FBI captured me.' Hoover boiled, and told those guys to get Karpis up to St. Paul; Alvin had embarrassed Hoover in front of his own FBI crew!"[5]

The bureau claimed that while Karpis was a fugitive, he sent a letter to Hoover in Washington, D.C., "threatening to come to FBI headquarters with a machine gun and kill the Director, thus striking a crippling blow to law enforcement." Grooms said that the message his uncle sent the director was of a very different character: "The letter said he knew that Hoover was as queer as a three-dollar bill. Alvin and Ma

J. Edgar Hoover, seen here in a 1942 photograph with his assistant Clyde Tolson, flew to St. Paul to supervise the interrogation of Karpis.

[Barker] laughed and laughed in my folks' kitchen about that letter. Alvin said, 'Just imagine how that queer blew his stack!'" Asked in 1994 to produce a copy of Karpis's death threat against Hoover, the FBI admitted that it could not find such a letter.[6]

Karpis got along well with members of organized crime, including the American Mafia, Grooms said: "It was a mutual admiration society—the Italians had their thing and Alvin knew people who could help the Italians out in various cities. . . . Alvin tipped off Lucky Luciano and Meyer Lansky while they were meeting in Toledo, Ohio . . . about J. Edgar Hoover being queer. Lansky, who was going to be deported, got the idea of getting a photograph of Hoover with his boyfriend, Clyde [Tolson, assistant director of the bureau]. After that, Hoover lost all interest in deporting Lansky."[7]

Grooms's account dovetails with the research of Hoover biographer Anthony Summers, who learned that two Nevada hoods had boasted that Lansky "nailed J. Edgar Hoover" with, according to writer Pete Hamill, "pictures of Hoover in some kind of gay situation with Clyde Tolson. . . . That was the reason, they said, that for a long time they had nothing to fear from the FBI."[8]

Karpis was flown 1,530 miles to St. Paul, accompanied by Hoover and Tolson. Remembering the Kansas City Massacre, the FBI took no chances with Karpis; he was bound hand and foot with fifteen-pound chains. Accounts of

Alvin Karpis (in white shirt) arriving at St. Paul's Holman Municipal Airport with Hoover and FBI agents from New Orleans

the words passed between Hoover and Karpis during the flight to St. Paul vary. The pilot told journalists that Hoover treated the gangster like "a little boy," saying, "Now come in here, Alvin." Karpis claimed that the FBI men played terrifying games with him, intimating that unless he cooperated they might toss him out of the airplane. At one point, Hoover said, Karpis talked about his life: "Everybody I knew had to work for a living," he told Hoover. "They didn't get much out of it. What I wanted was big automobiles like rich people had and everything like that. I didn't see how I was going to get them by making a fool of myself and working all my life. So I decided to take what I wanted."[9]

Hoover's publicist, Courtney Ryley Cooper, wrote that Karpis told Hoover, "I'm no hood, and I don't like to be called a hood. I'm a thief. . . . A thief is anybody who gets out and works for his living—like robbing a bank . . . or kidnapping somebody. He really gives some effort to it. A hoodlum is a pretty lousy sort of scum. He works for gangsters and bumps guys off." Hoover responded, "You're still a hoodlum."[10]

Karpis arrived at Holman Municipal Airport at 8:47 A.M. on May 2, 1936, surrounded by thirty FBI agents bristling with machine guns. *Daily News* reporter Nate Bomberg described the scene: "Finally the plane came in. It was the biggest plane I'd ever seen at that time. Gigantic. It pulled up to the administration building and finally the doors opened and down the ramp came a flock of FBI agents led by J. Edgar Hoover. . . . Karpis was wrapped in leg irons and arm irons and he was irons all over. Mr. Hoover was holding the irons and led Karpis to a waiting car."[11]

For the next half century, Karpis would argue that Hoover had been no hero—that the director had arrested him after Karpis was disarmed by other bureau agents. "That May day in 1936, I made Hoover's reputation as a fearless lawman," wrote Karpis. "It's a reputation he doesn't deserve. I have nothing but contempt for J. Edgar Hoover."[12]

66 'We Have the Right People, I Think'

St. Paul City Hall and Ramsey County Courthouse
15 Kellogg Boulevard West, St. Paul

For the November 1933 trial of the accused kidnappers of William Hamm Jr., the FBI had almost everything lined up—eyewitnesses, expert testimony, and forensic evidence. Only one thing was lacking—the right culprits.

The trial of Roger "the Terrible" Touhy, Chicago bootlegger and arch rival of Al Capone, unfolded on the eighth floor of the twenty-story St. Paul City Hall and Ramsey County Courthouse, a stunning Art Deco building that had just been completed the previous year. The Justice Department decided to use this courtroom, rather than the Federal Courts Building two blocks away, because the Touhy gang could be brought from the Ramsey County Jail to the courtroom via a tunnel.[13]

In addition to Touhy, the defendants were robber "Gloomy" Gus Schaefer, burglar Willie Sharkey, and Eddie "Father" McFadden, twice arrested for, but never convicted of, robbery. The four were arrested after an auto accident on July 19, 1933, in Elkhorn, Wisconsin. Police seeking a hit-and-run driver found in Touhy's Chrysler sedan extras that were not automotive standard equipment: three loaded .38 revolvers, a .45 pistol, a .38 automatic, and, concealed under a golf bag filled with bullets, an automatic rifle.[14]

The mobsters were indicted on August 12 in St. Paul because, an FBI memo concluded, "it is believed that public opinion would be more in favor of the prosecution in Hamm's home town [than in Wisconsin]." During the trial, which lasted from November 9 to 28, the gang was guarded by federal agents, police detectives, deputy sheriffs, and U.S. marshal's deputies equipped with machine guns. "Detectives and deputy sheriffs, armed with pistols, rifles and tear gas bombs, took their stations to prevent any last-minute breaks for freedom," reported the *Dispatch*. "Telegraphers sat at their keys, wires cleared, ready to flash to the world the word 'guilty' or 'not guilty'. . . . Machine guns were added to the armament to forestall violence." Kidnap conspirator Fred Goetz, the FBI learned from his wife, Irene, surfaced in the Twin Cities during the Touhy trial to help the gangsters get an acquittal, "not because he was friendly with them, but. . . [because] he did not wish to see them take a 'rap' for a crime they did not perform."[15]

Ramsey County Courthouse and St. Paul City Hall, site of the 1933 trial of Roger "the Terrible" Touhy (inset) for the Hamm kidnapping

The FBI was under tremendous pressure to solve the Hamm kidnapping case quickly. Under its prodding, several witnesses to the abduction tentatively identified the Touhy gang, saying they resembled the men who had abducted Hamm and delivered the ransom notes. Privately, Justice Department officials knew the evidence was tenuous at best. It included white linen bandages found in Touhy's car that the FBI referred to as "appropriate for use in blindfolding kidnaped persons." When William Hamm was introduced to the Touhy gang, he admitted that they neither sounded nor looked like the men who had kidnapped him, but Hoover nevertheless determined to press on. In a confidential August 1933 memo regarding U.S. attorney Lewis Drill's doubts that the Touhy gang could be identified by witnesses, Hoover scrawled, "I don't like Drill's attitude. We have the right people, I think."[16]

After nineteen hours of deliberation, the jury disagreed, acquitting all four gangsters of any involvement in the kidnapping of William Hamm. The only bright spot for the law enforcement officers was Sharkey's hanging himself with a necktie in Ramsey County Jail on November 30. "By dying as he did, Sharkey has done a service to society," said Illinois state attorney Tom Courtney.[17]

To the FBI's credit, the subsequent detective work on the Bremer and Hamm kidnap cases was extraordinary. Their mistake with the Touhy gang behind them, the FBI tracked down the wallpaper Hamm remembered from the Bensonville hideout where he had been held and identified the siren he heard there. Agents researched the source of hundreds of socks to identify the ones given to Edward Bremer by his kidnappers. Within twenty-four months, the FBI would have identified and arrested more than a dozen conspirators for the Bremer and Hamm kidnappings.

Touhy, whom Al Capone believed to be an obstacle to his control of Chicago crime, had no similar run of good fortune. He was convicted in February 1934 of the "kidnapping" of con man Jake "the Barber" Factor, an ally of Capone. The FBI "assumed from the start, with no material evidence, that the Touhy gang was responsible" for kidnapping Factor, wrote FBI agent Melvin Purvis. "Every fact was fitted to the theory and the theory was correct." Touhy served two decades in prison for the kidnapping, until a federal judge declared him innocent, framed through perjured testimony, and freed the fifty-five-year-old bootlegger. In December 1959, less than a month after being released, Touhy was shot to death by Chicago crime figures. "I've been expecting it," moaned the dying Touhy, certain that Capone loyalists were behind the shotgun blasts. "The bastards never forget."[18]

67 'Before They Kill Me, I'll Kill Karpis'

Old Ramsey County Jail
St. Peter and Fourth Streets, St. Paul

Doc Barker, Alvin Karpis, Roger Touhy, and Edna "the Kissing Bandit" Murray were among the gangsters who were secured inside the Ramsey County Jail, a sandstone-and-granite structure built in 1903. Dillinger's girlfriend Evelyn Frechette, being held there on charges of harboring a fugitive, complained to reporters in April 1934 that the jail prevented her from practicing dances: "It's kind of close quarters for it in this cell," she quipped, "and besides, there isn't any music."[19]

Virginia Gibbons Schwietz, a secretary in the jail in 1935 for Sheriff Tommy Gibbons, her uncle, recalled the excitement as the nation's public enemies were brought to the jail in handcuffs: "It was a romantic time," said Schwietz. The gangsters "were like celebrities. Every time they came down the jail steps to go to federal court . . . shackled with FBI guys—oh, God, newsmen all over."[20]

A lower profile was sought for gangster Byron Bolton, the Bremer kidnap conspirator who turned government informant. Captured January 8, 1935, by Justice Department agents, he pleaded guilty to kidnapping and inspired some of the FBI's most cryptic public statements. Asked about Bolton's confession, FBI assistant director Harold Nathan explained, "I am not even admitting that there is such a man as Bolton or that he is in St. Paul. However, if there is, and if he is in St. Paul, I know nothing about any such confession."[21]

After his January 8 arrest in Chicago, Doc Barker was also installed in the Ramsey County Jail, locked alone in a cell block guarded by machine gun-equipped federal agents; when he was taken to the Federal Courts Building, he was chained and handcuffed to three different agents.

The Ramsey County Jail, which harbored gangsters such as Alvin Karpis and Doc Barker; (inset) Arthur "Doc" Barker (left), with Ramsey County jailer William Gates in 1935

Barker "slept . . . like a baby elephant—trumpeting," jailer William Gates told a newspaper. "He snored all night." Barker volunteered to teach Ramsey County sheriff Tommy Gibbons how to load and fire the new machine guns supplied to guard the Barker-Karpis gang, but the sheriff declined the offer.[22]

A talkative Karpis was brought to the jail on May 6, 1936. He told the FBI that he had turned down Al Capone's invitation to join the Chicago syndicate, which would have earned Karpis $250 a week for "strong arm work." When he asked to speak with defense attorney Archibald Cary, the FBI brought the lawyer to the jail and attempted to eavesdrop on the conversation. Before Cary arrived, "confidential arrangements were made to place a microphone near the place where the conference . . . was to take place. Special agent J. E. Brennan concealed himself in the adjoining cell tier." But Cary, the lawyer for Minneapolis gangster Isadore Blumenfeld, was no fool: he "began thumping on the table," reported the FBI, "and it was difficult for Agent Brennan to over hear the exact nature of the conversation." Later, when attorney Tom Newman conferred with Karpis, the FBI fussed that "efforts to overhear the conversation between Karpis and Newman were made by this office through the use of a dictaphone, but the results were not successful to any extent."[23]

J. Edgar Hoover personally ordered a guard be placed around Karpis, then held in solitary confinement, twenty-four hours a day. Hoover decreed that Karpis could not receive newspapers, have visitors, or even meet with his attorney without written permission from the prosecutors. "In view of the extremely dangerous character of this man, with a record of fifteen bank robberies, three kidnapings, four murders and three jail breaks," wrote Hoover to the U.S. attorney general, "I considered it imperative that every precaution be taken to prevent a possible escape."[24]

When Hoover learned that postal inspectors wished to interview Karpis without FBI agents monitoring the meeting, Hoover issued an ultimatum to the attorney general: let the agents remain or Hoover would withdraw them from the detail guarding "this extremely dangerous prisoner."[25]

Robert Schwietz, then a young deputy sheriff, recalled the rumor that Karpis might be sprung from his cell by the Barker-Karpis gang: "I received a phone call in the jail at around two in the morning, saying that they were going to break Alvin Karpis out. I got ahold of [jailer] Emory Clewett and Emory called the FBI. . . . Now I'm 21 years old and scared to death, shaking like a leaf. The FBI agent came into the jail at 2:30 A.M. and told me 'If the gang comes in, they're going to come in shooting.' So the FBI agent puts a machine gun on my desk, aiming toward the door. I'd never *seen* a

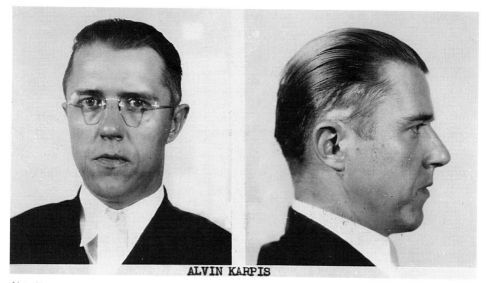

ALVIN KARPIS

Alvin Karpis in custody, 1936

machine gun before. The FBI [agent] told me, 'If they come in, just aim at the door and keep pulling that trigger.'"

Schwietz knew that everyone who entered the jail had to check their guns, even FBI agents. "The agent asked for his pistol," and Schwietz asked, "What good is a pistol?" The agent answered, "If the gang comes in, they're going to kill me. But before they kill me, I'm going to kill Karpis."

"So I'm sitting there," said Schwietz, "thinking 'Oh, Jesus—they'd have to get by me first!' I signed up for vacation in Texas the next morning and got out of town!"[26]

Easily the most dramatic exit from the jail was that of Jack Peifer, the Hollyhocks Club proprietor who had first proposed kidnapping William Hamm. On April 17, 1936, two teams of FBI agents stationed themselves outside the Hollyhocks and arrested Peifer, "in a semi-intoxicated condition," for his part in the kidnapping. By April 22 he was in Ramsey County Jail, forced to put up the Hollyhocks, then worth an estimated $40,000, to secure the $100,000 bail bond that won his temporary release. Peifer was vigorously defended by lawyer Archie Cary and former Minnesota Supreme Court justice Samuel Wilson, who said his client was "an ordinary citizen from a typical good Minnesota family . . . a man about town, a gambler, a wet, if you will, whom the government of the United States is trying to send to prison by innuendo."[27]

Peifer's claim to being an "ordinary citizen" was undermined by his co-defendants, many of whom identified him as the "fingerman" who selected William Hamm for kidnapping. After a ten-day trial, the jury declared Peifer guilty of kidnapping and he was sentenced to thirty years in prison.

"I am sorry for your relatives and friends," said the judge, as Peifer held his face, and Vi, his wife of one year, fell to the floor of the courtroom in shock.[28]

Awaiting the ride to Leavenworth, Peifer, according to the FBI, "is said to have walked into the cell, made some statement about it being pretty tough that he had gotten thirty years, and then walk[ed] over to get a drink. When he did not come right back, the others went over to him, and found that he had taken poison."[29]

"I put Jack in his cell the day he went to court," recalled Robert Schwietz. Peifer "scared the hell out of me. . . . I was walking through the cellblocks checking and someone said, 'Peifer fell asleep—but he looks like he's dead!' And I wasn't going into the cell. . . . I first called Emory Clewett and got the police department and they went in and found he was dead. Definitely, it was a suicide." After a forty-five minute effort to resuscitate him, Peifer was pronounced dead from the effects of a potassium cyanide pill on July 31, 1936.[30]

On hearing of his suicide, Vi Peifer told reporters, "I know Jack was innocent and he took his case to a higher court." According to at least one source, provided for his widow with a bundle of cash. Around the time of the Hamm kidnapping, Peifer told his wife that if anything happened to him, she should pull up a board in the floor of the Hollyhocks, where she would find some money so she could go on with her life. According to Vi's attorney, William Walsh, after Peifer's death she did just that, and she found $25,000 in cash hidden there.[31]

Not everyone accepts the official verdict that Peifer killed himself with poison just hours after defense lawyers had announced an appeal of his conviction. Clewett, the jailer, insisted that he had personally searched Peifer and found nothing that he could have used to kill himself. Could someone have assisted Peifer into the hereafter?[32]

The *Daily News* estimated that almost a thousand people jammed the service at Sunset Memorial Park, where Peifer was buried with military honors. Among the pallbearers were Minneapolis syndicate boss Tommy Banks, gambler Robert Hamilton from the Hollyhocks, bank robber John Davenport, and restaurant owner Charlie Saunders. Slot machine czar Tom Filben, liquor baron Frank McCormick, and nightclub owner Ben Harris were honorary pallbearers.[33]

"I've tried to figure out who could have smuggled that poison pill to Jack," said Martin Rohling, doorman for Peifer's Hollyhocks Club. "I was surprised when Jack committed suicide. He'd been laughing [just before], saying, 'I didn't do the kidnapping.'"[34]

'Hearts as Cold as Crystal'

Old Federal Courts Building (also site 5)
75 West Fifth Street, St. Paul

Two agents hid a microphone in the FBI's St. Paul field office, located on the second floor of what is now Landmark Center. They then left Hamm kidnapping suspect Charles Fitzgerald "alone" with racketeer Jack Peifer—before Peifer's suicide. Who knew what admissions of underworld skullduggery the pair might blurt out? As they bent over their surveillance apparatus, the agents were startled to hear an ear-splitting pounding. Peifer was rhythmically smashing the FBI's furniture with Fitzgerald's cane, completely obscuring the whispered conversations with his fellow gangster.[35]

At the old Federal Courts Building the last members of the Barker-Karpis and Dillinger gangs faced their victims, and, as some members turned into government informants, often faced each other. Suite 529 had been the headquarters of the Prohibition Bureau, which employed former Congressman Andrew Volstead, author of the Prohibition law. The federal grand jury investigating the Edward Bremer kidnapping in May 1934 met on the fourth floor; FBI inspector H. H. Clegg had to threaten reporters with contempt to keep them from loitering in search of a story. The U.S. marshal's office and the federal courtrooms, lush with marble and hand-carved cherry wood, were on the third floor. The most impressive space is courtroom 317, where Judge Matthew Joyce presided over the Hamm kidnapping trials. Room 203 was the St. Paul office of the FBI, where Alvin Karpis, Doc Barker, and other gangsters were interrogated.[36]

Most of the male associates of the John Dillinger gang—Homer Van Meter, John Hamilton, Tommy Carroll, and Eddie Green—were dead by spring 1934, when the FBI targeted the girlfriends, doctors, and errand boys who made the gang's stay in St. Paul so comfortable. Beth Green pleaded guilty to harboring a fugitive and was sentenced to fifteen months in the federal women's prison in Alderson, West Virginia. Dr. Clayton May, who had cared for Dillinger's gunshot wounds, was tried in St. Paul in May 1934 and sentenced to two years in Leavenworth. Evelyn Frechette was tried at the same time for harboring her boyfriend, John Dillinger. Attorney Louis Piquett, who defended Frechette, walked out of the courthouse and heard someone whisper his name. There, sitting in an automobile just a few dozen yards from the FBI's St. Paul offices, was Dillinger, smiling. "What the hell are you doing here?" Piquett asked. "Just thought I'd run up and see how the trial was coming along," quipped Dillinger—who then drove off.[37] Frechette received a two-year prison sentence.

In the spring of 1935, Judge Joyce presided over the first trial of the

The third-floor courtroom of the old Federal Courts Building, where surviving Dillinger and Karpis gang members were tried, with the assistance of gangster Byron Bolton (inset)

Bremer kidnapping conspirators, including Doc Barker and nine others. Fred Barker, however, did not live to face a jury. When they searched Doc Barker's Chicago apartment, agents found a map with a circle around Oklawaha, Florida, the site of Ma Barker's Lake Weir hideout. On January 16, 1935, FBI agents engaged in a six-hour machine-gun battle with Fred and his mother. The firing stopped after an estimated fifteen hundred rounds of ammunition had been fired at the Barkers. Fred Barker was found dead with a machine gun gripped in his left hand and a pistol in his right hand. "Close-by was 'Ma,'" claimed the FBI, "lying on her back, with a machine gun beside her lifeless body. The barrel was still smoking."[38]

After Kate Barker's death, the FBI took steps to convince the public that she had been the criminal mastermind behind the Barker-Karpis gang. In a *Chicago Tribune* series, Doris Lockerman, secretary to FBI special agent Melvin Purvis, wrote: "The Bremer kidnaping was Ma Barker's idea . . . [Fred] Goetz tried to talk her out of it . . . but Ma overruled him. . . . There were a hundred details to be arranged. Ma Barker and Goetz arranged them, planning the crime as carefully as a general staff ever planned a battle." Yet according to the FBI's internal files, the bureau knew all along that Goetz and Harry Sawyer, not Ma Barker, had planned the Bremer kidnapping. In fact, FBI interviews with surviving gang members and their girlfriends indicated that Ma Barker was not present at the key planning sessions before, during, or after Bremer's abduction. The files tend to support the claims of crime historians such as William J. Helmer, who suggest that the FBI—stunned to find a grandmotherly corpse on their hands—may have attempted to justify her death by transforming Kate Barker into a Medusa of gangland crime.[39]

The trial of Doc Barker and his accomplices began on April 15, 1935, at the Federal Courts Building. Government witness Bolton pleaded guilty to kidnapping and received four concurrent three-year prison sentences as a reward for betraying the gang. When Karpis heard that Bolton had informed against him, the FBI reported, Karpis said that he "would like to see Bolton run over by an automobile . . . and linger with a broken back for months and then die." Bolton was sent to a Milan, Michigan, prison in 1936 and released in December 1938.[40]

Kidnapping charges against gang members Jess Doyle and Edna Murray were dismissed on May 6, 1935, but Murray returned to Missouri State prison to continue her twenty-five-year sentence for robbery. Doyle, captured when his car got stuck in the mud in Kansas, was returned to the Nebraska state penitentiary for his role in the 1933 Fairbury National Bank robbery.

Assistant U.S. attorney George Heisey's final plea to the Bremer jury in mid-May 1935 was intense: "The kidnapping of Edward Bremer was not the crime of the century, but the crime of the ages. For every day of anguish and torture that Bremer went through, and for every day that his wife and daughter and father suffered, somebody ought to be made to suffer. And I think you know who it is!"[41]

On May 17, the jury issued guilty verdicts against Doc Barker and four others. Sentenced to spend the rest of his life in prison, Barker was sent to Leavenworth, and later transferred to Alcatraz. A few days earlier, Harry Campbell was arrested in Toledo, Ohio, and pleaded guilty to his part in the Bremer kidnapping; he, too, was sentenced to life and sent to Leavenworth. Pat Reilly received a twenty-one-month sentence in the El Reno, Oklahoma, reformatory for harboring a fugitive and for helping to set up medical care and other services for Dillinger.[42]

J. Edgar Hoover continued to campaign for longer prison sentences for the women who had harbored the public enemies, even those who had relatively little contact with the men's criminal activities. Helen Gillis, wife of Babyface Nelson, was sentenced to prison in Milan, Michigan. A 1934 FBI memo noted that "every method of attack has been used by agents in an effort to get this woman to talk, but without avail. It was thought that possibly her weak point would be her children . . . when discussing her children, she broke down and wept at length, but would not give in." Jean Delaney,

The Bremer kidnapping jury, guarded by deputy marshals, crosses Fifth Street on its return to the old Federal Courts Building after a break.

Tommy Carroll's lover, was found guilty of harboring Dillinger and sentenced to the women's prison in Alderson, West Virginia. Myrtle Eaton, whose Kennington apartment had been a planning center for the Bremer kidnapping, was found guilty in Jacksonville, Florida, in June 1936 and sentenced to six months in jail for harboring William Weaver.[43]

A second trial of Bremer kidnapping suspects began in St. Paul federal court on January 6, 1936: Edna Murray testified as a government witness against Harry Sawyer and William Weaver. The forty-four-year-old Sawyer, once the most powerful underworld fixer in Minnesota, had fled to Florida, Michigan, Wisconsin, Ohio, Nevada, Iowa, and finally to Mississippi, where he was arrested in Pass Christian on May 3, 1935.[44]

Pleading innocent, Sawyer enjoyed superb legal representation from former U.S. attorney Lewis L. Drill and lawyer Robert Rensch, but the evidence against him was overwhelming. Prosecutor George Heisey said that

Sawyer and Weaver had "hearts as cold as crystal and as hard as granite," that they were willing to commit "the most horrendous crime known to man." Building steam, Heisey roared that Bremer "still is suffering from his harrowing experience. Every day, every hour, every minute, while he was being held prisoner was a living hell. There was not a minute when he did not see death staring him in the face." The trial ended on January 24, when both Weaver and Sawyer were found guilty and sentenced to life imprisonment.[45]

Harry Sawyer's wife, Gladys, turned FBI informant against the Barker-Karpis gang in 1936. She told the FBI that, in the words of its report, "her husband is serving a life sentence . . . mainly because he was faithful to his friends and associates and because those friends deserted both him and her when they were needed." An FBI official wrote Hoover in July 1936 that Gladys Sawyer feared that gangsters would "knock her off." He suggested that the bureau "endeavor to instill a proper degree of confidence in this woman so that she will make a satisfactory witness. I don't believe, however, that we should waste any time attempting to protect Gladys Sawyer after the various attempts which she has made to embarrass the Bureau."[46]

Gladys begged Harry to blow the whistle on the St. Paul underworld in order to avoid a transfer from Leavenworth to Alcatraz: "With the deal that you got . . . why should we try any longer to protect some people," she wrote. "You know you shouldn't be there, so why stay if you can help yourself. . . . Life isn't worth living the way it is now. All my love. Gladys Sawyer." He refused to talk and was transferred.[47]

Alvin Karpis also refused to turn informer. During the airplane trip from New Orleans to St. Paul, he spoke freely about the shootouts he had participated in and other subjects, but drew the line at "ratting" on his friends. Karpis "frankly admits that this is the code of the underworld; that he has operated outside of the law since he was about fifteen years of age, and that he intends to abide by this code," the FBI reported.[48]

At the FBI's St. Paul field office, J. Edgar Hoover had him chained to a radiator, according to Karpis's account. Hoover reportedly demanded of his agents: "I want a signed confession from this man for every crime he ever committed in his life. I want to know the names of all the people who were in on his crimes. . . . If he starts to lie, kick his teeth in for him." In his autobiography, Karpis later described the experience: "They put handcuffs on me —real cuffs, not a necktie—and they chained shackles around my ankles and locked the other ends of the shackles to a steam radiator. I felt like an animal."[49]

Karpis told FBI agents that he would be willing to plead guilty to the Hamm kidnapping but might still testify to exonerate his friend Jack Peifer. "Karpis then laughingly remarked that he did not mind helping out anybody, and that 'a fellow can't get life for perjury.'" The FBI knew that Karpis's weak spot was the safety of his girlfriend, Delores Delaney, who had been captured in Atlantic City, New Jersey, and had been imprisoned in 1935 at Milan, Michigan. Karpis insisted that he had not told Delaney about his business and said he had considered offering the judge a $10,000 bribe to give Delaney a bench parole but was unable to figure out how to reach the jurist.[50]

Delaney gave birth to a son, named Raymond Alvin after Karpis's alias Raymond Hadley, in February 1935, while she was in federal custody. "I wish Al could see him," Delaney told reporters. "But I don't know where he is and if I found him, it would only mean Al's arrest. . . . My baby positively will never go inside a jail—no matter what happens to me." With his father and mother in prison, the boy was given to Karpis's parents to raise.[51]

"The FBI kept Karpis in a little detention room—still marked "U.S. Marshal"—on the third floor of the Federal Courts Building," reported Landmark Center tour guide Woody Keljik, and "when the trial was about to start, J. Edgar Hoover walked into the detention room and had Karpis handcuffed to him, so he could personally walk him the thirty feet to the trial!"[52]

On July 14, Karpis stood in the sweltering heat of judge Matthew Joyce's courtroom and pleaded guilty to the Hamm kidnapping. "I don't want to stay in that hot courtroom for three weeks," he joked, before being sentenced to life in prison. In the three-year span ending in the fall of 1936, with Karpis locked in Leavenworth, Hoover had succeeded in killing or imprisoning most members of the Barker-Karpis, Keating-Holden, Harvey Bailey, Frank Nash, and Dillinger gangs.

After Karpis was captured, he wrote to Delores Delaney:

I received your letter and was certainly surprised as I realize that I am unworthy of any kind thoughts that you have of me. I don't know how to express my feelings toward you in words, but when I lost you the light just seemed to go out.

As I slowly read your letter, it seemed as though I could see your laughing Irish eyes, but this time they didn't seem to be laughing. I can truthfully say that I have never received a letter in my life that has made me realize how selfish and inconsiderate I have been ever since I was a child.

I am not getting religious, or crying the blues, but it woke me up quicker than all the time I will do if I live to be one hundred years old. If a person like myself is capable of loving any one or having any affection for another, I certainly feel that way about you. Alvin Karpis.[53]

• • • • • • • • • • •

EPILOGUE

Hit man Joey Schaefer, released from Stillwater Prison after serving thirty-one years; Alvin Karpis at McNeil Island prison in November 1968, about to be paroled

More than half a century has passed since the slaying of Dillinger gunman Homer Van Meter and the suicide of Jack Peifer, two deaths that capped what the *St. Paul Daily News* called "an unsavory, ugly epoch" in St. Paul stretching from 1920 to 1936. "We did it all ourselves," said the *Daily News* on July 25, 1934. "We brought on the era of high crime and we cut it off. . . . We tolerated slums, crooked politics, fixers of high and low degree, four-flushers and go-getters, we got just about what we asked for, and we had nobody to blame but ourselves."

While St. Paul struggled to bury its gangster past, the FBI's newsreels, television and radio shows, books, and tours have turned minor thugs with colorful nicknames into legends who eclipsed far more powerful organized-crime figures. So vivid were the FBI's larger-than-life images of Dillinger-era outlaws that people found it hard to believe that criminals who survived so many shootouts could actually be dead. Crime historian Jay Robert Nash, for example, claimed that inconsistencies in John Dillinger's autopsy report prove that he was not the man killed by the FBI outside Chicago's Biograph Theater in 1934.[1]

"I think about him every day," Dillinger's sister Audrey Hancock told a

John Dillinger Sr., the bank robber's seventy-year-old father, shown here (in dark suit) with family members, who toured vaudeville theaters after Dillinger Jr.'s death in 1934

reporter, "and I wonder what I would do if he came in that door. I dreamed about him one night. I heard him calling, 'Sis!' just so plain and I got out of bed and swung that door wide open, expecting to find my brother there. But it wasn't; it was a dream. I never have had a dream as real as that one."[2]

Bruce Hamilton of Shiprock, New Mexico, claimed that his uncle, Dillinger gang member John "Three Fingered Jack" Hamilton, did not die of the wounds he suffered during the Hastings Spiral Bridge shootout in April 1934. Rather, Hamilton was smuggled to Chicago and then into Canada for medical attention—said his nephew—and returned to his family in South Bend, Indiana, eighteen months later with his face altered by surgery. What of the mutilated body found in August 1935 in an Oswego, Illinois, gravel pit? What of Hamilton's teeth, displayed by the FBI at a 1939 Chicago Dental Society meeting? The Dillinger gang obtained a corpse of appropriate size, explained Bruce Hamilton, and poured lye over the body to disfigure identifying marks. "The FBI got my grandfather, William Hamilton, to identify my uncle's body," added Hamilton. But "everyone in my family knew that my uncle was alive and back in South Bend."[3]

In fact, John Hamilton had "died" and been resurrected once before. Dillinger told newspaper reporters in early 1934 that Hamilton had been killed during the robbery on January 15, 1934, of the First National Bank of East Chicago. "Poor Red . . . he died from the wounds he received in East Chicago," mourned Dillinger. "Caught a whole flock of bullets in his stomach. . . . They dumped his body in the Calumet River." Dillinger was lying to reduce police interest in apprehending Hamilton; although he was wounded in the robbery, Hamilton was very much alive at the time.[4]

There are clues that support Bruce Hamilton's story. In September 1934, the FBI interrogated thief Frank Kirwin, one of the Dillinger gang's contacts in Minnesota. He told the FBI that Hamilton had indeed been severely wounded during the Hastings shootout. But, Kirwin insisted, "Hamilton was not killed and buried as reported."[5]

In his autobiography, FBI agent Melvin Purvis added another note of support for the rumors. He wrote of a man who brought photographs to the FBI, claiming the gentleman pictured was a very much alive John Hamilton. "The amazing part of his story was that he had recently taken the photographs, had made Hamilton pose in various positions so that there could be no doubt as to the identity of the person in the picture," marveled Purvis. "He even had the man holding a cap in his hand so that it appeared that his fingers were amputated in the same way as were those of Hamilton. He told us that Hamilton was at that time fully recovered from his wounds and was hiding out in the country somewhere in Missouri." Yet Purvis spurned the

The body of Dillinger gang member John Hamilton being exhumed from a grave in Oswego, Illinois, in August 1935

account as "obviously false," based on "faked photographs," and thus "no action was taken by the government."[6]

What of the other members of the Dillinger and Barker-Karpis gangs—and their victims?

Arthur "Doc" Barker, serving a life sentence in Alcatraz for the Bremer kidnapping, was slain by prison guards in January 1939. He had scaled a wall and tried to reach San Francisco Bay. "I am crazy as hell," said Barker to a guard as he expired, "I should never have tried it." John Knutson, an Alcatraz guard, insisted that the felon took his own life: "Barker got depressed—his relatives were all gone—so when he was out on the yard he ran across, scaled the wall, and started climbing the fence," recalled Knutson. "The guards yelled at him to let go. He wouldn't and they shot him off. It was suicide.[7]

George "Machine Gun Kelly" Barnes died of coronary failure in Leavenworth prison in July 1954 after serving nearly two decades for the kidnapping of Charles Urschel. "My dad was something of a braggart. He didn't express any remorse," said Kelly's son Bruce Barnes. "My Dad was *proud* that he got away with so much and the police never knew he even existed. In fact, the police were blaming those bank jobs on someone else. Dad told me he never made less than $125,000 a year on bank jobs, and yet he wasn't even on the list of the bank robbers they were looking for!"[8]

Kelly's wife, Kathryn, was also sentenced to life imprisonment, chiefly on the basis of testimony by a government handwriting expert that she had written threatening letters to Charles Urschel. J. Edgar Hoover condemned her as the mastermind behind the kidnapping, pointing to the "feminine thought and psychology" in the ransom letters.[9]

In 1970, however, former FBI agent William Turner released the text of a suppressed 1933 FBI laboratory test that would have exonerated her. The agency's analyst admitted that "detailed analysis indicated that Mrs. Kelly did not write these letters." Turner also released a 1959 memo from the special agent in charge of the FBI's Oklahoma City field office that suggested the lab report not be released to the U.S. attorney because it could be "a source of embarrassment to the Bureau." Kelly, who had protested her innocence for decades, appealed her conviction and was released from prison in 1958. She moved to Oklahoma and is now living at an undisclosed location.[10]

George "Machine Gun Kelly" Barnes in front of his Alcatraz jail cell

Harvey Bailey, dean of the 1920s bank robbers and associate of St. Paul's "Dapper Dan" Hogan, survived thirty years of a life sentence in Alcatraz and Leavenworth. After the seventy-six year-old Bailey was paroled in 1964, he collaborated with author J. Evetts Haley on his memoir, *Robbing Banks Was My Business*, and became a woodworker in a furniture factory. He died of a kidney ailment in 1979 in Joplin, Missouri, at the age of ninety-one.[11]

George Young and Joey Schaefer, the Murder Inc. hit men who killed bootlegger Abe Wagner in 1932, remained locked in Stillwater Prison for more than thirty years. Schaefer, sixty-five, was paroled in December 1963, and Young, fifty-four, was paroled shortly afterward. Neither broke his vow of silence about who paid them to murder Wagner. "It was me or him," Schaefer told reporters as he was taken to the Minneapolis–St. Paul airport for a flight to Philadelphia. "Loeb [Wagner] was trying to kidnap me."

"These were tough guys. . . . Mentally and physically, they had toughness that even someone in law enforcement has to grudgingly admire," said captain Joseph O'Connor of the Philadelphia Police Department's Organized Crime Unit, which monitored Young and Schaefer's activities in Pennsylvania after their release. "Thirty years hard time. . . . He never talked," added O'Connor. "They don't make people like this anymore!" Young died in 1971, and Schaefer died in 1982, both in Philadelphia.[12]

Leon Gleckman, the liquor czar who dreamed of becoming mayor of St. Paul, died in a bizarre car accident in July 1941. En route to his home, contemplating yet another prison term, he drove his Chevrolet into an abutment at Kellogg Boulevard and Wacouta Street, adjacent to St. Paul's Depot Bar. He died of a fractured skull; his blood alcohol level was .23—the equivalent of drinking thirteen ounces of 90-proof liquor. The death certificate called Gleckman's death "probably accidental." "You can't prove it, but in my heart, as a policeman, I think [he] wanted to do himself in," said Joe Sherin, then a St. Paul patrolman. "We all think Leon killed himself. . . . He was due to go to federal prison. He was the king of the bootleggers and he didn't fancy sitting in the Can."[13]

Harry Sawyer, the Green Lantern saloon proprietor who chose Edward Bremer for kidnapping by the Barker-Karpis gang, was transferred in 1936 from Leavenworth to Alcatraz. He was returned to Leavenworth in 1943 for another twelve years of imprisonment. The U.S. attorney vigorously opposed parole for Sawyer, warning that he was a "confirmed public enemy and has devoted his entire life to the commission of crime." Yet prison authorities hailed his "remarkable conduct record"—not a single disciplinary action was taken against him while he was behind bars. Sawyer became as indispensable in prison as he had been at the Green Lantern. He worked seven days a week, eight to nine hours a day, as a baker, kitchen helper, and server in the Leavenworth cafeteria, even filling in for absent inmates and volunteering for extra duty.[14]

Harry and Gladys Sawyer had begun efforts to adopt Francine, the five-year-old girl who had inadvertently led authorities to the Barker-Karpis gang hideout in Cleveland. But in September 1934 the adoption was stopped, and the girl was taken from them by the Minnesota Children's Bureau. A heartbroken Gladys moved back to Nebraska, and then to Denver, Colorado, where she divorced her incarcerated husband.

Sam Sandlovich was one of the only members of the family to keep in touch with Harry Sawyer while he was in prison. "My mother said that the Sandlovich family disowned Harry," said Carole DeMoss, Sandlovich's daughter and Sawyer's niece. "First for running a saloon in St. Paul, and then when he became involved with the Barker-Karpis gang, they severed all ties with him. I didn't even know I *had* an uncle Harry until he died."[15]

Sawyer's wealthy family in Nebraska was mortified by his notoriety. Most of his relatives refused to visit him or answer his letters; one offered Gladys Sawyer a thousand dollars to keep quiet about her husband's prison sentence. "It is apparent that there has been a deep family pride," said a caseworker, "and Harry's behavior has wounded them greatly." In 1955, after Sawyer suffered through years of chronic liver disease and arthritis, doctors found cancer attacking his spinal cord. He was paroled in February 1955 and sent to a Chicago hospital, where he died in June; his body was taken for burial in Chicago's Westlawn Cemetery. Even in death, Sawyer remained an outcast from his family.[16]

Kidnap victim William Hamm Jr. led the Hamm Brewing Company as president and then chairman of the board until 1965. "Bill Hamm didn't talk a lot. He was not a very demonstrative man and held everything into himself," recalled William Figge, former president of the company. "But one time, I drove with him to a brewing convention in Duluth. Just outside St. Paul, Hamm started to tell me all the details of his kidnapping. He wanted to talk to someone about it."[17]

Hamm's cousin John Flanagan wrote that Hamm was perceived as being "gloomy and possibly a bit fearful of the future. He apparently had thought about the possibility of being kidnapped . . . before the dreaded event occurred. Undoubtedly the kidnapping affected his later life and [he] developed a tendency to brood and even to be laconic in business meetings. . . . My cousin avoided unnecessary travel and even employed bodyguards when he visited the homes of relatives in the Lake Minnetonka area." Hamm died in Minneapolis in August 1970.[18]

Edward Bremer, victim of the Barker-Karpis gang's second kidnapping, died of a heart attack in Pampano Beach, Florida, in 1965 at the age of sixty-seven. His daughter, Betty Bremer Johnson, said her father did not speak about the event that had so traumatized him. Still, the obituary of the Commercial State Bank president and chairman described him as "the central figure in St. Paul's most famous kidnapping case in the 1930s."[19]

Most of the Dillinger and Barker-Karpis gang girlfriends put their criminal past behind them, sinking into anonymity. Evelyn Frechette, who was released in 1936 after serving two years for harboring John Dillinger, died of cancer in 1969. As Evelyn Tic, she had lived with her husband, Art, a state game warden and barber, in Shawano, Wisconsin. "I got the impression that Evelyn was glad to get out of it, with the guns and all, that it wasn't an easy life," said Bernice Tic, widow of Evelyn's stepson. "She liked the peace and quiet, taking care of my four daughters and cooking fish and venison that Art caught. She didn't speak about Dillinger much, and we let it go at that."[20]

Delores Delaney, Alvin Karpis' girlfriend, was released from prison and returned in 1938 to her family in St. Paul. Raymond Karpovicz, her son by Karpis, was born while she was in FBI custody and raised by family members in Chicago.[21]

No other gangster of the public enemies era endured as many years in prison as Alvin Karpis. He was incarcerated for thirty-three years—first in Alcatraz and then in McNeil Island prison on Puget Sound. Minneapolis defense attorney Eugene Rerat met him in Alcatraz in 1937: "I had expected to find a savage, snarling brute, a man filled with hate, an illiterate animal, dangerous even in prison," Rerat recalled. "Instead, I talked with one who had all the poise and polish of a business executive. Karpis was soft-spoken, extremely intelligent, and completely dignified in his conduct. What a success he might have been if he had turned those talents to business instead of crime!"[22]

Karpis secretly delivered his portion of the bank robbery and kidnapping loot to his family during the 1930s, according to his nephew Albert Grooms. The ill-gotten gains were deposited, with full interest accruing during his imprisonment, in savings accounts in Des Moines, Kansas City, and Duluth. "Those banks were just tickled as hell to have the money," said Grooms. "You didn't need a Social Security number in those days."

After Karpis was paroled, Grooms met with him in Port Arthur, Canada, and handed him a large check—the principal and interest from the crimes he had committed nearly half a century before. "It was a bundle, you damned well bet it was," says Grooms. "It was all the money he'd squirreled away during the 1930s!"[23]

When Karpis's autobiography, *The Alvin Karpis Story*, was published in 1971, Thomas McDade, a retired FBI agent who had investigated the Barker-Karpis gang, wrote Karpis a friendly note: Would the aging gangster like to meet the elderly agent who had hunted him four decades earlier? From his home in Spain, Karpis agreed to the interview. "I was pleased by his readiness to accept my note in the spirit intended—the nostalgia of a long retired lawman," recalled McDade. To his surprise, Karpis's letter "exuded energy, intelligence, enterprise and imagination. . . . He welcomed correspondence and so between us began an international exchange of letters." When Karpis and McDade met in Spain, Karpis recalled how irritating it had been to guard Ed Bremer. ("Oh, that fellow Bremer. How tired I got of him. All he did was complain about the food.") Karpis displayed his printless fingers, a legacy from the operations of Dr. Moran years before.[24]

Karpis died from an overdose of sleeping pills in the summer of 1979 in Torremolinos, Spain, at the age of seventy-one. He had outlived his nemesis, J. Edgar Hoover, by seven years.[25]

The golf-loving, fugitive Evergreen bandits, Francis "Jimmy" Keating and Tommy Holden, who had been recaptured at the Mission Hills golf course in 1934, were transferred to Alcatraz, locked in solitary confinement, and put to work breaking rock in an underground quarry. Holden was only disciplined once—when he asked for two extra pieces of turkey from the prison steam table. Prison officials warned, however, that "since return from escape, he [Holden] has been a constant plotter," seeking a way to break out again. After being released from prison, he died awash in violence and despair. Driving home on June 5, 1949, after drinking beer in a Chicago tavern, the fifty-three-year-old Holden got into a quarrel with his wife, Lillian. He slapped her face and she dashed up to her apartment. Holden chased after her with a .38-caliber revolver and shot her and two others dead. Once again a federal fugitive, he was hunted by the FBI and captured in Oregon in 1951. He died of heart failure in 1953 at Stateville Hospital, after being sentenced to serve twenty-five years in the Illinois State Penitentiary for the triple murder.[26]

Jimmy Keating, in contrast, achieved a rare form of gangster redemption. Working in a prison brush factory as a bristle clerk, he received high marks from both Leavenworth and Alcatraz officials for his good nature and intelligence. Although Keating was punished for nine disciplinary violations, his infractions were pranks: taking an unauthorized bowl of ice cream, playing baseball in the prison yard, laughing too loudly in the mess hall, making faces at the prison guards. After being released from prison in the late 1940s, Keating retired to Minneapolis, where he befriended former prizefighter Ernie Fleigel, one of the founders of the 620 Club (its motto: "Where Turkey is King") on the downtown Hennepin Avenue strip.

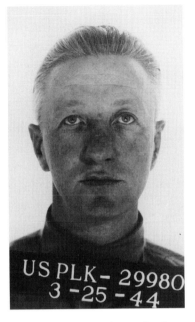

Veteran bank robber Jimmy Keating in 1944, twelve years after his return to custody

Every Sunday, Keating had brunch at Fleigel's home with another guest, former FBI agent John Roberts. "Keating believed he'd paid his debt and Roberts. . . . knew of his background and had come to terms with it," said Robert Fleigel, Ernie's son. "Keating was a soft-spoken, white-haired gentlemanly fellow. What few people knew was that he was the most successful train robber of the '20s and '30s. . . . Dad cautioned me not to bring up [Keating's] past, and I never did. I knew him only as a kindly old gentleman who had a way with kids."[27]

During the 1950s, Keating tended a floral shop in the Calhoun Beach Club in Minneapolis. He befriended Charlie Reiter, a former St. Paul Police officer and Bureau of Criminal Apprehension agent. He spoke little of prison or of his years as a bank robber, simply confessing that as a young man he had hungered for excitement—and bank robbery was how he got it. "I made lots of money," Keating told Reiter. "But the lawyers got the money and I got the time."[28]

Through the 1960s and 1970s, Keating remarried, became a grandparent, and found success as an organizer for the machinists union based in St. Paul. "When Jimmy got out of prison . . . someone directed him back to the Twin Cities, where he hooked up with a union. . . . It was his chance to be legitimate," said his friend "Shy" Troupe. "Jimmy's specialty had been anything that was illegal, and that specialty was *over* with; so what's a guy to do?"[29]

"Jimmy would say to me, 'I always wanted to be a banker,'" recalled Charlie Reiter. "'But the bankers wouldn't hire me. So I took my own banks.'"[30]

Keating died of heart failure in July 1978 in a nursing home in St. Louis Park, Minnesota. He was seventy-nine and had outlived virtually every public enemy he had golfed with back in 1931.[31]

Before his death, Keating was introduced by Ernie Fleigel at the 620 Club to a prominent Republican financier. "I don't think you've met my friend . . . he's a banker up in North Dakota," said Fleigel to Keating.

"Oh, really?" said an amused Keating. "What bank is that?" The financier identified his institution as the Fargo National Bank and asked if Keating had been there.

"Oh, I think I've done some business up there," chuckled Keating. Fleigel later told the banker that the business Keating had undertaken decades before in Fargo had involved a getaway car, a submachine gun, and thousands of dollars in cash withdrawn hastily in canvas bags.[32]

With the benefit of hindsight, former FBI agent William Turner, crime historian Carl Sifakis, and others have questioned whether the FBI's obsession with criminals like John Dillinger and Ma Barker (who was never convicted of, nor even arrested for, any crime) distracted the bureau from tracking a far more insidious foe. "No one argues that the Dillinger-style criminals were not genuine desperadoes," wrote Turner, "but the G-men's quarry was, essentially, the 'few preying on a few.' While all eyes were riveted on the blazing chases of Prettyboy Floyd, Babyface Nelson, et al., the Mafia and its allies were quietly building a criminal cartel preying on the nation."[33]

In contrast to the manpower lavished in 1934 on chasing Dillinger (who was personally accused of killing only one man), FBI agents ignored syndicate leaders such as Al Capone, who directed hundreds of murders. It was, after all, the accountants in the Special Intelligence Unit of the Treasury Department, not the FBI, that sent Capone to Alcatraz. "Had the full energies of Hoover's agency been turned on the major menace of the Capone-Luciano-Lansky organizations," Sifakis wrote, "it has been argued by many crime experts [that] organized crime today would be far less effective and pervasive, if not totally eliminated."[34]

For years, J. Edgar Hoover denied that the Mafia existed. In choosing to target Dillinger rather than the Mafia, Hoover showed a canny sense of how newspapers would cover—and history books would remember—the crime fighters at the bureau. Few recall today the names of Treasury agents Frank Wilson or Elmer L. Irey, the men who successfully prosecuted Al

Capone. Yet Hoover and his Chicago agent Melvin Purvis were lauded in newsreels, films, and front-page headlines for slaying Dillinger.

The official tour of FBI headquarters in Washington, D.C., kept the Dillinger myth alive with a shrine containing his guns, bulletproof vest, eyeglasses, and straw hat, along with a death mask, molded from the bank robber's face.

In Wisconsin today, tourists visit the Little Bohemia resort to see the bullet holes, the bed that Dillinger slept in, a bullet-shattered tin can used by the gang for target practice, and the shirts, underwear, and suitcases the gang left behind when the FBI raided the Rhinelander lodge.

In Minnesota, many ask what has become of the Dillinger door, a slab of veneered mahogany removed from apartment 303 after the March 1934 shootout at the Lincoln Court Apartments.

Lincoln Court landlord Daisy Coffey presented the bullet-riddled door to the family that ran the Brigham Inn, a resort, country store, and gas station near Remer, Minnesota.[36]

A St. Paul policeman points to bullet holes in the door of the Lincoln Court's apartment 303.

For twenty years, tourists gawked at the door, stuck their fingers through the holes, and listened to stories of the day when Dillinger answered the FBI's knock with a fusillade of bullets.[35] Eventually, the door began to disintegrate and was abandoned behind the Remer resort, where the wooden panels from Dillinger's apartment crumbled into dust.

Sites are in St. Paul, unless otherwise noted.

1 Dan Hogan's home, 1607 W. Seventh St.
(near May St. and I-35W entrance), private residence. (Map A)
*A bomb planted in Dan Hogan's Paige coupe in the white stucco garage
behind this home exploded on December 4, 1928, killing St. Paul's Irish
Godfather.*

2 Old St. Paul police headquarters (demolished),
110 W. Third St. (Kellogg Blvd. W., near Washington St.),
across from the St. Paul Public Library. (Map C)
*Police chief John J. "the Big Fellow" O'Connor supervised his "layover
agreement" with the underworld from police headquarters. O'Connor lived
nearby at 144 West Fourth St. (demolished)*

3 Nina Clifford's brothel and home (both demolished),
147 and 145 S. Washington St.
(now Hill St. near Kellogg Blvd. W.). (Map C)
*The two-story brick mansion that served as St. Paul's most elegant brothel
was demolished in the late 1930s. The site of madam Nina Clifford's home,
at the corner of Hill and Washington, was next to the old Ramsey County
morgue (164 S. Washington St.). The brothel site is below the Kellogg Blvd.
underpass. The entrance to the tunnel that may have run between
Clifford's back door and the Minnesota Club (317 Washington St.) is
visible on new Hill St. below Kellogg Blvd., near the medical examiner's
office at 155 Hill St.*

4 Dan Hogan's grave, Calvary Cemetery, 753 Front Ave.
(near N. Grotto St.). (Map A)
*Gangster Dan Hogan's grave is marked with a red granite monument and
footstone in lot A, block 6, section 59. Other architects of the O'Connor
system are buried nearby: fixer William "Reddy" Griffin's red granite
monument is in lot 15, block 19, section 51; police chief John O'Connor's
family mausoleum is in lots 2–3, block 52, section 6.*

5 Old Federal Courts Building (now Landmark Center),
75 W. Fifth St. (Map C)
*A brown-granite Romanesque masterpiece that cost nearly $2.5 million,
the Federal Courts building opened in 1902. The Prohibition Bureau,
which employed former Congressman Andrew Volstead, author of federal*

Prohibition legislation, had an office on the fifth floor in suites 528–529. The FBI pursued kidnappers and bank robbers from its second-floor field office in room 203. The Barker-Karpis gang's trials for kidnapping were held in Judge Matthew Joyce's federal courtroom, room 317, lush with marble and hard-carved cherry wood. Alvin Karpis was held during his trial in the third-floor detention center, room 323.

6 Dreis Brothers' Drug Store (demolished),
465 St. Peter St. (at W. Seventh St./Old W. Ninth);
the site is adjacent to Mickey's Diner. (Map C)
Liquor hijacker Burt Stevens was murdered by a "phantom gunman" at the southwest corner of this intersection in 1925, setting off a chain of events that would destroy one of the nation's biggest bootlegging rings.

7 Hotel St. Paul, 363 St. Peter St.
(southwest corner at Fifth St.). (Map C)
Built in 1910 (and reopened in 1989 after renovation), the hotel contained the third-floor headquarters of underworld figure Leon Gleckman, "the Al Capone of St. Paul."

8 Leon Gleckman's home, 2168 Sargent Ave. (near Cretin Ave.),
private residence. (Map A)
On September 24, 1931, gangsters kidnapped liquor czar Gleckman from this two-story residence, where he lived with his wife and three daughters.

9 Merchants Bank Building,
northwest corner of Fourth and Robert Sts.,
now First National Bank, St. Paul. (Map C)
The seventh floor of this white-brick skyscraper, built in 1915, provided a luxurious office for liquor baron Leon Gleckman and for the Justice Department agents determined to wiretap his suite 713.

10 Mystic Caverns nightclub (demolished), 676 Joy Ave.
(near the entrance to the former Twin City Brickyard),
now W. Water St. (Map A)
Built into a mushroom cave along the Mississippi River, the Mystic Caverns featured strippers, roulette wheels, and blackjack tables. Now abandoned (and known to cavers as Horseshoe Cave), the ruins of Mystic Caverns can be identified by the crumbling entrance .6 mile southwest of the new High Bridge, adjacent to the Lilydale Regional Park sign.

11 Castle Royal nightclub, 6 W. Channel St.,
now 215 S. Wabasha St. (near Plato Blvd.). (Map A)
With rich oriental carpets, crystal chandeliers, and seats for 300 revelers, the underground Castle Royal hosted performers like Cab Calloway, Harry James, and the Dorsey brothers in the front rooms and illicit gambling in the back rooms.

12 The Boulevards of Paris and the Coliseum Ballroom
(both demolished), 1100 W. University Ave.
(at N. Lexington Pkwy.). (Map A)
At the Boulevards of Paris, tuxedoed and gowned patrons could enjoy European cuisine, big-band jazz, and a full-scale reproduction of the American Bar in Paris, as well as the thrill of dancing side-by-side with notorious gangsters. The Coliseum, once an ice rink, claimed to have the largest dance floor in the world (100-by-250 feet).

13 The Green Dragon Cafe (demolished), 469 N. Snelling Ave.
(at W. University Ave.), now site of the Spruce Tree Center. (Map A)
On July 25, 1932, two hit men from the Murder Inc. syndicate gunned down bootlegger Abe Wagner and his partner, Al Gordon, here in broad daylight.

14 Lowry Hotel, 339 N. Wabasha St. (between Fourth and Fifth Sts.),
now Lowry Office Building. (Map C)
Opened in 1927, the Lowry had a long history of association with the underworld, providing a haven for Bugsy Siegel, Alvin Karpis, and other gangsters.

15 Harry "Dutch" Sawyer's home, 1878 Jefferson Ave.
(near Fairview Ave.), private residence. (Map A)
Underworld banker Sawyer, who supervised St. Paul's O'Connor system after the murder of Danny Hogan, hosted underworld parties in this two-story house.

16 Green Lantern saloon (demolished), 545 N. Wabasha St.
(between W. Tenth and W. Eleventh Sts.),
now site of the Wabasha Street Apartments. (Map C)
The Green Lantern was St. Paul's premier criminal hangout—a saloon for safecrackers and bankrobbers which "Creepy" Karpis called "my personal headquarters." The Lantern was turned over to Dillinger gang members Tommy Gannon and Pat Reilly in 1933, closed in 1934, and became a photography studio and a beauty shop in the 1950s before being razed.

17 Hotel St. Francis, Old W. Seventh St.

(between Wabasha and St. Peter Sts.), now 7th Place Residences, Francesca's restaurant, and the old Orpheum Theatre. (Map C)

Slot machine king and Dillinger gang patron Tom Filben used the St. Francis, built in 1916, as his base of operations. At the height of his power as an underworld fixer in the early 1930s, Filben lived in the two-story, stucco home at 2133 Fairmount Ave. (near S. Finn St.); his slot machine company, Patrick Novelty, was at 518 St. Peter St. (demolished), just a few blocks from the Hotel St. Francis.

18 Edgecumbe Court Apartments, 1095 Osceola Ave.

(at S. Lexington Pkwy.). (Map B)

Known to the FBI as a "lamsters' hideout," these apartments were home to many of America's most-wanted bank robbers and prison escapees from 1931 to 1933.

19 Lincoln Oaks Apartments, 572 Lincoln Ave. (near Grand Ave.). (Map B)

The "unlucky" bank robber Charlie Harmon and his wife, Paula, lived in apartment 1 of this brown-brick building while on the run from the FBI.

20 Cretin Court Apartments, 50 S. Cretin Ave. (at Grand Ave.). (Map A)

This three-and-a-half story brick building was once the home of bank robber Francis "Jimmy" Keating, one of the "Evergreen bandits" hunted by the FBI.

21 Summit-Dale Apartments, 616 Summit Ave. (at Dale St.),

now Hawthorne Apartments. (Map B)

Keating's bank robbing partner, Tommy Holden, hid under an alias in this handsome four-story red-brick structure.

22 Wildwood triple-murder site,

near Wildwood and Katherine Abbott Parks, Mahtomedi. (Map D)

On August 13, 1930, authorities discovered the bodies of three Kansas City gangsters hanging from willow trees about a half-mile southeast of the entrance to Wildwood Park, located at the intersection of Highway 244 and Birchwood Rd. A few hundred yards away at 92 Mahtomedi Ave. (at Stillwater Rd./County Rd. 12) is Big Ben Restaurant, on the site of the original Picadilly, a favorite diner for the John Dillinger gang.

23 Plantation nightclub (demolished), Old White Bear Ave.

(at Cottage Park Rd.), White Bear Lake;

the site is now Lion's Park. (Map D)

The gangsters who vacationed around White Bear Lake—including Al Capone's gunman Fred "Shotgun George Ziegler" Goetz—spent their evenings at the Plantation, where, in the words of the FBI, they indulged in a "riotous nightlife."

24 Keller Golf Course, 2166 Maplewood Dr.
(near County Rd. B), Maplewood. (Map A)
Founded in 1929, this eighteen-hole course was so popular with bank robbers such as "Evergreen bandit" Jimmy Keating that the FBI used its golf caddies as informants.

25 Ma Barker's hideout, 1031 S. Robert St. (near Bernard St.),
West St. Paul, private office. (Map A)
The Barker-Karpis gang, which rented this house from the Hannegraf family in February 1932, escaped a police raid after being tipped off by corrupt officers. Owner Helen Hannegraf lived next door at 1035 S. Robert.

26 John Lambert cottage, 148 Dellwood Ave.,
Dellwood, private residence. (Map D)
Located on the east shore of White Bear Lake near the intersection of Tamarack St. and Mahtomedi Ave./Highway 244, this eight-room cottage provided a vacation spot for the Barker-Karpis gang in the summer of 1932. The underworld gambled at the Silver Slipper roadhouse at 230 Warner Ave. in Mahtomedi, now a private residence near the corner of Warner and Greenwood, and socialized at Elsie's speakeasy at 159 Dahlia. Babyface Nelson and his wife lived in a Mahtomedi cottage and ate at Vince Guarnera's Italian restaurant at 959 Mahtomedi Ave.; bank robber Frank "Jelly" Nash lived in a Mahtomedi home near Rose and Spruce Sts.

27 Third Northwestern National Bank (demolished),
430 E. Hennepin Ave. (at S.E. Fifth St.), Minneapolis;
the site is now a parking lot. (Map E)
The triangular bank building that stood at this spot was the scene of one of the most violent bank robberies in Minnesota history. On December 16, 1932, the Barker-Karpis gang took more than $120,000 from the bank and left two Minneapolis policemen dead.

28 Como Park Zoo (off N. Lexington Pkwy.). (Map A)
During the getaway from their December 16, 1932, bank robbery in Minneapolis, the Barker-Karpis gang stopped near this spot to switch cars. Unaware of the robbery, Christmas tree salesman Oscar Erickson slowed down to look and was shot to death by Fred Barker.

29 Annbee Arms Apartments, 928 Grand Ave. (near S. Milton St.),
now Kensington Hall. (Map B)
*Two days after the Third Northwestern National Bank robbery, police
captured an intoxicated Larry DeVol at his apartment in this twenty-one-
suite, red-brick building.*

30 Cle-mar Apartments, 2062 Marshall Ave. (at N. Cleveland Ave.). (Map A)
*This four-story red-brick apartment building was home to Katherine "Ma"
Barker, con man Earl Christman, kidnapper Bernard "Big Phil" Phillips,
and other members of the Barker-Karpis gang.*

31 Grand Avenue Apartments, 1290 Grand Ave.
(near S. Syndicate St.). (Map B)
*In February 1933, the Barker-Karpis gang set up headquarters in this
four-story brick apartment building—but were forced to flee in March after
a tip-off of an impending police raid.*

32 Commodore Hotel, 79 Western Ave. (at Holly Ave.). (Map B)
*Opened in 1920, the hotel and its elegant art deco bar attracted literary
figures F. Scott and Zelda Fitzgerald as well as gangsters Al Capone and
Fred Barker. The hotel was renovated in the 1970s but still looks much like
it did when Ma Barker met her son Fred's girlfriend here.*

33 Hollyhocks Club casino, 1590 S. Mississippi River Blvd.
(white home between 1606 and 1616 S. Mississippi River Blvd.
near S. Cleveland Ave.), private residence. (Map A)
*Hosted by fixer Jack Peifer, this club overlooking the river bluffs was a
favorite haven for members of the Dillinger and Barker-Karpis gangs. The
facade was significantly renovated in the early 1990s, but the circular
driveway and expansive lawn still evoke its gangster-era splendor.*

34 Idlewild cottage, 5500 E. Bald Eagle Blvd.
(at Taylor Ave. near Highway 61),
White Bear Lake Township, private residence. (Map D)
*This one-and-a-half-story cottage provided an ideal hideout for the
Barker-Karpis gang to plan the kidnapping of William Hamm Jr. in 1933.*

35 Hamm Brewing Company, 681 E. Minnehaha Ave.
(at Payne Ave.), now Stroh Brewery Company. (Map A)
*On June 15, 1933, William Hamm Jr., grandson of the brewery's founder,
was kidnapped near the brewery (at the corner of Minnehaha and
Greenbrier, now obscured by the Stroh buildings) while he was walking
toward his home at 671 Cable Ave. for lunch. The Hamm mansion at what
is today the intersection of Greenbrier and Margaret Sts. was destroyed by
fire in 1954; a nine-foot-high brick column on the site, overlooking the*

entrance to Swede Hollow Park, marks the southeast corner of what was once the Hamm estate.

36 William W. Dunn home, 1916 Summit Ave. (near Prior Ave.),
private residence. (Map A)
William Dunn, the intermediary between William Hamm's kidnappers and the Hamm family, lived in this two-story stucco home. Unbeknownst to Hamm, Dunn had also served as the conduit for underworld payoff money to corrupt policemen.

37 Rosedale Pharmacy, 1941 Grand Ave. (at Prior Ave.),
now Thomas Liquors. (Map A)
On June 16, 1933, kidnapper Fred Goetz left a ransom note for the Hamm family at a soda booth in Clarence Thomas's drugstore. A portrait of Thomas now hangs at the back of the liquor store managed by his son.

38 Hideout of the Vernon Street Gang, 204 Vernon St. (near St. Clair Ave.),
private residence. (Map A)
During the Hamm kidnapping, this two-story house near Macalester College housed a convention of public enemies, including Fred and Doc Barker, Frank "Jelly" Nash, and Alvin Karpis.

39 Tom Brown's home, 759 E. Maryland Ave. (near Weide St.),
private residences. (Map A)
Former St. Paul police chief Tom Brown and his family resided in this two-story stucco house during the years when he used his position to aid some of the country's most notorious criminals.

40 South St. Paul Post Office, 236 N. Concord St.
(near Grand Avenue), South St. Paul. (Map A)
On August 30, 1933, the Barker-Karpis gang stole $33,000 from a South St. Paul stockyards payroll brought by rail to this two-story brick building from the Federal Reserve Bank of Minneapolis. The bandits severely wounded one police officer and shot another dead.

41 Dale Apartments, 628 Grand Ave. (at S. Dale St.). (Map B)
In December 1933 and January 1934, the Barker-Karpis gang used this imposing three-story building as its headquarters for planning the Edward Bremer kidnapping.

42 Jacob Schmidt Brewery, 882 W. Seventh St. (at Webster St.),
now Minnesota Brewing Company. (Map A)
Founded in 1855, this brewery helped make the Bremers one of Minnesota's wealthiest families—and a target for kidnappers. During

Prohibition, Schmidt beer was delivered to the underworld's Green Lantern saloon via a tunnel to a brewery employee's house on Erie St.

43 The Kennington, 565 Portland Ave. (at N. Kent St.). (Map B)
Shoplifter Myrtle Eaton offered her apartment 104 in this red brick building as a hideout for the Barker-Karpis gang before the Bremer kidnapping.

44 Holly Falls Apartments, 562 Holly Ave. (at N. Kent St.). (Map B)
On January 13, 1934, Roy McCord, wearing his Northwest Airlines radio operator's uniform, was mistaken for a police officer by Alvin Karpis and severely wounded near this four-story brick building in a hail of gunfire.

45 Bremer kidnapping site, intersection of
S. Lexington Pkwy. and Goodrich Ave. (Map B)
On the morning of January 17, 1934, banker Edward Bremer, who had just dropped his daughter off at the Summit School at 1150 Goodrich, was seized here by the Barker-Karpis gang.

46 Walter W. Magee's home, 1295 Lincoln Ave.
(near S. Syndicate St.), private residence. (Map B)
Magee, contacted by the Bremer kidnappers to act as intermediary between the gang and the Bremer family, had his two-story stucco home placed under police surveillance.

47 Bremer's abandoned automobile, outside 1910 Edgecumbe Rd.
(near Montreal Ave.), private residence. (Map A)
Hours after he was kidnapped, Edward Bremer's Lincoln sedan was found here in the Highland Park neighborhood, its interior stained with blood.

48 Edward Bremer home, 92 N. Mississippi River Blvd.
(near Otis Ave.), private residence. (Map A)
Protected by FBI agents, the Bremer family waited at their two-and-one-half-story brick mansion near the Lake St. bridge for word on the fate of Edward Bremer. The home of Edward's uncle, Otto Bremer, is at 1344 Summit Ave. (at Hamline Ave.).

49 Dr. Henry T. Nippert home, 706 Lincoln Ave.
(near S. St. Albans St.), private residence. (Map B)
After abducting Edward Bremer, the kidnappers placed a ransom note in a bottle and threw it through the front-door window of the three-story red-brick home owned by the Bremer family doctor.

50 Adolf Bremer Sr. mansion, 855 W. Seventh St. (near Oneida St.), now a private social service agency. (Map A)

Before paying the $200,000 ransom, Adolf Bremer Sr. called reporters to his two-story home to appeal for the safe return of his kidnapped son. Later the family built a tunnel from the house to the basement of the Schmidt brewery's Rathskeller bar across the street. Visitors to the Rathskeller can identify the tunnel, now sealed off to protect children who might be attracted by the underground passage, by a six-foot-high wooden door.

51 Harry "Dutch" Sawyer's farm, 305 Snail Lake Rd., Shoreview, private residence. (Map D)

Surrounded by groves of cottonwood trees, this small farm—in part financed with loot stolen in 1933 from the First National Bank of Fairbury, Nebraska—served as a hideout and conference center for underworld friends of nightclub owner Harry Sawyer. The two-story home across from Sitzer Park harbored such gangsters as Fred Barker, Alvin Karpis, and Edna "the Kissing Bandit" Murray.

52 Santa Monica Apartments, 3252 S. Girard Ave., Minneapolis. (Map E)

Just after his March 1934 escape from an Indiana jail, John Dillinger and his lover, Evelyn Frechette, moved into apartment 106 of this four-story building. Babyface Nelson and other Dillinger gang members reunited here to plan a wave of bank robberies.

53 Charlou and Josephine Apartments, 3300 and 3310 S. Fremont Ave., Minneapolis, now Fremont Apartments. (Map E)

These two four-story apartment buildings were home to several Dillinger gang members in 1934. Gunman Homer Van Meter and his girlfriend Marie Conforti lived in apartment 201 of the Josephine Apartments, while bank scout Eddie Green used the Charlou's apartment 207 to stash machine guns and bulletproof vests.

54 Dr. Nels Mortensen's home, 2252 Fairmount Ave. (near Woodlawn Ave.), private residence. (Map A)

Just after midnight on March 13, 1934, Dr. Nels Mortensen answered his doorbell and found wounded gangsters John Dillinger and John Hamilton on his front steps.

55 Lincoln Court Apartments, 93 S. Lexington Pkwy. (at Lincoln Ave.). (Map B)

On the morning of March 31, 1934, FBI agents and police knocked on the door of Lincoln Court apartment 303 on a landlady's hunch—

inadvertently stumbling into a gun battle with John Dillinger and Homer Van Meter. Dillinger's third-floor apartment, where he lived with girlfriend Evelyn Frechette, overlooked Lexington Pkwy.

56 Dillinger's getaway garage, 1123 Goodrich Ave.
(near S. Lexington Pkwy.), private. (Map B)
Evelyn Frechette—covered by the machine gun-wielding Dillinger— backed Dillinger's Hudson sedan out of this garage near the Lincoln Court shootout and drove the bank robber to safety.

57 The Dillinger doctor's clinic, 1835 Park Ave. (near E. Nineteenth St.), Minneapolis, private residence. (Map E)
Accompanied by girlfriend Frechette and fellow gang members, the wounded Dillinger sought help from underworld doctor Clayton May. The outlaw recuperated in apartment 1, on the south side of this two-story red-brick building.

58 Tommy Carroll's hideout (demolished), 35 W. Isabel St.
(at Hall Ave.). (Map A)
Post office robber and auto thief Tommy Carroll rented the upper floor of this house from the Vogel family during the spring and summer of 1932. He lived there with singer "Radio Sally" Bennett.

59 The Dillinger gang's Minneapolis mail drop, 3242 S. Sixteenth Ave.
(near E. Thirty-third St.), Minneapolis, private residence. (Map E)
Dillinger gang member Tommy Carroll received his mail-order submachine guns at this duplex, where the brother of his girlfriend Sally Bennett lived. The residence is opposite the Powderhorn Park Baptist Church. Carroll is buried at Oakland Cemetery, 927 Jackson St., St. Paul.

60 The Dillinger gang's weapons depot, 2214 Marshall Ave.
(near N. Cretin Ave.). (Map A)
In his hasty escape from the Lincoln Court shootout, John Dillinger left behind a note with the telephone number of gang member Eddie Green, traced by FBI agents to this three-story red-brick building in the Merriam Park neighborhood. Green rented apartment 106, on the east side of the building, for two weeks in March 1934. The Dillinger gang sought automotive repairs at the nearby gas station at 2178 Marshall.

61 Eddie Green's ambush house (demolished), 778 Rondo Ave.
(Concordia Ave. at S. Avon St.), today Interstate-94. (Map A)
FBI agents ambushed Dillinger gang member Green at this house, which was demolished—along with much of the Rondo neighborhood—for construction of I-94. Backup agents were hidden at Avon St. and

St. Anthony Ave., adjacent to what is today the baseball field at Maxfield Elementary School.

62 Homer Van Meter's death site, University Ave. and Marion St. (Map A)
Tipped off by underworld informants, St. Paul police officers surprised Dillinger gang member Van Meter at an auto dealership here on August 23, 1934. Van Meter, firing his .38 Colt automatic, was cut down by police gunfire when he ran into a blind alley between Aurora Ave. and Marion St., just two blocks from the state capitol.

63 New St. Paul police headquarters, 100 E. Eleventh St.
(between Minnesota and Robert Sts.). (Map C)
The St. Paul police headquarters was renovated in the mid-1980s, but the facade is similar to that of the 1930s, when a St. Paul Daily News *wiretap of police telephone lines exposed ties between gangsters and law enforcers.*

64 Hamm Building, 408 St. Peter St.
(between W. Sixth St. and Seventh Pl.). (Map C)
Fronted by the St. Paul Recreation Company—a billiard room, cigar stand, gym, boxing ring, and bowling alley—the basement of this Chicago-styled building housed one of the city's biggest illegal gambling operations. The gambling dens have long since been converted into offices.

65 Holman Municipal Airport, 644 Bayfield St.,
now St. Paul Downtown Airport. (Map A)
After his capture in New Orleans on May 1, 1936, Alvin Karpis, accompanied by FBI director J. Edgar Hoover and scores of special agents, was flown to St. Paul's Holman Airport to stand trial for the Hamm and Bremer kidnappings.

66 St. Paul City Hall and Ramsey County Courthouse,
15 Kellogg Blvd. W. (between Wabasha and St. Peter Sts.). (Map C)
Connected to the nearby Ramsey County jail by an underground tunnel, the Art Deco courthouse was the site of the 1933 trial of Roger Touhy, which took place on the eighth floor. The 1935 police corruption trials, sparked by wiretaps, occurred in the eleventh-floor courtrooms.

67 Old Ramsey County Jail (demolished),
St. Peter and W. Fourth Sts. (Map C)
This sandstone-and-granite structure on the southeast corner of the intersection of Fourth and St. Peter, completed in 1903, had an Italian Renaissance exterior. It held some of the most wanted criminals of the gangster era, including Alvin Karpis, Doc Barker, Roger Touhy, and Edna "the Kissing Bandit" Murray.

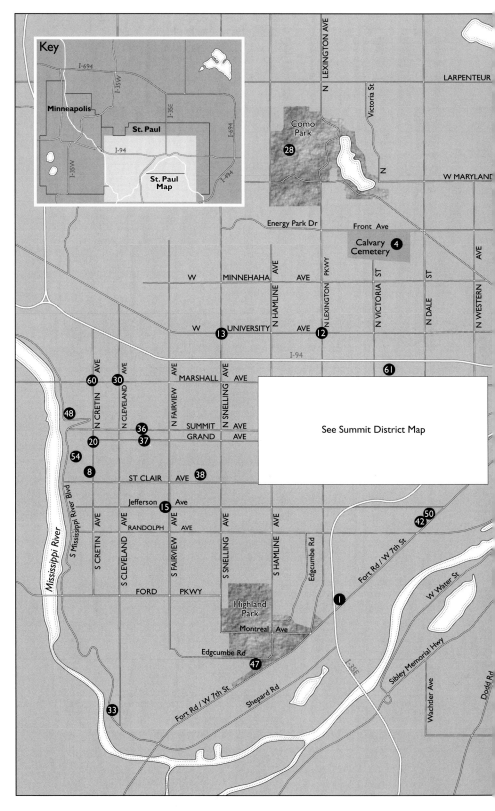

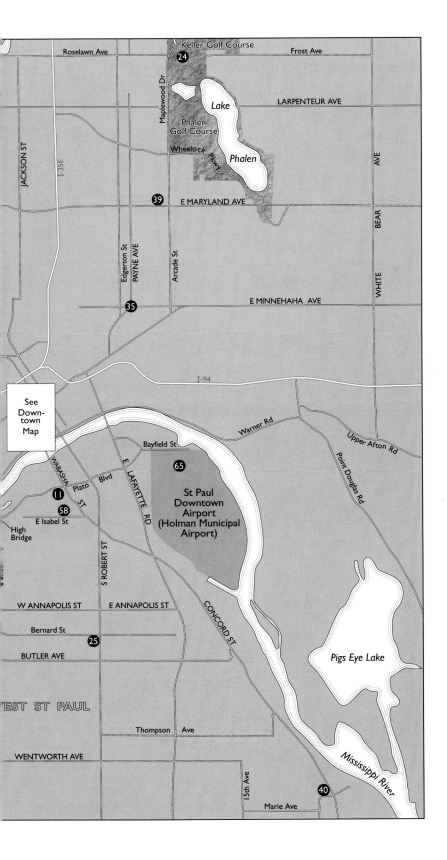

B. ST. PAUL'S SUMMIT DISTRICT • • • • • •

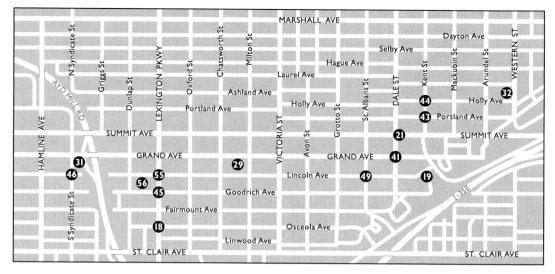

Key

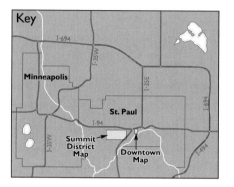

C. DOWNTOWN ST. PAUL • •

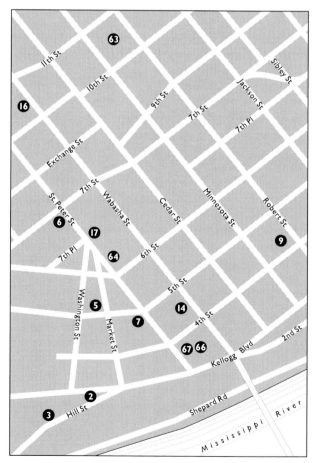

D. WHITE BEAR LAKE DISTRICT • • • • • • •

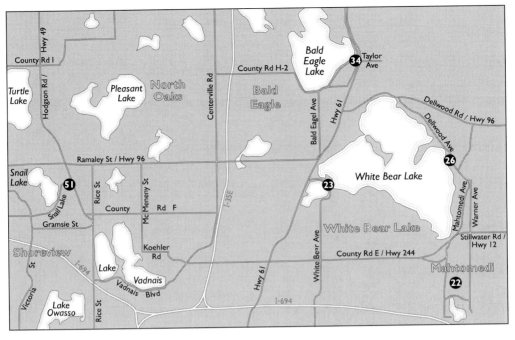

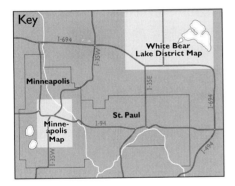

E. MINNEAPOLIS • • • •

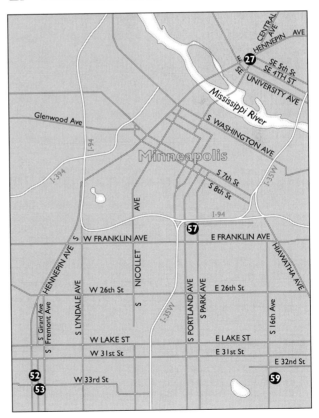

ROGUES AND REFORMERS GALLERY • • • •

ROGUES

Harvey Bailey Oklahoma bootlegger turned bank robber whose 1920s crime spree netted nearly $1 million in stolen cash and bonds, much of which was laundered through the St. Paul syndicate.

Arthur "Doc" Barker Convicted murderer and, as a member of the Barker-Karpis gang, a principal in the kidnappings of brewing company president William Hamm and bank president Edward Bremer.

Fred Barker Bank robber, jewel thief, and kidnapper from Tulsa, Oklahoma; founding member of Barker-Karpis gang.

Katherine "Ma" Barker Born Arizona "Donnie" Clark, mother of Fred and Arthur Barker; after her death named by J. Edgar Hoover as the mastermind of Barker-Karpis gang.

George "Machine Gun Kelly" Barnes Minor bootlegger and bank robber who earned notoriety as "Machine Gun Kelly" through publicity over his kidnapping of Oklahoma oilman Charles Urschel.

Sally "Radio Sally" Bennett St. Paul nightclub singer and girlfriend of Dillinger gang member Tommy Carroll.

Isadore "Kid Cann" Blumenfeld Romanian immigrant who headed the Minneapolis combination liquor syndicate; prosecuted but acquitted for laundering George "Machine Gun Kelly" Barnes's kidnapping money.

William Byron "Monty Carter" Bolton Driver for Al Capone's Chicago syndicate; partner of gunman Fred Goetz; took part in Hamm kidnapping and later turned government witness.

Thomas A. Brown St. Paul police chief from 1930 to 1932 and later head of elite police kidnap squad; suspected by FBI of leaking information to members of the Dillinger and Barker-Karpis gangs.

Alphonse "Scarface" Capone Legendary Chicago racketeer who reportedly stayed at St. Paul's Commodore Hotel.

Thomas L. Carroll Chicago-area auto thief, post office robber, and sometime Dillinger gang associate; suspected of joining Babyface Nelson and Homer Van Meter in the October 1933 robbery of the First National Bank of Brainerd, Minnesota.

Earl Christman Con man and freelance bank robber for Barker-Karpis gang; mortally wounded during 1933 robbery of First National Bank of Fairbury, Nebraska.

Nina Clifford St. Paul's most prominent madam, whose elegant brothel on Washington Street attracted the city's wealthiest businessmen and politicians.

Marie Conforti Girlfriend of Dillinger gang member Homer Van Meter.

James P. Crumley St. Paul police inspector and former head of the morals squad; onetime ally of police chief Thomas Brown; dismissed in 1935 after wiretaps exposed his tip-offs to the underworld.

Harry "Gorilla Kid" Davis Philadelphia hoodlum slain near St. Paul in 1932 by Murder Inc. assassins George Young and Joey Schaefer.

Volney "Curly" Davis Convicted murderer, Oklahoma prison escapee, burglar, and fringe member of Barker-Karpis gang.

Jean Delaney St. Paul girlfriend of Dillinger gang member Tommy Carroll; sister of Delores and Helen Delaney.

Delores Delaney Girlfriend of Alvin Karpis; sister of Jean and Helen Delaney.

Helen "Babe" Delaney Wife of Dillinger gang member William "Pat" Reilly; sister of Delores and Jean Delaney.

Lawrence "the Chopper" DeVol Mentally unstable bank robber, jail escapee, cop killer, and freelance machine gunner for the Barker-Karpis gang.

John Dillinger Indiana bank robber, jail escapee, and folk hero, named Public Enemy Number One by J. Edgar Hoover.

Jess Doyle Bank robber, auto thief, and minor member of Barker-Karpis gang; participant in 1933 robbery of First National Bank of Fairbury, Nebraska.

Arthur "Old Man" Dunlop Indiscreet boyfriend of Katherine "Ma" Barker; gangland murder victim.

William W. Dunn Hamm Brewing Company sales manager who served as intermediary during kidnapping of William Hamm Jr.; reported bribe collector for St. Paul police and friend of liquor czar Leon Gleckman.

Myrtle Eaton Shoplifter and girlfriend of Barker-Karpis gang member William Weaver.

Helen Ferguson Girlfriend of ill-fated Barker-Karpis gang member Earl Christman.

Thomas P. Filben Slot machine king and underworld fence working through his Patrick Novelty company; gangland supplier of automobiles, banking services, and political clout.

Charles "Old Charlie" Fitzgerald Veteran bank robber and burglar, employed as "greeter" by Barker-Karpis gang during William Hamm kidnapping.

Evelyn "Billie" Frechette Wisconsin-born girlfriend of bank robber John Dillinger.

Thomas E. Gannon St. Paul contact for Dillinger gang, one-time proprietor of underworld's Green Lantern Saloon.

Lester "Babyface Nelson" Gillis Bank robber, machine gun aficionado, and casual murderer who participated in crimes involving both Dillinger and Barker-Karpis gangs.

Leon Gleckman Liquor syndicate head and political fixer for St. Paul underworld with close ties to police chief Thomas Brown.

Benjamin and Abraham Gleeman St. Paul bootleggers wrongly convicted of killing hijacker Burt Stevens; their testimony helped expose the multimillion-dollar Cleveland liquor syndicate.

Fred "Shotgun George Ziegler" Goetz Chicago killer for Al Capone's syndicate, reputed triggerman at St. Valentine's Day Massacre, and freelancer with Barker-Karpis gang on St. Paul kidnappings.

Beth Green (aka Bessie Skinner) Government informant and girlfriend of Dillinger gang member Eddie Green.

Harry Eugene "Eddie" Green St. Paul contact man, convicted payroll robber, and "jug marker" (bank scout) for Dillinger gang.

John "Three Fingered Jack" Hamilton Indiana prison escapee and member of Dillinger gang; mortally wounded during 1934 Hastings shootout after FBI's Little Bohemia raid.

Robert B. Hamilton Gambling impresario who directed casino operations at the Hollyhocks Club, the Plantation nightclub, and the Boulevards of Paris.

Charles P. Harmon Unlucky bank and post office robber; friend of Frank Nash and hanger-on with Barker-Karpis gang until his death during the robbery of Wisconsin's Kraft State Bank in 1931.

Paula Harmon Widow of bank robber Charlie Harmon and girlfriend of Fred Barker.

Ben Harris Twin Cities gambling figure and operator of the Plantation nightclub, believed by FBI to be connected to the Barker-Karpis gang.

Daniel "Dapper Dan" Hogan Owner of underworld's Green Lantern saloon and fence of stolen merchandise; recognized as unofficial head of St. Paul underworld until his car-bomb murder.

Thomas Holden One of the Chicago-area "Evergreen bandits" who escaped with partner Jimmy Keating from Leavenworth prison in 1930, sparking a nationwide FBI manhunt focusing on golf courses.

Alvin "Creepy" Karpis Montreal-born bank robber, kidnapper, jewel thief, prison escapee, safe blower, and founding member of Barker-Karpis gang.

Francis L. "Jimmy" Keating Chicago-area railroad and bank robber and inveterate golfer, known for his 1930 escape from Leavenworth prison; he and partner Tommy Holden were known as the "Evergreen bandits."

Machine Gun Kelly—See George Barnes.

Vivian Mathis Girlfriend of Barker-Karpis gang machine gunner Verne Miller; lived near Brainerd, Minnesota .

Dr. Clayton E. May Minneapolis underworld physician for members of the Dillinger gang.

Morrie "the Phantom Gunman" Miller St. Paul liquor syndicate hit man and killer of hijacker Burt Stevens.

Vernon C. "Verne" Miller South Dakota sheriff who became a freelance machine gunner, embezzler, bootlegger, bank robber, and perpetrator of the June 1933 Kansas City Massacre.

Edward C. "Big Ed" Morgan   Minneapolis slot machine czar and boss of the city's Irish liquor and gambling syndicate during the 1920s.

Edna "the Kissing Bandit" Murray   Holdup artist, liquor hijacker, and Missouri prison escapee; girlfriend of Barker-Karpis gang member Volney Davis.

Frank "Jelly" Nash   Oklahoma bank and train robber, burglar, and convicted murderer (nicknamed "the Gentleman Bandit"), whose capture precipitated the Kansas City Massacre.

Babyface Nelson   See Lester Gillis.

John J. "the Big Fellow" O'Connor   St. Paul police chief, 1900–12 and 1914–20; architect of the O'Connor system, or layover agreement, which guaranteed safe haven for gangsters.

John "Jack" Peifer   Underworld banker and police fixer, operator of Hollyhocks Club casino, and key strategist for Barker-Karpis gang's kidnappings of Edward Bremer and William Hamm.

Bernard "Big Phil Courtney" Phillips   Auto thief, kidnapper, bank robber, and ex-police officer; mistrusted by Barker-Karpis gang, Phillips disappeared in 1932.

William Albert "Pat" Reilly   St. Paul gambler, bootlegger, and Green Lantern saloon bartender who served as an errand boy for John Dillinger.

Gladys Rita Sawyer   Wife of underworld fixer Harry Sawyer and government informant against Barker-Karpis gang.

Harry "Dutch" Sawyer   Bootlegger, fence, gangland banker, protégé of fixer Dan Hogan, and St. Paul contact for Dillinger and Barker-Karpis gangs.

Joseph Schaefer   Murder Inc. hit man, formerly employed by Irving "Waxey Gordon" Wexler's mob, who killed bootlegger Abe Wagner in St. Paul.

Benjamin "Bugsy" Siegel   Organized crime executive, murderer, and casino entrepreneur who lobbied in 1939 for release of two Murder Inc. killers from Minnesota's Stillwater Prison.

Sammy "Ten Dollar Kid" Silverman   Minneapolis gangster slain near Mahtomedi, Minnesota, in August 1930.

Frank Sommers   St. Paul police chief with ties to gangster Danny Hogan; forced to resign in 1920s over "vice investigation" scandal.

Robert "Frisco Dutch" Steinhardt   Chicago pickpocket employed at St. Paul's Boulevards of Paris nightclub and the Plantation nightclub in White Bear Lake.

Burton Stevens   Liquor hijacker whose 1925 murder in St. Paul led to exposure of a nationwide liquor conspiracy.

Roger "the Terrible" Touhy   Chicago bootlegger and rival of Al Capone; tried and aquitted in St. Paul federal court for the kidnapping of William Hamm.

Homer Van Meter   Train robber from Fort Wayne, Indiana, who served as lieutenant for Dillinger's bank robbery gang.

Abe Wagner (aka Abe Loeb)   New York bootlegger; victim of 1932 Murder Inc. assassination in St. Paul's Midway district.

William "Lapland Willie" Weaver   Arkansas bank robber, kidnapper, convicted murderer, and Bremer kidnapping conspirator with Barker-Karpis gang.

George Young   Murder Inc. killer allied with syndicate chieftain Meyer Lansky; murdered bootlegger Abe Wagner in St. Paul.

REFORMERS

Gustave "Gus" H. Barfuss   St. Paul policeman and public safety commissioner who lobbied to eliminate politics from police department.

Thomas E. Dahill   Reformer and St. Paul police chief during investigation of John Dillinger's robberies; foe of former chief Thomas Brown.

Clinton A. Hackert   St. Paul police chief and ally of reformer Thomas Dahill in fight against corrupt officers with ties to organized crime.

Wallace Ness Jamie   Criminologist nephew of Eliot Ness (of "the Untouchables"), who was hired by the *St. Paul Daily News* to expose police-underworld corruption.

Howard Kahn   Anticrime crusader and editor of *St. Paul Daily News*, who joined with investigator Wallace Jamie to expose police corruption in mid-1930s.

H.E. "Ned" Warren   Public safety commissioner who joined editor Kahn and investigator Jamie in exposing police-underworld corruption.

TWIN CITIES CRIME CHRONOLOGY • • • •

June 11, 1900 John J. O'Connor becomes chief of St. Paul police; his "layover agreement" with visiting gangsters establishes the foundation for a crime wave based in St. Paul.

October 28, 1919 Eighteenth Amendment, the Prohibition initiative written by Minnesota congressman Andrew Volstead, passes, nurturing organized crime syndicates in all major U.S. cities.

September 28, 1922 Harvey Bailey gang robs the Hamilton County Bank in Cincinnati of $265,000; portions of the money later surface in St. Paul.

December 18, 1922 Harvey Bailey gang robs the Denver Mint of $200,000; the stolen Denver bonds are traced to St. Paul.

February 16, 1925 Murder of bootlegger Burt Stevens in downtown St. Paul leads to exposure of $140 million nationwide liquor syndicate.

November 4, 1928 Fixer Arnold "the Brain" Rothstein is murdered in New York; murder weapon is traced to St. Paul.

December 4, 1928 Crime kingpin Daniel Hogan is slain by car bomb; protégé Harry "Dutch" Sawyer takes over Hogan's Green Lantern saloon.

February 14, 1929 St. Valentine's Day Massacre in Chicago, in which seven members of George "Bugs" Moran's gang are murdered by members of Al Capone's gang.

January 18, 1930 Bootlegger Leon Gleckman moves into Hotel St. Paul, which becomes the city's headquarters for corruption and graft.

February 28, 1930 Bank robbers Thomas Holden and Francis "Jimmy" Keating, the "Evergreen bandits," escape from Leavenworth prison and hide out in Minnesota.

June 3, 1930 Thomas A. Brown, once a defendant in the Cleveland liquor syndicate case, is appointed chief of St. Paul police.

July 15, 1930 Bank of Willmar, Minnesota, is robbed by George "Machine Gun Kelly" Barnes and the Keating-Holden gang.

August 13, 1930 Three Kansas City mobsters, Sammy "Ten Dollar Kid" Silverman, Michael Rusick, and Frank "Weanie" Coleman, are slain near White Bear Lake, Minnesota.

September 17, 1930 Harvey Bailey robs $2.6 million from National Bank and Trust Company of Lincoln, Nebraska, laundering the stolen bonds in St. Paul.

May–September 1931 Jimmy Keating and Tommy Holden hide out in St. Paul during nationwide FBI manhunt.

May 2, 1931 Gangster Alvin "Creepy" Karpis is released from state penitentiary at Lansing, Kansas.

June 1, 1931 Legendary bank robber Frank "Jelly" Nash of Oklahoma moves to St. Paul with members of the Barker-Karpis gang.

August 17, 1931 Bank robber Harry "Slim Jones" Morris is found dead near Red Wing, Minnesota.

September 24, 1931 Liquor czar Leon Gleckman is kidnapped and held for ransom; he is released eight days later; his kidnappers are either imprisoned or killed.

October 20, 1931 Bank robber Charlie Harmon is slain during Keating-Holden gang's holdup of Kraft State Bank of Menomonie, Wisconsin.

October 1931–January 1932 Bank robber Bernard "Big Phil Courtney" Phillips hides in St. Paul's Merriam Park neighborhood.

December 19, 1931 Fred Barker murders Sheriff C. Roy Kelly in West Plains, Missouri, and flees to St. Paul.

January 5, 1932 Barker-Karpis gang holds town of Cambridge, Minnesota, hostage, stealing $3,000 in goods and kidnapping the town marshal.

March 7, 1932 Bodies of Margaret "Indian Rose" Perry and Sadie Carmacher are found in burned-out car near Balsam Lake, Wisconsin, just before they are to inform on Barker-Karpis gang.

March 29, 1932 Barker-Karpis gang robs the Northwestern National Bank and Trust Company in Minneapolis.

April 25, 1932 Barker-Karpis gang, tipped off by police, escapes from Hannegraf family home; body of Arthur Dunlop, companion of Katherine "Ma" Barker, is later found at Frenstad Lake in Wisconsin.

May 3, 1932 William Mahoney is elected mayor of St. Paul, promising to eliminate influence of "organized, sinister, and invisible" gangsters.

June 7, 1932 St. Paul police chief Thomas Brown is demoted to detective on suspicion of having warned Barker-Karpis gang of April raid.

June 17, 1932 Members of Barker-Karpis and Keating-Holden gangs rob the Citizens National Bank of Fort Scott, Kansas, of $47,000.

July 7, 1932 Bank robbers Jimmy Keating, Tommy Holden, and Harvey Bailey are arrested by FBI agents at a golf course in Kansas City.

July 25, 1932 Murder Inc. hit men George Young and Joey Schaefer hunt down and kill bootlegger Abe Wagner and his partner, Al Gordon, in St. Paul's Midway district.

July 26, 1932 Barker-Karpis gang robs Cloud County Bank of Concordia, Kansas, then escapes to White Bear Lake, Minnesota, to divide $240,000 in stolen bonds and cash.

August 5, 1932 New St. Paul police chief Thomas Dahill announces war against "hoodlums" and "gun-toters."

September 10, 1932 Arthur "Doc" Barker is freed from Oklahoma state prison and rejoins the Barker-Karpis gang in Minnesota.

September 23, 1932 Barker-Karpis gang robs State Bank and Trust Company of Redwood Falls, Minnesota, of $35,000.

September 30, 1932 Citizens National Bank of Wahpeton, North Dakota, is robbed of $6,900, allegedly by the Barker-Karpis gang.

November 3, 1932 Volney "Curley" Davis of Barker-Karpis gang is released from Oklahoma state prison and moves to St. Paul.

December 16, 1932 Barker-Karpis gang robs Third Northwestern National Bank of Minneapolis. Two policemen are killed; bystander Oscar Erickson is murdered by Fred Barker in St. Paul's Como Park.

December 18, 1932 Larry "the Chopper" DeVol of the Barker-Karpis gang is arrested by police in St. Paul for the December 16 bank robbery.

March 22, 1933 Volstead Act is repealed.

February–March 1933 Barker-Karpis gang hides out in Grand Avenue apartment, escaping after tip-off by St. Paul police.

April 4, 1933 Barker-Karpis gang robs First National Bank of Fairbury, Nebraska; gang member Earl Christman is mortally wounded during the getaway.

May 1933 Ma Barker moves into St. Paul's Commodore Hotel; John Dillinger is released on parole from Indiana state prison at Michigan City, Indiana.

May 28, 1933 Barker-Karpis gang members Fred Barker and Alvin Karpis move to 204 Vernon Street in St. Paul, making plans to kidnap a prominent businessman.

June 9, 1933 Bank robber Frank Nash of Oklahoma visits St. Paul for the last time.

June 15, 1933 Brewing company executive William Hamm Jr. is kidnapped by Barker-Karpis gang in St. Paul.

June 17, 1933 Bank robber Frank Nash, an FBI agent, and three police officers are killed by Verne Miller in Kansas City Massacre at Union Station.

June 19, 1933 Kidnap victim William Hamm is released near Wyoming, Minnesota, after payment of $100,000 ransom.

July 22, 1933 George "Machine Gun Kelly" Barnes kidnaps Oklahoma oilman Charles Urschel and demands $200,000; portions of ransom money are laundered through Minneapolis syndicate.

August 30, 1933 Barker-Karpis gang robs $33,000 from stockyards payroll delivered by train to South St. Paul Post Office, killing one policeman and seriously wounding another.

September 1933 Eddie Green rents Charlou Apartment suite as Minneapolis headquarters for John Dillinger's bank robbery gang.

September 4, 1933 Dillinger gang member Tommy Carroll is arrested after auto accident in St. Paul; police release Carroll, despite finding a loaded revolver in his car.

October 23, 1933 First National Bank of Brainerd, Minnesota, is robbed of $32,000 by a group believed to include Babyface Nelson, Tommy Carroll, and other members of the Dillinger gang.

November 9–28, 1933 Roger "the Terrible" Touhy and associates are tried in St. Paul for William Hamm kidnapping; they are acquitted of all the charges.

November 29, 1933 Verne Miller, hunted by both the FBI and organized crime figures for the Kansas City Massacre, is found murdered in Detroit.

December 7, 1933 Fred Barker of the Barker-Karpis gang moves to St. Paul's Grand Avenue to plan next kidnapping.

January 13, 1934 Northwest Airlines employee Roy McCord, wearing his radio operator's uniform, is mistaken for a policeman and shot by the Barker-Karpis gang in St. Paul.

January 17, 1934 Barker-Karpis gang kidnaps banker Edward Bremer in St. Paul; Bremer is released February 7 near Rochester, Minnesota, after payment of the $200,000 ransom.

March 4, 1934 Lester "Babyface Nelson" Gillis murders an innocent motorist, Theodore Kidder, in St. Louis Park, a Minneapolis suburb.

March 5, 1934 John Dillinger, with girlfriend Evelyn Frechette, moves to Minneapolis after escaping from jail in Crown Point, Indiana.

March 6, 1934 Dillinger robs Sioux Falls, South Dakota, bank of $49,500, leaving one policeman dead, and returns to Minneapolis.

March 13, 1934 Dillinger gang robs First National Bank of Mason City, Iowa, of $52,000, then flees to Minneapolis. Dillinger and John Hamilton seek medical care from Dr. Nels Mortensen of St. Paul.

March 19, 1934 Dillinger moves into Lincoln Court Apartments in St. Paul to recuperate from gunshot wounds suffered during the Mason City, Iowa, bank robbery.

March 20, 1934 Fred "Shotgun George Ziegler" Goetz of Al Capone's syndicate, a key participant in the Bremer kidnapping, is shot to death in Cicero, Illinois.

March 31, 1934 John Dillinger and Homer Van Meter evade capture by FBI and St. Paul police during a shootout at the Lincoln Court Apartments; Dillinger takes shelter at the Minneapolis clinic of Dr. Clayton May.

April 3, 1934 Dillinger gang member Eddie Green is mortally wounded by FBI agents in St. Paul; he dies April 11.

April 23–24, 1934 Dillinger gang escapes from FBI raid at resort in Little

Bohemia, Wisconsin, killing one agent; Dillinger evades police roadblock in Hastings, Minnesota, but John Hamilton is mortally wounded by police fire.

May 1934 Investigator Wallace Jamie arrives in St. Paul to explore police corruption at the invitation of the *St. Paul Daily News*; he installs telephone taps in police offices.

June 7, 1934 Dillinger gang member Tommy Carroll is killed by police detectives near Waterloo, Iowa.

July 22, 1934 Dillinger is shot to death by FBI agents outside Chicago's Biograph Theater.

August 23, 1934 Dillinger gang member Homer Van Meter is shot to death in a police ambush in St. Paul.

September 5, 1934 Three girlfriends of Barker-Karpis gang members, including Fred Barker's lover, Paula Harmon, are arrested by police in Cleveland, Ohio.

November 27, 1934 Babyface Nelson is shot to death by FBI agents near Fox River Grove, Illinois.

January 8, 1935 Doc Barker is captured by FBI agents in his Chicago apartment and taken to St. Paul for kidnapping trial.

January 16, 1935 Fred and Ma Barker are killed in a gun battle with the FBI at Lake Weir, Florida.

May 17, 1935 Doc Barker and four other gang members are convicted in St. Paul federal court of the kidnapping of Edward Bremer; Barker is incarcerated at Leavenworth prison.

June 7, 1935 Volney Davis and four others are convicted in St. Paul federal court of the kidnapping of Edward Bremer, receiving sentences ranging from five years to life.

August 28, 1935 Body of Dillinger gang member John Hamilton is discovered by the FBI in Oswego, Illinois.

January 24, 1936 Underworld fixer Harry Sawyer and William Weaver are convicted in St. Paul federal court of kidnapping Edward Bremer.

May 1, 1936 Alvin Karpis is arrested in New Orleans and brought by J. Edgar Hoover to St. Paul in chains for trial.

June 8, 1936 Larry DeVol of the Barker-Karpis gang escapes from the prison hospital at St. Peter, Minnesota, and is shot to death by police in Enid, Oklahoma, on July 8.

July 31, 1936 Fixer Jack Peifer commits suicide in St. Paul's Ramsey County jail after being convicted of participating in the William Hamm kidnapping.

October 9, 1936 Former St. Paul police chief Thomas Brown is permanently removed from the force after evidence of his corruption and contact with the Barker-Karpis gang is released.

Stacked on shelves in the J. Edgar Hoover Building's reading room in Washington, D.C., are the documents that form the core of *John Dillinger Slept Here*—the FBI's voluminous files on Hoover's crusade against gangsters in the 1930s.

The FBI files on the Barker-Karpis gang (76,159 pages), Alvin "Creepy" Karpis (2,360 pages), Charles "Pretty Boy" Floyd, Frank Nash, and the Kansas City Massacre (15,786 pages), and John Dillinger and his gang (36,795 pages) are of special value to historians. In addition, the FBI's Crime Conditions files, covering 1930s underworld activity in Minneapolis and St. Paul, proved helpful. The verbatim transcripts of FBI interviews (1934–1936) with girlfriends of Barker-Karpis and Dillinger gang members were particularly useful, as were interviews with eyewitnesses and, in some cases, the gangsters themselves.

U.S. Prohibition Bureau, Treasury Department/Internal Revenue Service, U.S. Post Office, U.S. Attorneys Office, and other federal records stored in the National Archives in Washington, D.C., helped reconstruct the Leon Gleckman, Dan Hogan, Frank Nash/Kansas City Massacre, and Cleveland Syndicate cases.

Notes from the author's interviews and photocopies of documents from the FBI, the National Archives, and many other sources that were used in researching this work are held in the Paul Maccabee St. Paul Gangster History Research Collection at the Minnesota Historical Society (MHS), St. Paul.

GOVERNMENT PAPERS AND REPORTS

Federal

Department of Justice. Bureau of Prisons. Escaped Prisoners file, 1932–33. RG 129, National Archives, Washington, D. C.

———.Bureau of Prisons. Inmate Records. Inmate Locator Service, Department of Justice, Washington, D.C.

———. Bureau of Prohibition. Records, 1920–1933. RG 60, National Archives, Washington, D. C.

———. Federal Bureau of Investigation. Bremer Kidnap files, 1934–84; Dillinger files, 1934, 1954; Hamm Kidnap files, 1933–64; Kansas City Massacre files, 1933–34. Freedom of Information Act Reading Room, FBI Headquarters, Washington, D.C.

———. Federal Bureau of Investigation. Crime Conditions files, 1934–45; Leon Gleckman files. Paul Maccabee St. Paul Gangster History Research Collection, MHS.

———. Mail and Files Division. Postal Service Investigation Records, 1921–35. RG 60, National Archives, Washington, D. C.

National Commission on Law Observance and Enforcement. *Enforcement of the Prohibition Laws.* 71st Cong., 3d sess. Washington, D.C.: Government Printing Office, 1931.

U.S. District Court, Third Division. *U.S.A. v. Clayton E. May, Evelyn Frechette et al.,* 1934. MHS.

U.S. District Court, Third Division. *U.S.A. v. Albert (Pat) Reilly,* 1934.

U.S. District Court, Third Division. *U.S.A. v. Alvin Karpavicz,* 1935.

State

Michigan Department of Health. Death Certificates.

Minnesota Bureau of Criminal Apprehension. Homicide and Investigation files, 1930–36.

Minnesota Bureau of Prisons. Stillwater State Prison Inmate files. MHS.

Minnesota Manuscript Census Schedules, St. Paul, 1895, 1905.

Minnesota Department of Health. Death Certificates.

South Dakota, State Penitentiary. Prison Inmate files. South Dakota State Archives.

Wisconsin Department of Health and Social Services. Death Certificates.

Local

Detroit Police Department. Homicide files.

Hennepin County, Minnesota. Probate records.

Lancaster County, Nebraska. Probate records.

Minneapolis Police Department. Homicide files.

Philadelphia Police Department. Organized Crime Intelligence files.

Ramsey County, Minnesota. Minnesota Medical Examiner's records.

Ramsey County, Minnesota. Probate records.

Ramsey County, Minnesota, District Court. Indictment records.

Ramsey County, Minnesota, District Court. *State of Minnesota v. James Crumley et al.*, 1935. MHS.

St. Paul City Water Department. Sewer maps.

St. Paul Police Department. Homicide and accident files.

NEWSPAPERS

Brainerd Daily Dispatch, Oct. 1933.

Brainerd Journal Press, Oct. 1933.

Hastings Gazette, Apr. 1934.

Minneapolis Journal, 1919–40.

Minneapolis Tribune, 1919–60.

St. Paul Daily News, 1929–39.

St. Paul Dispatch, 1914–93 (merged with *Pioneer Press* in 1985).

St. Paul Pioneer Press, 1919–93 (merged with *Dispatch* in 1985).

St. Paul Pioneer Press-Dispatch morgue file, 1914– . St. Paul Public Library.

South St. Paul Daily Reporter, Aug.–Sept. 1933.

Willmar Tribune, July 1930.

SPEECHES AND MEMOIRS

Hoover, J. Edgar. "Patriotism and the War Against Crime." Speech before the Daughters of the American Revolution, Apr. 23, 1936. Washington, D.C.: Government Printing Office, 1936 (SUDOC J1.14/2:P27).

Minnesota Bankers Association. Speeches at the 44th Annual Convention, June 13–14, 1933, Minneapolis.

Pranke, Richard N. "Autobiography of Richard N. Pranke." Pranke Family Records, MHS.

Rohlfing, Althea. Speech at the Mahtomedi Club, Mar. 1984, copy in author's possession.

PRIMARY INTERVIEWS (partial list)

Interviews are by the author unless otherwise noted.

Bailey, Harvey. Interviews by J. Evetts Haley, Oct. 31, 1965, May 16, 1966, Sept. 18, 1966, and May 23, 1967. Nita Stewart Haley Memorial Library, Midland, Texas.

Barnes, Bruce. Jan. 11, 1994.

Benz, Louise. Oct. 30, 1992.

Bergaus, Mercia. May 1993.

Boardsen, Dirk. Sept. 5, 1992.

Bomberg, Nate. Interview by Ms. Cherry, ca. 1975. Ramsey County Historical Society, St. Paul.

Bowser, John. May 5, 1989, May 19, 1989.

Bremer, Donna. Dec. 29, 1993.

Brigham, Christine. N.d.

Bullert, Bernie. Dec. 17, 1993.

Cardozo, Ted. Dec. 29, 1993.

Charlton, Mary. Jan. 23, 1993, May 15, 1993.

Coleman, Jim. Apr. 24, 1992.

Comstock, Paul G. Sept. 4, 1992, Sept. 6, 1992.

Comstock, Virginia. Sept. 21, 1992.

Cravath, Calvert. June 1991, Aug. 7, 1991.

Delaney, Thomas. May 9, 1992.

DeMoss, Carole. Dec. 16, 1993.

Deyo, Evelyn M. May 1993.

DuPont, Horace. Oct. 31, 1992, Jan. 7, 1994.

Ehrlich, Max. Oct. 30, 1992.

Eue, Donna. Apr. 15, 1993.

Fahey, Ted. July 19, 1991.

Fenn, Ralph. N.d.

Figge, William. Jan. 6, 1994.

Filben, Bill. June 13, 1992.

Fish, Donald. Jan. 23, 1993.

Fleigel, Robert. Dec. 10, 1991.

Geisenheyner, Bob. N.d.

Gibson, Janet. Aug. 27, 1993.

Gibson, Michael. Apr. 9, 1993.

Gillespie, Eben. Jan. 15, 1992, Jan. 6, 1994.

Graves, Mary. May 28, 1992, Jan. 22, 1994.

Grooms, Albert. June 18, 1993.

Grossman, Bernice. May 30, 1992.

Guarnera, Marge. Apr. 1993.

Hamilton, Bruce. Dec. 17, 1993.

Hannegraf, Nick Jr. Dec. 19, 1991.

Harrington, Gladys. June 1993.

Heaberlin, Fred. Jan. 6, 1994.

Herschler, Kenneth. May 21, 1993.

Hesse, Howard. Interview by Tim Albright, Mar. 27, 1992.

Hiebert, Gareth. Dec. 3, 1993.

Holsapple, Janice. Apr. 9, 1993.

Hornig, David. N.d.

Horton, Norman Sr. May 15, 1991.

Hurley, George Jr. June 11, 1994.

Hurley, Harold. Aug. 27, 1993, June 10, 1994.

Jamie, Louise. Mar. 12, 1992.

Johnson, Betty Bremer. Jan. 27, 1992.

Johnson, Marien. Dec. 19, 1991, May 30, 1992.

Johnson, Mary. May 12, 1993.

Johnson, Walter "Buster." N.d.

Junterman, Marguerite. Aug. 8, 1993.

Keljik, Woody. Jan. 22, 1993.

Kohrt, Bonnie. Jan. 1993.

Koontz, Hope Healy. Dec. 3, 1993.

Knox, Jep. Dec. 3, 1993.

Knutson, John. Mar. 1993.

Lannon, Pat Sr. May 13, 1993, June 14, 1993, Aug. 27, 1993.

Lehman, Jim. N.d.

Lindholm, Clifford Allen. Dec. 1992.

McBride, Irene. N.d.

McCalla, Colleen. July 9, 1993.

Macey, John W. Jan. 3, 1992.

McCord, Roy Norman Jr. Dec. 23, 1992.

McGree, Aloysius. Apr. 11, 1992.

McLaughlin, J. T. N.d.

McLean, Ellie (Halberg). Apr. 15, 1993.

McMahon, Marie. Mar. 1993.

McNamara, Sally. Apr. 30, 1993.

Magine, Julio. July 1993.

Mattlin, Carroll. May 21, 1992.

Merrick, Gordon L. Dec. 11, 1992.

Merrill, Ralph. Oct. 10, 1990.

Michaud, Ann. Nov. 20, 1993.

Miller, Fred Jr. May 14, 1993.

Morgan, David J. June 8, 1993.

Murphy, Lorretta. Interview by relative, Apr. 1985. In the posession of Jim Vogel, Anoka, Minnesota.

Nemerov, Irving. May 17, 1991.

O'Connor, Joseph. Feb. 26, 1991.

Opsahl, Ross. N.d.

Orth, Earl. Mar. 14, 1993.

Patch, Earl A. July 20, 1993.

Paul, Francis MacLaren. April 13, 1993.

Pavlak, Robert. Feb. 6, 1993.

Peters, Vera. Mar. 27, 1993.

Phillips, Vern. Apr. 30, 1993.

Pranke, Richard N. Mar. 23, 1985, Oct. 23, 1992.

Preston, Jean. June 6, 1992.

Purcell, Tom. Apr. 1992.

Ramaley, Jack. May 22, 1992.

Rautenberg, Bunny. May 14, 1993.

Reiter, Charlie. May 2, 1991, Sept. 24, 1993, Oct. 12, 1993, Sept. 1, 1994.

Resler, Jane. Sept. 9, 1994.

Rohlfing, Althea. Apr. 16, 1993.

Rohling, Martin. June 16, 1991, May 22, 1992.

Roy, Elizabeth. Dec. 17, 1994.

Scarlett, Vicenta Donnelly. May 14, 1994.

Schroth, Louis. Apr. 2, 1993.

Schude, Blanche Carter. May 5, 1992.

Schwietz, Robert. Dec. 30, 1992.

Schwietz, Virginia Gibbons. Dec. 30, 1992.

Senesac, Peggy. Nov. 20, 1992.

Seng, Robert J. and Barbara. Sept. 24, 1993, Oct. 30, 1993.

Sherin, Joe. 1992.

Sinykin, Beverly. Apr. 12, 1992.

Smith, Zane. Apr. 1993.

Thomas, James. July 16, 1993, Jan. 14, 1994.

Tic, Bernice. Feb. 1994.

Tiemann, Tony. Nov. 20, 1992.

Troupe, "Shy." Nov. 3, 1993.

Tuttle, Steve. Jan. 30, 1993.

Vogel, Jim. Mar. 1993.

Vogel, John. May 14, 1993.

Vogelgesang, Anita. May 5, 1992.

Walsh, William. Jan. 6, 1995.

Wybest, Robert H. Oct. 10, 1993.

Yeaman, Jack. Aug. 24, 1993.

AUDIO AND VIDEO SOURCES

Brede, Neil. "St. Paul Gangster Days." Video documentary. First broadcast on public access television, St. Paul, 1987.

Heistad, Mark. "A Story of Crime, Criminals, and Corruption." Minnesota Public Radio. Broadcast Nov. 8, 1985.

"John Dillinger." *Biography.* Arts and Entertainment Channel. Broadcast April 4, 1995.

BOOKS

Barnes, Bruce. *Machine Gun Kelly: To Right a Wrong.* Perris, Calif: Tipper Publications, 1991.

Bergreen, Laurence. *Capone: The Man and the Era.* New York: Simon and Schuster, 1994.

Callahan, Clyde C. and Byron B. Jones. *Heritage of an Outlaw: The Story of Frank Nash.* Hobart, Okla.: Schoonmaker Publishers, 1979.

Cooper, Courtney Ryley. *Here's to Crime.* Boston: Little, Brown and Company, 1937.

———. *Ten Thousand Public Enemies.* Foreword by J. Edgar Hoover. Boston: Little, Brown and Company, 1935.

Cromie, Robert and Joseph Pinkston. *Dillinger: A Short and Violent Life.* Evanston, Ill.: Chicago Historical Bookworks, 1990; reprint of 1962.

Edge, L. L. *Run the Cat Roads: True Story of Bank Robbers in the 30s.* New York: Dembner Books, 1981.

Empson, Donald. *On the Street Where You Live.* St. Paul: Witsend Press, 1975.

Enright, Richard T. with Ray Cowdery. *Capone's Chicago.* Lakeville, Minn.: Northstar-Maschek Books, 1987.

Fenwick, A. R., ed. *Sturdy Sons of Saint Paul.* St. Paul: Junior Pioneer Association, n.d. [1899].

Fish, Donald E. *The Dillinger Connection: What Part Did John Dillinger Play in the Brainerd Bank Robbery?* St. Paul: Bywords Printing, 1986.

Flanagan, John T. *Theodore Hamm in Minnesota: His Family and Brewery.* St. Paul: Pogo Press, 1989.

Fox, Stephen R. *Blood and Power: Organized Crime in Twentieth-Century America.* New York: William Morrow, 1989.

Gentry, Curt. *J. Edgar Hoover: The Man and the Secrets.* New York: Norton, 1991.

Girardin, G. Russell, with William J. Helmer. *Dillinger: The Untold Story.* Bloomington: Indiana University Press, 1994.

Guilford, H[oward]. A. *Holies of Holies of the White Slave Worshipper.* [St. Paul,] Minn.: By the author, n.d. [ca. 1915].

———. *A Tale of Two Cities: Memoirs of 16 Years Behind a Pencil.* Robbinsdale, Minn.: By the author, 1929.

Haley, J. Evetts. *Robbing Banks Was My Business: The Story of J. Harvey Bailey.* Canyon, Texas: Palo Duro Press, 1973.

Hollatz, Tom. *Gangster Holidays: The Lore and Legends of the Bad Guys.* St. Cloud, Minn.: North Star Press, 1989.

Hoover, J. Edgar. *Persons in Hiding.* Boston: Little, Brown and Company, 1938.

Jennings, Dean. *We Only Kill Each Other: The Life and Bad Times of Bugsy Siegel.* Englewood Cliffs, N.J.: Prentice-Hall, 1967.

Karpis, Alvin, with Bill Trent. *The Alvin Karpis Story.* New York: Coward, McCann and Geoghegan, 1971.

Koblas, John J. *F. Scott Fitzgerald in Minnesota: His Homes and Haunts.* St. Paul: Minnesota Historical Society Press, 1978.

Kobler, John. *Capone: The Life and World of Al Capone.* New York: G. P. Putnam and Sons, 1971.

Koeper, H. F. *Historic St. Paul Buildings.* St. Paul: St. Paul City Planning Commission, 1964.

Kunz, Virginia Brainerd. *Saint Paul: The First 150 Years.* St. Paul: St. Paul Foundation, 1991.

———. *The Mississippi and St. Paul: A Short History of the City's 150-year Love Affair with Its River.* St. Paul: Ramsey County Historical Society, 1987.

Lacey, Robert. *Little Man: Meyer Lansky and the Gangster Life.* Boston: Little, Brown and Company, 1991.

Michels, Eileen, with Nate Bomberg. *A Landmark Reclaimed.* St. Paul: Minnesota Landmarks, 1977.

Millet, Larry. *Lost Twin Cities.* St. Paul: Minnesota Historical Society Press, 1992.

Nash, Jay Robert. *Almanac of World Crime.* Garden City, N.Y.: Anchor Press/Doubleday, 1981.

———. *Bloodletters and Badmen: A Narrative Encyclopedia of American Criminals from the Pilgrims to the Present.* New York: M. Evans and Company, 1973.

———. *The Dillinger Dossier.* Highland Park, Ill.: December Press, 1983.

Perkins, A. H. S. *All About White Bear Lake: Minnesota's Popular Summer Resort.* White Bear Lake, Minn.: n.p., 1890.

Powers, Richard G. *Secrecy and Power: The Life of J. Edgar Hoover.* New York: Free Press, 1987.

Purvis, Melvin. *American Agent.* Garden City, N.Y.: Doubleday, Doran and Company, 1936.

Schoenburg, Robert J. *Mr. Capone.* New York: William Morrow and Company, 1992.

Sevareid, Paul A. *The People's Lawyer: The Life of Eugene A. Rerat.* Minneapolis: Ross and Haines, 1963.

Sifakis, Carl. *The Mafia Encyclopedia.* New York: Facts on File, 1987.

Smith, Alice R., Sharon F. Wright, and Judy Kaiser. *Mahtomedi Memories.* [Mahtomedi?]: n.p., 1976.

Spiering, Frank. *The Man Who Got Capone.* Indianapolis: Bobbs-Merrill Company, 1976.

Summers, Anthony. *Official and Confidential: The Secret Life of J. Edgar Hoover.* New York: G. P. Putnam's Sons, 1993.

Thayer, Steve. *Saint Mudd: A Novel of Gangsters and Saints.* St. Paul: Birchwood Page Publishing, 1988.

Theoharis, Athan G. and John Stuart Cox. *The Boss: J. Edgar Hoover and the Great American Inquisition.* Philadelphia: Temple University Press, 1988.

Toland, John. *Dillinger Days.* New York: Random House, 1963.

Touhy, Roger and Ray Brennan. *The Stolen Years.* Cleveland: Pennington Press, 1959.

Turkus, Burton B. and Sid Feder. *Murder Inc.: The Story of "the Syndicate".* New York: Farrar, Straus and Young, 1951.

Turner, William W. *Hoover's FBI: The Men and the Myth.* New York: Dell Publishing Co., 1971; reprint of 1970.

Wallis, Michael. *Pretty Boy: The Life and Times of Charles Arthur Floyd.* New York: St. Martin's Press, 1992.

Weir, William. *Written with Lead: Legendary American Gunfights and Gunfighters.* Hamden, Conn.: Archon Books, 1992.

Wing, Frank. *Brewers Handbook of the U.S. and Canada.* New York: J. M. Wing Co., 1887.

Woolworth, Nancy L. *The White Bear Lake Story.* White Bear Lake, Minn.: White Bear Avenue Chamber of Commerce, 1968.

ARTICLES

Allenspach, Kevin. "It Was No Gangster Movie." *Brainerd Daily Dispatch*, Dec. 4, 1988, p. 1C.

Baker, Robert Orr. "The Minnesota Club: St. Paul's Enterprising Leaders and Their 'Gentlemen's Social Club.'" *Ramsey County History* 19, no. 2 (1984–85): 3–21.

Bellville, Lance. "Nina." *Minnesota Monthly*, October 1981, p. 15–17.

Best, Joel E. "Long Kate, Dutch Henriette and Mother Robinson: Three Madames in Post-Civil War St. Paul." *Ramsey County History* 15, no. 2 (1979–80): 3–10.

Bomberg, Nate. "The Day Karpis Returned." *Capital: St. Paul Pioneer Press and Dispatch Sunday Magazine*, Mar. 28, 1971, p. 6, 10.

Brueggemann, Gary J. "Beer Capital of the State—St. Paul's Historic Family Breweries." *Ramsey County History* 16, no. 2 (1980–81): 3–15.

Clark, Bernice. "My Adventures with the Dillinger Gang." *Chicago Herald and Examiner*, Sept. 10, 1934.

Dahill, Thomas E. and J. O. Myers. "When St. Paul Silenced New Jersey's Hired Guns." *Startling Detective Adventures* 10, no. 60 (July 1933): 40–43, 54.

"The Dillinger Man-Hunt." *True Detective*, July 1934, p. 65–66.

Ernst, Robert R. "The Last Days of Lawrence DeVol." *OklahombreS*, Winter 1991, p. 10–12.

Ex-Operative 48. "Sterilization: Preston Paden, Whelp of a Gun Moll," *Official Detective Stories*, Apr. 1, 1937.

Ferris, Joseph A. "How Barton 'The Chopper' Was Captured." *True Detective Mysteries* 20, no. 4 (July 1933): 20–25, 104–107.

Frechette, Evelyn. "Evelyn Tells Life with Dillinger." *Chicago Herald and Examiner*, Aug. 28, 29, 1934.

———. "What I Knew About Dillinger." *Chicago Herald and Examiner*, Aug. 30, 31, 1934.

"Gangsters: An Interview with Will Greer." *Scattered Seeds* (Central High School, St. Paul) 8 (1976): 2–9.

Hale, Avery, "The Inside Story of Dillinger at Last." *True Detective Mysteries* Dec. 1934, p. 6–13, 86–89; and Jan. 1935, p. 4, 54–57, 112–116, 118.

High, Stanley. "St. Paul Wins a War." *Current History* 49, no. 1 (1938): 18–20.

Kahlstrom, Jonathan. "Renovating the First National Bank Building." *Minnesota Real Estate Journal*, Dec. 23, 1991 (supplement), p. 2.

Karpis, Alvin. "Karpis Recalls St. Paul." *Capital: St. Paul Pioneer Press and Dispatch Sunday Magazine*, Mar. 27, 1971, p. 4–6, 9.

Liggett, Walter W. "Minneapolis and Vice in Volsteadland." *Plain Talk*, Apr. 1930, p. 385–399.

McDade, Thomas M. "Karpis Recalls His Crime Spree of the 1930s in Talks with McDade." *Grapevine*, May 1980, p. 36–38.

Nash, Alanna. "Memories of John Dillinger." *Chicago Reader*, July 20, 1984, p. 9, 32–38.

Negri, "Fatso," with Bennett Williams. "In the Hinges of Hell: How G-Men Ended Crime's Reddest Chapter." *True Detective Mysteries*, Dec. 1940, p. 14–19, 90–91; Jan. 1941, p. 16–19, 108–10; Feb. 1941, p. 30–32, 112–15; Mar. 1941, p. 66–69, 87–89; Apr. 1941, p. 30–32, 114–16; May 1941, p. 30–32, 102–105; July 1941, p. 30–32, 104–107; Aug. 1941, p. 30–32, 74–76.

Nienaber, Craig. "Gangsterland in the '30s." *Hennepin County History* 36, no. 4 (Winter 1977–78): 3–9; and 37, no. 1 (Spring 1978): 15–19.

Opsahl, Ross. "South St. Paul, Minnesota, Machine Gun Raid," *Thompson Collectors News* 10 (Aug. 15, 1991); and 12 (Oct. 15, 1991).

Pegler, Westbrook. "Fair Enough." *New York World-Telegram*, Feb. 19, 1934.

Pfleger, Helen Warren, as told to George A. Rea. "Volstead and Prohibition: A Roaring '20's Memoir." *Ramsey County History* 12, no. 1 (Spring–Summer 1975): 19–22.

Powner, John. "On the Scarlet Trail of the Twin City Terrorists." *Startling Detective Adventures*, July 1935, p. 28–35, 71–75.

Price, Mollie. "Swede Hollow: Sheltered Society for Immigrants to St. Paul." *Ramsey County History* 17, no. 2 (1981–82): 12–22.

"Rufus C. Coulter." *Grapevine*, Nov. 1975, p. 28.

Russell, John M. "Scenes from Yesteryear," *Dunn County News* (Menomonie, Wis.), Apr. 25, 1985.

Snider, John. "The Great Denver Mint Robbery." *Denver Post*, Aug. 18, 23, and 30, 1959.

Trohan, Walter. "J. Edgar Hoover, the One-Man Scotland Yard." *Chicago Tribune*, June 21, 1936, pt. 7, p. 1, 8, 11.

Yandle, Jim. "The Bloody End to Ma Barker's Crime Spree." *Orlando Sentinel*, Jan. 19, 1988, p. 4.

NOTES • • • • • • • • • • •

Abbreviations:

BCA   Bureau of Criminal Apprehension (Minnesota)

FBI   Federal Bureau of Investigation (includes Bureau of Investigation, U.S. Bureau of Investigation, and Division of Investigation)

MHS   Minnesota Historical Society

NARG   National Archives Record Group

SPPD   St. Paul Police Department

Many FBI documents are held in the FBI's Freedom of Information Act Reading Room in named file sets. The abbreviations listed below stand for the name of the set and the prefix that is common to all documents in the set. Most documents also have file numbers; many have both file and section numbers. Citations in the notes below use the given abbreviation for file set and prefix, as well as any file and section numbers available.

BKF   Bremer Kidnap file 7–576–

CCF   Crime Conditions file 62–30930–

DF   Dillinger file 62–29777–

HKF   Hamm Kidnap file 7–77–

KCMF   Kansas City Massacre file 62–28915–

Notes from the author's interviews and photocopies of documents from the FBI, the National Archives, and many other sources that were used in researching this work are held in the Paul Maccabee St. Paul Gangster History Research Collection, MHS.

The *St. Paul Pioneer Press* and the *St. Paul Dispatch* are cited as *Pioneer Press* and *Dispatch* respectively.

Notes for Preface

1. Alvin Karpis with Bill Trent, *The Alvin Karpis Story* (New York: Coward, McCann, and Geoghegan, 1971), 100.

2. Avery Hale, "The Inside Story of Dillinger at Last," *True Detective Mysteries*, Dec. 1934, p. 9.

3. Anthony Summers, *Official and Confidential: The Secret Life of J. Edgar Hoover* (New York: G. P. Putnam's Sons, 1993), 43–44, 65–66, 225–34; Curt Gentry, *J. Edgar Hoover: The Man and the Secrets* (New York: Norton, 1991), 327–32.

4. Errol Stuart, Chicago police records officer, and Dennis Bingham, Chicago police executive, interviews by author, July 22, 1994.

5. Johnny "Dollar" Douthit, BCA agent, interview by author, May 14, 1993; Marcia Cummings, BCA staff member, interview by author, Feb. 1991.

6. Federal Bureau of Prisons archivist, to author, Anne Diestel, July 25, 1994; Mike Robar, Federal Bureau of Prisons staff member, interview by author, n.d.

Notes for Chapter 1

1. William Schader, deputy fire inspector, Division of Fire Prevention report, Dec. 4, 1928, Re: Danny Hogan, SPPD.

2. *Dispatch*, Dec. 6, 1928, p. 1; *Minneapolis Morning Tribune*, Dec. 7, 1928, p. 1.

3. Danny Hogan homicide report, Dec. 11, 1928, p. 1, SPPD. See also, Daniel Hogan death certificate, no. 2881, Dec. 5, 1928, City of St. Paul.

4. Daniel Hogan, San Quentin Prison record, California State Archives, Sacramento; FBI memo, May 31, 1927, p. 7, file 48–39–10, NARG 60.

5. Special assistant to Attorney General Pratt, to Assistant Attorney General Luhring, Justice Dept. memo, May 4, 1927, p. 3–4, 7–8, file 48–39–10, NARG 60.

6. Mark Heisted, "A Story of Crime, Criminals, and Corruption," Minnesota Public Radio documentary, Nov. 8, 1985.

7. Max F. Burger, FBI report, June 25, 1926, p. 9, FBI file 62–11743–13, file 48–39–10, NARG 60.

8. Here and preceding paragraph, see Burger report, June 25, 1926, file 48–39–10, NARG 60.

9. Office of the Inspector, Post Office Dept. memo, July 8, 1926, file 48–39–10, NARG 60.

10. John Pratt to Assistant Attorney General Lurhing, Justice Dept. memo, May 4, 1927, p. 18, file 48–39–10, NARG 60.

11. L. L. Edge, *Run the Cat Roads: The True Story of Bank Robbers in the 30s* (New York: Dembner Books, 1981), 35; J. Evetts Haley, *Robbing Banks Was My Business: The Story of J. Harvey Bailey, America's Most Successful Bank Robber* (Canyon, Tex.: Palo Duro Press, 1973), 48–50.

12. L. B. Reed, FBI report, May 31, 1927, p. 4, FBI file 62–14440–4, file 48–39–10, NARG 60; John Snider, "The Great Denver Mint Robbery," *Denver Post*, Aug. 18, 23, 30, 1959, quoted in Haley, *Robbing Banks*, 39; Dow Helmars, "The Denver Mint Robbery, 1927," *Denver Post Empire*, Dec. 7, 1975.

13. Edge, *Run the Cat Roads*, 37; Haley, *Robbing Banks*, 47 (quote), 48, 63–65; Reed report, May 31, 1927, p. 4, file 48–39–10, NARG 60.

14. Harvey Bailey, interview by J. Evetts Haley, Oct. 31, 1965, p. 7, 16–17, and Sept. 18, 1966, p. 4, J. Evetts Haley Collection, Nita Haley Library, Midland, Tex. (cited hereafter as Haley Collection); Haley, *Robbing Banks*, 50–51.

15. Pratt to Luhring memo, May 4, 1927, p. 4–5, file 48–39–10, NARG 60.

16. "Application for Reducing Hogan Bond is Denied," newspaper clipping dated Jan. 29, 1929, *St. Paul Pioneer Press* morgue file, St. Paul Public Library; *Minneapolis Morning Tribune*, Feb. 2, 1927, p. 2; *Dispatch*, July 5, 1927, p. 1.

17. Reed report, May 31, 1927, p. 1, 3, file 48–39–10, NARG 60.

18. E. L. Dole, FBI memos, Jan. 4, 1928, July 20, 1927, p. 12, file 48–39–10, NARG 60; FBI report, Apr. 7, 1928, FBI file 62–14440–21, file 48–39–10, NARG 60; John L. Talty, Statement to St. Paul Police, July 8, 1927, Ann Grenville and Teddy DuBois homicide file, SPPD.

19. Luhring to attorney general, Justice Dept. memo, July 12, 1926, p. 1–2, file 48–39–10–2, and Pratt to Luhring memo, May 4, 1927, p. 18, file 48–39–10, both NARG 60.

20. Ann Michaud, interview by author, Nov. 20, 1993.

21. *Minneapolis Journal*, Dec. 5, 1928, p. 1, 4; Michaud interview, Dec. 7, 1993.

22. *Pioneer Press*, Dec. 5, 1928, p. 1.

23. Special agent _____, St. Paul, to Werner Hanni, FBI memo, Feb. 19, 1934, p. 2, CCF 16, vol. 1. See also Nate Bomberg, interview transcript, Council of Arts and Sciences, Ramsey County Historical Society, St. Paul.

24. "Gangsters: An Interview with Will Greer," *Scattered Seeds* (Central High School, St. Paul) 8 (1976): 3–4.

25. *St. Paul City Directory, 1915*, 89; Maurice E. Doran, *History of the St. Paul Police Department* (St. Paul: Police Benevolent Society, 1912), viii, 29, 37, 45–50; A. R. Fenwick, *Sturdy Sons of St. Paul* (St. Paul: Junior Pioneer Association, 1899), 142–43; *St. Paul Daily News*, Jan. 17, 1922, p. 1.

26. *St. Paul Daily News*, July 4, 1924, p. 2; *Souvenir Book of the St. Paul Police Department* (St. Paul: Perkins-Thomas Printing Co., 1904), p. 3.

27. George C. Rogers, "Life of Dick O'Connor (Chapter 2)," *St. Paul Daily News*, Jan. 10, 1933, p. 1.

28. *Dispatch*, Mar. 21, 1913, p. 1; William H. Griffin death certificate, Mar. 20, 1913, Minnesota Department of Health; Ramsey County, William H. Griffin probate file, no. 20903, St. Paul City Hall; *St. Paul City Directory, 1912*, 727.

29. Paul Light (pseud. Howard Kahn), "So What," *Pioneer Press*, Sept. 7, 1943.

30. *Pioneer Press*, Nov. 27, 1912, p. 1.

31. "Long Career of Famous Sleuth Closes on Coast," newspaper clipping [ca. July 1924], *St. Paul Pioneer Press* morgue files; *Minneapolis Journal*, July 4, 1924, p. 1.

32. David J. Morgan, interview by author, June 8, 1993.

33. *Pioneer Press*, Feb. 24, 1910, p. 1 (dice), Dec. 14, 1916, p. 1 (haven); *Dispatch*, Mar. 3, 1910, p. 1 (liquor).

34. Westbrook Pegler, "Fair Enough," *New York World-Telegram*, Feb. 19, 1934; J. Edgar Hoover to Mr. Clegg, FBI memo, Feb. 28, 1934, CCF 26, vol. 1.

35. Heisted, "A Story of Crime."

36. Morgan interview, June 8, 1993.

37. *Pioneer Press*, July 5, 1924, p. 6.

38. *Pioneer Press*, May 21, 1922, p. 1; Luhring memo, July 12, 1926, p. 8, file 48–39–10–2, NARG 60. See also *Dispatch*, Dec. 15, 1923, p. 1; "Sommer Sketch," unpublished notes from *Pioneer Press* newspaper morgue file.

39. *Pioneer Press*, Dec. 5, 1928, p. 10.

40. Fred Heaberlin, interview by author, Jan. 6, 1994.

41. Pat Lannon Sr., interviews by author, June 14, Aug. 27, 1993.

42. Hanna Steinbracker [sic] death certificate, no. 10485, July 14, 1929, Wayne County (Detroit, Mich.); U.S. Manuscript Census Schedules, 1900, 1920, Precinct 1, St. Paul; Minnesota Manuscript Census Schedule, 1895, 1905, St. Paul, Precinct 1, Ward 4; Map of Mt. Elliott Cemetery Plots, lot 266N.

43. *St. Paul City Directories, 1889–1929*; St. Paul, "Detailed Statement of Specifications for New Buildings, 147 Washington Street South, June 9, 1888."

44. Joel E. Best, "Long Kate, Dutch Henriette and Mother Robinson: Three Madames in Post-Civil War St. Paul," *Ramsey County History* 15 (1979–80): 3–10.

45. *St. Paul City Directories, 1899–1931*; Oliver Towne column, "Fabulous Hill Street," *Dispatch*, Aug. 11, 1958.

46. U.S. Manuscript Census Schedule, 1900, Precinct 1, St. Paul.

47. Morgan interview, June 8, 1993.

48. Oliver Towne, "Madame of Madames," *Dispatch*, Dec. 1, 1973.

49. *Pioneer Press*, Dec. 18, 1923, p. 2.

50. Oliver Towne, "Nina Clifford's Legacy," *Dispatch*, July 4, 1963.

51. H. A. Guilford, *Holy of Holies of the White Slave Worshipper* (St. Paul: n.p., n.d. [ca. 1915]), 5, 8.

52. Horace Dupont, interview by author, Jan. 7, 1994.

53. Hanna Steinbracker death certificate, July 14, 1929; Map of Mt. Elliott Cemetery Plots, lot 266N.

54. *St. Paul Daily News*, July 17, 1929, p. 1; *Pioneer Press*, July 18, 1929, p. 16; Death notice for Hanna Steinbrecher, *Detroit News*, July 16, 1929.

55. Ramsey County, Hannah Steinbrecher probate file, no. 44961, July 1929; Wayne County, Hanna Steinbrecher Probate Court record (reviewed by Sal Giacona); Gareth Hiebert, interview by author, Nov. 17, 1993.

56. Heaberlin interview, Jan. 6, 1994.

57. Dupont interview; *St. Paul City Directories, 1931–1934*.

58. City of St. Paul, Div. of Building Inspection, Permit Application, May 3, 1933, 147 S. Washington; Oliver Towne, "Ode to Nina Clifford," *Dispatch*, Jan. 9, 1960; *Dispatch*, June 7, 1933, p. 1.

59. Bernie Bullert, St. Paul Water Utility general manager, interview by author, Dec. 17, 1993, quoting from *City Water Utility Standard Mains Book*, 1934, 239–240.

60. Robert O. Baker, "The Minnesota Club: St. Paul's Enterprising Leaders and their 'Gentlemen's Social Club' " *Ramsey County History* 19, no. 2 (1984): 15–16; author's interviews with Gareth Hiebert and Jep Knox, Dec. 3, 1993.

61. Donald Empson, *The Street Where You Live: A Guide to the Street Names of St. Paul* (St. Paul: Witsend Press, 1975), 158–59; Virginia Brainerd Kunz, *St. Paul: The First 150 Years* (St. Paul: St. Paul Foundation, 1991), 62–63; *St. Paul City Directory, 1887, 1889*; Charles Reiter, former police officer, interview by author, Sept. 24, 1993.

62. *Dispatch*, Dec. 8, 1928, p. 1, Dec. 7, 1928, p. 1.

63. Heaberlin interview, Jan. 6, 1994; *Minneapolis Morning Tribune*, Dec. 8, 1928, p. 15.

64. *Minneapolis Morning Tribune*, Dec. 6, 1928, p. 1–2.

65. *Dispatch*, Dec. 5, 1928, p. 1; Michaud interview, Dec. 7, 1993.

66. Gene DiMartino, Calvary Cemetery superintendent, interview by author, Oct. 8, 1993.

67. Lannon interview, June 14, 1993.

68. "Scores of Friends Offer Selves for Blood Transfusion," newspaper clipping dated Dec. 4, 1928, *Pioneer Press* morgue file; *Minneapolis Morning Tribune*, Dec. 6, 1928, p. 1–2.

69. "Hogan-Rothstein Link is Revived," newspaper clipping dated Dec. 19, 1928, *Pioneer Press* morgue file.

70. Michaud interviews, Nov. 20 and Dec. 7, 1993.

71. S. K. McKee, FBI report, May 20, 1936, p. 10, HKF 732, sec. 8.

72. McKee report, May 20, 1936, p. 10, HKF 732.

73. Woody Keljik, interview by author, Jan. 22, 1993.

Notes for Chapter 2

1. *Pioneer Press*, June 29, 1919, sec. 2, p. 4.

2. Dean Jennings, *We Only Kill Each Other: The Life and Bad Times of Bugsy Siegel* (Englewood Cliffs, N.J.: Prentice-Hall, 1967), 35.

3. Helen Warren Pfleger as told to George A. Rea, "Volstead and Prohibition: A Roaring '20s' Memoir," *Ramsey County History* 12 (Spring/Summer 1975): 21.

4. *Dispatch*, Nov. 25, 1920, p. 1–2; *Dispatch*, Nov. 26, 1920, p. 1; *Dispatch*, Nov. 27, 1920, p. 1.

5. Frank Wing, *Brewers Handbook of the U.S. and Canada* (New York: J. M. Wing Co., 1887), 67–73, cited in Gary J. Brueggemann, "Beer Capital of the State—St. Paul's Historic Family Breweries," *Ramsey County History* 16 (1980–81): 3; McKee report, May 20, 1936, p. 9, HKF 732. *Pioneer Press*, Jan. 17, 1926, p. 1.

6. Bomberg interview, Ramsey County Historical Society.

7. *Dispatch*, Mar. 21, 1922, p. 1; *Pioneer Press*, Dec. 23, 1926, p. 1.

8. Frank Buckley, "Prohibition Survey of Minnesota," in *Enforcement of the Prohibition Laws*, Official Records of the National Commission on Law Observance and Enforcement, 71st Cong., 3d sess. (Washington, D.C.: Government Printing Office, 1931), 4:598–99.

9. C. W. Hitsman and Ray J. Casserly, Bureau of Prohibition report, Dec. 6, 1932, p. 3, file 23–39–140, NARG 60.

10. *Pioneer Press*, Oct. 20, 1921, p. 1, Aug. 8, 1930, p. 1.

11. Judge John F. McGee, Minneapolis, to U.S. attorney general, Mar. 4, 1924, p. 2–3, file 23–05–39–46, NARG 60.

12. *Pioneer Press*, May 8, 1921, p. 1, Oct. 20, 1921, p. 1; *Dispatch*, Sept. 14, 1927, p. 1, Dec. 9, 1922, p. 1.

13. *Pioneer Press*, Mar. 21, 1922, p. 1, Aug. 3, 1923, p. 1, Apr. 13, 1924, p. 1; *Dispatch*, Feb. 1, 1922, p. 1.

14. Walter W. Liggett, "Minneapolis and Vice in Volsteadland," *Plain Talk*, Apr. 1930, p. 390, in possession of Marda Woodbury, daughter of Walter Liggett; Heisted, "A Story of Crime."

15. Bomberg interview, Ramsey County Historical Society; Liggett, "Minneapolis and Vice in Volsteadland," 389.

16. *Dispatch*, Sept. 16, 1922, p. 1; *Pioneer Press*, Sept. 3, 1922, p. 1.

17. Lafayette French Jr., U.S. attorney, St. Paul, to U.S. attorney general, Justice Dept. memo, Nov. 27, 1925, file 23–39–51, NARG 60.

18. *Pioneer Press*, June 27, 1925, p. 1, Oct. 22, 1925, p. 1.

19. *Dispatch*, Sept. 13, 1920, p. 1; H. H. Clegg to director, FBI memo, May 8, 1934, p. 5, DF 1310, sec. 25.

20. *Dispatch*, Sept. 26, 1925, p. 4.

21. Affidavit of Abe Gleeman, Ramsey County Court, Sept. 15, 1925, sec. 1–6, Dispatch-Pioneer Press Papers, MHS. This affidavit also appears in full in the *Pioneer Press*, Sept. 26, 1925, p. 1.

22. *Pioneer Press*, Mar. 16, 1926, p. 1; Affidavit of Bennie Gleeman, Ramsey County Court, Sept. 15, 1925, sec. 1–3, Dispatch-Pioneer Press Papers, MHS; Burger report, June 25, 1926, p. 6, file 48–39–10, NARG 60. The Gleeman affidavit also appears in full in the *Pioneer Press*, Sept. 26, 1925, p. 1.

23. Max F. Burger, Justice Dept. report, July 23, 1926, p. 16–21, file 48–39–10, NARG 60.

24. P. W. to director, FBI memo, July 29, 1926, p. 3–5, file 23–39–50, NARG 60; Burger report, June 25, 1926, p. 1–7, July 23, 1926, p. 19, file 48–39–10, NARG 60.

25. Bennie Gleeman affidavit, sec. 6, 14–16; *Pioneer Press*, Sept. 26, 1925, p. 2.

26. Bennie Gleeman affidavit, sec. 26; Burton Stevens death certificate, no. 6257, Feb. 18, 1925, Minnesota Department of Health.

27. Bennie Gleeman affidavit, sec. 21.

28. Bennie Gleeman affidavit, sec. 22–24.

29. Bennie Gleeman affidavit, sec. 24–27, 31; Abe Gleeman affidavit, sec. 34–37, 40, 44.

30. *Pioneer Press*, Sept. 26, 1925, p. 1, Sept. 28, 1929, p. 10.

31. *Pioneer Press*, Sept. 26, 1925, p. 1.

32. *Pioneer Press*, Feb. 17, 1926, p. 1–2.

33. *Pioneer Press*, Mar. 23, 1926, p. 2; *Dispatch*, Feb. 19, 1926, p. 1; *Pioneer Press*, Feb. 24, 1926, p. 1, 3.

34. *Dispatch*, Sept. 26, 1925, p. 4.

35. *Pioneer Press*, Sept. 28, 1925, p. 1, June 20, 1923, p. 1 (McGee); Buckley, "Prohibition Survey of Minnesota," 4:595–97.

36. Liggett, "Minneapolis and Vice in Volsteadland," 388.

37. *Pioneer Press*, Sept. 28, 1929, p. 1.

38. *Pioneer Press*, Oct. 1, 1929, p. 10, July 8, 1933, p. 3; *Dispatch*, Jan. 14, 1930, p. 1.

39. M. E. Evans (Ohio), assistant U.S. attorney, to M. D. Kiefer, special assistant U.S. attorney general, Justice Dept. memo, May 4, 1926, file 23–57–142–57, NARG 60.

40. Morris Roisner, Prison Admission Summary, file 51308–1, Leavenworth, Kans., July 2, 1937, Federal Bureau of Prisons; *Pioneer Press*, Nov. 16, 1927, p. 1, Sept. 13, 1935, p. 1.

41. C. W. Stein to J. Edgar Hoover, FBI memo, Mar. 18, 1936, HKF 444, sec. 6; *Dispatch*, Mar. 10, 1926, p. 1.

42. J. D. Glass, FBI report, June 28, 1932, p. 6, file 4–2–11–0, NARG 129.

43. Drill to U.S. attorney general, Justice Dept. memo, Mar. 15, 1933, p. 1–2, NARG 60; *Pioneer Press*, May 5, 1934, p. 1; Rep. Einar Hoidale to U.S. Attorney General Homer Cummings, letter, Sept. 17, 1934, file 5–39–54, and Hoidale to Cummings, telegram, Oct. 4, 1934, file 5–39–52, both in NARG 60.

44. "In re: Leon Gleckman, St. Paul, Minnesota," IRS memo, Feb. 9, 1933, Chicago, SI-8369-F, NARG 60; Leon Gleckman, Prison Admission Summary, file 48710–L, Leavenworth, Kans., Apr. 22, 1936, p. 2, Federal Bureau of Prisons.

45. Gleckman admission summary, p. 4–5.

46. "Raid Yields 13 Stills, 1,000 Gallons Liquor," newspaper clipping, ca. Aug. 1922, *Pioneer Press* morgue file; *Dispatch*, Nov. 6,

1922, p. 5; *U.S. v. Leon Gleckman*, Federal district court, Minneapolis, 1922.

47. FBI memo for the director, July 29, 1926, p. 1–2, FBI file 62–11743, file 23–39–50, NARG 60; *Leon Gleckman v. U.S.A.*, Affidavit for Withdrawal of Confession of Error, no. 6506 (8th Cir. 1923).

48. FBI memo, July 29, 1926, p. 1, file 23–39–50; Gleckman admission summary, p. 1.

49. L. B. Nichols to Clyde Tolson, FBI memo, July 17, 1939, containing Treasury Dept. report of Elmer Irey on Leon Gleckman, p. 4, file 51–39–2, NARG 60; H. M. Slater, FBI report, Mar. 11, 1932, p. 3, and R. J. Caffrey, FBI report, July 29, 1932, p. 30 (quote), both in file 4–2–11–0, NARG 129; Frank Spiering, *The Man Who Got Capone* (Indianapolis: Bobbs-Merrill, 1976), 85.

50. S. K. McKee, FBI report, June 3, 1936, p. 3, HKF 776, sec. 9; Stein to director, FBI teletype, May 1, 1936, HKF 629.

51. R. T. Noonan, FBI report, May 27, 1936, p. 5, HKF 759, sec. 9; K. R. McIntire to director, FBI memo, June 15, 1936, HKF 834, sec. 10. The relationship between Gleckman and Brown is confirmed by the author's interview with retired St. Paul Police Lt. Ralph Merrill, Oct. 10, 1990.

52. McKee report, June 3, 1936, p. 3, HKF 776.

53. Calvert Cravath, interviews by author, June 1991 and Aug. 7, 1991; Calvert Cravath to Ann DeJoy of the Hotel St. Paul, July 5, 1985, letter in author's possession.

54. Cravath interviews, June 1991 and Aug. 7, 1991; Cravath to DeJoy, July 5, 1985; John S. Hurley, assistant director, Bureau of Prohibition report, Feb. 28, 1934, p. 6–9, NARG 60.

55. R. T. Noonan, report, June 18, 1936, p. 43, HKF 880, sec. 10; *Pioneer Press*, Oct. 3, 1931, p. 1, 6.

56. Noonan report, June 18, 1936, p. 40–41, 44, HKF 880.

57. Noonan report, June 18, 1936, p. 50, HKF 880; McKee report, June 3, 1936, p. 4–5, HKF 776.

58. Frank LaPre death certificate, Oct. 7, 1931, Minnesota Department of Health; Ramsey County Medical Examiner, Frank LaPre

autopsy report, file 9536, Oct. 3, 1931; *Pioneer Press*, Oct. 5, 1931, p. 1–2.

59. Noonan report, June 18, 1936, p. 41, HKF 880, and Lannon interview, May 13, 1993 (Tallerico information); anonymous former St. Paul police officer, interview by author, June 1993.

60. Noonan report, June 18, 1936, p. 47, 51, HKF 880.

61. *Dispatch*, June 29, 1932, p. 1.

62. Special agent ____, St. Paul, to Werner Hanni, FBI memo, Feb. 19, 1934, p. 3, CCF 16, vol. 1.

63. McKee report, June 3, 1936, p. 5, HKF 776.

64. Gertrude Sletner, interview by author, July 30, 1993.

65. Director A. W. W. Woodcock to Mr. Youngquist, Bureau of Prohibition memo, July 22, 1932, p. 1–2, file 23–39–140, NARG 60.

66. Max Ehrlich, interview by author, Oct. 30, 1992.

67. *Dispatch*, Jan. 29, 1932, p. 1; Nichols to Tolson, July 17, 1939, p. 1–2, file 51–39–2, NARG 60.

68. Leo E. Owens, *Dispatch* publisher, to U.S. Attorney General William D. Mitchell, Oct. 6, 1931, file 5–39–52, NARG 60.

69. Heisey to L. L. Drill, U.S. attorney, Justice Dept. memo, May 18, 1933, p. 2, file 5–39–52, NARG 60.

70. Norman J. Morrison, special assistant, to attorney general, St. Paul, Justice Dept. memo, Nov. 11, 1933, NARG 60.

71. E. C. Crouter to Mr. Key, Justice Dept. memo, Mar. 27, 1933, p. 2–3, file 5–39–52, NARG 60.

72. *St. Paul City Directory, 1932*, 10.

73. Noonan report, May 27, 1936, p. 6, HKF 759; Reiter interview, Sept. 24, 1993; D. P. Sullivan, FBI report, June 11, 1936, p. 5, HKF 823, sec. 10.

74. Sarah Knutson, interview by author, Nov. 1993; *State of Minnesota v. Doc Jones et al.*, Jan. 11, 1935, Ramsey County District Court Indictment Record, MHS.

75. Donna Bremer, interview by author, Dec. 29, 1993; *Pioneer Press*, Feb. 8, 1994, p. 1C, 4C; Jim George, "Castle Royal: In the Spotlight Again," *Dispatch*, July 20, 1977, p. 33–34.

76. Lannon interview, June 14, 1993.

77. Castle Royal advertisement, *Dispatch*, Oct. 27, 1933, sec. 2, p. 5.

78. Marguerite Junterman, interview by author, Aug. 8, 1993.

79. Junterman interview; *Dispatch*, July 23, 1958, p. 38.

80. Boulevards of Paris advertisement, *St. Paul Daily News*, Sept. 8, 1929, rotogravure section, p. 4–5.

81. Sullivan report, June 11, 1936, p. 5, HKF 832; Junterman interview; McKee report, May 20, 1936, p. 8, HKF 732.

82. Junterman interview; Noonan report, June 18, 1936, p. 49–50, HKF 880.

83. *Pioneer Press*, Oct. 31, 1926, p. 1; *Dispatch*, Dec. 25, 1926, p. 1; Junterman interview; Marie McMahon, John Lane's granddaughter, interview with author, Mar. 1993.

84. Junterman interview; *Dispatch*, July 23, 1958, p. 38.

85. Noonan report, May 27, 1936, p. 8, HKF 759; *Pioneer Press*, Jan. 21, 1936, p. 1; Statement of Thomas E. Gannon, undated, p. 3, Walter Liggett homicide file, BCA.

86. McMahon interview; Junterman interview; *Dispatch*, Sept. 18, 1929, p. 1.

87. John E. Brennan, FBI report, Feb. 15, 1936, p. 7, HKF 423, sec. 5; Noonan report, May 27, 1936, p. 6, HKF 759; St. Paul Street Address Index, MHS; *Dispatch*, June 2, 1952, July 23, 1958, p. 38.

88. *Pioneer Press*, Nov. 4, 1932, p. 1–2.

89. William Weir, *Written with Lead: Legendary American Gunfights and Gunfighters* (Hamden, Conn.: Archon Books, 1992), 200–201.

90. Abe Loeb death certificate, no. 1752, July 29, 1932, Minnesota Department of Health; Burton B. Turkus and Sid Feder, *Murder, Inc.: The Story of "the Syndicate"* (New York: Da Capo Press, 1992, reprint of 1951), 16–18.

91. Excerpts from Philadelphia Police Dept. intelligence files, supplied by Capt. Joseph O'Connor, interview by author, Feb. 26, 1991.

92. R. E. Newby to director, FBI memo, July 15, 1935, p. 3–4, BKF 240x, sec. 3; *Dispatch*, Nov. 9, 1932, sec. 2, p. 1; Statement of

Gustav Enaas, Sept. 2, 1932, Abe Loeb, Al Gordon homicide file 6970, SPPD.

93. Harry Davis murder file, no. 1193, July 21, 1932, BCA; Richard N. Pranke, "Autobiography: Travels and Genealogy," p. 173, Pranke Family Records, MHS; R. E. Newby to M. Nathan, FBI memo, Feb. 26, 1934, p. 13, CCF 46, vol. 1.

94. Statement of Lila Danz, July 26, 1932, Loeb and Gordon homicide file, SPPD; Thomas E. Dahill and J. O. Meyer, "When St. Paul Silenced New Jersey's Hired Guns," *Startling Detective Adventures* 10, no. 60 (July 1933): 40–43, 54.

95. Ellie (Hallberg) McLean, interview by author, Apr. 15, 1993.

96. Dahill and Meyer, "When St. Paul Silenced," 40, 43; Statement of Mrs. Helen Schultz, July 26, 1932, and Report of Officer Kahler, July 25, 1932, Loeb and Gordon homicide file, SPPD; Ramsey County coroner, Abe Loeb file, no. 9950, Ancker Hospital autopsy record, July 26, 1932; Thomas Delaney, interview by author, May 9, 1992.

97. Richard N. Pranke, former FBI special agent, interview by author, Oct. 23, 1992.

98. Statements of Pauline Poetz, Sept. 17, 1932, Dr. Henry H. Hall, Aug. 13, 1932, Mrs. T. W. Edwards, Aug. 24, 1932, Mrs. Hortense Nickolaus, Aug. 24, 1932, Loeb and Gordon homicide file, SPPD.

99. Dupont interview, Oct. 31, 1992; *Dispatch*, Nov. 3, 1932, p. 1, 3.

100. *Pioneer Press*, Nov. 11, 1932, p. 1, 3; Turkus and Feder, *Murder, Inc.*, 20.

101. Special agent in charge, St. Paul, to director, FBI memo, June 15, 1949, BKF 1528, sec. 273.

102. Special agent in charge to director memo, June 15, 1949, p. 2, BKF 1528; Roy Farnham, retired head of Stillwater Records and Identification, interview by author, 1985; statement of Thomas E. Gannon, undated, p. 2, Liggett homicide file, BCA; Philadelphia Police Dept. intelligence files, quoted in O'Connor interview, Feb. 26, 1991. These files included the 1956 letter from Stillwater Warden Douglas C. Rigg to Senator Hubert H. Humphrey.

103. M. B. Rhodes to director, FBI memo, Sept. 12, 1944, p. 6, BKF 15266, sec. 272; spe-

cial agent in charge to director, FBI memo June 15, 1949, p. 3. See also transcription of letter from Stillwater inmate Tommy Gannon, Liggett homicide file, BCA.

104. Special agent in charge to director memo, June 15, 1949, p. 2; Rhodes to director memo, Sept. 12, 1934, p. 1, 7–8, BKF 15266; Jennings, *We Only Kill Each Other*, 36.

105. Karpis with Trent, *Karpis Story*, 243; S. W. Hardy, FBI report, Apr. 6, 1932, p. 6, file 4–2–11–0, NARG 129.

106. Jay Robert Nash, *Bloodletters and Badmen: A Narrative Encyclopedia of American Criminals from the Pilgrims to the Present* (New York: M. Evans and Co., 1991; reprint of 1973), 500–501; "Vice Conditions—Minneapolis and St. Paul, Minnesota," FBI report, July 19, 1943, p. 84, CCF 315, vol. 6.

107. Rhodes to director memo, Sept. 12, 1944, p. 8, BKF 15266; "Vice Conditions—Minneapolis and St. Paul," July 19, 1943, p. 78; Joe Sherin, former St. Paul police officer, interview by author, 1992.

108. Jennings, *We Only Kill Each Other*, 4.

Notes for Chapter 3

1. Karpis with Trent, *Karpis Story*, 98.

2. Karpis with Trent, *Karpis Story*, 99–100; Michael Wallis, *Pretty Boy: The Life and Times of Charles Arthur Floyd* (New York: St. Martin's Press, 1992), 170–71; FBI interview with Edna Murray, Feb. 12, 1935, p. 10–11, BKF 4546, sec. 69; R. C. Suran, FBI report, May 18, 1936, p. 2, BKF 11653, sec. 203.

3. John E. Brennan, FBI report, May 22, 1936, p. 3, BKF 11766, sec. 204; Wallis, *Pretty Boy*, 171.

4. Special agent _____ to Werner Hanni memo, Feb. 19, 1934, CCF vol. 1; Lannon interview, June 14, 1993; S. P. Cowley to director, FBI memo, Apr. 24, 1934, p. 5, DF 1010, sec. 19.

5. Courtney Riley Cooper, *Here's to Crime* (Boston: Little, Brown and Co., 1937), 81–82.

6. Cowley to director memo, Apr. 24, 1934, p. 5, DF 1010; Karpis with Trent, *Karpis Story*, 101, 110–11.

7. Statement of Delores Delaney to FBI, Jan. 22, 1934, p. 1–3, BKF, NR Bulky Box 3,

pt. 1; Karpis with Trent, *Karpis Story,* 110–11, 113.

8. Haley, interview with Harvey Bailey, Sept. 18, 1966, p. 18, Haley Collection.

9. Clegg to director memo, May 8, 1934, p. 4, DF 1310; Lannon interview, June 14, 1993; Heaberlin interview, Jan. 6, 1994.

10. Harry Sawyer, FBI wanted poster, Feb. 12, 1935, identification order 1240; Carole J. DeMoss, Harry Sawyer's niece, interview by author, Jan. 19, 1994; "Aunt Billie," DeMoss family letter, n.d., copy in author's possession; *Pioneer Press,* Jan. 25, 1936, p. 3; Harry Sawyer, Leavenworth and Alcatraz prison files, Federal Bureau of Prisons.

11. Harry Sawyer, FBI file, fingerprint record, R44401, Feb. 28, 1958; *Pioneer Press,* Jan. 25, 1936, p. 3.

12. Clegg to director memo, May 8, 1934, p. 1, DF 1310; *Pioneer Press,* Jan. 21, 1936, p. 1, 7; McKee report, May 20, 1936, p. 8, HKF 732.

13. Hardy report, Apr. 6, 1932, p. 6, file 4–2–11–0, NARG 129; *Pioneer Press,* Nov. 4, 1932, p. 1; *Dispatch,* Nov. 4, 1932, p. 1; "Gangsters: An Interview with Will Greer," p. 3–4; Noonan report, June 18, 1936, p. 50, HKF 880.

14. J. D. Glass, FBI report, June 28, 1932, p. 4, file 4–2–11–0, NARG 129; R. C. Suran, FBI report, Oct. 6, 1934, p. 40–41, 48, KCMF 2655, sec. 63; R. C. Suran, FBI report, Sept. 1, 1934, p. 30, KCMF 2366, sec. 57.

15. Jane Resler, interview by author, Sept. 9, 1993.

16. O. G. Hall, FBI report, Dec. 7, 1933, p. 2, KCMF 950, sec. 28; Resler interview.

17. Karpis with Trent, *Karpis Story,* 101–2; Earl Van Wagoner, FBI report, Apr. 11, 1934, p. 9, DF 538, sec. 11.

18. Karpis with Trent, *Karpis Story,* 101–3.

19. *Pioneer Press,* Jan. 21, 1936, p. 1, 7; Lannon interview, June 14, 1993.

20. Harold J. Hurley, son of Green Lantern manager George Hurley, interview by author, June 10, 1994; McKee report, May 20, 1936, p. 3, HKF 732; Statement of Claire Lucas, Mar. 21, 1931, and statement of Isaac Goodman, Mar. 20, 1931, Frank Ventress homicide file, SPPD.

21. *Pioneer Press,* Nov. 4, 1923, p. 1, 8;

Heaberlin interview, Jan. 6, 1994; Heisted, "A Story of Crime"; George Hurley, interview by author, June 11, 1994; Hardy report, Apr. 6, 1932, p. 6, file 4–2–11–0, NARG 129.

22. K. R. McIntire to director, FBI memo, May 26, 1936, p. 2, HKF 769, sec. 9; McKee report, May 20, 1936, p. 9, HKF 732.

23. Edge, *Run the Cat Roads,* 39–40; Haley, interview with Harvey Bailey, Oct. 31, 1965, p. 3–4, 16, Haley Collection. See also Haley, *Robbing Banks,* 81.

24. Haley, *Robbing Banks,* 8, 24, 107–14.

25. S. K. McKee, FBI report, Apr. 27, 1936, p. 14, HKF 647; K. R. McIntire, FBI report, Apr. 10, 1935, p. 96, BKF, sec. 96.

26. D. L. Nicholson, FBI report, June 27, 1934, p. 18, DF 2274, sec. 40; D. L. Nicholson, FBI report, Sept. 19, 1934, p. 2, St. Paul file 26–2434, in Albert Reilly Leavenworth prison file, no. 48037, Federal Bureau of Prisons; Van Wagoner report, Apr. 11, 1934, p. 4, DF 538.

27. Harold Hurley interview, Aug. 27, 1993.

28. *Dispatch,* June 21, 1926, p. 1; *Pioneer Press,* Mar. 14, 1930, p. 1, 2; Harold Hurley interview, Aug. 27, 1993.

29. Blanche Schude Carter, interview by author, May 5, 1992.

30. Heaberlin interview, Jan. 6, 1994.

31. Frank Ventress file 9250, Mar. 23, 1931, Ramsey County coroner; statement of Mrs. Dorothy Van [Ventress], Mar. 21, 1931, and statement of Harry Kramer, Mar. 26, 1931, Ventress homicide file, SPPD; *Pioneer Press,* May 29, 1931, p. 1, 2; *Dispatch,* Mar. 20, 1931, p. 1, 2; O. G. Hall to Werner Hanni, FBI memo, Feb. 12, 1934, p. 1, BKF 334, sec. 4.

32. D. L. Nicholson, FBI report, Sept. 22, 1934, p. 6, 8, DF 4004, sec. 66.

33. Noonan report, June 18, 1936, p. 21, HKF 880.

34. FBI memo on Thomas A. Brown, Nov. 10, 1936, p. 16, HKF 1082, sec. 11.

35. Clegg to director memo, May 8, 1934, p. 4, DF 1310; R. L. Nalls to Werner Hanni, FBI memo, Jan. 31, 1934, BKF 143, sec. 2.

36. H. H. Clegg to director, FBI memo, June 9, 1934, p. 5, DF 1956, sec. 35; Jack Ramaley, interview by author, May 22, 1992.

37. Special agent in charge _____, Minneapolis, to director, FBI memo, May 22,

1950, FBI file 62–32578–1087; R. C. Coulter, FBI report, Aug. 31, 1934, p. 1, 7–8, KCMF 2355, sec. 57.

38. Coulter report, Aug. 31, 1934, p. 4, KCMF 2355; special agent in charge to director memo, May 22, 1950, FBI file 62–32578–1087; *Dispatch*, Apr. 3, 1934, p. 1, 4; Dupont interview, Oct. 31, 1992.

39. Coulter report, Aug. 31, 1934, p. 10, KCMF 2355.

40. Thomas Patrick Filben death certificate, no. 3397, Sept. 13, 1973, State of California; Jean Preston, niece of Tom Filben, interview by author, June 6, 1992; Dupont interview, Oct. 31, 1992; Bill Filben, nephew of Tom Filben, interview by author, June 13, 1992.

41. Vogelgesang, interview by author, May 5, 1992.

42. Preston interview.

43. Dupont interviews, Oct. 31, 1992, and Jan. 7, 1994.

44. Clegg to director memo, May 8, 1934, p. 4, DF 1310; Clegg to Purvis, FBI teletype, May 6, 1934, HKF 318, sec. 4.

45. Dupont interviews, May 1991 and Oct. 31, 1992; Filben interview.

46. Eben Gillespie, son of George Gillespie, interviews by author, Jan. 15, 1992, and Jan. 6, 1994; S. W. Hardy, FBI report, Jan. 17, 1940, p. 2, BKF 1542, sec. 270; *Dispatch*, Jan. 5, 1932, p. 1, 2.

47. Gillespie interview, Jan. 6, 1994; Hardy report, Jan. 17, 1940, p. 2–3, BKF 1542.

48. Karpis with Trent, *Karpis Story*, 162; Hardy report, Jan. 17, 1940, p. 1, 6–7, BKF 1542; Dupont interview, Oct. 31, 1992; Noonan report, May 27, 1936, p. 10, HKF 759.

49. Hardy report, Jan. 17, 1940, p. 4–5, BKF 1542; Preston interview; John Bowser, interviews by author, May 5 and 19, 1989, May 28, 1992.

50. Bowser interview, May 5, 1989; Filben interview; Mary Graves, historian at Voyageurs National Park, interview by author, May 28, 1992; O. G. Hall, FBI report, July 27, 1933, p. 28, KCMF 401, sec. 13.

51. Glass report, June 28, 1932, p. 6, file 4–2–11–0, NARG 129.

52. Ted Fahey, former St. Paul police officer, interview by author, July 19, 1991.

53. Glass report, June 28, 1932, p. 6–8, file 4–2–11–0, NARG 129.

54. Noonan report, May 27, 1936, p. 9–11, HKF 759; Dupont interview, Oct. 31, 1992.

Notes for Chapter 4

1. H. H. Clegg to special agent in charge, Kansas City, FBI memo, May 31, 1934, DF 1733, sec. 32; J. D. Glass, FBI report, June 27, 1932, p. 3, file 4–2–11–0, NARG 129; R. C. Suran, FBI report, Sept. 22, 1934, p. 4, KCMF 2502, sec. 60; W. R. Ramsey Jr., FBI report, Aug. 8, 1934, p. 12, KCMF 2178, sec. 53.

2. Glass report, June 27, 1932, p. 3, file 4–2–11–0, NARG 129; Robert J. Seng and daughter Barbara Seng, interviews by author, Sept. 24 and Oct. 30, 1993.

3. *Dispatch*, Sept. 22, 1930, p. 1, May 8, 1930, p. 1.

4. V. A. Batzner (National Citizens Bank, Mankato), speech to Minnesota Bankers Association 44th annual convention, Minneapolis, June 13–14, 1933, Minnesota Bankers Association files, Minneapolis.

5. *Pioneer Press*, Sept. 17, 1932, p. 2, Oct. 13, 1931, p. 1.

6. Glass report, June 27, 1932, p. 1, 3–5, file 4–2–11–0, NARG 129.

7. Clyde C. Callahan and Byron B. Jones, *Heritage of an Outlaw: The Story of Frank Nash* (Hobart, Okla.: Schoonmaker Publishers, 1979), 19, 29.

8. Callahan and Jones, *Heritage of an Outlaw*, v, 1, 135 (quote from Hobart, Oklahoma, *Republican*).

9. Callahan and Jones, *Heritage of an Outlaw*, 27, 28–29, 34; D. O. Smith, FBI report, Aug. 18, 1932, file 4–2–11–0, NARG 129.

10. Kansas City Massacre, FBI Case Summary, revised May 1984, p. 1.

11. Frank Nash, FBI wanted poster, Mar. 21, 1932, identification order 1166, KCMF 542, sec. 18; Glass report, June 27, 1932, p. 4, file 4–2–11–0, NARG 129.

12. Suran report, Oct. 6, 1934, p. 39, 47, KCMF 2655; Callahan and Jones, *Heritage of an Outlaw*, 23.

13. Callahan and Jones, *Heritage of an Outlaw*, 56.

14. Glass report, June 27, 1932, p. 5, file

4–2–11–0, NARG 129; Suran report, Oct. 6, 1934, p. 47, KCMF 2655.

15. Hall report, July 27, 1933, p. 31, KCMF 401; Glass report, June 27, 1932, p. 5–9, and J. D. Glass, FBI report, June 8, 1932, p. 9, both in file 4–2–11–0, NARG 129.

16. Glass report, June 27, 1932, p. 5, file 4–2–11–0, NARG 129.

17. *Pioneer Press*, Jan. 10, 1936, p. 1–2; Murray, Statement to FBI, Feb. 12, 1935, p. 1, BKF 4546; H. H. Clegg to director, FBI memo, Apr. 16, 1934, p. 1, DF 601, sec. 13.

18. Ex-Operative 48, "Sterilization: Preston Paden, Whelp of a Gun Moll," *Official Detective Stories*, Apr. 1, 1937, p. 42; Barker-Karpis gang—Bremer Kidnapping, FBI case summary, Nov. 19, 1936, p. 12, BKF.

19. Murray statement to FBI, Feb. 12, 1935, p. 3, 5, BKF 4546.

20. Murray statement to FBI, Feb. 12, 1935, p. 4, 5, 11, BKF 4546.

21. FBI memo on Thomas A. Brown, Nov. 10, 1936, p. 11, HKF 1082.

22. Glass report, June 27, 1932, p. 4–5, file 4–2–11–0, NARG 129.

23. Charles P. Harmon, U.S. Penitentiary, Leavenworth, Kansas, prison inmate file, no. 30676, Federal Bureau of Prisons.

24. Callahan and Jones, *Heritage of an Outlaw*, 149.

25. Suran report, Sept. 22, 1934, p. 13, KCMF 2502; H. H. Clegg to director, FBI letter, May 4, 1934, p. 2, DF 1177, sec. 22; Paula Harman to Chas. P. Harman [*sic*], telegram, July 20, 1929, Harmon prison file, Federal Bureau of Prisons; Callahan and Jones, *Heritage of an Outlaw*, 149–50.

26. J. D. Glass, FBI report, June 10, 1932, p. 3, file 4–2–11–0, NARG 129.

27. Special agent _____, St. Paul, to special agent in charge Werner Hanni, FBI memo, Feb. 19, 1934, p. 3, CCF 16, vol. 1; Paul A. Sevareid, *The People's Lawyer: The Life of Eugene A. Rerat* (Minneapolis: Ross and Haines, 1963), 79–81; John M. Russell, "Scenes from Yesteryear," *Dunn County News* (Menomonie, Wis.), Apr. 25, 1985.

28. J. J. Keating, FBI report, Feb. 24, 1932, p. 10–11, file 4–2–11–0, NARG 129.

29. Glass report, June 27, 1932, p. 8, file 4–2–11–0, NARG 129; Francis Keating and Thomas Holden, prison inmate files, Federal Bureau of Prisons.

30. Callahan and Jones, *Heritage of an Outlaw*, 47, 152.

31. S. W. Hardy, FBI report, Apr. 6, 1932, p. 10, and Keating report, Feb. 24, 1932, p. 10, both file 4–2–11–0, NARG 129; Callahan and Jones, *Heritage of an Outlaw*, 144; Irving Nemerov, interview by author, May 17, 1991.

32. Haley, *Robbing Banks*, 77; R. J. Caffrey, FBI report, Aug. 1, 1932, p. 2–3, 8, file 4–2–11–0, NARG 129; D. P. Sullivan, FBI report, May 19, 1936, p. 5, HKF 723, sec. 8; Glass report, June 27, 1932, p. 8, file 4–2–11–0, NARG 129.

33. Special agent to Hanni memo, Feb. 19, 1934, p. 2, CCF 16, vol. 1; Glass report, June 8, 1932, p. 7, file 4–2–11–0, NARG 129.

34. E. E. Conroy to director, Apr. 4, 1934, p. 3, KCMF 1523, sec. 40; H. E. Anderson to director, FBI letter, Mar. 7, 1934, p. 3, KCMF 1374, sec. 38.

35. J. D. Glass, FBI report, May 11, 1932, p. 23–25, file 4–2–11–0, NARG 129.

36. Glass reports, June 8, 1932, p. 5, May 11, 1932, p. 26, file 4–2–11–0, NARG 129.

37. Earl Orth, interview by author, Mar. 14, 1993.

38. Reiter interview, Sept. 24, 1993.

39. Newby to Nathan memo, Feb. 26, 1934, CCF 46, vol. 1.

40. J. D. Glass, FBI report, June 2, 1932, p. 5–6, 7–10, file 4–2–11–0, NARG 129.

41. Special agent to Hanni memo, Feb. 20, 1934, p. 1, CCF 16, vol. 1; Hardy report, Apr. 6, 1932, p. 7, file 4–2–11–0, NARG 129.

42. Haley, *Robbing Banks*, 81–82; Wm. Larson to special agent in charge, St. Paul, FBI letter, Feb. 9, 1934, p. 7, BKF 206, sec. 3; McIntire report, Apr. 10, 1935, p. 95, BKF sec. 96.

43. Keating report, Feb, 24, 1932, p. 11, file 4–2–11–0, NARG 129; special agent to Hanni memo, Feb. 19, 1934, p. 2, CCF 16, vol. 1.

44. *Pioneer Press*, Dec. 3, 1931, p. 1–2, July 15, 1932, p. 18.

45. Ray Cowdery, *Capone's Chicago* (Küsnacht, Switzerland: Northstar-Maschek, 1987), 68.

46. Edge, *Run the Cat Roads*, 39; *Pioneer Press*, July 16, 1930, p. 1, 3.

47. *Pioneer Press*, July 16, 1930, p. 1, 3; *Dispatch*, July 15, 1930, p. 1–2.

48. *Dispatch*, July 15, 1930, p. 1–2.

49. Bailey interview, Sept. 18, 1966, p. 16–17, Haley Collection; Haley, *Robbing Banks*, 77–79.

50. *Dispatch*, Aug. 28, 1930, p. 2.

51. St. Paul agent, FBI report, Apr. 2, 1938, p. 11–12, FBI file 60–1501–1556.

52. Althea Rohlfing, transcript of speech given to Mahtomedi Club, 1984, copy in author's possession; *Pioneer Press*, Aug. 15, 1930, p. 1–2; *Dispatch*, Aug. 14, 1930, p. 1.

53. Earl Switzer to John I. Navarre, Detroit Police Dept. memo, Feb. 21, 1934, p. 3, Verne Miller homicide file, Detroit Police Dept.

54. *Dispatch*, Jan. 6, 1932, p. 1, Aug. 17, 1931, p. 1; Bailey interview, Sept. 18, 1966, p. 15, Haley Collection; McKee report, May 20, 1936, p. 9, HKF 732.

55. Bailey interview, Sept. 18, 1966, p. 15, Haley Collection; *Dispatch*, Aug. 17, 1931, p. 1.

56. Rorer to director, FBI telegram, Apr. 1, 1934, DF 386, sec. 9.

57. Barker-Karpis gang, FBI case summary, revised Apr. 1984, p. 5, FBI file IC 7–579.

58. Glass report, June 27, 1932, p. 4, file 4–2–11–0, NARG 129.

59. Glass report, June 10, 1932, p. 2, June 27, 1932, p. 4–5, file 4–2–11–0, NARG 129; Gladys Harrington, interview by author, June 1993; S. K. McKee, FBI report, Mar. 5, 1936, p. 15, HKF 400, sec. 5.

60. Glass report, June 8, 1932, p. 6, file 4–2–11–0, NARG 129.

61. Walter "Buster" Johnson, interview by author, n.d.; Glass report, June 27, 1932, p. 2, file 4–2–11–0, NARG 129.

62. ____, FBI report, July 19, 1943, p. 50, CCF 315, vol. 6; Noonan report, May 27, 1936, p. 6, HKF 759.

63. Robert Schmidt ("Frisco Dutch" Steinhardt) criminal history file, July 1, 1934, BCA; Joseph Wokrol homicide file C–5813, Chicago Police Dept. (contains information on Steinhardt).

64. D. P. Sullivan, FBI report, June 11, 1936, p. 5, HKF 823, sec. 10; *Dispatch*, Apr. 20, 1934, p. 1, 4.

65. Noonan report, May 27, 1936, p. 6, HKF 759; *Dispatch*, Apr. 14, 1934, p. 1.

66. E. A. Tamm to director, FBI report, June 5, 1936, HKF 794, sec. 9.

67. John W. Macey, Keller Golf Course caddy, interview by author, Jan. 3, 1992; crime buff Tim Albright, interview with Dillinger caddy Howard Hesse, Mar. 27, 1992, notes in author's possession; Tom Purcell, Keller Golf Course professional, interview by author, Apr. 1992.

68. Glass report, May 11, 1932, p. 42, file 4–2–11–0, NARG 129.

69. Hardy report, Apr. 6, 1932, p. 10, file 4–2–11–0, NARG 129; *Pioneer Press*, July 15, 1932, p. 18.

70. Special agent to Hanni memo, Feb. 19, 1934, p. 2, CCF 16, vol. 1.

71. Glass report, June 2, 1932, p. 20–24, file 4–2–11–0, NARG 129.

72. Glass report, June 27, 1932, p. 8, file 4–2–11–0, NARG 129.

73. Glass report, June 27, 1932, p. 4, file 4–2–11–0, NARG 129.

74. Callahan and Jones, *Heritage of an Outlaw*, 65–66, 142; Cooper, *Here's to Crime*, 241–42.

75. Harvey Bailey interview, May 23, 1967, p. 1, Haley Collection.

76. *Pioneer Press*, July 9, 1932, p. 1; *Minneapolis Journal*, July 19, 1932, p. 1.

Notes for Chapter 5

1. Interviews by author with Marian Johnson, Dec. 19, 1991, and May 30, 1992, Bernice Grossman, May 30, 1992, and Nick Hannegraf Jr., Dec. 19, 1991; J. Edgar Hoover, *Persons in Hiding* (Boston: Little, Brown, and Co., 1938), 8.

2. [Unsigned, untitled] FBI memo, Apr. 24, 1936, p. 1, BKF 11635, sec. 202; Karpis with Trent, *Karpis Story*, 26–30; Alvin Karpis file, May 10, 1932, BCA.

3. Albert Grooms, interview by author, June 18, 1993.

4. FBI memo, Apr. 24, 1936, p. 2–3, BKF 11635.

5. S. K. McKee, FBI report, June 9, 1936,

p. 198, HKF 810, sec. 9; Karpis file, BCA; Karpis with Trent, *Karpis Story*, 39–44.

6. Fred Barker file, May 10, 1932, BCA; Karpis with Trent, *Karpis Story*, 56, 81–82; Barker-Karpis gang, FBI summary, Apr. 1984, p. 1.

7. Bremer kidnap, FBI summary, Nov. 19, 1936, p. 1–2; Nash, *Bloodletters and Badmen*, 33–35.

8. Anthony Summers, *Official and Confidential: The Secret Life of J. Edgar Hoover* (New York: G. P. Putnam and Sons, 1993), 74–75.

9. Bremer kidnap, FBI summary, Nov. 19, 1936, p. 2.

10. M. A. Jones to Mr. Bishop, FBI memo, Mar. 5, 1971, p. 4, BKF 15562, sec. 277; Barker-Karpis gang, FBI summary, Apr. 1984, p. 1; Edge, *Run the Cat Roads*, 21.

11. Barker-Karpis gang, FBI summary, Apr. 1984, p. 3; Arthur W. Dunlop file, May 2, 1932, BCA; Karpis with Trent, *Karpis Story*, 84, 87–88.

12. Arthur R. Barker, FBI wanted poster, Mar. 23, 1934, identification order 1219; Grooms interview.

13. McKee report, May 20, 1936, p. 7, HKF 732.

14. Marian Johnson interview; Hannegraf interview.

15. Karpis with Trent, *Karpis Story*, 85–87; Bremer kidnap, FBI summary, p. 5; undated newspaper clipping, *West Plains Daily Quill*, Karpis file, BCA.

16. Grooms interview.

17. McKee report, May 20, 1936, p. 3, HKF 732; Barker-Karpis gang, FBI summary, Apr. 1984, p. 4.

18. Marian Johnson interview; Grossman interview.

19. Grossmann interview.

20. Karpis with Trent, *Karpis Story*, 44–45.

21. Hardy report, Apr. 6, 1932, p. 2, file 4-2-11-0, NARG 129; Karpis with Trent, *Karpis Story*, 45–46.

22. S. K. McKee, FBI report, May 8, 1936, p. 20–21, BKF 11529, sec. 200.

23. Marian Johnson interview.

24. Memo for the director, FBI memo, Feb. 21, 1934, p. 4, BKF 706, sec. 8; Marian Johnson interview; C. W. Stein to director, FBI memo (Raasch statement), Aug. 18, 1936, p. 1, HKF 1037, sec. 11.

25. Stein to director memo (Raasch statement), Aug. 18, 1936, p. 5, HKF 1037; Noonan report, May 27, 1936, p. 20, HKF 759.

26. Karpis with Trent, *Karpis Story*, 88–89; McKee report, May 20, 1935, p. 4, HKF 732.

27. Agents Vall and Mallette to Melvin Passolt, BCA memo, Apr. 30, 1932 (a), Arthur Dunlop file, BCA; Noonan report, May 27, 1936, p. 25–26, HKF 759.

28. Agents Vall and Mallette to Melvin Passolt, Apr. 30, 1932 (b), and Irie Mallette to Melvin Passolt, BCA memo, May 14, 1932, memos in Dunlop file, BCA; Grossman interview; Hannegraf interview.

29. Stein to director memo (Raasch statement), p. 2–3, HKF 1037.

30. Karpis with Trent, *Karpis Story*, 89.

31. Agent Mallette to Melvin Passolt, BCA memo, Apr. 30, 1932, Dunlop file, BCA.

32. Mallette to Passolt, Apr. 30, 1932, BCA; McKee report, May 27, 1936, p. 27, HKF 759; Karpis with Trent, *Karpis Story*, 89.

33. *Pioneer Press*, Apr. 28, 1932, p. 1, 3.

34. *Dispatch*, Apr. 28, 1932, p. 1; Thomas A. Brown, personnel file, SPPD.

35. Marian Johnson interview; Hannegraf interview.

36. A. H. S. Perkins, *All About White Bear Lake: Minnesota's Popular Summer Resort*, (White Bear: n.p., 1890), 50.

37. McKee report, Mar. 5, 1936, p. 15, HKF 400; Hope Healy Koontz, former Mahtomedi neighbor of John Lambert, interview by author, Dec. 3, 1993; *Dispatch*, Apr. 22, 1936, p. 1; McIntire report, Apr. 10, 1935, p. 95, BKF sec. 96; Karpis with Trent, *Karpis Story*, 47.

38. McIntire report, Apr. 10, 1935, p. 95, BKF sec. 96; Barker-Karpis gang, FBI summary, Apr. 1984, p. 5.

39. Interviews by author of Vern Phillips, Lincoln Township constable and White Bear Police Dept. employee, Apr. 30, 1993, and Fred Miller Jr., Mahtomedi resident, May 14, 1993; Rohlfing speech, Oct. 1, 1984.

40. "General Crime Survey: Semi-Annual Report," FBI report, Oct. 15, 1944 to Apr. 15,

1945, p. 127, CCF 62–75147–43, vol. 2; *Dispatch*, Oct. 8, 1931, p. 1–2; Oct. 9, 1931, p. 1–2; Rohlfing speech, Oct. 1, 1984; Rohlfing interview, Apr. 16, 1993; Marge Guarnera, co-owner of Guarnera's restaurant, interview by author, Spring 1993.

41. Evelyn M. Deyo, interview by author, May 1993; *Dispatch*, Apr. 22, 1936, p. 1, 3.

42. Walter Johnson interview.

43. McIntire report, Apr. 10, 1935, p. 95, BKF sec. 96; Karpis with Trent, *Karpis Story*, 19, 45–46; Ramsey report, Aug. 8, 1934, p. 12, KCMF 2178; Barker-Karpis gang, FBI summary, Apr. 1984, p. 5.

44. Karpis with Trent, *Karpis Story*, 18, 24.

45. Ramsey report, Aug. 8, 1934, p. 12, KCMF 2178.

46. M. F. Trainor, FBI report, Feb. 20, 1934, p. 14, BKF 676, sec. 7; *Pioneer Press*, Jan. 1, 1933, p. 1–2.

47. Memo for director, Feb. 21, 1934, p. 5, BKF 706; Paul Cromer, interview by author, Mar. 12, 1993.

48. *Dispatch*, Apr. 22, 1936, p. 1, 3.

49. Rohlfing interview.

50. Karpis with Trent, *Karpis Story*, 63.

51. C. W. Stein to director, FBI memo, June 13, 1936, p. 4–5, HKF 853, sec. 10.

52. S. K. McKee, FBI report, July 30, 1936, p. 6, HKF 1002, sec. 11.

53. McIntire report, Apr. 10, 1935, p. 96, BKF sec. 96; McKee report, May 8, 1936, p. 4, BKF 11529.

54. *Dispatch*, Sept. 23, 1932, p. 1–2.

55. Karpis with Trent, *Karpis Story*, 15, 16–17.

56. *Dispatch*, Sept. 30, 1932, p. 1.

57. Bremer kidnap, FBI summary, Nov. 19, 1936, p. 10–11.

58. Grooms interview.

59. M. A. Jones to L. B. Nichols, FBI memo, May 9, 1950, p. 1, BKF, sec. 273; Lawrence DeVol to L. F. Utecht et al., Stillwater prison statement, Dec. 13, 1934, Lawrence DeVol Stillwater prison file, MHS; Followup report on William Weaver, Jan. 27, 1936, Leo Gorski homicide file, Minneapolis Police Dept.; John Powner, "On the Scarlet Trail of the Twin City Terrorists," *Startling Detective Adventures*, July 1935, p. 28–33, 71–75.

60. Earl A. Patch, interview by author, July 20, 1993.

61. Patch interview; *Pioneer Press*, Dec. 17, 1932, p. 1–2.

62. Gorski homicide file, Dec. 18, 1932, Minneapolis Police Dept.; Joseph A. Ferris, "How Barton 'The Chopper' Was Captured," *True Detective Mysteries* 20, no. 4 (July 1933): 20–25, 104–107; Patch interview.

63. Karpis with Trent, *Karpis Story*, 64–66; Minneapolis Police Dept. reward poster, Apr. 8, 1932; *Pioneer Press*, Dec. 17, 1932, p. 1–2.

64. Karpis with Trent, *Karpis Story*, 64–65; *Pioneer Press*, Dec. 17, 1932, p. 1–2; Oscar Erickson homicide file 10132, Dec. 16, 1932, SPPD.

65. Arthur Zachman statement, Erickson homicide file, SPPD; *Pioneer Press*, Dec. 17, 1932, p. 1–2.

66. Karpis with Trent, *Karpis Story*, 65.

67. Zachman statement, Erickson homicide file, SPPD; *Pioneer Press*, Dec. 17, 1932, p. 1–2.

68. Jack Mackay, "State Lifer Is Termed Innocent," *Minneapolis Tribune*, Apr. 7, 1950, p. 1, 9; Karpis with Trent, *Karpis Story*, 64–65.

69. *Pioneer Press*, Dec. 17, 1932, p. 1–2; Ancker Hospital autopsy report, Dec. 17, 1932, Offense Report 8656, Erickson homicide file, SPPD.

70. Ferris, "How Barton 'The Chopper' Was Captured," 105.

71. Powner, "On the Scarlet Trail," 32–33.

72. Powner, "On the Scarlet Trail," 33, 71; Hammgren, Kast, Soderburg, and Kane reports, Dec. 18, 1932, Erickson homicide file, SPPD.

73. Ferris, "How Barton 'The Chopper' Was Captured," 104; *Minnesota v. Lawrence Barton*, Jan. 9, 1933, p. 3.

74. Lawrence M. DeVol, deputy warden's examination sheet, Stillwater prison file, MHS; Lawrence DeVol, FBI fingerprint file, July 16, 1936, BCA.

75. J. E. Risden, Des Moines, Iowa, to Minneapolis Police Dept. chief of detectives, Justice Dept. letter, Dec. 24, 1932, Gorski homicide file, Minneapolis Police Dept.; DeVol fingerprint file, BCA.

76. Lawrence DeVol criminal history file, BCA; Lawrence DeVol, St. Peter State Hospital wanted poster, Larry DeVol, Stillwater prison file, MHS.

77. DeVol, Stillwater prison statement; special agent in charge, St. Paul, to director, FBI memo, Dec. 31, 1948, p. 1, BKF 15287, sec. 273; McIntire report, Apr. 10, 1935, p. 96, BKF sec. 96.

78. Sevareid, *The People's Lawyer*, 40–41; John J. Sullivan, warden, to C. R. Carlgren, Stillwater prison letter, July 25, 1935, DeVol Stillwater prison file, MHS.

79. *Minneapolis Journal*, June 11, 1936, p. 1, 11, June 8, 1936, p. 1, 6; Robert R. Ernst, "The Last Days of Lawrence DeVol," *OklahombreS*, Winter 1991, p. 10–12.

80. R. T. Noonan, FBI report, Mar. 20, 1936, p. 25, HKF 431, sec. 5.

81. Jim Lehman, interview by author, 1992.

82. McKee report, July 30, 1936, p. 3, HKF 1002; S. K. McKee, FBI report, July 13, 1936, p. 2, HKF 922, sec. 10.

83. Ramsey report, Aug. 8, 1934, p. 13, KCMF 2178; J. Edgar Hoover to special agent in charge, St. Paul, FBI letter, June 17, 1936, HKF 845, sec. 10.

84. Anne Diestel (Federal Bureau of Prisons) to author, June 13, 1994, letter in author's possession; Edwin Wiechman statement, Dec. 19, 1932, Erickson homicide file, SPPD; R. J. Caffrey, FBI report, July 29, 1932, p. 2–3, file 4–2–11–0, NARG 129; Switzer to Navarre, Feb. 21, 1934, p. 1, Miller homicide file, Detroit Police Dept.; McIntire report, Apr. 10, 1935, p. 95, BKF sec. 96.

85. Ramsey report, Aug. 8, 1934, p. 29, KCMF 2178; Suran report, Sept. 22, 1934, p. 11, KCMF 2502.

86. Switzer to Navarre, Feb. 21, 1934, p. 2, Miller homicide file, Detroit Police Dept.

87. Karpis with Trent, *Karpis Story*, 161–162.

88. C. O. Lawrence, FBI report, Sept. 27, 1934, p. 1–2, KCMF 2548, sec. 61; McKee report, May 20, 1936, p. 11, HKF 732.

89. Switzer to Navarre, Feb. 21, 1934, p. 2, May 7, 1935, p. 3, Miller homicide file, Detroit Police Dept.; Ramsey report, Aug. 8, 1934, p. 28–29, KCMF 2178; Bernard Phillips, FBI

wanted poster, July 13, 1933, identification order 1196.

90. A. Rosen to director, FBI memo, Apr. 3, 1936, p. 3, HKF 469x, sec. 6.

91. Murray statement, Feb. 12, 1935, p. 2, BKF 4546.

92. McKee report, May 20, 1936, p. 3, HKF 732; McIntire report, Apr. 10, 1935, p. 96, BKF sec. 96.

93. McIntire report, Apr. 10, 1935, p. 96, BKF sec. 96.

94. J. R. Green and R. B. Smith, FBI report, Sept. 21, 1934, p. 1–3, BKF 2932, sec. 36.

95. Karpis with Trent, *Karpis Story*, 79; Suran report, May 22, 1936, p. 4, BKF 11766; Suran report, Oct. 6, 1934, p. 12, KCMF 2655. See also Ramsey report, Aug. 8, 1934, p. 4, KCMF 2178.

96. Ramsey report, Aug. 8, 1934, p. 10–15, KCMF 2178.

97. *St. Paul City Directory, 1920*, p. 6.

98. Glass report, May 11, 1932, p. 21, file 4–2–11–0, NARG 129 (Keating): Bremer kidnap, FBI summary, Nov. 19, 1936, p. 3. See also R. D. Brown, FBI report, Sept. 19, 1934, p. 49, BKF 2919, sec. 36.

99. R. C. Suran, FBI report, Mar. 3, 1936, p. 11, HKF 401, sec. 5.

100. S. K. McKee, FBI report, Apr. 14, 1936, p. 5, HKF 520, sec. 6; Karpis with Trent, *Karpis Story*, 59.

101. Suran report, Sept. 22, 1934, p. 15, KCMF 2502.

102. Hoover, *Persons in Hiding*, 9; Suran report, Sept. 22, 1934, p. 15–16, KCMF 2502;

103. Karpis with Trent, *Karpis Story*, 90; Suran report, Sept. 22, 1934, p. 10, KCMF 2502; R. C. Suran, FBI report, Sept. 1, 1934, p. 19, KCMF 2366. See also Brown report, Sept. 19, 1934, p. 40, BKF 2919.

104. "Gangsters: An Interview with Will Greer," p. 9.

Notes for Chapter 6

1. McKee report, Apr. 27, 1936, p. 65–66, HKF 647.

2. Director to special agent in charge, St. Paul, FBI memo, Feb. 12, 1934, p. 1, file 62–30819–3; Jack Peifer file, 1936, BCA; *Dispatch*, Aug. 5, 1936, p. 1.

3. S. K. McKee, FBI report, Apr. 3, 1936, p. 2, HKF 468, sec. 6; Sullivan report, May 19, 1936, p. 5, HKF 723; Sullivan report, June 11, 1936, p. 6, HKF 823; McKee reports, July 30, 1936, p. 2–3, HKF 1002, and June 9, 1936, p. 206, HKF 810.

4. McKee report, July 30, 1936, p. 6–7, HKF 1002.

5. McKee report, Apr. 27, 1936, p. 67, HKF 647; Delaney statement, Jan. 22, 1934, p. 2, BKF NR Bulky Box 3, pt. 1.

6. R. T. Noonan, FBI report, May 14, 1936, p. 9–10, HKF 761, sec. 9.

7. Ramsey County Probate Court, Petition for General Administration, John P. Peifer, Decedent, July 21, 1937 (see also McKee report, Apr. 27, 1936, p. 65, HKF 647); C. W. Stein to director, FBI letter, Apr. 30, 1936, p. 1, BKF 11564, sec. 201 (see also Noonan report, May 14, 1936, p. 8, HKF 761).

8. McKee report, Apr. 27, 1936, p. 6–7, HKF 647.

9. Elizabeth Roy, interview by author, Dec. 17, 1994.

10. McKee report, July 30, 1936, p. 2, 4, HKF 1002; Harry Kramer statement, Mar. 26, 1931, Ventress homicide file, SPPD; C. W. Stein to director memo, June 13, 1936, p. 7, HKF 853.

11. *Pioneer Press*, May 17, 1931, p. 1; McKee report, Apr. 27, 1936, p. 6, 10, 17, HKF 647.

12. Fred Heaberlin interview, Jan. 6, 1994.

13. Bryan [Byron] Bolton, statement to FBI, Jan. 27, 1936, p. 30, HKF 365x, sec. 4; McKee report, June 9, 1936, p. 90, HKF 810; Schude interview; Nicholson report, Sept. 22, 1934, p. 4, DF 4004.

14. Martin Rohling, interviews by author, June 16, 1991, and May 22, 1992; *Pioneer Press*, July 23, 1934, p. 1. A 1936 FBI letter noted that in July 1934 "the Hollyhocks Inn was raided and numerous gambling devices seized by the police, but later returned to the Hollyhocks presumably to Peifer for some unknown reason." See C. W. Stein to George F. Sullivan, U.S. attorney, FBI letter, p. 2, HKF 613.

15. Noonan report, May 14, 1936, p. 10, HKF 761.

16. Stein to Director memo, June 13, 1936, p. 7–8, HKF 853.

17. R. C. Suran, FBI report, May 15, 1936, p. 10–11, BKF 11619, sec. 202.

18. Nate Bomberg, "St. Paul and the Federal Building in the Twenties and Thirties," in Eileen Michaels, *A Landmark Reclaimed* (St. Paul: Minnesota Landmarks, 1977), 55.

19. *Minneapolis Journal*, Nov. 23, 1936, p. 1.

20. Rohling interviews.

21. Glass report, May 11, 1932, p. 31, file 4–2–11–0, NARG 129; *Dispatch*, Aug. 5, 1932, p. 1, Aug. 9, 1932, p. 1; Stein to director memo (Raasch statement), Aug. 18, 1936, p. 3, HKF 1037.

22. Stein to director memo (Raasch statement), Aug. 18, 1936, p. 3, HKF 1037.

23. Karpis with Trent, *Karpis Story*, 127, 130; J. Edgar Hoover to assistant attorney general McMahon, FBI memo, May 13, 1936, p. 2–3, HKF 724, sec. 8; *Pioneer Press*, Aug. 8, 1936, p. 1–2.

24. John T. Flanangan, *Theodore Hamm in Minnesota* (St. Paul: Pogo Press, 1989), 108–22; "Denials Stand Unaltered by Grilling," newspaper clipping dated July 23, 1936, *Pioneer Press* morgue file.

25. *Dispatch*, July 31, 1936, p. 1, 8.

26. Lannon interview.

27. *St. Paul Daily News*, June 17, 1933, p. 1–2; Karpis with Trent, *Karpis Story*, 159.

28. Suran reports, Oct. 6, 1934, p. 48, KCMF 2655, Sept. 22, 1934, p. 59, KCMF 2502; Harold Nathan, FBI report, Feb. 21, 1934, p. 17, BKF 721, sec. 8.

29. Werner Hanni to director, FBI memo, Feb. 21, 1934, FBI file 62–12114–66; Hall report, July 27, 1933, p. 32, KCMF 401.

30. Hall report, July 27, 1933, p. 33–34, KCMF 401.

31. McKee report, Apr. 27, 1936, p. 7, HKF 647.

32. Special agent to Hanni memo, Feb. 19, 1934, CCF 16, vol. 1.

33. Nathan report, Feb. 21, 1934, p. 17, BKF 7210.

34. *Pioneer Press*, Aug. 8, 1936, p. 1–2.

35. Perkins, *All About White Bear Lake*, 3, 5, 9; John J. Koblas, *F. Scott Fitzgerald in Minnesota: His Homes and Haunts* (St. Paul:

Minnesota Historical Society, 1, 3, 25–26, 35, 39–41.

36. McKee reports, June 9, 1936, p. 93–94, HKF 810, and Mar. 5, 1936, p. 18, HKF 400.

37. Karpis with Trent, *Karpis Story*, 134.

38. Clifford Allen Lindholm, interview by author, Dec. 1992.

39. Steve Tuttle, interview by author, Jan. 30, 1993.

40. Sally McNamara, interview by author, Apr. 30, 1993; Lindholm interview.

41. McKee report, June 9, 1936, p. 90–92, 99, HKF 810; S. K. McKee, FBI report, Mar. 30, 1936, p. 7–8, HKF 458, sec. 6.

42. McKee reports, Apr. 27, 1936, p. 70–71, HKF 647, and June 9, 1936, p. 92, HKF 810.

43. McKee report, June 9, 1936, p. 99, 105, HKF 810.

44. McKee reports, Mar. 5, 1936, p. 21, HKF 400, and June 9, 1936, p. 92, HKF 810; Noonan report, May 14, 1936, p. 19, HKF 761.

45. Tuttle interview.

46. *Pioneer Press*, Aug. 8, 1936, p. 1–2.

47. Brueggeman, "Beer Capitol of the State," 12–13.

48. McIntire report, Apr. 10, 1935, p. 179; John L. Madala, FBI report, May 19, 1936, p. 10, HKF 738, sec. 9 (quote; see also Nash, *Bloodletters and Badmen*, 520–22); Schoenberg, *Mr. Capone*, 227; Brown report, Sept. 19, 1934, p. 51, BKF 2919; Suran report, Sept. 22, 1934, p. 5, KCMF 2502; Bilek, Arthur J., "St. Valentine's Day Massacre, Part II," *Real Crime Book Digest*, Spring 1995, p. 4–7.

49. Ramsey report, Aug. 8, 1934, p. 2, KCMF 2178; Melvin Purvis, *American Agent* (Garden City, N.Y.: Doubleday, Doran and Co., 1936), 151; Callahan and Jones, *Heritage of an Outlaw*, 155–56; M. H. Purvis to director, FBI memo, Mar. 21, 1934, KCMF 1475, sec. 40; McIntire report, Apr. 10, 1935, p. 177; M. H. Purvis to director, FBI memo, Mar. 23, 1934, KCMF, sec. 40.

50. Purvis, *American Agent*, 151–52.

51. E. P. Guinane, FBI report, July 21, 1934, p. 4, KCMF 2037, sec. 50 (quote); Ramsey report, Aug. 8, 1934, p. 2, KCMF 2178; Suran report, Sept. 22, 1934, p. 8, KCMF 2502.

52. Hoover to McMahon memo, May 13,

1936, p. 2, HKF 738; John W. Anderson, FBI report, Aug. 31, 1936, p. 5, HKF 1053, sec. 11.

53. S. K. McKee, FBI report, July 8, 1936, p. 6, HKF 913, sec. 10; Madala report, May 19, 1936, p. 11, HKF 738.

54. McKee report, May 8, 1936, p. 5, BKF 11529.

55. Bolton statement, Jan. 27, 1936, p. 3–4, HKF 365x.

56. McKee report, June 9, 1936, p. 9, HKF 810; Hoover to McMahon memo, May 13, 1936, p. 2–4, HKF 724; Stein to director memo, June 13, 1936, p. 1, HKF 853.

57. Bolton statement, Jan. 27, 1936, p. 5–6, HKF 365x; FBI memo, May 4, 1936, p. 2, HKF 650x; S. K. McKee, FBI report, July 28, 1936, p. 2–3; HKF 989, sec. 11; Charles Fitzgerald file, May 1936, BCA.

58. A. Rosen to director memo, Apr. 3, 1936, p. 6, HKF 469x, sec. 6; McKee report, July 8, 1936, p. 2, HKF 913.

59. Hoover to McMahon memo, May 13, 1936, p. 3, HKF 724; Werner Hanni, FBI report, June 26, 1933, p. 21, HKF 20, sec. 1.

60. McKee reports, July 8, 1936, p. 3, HKF 913 and June 9, 1936, p. 13, HKF 810; Hoover to McMahon memo, May 13, 1936, p. 3–4, HKF 724; S. K. McKee, FBI report, July 1, 1936, p. 7, HKF 891, sec. 10.

61. R. T. Noonan, FBI report, Oct. 10, 1933, p. 4, HKF 176, sec. 2; Hanni report, June 26, 1933, p. 22, 26, HKF 20.

62. Hoover to McMahon memo, May 13, 1936, p. 4, HKF 724; Hanni report, June 26, 1933, p. 22, 23, HKF 20; McKee reports, June 9, 1936, p. 14, HKF 810, and July 8, 1936, p. 3, HKF 913.

63. V. W. Hughes, FBI report, Aug. 10, 1933, p. 2, HKF 127, sec. 2.

64. Stein to director memo, June 13, 1936, p. 2, HKF 853. See also Noonan report, June 18, 1936, p. 49, HKF 880.

65. Noonan report, May 27, 1936, p. 3, HKF 759.

66. Stein to director memo, Apr. 30, 1936, p. 1, BKF 11564; K. R. McIntire to director, FBI memo, June 3, 1936, p. 1, HKF 800, sec. 9. See also Stein to director, FBI telegram, May 4, 1936, HKF 657, sec. 8; Noonan report, May 27, 1936, p. 9, HKF 759; "Peifer Named as Visitor to Karpis' House," newspaper clip-

ping dated July 16, 1936, *Pioneer Press* morgue file.

67. Noonan report, May 27, 1936, p. 5, 17, HKF 759; McKee report, June 3, 1936, p. 3, HKF 776 (quote). See also Stein to director teletype, May 1, 1936, HKF 629.

68. William C. Figge, interview by author, Jan. 6, 1994.

69. Noonan report, May 27, 1936, p. 4, HKF 759.

70. Hughes report, Aug. 10, 1933, p. 2, HKF 127.

71. Hanni report, June 26, 1933, p. 3–4, HKF 20.

72. FBI memo on Thomas Brown, Nov. 10, 1936, p. 7, HKF 1082; McKee report, June 9, 1936, p. 47, HKF 810.

73. Hanni report, June 26, 1933, p. 5, HKF 20.

74. Hughes report, Aug. 10, 1933, p. 2, HKF 127; R. L. Walls, FBI report, June 29, 1933, p. 2–3, HKF 30, sec. 1.

75. McKee report, June 9, 1936, p. 32–34, HKF 810; Hanni report, June 26, 1933, p. 30–32, HKF 20.

76. Hoover to McMahon memo, May 13, 1936, p. 5, HKF 724; McKee reports, June 9, 1936, p. 54, HKF 810, July 8, 1936, p. 3, HKF 913, June 9, 1936, p. 16, HKF 810, and Apr. 27, 1936, p. 86, HKF 759.

77. FBI reproduction of ransom note, HKF 1131, sec. 12.

78. FBI reproduction of ransom note, HKF 1131.

79. McKee report, June 9, 1936, p. 15, HKF 810; Hoover to McMahon memo, May 13, 1936, p. 6, HKF 724; McKee report, June 9, 1936, p. 50, HKF 810.

80. Bolton statement, Jan. 27, 1936, p. 11, HKF 365x.

81. McKee report, June 9, 1936, p. 83–87, HKF 810.

82. McKee report, June 9, 1936, p. 61, HKF 810; Frances MacLaren Paul, interview by author, Apr. 3, 1993.

83. Hall report, July 27, 1933, p. 4–6, KCMF 401.

84. Hall report, July 27, 1933, p. 3–4, KCMF 401; McKee report, July 8, 1936, p. 3, HKF 913.

85. Noonan report, May 14, 1936, p. 26–27,

HKF 761; McKee report, June 9, 1936, p. 67, HKF 810.

86. E. E. Conroy to director, FBI letter, Mar. 13, 1934, p. 1, HKF 302, sec. 4; McKee reports, June 9, 1936, p. 69, HKF 810, and Mar. 5, 1936, p. 13, HKF 400. See also Suran report, Oct. 6, 1934, p. 48, KCMF 2655.

87. Hall report, July 27, 1933, p. 13, KCMF 401.

88. Paul interview; McKee report, Mar. 5, 1936, p. 7, HKF 400.

89. McKee report, June 9, 1936, p. 1, 56, HKF 810; Hoover to McMahon memo, May 13, 1936, p. 6, HKF 724.

90. Karpis with Trent, *Karpis Story*, 141.

91. McKee report, June 9, 1936, p. 17, 34–36, HKF 810.

92. Noonan report, June 18, 1936, p. 34, HKF 880.

93. Noonan report, May 14, 1936, p. 21, 24, HKF 761.

94. McKee report, Apr. 27, 1936, p. 29, HKF 647; Noonan report, June 18, 1936, p. 5, HKF 880. See also FBI memo on Brown, Nov. 10, 1936, HKF 1082.

95. O. G. Hall to W. A. Rorer, FBI memo, Mar. 7, 1934, p. 2, KCMF, sec. 39. See also Hall report, July 27, 1933, p. 13–14, KCMF 401.

96. McKee report, June 9, 1936, p. 23, HKF 810.

97. W. A. Rorer to director, FBI letter, Mar. 27, 1934, p. 2–3, KCMF, sec. 40. See also Noonan report, May 27, 1936, p. 16, HKF 759.

98. Hall report, July 27, 1933, p. 9, KCMF 401.

99. Hanni to Hoover memo, Feb. 20, 1934, p. 2, CCF 16, vol. 1.

100. *Dispatch*, July 21, 1936, p. 1, italics in original.

101. FBI memo on Brown, Nov. 10, 1936, p. 1, HKF 1082; Thomas A. Brown personnel file, SPPD; Thomas Archibald Brown death certificate, no. 16132, Jan. 8, 1959, Minnesota Department of Health.

102. Vera Peters, interview by author, Mar. 27, 1993.

103. *Dispatch*, June 10, 1930, p. 1.

104. Noonan report, June 18, 1936, p. 48, HKF 880.

105. Peters interview.

106. *Pioneer Press*, Dec. 15, 1923, p. 5.

107. Glass report, June 28, 1932, p. 6, file 4–2–11–0, NARG 129.

108. Stein to director memo, Mar. 18, 1936, HKF 444 (containing district court document dated July 23, 1926).

109. *Dispatch*, Nov. 6, 1930, p. 1, 4; *Dispatch*, Nov. 20, 1930, p. 1–2.

110. Stein to director memo (Raasch statement), Aug. 10, 1936, p. 3–4, HKF 1037.

111. *Dispatch*, June 24, 1933, p. 1.

112. FBI memo on Brown, Nov. 10, 1936, p. 7, HKF 1082; Noonan report, May 27, 1936, p. 5, HKF 759.

113. FBI memo on Brown, Nov. 10, 1936, p. 5, 10, HKF 1082.

114. Hanni to Hoover memo, Feb. 20, 1934, p. 2, CCF 16, vol. 1; Harold Nathan to director, FBI letter, Feb. 20, 1934, p. 1, BKF, sec. 7.

115. McKee report, June 9, 1936, p. 21, 22, HKF 810.

116. John Edgar Hoover to Mr. Tamm, FBI memo, May 16, 1936, BKF 11575x, sec. 201; McKee to director, FBI teletype, May 15, 1936, HKF 726, sec. 8.

117. Rosen to director memo, Apr. 3, 1936, p. 7, 8, HKF 469x.

118. T. G. Melvin, FBI report, June 16, 1936, p. 2, HKF 864, sec. 10.

119. Clegg to director memo, May 8, 1934, p. 4, DF 1310.

120. Suran report, May 22, 1936, p. 3, BKF 11766.

121. C. W. Stein to director, FBI memo, Mar. 16, 1936, p. 1–3, HKF 414, sec. 5.

122. Brennan report, Feb. 15, 1936, p. 4, HKF 423.

123. Stein to director memo, Apr. 30, 1936, p. 3, BKF 11564; Noonan report, June 18, 1936, p. 4, HKF 880; Stein to director telegram, May 4, 1936, HKF 657. See also Ramsey County Real Estate records, title and abstract for the Hollyhocks Club; McKee report, June 9, 1936, p. 57–58, HKF 810. Walt McKenna informed the FBI that Peifer told him to tell Benz to warn Hamm. Benz also admitted to the conversation.

124. Noonan report, May 27, 1936, p. 7, HKF 759.

125. Noonan report, May 27, 1936, p. 4, HKF 759.

126. Galen M. Willis to E. A. Tamm, FBI memo, Mar. 18, 1940, p. 2–3, HKF 1125, sec. 12; McKee report, July 8, 1936, p. 4, HKF 913; McKee report, June 9, 1936, p. 21, HKF 810.

127. McKee report, July 8, 1936, p. 5, HKF 913; *Dispatch*, July 21, 1936, p. 1–2.

128. Willis to Tamm memo, Mar. 18, 1940, p. 2, HKF 1125.

129. McKee report, July 8, 1936, p. 6, HKF 913.

130. *South St. Paul Daily Reporter*, Aug. 30, 1933, p. 1, 3.

131. Ross Opsahl, "South St. Paul, Minnesota Machine Gun Raid," *Thompson Collectors News* 10 (Aug. 15, 1991): 3; *Pioneer Press*, Apr. 22, 1936, p. 1, 2.

132. Irie Mallette and Herman Vall to Melvin Passolt, memo, "South St. Paul Hold-Up," Aug. 30, 1933, p. 2, BCA.

133. *Pioneer Press*, Apr. 22, 1936, p. 1, 2.

134. Jack Yeaman, interview by author, Aug. 24, 1993.

135. *Pioneer Press*, Aug. 31, 1933, p. 1.

136. Karpis with Trent, *Karpis Story*, 149.

137. Mallette and Vall to Passolt memo, Aug. 30, 1933, p. 1.

138. Clegg to director, Apr. 16, 1934, p. 5, DF 601.

139. Noonan report, May 27, 1936, p. 11, 18, HKF 759.

140. O. G. Hall to Werner Hanni, FBI memo, Feb. 20, 1934, p. 7, BKF, sec. 9; Yeaman interview.

141. Ross M. Opsahl, "South St. Paul Machine Gun Raid, Part II, Epilogue," *Thompson Collectors News* 12 (Oct. 15, 1991).

142. Robert Pavlak, interview by author, Feb. 6, 1993.

143. *South-West Review*, Aug. 15, 1993, p. 1; Yeaman interview.

Notes for Chapter 7

1. Callahan and Jones, *Heritage of an Outlaw*, 152.

2. Janet Gibson, interview by author, Aug. 27, 1993.

3. Janet Gibson interview; Verne Miller, FBI wanted poster, July 11, 1933, Identification Order 1195.

4. Michael Gibson, interview by author,

Apr. 9, 1993; Janice Holsapple, interview by author, Apr. 9, 1993.

5. Verne Miller, South Dakota State Prison file, Apr. 1923, State Archives, Pierre, S.D; Purvis, *American Agent*, 37.

6. Verne Miller, South Dakota State Prison file.

7. Miller, FBI wanted poster, July 11, 1933; Purvis, *American Agent*, 38.

8. *Dispatch*, Feb. 3, 1928, p. 1; *Minneapolis Journal*, Feb. 3, 1928, p. 1, 18, Feb. 5, 1928, p. 1; Switzer to Navarre, Feb. 21, 1934, p. 1, Miller homicide file, Detroit Police Dept.

9. Suran report, Oct. 6, 1934, p. 10, KCMF 2655; Callahan and Jones, *Heritage of an Outlaw*, 92, 152; Warden of the South Dakota Penitentiary to Melvin Passolt, letter, Sept. 5, 1933, in South St. Paul Payroll file, BCA.

10. Barnes, *Machine Gun Kelly*, 191–92.

11. Madala report, May 19, 1936, p. 11–12, Hamm 738.

12. Callahan and Jones, *Heritage of an Outlaw*, 54–55.

13. McKee report, May 8, 1936, p. 31, BKF 11529.

14. Switzer to Navarre, Feb. 21, 1934, p. 3, Miller homicide file, Detroit Police Dept.

15. Haley, *Robbing Banks*, 117; Switzer to Navarre, Feb. 21, 1934, p. 1, Miller homicide file, Detroit Police Dept.

16. Hall report, July 27, 1933, p. 25, KCMF 401.

17. Glass report, June 28, 1932, p. 3, file 4-2-11-0, NARG 129; Hall report, July 27, 1933, p. 25–26, KCMF 401; Michael Gibson interview.

18. Michael Gibson interview; Holsapple interview.

19. Janet Gibson interview.

20. Suran report, Oct. 6, 1934, p. 14–15, KCMF 2655.

21. Wallis, *Pretty Boy*, 312–14; Earl C. Switzer to inspector, May 7, 1935, p. 1, Miller homicide file, Detroit Police Dept.

22. Callahan and Jones, *Heritage of an Outlaw*, 76–78.

23. Kansas City Massacre, FBI case summary, revised May 1984, KCMF; Wallis, *Pretty Boy*, 314–17.

24. Madala report, May 19, 1936, p. 13, HKF 738.

25. Janet Gibson interview.

26. Wallis, *Pretty Boy*, 322.

27. Hall report, July 27, 1933, p. 30–31, KCMF 401.

28. McKee report, June 9, 1936, p. 42, HKF 810; Donna Eue, niece of Vivian Mathis, interview by author, Apr. 15, 1933.

29. William H. Schoemaker to Fred W. Frahm, Chicago Police Dept. letter, Jan. 6, 1934, Miller homicide file, Detroit Police Dept.; *Pioneer Press*, Nov. 2, 1933, p. 1, Nov. 30, 1933, p. 1–2.

30. Switzer to inspector, May 7, 1935, p. 1, and handwritten notes on Miller homicide, Dec. 14, 1933, p. 166–72, both in Miller homicide file, Detroit Police Dept.

31. Switzer to Navarre, Feb. 21, 1934, p. 1–2, Miller homicide file, Detroit Police Dept.

32. Louis Buchalter, interview by FBI, Nov. 29, 1933, p. 57, handwritten notes in Miller homicide file, Detroit Police Dept.

33. Wayne County, autopsy report on Verne Miller, Dec. 1, 1933, p. 188, and handwritten notes on Miller homicide, Dec. 14, 1933, p. 168, both in Miller homicide file, Detroit Police Dept.

34. Switzer to Navarre, Feb. 21, 1934, p. 3, Miller homicide file, Detroit Police Dept.

35. Purvis, *American Agent*, 40–43.

36. Kansas City Massacre, FBI summary, May 1984, p. 5; Suran report, Oct. 6, 1934, p. 1, KCMF 2655; Janet Gibson, letter to author, Apr. 28, 1994; Janet Gibson interview; Mike Gibson interview; Holsapple interview.

37. *Pioneer Press*, Dec. 7, 1933, p. 10; *Pioneer Press*, Dec. 4, 1933, p. 11.

38. Eue interview; Janet Gibson interview.

39. Athan G. Theoharis and John Stuart Cox, *The Boss: J. Edgar Hoover and the Great American Inquisition* (Philadelphia: Temple University Press, 1988), 123; Cooper, *Ten Thousand Public Enemies*, 270–72; Gentry, *Hoover*, 168–69; Purvis, *American Agent*, 35–36.

40. Purvis, *American Agent*, 45, 58–59; Theoharis and Cox, *The Boss*, 128–30; Gentry, *Hoover*, 168–69.

41. Theoharis and Cox, *The Boss*, 123–30.

42. J. Edgar Hoover, "Patriotism and the War Against Crime," speech to the Daughters of the American Revolution, Apr. 23, 1936, p. 6, Government Printing Office, JI.14/2:P27.

43. Walter Trohan, "J. Edgar Hoover, the One-Man Scotland Yard," *Chicago Tribune*, June 21, 1936, pt. 7, p. 1, 8, 11.

Notes for Chapter 8

1. Suran report, Sept. 1, 1934, p. 20, KCMF 2366; Director to attorney general, FBI memo, Jan. 20, 1934, BKF 13, sec. 1.

2. Suran report, Sept. 1, 1934, p. 19–20, KCMF 2366.

3. Bremer kidnapping, FBI summary, Nov. 9, 1936, p. 19–20.

4. George "Machine Gun Kelly" Barnes et al., kidnapping of Charles F. Urschel, FBI case summary, Oct. 15, 1935, revised July 1989; H.E. Anderson to director, FBI memo, Mar. 7, 1934, p. 2, KCMF 1374, sec. 38.

5. "Machine Gun Kelly" et al., FBI summary, July 1989.

6. *Dispatch*, Sept. 30, 1933, p. 1, 5.

7. R. C. Coulter, FBI report, Feb. 24, 1934, 2–4, BKF 771, sec. 9; *Pioneer Press*, Feb. 11, 1934, p. 1–2; *Dispatch*, Feb. 10, 1934, p. 1, 3.

8. Noonan report, May 27, 1936, p. 20, HKF 759.

9. *Your Visit to the Jacob Schmidt Brewing Company* ([St. Paul]: Jacob Schmidt Brewing Company, 1950), 3–5. See also Brueggemann, "Beer Capital of the State," p. 11.

10. Gordon L. Merrick, interview by author, Dec. 11, 1992.

11. Karpis with Trent, *Karpis Story*, 163; Suran report, Sept. 1, 1934, p. 23–24, KCMF 2366; Director to all field offices, FBI memo, Feb. 21, 1934, p. 49, BKF 711, sec. 8.

12. McKee report, May 20, 1936, p. 9, HKF 732.

13. Brown report, Sept. 19, 1934, p. 50, BKF 2919; Merrick interview; *St. Paul Daily News*, Sept. 23, 1936, p. 1.

14. Brown report, Sept. 19, 1934, p. 51, BKF 2919; Glass report, May 11, 1932, p. 22,

file 4–2–11–0, NARG 129; Brennan report, Feb. 15, 1936, p. 6, HKF 423.

15. Director to field offices memo, Feb. 21, 1934, p. 16, BKF 711.

16. Karpis with Trent, *Karpis Story*, 167–68; D. L. Nicholson, FBI report, Apr. 14, 1934, p. 15, DF 688, sec. 14.

17. McIntire report, Apr. 10, 1935, p. 173, BKF sec. 96.

18. McIntire report, Apr. 10, 1935, p. 82, 173, BKF sec. 96.

19. Bremer kidnapping, FBI summary, Nov. 19, 1936, p. 18–19; Clegg to special agent in charge memo, May 31, 1934, DF 1733; *St. Paul City Directory, 1932*, 347; William Weaver, FBI wanted poster, Feb. 12, 1935, order no. 1238, BKF 4582, sec. 69; Bremer kidnapping, FBI summary, Nov. 19, 1936, p. 5–6; McIntire report, Apr. 10, 1935, p. 82, BKF sec. 96.

20. McIntire report, Apr. 10, 1935, p. 82–83, BKF sec. 96; Bremer kidnapping, FBI summary, Nov. 19, 1936, p. 51.

21. McIntire report, Apr. 10, 1935, p. 97, BKF sec. 96. Murray statement, Feb. 12, 1935, p. 4, BKF 4546.

22. Hall to Hanni memo, Jan. 27, 1936, p. 1, BKF 104.

23. *Pioneer Press*, Apr. 24, 1935, p. 1, 5; Roy Norman McCord Jr., interview by author, Dec. 23, 1992; Mary Johnson, interview by author, May 12, 1993; O. G. Hall to Werner Hanni, FBI memo, Feb. 6, 1934, p. 3, BKF 264, sec. 3.

24. Hall to Hanni memo, Feb. 6, 1934, p. 4; Karpis with Trent, *Karpis Story*, 165.

25. McCord interview.

26. Mary Johnson interview.

27. Lannon interview.

28. Colleen McCalla, interview by author, July 9, 1993.

29. *Pioneer Press*, Jan. 10, 1936, p. 1–2.

30. Director to field offices memo, Feb. 21, 1934, p. 23–24, 47, BKF 711.

31. Vicenta Donnelly Scarlett, interview by author, May 14, 1994.

32. Director to field offices memo, Feb. 21, 1934, p. 23–24, 47, BKF 711.

33. Bomberg interview, Ramsey County Historical Society.

34. *Minneapolis Journal*, Jan. 18, 1934, p. 1–2.

35. McIntire report, Apr. 10, 1935, p. 32–33, BKF sec. 96.

36. *Pioneer Press*, Apr. 5, 1952, p. 4; Director to field offices, Feb. 21, 1934, p. 16, BKF 711.

37. *Dispatch*, Jan. 19, 1934, p. 1, 7; *Dispatch*, Jan. 20, 1934, p. 1, 5; *Dispatch*, Jan. 25, 1934, p. 1–2, BKF sec. 96.

38. McIntire report, Apr. 10, 1935, p. 34–35, BKF sec. 96; Bremer kidnapping, FBI summary, Nov. 19, 1936, p. 21–22.

39. McIntire report, Apr. 10, 1935, p. 34–35, BKF sec. 96; Bremer kidnapping, FBI summary, Nov. 19, 1936, p. 21–22; Betty Bremer Johnson, interview by author, Jan. 27, 1992. See also *Dispatch*, Jan. 19, 1934, p. 1, 7.

40. Bremer kidnapping, FBI summary, Nov. 19, 1936, p. 23.

41. Director to Hanni memo, Jan. 19, 1934, BKF 10.

42. Joseph B. Keenan to attorney general, Justice Dept. memo in FBI files, Jan. 22, 1934, BKF 100, sec. 2.

43. Memo to Werner Hanni, FBI memo, Jan. 19, 1934, p. 1–2, BKF, sec. 1.

44. Bremer Johnson interview.

45. Werner Hanni to St. Paul office, FBI memo, Jan. 27, 1934, BKF, sec. 2.

46. *Pioneer Press*, Jan. 10, 1936, p. 1–2.

47. McIntire report, Apr. 10, 1935, p. 36–37, BKF sec. 96; *St. Paul Dispatch*, Feb. 8, 1934.

48. Director to field offices memo, Feb. 21, 1934, p. 26–27, BKF 711.

49. Director to field offices memo, Feb. 21, 1934, p. 31, BKF 711.

50. Edward G. Bremer, statement to FBI, Feb. 8, 1934, p. 2, BKF, sec. 3; Bremer Johnson interview.

51. Bremer statement, Feb. 8, 1934, p. 2, BKF sec. 3.

52. Director to field offices memo, Feb. 21, 1934, p. 23, BKF 711.

53. McIntire report, Apr. 10, 1935, p. 41–42, BKF sec. 96.

54. McIntire report, Apr. 10, 1935, p. 65, BKF sec. 96.

55. Bremer kidnapping, FBI summary, Nov. 19, 1936, p. 28; Purvis, *American Agent*, 149.

56. Tony Tiemann, interview by author, Nov. 20, 1992.

57. McIntire report, Apr. 10, 1935, p. 34–35, BKF sec. 96; *Dispatch*, Feb. 8, 1934, p. 1.

58. J. Edgar Hoover to attorney general, FBI memo, Feb. 8, 1934, BKF 212, sec. 3; S. L. Fortenberry to Werner Hanni, FBI memo, n.d., p. 1, BKF 310, sec. 4; Louise Benz, interview by author, Oct. 30, 1992.

59. Bremer Johnson interview.

60. Hoover to field offices memo, Feb. 21, 1934, p. 11/2, BKF 711.

61. H. H. Clegg to Director, FBI memo, May 8, 1934, HKF 317, sec. 4.

62. McIntire report, Apr. 10, 1935, p. 35, BKF sec. 96; R. G. Harvey to director, FBI memo, Feb. 11, 1934 (with enclosed memo dated Feb. 10, 1934), BKF 281, sec. 3; Nathan report, Feb. 21, 1934, p. 1, BKF 721.

63. Barker-Karpis gang, FBI summary, Apr. 1984, p. 8; Bremer kidnapping, FBI summary, Nov. 19, 1936, p. 29; Director to special agent in charge, St. Paul, FBI memo, Feb. 12, 1934, p. 2, BKF 310, sec. 4; R. E. Newby to director, FBI memo, Mar. 29, 1934, p. 3, BKF 1558.

64. Stein to director memo (enclosing statement of Byron Bolton to FBI), Aug. 18, 1936, p. 1, HKF 1037.

65. Callahan and Jones, *Heritage of an Outlaw*, 156; Purvis to director letter, Mar. 21, 1934, KCMF 1475.

66. Madala report, May 19, 1936, p. 15, HKF 738; Karpis with Trent, *Karpis Story*, 173–74; McIntire report, Apr. 10, 1935, p. 178, BKF sec. 96.

67. FBI memo, Apr. 24, 1936, p. 2, BKF 11635; McIntire report, Apr. 10, 1935, p. 175–77, BKF sec. 96.

68. McKee report, May 8, 1936, p. 8, BKF 11529.

69. Murray statement, Feb. 12, 1935, p. 12–13, BKF 4546.

70. Purvis, *American Agent*, 138.

71. *Pioneer Press*, Jan. 10, 1936, p. 1–2.

72. H. H. Clegg to director memo, May 8, 1934, p. 1, DF 1310.

73. D. L. Nicholson, FBI report, Sept. 11, 1934, p. 3, DF 3813, sec. 64; Ramsey County Register of Deeds, Abstract of Title, Lot 23, Eisenmenger's Lake Villas, since July 29,

1929; FBI memo on Thomas Brown, Nov. 10, 1936, p. 11, HKF 1082;; S. P. Cowley to Director, FBI memo, Apr. 11, 1934, DF 514, sec. 11; Suran report, Oct. 6, 1934, p. 48, KCMF 2655.

74. H. H. Clegg to Director, FBI memo, Apr. 13, 1934, p. 6, DF 560, sec. 12.

75. FBI memo on Thomas Brown, Nov. 10, 1936, p. 10, HKF 1082; R. E. Newby to Director, FBI memo, Sept. 12, 1934, and D. L. Nicholson, FBI report, Sept. 13, 1934, p. 2–3, both in DF 3904, sec. 65.

76. Gladys Sawyer, statement to FBI, Sept. 13, 1934, p. 5, BKF 2869, sec. 35; Bremer kidnapping, FBI summary, Nov. 19, 1936, p. 38–40.

77. Karpis with Trent, *Karpis Story*, 178; D. M. Ladd to special agent in charge, Detroit, FBI memo, Sept. 29, 1934, BKF 3029, sec. 37; McKee report, May 20, 1936, p. 2, 6, HKF 732; Bremer Kidnapping, FBI summary, Nov. 19, 1936, p. 37–40.

78. *Pioneer Press*, May 9, 1936, p. 2; Bonnie Kohrt, interview by author, Jan. 1993.

79. Paul G. Comstock, interviews by author, Sept. 4 and Sept. 6, 1992.

80. Dirk Boardsen, interview by author, Sept. 5, 1992.

Notes for Chapter 9

1. *U.S.A. v. Clayton E. May, Evelyn Frechette et al.*, 129–30 (U.S. 3d Dist., 1934), MHS; Clegg to director memo, Apr. 13, 1934, p. 8, DF 568.

2. Robert Cromie and Joseph Pinkston, *Dillinger: A Short and Violent Life* (Evanston, Ill.: Chicago Historical Bookworks, 1990; reprint of 1962), 133–35, 159–62; Evelyn Frechette, "Evelyn Tells Life with Dillinger" (part 3), *Chicago Herald and Examiner*, Aug. 29, 1934.

3. H. H. Clegg, FBI report, May 25, 1934, p. 4, DF 1712, sec. 32.

4. Evelyn Frechette, "Evelyn Tells Life with Dillinger" (part 2), *Chicago Herald and Examiner*, Aug. 28, 1934; *USA v. Clayton E. May et al.*, 581, 613–15.

5. H. H. Reinecke, FBI report, Apr. 20, 1934, p. 2 DF 672, sec. 14; Evelyn Frechette, "My Wild Flight with Dillinger," *Startling Detective Adventures*, 1934, p. 60, in DF

3771x, sec. 62; Cromie and Pinkston, *Dillinger*, 163–64, 170–72, 175.

6. Cromie and Pinkston, *Dillinger*, 5, 8, 172–74, 136–41, 176.

7. Homer Van Meter, FBI wanted poster, Apr. 11, 1934, DF 473, sec. 11; Russell G. Girardin with William J. Helmer, *Dillinger: The Untold Story* (Bloomington: Indiana University Press, 1994), 19.

8. Bernice Clark, "My Adventures with the Dillinger Gang," *Chicago Herald and Examiner*, Sept. 10, 1934, pt. 2, p. 1, 6; V. W. Peterson, FBI report, May 17, 1934, p. 3–4, DF 1478, sec. 28.

9. Eddie Green, St. Cloud State Reformatory file 5774, MHS.

10. Green, St. Cloud State Reformatory file.

11. Green, St. Cloud State Reformatory file; Cooper, *Here's to Crime*, 85–87.

12. Bruce Hamilton, nephew of John Hamilton, interview by author, Dec. 17, 1993; Girardin with Helmer, *Dillinger*, p. 26, 45; Cromie and Pinkston, *Dillinger*, 59–60, 83–84, 105–11.

13. Clark, "My Adventures with the Dillinger Gang," p. 6.

14. Lester M. Gillis, FBI wanted poster, Apr. 25, 1934, no. 1223, DF 1340, sec. 25; Nash, *Bloodletters and Badmen*, 402.

15. Nash, *Bloodletters and Badmen*, 403; John Herbert Dillinger, FBI case summary, July 12, 1954, 18; *Dispatch*, Mar. 5, 1934, p. 1, 9; *Pioneer Press*, Mar. 5, 1934, p. 1; Fatso Negri with Bennett Williams, "In the Hinges of Hell: How G-Men Ended Crime's Reddest Chapter" (part 6), *True Detective Mysteries*, May 1941, p. 102.

16. Cromie and Pinkston, *Dillinger*, 9–14; "The Dillinger Man-hunt," *True Detective*, July 1934, p. 66.

17. Girardin with Helmer, *Dillinger*, 271–74.

18. Frechette, "My Wild Flight with Dillinger," p. 60, DF 3771x.

19. H. H. Clegg to director, FBI memo, Apr. 4, 1934, p. 2, DF 402, sec. 9.

20. Clegg to director, FBI memo, Apr. 19, 1934, p. 1, DF 662, sec. 14.

21. Marie Marion Conforti, statement to FBI, Apr. 26, 1934, p. 1–2, DF 948, sec. 19.

22. John Herbert Dillinger, FBI summary, p. 6; *Pioneer Press*, Mar. 14, 1934, p. 1; Purvis to director, FBI teletype, Apr. 8, 1934, DF 393, sec. 9.

23. Marie Conforti, statement to FBI, Aug. 29, 1934, p. 1, DF 3702, sec. 61.

24. Clegg to director memo, Apr. 13, 1934, p. 12, DF 560.

25. Hoover, *Persons in Hiding*, p. 36. See also Suran report, Sept. 1, 1934, p. 36–37.

26. Nicholson report, Sept. 22, 1934, p. 9, DF 4004.

27. Evelyn Frechette, "What I Knew about Dillinger," *Chicago Herald and Examiner*, Aug. 30, 1934.

28. Clegg to director memo, Apr. 13, 1934, p. 5; Frechette, "Evelyn Tells Life with Dillinger" (part 1); D. L. Nicholson, FBI report, May 29, 1934, p. 3, DF 1714, sec. 32.

29. Reiter interviews, Sept. 1 and 24, 1994; V. W. Peterson, FBI report, June 23, 1934, p. 45–46, DF 2211, sec. 39.

30. Reiter interviews, May 2, 1991 and Sept. 24, 1993; Cowley to director memo, Apr. 11, 1934, DF 514.

31. John Herbert Dillinger, FBI case summary (revised), Feb. 1, 1984, p. 1; Peterson report, May 17, 1934, p. 5, DF 1478.

32. D. L. Nicholson, FBI report, Apr. 9, 1934, p. 33–34, DF 466, sec. 10.

33. Peterson report, May 17, 1934, p. 6, DF 1478.

34. *Dispatch*, Apr. 26, 1934, p. 1–2.

35. H. H. Clegg, FBI report, Apr. 21, 1934, p. 1, DF 670, sec. 14; D. L. Nicholson, FBI report, Sept. 19, 1934, p. 1–2, DF.

36. Clegg report, Apr. 21, 1934, p. 5–6, DF 670; Nels George Mortensen death certificate, no. 3146, Oct. 23, 1971, Minnesota Department of Health; *Pioneer Press*, Jan. 17, 1934, p. 8; *Pioneer Press*, Apr. 10, 1934, p. 1.

37. Nicholson report, Sept. 11, 1934, p. 1–2, DF 3813; *Dispatch*, July 19, 1934, p. 1; Albert Reilly, Leavenworth prison file 48037, Federal Bureau of Prisons; Pat Reilly, Minnesota Prison file 17141, MHS.

38. H. H. Clegg to special agent in charge, Cincinnati, FBI memo, June 9, 1934, p. 4, DF 1880, sec. 35.

39. Clegg report, Apr. 21, 1934, p. 3, DF 670.

40. Clegg report, Apr. 21, 1934, p. 2–3, 4, DF 670; Hall report, July 27, 1933, p. 17, KCMF 401; Suran report, Mar. 3, 1936, p. 16–17, HKF 401. See also Cowley to director memo, Apr. 24, 1934, p. 4, DF 1010.

41. Director to S. P. Cowley, FBI memo, Apr. 24, 1934, DF 754, sec. 16; Cowley to director memo, Apr. 24, 1934, p. 5, 6, DF 1010.

42. Cowley to director memo, Apr. 24, 1934, p. 3, 4–5, DF 1010; *Dispatch*, May 3, 1934, p. 1, 6.

43. Nels Mortensen death certificate, Oct. 23, 1971.

44. John Herbert Dillinger, FBI summary, July 12, 1954, p. 4.

45. Louis Schroth, interview by author, Apr. 2, 1993.

46. Letter of Mar. 1934 quoted in Alanna Nash, "Memories of John Dillinger," *Chicago Reader*, July 20, 1984, p. 33–34.

47. *USA v. Clayton E. May et al.*, 292; Cromie and Pinkston, *Dillinger*, 186.

48. J. T. McLaughlin, Lincoln Court Apts. caretaker, interview by author; D. L. Nicholson, FBI report, Apr. 2, 1934, p. 5–7, 10, DF 299, sec. 8.

49. Obituary of Rufus C. Coulter, *Grapevine*, Nov. 1975, p. 28; Nicholson report, Apr. 2, 1934, p. 11–13, DF 299; *USA v. Clayton E. May et al.*, 187. See also H. H. Reinecke report, Apr. 20, 1934, p. 2, DF 672.

50. *USA v. Clayton E. May et al.*, 177–79.

51. *USA v. Clayton E. May et al.*, 594; John Herbert Dillinger, FBI summary, July 12, 1954, p. 5; *Dispatch*, Mar. 31, 1934, p. 1.

52. *USA v. Clayton E. May et al.*, 95.

53. *USA v. Clayton E. May et al.*, 95–96; Bob Geisenheyner, interview by author, n.d.

54. Schroth interview; *USA v. Clayton E. May et al.*, 595; Cromie and Pinkston, *Dillinger*, 188.

55. Geisenheyner interview.

56. D. L. Nicholson, FBI report, Apr. 28, 1934, p. 5–7, DF 1144, sec. 22.

57. *Pioneer Press*, Apr. 2, 1934, p. 10, Apr. 3, 1934, p. 4; *St. Paul Daily News*, Mar. 31, 1934, p. 1.

58. *Dispatch*, Apr. 5, 1934, p. 12, Apr. 4, 1934, p. 1, 12, Apr. 2, 1934, p. 1; Cromie and Pinkston, *Dillinger*, 188.

59. *U.S.A. v. Clayton E. May et al*,

227–241; Cromie and Pinkston, *Dillinger*, 188; Nicholson report, Apr. 2, 1934, p. 9, DF 299.

60. *Dispatch*, Apr. 6, 1934, p. 1–2; *Dispatch*, Apr. 30, 1934, p. 1; Director to S. P. Cowley, FBI memo, Apr. 4, 1934, p. 4, DF 325, sec. 8.

61. Mary Charlton, interview by author, Jan. 23, 1993; F. A. Tamm to director, FBI memo, June 13, 1934, p. 1, DF 2072, sec. 37.

62. *Dispatch*, Apr. 4, 1934, p. 1, 12; Director to H. H. Clegg, FBI memo, Mar. 31, 1934, p. 2, DF 323, sec. 8.

63. Memoranda of conversations between Mr. Hoover and Mr. Purvis and between Mr. Hoover and Mr. Rorer, both Apr. 1, 1934, DF 264, sec. 7.

64. Werner Hanni to H. H. Clegg, FBI memo, May 1, 1934, p. 6, DF 1513, sec. 29.

65. *Dispatch*, Apr. 31, 1934, p. 1; *Dispatch*, May 3, 1934, p. 1, 6.

66. Director to Mr. Cowley, FBI memo, Apr. 2, 1934, DF 324, sec. 8.

67. *USA v. Clayton E. May et al.*, 475, 486.

68. *USA v. Clayton E. May et al.*, 352. See also *Pioneer Press*, Apr. 21, 1938, p. 1; H. H. Clegg, FBI report, Apr. 21, 1934, p. 3–4, DF 677, sec. 14.

69. *USA v. Clayton E. May et al.*, 479–82, 486–87.

70. *USA v. Clayton E. May et al.*, 545; *Pioneer Press*, Apr. 27, 1934, p. 1–2.

71. Clayton E. May, statement to FBI, Apr. 17, 1934, DF 673, sec. 14.

72. Clegg report, Apr. 21, 1934, p. 2–4, DF 677; *Pioneer Press*, Apr. 21, 1938, p. 1.

73. Thomas Leonard Carroll, FBI wanted poster, Apr. 25, 1934, Identification Order 1224.

74. Thomas L. Carroll, Ramsey County Probate file 53032, 1934; Thomas L. Carroll, Leavenworth prison file 36697, Federal Bureau of Prisons.

75. Carroll prison file.

76. Thomas Carroll, wanted poster, Post Office Dept., Dec. 1, 1933, BCA.

77. Carroll, FBI wanted poster.

78. Dan Lambert, "How Iowa 'Rubbed Out' Dillinger's Ace Gunman," *Startling Detective Adventures*, 1934, p. 9–10, in DF 3771x, sec. 62; *Dispatch*, June 8, 1934, p. 1–3.

79. Peterson report, June 23, 1934, p. 45,

DF 2211; Kenneth Herschler, interview by author, May 21, 1993; Mercia Bergaus, who raised Kenneth, son of "Radio Sally" Bennett, interview by author, May 1993.

80. Interviews by author with Jim Vogel, Mar. 1993, and John Vogel, May 14, 1993.

81. Jim Vogel interview.

82. John Vogel interview.

83. Loretta Murphy, interview by relative, Apr. 1985, audiotape in the possession of Jim Vogel, Anoka, Minn.

84. Jim Vogel interview.

85. Peterson report, June 23, 1934, p. 46–47, DF 2211.

86. Carroll, FBI wanted poster, Apr. 25, 1934; *Pioneer Press*, June 8, 1934, p. 1, 3; Lambert, "How Iowa 'Rubbed Out' Dillinger's Ace Gunman," p. 11, DF 3771x.

87. Janet Gibson interview; *Brainerd Daily Dispatch*, Oct. 23, 1933, p. 1.

88. Fatso Negri with Bennett Williams, "In the Hinges of Hell: How G-Men Ended Crime's Reddest Chapter" (part 4), *True Detective Mysteries*, Mar. 1941, p. 89.

89. Donald Fish, interview by author, Jan. 23, 1993; Donald Fish, *The Dillinger Connection* (St. Paul: ByWords Printing, 1986), 3–4.

90. Fish interview.

91. *Brainerd Journal Press*, Oct. 27, 1933, p. 1.

92. Zane Smith, interview by author, Apr. 1993; Kevin Allenspach, "It Was No Gangster Movie," *Brainerd Daily Dispatch*, Dec. 4, 1988, p. 1C.

93. FBI memo, May 13, 1934, p. 11, DF 1415, sec. 27.

94. H. H. Clegg, FBI report, May 3, 1934, p. 3, DF 1219, sec. 23; *Dispatch*, Nov. 11, 1933, p. 1.

95. D. L. Nicholson, FBI report, May 14, 1934, p. 9, 30 DF 1410; R. C. Coulter to H. H. Clegg, FBI memo, June 10, 1934, p. 3, DF 1410, sec. 38.

96. Carroll, FBI wanted poster; *Pioneer Press*, June 8, 1934, p. 1, 3; D. L. Nicholson, FBI report, Sept. 28, 1934, p. 1, DF 4027, sec. 67; H. H. Clegg to director, FBI memo, June 20, 1934, p. 1–2, DF 2144, sec. 38.

97. Clegg to Purvis teletype, May 6, 1934, HKF 318.

98. R. C. Coulter to H. H. Clegg, FBI memo, June 10, 1934, p. 1, DF 2097, sec. 38; Clegg to director memo, June 20, 1934, p. 2, DF 2144.

99. Coulter to Clegg memo, June 10, 1934, p. 1, DF 2097; *Pioneer Press*, June 8, 1934, p. 1, 3.

100. Loretta Murphy interview.

101. June Bock, secretary, Oakland Cemetery, to Robert E. Bates, Sept. 17, 1987, letter in author's possession.

102. Lambert, "How Iowa 'Rubbed Out' Dillinger's Ace Gunman," p. 670, DF 3771x.

103. Clegg to Director memo, Apr. 4, 1934, p. 1, DF 402.

104. *Dispatch*, Mar. 13, 1934, p. 1; Robert H. Wybest, interview by author, Oct. 10, 1993.

105. Wybest interview; *Dispatch*, Mar. 13, 1934; Clegg to director memo, Apr. 13, 1934, p. 8, DF 560.

106. S. P. Cowley to director, FBI memo, Apr. 8, 1934, p. 1, DF 468, sec. 11; W. A. Rorer, FBI report, Apr. 9, 1934, p. 10, DF 491, sec. 11; S. P. Cowley, FBI memo, Apr. 4, 1934, p. 1, DF 294, sec. 7; Clegg to director memo, Apr. 19, 1934, DF 662; Nicholson report, Apr. 9, 1934, p. 28, DF 446.

107. H. H. Clegg to director, FBI memo, Apr. 4, 1934, p. 1–5, DF 467, sec. 10.

108. E. N. Notesteen to H. H. Clegg, FBI memo, Apr. 3, 1934, p. 1–2, DF 467, sec. 10.

109. Clegg to director memo, Apr. 4, 1934, p. 2, DF 402; Notesteen to Clegg memo, Apr. 3, 1934, p. 2–3, DF 467; *Pioneer Press*, Apr. 4, 1934, p. 1, 5.

110. Lannon interview; Thomas Delaney, an acquaintance of Eddie Green's brother, interview by author, May 9, 1992; H. H. Clegg to director, FBI memo, Apr. 17, 1934, p. 3, DF 664, sec. 14.

111. Cowley to director memo, Apr. 8, 1934, p. 5, DF 468; S. P. Cowley to director, FBI memo, Apr. 19, 1934, p. 4, DF 1584, sec. 30.

112. Nicholson report, Apr. 28, 1934, p. 50, DF 1144.

113. *Pioneer Press*, Apr. 8, 1934, p. 1; John Herbert Dillinger, FBI summary, July 12, 1954, p. 6; Harry Eugene Green file 10819–N, Apr. 11, 1934, Ramsey County coroner.

114. Cromie and Pinkston, *Dillinger*, 192–97, 206–7.

115. Clegg to director memo, Apr. 4, 1934, p. 3, DF 402; FBI memo, Apr. 16, 1934, p. 3, DF 1524, sec. 29.

116. S. P. Cowley to director, FBI memo, Apr. 19, 1934, DF 689, sec. 14; Director to S. P. Cowley, FBI memo, Apr. 18, 1934, DF 1537, sec. 29.

117. Cowley memo, Apr. 4, 1934, p. 1, DF 294; Cowley to director memo, Apr. 19, 1934, DF 689.

118. S. P. Cowley to director, FBI memo, Apr. 3, 1934, DF 292, sec. 7.

119. L. J. Rauber, FBI memo, Apr. 7, 1934, DF 407, sec. 9; Erik G. Peterson to director, FBI memo, Apr. 6, 1934, p. 2, DF 341, sec. 8.

120. Purvis, *American Agent*, 1, 10–14.

121. Purvis, *American Agent*, 15–18; Director to attorney general, FBI memo, June 27, 1934, DF 2224, sec. 40.

122. Purvis, *American Agent*, 16–19.

123. *Pioneer Press*, June 21, 1934, p. 1.

124. Gentry, *Hoover*, 172.

125. Aloysius "Ollie" McGree, Hastings resident, interview by author, Apr. 11, 1992.

126. Larry H. Johns, "The Hastings Spiral Bridge: Gone But Not Forgotten," *Minnesota Calls* 5, no. 3 (May/June 1992): 10.

127. *Hastings Gazette*, Apr. 27, 1934, p. 1; D. L. Nicholson, FBI report, May 11, 1934, p. 13, DF 1356, sec. 26.

128. Edwin J. Riege, "The Dillinger Case" (part 2), *The Investigator*, Dec. 1988, p. 3; John Herbert Dillinger, FBI summary, July 12, 1954, p. 10; *Hastings Gazette*, Apr. 27, 1934, p. 1.

129. *Minneapolis Journal*, Apr. 24, 1934, p. 1–2.

130. Bremer kidnapping, FBI summary, Nov. 19, 1936, p. 36; John Herbert Dillinger, FBI summary, July 12, 1954, p. 27; Cromie and Pinkston, *Dillinger*, 265; Girardin with Helmer, *Dillinger*, 156.

131. Cromie and Pinkston, *Dillinger*, 1–4, 250–56. Crime historian Jay Robert Nash, it should be noted, has argued that coroner's records suggest a "patsy" substitute, and not John Dillinger, was killed at the Biograph that day. See Nash, *Bloodletters and Badmen*, 176–78.

132. Summers, *Official and Confidential*, 72–73.

133. D. L. Nicholson, FBI report, Sept. 6, 1934, p. 3–4, DF 3788, sec. 62.

134. Jim Coleman, interview by author, Apr. 24, 1992; Nicholson report, Sept. 11, 1934, p. 7–8, 12, DF 3813.

135. Cowley to director memo, Apr. 8, 1934, p. 4, DF 468.

136. S. P. Cowley to special agent in charge, St. Paul, FBI memo, Sept. 5, 1934, DF 3786, sec. 62.

137. E. A. Tamm to director, FBI memo, Aug. 24, 1934, p. 1–2, DF 3630, sec. 59.

138. Nicholson report, Sept. 6, 1934, p. 19, DF 3788.

139. Dupont interview, May 1991; *St. Paul Daily News*, Aug. 25, 1934, p. 1–2. This version of Van Meter's death was also cited in Cromie and Pinkston, *Dillinger*, 263. See also Keljik interview.

140. Girardin with Helmer, *Dillinger*, 321.

141. S. P. Cowley to special agent in charge, St. Paul, FBI memo, Sept. 10, 1934, DF, sec. 64.

142. D. M. Ladd to director, FBI letter, Aug. 24, 1934, p. 3, DF 3595, sec. 59.

143. *Pioneer Press*, Aug. 24, 1934, p. 1.

144. Van Meter file 11023E, Aug. 23, 1934, Ramsey County coroner; *Minneapolis Tribune*, Aug. 24, 1934, p. 1–2; *Pioneer Press*, Aug. 24, 1934, p. 1.

145. Keljik interview.

146. St. Paul resident Norm Horton Sr., interview by author, May 15, 1991; *Dispatch*, Aug. 24, 1934, p. 1; Cromie and Pinkston, *Dillinger*, 239–40.

147. D. L. Nicholson, FBI report, Aug. 28, 1934, p. 1, DF 3676, sec. 61; E. A. Tamm to director, FBI memo, Aug. 24, 1934, p. 2, DF 3639, sec. 60; *Minneapolis Tribune*, Aug. 24, 1934, p. 1–2; Tamm to director memo, Aug. 24, 1934, p. 1–2, DF 3630.

148. Ladd to director memo, Aug. 24, 1934, 1–2, DF 3595; Nicholson report, Aug. 28, 1934, p. 6, DF 3676.

149. Nicholson report, Aug. 28, 1934, p. 6–7, DF 3676; Noonan report, June 18, 1936, p. 48, HKF 880.

150. Nicholson report, Aug. 28, 1934, p. 8, DF 3676.

151. Nicholson report, Sept. 6, 1934, p. 19.

152. Lannon interview; Noonan report, June 18, 1936, p. 48, HKF 880.

153. *Dispatch*, Aug. 27, 1934, p. 1.

154. Clegg to director memo, May 8, 1934, p. 4, DF 1310; Rosen to director memo, Apr. 3, 1936, p. 7, HKF 469x; Stein to director memo (Bolton statement), Aug. 18, 1936, p. 1, HKF 1037.

155. Pranke interview, Oct. 23, 1992.

156. Pranke, "Autobiography," 277; Nicholson report, Aug. 28, 1934, p. 3–4, DF 3676.

157. Nicholson report, Aug. 28, 1934, p. 2, DF 3676; J. Edgar Hoover to E. A. Tamm, FBI memo, Sept. 6, 1934, DF 3783, sec. 62.

158. *Pioneer Press*, Aug. 25, 1934, p. 1.

159. Nash, *Bloodletters and Badmen*, 404–5.

160. Hoover, *Persons in Hiding*, xvii; Avery Hale, "The Inside Story of Dillinger at Last," *True Detective Mysteries*, Dec. 1934, p. 7–8.

161. John Herbert Dillinger, FBI summary, July 12, 1954, p. 1, 12.

162. *Pioneer Press*, Aug. 24, 1934, p. 1; *Minneapolis Tribune*, Aug. 25, 1934, p. 8.

Notes for Chapter 10

1. Pranke, "Autobiography" 138–42.

2. *Pioneer Press*, Feb. 16, 1934, p. 1–2. On cleanup campaigns, see, for example, *Dispatch*, Nov. 7, 1922, p. 1, Nov. 22, 1929, p. 1, Dec. 9, 1929, p. 1.

3. Hanni to director memo, Feb. 20, 1934, p. 1, CCF 16, vol. 1.

4. *Dispatch*, Mar. 28, 1951, p. 25.

5. *St. Paul Daily News*, Mar. 31, 1934, p. 1.

6. *St. Paul Daily News*, Feb. 16, 1934, p. 1, and Feb. 24, 1934, p. 1.

7. *St. Paul Daily News*, Feb. 23, 1934, p. 1.

8. Thomas E. Dahill to John Edgar Hoover, SPPD letter, Feb. 17, 1934, CCF 20, vol. 1; R. T. Harbo to Mr. Tolson, FBI memo, Feb. 20, 1934, CCF 20, vol. 1.

9. J. Edgar Hoover to Thomas E. Dahill, FBI letter, Feb. 28, 1934, CCF 20, vol. 1; J. Edgar Hoover to William Stanley, FBI memo, Mar. 9, 1934, CCF 37, vol. 1.

10. *St. Paul Daily News*, Mar. 8, 1934, p. 1.

11. Purvis, *American Agent*, 140.

12. Lannon interview; Reiter interview; special agent ____ to Hanni memo, Feb. 19, 1934, p. 4, CCF 16, vol. 1.

13. *Pioneer Press*, June 27, 1934, p. 4.

14. H. H. Clegg to director, FBI memo, June 22, 1934, HKF 326, sec. 4.

15. C. W. Stein to director, FBI memo, June 12, 1936, p. 1, HKF 824, sec. 10; Louise Jamie, widow of Wallace Jamie, interview by author, Mar. 12, 1992. See also Stanley High, "St. Paul Wins a War," *Current History* 49, no. 1 (1938): 18–20.

16. High, "St. Paul Wins a War," 19.

17. *St. Paul Daily News*, June 27, 1935, p. 1, 5, June 29, 1935, p. 1–2; *Minnesota v. James P. Crumley et al.*, 344–45; *Pioneer Press*, June 26, 1935, p. 1. Although the present location of the wire recordings is unknown, transcripts of many of the wiretaps are contained *Minnesota v. James P. Crumley et al.*, Ramsey County District Court, Dec. 1935, MHS. Other excerpts appeared in the *St. Paul Daily News* in June 1935.

18. *Minnesota v. James P. Crumley et al.*, 369; *Dispatch*, Feb. 7, 1939, p. 1.

19. Noonan report, May 27, 1936, p. 3, HKF 759; *Minnesota v. James P. Crumley et al.*, 369, 373–76.

20. *St. Paul Daily News*, June 27, 1935, p. 1–3; *St. Paul Daily News*, June 24, 1935, p. 1–2.

21. *Dispatch*, Feb. 7, 1939, p. 1; Minnesota Police Association Official Bulletin, vol. 4, no. 8 (Mar. 1931).

22. Stein to director and Sal Connelly, FBI teletype, May 18, 1936, HKF 710, sec. 8; *Pioneer Press*, Apr. 23, 1936, p. 1–2, Apr. 25, 1935, p. 1, 3; *Dispatch*, Feb. 7, 1939, p. 1.

23. Brennan report, Feb. 15, 1936, p. 4, HKF 423.

24. Wills to Tamm memo, Mar. 18, 1940, p. 3–4, HKF 1125. See also John L. Connolly to J. Edgar Hoover, city of St. Paul letter, July 25, 1936, HKF 972, sec. 10.

25. Stein to director memo, June 12, 1936, p. 1–2, HKF 842.

26. T. D. Quinn to Mr. Tolson, FBI memo, Apr. 30, 1936, HKF 664, sec. 8; C. A. Hackert to G. H. Barfuss, SPPD letter, July 17, 1936, and H. E. Warren to Thomas A. Brown, City of St. Paul letter, Aug. 5, 1936, both in Thomas Brown file, SPPD.

27. C. A. Hackert to Personnel Division, memo, Nov. 4, 1936, Thomas Brown file, SPPD. S. W. Hardy, FBI report, Jan. 17, 1940, p. 4, BKF 15142, sec. 270.

28. Peters interview; Thomas A. Brown death certificate, Jan. 8, 1959, Minnesota Department of Health; *St. Paul Daily News*, Sept. 29, 1936, p. 1, 10.

29. *St. Paul Daily News*, June 3, 1936, p. 1, Aug. 1, 1936, p. 1; *Pioneer Press*, June 7, 1936, p. 1.

30. Sherin interview.

31. *Chicago Daily News*, Apr. 16, 1940, p. 1.

32. Mayor Mark E. Gehan to Senator Royal Copeland, city of St. Paul letter, Apr. 27, 1937, CCF 238, vol. 4.

33. J. Edgar Hoover to attorney general, FBI memo, May 7, 1937, CCF 238, vol. 4.

Notes for Chapter 11

1. *Pioneer Press*, Sept. 3, 1935, p. 1, 4.

2. Hoover to McMahon memo, May 13, 1936, p. 7, HKF 724; E. J. Connelley, FBI report, May 18, 1936, p. 1–3, BKF 11665, sec. 203; Karpis with Trent, *Karpis Story*, 190–98, 202–19, 223.

3. Karpis with Trent, *Karpis Story*, 230–33; *Pioneer Press*, May 2, 1936, p. 1–2; Gentry, *Hoover*, 185–87.

4. Gentry, *Hoover*, 185–87, 188.

5. Gentry, *Hoover*, 179–80; Ray Tucker, "Hist! Who's That?" *Colliers* 92, no. 8 (Aug. 19, 1933): 15, 48; Grooms interview.

6. Barker-Karpis gang, FBI summary, Apr. 1984, p. 10; Richard G. Powers, *Secrecy and Power: The Life of J. Edgar Hoover* (New York: Free Press, 1987), 208; Grooms interview; J. Kevin O'Brien, chief, FBI Freedom of Information section, to author, Oct. 24, 1994, letter in author's possession.

7. Grooms interview.

8. Summers, *Official and Confidential*, 241–42.

9. Connelley report, May 18, 1936, p. 9, BKF 11665; *Dispatch*, May 2, 1936, p. 1, 3; Karpis with Trent, *Karpis Story*, 240; Hoover, *Persons in Hiding*, 45.

10. Cooper, *Here's to Crime*, 112–113.

11. *Dispatch*, May 2, 1936, p. 1, 3; Nate Bomberg, "The Day Karpis Returned," *Capital: St. Paul Pioneer Press and Dispatch Sunday Magazine*, Mar. 28, 1971, p. 6, 10.

12. Karpis with Trent, *Karpis Story*, 256.

13. *Dispatch*, Nov. 10, 1935, p. 3; Larry Millett, *Lost Twin Cities* (St. Paul: Minnesota Historical Society, 1992), 258.

14. Hughes report, Aug. 10, 1933, p. 1, HKF 127; Noonan report, Oct. 10, 1933, p. 7, HKF 176.

15. Hughes memo, Aug. 10, 1933, p. 2, HKF 127; Noonan report, Oct. 10, 1933, p. 4, HKF 176; *Dispatch*, Nov. 10, 1933, p. 3, Nov. 28, 1933, p. 1–2; McIntire report, Apr. 10, 1935, p. 173, 178, BKF sec. 96.

16. Noonan report, Oct. 10, 1933, p. 7, HKF 127; Parrish to Hoover, FBI memo, Aug. 3, 1933, HKF 89, sec. 1.

17. *Pioneer Press*, Dec. 2, 1933, p. 1.

18. Nash, *Bloodletters and Badmen*, 561–65; Purvis, *American Agent*, 74; Carl Sifakis, *The Mafia Encyclopedia* (New York: Facts on File, 1987), 325; Nash, *Bloodletters and Badmen*, 564–65.

19. *Dispatch*, Apr. 28, 1934, p. 1, 5.

20. Virginia Gibbons Schwietz, interview by author, Dec. 30, 1992.

21. Bremer kidnapping, FBI summary, Nov. 19, 1936, p. 43, 52; *Dispatch*, Jan. 23, 1935, p. 1–2.

22. *Dispatch*, Jan. 19, 1935, p. 1, 3; *Pioneer Press*, Oct. 17, 1935, p. 8.

23. McKee report, May 8, 1936, p. 25, BKF 11529; Suran report, May 18, 1936, p. 3, BKF 11653; C. W. Stein to director, FBI memo, May 22, 1936, p. 2, BKF 11755, sec. 204.

24. C. W. Stein to director, FBI memo, May 11, 1936, BKF 11541, sec. 201; J. Edgar Hoover to attorney general, FBI memo, June 29, 1936, HKF 885, sec. 10.

25. Hoover to attorney general memo, June 29, 1936, HKF 885.

26. Robert Schwietz interview.

27. *Dispatch*, Apr. 17, 1936, p. 1, 5, Apr. 28, 1936, p. 1–2; *Minneapolis Tribune*, July 25, 1936, p. 1, 4.

28. McKee report, July 28, 1936, HKF 991: *Dispatch*, July 31, 1936, p. 1–2.

29. E. A. Tamm to director, FBI memo, July 31, 1936, HKF 1013, sec. 11.

30. Robert Schwietz interview; Dr. Raymond Bieter, M.D., to coroner C. A. Ingerson, Aug. 7, 1936, University of Minnesota letter, John Peter Peifer file 12127, July 31, 1936, Ramsey County coroner.

31. *St. Paul Daily News*, July 31, 1936, p. 1; William Walsh, interview by author, Jan. 6, 1995.

32. S. K. McKee, FBI report, Aug. 1, 1936, p. 2, HKF 1005, sec. 11.

33. *St. Paul Daily News*, Aug. 3, 1936, p. 2; *Minneapolis Journal*, Aug. 3, 1936, p. 1–2.

34. Martin Rohling interview, June 1991.

35. McKee report, Apr. 27, 1936, p. 63, HKF 647.

36. Eileen Michels, "Old Federal Courts Building—Beautiful, Unique—Its Style of Architecture Faces Extinction," *Ramsey County History* 9, no. 1 (Spring 1972): 3–9.

37. Director to attorney general memo, June 27, 1934, DF sec. 40; Girardin with Helmer, *Dillinger*, 161.

38. Barker-Karpis gang, FBI summary, Apr. 1984, p. 9–10; Jim Yandle, "The Bloody End to Ma Barker's Crime Spree," *Orlando Sentinel*, Jan. 19, 1988, p. 4.

39. Doris Lockerman, "G-Men on the Trail of the Desperadoes," *Chicago Tribune*, Oct. 18, 1935; Helmer, *Dillinger*, 268.

40. *New York Times*, Aug. 26, 1936, p. 11; McKee report, July 10, 1936, p. 10, HKF 891; Anne Diestel to author, July 25, 1994, in author's possession.

41. *Dispatch*, May 14, 1935, p. 1–2; Ex-Operative 48, "Sterilization," 42.

42. Anderson report, Aug. 31, 1936, p. 3, HKF 1053; *Dispatch*, May 25, 1935, p. 1; Bremer kidnapping, FBI summary, Nov. 19, 1936, p. 63–64; Nicholson report, Sept. 28, 1934, p. 1–2, DF 4027.

43. Nicholson report, May 14, 1934, p. 12, DF 1410; Director to attorney general memo, June 27, 1934, DF sec. 40; *Pioneer Press*, June 4, 1936, p. 4.

44. *Dispatch*, May 4, 1935, p. 1, 3.

45. Anderson report, Aug. 31, 1936, p. 3, HKF 1053.

46. McKee report, May 20, 1936, p. 2, HKF

732; E. A. Tamm to director, July 15, 1936, HKF 941, sec. 10.

47. McKee report, May 20, 1936, p. 13–14, HKF 732.

48. McKee report, May 8, 1936, p. 12, BKF 11529.

49. Karpis with Trent, *Karpis Story*, 241–43.

50. S. K. McKee reports, July 30, 1936, p. 8, HKF 1002, and May 8, 1936, p. 8, 31, BKF 11529.

51. *Pioneer Press*, Feb. 2, 1935, p. 3.

52. Keljik interview.

53. McKee report, July 28, 1936, p. 1, HKF 989; *St. Paul Daily News*, July 14, 1936, p. 1; Richard Hirsch, "Killers Call Him 'Creepy'," *True Detective*, June 1940, p. 111.

Notes for Epilogue

1. *St. Paul Daily News*, July 25, 1934, p. 1; Nash, *Bloodletters and Badmen*, 176–78.

2. Nash, "Memories of John Dillinger," p. 38.

3. Hamilton interviews; Girardin with Helmer, *Dillinger*, 298.

4. Girardin with Helmer, *Dillinger*, 63.

5. Nicholson report, Sept. 11, 1934, p. 23, DF 3813.

6. Purvis, *American Agent*, 264.

7. Barker-Karpis gang, FBI summary, Nov. 19, 1936, p. 10; John Knutson, interview by author, Mar. 1993.

8. Bruce Barnes, interview by author, Jan. 11, 1994.

9. Hoover, *Persons in Hiding*, 143; William W. Turner, *Hoover's FBI: The Men and the Myth* (New York: Dell Publishing Co., 1970), 21.

10. Turner, *Hoover's FBI*, 21–23, Appendix.

11. Haley, *Robbing Banks*, 176–202.

12. *Minneapolis Tribune*, Dec. 27, 1963, p. 1; Joseph O'Connor interview; Social Security Administration locator service, 1995.

13. Minnesota Department of Health, Leon Gleckman death certificate, July 14, 1941, no. 14784; St. Paul police report on death of Leon Gleckman, July 15, 1941, Ram-

sey County medical examiner's files; Sherin interview.

14. Harry Sawyer, Leavenworth/Alcatraz prison file, Federal Bureau of Prisons.

15. DeMoss interview.

16. Inmate Locator Service, Harry Sawyer file; Carole J. DeMoss to author, Jan. 4, 1994, letter in author's possession; Sawyer prison file.

17. Figge interview.

18. Flanagan, *Theodore Hamm in Minnesota*, 108, 122.

19. *Pioneer Press*, May 5, 1965, p. 1–2; Bremer Johnson interview.

20. Evelyn Tic death certificate, Jan. 13, 1969, Wisconsin Department of Health and Social Services; Bernice Tic, interview by author, Feb. 1994.

21. *Chicago Tribune*, Jan. 6, 1961, p. F2, Oct. 7, 1973, p. F4.

22. Sevareid, *The People's Lawyer*, 107.

23. Grooms interview.

24. Thomas M. McDade, "Karpis Recalls His Crime Spree of 1930s in Talks with McDade," *Grapevine*, May 1980, p. 36–38.

25. Barker-Karpis gang, FBI summary, Apr. 1984, p. 12.

26. Thomas Holden, Leavenworth/Alcatraz prison file, Special Progress report, Dec. 1946, Federal Bureau of Prisons; Lillian Holden homicide report, June 1949, Chicago Police Dept.; Thomas Holden file, n.d., Illinois Dept. of Corrections.

27. Francis Keating, Leavenworth/Alcatraz prison file, Federal Bureau of Prisons; Robert Fleigel, interview by author, Dec. 10, 1991; Robert Fleigel to author, Nov. 19, 1991, letter in author's possession.

28. Fleigel letter; Reiter interview.

29. "Shy" Troupe, interview by author, Nov. 3, 1993.

30. Reiter interview.

31. State of Minnesota, Francis Keating death certificate, July 25, 1978.

32. Fleigel interview.

33. Turner, *Hoover's FBI*, 147.

34. Sifakis, *Mafia Encyclopedia*, 268.

35. Interviews by author with Christine Brigham and Irene McBride, n.d.

INDEX • • • • • • • • • • • • •

Geographic places are in Minnesota unless otherwise noted. Italicized page numbers indicate photographs.

Alberts, Joseph "Two Gun," agent, 26
Alcorn, Truman, police officer, 169
Anderson, William, attorney, 30
Annbee Arms Apartments (Kensington Hall), St. Paul, 122, 296, 304
Anti-Semitism, toward bootleggers, 33
Arone's Bar, Minneapolis, 119

Babyface Nelson, *see* Gillis, Lester M.
Bachellor, William R., contractor, 68
Bailey, Harvey, bank robber, xx, 4, 5, 24, 60, 61, 65–66, *66*, 74, 82, 94, 106, 112, 283; feuds, 174, 306, 309, 310
Bald Eagle Boulevard, White Bear Lake Township, 141, 296
Bald Eagle Lake, 155, 156. *See also* Idlewild cottage
Bank robberies, *1932*, 78–79; map, *116*. *See also* individual banks
Banks, Tommy, bootlegger, 3, 134, 140, 162
Barfuss, Gustave "Gus" H., police official, 252, *258*, 308
Barker, Arthur "Doc," xi, 55, 65, 78, 105, 107, 163, 306, 311, 313; family, 106; gun, 168–69; captured, 268–69, *268*, 274; death, 282. *See also* Barker-Karpis gang
Barker, Fred, gangster, xi, xiii, 55, 63, 65, *102*, 105–6, 108, 109, 110, *121*, 130, 166, 217, 295, 296, 306, 310–13; family, 106; girlfriends, 130–31; death, 273. *See also* Barker-Karpis gang
Barker, Katherine "Ma," gangster, xi, 45, 65, *103*, *107*, *130*, 306, 311; police files, xiv; family, 106; relationships, 129–31; death, 273, 313. *See also* Barker-Karpis gang
Barker-Karpis gang, xi, xiii, xvii, 34, 60, 61, 63, 67, 75, 134, 135, 138, 245; Bremer kidnapping, xvi, 161–62, 298; Hamm kidnapping, xvi–xvii, 134, 139, 141–44, 147–49, 150, 155–59, 161–62, 164–65, 296; robberies, xix, 54, *116*, 117–20, 166, 167, 295, 297, 310, 311; girlfriends, 72–73, 197, 285; residences, 78, 104–8, 110, 112–15, 124, 127, *130*, 155–59, *158*, 184, 186, 293, 295, 296, 297, 298, 302, 304, 311; breakup, 202; trials, 292. *See also* individual members
Barker, Lloyd, 106
Barnes, Bruce, gangster's son, xx, 173–74, 282
Barnes, George, *see* Kelly, George
Baum, W. Carter, agent, xvii, 231, 237
Bayfield Street, St. Paul, 262, 301
BCA, *see* Minnesota Bureau of Criminal Apprehension
Bear Island View Resort, Longville, 241
Beer, 25, 65, 187–88. *See also* Hamm Brewing Company, Schmidt Brewing Company
Belle Plaine, bank robbery, 78
Bennett, Joseph, 230
Bennett, Sally, gangster's girlfriend, 227–28, *227*, 230, 300, 306
Bensonville, Ill., hideout, 149, 153, 156
Bentz, Eddie, robber, 61, 210
Benz, Herbert G., businessman, 150, 164–65
Berman, Edward "Barney," gangster, 30, 184–85
Bernstein, A. E., attorney, 33
Big Lake, hideout, 94
Biograph Theater, Chicago, 241
Birches Camp Resort, Grand Rapids, 242
Bixby, bank robbery, 78
Blue Room, St. Paul, speakeasy, 65
Blumenfeld, Isadore, gangster, xiii, xiv, 3, 16, 30, 38, 47, 65, 185, 173, 306; Urschel kidnapping, 136
Boardman, Henry, 135
Boardman, Cornelia, 135
Boardsen, Dirk, contractor, 205
Bolton, William Byron, gangster, 146–47; Hamm kidnapping, 148, 153, 157, 162, 163, 165, 245, 268, *273*, 274, 306; St. Valentine's Day Massacre, 146–47; robbery, 166
Bomberg, Nate, journalist, 25, 74–75, 138, *260*
Bootlegging, 27–28, 31, 49–50, 107, 187; criminal activities, 4, 24; role of railroads, 25, 26–27; folk heroes, 26. *See also* Liquor, Prohibition
Boulevards of Paris, St. Paul, nightclub, xii, 44, 46–49, 98, 152, 215, 227, 293, 302

Bowser, John, 74

Bradley, Charles, 157

Bradley, George, 251

Brady's Bar, Minneapolis, 3

Brainerd, robbery site, 116, 229–30; hideout, 172, 176

Bremer, Adolf, brewery president, *182*, 186–87, 199; residence, 299, 302

Bremer, Adolph, Jr., 199

Bremer, Donna, nightclub owner, 45–46

Bremer, Edward, kidnapped, xi–xii, xvi, xvii, 69, 71, 83, 116, 161, 162, 163, 164, *182*, 182–205, 301, 302, 304, 306, 312; residence, *183*, *196*, 298, 302; kidnapping reenactment, *193*; kidnapping trial, 272–75, *275*; death, 285

Bremer, Emily E., 198, *199*

Bremer, Louise, 198, 200

Bremer, Otto, 196, 298

Bremer, Steve, nightclub owner, 45–46

Breweries, *see* Beer, individual companies

Brown and Bigelow, St. Paul, 55

Brown Derby, St. Paul, nightclub, 63

Brown, Mary, 159

Brown, Thomas Archibald, police official, xvii, 34, 36, 46, 47, 63, 69, 110, 112–13, 137, 139, 150, 159–61, *160*, 169, *182*, 187, 243, 245–46, 252, 306, 309, 310, 313; Gleckman kidnapping, 39, 40; sheriff campaign, 72, *164*; cabin, 74; Hamm kidnapping, 152, 153, 157, 161–65; liquor syndicate, 160; home, 159, 297, 303; Bremer kidnapping, 163; investigated, 201, 256–58

Brownstein, Abe "Brownie," bootlegger, 30

Brunskill, Frank, police official, 6

Bruton, Haskett, 122

Buchalter, Betty, racketeer's wife, 173

Buchalter, Louis "Lepke," racketeer, 50, 173

Buckbee, Charles E., mayor, 98

Bucket of Blood, St. Paul, 13

Bugsy Siegel, *see* Siegel, Benjamin

Builders Exchange Building, St. Paul, 29

Burdette, Wynona, gangster's girlfriend, 63, 138, 184, 186, 197

Bureau of Criminal Apprehension, *see* Minnesota Bureau of Criminal Apprehension

Burke, Fred, 146

Burns, Bob, musician, 27

Butler, Pierce, Jr., attorney, 31

Cabins, gangster, 74–75; map, *116*

Caffrey, Raymond, agent, 176

Calhoun Beach Club, Minneapolis, 287

Callahan, Clyde, biographer, 88, 174

Calvary Cemetery, St. Paul, 17–18, 291, 302

Cambridge, 72–73, 116, 310

Cameron, "Dutch" Otto, gambler, 254

Campbell, Harry "Limpy," robber, 63, 106, 138, 274

Cann, Kid, *see* Blumenfeld, Isadore

Canner, William "Dutch," robber, 39, 74

Capone, Alphonse "Al," 26, 60, 131, 135, 288, 306; bootlegger, 34, 36, 39, 43; syndicate, 71, 88, 189

Carmacher, Sadie, murdered, 73–74, 125, 310

Carroll, Thomas L. "Tommy," gang member, 67, 215, 222, *226*, 229–32, 238, 306, 312, 313; death, 116, 232; hideout, 226, 227–28, 300, 303

Cary, Archibald, attorney, 62, 140, 270

Castle Royal, St. Paul, 44–46, *45*, 293, 303

Central State Bank, Sherman, Tex., 82

Charles, Herbert, 156

Charles Street, St. Paul, *28*

Charlou (Fremont) Apartments, Minneapolis, 213–16, 299, 305, 311

Charlton, Mary, 223

Charrington, Pat, 220

Chase, John Paul, gang member, 211, 229

Chicago Great Western Railroad, robbery, 5

Christman, Earl, con man, 65, 78, 113, 124, 296, 306, 311; death, 128, 130

Church of the Assumption, St. Paul, 232

Cicero, Ill., safe city, 60

Citizens National Bank, Fort Scott, Kans., robbery, 112, 310

Citizens National Bank, Wahpeton, N.D., robbery, 118

Clare, Red, 19

Clark, Bernice, 67, 209, 211, 214, 220

Clark, Russell, gangster, 209

Cle-mar Apartments, St. Paul, 124–25, 296, 302

Clements, bank robbery, 78

Clements Auto, Mankato, 222

Clifford, Nina, madam, xx, 12, 13, *14*, 15–17, *17*, 71, 291, 304, 306

Cloud County Bank, Concordia, Kans., 113–15, 310

Coffey, Daisy, landlord, 218, 289

Coleman, Delia, resort owner, 241

Coleman, Frank "Weanie," gangster, 92, 95, *95*, 309

Coleman, James, resort owner, 241

Coliseum Ballroom, St. Paul, 44, 46–49, *47*, 293, 302

Colton, Clarence, gunman, 68, 139

Commercial State Bank, St. Paul, 184

Commodore Hotel, St. Paul, 129–31, *130*, 296, 304, 311

Como Park Zoo, St. Paul, 295, 302

Comstock, Paul, 204

Comstock, Virginia, 204

Concord Street, South St. Paul, 165, 204, 297

Conforti, Marie, gangster's girlfriend, 214, 215, 237, 241, 299, 306

Cooper, Courtney Ryley, 181, 264

Copeland, Royal, senator, 237, 250, 259

Costello, Frank, gangster, 4, 55

Cotton Club, Minneapolis, 173

Coulter, Rufus, agent, 220–21

Courtney, Big Phil, *see* Phillips, Bernard

Courtney, James, *see* Keating, Francis L.

Courtney, John, druggist, 51, 52

Courtney, Tom, attorney, 267

Cowley, Samuel, agent, xvii, 246

Cranberry Lake, Wisconsin, 145

Crane Lake, gangster cabins, 74–75

Cravath, Austin, bootlegger, 38–39

Cravath, Calvert, 38

Cretin Court Apartments, St. Paul, 88–90, 294, 302

Crowe, Ann, 13

Crowe, Hannah, *see* Clifford, Nina

Crowe, Patrick, 13

Crumley, James P., police official, 109, 110, 163, 169, 187, 255, 256, 306

Cullen, Frank, police official, 160, 243, 244, 245

Culligan, Michael J., 256

Cummings, Henry, police officer, 220–21

Cummings, Homer, attorney general, 218, 224, 250

Cushing, bank robbery, 78

Dahill, Thomas E., police official, 16, 36, 64, 150–52, 157, 161, 162, 195, 220; reformer, 139, 164, 223, 224, 233, 252, *253*, 308, 310

Dale Apartments, St. Paul, 184, 186, 297, 304

Dandy Jack, gangster, 54

Davenport, Jack, robber, 162

Davis, Harry, hoodlum, 51; murdered, 139, 306

Davis, Volney "Curly," robber, xiii, 65, 78, 83, 84, 106, 138, 155, 197, 239, 306, 311, 313

Delaney, Delores, gangster's girlfriend, *61*, 61–62, 64, 135, 217, 231, 306; captured, 274–75, 277; released, 285

Delaney, Helen "Babe," gangster's wife, 217, 306

Delaney, Jean, gangster's girlfriend, 215, 217, 231–32, 237, 306

Dellwood, 112, 295

DeMoss, Carole, gangster's niece, xx, 284

Dempsey, Jack, in Minnesota, 5

Denver, mint robbed, 4–5

Depot Cafe, St. Paul, 166

DeVol, Clarence, 61–62

DeVol, Lawrence "the Chopper," robber, 61, 65, 101, *105*, 109, 112, 113, 121, *123*, 134, 139, 163, 296, 306, 311, 313; background, 122–23; death, 124

Dexheimer farm, Mendota, 38

Deyo, Evelyn, 113

Dillinger, Beryl, 213

Dillinger, John, *x*, xi, xii, 29, 34, 49, 51, 65, 71, 135, *206*, *219*, 251, 299, 306, 312; captured, xii; police files, xiv; gang, 62, 67, 69, 118, 272, 311; robbery sites mapped, 116; doctors, 155, 216–18, 224–25, 299, 300, 302, 305; residences, 208–16; shootout, 218–21; girlfriends, 220, 285; garage, 221–24, 304; mail drop, 226, 230–31; weapons depot, 232–33; death, 241, 313

Dillinger, John, Sr., gangster's father, *280*

Dittrich, Jeff, police official, 169

Dodd, Thomas, agent, 225, 234

Doran, Frank, barber, 89

Doran, Jerk, promoter, 69–70

Doyle, Doris, robber's sister, 190

Doyle, Jess, robber, 113, 118, 127–28, *128*, 148, 190, 306; captured, 274

Dreis Brothers' Drug Store, St. Paul, 29, 31, 292, 304

Drill, Lewis L., attorney, 35, 266

Drover's Tavern, South St. Paul, 104, 107

Drugstores, selling liquor, 25, 27, 128, 156

Du Bois, Teddy, gangster's girlfriend, 6

Duffing, Susie Friermuth, bootlegger, *22*

Dunlap, Roy, newspaperman, 16
Dunlop, Arthur "Old Man," *107*, 107, 110, 307, 310; murdered, 111
Dunn, William W., businessman, 297, 302, 307; intermediary, 137, 150, 152, 165, 151–53, *151*, 156, 165, 255
Dupont, Horace "Red," xx, 53, 68, 72, 242
Dutch Schultz, *see* Flegenheimer, Arthur
Dyckman Hotel, Minneapolis, 3

East Side Ice Company, St. Paul, 115
Eaton, Myrtle, gangster's girlfriend, 189–91, *190*, 214, 298, 307; captured, 262
Edgecumbe Court Apartments, St. Paul, 78–80, *79*, 83, 84, 186, 294, 304
Edgecumbe Road, St. Paul, 195, 298
Edwards, Thomas, 53
Ehrlich, Max, 42
Eighteenth Amendment, 24, 309; repealed, 43. *See also* Prohibition
Electronic surveillance, 196, *248*, 252, 254, *254*, 255, *257*, 258
Eleventh Street, St. Paul, 250, 301
Elk River, bank robbery, 78
Elmwood Apartments, St. Paul, 9
Elsie's, White Bear Lake, speakeasy, 295
Erickson, Delvina, 121
Erickson, Oscar, murder victim, 119, 120–21, 295, 311
Eue, Donna, 179
Evan, Ira, police officer, 119
Evans, M. E., attorney, 34
Evergreen bandits, *see* Holden, Thomas; Keating, Francis L.

Factor, Jake "the Barber," 267
Fahey, Ted, police officer, 75
Fairbury National Bank, Neb., robbery, 274
Fairmount Avenue, St. Paul, 71, 216, 294, 299
Fairview Avenue, St. Paul, 60
Farmer, Herbert "Deafy," 60, 108, 130
Farmers Savings Bank, Alden, Iowa, 110
Federal Acceptance Corporation, 71, 135
Federal Bureau of Investigation (FBI), xii–xiii, xiv, xvi, xvii, 4, 60, 64, 69; investigates St. Paul police, 69, 236, 244–47, 251–52; investigates Kansas City Massacre, 140, 177–78; investigates kidnappings, 158, 160–63, 188, 200–203, 266–67, 273, 275–76; hunts Dillinger, 209, 213, 215, 217–24, 231,

232–33; field office, 224, 272, 292; criticized, 237, 288. *See also* Hoover, J. Edgar
Federal Bureau of Prisons, xiv, xvi
Federal Courts Building (Landmark Center), St. Paul, 19, 24, 55, 222, 224, 262, *273*, 291–92, 304
Ferguson, Helen, gangster's girlfriend, 114, 124, 128–29, 130, 307
Ferrick, Jack, gangster, 113
Fifth Street, St. Paul, 24, 291
Figge, William, 152, 285
Filben, Delia, 71
Filben, Patrick, 71
Filben, Thomas P., 53, 68, 69–75, *70*, 164, 242, 307; purchases Hollyhocks, xx, 135; headquarters, 294
Finch Drug Store Building, Hastings, 236, 237
Finiello, John, murder victim, 50
Finkelstein and Ruben, business, 3
Finn, Nicholas J., priest, 17
First National Bank, Brainerd, 229–30
First National Bank, Fairbury, Neb., robbery, 127–28
Fish, Don, resort owner, 229
Fisher, Charles, 229
Fitzgerald, Charles "Old Charlie," 96, 146–47, 307; Hamm kidnapping, 148–49, *148*, 153, 155–57, 162, 165; robber, 166, 167
Fitzgerald, F. Scott, novelist, xi, 129, 142, 296
Flamingo Hotel, Las Vegas, 57
Flanagan, John, 285
Flegenheimer, Arthur "Dutch Schultz," 34, 49
Fliegel, Ernie, prizefighter, 287
Floyd, Arthur "Pretty Boy," robber, 60
FOIA, *see* Freedom of Information Act
Fort Scott, Kans., bank robbery, 91
Fourth Street, St. Paul, 41, 267, 292, 301
Francis, Roy, 239
Fransmeyer farm, 38
Frechette, Evelyn "Billie," Dillinger's girlfriend, 208, 213, 215, 218–22, *219*, 225, 272, 285, 299, 300, 307, 312
Freedom of Information Act, xii, xiii
Fremont Apartments, Minneapolis, *see* Charlou Apartments, Josephine Apartments
Fremont Avenue, Minneapolis, 51, 213, 299
French, Lafayette, attorney, 27, 33
French Cafe, St. Paul, 90
Friermuth, Florence, bootlegger, *22*
Frisco Dutch, *see* Steinhardt, Robert

Front Avenue, St. Paul, 17, 291
Fullerton, Helen, 156

G-Men, film, 191
Gannon, Thomas E., gang member, 49, 68–69, 214–15, 242, 293, 307
Gates, William, jailer, *268*, 269
Gebhardt, Michael, police official, 25
Gehan, Mark, mayor, 256, 259
Geisenheyner, Bob, 222
Gellman, Harry, bootlegger, 29, 34
Gibbons, Tom, sheriff, 267, 269
Gibson, Janet, 172, 175, 176, 229
Gibson, John, farmer, 229
Gibson, Mike, 175
Gillespie, George, 72
Gillespie Auto Company, 72
Gillis, Helen, gangster's wife, 231–32, 237, 274
Gillis, Lester M. "Babyface Nelson," robber, xi, xii, xvii, 61, 67, 71, 78, 113, 209, 211, 229–32, 237, 246, 295, 307, 312, 313; bootlegger, 24; wanted poster, *212*
Ginsberg, Abe, attorney, 29, 31
Girard Avenue, Minneapolis, 208, 299
Gleckman, Florence, 40–41
Gleckman, Gershon, 35
Gleckman, Helen Mae, *42*
Gleckman, Leon, syndicate head, xii, 12, 24, 29–31, *37*, *42*, 90, 137–38, 160, 161, 283–84, 307; headquarters, 34, 36–39, 152, 292, 304, 309; kidnapped, 39–41, 55, 138, 292, 310; residence, 302
Gleckman, Lorraine, *42*
Gleckman, Nechama "Nettie," 35
Gleckman, Rose, 35, 41, *42*
Gleeman, Abraham, bootlegger, 30–33, *32*, 67, 160, 161, 307
Gleeman, Benjamin, bootlegger, 29–33, *32*, 67, 160, 161, 307
Goetz, Fred, *see* Ziegler, Shotgun George
Goetz, Irene Dorsey, gangster's wife, xiii, 145, 146, 201
Golder, Ben, 53
Golf courses, patronized by gangsters, 99–101. *See also* Keller Golf Course, Mission Hills Country Club
Goodman, Isaac, bootlegger, 65
Goodman, Leona, maid, 233–34
Goodrich Avenue, St. Paul, 221, 300
Gordon, Al, bootlegger, 51, 53, 293

Gordon, W. S., detective, 115
Gordon, Waxey, *see* Wexler, Irving
Gorilla Kid, *see* Davis, Harry
Gorski, Leo, police officer, 119, 120
Grand Avenue, St. Paul, 67, 122, 153, 296, 297. *See also* individual buildings
Grand Avenue Apartments, St. Paul, 296, 304
Gray, William, caretaker, 204
Green, Beth "Bessie," *see* Skinner, Beth
Green, Frank, 234
Green, Harry Eugene "Eddie," gang member, 62, 164, 167, 210, *210*, 213, 215, 222, 225, 232, 233, 299, 300, 307, 311, 312; ambushed, 234–36, 300–301, 302
Green Dragon Cafe, St. Paul, 49, 51, *52*, 53, 293, 302
Green Gables, St. Paul, nightclub, 227
Green Gables Tourist Camp, Minneapolis, 242
Green Lantern Saloon, St. Paul, 2, 5, 11, 19, 63, 64–69, 136, 139, 140, 187–88, 216, 293, 298, 304
Greenwood Lodge, 146
Greer, Bill, reporter, 8, 11, 63
Grenville, Ann, 6
Griffin, Cora, 9
Griffin, William H. "Reddy," fixer, 9–10; grave, 18, 291, 302
Grooms, Albert, gangster's nephew, xx, 104–5, 107, 263, 286
Grooms, William, police officer, 176
Guarnera, Vince, 295
Guild of Catholic Women, 16
Guilford, Howard, editor, 15

Hackert, Clinton A., police official, 252, *253*, 258, 308
Haley, J. Evetts, biographer, 94, 283
Hall, Oscar G., agent, 99, 140
Hamill, Pete, quoted, 263
Hamilton, Bruce, gangster's nephew, xx, 261
Hamilton, John, gangster, xx, 24, 67, 209, 210–11, 213, 216, 217, 220, 236–41, *238*, *239*, 299, 307, 312; death, 281–82, *282*, 313
Hamilton, Robert Brooks, casino operator, 44, 46, 138, 307
Hamilton, William, gangster's father, 281
Hamilton County Bank, Cincinnati, robbery, 4, 5
Hamm, William, Sr., 150
Hamm, William, Jr., kidnapped, xi–xii, xvii,

41, 69, 71, 83, 116, 132, 134, 139–40, 141–65, *151*, 265–67, 285, 296, 297, 302, 306, 311

Hamm Brewing Company, St. Paul, 144, *145*, 165, 296–97, 303

Hamm Building, St. Paul, 150, *249*, 255, 301, 304

Hancock, Audrey, gangster's sister, 280–81

Hanft, Hugo, judge, 28

Hankins, Leonard, gambler, 54–55

Hannegraf, Helen, landlord, 104, 107, 109, 112, 295, 310

Hannegraf, Nick, tavern owner, 104, 107, 109, 112

Hanni, Werner, agent, xv, 158, 162, 195, 224, 251

Hardy, Fremont, *6*

Hardy, Sam, agent, 218

Harmon, Charles Preston "Charlie," robber, 78, 80, 82, 84, 85–87, *86*, 134, 307, 310; death, 116, 130–31; residence, 294, 304

Harmon, Paula, robber's wife, xiii, 63, 78, 130, 138, 155–56, 184, 197, 307, 313; home, 294, 304

Harney, Malachi "Mel," agent, 26

Harris, Ben, casino manager, 46–47, 98, 165, 307

Harris, Sammy, 34

Haskell, Benny, bootlegger, xii, 26

Hastings, shootout, 116, 236–41

Hawthorne Apartments, St. Paul, 294, 304

Haybeck, Esther, 78

Heaberlin, Fred, journalist, 3, 13, 16, 17, 65, 68, 136

Heisey, George A., attorney, 43, 274

Heller, Harold, hijacker, 161

Hennepin Avenue, Minneapolis, 115, 295

Hermanson, Frank, police officer, 176

Herschler, Arthur, 227

Hesselroth, Paul, teller, 118

Hiebert, Gareth, journalist, 14, 17, 49

Hogan, Daniel, underworld czar, xi, xix, xx, 2–6, 7, *6*, *19*, 29, 63–65, 307; murdered, *xxii*, 2, 7, 17–19, *21*, 291, 302, 309; residence, 3, 291; burial site, 17, 291

Hogan, Leila, *6*, 18

Hoidale, Einar, congressman, 35

Holden, Lillian, robber's wife, 90

Holden, Thomas, robber, 36, 48, 63, 72, 75, *76*, 88–89, 109, 112, 138, 286–87, 307, 309, 310; residences, 78, 90–91, 186, 294, 304; golfer, 99–101, 286. *See also* Keating-Holden gang

Hollis, Herman, agent, xvii, 246

Holly Avenue, St. Paul, 191, 298

Holly Falls Apartments, St. Paul, *190*, 191, 298, 304

Hollyhocks Club Casino, St. Paul, xii, 36, 39, 44, 61, 67, 96, 134–41, *135*, 164–65, 187, 296, 302

Hollywood Inn, Mendota, 19

Holman Municipal Airport, St. Paul, 53, 262–64, *264*, 301, 303

Hoover, J. Edgar, xii, xvi, xvii, 4, 11, *207*, 214, 218, 222, 223–24, 235–36, 241, 244, 246; views on Barker-Karpis gang, 104, 106, 201; views on Kansas City Massacre, 176, 179; views on Bremer kidnapping, 195–96; publicity, 180–81, *180*, 222, 224, 235, 280; views on gangster girlfriends, 214, 274; views on Dillinger, 218, 222–24, 246–47; hunts Karpis, 262–65, *263*, 269, 276–77; homosexuality, 263; ignores Mafia, 263, 288. *See also* Federal Bureau of Investigation, St. Paul police

Horn, Tommy, detective, 11

Horseshoe Cave, St. Paul, 292

Hot Springs, Ark., safe city, 60

Hotel St. Francis, St. Paul, 69–71, *70*, 294, 304

Hotel St. Paul, St. Paul, 51, 137; Gleckman's headquarters, 34, 36–39, *37*, 152, 292, 304, 309

Hotel Savoy, St. Paul, 9

Hugo, bank robbery, 78

Hurley, George, saloon manager, 67–68

Hurley, Harold, 67

Idlewild cottage, Bald Eagle Lake, 141–44, *142*, 157, 296, 305

Irey, Elmer L., agent, 288

Irvine Park, St. Paul, 7

Isabel Street, St. Paul, 226, 300

Iten's Auto Center, Cambridge, 72

Jackson, Lucy, maid, 233

Jackson Investment Company, 164–65

Jamie, Alexander, investigator, 253

Jamie, Wallace Ness, investigator, 250, 253–55, *254*, 256, 308, 313

Jefferson Avenue, St. Paul, 60, 61, 293

Jennings, Dean, writer, 24

Johnson, Betty Bremer, 195, 200, 285

Johnson, Marian, 108, 109–10

Johnson, Mary, 192
Johnson, Walter "Buster," 97, 113
Jones, Byron, biographer, 88, 174
Joplin, Mo., safe city, 60
Josephine (Fremont) Apartments, Minneapolis, 213–16, 299, 305
Joyce, Matthew, judge, 272–73, 292
Junterman, Marguerite Lane, 46, 47, 48

Kahn, Howard, editor, xvii, 251, *251*, 308. *See also St. Paul Daily News*
Kansas City, Mo., safe city, 60. *See also* Mission Hills Country Club
Kansas City Massacre, xi, xii, xiv, 83, 140, 155, 165, 172, 175–77, 179, 307, 308, 311
Kansas State penitentiary, prison break, 67
Karpis, Alvin "Creepy," gangster, xi, xx, 55, 60, 61–65, *102*, 104–6, *105*, 109, 110, 120, 125, 140, 163, 164, 217, 293, 298, 301, 307, 310; police file, xiv; bootlegger, 24; family, 104, 285; captured, *260*, 262–65, *264*, 268, 269–70, *270*, 276–77, 285–86; paroled, *279*, 286; autobiography, 286; trials, 292, 301, 313. *See also* Barker-Karpis gang
Karpovicz, Albin Francis, *see* Karpis, Alvin
Keating, Francis L. "Jimmy," robber, xi, 36, 48, 60, 61, 63, 72, 75, *77*, 88–90, 138, 286–88, *287*, 295, 307, 309, 310; residences, 78, 129, 186, 294, 302; golfer, 99–101, 286
Keating-Holden gang, *see* Holden, Thomas; Keating, Francis L.
Kedney warehouse, Minneapolis, 30
Keenan, Joseph, attorney general, 196
Keljik, Woody, 19, 244
Keller, Paul D., 28
Keller Golf Course, Maplewood, 99–101, *100*, 295, 303
Kellogg Boulevard, St. Paul, 7, 265, 291, 301
Kelly, C. Roy, sheriff, 108, 310
Kelly, George "Machine Gun," xi, xix, xx, 82, 88, 95, 125, 173–74, *283*, 306, 309; bootlegger, 24; Urschel kidnapping, 136, 184–85, *185*, 282, 311
Kelly, Kathryn, gangster's wife, 184–85, *283*
Kennington Apartments, St. Paul, 189–91, *190*, 275, 298, 304
Kensington Hall, St. Paul, *see* Annbee Arms Apartments
Kevin Sweet Grass Developing Company, St. Paul, 29

Kid Cann, *see* Blumenfeld, Isadore
Kidder, Theodore, murder victim, xvii, 211, 312
Kidnapping, FBI investigations, 69, 71; Lindbergh laws, 185; protection, 186–87. *See also* specific kidnappings
King's Horses, Mahtomedi, roadhouse, 113
Kinkead, Michael, attorney, 46, 137
Kirwin, Frank, 204, 241, 242, 245, 281
Kissing Bandit, *see* Murray, Edna
Knutson, Sarah, 44–45
Kraft, James, banker, 87
Kraft, William, banker, 87
Kraft State Bank, Menomonie, Wisc., robbery, 87, 130–31
Krause, Otto, iceman, 144

Lachowitzer, Frank, iceman, 156
Ladd, D. Milton "Mickey," agent, 246
Lake McCarron, Roseville, 14
Lake Minnetonka, hideout, 94
Lake Weir, Fla., hideout, 273
Lally, Jack, police officer, 141
Lambert, John, cottage, 112, *114*, 295, 305
Lancaster, Silas, janitor, 208
Landmark Center, *see* Federal Courts Building
Lane, John, nightclub owner, 46–49, *47*, 98
Lannon, Pat, Sr., police officer, xx, 13, 18, 45–46, 65, 140, 192, 245
Lansky, Meyer, gangster, 4, 50, 53–54, 55, 263
Lapland Willie, *see* Weaver, William
LaPre, Frank, 39–40
Layover agreement, *see* O'Connor system
Leckerman, Doris, secretary, 273
LeClaire's Resort, Longville, 241
Lee, Lillian, 16
Leech Lake, hideouts, 204, 241
Lehman, Erma, 124
Lehman, Jim, 124
Lexington Parkway, St. Paul, 218, 224, 295, 298, 299
Ligget, Walter, journalist, 25–26, 33; murdered, 49
Lincoln Avenue, St. Paul, 53, 194, 294, 298
Lincoln Court Apartments, St. Paul, 71, 213, 218–21, *219*, 251, *289*, 299–300, 304, 312
Lincoln Oaks Apartments, St. Paul, 294, 304
Lindbergh, Charles, Jr., kidnapping, 50, 185
Lindholm, Clifford, 143

Lindvall, R. C., police officer, *120*
Lion's Park, White Bear Lake, 294, 305
Liquor, distilleries, *22*, 25, 27; syndicate, 107.
    See also Bootlegging, Prohibition
Little Bohemia Lodge, Rhinelander, Wisc.,
    raid, 116, 224, 231, 235, 237, 289, 307, 312–13
Little Canada, 63
Loeb, Abe, *see* Wagner, Abe
Long, Opal, *see* Clark, Bernice
Lowry Hotel, St. Paul, 16, 55, *56*, 293, 304
Lowry Office Building, St. Paul, 55, 293, 304
Lucas, Claire, auto thief, 65
Luciano, Charles "Lucky," gangster, 4, 55, 60,
    263

Machine Gun Kelly, *see* Kelly, George
MacLaren, Gertrude, 155, 156
MacLaren, James, salesman, 155
Mafia, xii, 50
Magee, Walter W., intermediary, *182*, 188,
    194–95, 197, 199–200; residence, 298, 304
Mahoney, William J., mayor, 16, 40, 42–43,
    111, 138, 222, 251, 310
Mahtomedi, hideouts, 92, 112–15, 294, 295
Maihori, Henry Kazo, 143, 144
Makley, Charles, gang member, 209
Malone, Michael, agent, 36, 43
Mamie Porter's Chicken Shack, St. Paul, 13
Maplewood Drive, Maplewood, 99, 295
Marshall Avenue, St. Paul, 124, 126, 232–33,
    296, 300
Martindale, A. L., 233
Maryland Avenue, St. Paul, 159, 297
Mason City, Iowa, robbery site, 116
Mathis, Bertha, 179
Mathis, Betty, 175, 176, 179
Mathis, Vivian, gangster's girlfriend, *170*, 172,
    174, 175, 176, 229, 307
May, Clayton E., doctor, 62, 224–25, 235, 272,
    300, 305, 307, 312
McCalla, Colleen, 192
McCarty, Mary, housekeeper, 204
McCord, Roy, xvii, *182*, 191–92, 298, 312
McCormick, Frank, 215
McDade, Thomas, agent, 286
McFadden, Eddie "Father," robber, 265
McGee, John, judge, 26, 33
McKellar, Kenneth, senator, 262
McKenna, Walter "Saph," boxer, 36, 135, 137,
    150

McLean, Ellie Hallberg, 51
McMeekin, Tommy, attorney, 62
McMullen, William, detective, 74, 163
Menke, Rose, 223
Menomonie, Wisc., robbery site, 116
Merchants Bank (First National Bank) Build-
    ing, St. Paul, 41, 292, 304
Merriam Park, St. Paul, 232–33
Merrick, Gordon "Curly," truck driver, 187
Michaud, Ann, xx, 7, 18, 19
Mickey's Diner, St. Paul, 29, 292
Midway area, St. Paul, 27–28
Midway Bank, St. Paul, 55
Mikulich, Frances, *see* Nash, Frances
    Mikulich
Miller, Eddie, porter, 69
Miller, John, 156
Miller, Morrie, hitman, 31–34, 307
Miller, Vernon C., gangster, xi, 63, 78, 82, 118,
    134, 165, *170*, *171*, 299, 307, 311, 312; mur-
    dered, xix, 175, 178; bootlegger, 24; mur-
    derer, 83, 95; background, 172–75; hunted,
    177–78. *See also* Kansas City Massacre
Milligan, Opal, gangster's girlfriend, 242
Millman, Ben, tailor, 89, 97
Milwaukee freight yards, St. Paul, 31
Minneapolis, inhospitable to gangsters, 89;
    map, 305
Minneapolis Combination, bootlegging group,
    30
Minnehaha Avenue, St. Paul, 144, 296
Minnesota Bankers Association, 78–79
Minnesota Blueing Company, Minneapolis,
    35–36
Minnesota Brewing Company, St. Paul, 297,
    302
Minnesota Bureau of Criminal Apprehension
    (BCA), xiii, xiv, xix, 51, 61, 74, 92, 99, 110,
    111, 115, 167, 215
Minnesota Children's Bureau, 284
Minnesota Club, St. Paul, 13, 16–17, 291
Minnesota Federation of Women's Clubs, 10
Minnesota *13*, whiskey, 27
Mission Hills Country Club, Kansas City,
    Mo., 101, 112, 126
Mississippi River Boulevard, St. Paul, 134,
    296, 298
Moeller, George, sheriff, 46
Moonlight Gardens, St. Paul, 84
Moran, George "Bugs," 18, 94, 95, 145, 146–47,
    309

Moran, John, informant, 6
Morgan, David, police officer, 10, 12, 14
Morgan, Edward G., syndicate boss, 3, 308
Morris, Harry, robber, 96, 310
Morrison County, distilleries, 27
Mortensen, Nels, doctor, 155, 216–18, *217*, 312; residence, 216, 299, 302
Murder Inc., 49, 50, 51, 54, 55, 63, 139
Murphy, Loretta, 228, 232
Murray, Edna, gangster's girlfriend, xiii, 78, 83–84, *83*, 138, 163, 186, 197, 202, 245, 308; captured, 274
Mystic Caverns, St. Paul, nightclub, 44–45, 292, 302

Nalls, Rosser, agent, 220–21
Nankin Cafe, Minneapolis, 143
Nash, Frances Mikulich, 81–82, *82*, 156
Nash, Frank "Jelly," gangster, 48, 60, 61, 75, 78, *79*, 80–81, 82, 97, 134, 140, 156, 308, 310, 311; bootlegger, 24; escape, 36; investigated by FBI, 82–83; Hamm kidnapping, 155, 156, 158; death, 176; residence, 295. *See also* Kansas City Massacre
Nathan, Harold, agent, 162, 268
Negri, Joseph "Fatso," 211, 229
Nelson, Arthur E., mayor, 160
Nelson, Babyface, *see* Gillis, Lester M.
Ness, Eliot, agent, 253
New Orleans, La., safe city, 60
Newman, Tom, attorney, 62, 141, 155
Nichols, Louis, executive, 263
Ninth Street, St. Paul, 29, 292
Nippert, Henry T., doctor, 162, 197, 298, 304
North Star Brewery, St. Paul, 187
Northwestern National Bank and Trust Company, Minneapolis, robbery, 108–9, 174, 310
Notesteen, E. N., agent, 234
Nye, Wallace, mayor, 11

Oakland Cemetery, St. Paul, 232, 300
O'Connor, Annie, 9
O'Connor, John J., police official, xi, *1*, 2, 7, 8–12, 109, 161, 283, 291, 308, 309; grave, 18, 291, 302
O'Connor, Richard T., 9
O'Connor, Tommy, 5–6
O'Connor system, xi, 1, 2, 3–4, 9–12, 19, 60–62, 75, 78, 96, 109–10, 158, 161, 165, 229, 291, 308, 309; violations, xvi, 11, 139; during

Prohibition, 28, 33, 34, 44; demise, 252–53, 258–59
O'Halloran and Murphy, St. Paul, funeral home, 17
Olmsted County Bank and Trust, Rochester, 5
Orpheum Theatre, St. Paul, 48, 304
Orth, Earl, 89–90
Osceola Avenue, St. Paul, 78, 294
Owasso Tavern, Little Canada, 63

Pantorium Cleaners and Shoe Repair, St. Paul, 67
Park Avenue, Minneapolis, 224, 300
Passolt, Melvin, agent, 99, 167
Patch, Earl, bookkeeper, 119
Patrick Novelty Company, St. Paul, 71–72, 242, 294, 307
Paul, Frances MacLaren, 155, 156
Pavlak, Leo, police officer, 166, 169
Pavlak, Robert, police officer, 169
Peifer, John "Jack," proprietor, 24, 61, 67, 73–74, 124, 133–41, *133*, *135*, 142, 161, 242, 296, 308, 313; Gleckman kidnapping, 39–40; Hamm kidnapping, 134, 139, 141, 146, 147, 150, 157, 159, 162–63, 165; Urschel kidnapping, 136; captured, 270; death, 271, 280
Peifer, Violet, gangster's wife, *133*, 134, 140, 141, 271
Penney, Lester, resort owner, 229
Perrow, H. C., police officer, 231
Perry, Margaret, informant, 72–73, 125, 310
Peter Iten's Auto Center, Cambridge, 72
Peters, Vera Brown, 159, 160
Pfleger, Helen Warren, clerk, 24–25
Phillips, Bernard, robber, 101, 109, 112, 124–27, *126*, 296, 308, 310
Picadilly, Mahtomedi diner, 294
Pierpont, Harry, gang member, 209
Pillsbury Street, St. Paul, 28
Piquett, Louis, attorney, 272
Plain Talk, magazine, 25, 33
Plantation, White Bear Lake, nightclub, 96–98, *97*, 294–95, 305
Police, corruption, 60, 62, 111–12, 127. *See also* Federal Bureau of Investigation; O'Connor system; St. Paul police
Porter, Mamie, 13
Portland Avenue, St. Paul, 189, 298

Post office, burglaries, 6–7. *See also* South St. Paul Post Office

Pranke, Richard, agent, 53, 246

Premo, Alex, 142

Presby, Paul, journalist, 243–44

Preston, Jean, 71–72

Prohibition, corruption, 4, 28, 29, 30, 32, 34, 38, 47, 65, 272; agents, 26. *See also* Bootlegging, Liquor

Prohibition Act, 24, 272; repealed, 311. *See also* Volstead, Andrew J.

Prohibition Bureau, St. Paul, 24–29, 41, 291

Prostitution, 10, 13–17

Public Safety Building, St. Paul, 250, *250*

Purple Gang, 173

Purvis, Melvin, agent, 146, 168, 179, 201, 203, 214, 223–24, 236, 237, 252, 262, 267, 281–82, 289

Quick, Lester, 157

Quinn, John, racketeer, 136

Raasch, Fred, police officer, 109, 110, 139, 161, 254–55

Radio Sally, *see* Bennett, Sally

Radisson Hotel, Minneapolis, 26, 134

Rafferty, George, taxi driver, 40

Railroads, during Prohibition, 25, 26–27

Ramaley, Jack, 69

Ramaleys' White Bear Castle, nightclub, 97

Ramsey County Courthouse (St. Paul City Hall), St. Paul, 265, *266*, 301, 304

Ramsey County Jail, St. Paul, xiv, 5, 267, *268*, 301, 304

Rand, Sally, stripper, 44

Randall, Theodore J., *see* Green, Eddie

Redwood Falls, robbery site, 116

Reed, Henry P. "Harry," 78, 255–56

Reed, Otto, police official, 176

Reilly, Frank, saloon keeper, 40, 47–48, 159, 245

Reilly, William Albert "Pat," 61, 67, *67*, 216–18, 238, 242, 245, 274, 293, 308

Reiter, Charlie, police officer, xx, 90, 215, 287

Reno, Nev., safe city, 60

Republic Finance Company, 41–43

Republican National Convention (*1928*), 94

Resler, Jane, 64

Rhinelander, Wisc., 116. *See also* Little Bohemia Lodge

Rising Sun Brewery, N.J., 50–51

Robert Street, St. Paul, 104, 108, 295

Rochester, kidnapping site, 116, 200

Rohling, Martin, doorman, xx, 137, 138, 271

Roisner, Morris, bootlegger, 29, 31, 34, 39

Rondo Avenue, St. Paul, 233, 234, 300

Rosedale Pharmacy, St. Paul, 297, 302; Hamm kidnapping, 153–55, *154*

Rothmeyer, Andrew, bar owner, 188

Rothstein, Arnold "the Brain," 18, 309

Roy Street, St. Paul, 53

Royal Cigar Store, St. Paul, 256

Runyan, Guy, mayor, 72

Rusick, Michael, mobster, 92, 95, *95*, 309

Rutman, Morris, bootlegger, 113

Safe cities, 60

St. Francis Hotel, *see* Hotel St. Francis

St. Paul, underworld haven, xi, xvi, 4–5, 7–12, 250; speakeasies, 25, 27, 44, 65; liquor syndicate, 29–34, 55; gambling, 36, 63, 71–72, 161; nightlife, 44–49, 90, 129, 134–35, 137; safe city, 60, 61, 62; maps, 302–4. *See also* O'Connor system, St. Paul police

St. Paul City Hall (Ramsey County Courthouse), 265, *266*, 301, 304

St. Paul Daily News, 251–55, 280

St. Paul Airport, *see* Holman Municipal Airport

St. Paul Hotel, *see* Hotel St. Paul

St. Paul police, 18, 44; records, xiv; corruption, 2–4, 5, 9, 17, 28–29, 157, 159–165, 187; headquarters, 7, *8*, 13, 28, 250, *250*, 291, 301, 304; reformers, 139, 251, 258–59; kill Van Meter, 240–44; cleaned up, 248–59. *See also* Brown, Thomas Archibald; Federal Bureau of Investigation; O'Connor system

St. Paul Recreation Company, 152, 255, 301, 304

St. Peter Street, St. Paul, 29, 34, 71, 292, 301

St. Peter's Cemetery, Mendota, 235

St. Valentine's Day Massacre, xiv, 145, 146, 307, 309

Salt, Augusta, nurse, 225

Sanborn, J. B. "John," judge, 160, 210

Sand Point Lake, cabins, 75

Sandlovich, Harry, *see* Sawyer, Harry

Sandlovich, Sam, gangster's brother, 284

Sandstone, bank robbery, 78

Santa Monica Apartments, Minneapolis, 208–13, 299, 305

Sargent Avenue, St. Paul, 39, 40–41, 42, 292

Savage, bank robbery, 78

Sawyer, Gladys Rita, 19, 47, *58*, 145, 162, 187–88, 204, 284, 308

Sawyer, Harry "Dutch," gangster, xvi, xx, 19, 21, 24, 47, *58*, *59*, 139, 141, 145, 150, 156, 161, 162–63, 217, 242, *261*, 308, 309, 313; harbors fugitives, 60–61; background, 62–64; homicide, 73; tips-off gangsters, 110, 127; Bremer kidnapping, 187–89; residences, 197, 203–5, 293, 299, 302, 305; captured, 275–76, 284–85

Schaefer, "Gloomy" Gus, robber, 265

Schaefer, Joseph, hitman, xix, 49, 50–51, 53–56, *53*, *278*, 283, 306, 308, 310

Schall, Thomas, senator, 35

Schmidt Brewing Company, St. Paul, 65, 184, 186–87, 297–98, 302; during Prohibition, 25

Schoen, Carl, 65, 188

Schroth, George, 221

Schroth, Louis, 219, 221–22

Schude, Blanche, 68, 132

Schultz, Dutch, *see* Flegenheimer, Arthur

Schwietz, Robert, 269–70

Schwietz, Virginia Gibbons, 267–68

Sebago Resort, Brainerd, 229

Seidel, Karl, chef, 46

Selby Avenue, St. Paul, 84

Senator Hotel, Minneapolis, 134

Seng, Robert, 78

Seven Corners, St. Paul, 63

Seventh Street, St. Paul, 2, 29, 69, 183, 291, 294, 297, 299

Shakopee, bank robbery, 78

Shanley, William T., police officer, 211

Sharkey, Willie, burglar, 265

Sherin, Joe, police officer, 56, 259

Shetsky, Rubin, 54

Shoreview, hideout, 197, 203–5, 299

Siegel, Benjamin "Bugsy," gangster, 50, 54, 55–57, *56*, 63, 293, 308

Sifakis, Carl, historian, 288

Silver, Harry, 135

Silver Slipper, Mahtomedi, roadhouse, 112–13, 295

Silverberg, Albert, *see* Young, George

Silverman, Maurice, agent, 26

Silverman, Sammy, gangster, 92–96, *95*, 308, 309

Sioux Falls, S.D., robbery site, 116

Sitzer Park, Shoreview, 299

Sixteenth Avenue, Minneapolis, 226, 230, 300

Skelly, Clifford, kidnapper, 184–85

Skinner, Beth, gangster's girlfriend, 29, 62, 67, 69, 164, 214, 215, 216, 217, 233, 234, 236, 272, 307

Sletner, Gertrude, maid, 41

Smith, Harry, 53

Smith, Zane, 230

Snail Lake Road, Shoreview, 203, 299

Snelling Avenue, St. Paul, 49, 293

Sommers, Frank, police official, 12, 15, 30, 160, 161, 308

South St. Paul, robberies, 5–7, 19, 165–69, *167*, *168*, 297, 303, 311

Speakeasies, St. Paul, 25, 27, 44

Spruce Tree Center, St. Paul, 51, 293

Stahlman Brewery, St. Paul, 187

Startling Detective Adventures, magazine, *52*, 213, 232

Stassen, Harold, attorney, 166, 169

Stearns County, distilleries, 27

Steffen, Emil, detective, 232

Stein, Clinton, agent, 258

Steinbrecher, Conrad, 13

Steinhardt, Robert, casino operator, 44, 46, 92, 98, 134–35, 162, 308

Stevens, Burton, hijacker, 29–34, 161, 292, 304, 308, 309

Stroh Brewery Company, St. Paul, 144, 296, 303

Sullivan, J. N., agent, 43

Sullivan, Thomas, attorney, 62

Summers, Anthony, biographer, 263

Summit Avenue, St. Paul, 7, 89, 90, 150, 187, 196, 294, 297

Summit-Dale Apartments, St. Paul, 90–92, *91*, 294, 304

Summit School, St. Paul, 298

Sundberg, Arthur, delivery boy, 14–15

Superior Industrial Alcohol Company, Cleveland, Ohio, 30, 32

Swede Hollow Park, St. Paul, 297

Tallerico, Albert, 39–40

Tamm, E. A., executive, 244

Tanaka, Sam, 137, 143

Taran, Sammy, bootlegger, 27–28

Telephones, gangsters' use, 62, 127

Ten Dollar Kid, *see* Silverman, Sammy

Ten Thousand Public Enemies (Cooper), 181

Theodore Hamm Brewing Company, *see* Hamm Brewing Company

Third Northwestern National Bank, Minneapolis, robbery, 54, 115–20, *119*, 295, 305

Third Street (Kellogg Boulevard), St. Paul, 7, 291

Thomas, Clarence, 153, 154, 297

Thomas Liquors, St. Paul, 154, 297, 302

Thompson, Tommy "Buck Tooth," journalist, 235

Three Fingered Jack, *see* Hamilton, John

Tierney, Charles, police officer, 36, 150, 152, 162, *182*

Toledo, Ohio, safe city, 60

Tolson, Clyde, agent, *180*, 263, *263*

Touhy, Roger "the Terrible," 135; bootlegger, 265–67, *266*; trial, 301, 304, 308, 312

Town Talk Sandwich Shop, St. Paul, 215

Trout Lake, gangster cabins, 74–75

True Detective, magazine, 213

True Detective Mysteries, magazine, 104, 246

Tulsa, Okla., safe city, 60

Turkus, Burton, attorney, 54, 56

Turner, William, agent, 283, 288

Tuttle, Steve, 143, 144

Tuttle, Virginia, 144

Ulrich, Fred, 19

University Avenue, St. Paul, 27, 35, 44, 240, 241, 242, 293, 301

Urschel, Charles F., kidnapped, 136, 184–85, 282, 306, 311

Utecht, Warden, 54

Vanity Fair, dance hall, St. Paul, 49

Van Lear, Ralph, mayoral candidate, 117

Van Meter, Homer, gangster, xiv, 67, 69, 137, 159, 204, 209–11, *209*, 213–16, 220–21, 222, 223, 229, 231, 233, 238, 280, 299, 300, 308, 312; death, *240*, 241–47, *243*, 301, 302, 313

Vannovich, Sam, 33

Ventress, Frank, 68, 136

Vernon Street, St. Paul, 155–58, 163, 297, 302, 311

Vernon Street gang, *see* Barker-Karpis gang

Vetloff, Zolly, 89

Vogel, Pete, family, 227–28

Vogelgesang, Anita, 71

Volstead, Andrew J., congressman, 23–25, *23*, 272, 291, 309

Volstead Act, *see* Prohibition Act

Voyageurs National Park, 74

Wabasha Street Apartments, St. Paul, 293, 304

Wabasha Street Caves, St. Paul, 45, 293, 303

Wabasha Street, St. Paul, 44, 55, 293

Wagner, Abe, bootlegger, *50*, 51; murdered, 50, 51–54, *52*, 56, 139, 283, 293, 308, 310

Wagner, Allie, 50

Wahpeton, N. D., robbery site, 116, 118

Walker, "Denver Bobbie," robber, 73

Walker, Paul E., detective, 232

Walsh, William, attorney, 271

Ward, Charlie, 54–55

Warner Road, Mahtomedi, 113

Warren, H. E. "Ned," commissioner, 253, 256, 258, 308

Washington Avenue, Minneapolis, 109

Washington Street, St. Paul, 13, 14, 291, 304

Water Street, St. Paul, 44, 292

Waterloo, Iowa, shooting site, 116

Waxey Gordon, *see* Wexler, Irving

Weaver, William, gunman, 68, 139, 155, 191, 214, 308; residence, 84; robs bank, 118; captured, 262, 276

Webber, Frank, gangster, 87

Webber, Tommie, gangster, 30–31

Weir, William, 49–50

Weisman, William, 53

West St. Paul, hideout, 104, 108, 295

Western Avenue, St. Paul, 129, 295

Wexler, Irving, bootlegger, 34, 50, 308

Wheeler Avenue, St. Paul, 27–28

White, Theodore H., quoted, xii

White Bear Castle, *see* Ramaleys' White Bear Castle

White Bear Lake, nightlife, 96–97, 113; map, 305. *See also* Idlewild cottage

Wiechman, Ed, janitor, 124

Wildwood Park, Mahtomedi, 294, 305

Williams, Winnie, gangster's girlfriend, 126–27

Willmar, bank robbery, 92–94, 116

Wilson, Frank, agent, 288

Winkler, Georgette, 145, 159, 176

Winkler, Gus, gangster, 145, 159, 176

Winthrop, bank robbery, 78

Wiretaps, *see* Electronic surveillance
Woodruff, Wisc., hideout, 39
Wybest, Robert, 233
Wyoming, kidnapping site, 116

Yeaman, Jack, 166, 169
Yeaman, John, police officer, 166, 169
You Can't Get Away with It, film, 180
Young, George, hitman, xix, 49, 50–51, 53–56, 283, 306, 308, 310

Zachman, Arthur, 120, 121
Ziegler, Shotgun George (Fred Goetz), gangster, xiii, 48, 135, *146*, 166, 294, 307; Hamm kidnapping, 144–47, 149, 153–57, 162, 189, 201, 265, 297; St. Valentine's Day Massacre, 145, 307; murdered, 312
Zumbrota, 200

PICTURE CREDITS

Photographs and other illustrations used in this book appear through the courtesy of the institutions or persons listed below. The name of the photographer, when known, is given in parentheses, as is additional information about the source and location of the item. Donors of photographs now at the Minnesota Historical Society are individually identified.

Minnesota Historical Society (MHS) collections, St. Paul—pages i, ii–iii (Peter Latner), vi (Northwest Photographic Studio), 1, 8, 14 (A. F. Raymond), 28, 37 (Kenneth Wright), 52 *top* (Arthur Lund), 56 (C. P. Gibson), 70 (Gibson), 79 (Gibson), 80, 91 (Wright), 130 (Gibson), 148, 149, 168 *top*, 168 *bottom* (Phillip Hutchens; South St. Paul Police Dept.), 183, 186, 193, 196, 212, 217, 219 (Hutchens), 243 (Richard Pranke Papers), 249, 250, 253 left, 260, 261, 266, 278; cover: gun (Latner), building (Hutchens)
Associated Press/Wide World—pages x, 179, 202, 264, 273 *inset*, 279
Barfuss Family—pages 164, 253 *right*, 258 (all MHS)
Jane Bonne—page 133 (MHS)

Chicago Tribune—pages 146, 282 (AP/Wide World)
Federal Bureau of Investigation, Washington, D.C.—pages xv, 56 *inset*, 58, 79 *inset*, 91 *inset*, 121, 130 *inset*, 132, 135 *inset*, 163, 206, 207, 219 *left inset*, 239 top, 270; cover: Dillinger poster, face
Federal Bureau of Prisons, Washington, D.C.—pages 86, 91 *inset*, 287
Janet Gibson—page 170 (MHS)
Hastings Gazette—page 238 (Apr. 27, 1934)
Kenneth Herschlar—page 227 (MHS)
Keller Golf Course, Maplewood—page 100
Kansas City Star—pages 171, 177
Landmark Center, St. Paul—page 273
Lane Family—page *47*, 47 *inset* (MHS)
Library of Congress, Washington, D.C.—page 154 *inset* (AP/Wide World)
Ann Michaud—page 6 (MHS)
Minneapolis Public Library, Minneapolis Collection—pages 37 *inset*, 42, 103, 120 (*Star Tribune*), 151, 158 *inset*, 199, 251, 275
Minnesota Bureau of Criminal Apprehension, St. Paul—pages *59*, 102, 123, 209, 219 *right inset*, 226 (all MHS)
Sue Mollner—page 126 (MHS)
National Archives, Washington, D.C.—pages 180, 180 *inset*
Jean Preston—page 70 *inset* (MHS)

Ramsey County Historical Society, St. Paul—pages 23, 83, 128, 145, 190 *inset*

St. Paul Daily News—pages *21* (St. Paul Police Dept.), 22, *32*, 45, 241 bottom (Aug. 25, 1934), 248 (June 24, 1935), 254 (June 27, 1935), 257 (June 24, 1935), 266 *inset*, 268, 268 *inset* (all MHS)

St. Paul Dispatch—pages 45 *inset* (Oct. 27, 1933), 95 (Aug. 14, 1930), 182 (Jan. 18, 1934)

St. Paul Health Department—page 20

St. Paul Pioneer Press—pages vi *inset*, xxii (Dec. 5, 1928), 19, 50, 73 (Mar. 8, 1932), 114, 119 (Dec. 17, 1932), 158, 190

St. Paul Police Department—pages 8 *inset*, *21*

South St.Paul Daily Reporter—page 167 (Aug. 30, 1933)

Star Tribune/Minneapolis-St. Paul—pages 17, 53, 120, 126, 135, 142, 160, 280, 289

Startling Detective Adventures—page 52 *bottom* (July 1933)

James Thomas—page 154 (MHS)

University of Oklahoma Library, Western History Collections, Norman—page 185

UPI/Bettman—pages 61, 66, 67, 76, 77, 82, 105, 107, 126 *inset*, 210, 235, 239 *bottom*, 241 top, 263, 283

White Bear Press—page 97 (June 26, 1930)

Willmar Tribune—page 93 (July 16, 1930)

Maps by Mui D. Le and Alan J. Willis, University of Minnnesota Cartography Laboratory, Minneapolis